THEODORE ROOSEVELT

and the Rise

of America

to World Power

HOWARD K. BEALE

THEODORE
ROOSEVELT

and the
Rise of America
to World Power

THE JOHNS HOPKINS UNIVERSITY PRESS
Baltimore and London

© 1956 by THE JOHNS HOPKINS PRESS

All rights reserved

Printed in the United States of America

The Johns Hopkins University Press, Baltimore, Maryland 21218
The Johns Hopkins Press Ltd., London

Originally published, 1956

Johns Hopkins Paperbacks edition, 1984

LIBRARY OF CONGRESS CATALOGING IN PUBLICATION DATA

Beale, Howard K. (Howard Kennedy), 1899-1959.
   Theodore Roosevelt and the rise of America to world
power.

   Reprint. Originally published: Baltimore: Johns
Hopkins Press, 1956. (The Albert Shaw lectures on diplo-
matic history; 1953)
   Includes bibliographical references and index.
   1. Roosevelt, Theodore, 1858-1919. 2. United States —
Foreign relations — 1901-1909. I. Title.
E757.B4 1984   973.91'1'0924   83-25584
ISBN 0-8018-3249-7

Contents

Preface

These lectures are the result of a good deal of questioning over a long period of years. For three decades the United States and other great powers have been pursuing policies that have not led to the better world for which men and nations have hoped. Obviously, no nation has wished to proceed to the present desperate state of international relations that threatens to destroy civilization itself; equally obviously, no one nation alone has brought the world to this state of things. Too little is known about historical causation to say what has led to this dénouement. It cannot be said with any certainty that the trend in international affairs has been inevitable or that the course of international events has been determined by forces over which man has no control. Nor yet can it be asserted, in the present state of historiography, that man by taking thought and making decisions has been fully responsible for what has happened. Yet there has been a certain inexorability about the sequence of events from World War I to the present. Decisions made by statesmen in each successive situation have been governed to a considerable extent by values already accepted and by decisions already made by predecessors under whom the direction foreign policy was to take had been established.

Often it has seemed that what was really needed was to change the direction, to abandon the road that led to the 1950's and start out in an entirely different direction. My first question therefore was: How did America get started down this road and was there a time, perhaps before World War I, when decisions were made that account for the direction national policy has taken? What decisions so affected the nation's course?

Closely related was a second baffling question to which historians seldom offer an answer, namely, whether individual men or only blind forces influence history. Leaders occupy important rôles in history as it is usually recounted, but historians often seem to assume that it is forces and not men who determine what happens. A thorough study a few years ago of what historians had written about the causes of the Civil War revealed that all the writers had told the story in terms of leaders of the day and many of them also in terms of forces, but that most of them had kept men and forces in separate compartments as if there were no inter-action between them. Not one had come to grips with the problem as to which was more important or whether the leaders had any effect upon history at all. So, too, in recent history. Consequently, the question is still to be faced whether there was a time at which a route different from the one taken in recent foreign policy could have been chosen by the people or their leaders.

A third question that has never been satisfactorily an-swered is why America shifted from the assumption in 1914 that war in Europe could not have serious meaning for America to her conviction three years later that she must enter that war. If events between 1914 and 1917 do not provide an entirely satisfying answer, what effect, if any, had the history of the years before 1914 upon this change of heart and America's ultimate support of France and England against Germany? And what accounted for Theodore Roosevelt's insistence earlier and more vigorously than most that we enter the war?

In view of later criticisms of imperialist powers in general and American imperialism in particular and in view, too, of the strength of opposition to expansion and imperialism among Americans at the turn of the century, an answer has long been needed to a fourth question: Why did America decide in favor of rather than against expansionism and imperialism? Or did her leaders not make the decision but merely find themselves pushed into policies by forces too big for them?

In so far as Roosevelt and other expansionists and imperialists did determine our policy, what were their motives? Was it national pride, a sense of the white man's burden, conviction about democracy, a sense of mission in the world, desire for economic gain, sheer love of power, or what, that propelled the men of 1900 into further extension of America's concern and influence to far parts of the world? This was a fifth question to which the answer could be found in part in Roosevelt.

A sixth question concerned Theodore directly. While he was alive and during the years following his death, literature on Roosevelt tended to reflect the popular admiration of his contemporaries for his handling of international problems. Then the tide turned and a series of studies appeared that questioned both his wisdom and his ability as an international statesman. His importance in events in which he unquestionably participated was denied. His veracity in telling of other events and his part in them was questioned. It seemed now time to ask whether the early admiration or the later depreciation or perhaps a third more balanced view was the soundest.

Finally, in several years of preparation of a biography of Theodore Roosevelt I have increasingly been preoccupied with the question as to what impact he did have upon world affairs. An answer to this seemed important, too, for all Americans interested in recent history.

The invitation to deliver a series of lectures at The Johns Hopkins University on some phase of the foreign policy of Theodore Roosevelt offered a chance to pursue answers to some of these questions. This volume is an expansion of the Albert Shaw lectures there given. The lectures are Roosevelt-centered. No attempt has been made to narrate the history of foreign relations during his time except where he was vitally concerned. The topics dealt with have been chosen for investigation because Roosevelt was involved in them. Important international happenings have been discussed, or little-known episodes described, or long-known stories retold in these lectures as part of an effort to view them as Roosevelt viewed them and to determine and evaluate his rôle. The hope has been that new light would be thrown on the foreign relations of the period by thus viewing them through the eyes of one of the leading participants.

Obviously, satisfactory answers have not been found to all the questions to which answers were sought. Some of the conclusions have had perforce to be tentative. Some of the questions may never be answered, but it is hoped that these lectures may make it possible to come nearer to finding answers, and that, in any case, they may bring new understanding of one of the most colorful and important actors in international affairs in recent times. Through him men may perhaps learn better to comprehend what determines history. Furthermore, new questions have arisen in the course of the study, some of them of fundamental importance to an understanding of American foreign policy in the later twentieth century; and it is hoped that the lectures may illuminate these new problems and may provoke others to pursue the problems further.

I am under obligation to many for courtesies or assistance while these lectures were being prepared. I wish to thank for permission to quote from the books here listed a number of holders of copyrights: Appleton-Century-Crofts, Inc., New York, for Thomas A. Bailey, *A Diplomatic History of the American People* (1940), M. A. DeWolfe Howe, *James Ford Rhodes* (1929), and Theodore Roosevelt, *The Strenuous Life: Essays and Addresses* (1899); George Allen and Unwin, Ltd., London, for John A. Hobson, *Imperialism: A Study* (1938); The Atlantic Monthly Press, Boston, for John D. Long, *America of Yesterday as Reflected in the Journal of John Davis Long* . . . (1923), Lawrence S. Mayo, ed.; The Bobbs-Merrill Co., Indianapolis, for Albert J. Beveridge, *The Meaning of the Times* (1908, 1936), used by special permission of the publishers; Brandt and Brandt, New York, for Oscar K. Davis, *Released for Publication* (1925, 1953); Cassell and Co., Ltd., London, for Bernhard H. von Bülow, *Imperial Germany* (1914), Marie A. Lewenz, tr., and George P. Gooch, *History of Modern Europe, 1898–1919* (1923); The University of Chicago Press, for Howard C. Hill, *Theodore Roosevelt and the Caribbean* (1927); The Columbia University Press, New York, for John W. Burgess, *Recent Changes in American Constitutional Theory* (1923); Constable and Co., Ltd., London, for Robert B. Mowat, *Life of Lord Pauncefote* (1929); Dodd, Mead, and Co., New York, for Tyler Dennett, *John Hay* (1933), William H. Edwards, *The Tragedy of Edward VII* (1928), Mark A. DeWolfe Howe, *George von Lengerke Meyer: His Life and Public Services* (1919), and Philip C. Jessup, *Elihu Root* (1938); Doubleday and Co., Inc., New York, for Archie Butt, *The Letters of Archie Butt* (1924), Lawrence F. Abbott, ed., Archie Butt, *Taft and Roosevelt: The Intimate Letters of Archie Butt* (1930), Rudyard Kipling, *Something of Myself: For My Friends Known and Unknown* (copyright 1937 by Caroline Kipling and reprinted by permission of Mrs. George Bambridge), and Serge Witte, *Memoirs* (1920, 1921); Gerald Duckworth and Co., Ltd., London, for the foreign rights to

George W. Smalley, *Anglo-American Memories* (1911, 1912);
E. P. Dutton and Co., Inc., New York, for Alfred L. P.
Dennis, *Adventures in American Diplomacy* (1928), and
John L. Heaton, *Cobb of " The World "* (1924); the trustees
of the estate of Frederick H. Gillett for Frederick H. Gillett,
George Frisbie Hoar (1934); Lloyd C. Griscom for *Diplo-
matically Speaking* (1940), published by Little, Brown and
Co., Boston; Sir Cecil Graves, London, for Viscount Edward
Grey, *Twenty-five Years, 1892–1916* (1925); Harcourt, Brace,
and Co., Inc., New York, for A. Whitney Griswold, *The Far
Eastern Policy of the United States* (1938), Henry F.
Pringle, *Theodore Roosevelt* (1931), and *The Letters of
Lincoln Steffens* (1938), Ella Winter and Granville Hicks,
eds.; Harper and Brothers, New York, for David J. Hill,
Impressions of the Kaiser (1918), *The Kaiser's Memoirs*
(1922), Thomas R. Ybarra, tr., Allan Nevins, *Henry White:
Thirty Years of American Diplomacy* (1930), Henry L.
Stoddard, *It Costs To Be President* (1938), *Mark Twain's
Autobiography* (1924), and *Mark Twain in Eruption* (1940),
Bernard DeVoto, ed.; The Harvard University Press, Cam-
bridge, for *The Letters of Theodore Roosevelt* (copyright
1951, 1952, 1954 by the President and Fellows of Harvard
College), Elting E. Morison, ed., Ralph Barton Perry, *The
Thought and Character of William James* (1935), and Elihu
Root, *Addresses on International Subjects* (1916); Dr. Ives
Hendrick, executor of the estate of Burton J. Hendrick, for
Burton J. Hendrick, *The Life of Andrew Carnegie* (1932);
Henry Holt and Co., Inc., New York, for Samuel F. Bemis,
A Diplomatic History of the United States (1936), and Mary
Coolidge, *Chinese Immigration* (1909); Hodder and Stough-
ton, Ltd., London, for Maurice F. Egan, *Ten Years near
the German Frontier* (1919); The Houghton Mifflin Co.,
Boston, for *The Letters of Henry Adams, 1892–1918* (1938),
Worthington C. Ford, ed., Stephen Gwynn, *The Letters and
Friendships of Sir Cecil Spring Rice* (1929), Mark A. De-

Wolfe Howe, *Portrait of an Independent: Moorfield Storey,
1845–1929* (1932), John J. Leary, *Talks with T. R.* (1920),
The Letters of Grover Cleveland, 1850–1908 (1933), Allan
Nevins, ed., *The Letters of Charles Eliot Norton* (1913),
Sara Norton and M. A. DeWolfe Howe, eds., *Theodore
Roosevelt, Thomas H. Benton* (1899), *The Intimate Papers
of Colonel House* (1926-1928), Charles Seymour, ed., William R. Thayer, *Life and Letters of John Hay* (1908), and
George Macauley Trevelyan, *Grey of Fallodon* (1937); The
Johns Hopkins Press, Baltimore, for Dexter Perkins, *The
Monroe Doctrine, 1867–1907* (1937); Bruce Humphries, Inc.,
Boston, for Francis M. Huntington Wilson, *Memoirs of an
Ex-Diplomat* (1945); Hutchinson and Co., Ltd., London, for
The Letters of Prince von Bülow (1930), Frederic Whyte,
tr.; The University of Illinois Press, Urbana, for Paul Varg,
Open Door Diplomat: The Life of W. W. Rockhill (1952);
Alfred A. Knopf, Inc., New York, for Herman Bernstein,
The Willy-Nicky Correspondence (1918), William H. Langer, *The Diplomacy of Imperialism, 1890–1902* (1935, 1951),
Baron Roman Romanovitch Rosen, *Forty Years in Diplomacy* (1922), and Oswald G. Villard, *Prophets True and
False* (1928); J. B. Lippincott Co., Philadelphia, for John
O. P. Bland, *Recent Events and Current Politics in China*
(1912); Paul List Verlag, Leipzig, for Hermann von Eckardstein, *Die Isolierung Deutschlands* (vol. III of *Lebenserrinnerungen und politische Denkwürdigkeiten*) (1919-1921);
Little, Brown, and Co., Boston, for Alfred T. Mahan, *The
Influence of Sea Power upon the French Revolution and
Empire, 1793–1812* (1898), *The Influence of Sea Power upon
History, 1660–1783* (1898), *The Interest of America in Sea
Power, Past and Future* (1898), and *The Problem of Asia*
(1905), and Dexter Perkins, *Hands Off: A History of the
Monroe Doctrine* (1941); Longmans, Green, and Co., Inc.,
New York, for George P. Gooch, *Before the War: Studies in
Diplomacy* (1936); The Macmillan Co., New York, for

Owen Wister, *The Pentacost of Calamity and a Straight
Deal* (1915); Macmillan and Co., Ltd., London, for the
foreign rights in Brooks Adams, *America's Economic Su-
premacy* (1900), Lord Newton, *Lord Lansdowne* (1929),
and Sidney Lee, *King Edward VII* (1927); Mr. Lyle Evans
Mahan, New York, for Alfred T. Mahan, *Lessons of the War
with Spain and Other Articles* (1899); John Murray, Ltd.,
London, for Charles C. Taylor, *The Life of Admiral Mahan:
Naval Philosopher* (1920); Thomas Nelson and Sons, Ltd.,
Edinburgh, and The Right Hon. Susan Lady Tweedsmuir,
for John Buchan, *Lord Minto: A Memoir* (1924); Mr. Allan
Nevins, for his rights in his *Henry White* (1930); The Odys-
sey Press, Inc., New York, for John H. Latané and David
W. Wainhouse, *A History of American Foreign Policy* (1940);
Putnam and Co., Ltd., London, for *Prince von Bülow:
Memoirs* (1931-1932); G. P. Putnam's Sons, New York, for
Blanche E. C. Dugdale, *Arthur James Balfour* (1936), for
Theodore Roosevelt, *African and European Addresses* (1910),
Lawrence F. Abbott, ed., T. Roosevelt, *Essays on Practical
Politics* (1888), and T. Roosevelt, *American Ideals and Other
Essays, Social and Political* (1902), for *Speeches, Corre-
spondence and Political Papers of Carl Schurz* (1913), Fred-
erick Bancroft, ed., and for the American rights to George
W. Smalley, *Anglo-American Memories* (1911, 1912); St.
Martin's Press, New York, for the American rights to Brooks
Adams, *America's Economic Supremacy* (1900); Charles
Scribner's Sons, New York, for Joseph B. Bishop, *Theodore
Roosevelt and His Time* (1920), Nicholas Murray Butler,
Across the Busy Years (1939-1940), Royal Cortissoz, *The
Life of Whitelaw Reid* (1921), *Letters from Theodore Roose-
velt to Anna Roosevelt Cowles, 1870–1918* (1924), Anna R.
Cowles, ed., George Dewey, *Autobiography of George Dewey:
Admiral of the Navy* (1916), Finley Peter Dunne, *Mr.
Dooley at His Best* (1938), *Selections from the Correspond-
ence of Theodore Roosevelt and Henry Cabot Lodge, 1884–*

1918 (1925), Henry C. Lodge, ed., Henry C. Lodge, *The Senate of the United States and Other Essays and Addresses, Historical and Literary* (1921), Edward S. Martin, *The Life of Joseph Hodges Choate* (1921), Corinne R. Robinson, *My Brother Theodore Roosevelt* (1922), Theodore Roosevelt, *Autobiography* (1913), *Letters to Kermit from Theodore Roosevelt, 1902-1908* (1946), Will Irwin, ed., and Theodore Roosevelt, *Literary Essays* (1890); Simon and Schuster, Inc., New York, for Don C. Seitz, *Joseph Pulitzer: His Life and Letters* (1924); Skeffington & Son Ltd., London, for Johann von Bernstorff, *My Three Years in America* (1920); The Stackpole Co., Harrisburg, for Alfred Lief, *Brandeis: The Personal History of an American Ideal* (1936); Mr. Charles M. Storey, trustee of the estate of Moorfield Storey, for his rights to Mark A. DeWolfe Howe, *Portrait of an Independent: Moorfield Storey, 1845–1929* (1932); Alfred Vagts for his *Deutschland und die Vereinigten Staaten in der Welt Politik* (1935); Verlag Ullstein, Berlin-Tempelhof, for *Die Denkwürdigkeiten des Fürsten von Bülow*, Franz von Stockhammern, ed., (1930-1931); and Mr. Henry H. Villard, for his rights to Oswald G. Villard, *Fighting Years* (1939).

For permission to quote from articles in periodicals I also wish to express thanks to: *The American Historical Review*, for Seward W. Livermore, " Theodore Roosevelt, the American Navy, and the Venezuelan Crisis of 1902-1903," LI (April, 1946), 452-471; Appleton-Century-Crofts, Inc., New York, for Theodore Roosevelt, " Fellow-Feeling as a Political Factor," *Century Magazine*, XXXVII (January, 1900), 466-471, and Theodore Roosevelt, " Military Preparedness and Unpreparedness," *Century Magazine*, XXXVII (November, 1899), 149-153; *The Atlantic Monthly*, for E. S., " Mr. Roosevelt," CIX (May, 1912), 577-581; *The Commercial and Financial Chronicle* for various quotations; *Current History*, for James Bryce, " The Policy of Annexation for America," *Forum*, XXIV (December, 1897), 385-395; *The Far Eastern*

Quarterly, for William R. Braisted, " The United States and the American China Development Company," xi (February, 1952) , 147-165; *The Nation* for various quotations; and *The Pacific Northwest Quarterly*, for Winston B. Thorson, " Pacific Northwest Opinion on the Russo-Japanese War of 1904-1905," xxv (October, 1944) , 317.

For permission to quote from manuscript letters I am deeply indebted to a number of persons to whom the literary property right has descended who have graciously granted me permission, in nearly every case unrestricted permission, to quote from the letters of Roosevelt's contemporaries: for Brooks Adams permission was granted by his grandnephew, Thomas B. Adams, on behalf of the trustees of the Adams Papers; for Horace N. Allen by his sons, Horace E. Allen and Maurice Allen; for Albert J. Beveridge by his wife, Catherine (Mrs. Albert J.) Beveridge; for Poultney Bigelow by his niece, Anne T. (Mrs. Simon C.) Eristoff; for William Jennings Bryan by his granddaughter, Ruth Owen (Mrs. Robert) Lehman; for Andrew Carnegie by his daughter, Margaret C. (Mrs. Roswell) Miller; for William E. Chandler by his daughter-in-law (widow of Lloyd H. Chandler) , Agatha B. E. (Mrs. Harley H.) Christy; for Joseph H. Choate by his daughter, Miss Mabel Choate; for Grover Cleveland by his son, Richard F. Cleveland; for John W. Foster by his grandson, Allen W. Dulles; for Lloyd C. Griscom by Mr. Griscom himself; for John Hay by his daughter, Alice H. (Mrs. James M.) Wadsworth; for Henry Higginson by his son, A. Henry Higginson; for Henry Demarest Lloyd by his grandson, Henry Demarest Lloyd, Jr. (III) ; for Henry Cabot Lodge by his grandson, Ambassador Henry Cabot Lodge, Jr. (II) ; for Alfred T. Mahan by his son, Lyle Evans Mahan; for George von L. Meyer by his daughter, Alice M. (Mrs. Philip O.) Coffin; for Joseph Pulitzer by his son, Joseph Pulitzer, Jr.; for Whitelaw Reid by his daughter-in-law, Helen Rogers (Mrs. Ogden Mills) Reid; for William W. Rockhill by his grandson, Courtland Hoppin; for Elihu Root by his son, Elihu Root, Jr.; for Charles S. Sperry by his grandson, Marcy L. Sperry, Jr.; for Oscar S. Straus by his son, Roger W. Straus; for Charles G. Washburn by his grandson, Charles G. Washburn, II; for Henry White by his son, John Campbell White; and for William Allen White by his son, William L. White.

For permission to quote from the Theodore Roosevelt letters, the letters of his sister Anna Roosevelt Cowles, those of his sister Corinne Roosevelt Robinson, and those of his brother, Elliott Roosevelt, I owe a very special debt of gratitude to William M. Cruikshank, literary executor of the Roosevelt estate, to Roosevelt's nephew Mr. W. Sheffield Cowles, to his niece Mrs. Corinne R. Alsop, and to his niece Mrs. Eleanor Roosevelt, respectively. In each case the permission was unrestricted permission to quote free of all censorship. Without this sort of freedom in the use of the Roosevelt papers it would have been impossible to publish these lectures. The generosity, the coöperation, and the understanding of the Roosevelt family in regard to this uncensored use of Roosevelt letters here, in the eight recently published volumes of letters, and elsewhere have contributed greatly to an understanding of Roosevelt and of his era. The attitude of the family is especially noteworthy in view of the outspokenness of many and the intimacy of some of the letters thus made available.

Finally, concerning permission to quote, I wish to thank the families of William B. Allison, of Moreton Frewen, of John C. Spooner, and of William Howard Taft for their exemplary action in dedicating the letters of these men to the public, thereby permanently eliminating the whole problem of literary property right for future historians.

During the research for these lectures many people were helpful. To the staffs of the Historical Society of Iowa in Iowa City, the Kansas State Historical Society in Topeka, and the Massachusetts Historical Society in Boston, and the staffs of the Bancroft Library of the University of California in Berkeley, the Clements Library of the University of Michigan in Ann Arbor, the Columbia University Library in New York, the Connecticut State Historical Library in Hartford, the Harper Library of the University of Chicago, the Henry E. Huntington Library in San Marino, California, the Indiana State Library in Indianapolis, the Historical, Memorial, and Art Department of Iowa in Des Moines, the Library of the Meadville Theological Seminary in Chicago, the Manuscripts Division of the New York Public Library, the Roosevelt House in New York City, the Leland Stanford University Library, and the Widener Memorial Library of Harvard University, I am indebted for use of materials and facilities for work. I feel a special debt of gratitude to the Baker Library of Dartmouth College, to the Library of Congress, and to the Memorial Library of the University of Wisconsin but especially its assistant director Louis Kaplan, the staff of its Reference Division, and Mary M. Kirsch in its Periodical Division. A large share of the research and writing for these lectures was done in these last three libraries. Mrs. Albert J. Beveridge, Mrs. Margaret Long Stanley, Mr. Raymond Robins, and Mr. and Mrs. William Allen White provided both gracious hospitality and interesting personal additions to my understanding of Theodore Roosevelt while I worked in the papers of Senators Albert J. Beveridge and Chester I. Long, of Raymond Robins, and of William Allen White. To David Mearns, chief, to Robert Land, assistant chief, to Thomas P. Martin, former assistant chief of the Manuscripts Division of the Library of Congress, to C. Percy Powell, long in charge of the Taft and Roosevelt papers in that division, and to Katharine E. Brand of the same division, whose knowledge of recent manuscript collections is unequalled, I am especially indebted. So, too, to Willard Webb, who has been more than generous with the facilities

of the Library of Congress and with his own wide knowledge
of men and affairs. John C. Jacques in charge of newspapers
and Ruth H. Davis and Litta B. Bascom in charge of government publications of the Wisconsin State Historical Society
were generous with their time and materials. Two reference
librarians, Georgia Faison of the University of North Carolina and Genevieve Winchester of the University of Wisconsin, have given me help of the sort that makes their skill,
their patience, and their devotion an essential part of books
published in their institutions. But above all others I am
indebted to Nora E. Cordingley, long librarian of Roosevelt
House in New York and later of the Theodore Roosevelt
Collection at Harvard. Her knowledge of Roosevelt materials, the information she had organized about Roosevelt,
and her generous giving of her time and herself to all workers
in Roosevelt materials combine to make her too early death
an irreparable loss to students of Roosevelt.

Before they died I had interviews of some length with a
number of friends and relatives of Theodore Roosevelt.
Among these were Mrs. Roosevelt, Theodore Roosevelt, Jr.,
Kermit Roosevelt, Cabinet Member James R. Garfield,
Senator Joseph L. Bristow of Kansas, Assistant Secretary of
State Francis B. Loomis, Poultney Bigelow, law school classmate and lifelong antagonist of Roosevelt, Philippe Bunau-
Varilla, director of the French Panama Canal Company,
Viscountess Bryce, whose husband was British Ambassador
in Roosevelt's day, and Viscount Lee of Fareham, who accompanied Roosevelt in the Cuban fighting and played host
to him in London. Especially helpful because of his close
acquaintance was William Loeb, Jr., Roosevelt's private
secretary at Albany and throughout the Presidency. To
Hermann Hagedorn, secretary of the Roosevelt Memorial
Association, I owe particular gratitude because of the understanding of Roosevelt that he has shared with me and because of his helpfulness in collecting and preserving and his

generosity in making available rich Roosevelt materials that might otherwise not have been accessible. Through their unusual human understanding and insights two personal friends of Roosevelt, William Allen White and Raymond Robins, with whom I had long discussions about Roosevelt, contributed much. And to Fola LaFollette I wish to voice thanks for stimulating and penetrating suggestions about Roosevelt in talks I have had with her about her father and Roosevelt.

For help of a different sort I wish to express appreciation to several. The Social Science Research Council gave a grant-in-aid. The Research Committee of the University of Wisconsin has generously provided research assistants and research leave. Several of these research assistants at the University of Wisconsin have in succession helped prepare the lectures. E. David Cronon now of Yale University spent a year with me in the Library of Congress; Herbert Gutman helped during the actual writing of the lectures and did a good deal of the research on the China lecture. Gerd Korman helped on the German chapters and Margaret Meehan, Alfred D. Sumberg, Loren Baritz, and Arthur I. Waskow did the painstaking checking of facts and references. All seven offered useful criticism. Mrs. Fred Pierce of Washington, D. C., has for years devotedly worked with me typing for me accurate copies of letters in the Library of Congress and Catherine H. Wikoff of Madison has helped generously in the last stages of preparing the manuscript for the press. R. Alan Lawson, Richard A. Thompson, and Arthur I. Waskow of the University of Wisconsin have helped with painstaking proof-reading. To the editing skill of Livia Appel, editor of the Wisconsin Historical Society, I am indebted for countless valuable suggestions. I have had help and suggestions, too, from various students and colleagues. Eugene Boardman of the University of Wisconsin, Robert A. Lively of Princeton University, William Neumann of Goucher

College, Henry Pelling of the Queen's College, Oxford, James Z. Rabun of Emory University, Charles Vevier of the University of Rochester, and William A. Williams of the University of Oregon have given each for a portion of the manuscript that most valuable of all assistance—criticism. My friends Alexander H. McLeod, Jr., of the Macmillan Company and John Hope Franklin of Brooklyn College have read the whole manuscript and have made detailed and intelligent suggestions by the hundred.

HOWARD K. BEALE

October, 1956
University of Wisconsin

THEODORE ROOSEVELT

and the Rise

of America

to World Power

Introduction

Theodore Roosevelt brought to the Presidency unusual equipment for dealing with foreign policy. He had grown up among people that knew Europe first hand. His Great Uncle James I. Roosevelt had lived in Paris, where he moved in fashionable circles and counted the Queen of Spain and Lafayette among his friends. One of Theodore's mother's brothers had lived abroad before the Civil War pursuing a love of art and literature, and two other uncles Theodore himself visited repeatedly in England, where they lived in voluntary exile after the Civil War. His father had traveled in Europe several times. Then during his own childhood his father and mother had twice taken the whole family to live and travel abroad, first for a year when Theodore was ten and eleven and then again for thirteen months from before his fourteenth to just after his fifteenth birthday. In consequence Theodore had made leisurely journeys not only through Europe but in Egypt and the Near East, had stayed long periods in Rome and Paris, and had learned to speak German by living in a family in Dresden. As a boy he had thus come to know and like foreign countries and their people. After each of his marriages he had enjoyed an exten-

1

sive honeymoon in Europe. His younger brother had made a
year's trip around the world in the early eighties. His older
sister on whom he frequently depended for counsel had spent
several years in the nineties as hostess to their cousin, Roosevelt Roosevelt, Franklin Roosevelt's brother, while Rosy, as
he was called, was American Secretary of Legation in London. Theodore himself had been married in London, where
his best man had been a young British diplomat, who was
one day to become Ambassador to the United States. And
in the nineties Theodore had hurriedly made one more trip
to England and France. Hence he brought to the White
House, for whatever it was worth, a direct knowledge of the
world and its people that no previous president save the
Adamses, Jefferson, and Monroe had possessed.

Besides, through his father and sister and because of his
own reform reputation and aristocratic status, he had had
entré to the highest British political, social, and intellectual
circles on his visits in England. He came to know members
of Parliament and Cabinet officers of the eighties and younger
men who were to be leaders in Parliament while he was President of the United States. In his twenties he dined, lunched,
or spent weekends with Sir Francis Jeune, judge of the High
Court of Justice, with Lord North, with such Cabinet officers
as the Earl of Carnarvon, Viscount Goschen, Earl Stanhope,
Sir John Gathorne-Hardy, and the Duke of Devonshire, and
with numerous members of Parliament—Liberals and Conservatives, Irish members, and " radicals " like Tim Healy,
Irish land reformer who had been several times in jail as an
agitator. Goschen was First Lord of the Admiralty, and
Theodore came also to know the Fourth Lord, Baron Beresford, so that he had opportunity as a very young man to talk
on one of his favorite topics with British naval experts. He
also made the acquaintance of Joseph Chamberlain, who as
a Cabinet member was to determine policies during the Boer
War and Theodore's own Presidency. With intellectuals, too,

like John Morley, George Otto Trevelyan, and James Bryce he formed at this time lasting friendships. From these days he carried through life affection for the British and admiration for many of their traits of character, though sometimes he deplored their national policies.

From his visits in London in the eighties dated also his friendship with young American diplomat Henry White, who was to be influential when Roosevelt rose to power. John Hay, who was Secretary of State, and Joseph Choate, who was Ambassador to Britain when Roosevelt was suddenly elevated to the Presidency, he had known from boyhood as friends of his father. In the gay social circle in which he moved for seven years in Washington (1889-1895 and 1897-1898), he dined, danced, rode horseback, discussed literature, argued about the affairs of the world, and formed permanent friendships with young diplomats serving apprenticeships at their legations in Washington who were to occupy more important posts while he was President. Among these were Cecil Spring Rice and Hermann Speck von Sternburg, through whom as President he was to carry on delicate personal negotiations. In Washington, too, in 1890, he came to know Rudyard Kipling and continued to see him through the nineties. His tent-mate in the Spanish War was the British military attaché Arthur Lee, who as a member of Parliament and later of the Government under Arthur J. Balfour and David Lloyd George, was to provide Roosevelt with a private line of communication to the British Cabinet.

Definite ideas and interests, too, Roosevelt brought out of his background to high office in Washington. His keen interest in the Navy stemmed from boyish admiration for his Bulloch uncles, both officers in the Confederate Navy. Uncle Irvine had been navigation officer under Raphael Semmes on the *Alabama* when it was sunk, but he had survived to command the *Shenandoah*. Uncle Jimmy had served under David G. Farragut in the American Navy before the Civil

War, and later, in the Confederate Navy, he had won fame
running rich cargoes through the Northern blockade. He had
obtained in England the naval vessels with which the Con-
federacy preyed on Northern shipping. Dangerous exploits
of these naval uncles thrilled Theodore as a small boy, and
the men themselves became heroes to the older boy and
young man, who visited them in their English exile where
they held him spellbound with their tales of the sea. Uncle
Jimmy, in particular, he loved and respected. Henry Cabot
Lodge described James Bulloch as " an attractive old man "
with " a sort of Philip Nolan air about him which is rather
pathetic," [1] but Theodore confided later in life to Archie Butt
that his Uncle Bulloch appealed to him more than any man
he had ever met. Throughout his life he was profoundly
influenced by these Bulloch uncles. At Harvard he refused
to do a traditional " distinction thesis " because he regarded
the subjects as dull, and hence he failed to win the high
honors to which his grades would have entitled him in more
than one subject. Instead under Uncle Jimmy's spell he
began as an undergraduate a *Naval History of the War of
1812.* By the time Roosevelt was four years out of college
this undergraduate labor of love was being used as a text in
several colleges and had run through four editions of the
eight ultimately published.

Another influence was an attractive younger brother,
Elliott, whom he adored. Elliott's superior skills in boating,
boxing, riding, hunting, and markmanship stimulated Theodore to emulate his brother's exploits. And Elliott as a youth
had gone big-game hunting in India and had lived and ridden
and fought the Indians with the cavalry in Texas. Theodore
was never content until he had, like Elliott, hunted big game
and fought in a battle. As part of outgrowing asthmatic
weakness Theodore took up boxing. Too near-sighted to see
well without glasses that he could not wear at combative
sports and lacking the physical grace and dexterity of his

brother, he suffered punishment, terrible punishment, in boxing, wrestling, horseback riding, single sticks, jiu-jitsu, and
broadswords, but he courageously took the punishment and
asked for more. Whether his belief was medically sound or
not, he credited his later robustness to the strenuosity he had
cultivated. The qualities he had developed in overcoming a
sickly body and the compensation he was always seeking for
years when he had been too frail to participate in boyish
games led him to cultivate the "manly arts," made him
admire fighting men, and gave him a desire to demonstrate
his own undoubted courage. All his life he gloried in a fight,
whether of words or of fisticuffs or of bullets.

Roosevelt was an aristocrat by birth and training. He
came of people accustomed for generations to wealth and
security and used to serving the public, often in minor offices,
but always faithfully. His father, who was the greatest influence on his early life, had devoted a large share of his time
to philanthropies and to personal work with the poor. His
father's children were brought up with a strong sense of responsibility of the sort represented in settlement-house work,
organizing clubs for poor boys, and conducting religious services in slum neighborhoods. There was no questioning of
poverty or the causes of poverty; it was the *noblesse oblige*
of aristocrats that in Theodore's boyhood dominated Roosevelt relations with less fortunate people. When he entered
public life it was with a sense of the responsibility of people
of culture, especially young men with college educations, to
enter public life and help run the nation. This idea he
preached to successive generations from his undergraduate
days at Harvard through the Presidency. It was easy then,
when he became concerned about foreign policy and America's place in the world, to make the transition from this
noblesse oblige that led his father to organize Bible classes
in the slums to a belief that America should take civilization
to the rest of the world. The white race, especially English-

speaking peoples, had the same advantages among nations
that his small group of college-educated aristocrats enjoyed
in the America of Roosevelt's youth. In leading America into
world politics to see that the world was properly conducted he
was repeating on a larger stage what he had done when as a
young dude he had entered the New York legislature. There
he argued against corrupt business men and dishonest politicians in Assembly debates and organized the decent legisla-
tors to effective action and then on occasion won the respect
of bullies contemptuous of his cultivated speech and good
manners by licking them in a boxing bout. Translated to a
larger stage, the later Roosevelt was impressed with the importance of skilled but informal diplomacy, which he personally directed, and of naval might to overawe bullies
among nations, but above all with America's moral obligation as a specially advantaged nation to play a major rôle in
the world of backward peoples.

Much as Roosevelt cherished the social amenities, the
American in him disliked the forms with which officials frequently hedged themselves about. He liked dignity. He had
a keen sense of respect due his office as head of a great nation.
He disliked the cheap forms of familiarity and rebuked pre-
sumptions of intimacy where none was warranted. But arti-
ficial formalities he found absurd; indirection he employed
with difficulty. He liked directness even in diplomacy.
Protocol irked him, and when he yielded to its demands he
did so under protest. He changed the title of the home of
the President from " Executive Mansion " to " The White
House," partly because, as he explained, every state had an
executive mansion and partly because the simplicity of a
" white house " appealed to him.[2] Similarly, he objected
strenuously to the title " Excellency," by which he found the
President had traditionally been addressed. The particular
title " Excellency " was so promiscuously used that he considered it unfitting for the President of his great country.

But he felt no need of any title to win respect for his office. Something American in him was offended by titles of whatever sort. He instructed Hay to request the diplomats not to use the title " Excellency." Three months later he wrote a little petulantly to Adee, then acting Secretary of State: " Let them call me ' The President,' or ' Mr. President,' or ' Sir,' but not a title to which I have no right (And one, incidentally, given to every third rate German potentate or beaurocrat)." When Assistant Secretary Adee, who handled such matters, let the Chinese Ambassador use the title in 1908, in spite of his repeated objections, the President called Adee aside on the way out and scolded him before the Ambassador had left and then indited a letter of protest to the State Department. " It is wholly improper," he exploded, " to permit the use of a silly title like ' Excellency ' (and incidentally if titles were to be allowed at all, this title is entirely unworthy of the position of the President). Any title is silly when given the President. This title is rather unusually silly. But it is not only silly but inexcusable for the State Department . . . to permit foreign representatives to fall into the blunder of using this title. I would like an immediate explanation of why the blunder was permitted." [3]

Again maintaining the dignity of his office, Roosevelt declined to address kings and emperors as did even their highest born subjects and the presidents of other republics as " Your Majesty," but wrote to them directly in the second person as an equal. At the time of the Portsmouth Conference this intimate form of addressing kings, kaiser, czar, and mikado as equals created discussion abroad, but from Roosevelt was accepted. [4]

Roosevelt battled constantly, though not too effectively, against the inanities the State Department put into his mouth. " Old Adee," as Roosevelt called him, had been writing the formal messages of presidents ever since Arthur's day. " I am always in correspondence with all the kings, princes, potentates, and powers around the earth," Roosevelt laughed. " It is not a personal correspondence, but merely the formal way in which the head of every State congratulates the head of every other State every time anything happens that calls for congratulations. . . . I write four or five letters or telegrams every day and old Adee does that for me. I never see them," the President explained, " unless there is something of special importance. But I am always sending a congratulation, or a felicitation, or a message of condolence or sympathy to somebody in a palace somewhere or other, and old Adee does that for me." " Why, there isn't a kitten born in a palace anywhere on earth," he chuckled, " that I don't have to write a letter of congratulation to the peripatetic Tomcat that might have been its sire, and old Adee does that for me! " [5] Roosevelt, however, seriously protested from time to time against the kind of letters Adee wrote in his name. In 1902, for instance, he sent Hay four examples where Adee had not " done at all well." " It seems to me," he protested, " that . . . my answer should have been as long and as cordial as their inquiries." To one of the four, Arthur Balfour, he overrode the State Department and sent his own telegram.[6] He persistently resisted invitations from heads of state and foreign princes because he was completely unimpressed with titles and rank, was bored with the formalities involved, and knew full well that no useful negotiation would be carried on through them. So, while he did not know how to escape German Prince Henry's visit, he did delicately but firmly resist other royal visits.[7]

Old Adee once got him into serious trouble. " President Pardo, of Peru, sent me a florid South American telegram about our navy visiting Peru," Roosevelt himself told the story. " I never saw it. Adee . . . prepared one of the usual fatuous answers, into which he unwarily put the statement that I extended to him all good wishes from ' me and my people.' Jaded, overworked Root did not have his attention attracted by the phrase, and as it was a routine telegram signed my name to it and sent it off. Thereupon all the New York papers had hysteria over this as showing marked imperialistic and megalomaniac tendencies on my part." " Of course," lamented the President, amused even while annoyed, " I could not possibly explain, because to do so meant that poor President Pardo would have had his feelings deeply hurt by learning that I had never seen his telegram or my answer! " " But," Roosevelt added, " I gave orders that hereafter nobody was to sign my name but me myself." [8]

Details of precedence irked Roosevelt. When he was about to have a simple family dinner for the Kaiser's brother he wrote Hay half exasperated, half amused, " How in the name of heaven will we avoid hurting various Teutonic susceptibilities? Will the Prince take Mrs. Roosevelt, while I walk in solemn state ahead by myself? . . . I am quite clear that I ought not to walk in with my wife on one arm and my daughter on the other and the Prince somewhere alongside— but further than this I do not go." [9] He persisted in telling American diplomats to use common sense in the dress they chose and to wear whatever—by pleasing the sovereign to whom they were assigned—would make their work most effective. When Adee, who took such matters solemnly, designed an American diplomatic uniform and proffered a report on the matter Roosevelt buried it " at the bottom of the drawer that was his special cemetery for unwelcome suggestions." With some delight he broke through tradition that prevented his inviting people of equal rank together lest offense be given. For example, he boldly invited to the same dinner diplomats and justices of the Supreme Court and seated the diplomats above the justices.[10]

Roosevelt's diplomatic appointments were on the whole traditional political choices, but, even among diplomats politically selected, he was irked by shirkers and incompetents and those unduly impressed with pomp and social status.

Assistant Secretary of State Francis B. Loomis carried on some investigations in Europe trying to evolve a plan for getting better and prompter reports from legations abroad. Roosevelt encouraged representatives abroad to send full reports to the State Department or to him personally.[11] He was particularly insistent that his representatives should stay on the job even at the expense of earned leave or their own convenience when important things needed doing. Robert McCormick was moved out of St. Petersburg and ultimately out of the service because Roosevelt could not get information out of him.[12] And in his own capital, when business was to be done, the President summoned foreign diplomats accredited to him to conferences without compunction even at inconvenient hours.[13]

Whenever Roosevelt could, he broke through the stiff, formal procedures that protocol required. Thus after he had formally received the credentials of German Ambassador Speck von Sternburg he took him shooting, tramping, and horseback riding on Long Island. Archie Butt recorded on the occasion of the reception of a special ambassador and an Imperial Prince from China: " The President read similar complimentary remarks prepared by Adee. After this formality the President made an extemporary address of welcome which really meant something." [14] When Jonkheer John Loudon was received as Minister from the Netherlands, the President read the response " prepared for him to say parrot-like." Then, " both looking very foolish," Archie Butt described the scene, " the President took him by the hand and said what he really wanted to say, that he knew the Dutch, that he could even sing some baby Dutch songs which had been handed down for generations in the Roosevelt family. . . . He repeated some of them . . . [and] the new Minister . . . almost danced with enjoyment." [15] When Jules Jusserand was presented, Roosevelt himself wrote, " Having the diplomats presented to me is an awful bore. . . . But this was a different matter. I kept him talking half an hour. Among other things we discussed [Thomas R.] Lounsbury's ' Shakespeare and Voltaire.' " [16]   Indeed, Roosevelt once shocked his military aide Archie Butt by inviting him to " draw up a chair " to chat with a Japanese ambassador and prince with whom he was chatting informally as he would have done in his own home.[17] Once he interrupted a luncheon at which the Swiss Minister, Fernand du Martheray, was a guest to demonstrate certain jiu-jitsu holds by throwing that diplomat one way and then another on the floor beside the luncheon table to everyone's amusement.[18]

While they were visiting the kings and emperors of Europe in 1910 Mr. and Mrs. Roosevelt won perhaps as much respect and acclaim among European aristocrats by an episode in Copenhagen as by anything they did on the whole tour. Somehow the trunks were delayed and Mrs. Roosevelt had to appear at a Court dinner in her traveling dress. She did so with such grace, poise, and complete freedom from embarrassment that the marshall of the Danish Court exclaimed in amazement that she was " vraiment royale." [19]

Roosevelt's informal hikes, rides, and swims on which he took the personal representatives of the heads of foreign governments were famous. Roosevelt got keen amusement out of taking the pompous younger brother of the Kaiser in immaculate riding clothes for a two-hour ride through the rain and mud of a Rock Creek storm until the mud-besplattered, drenched prince was a sorry sight.[20] Prince Henry proved sportsmanlike. Some, on the other hand, took it grimly. Some like Sir Michael Herbert and Sir Mortimer Durand had not the physical vigor to take it at all, though Sir Mortimer tried. For those ambassadors who could, however, there was an intimacy in diplomacy based on hikes, swims, and tennis with the head of the state that was unusual and useful. Speck von Sternburg, the German ambassador, and Jules Jusserand, the ambassador of France, played tennis, swam

the icy Potomac in springtime, scrambled through the mud
of Rock Creek Park, and scaled cliffs with an exuberant
president. This made possible an effectiveness of international negotiation that far transcended relationships of the
sort characterized by formal speeches written for president
and ambassador by " Old Adee " and his counterpart at a
legation.

Ambassador Meyer, in Russia, only with some difficulty
persuaded the President not to commit his blunt, indiscreet,
honest comments to the diplomatic pouch for Russian secret
police to read before they reached Meyer. Between them
they did work out codes and special couriers to maintain the
sanctity of their communications into and out of Russia.[21]
But generally Roosevelt spoke forthrightly, openly, and often
vigorously to foreign diplomats used to hypocrisies, circum-
locutions, and inane politeness. Indeed, Secretary of War
Root wrote: Roosevelt's successful handling " of very delicate diplomatic situations . . . has been so marked, in view
of the President's extraordinary candor and directness, that
it rather tends to create an impression that the traditional
arts of diplomacy, with all their finesse and circumlocution,
involve a good deal of humbug, after all." [22]

Roosevelt's and his wife's tastes and values account in
large part for the peculiar characteristics of Roosevelt's
methods. A combination of blunt directness and social graciousness, a mixture of aristocratic distinction and democratic disregard of caste, a blending of simplicity in taste and
regard for proprieties, and an amalgamation of his own love
of all sorts of humankind and his wife's concern about good
breeding together gave to the White House while the Roosevelts occupied it and to the conduct of foreign policy while
Theodore handled it the peculiar Roosevelt quality. In the
White House the social proprieties were rigorously observed,
the guest lists carefully scrutinized. People lacking character
were scrupulously excluded, social climbers were repelled,

and ungentlemanly conduct was firmly penalized. Yet Mrs. Roosevelt's code included, without regard to economic status or social position, graciousness that charmed her husband's friends, friends of great variety, sometimes exotic, frequently unused to the social climate to which Mrs. Roosevelt was born. Her code demanded conscientious performance without condescension of all the obligations of a President's wife however distasteful some of those duties were to a woman of her class and tastes. Coupled with the concern for the proprieties and the social perfection that Mrs. Roosevelt brought to the White House were a simplicity and freedom from ostentation that both Roosevelts cherished. Theodore and Edith Roosevelt accepted living in the White House as completely natural; not since the John Quincy Adamses had the White House been occupied by people born aristocrats. Out of their comfortable sense of being at home in a mansion that has overawed most occupants, the Roosevelts brought a fulness of enjoyment that the White House has rarely known. The President's residence became the home of warm-hearted people with great capacities for friendship, who entertained amazing numbers of guests without losing the quality of intimacy of a happy and hospitable home.[23] Without this setting in which to conduct business with representatives of foreign powers, Roosevelt could not have handled his foreign policy in the manner that became Rooseveltian. Simple folk felt comfortable and at ease; yet no foreign aristocrat failed to recognize aristocracy whose qualities he understood. Roosevelt needed no diplomatic forms to add dignity or cover social inadequacies or protect against social blunders. He managed therefore to deal with foreign problems and foreign agents as man to man, friend to friend, with the directness of a North Dakotan cowboy sheathed under the grace of aristocratic manners. His approach sometimes offended, often startled, but frequently pleased men used to artificialities and lack of candor. In any case, it was effective.

chapter **I**

ROOSEVELT *and the Rise of*
American Imperialism

During the last decade of the nineteenth century, Americans were making momentous decisions that would affect their nation into a distant future. The century had seen nations long established intensify their national loyalties and prides and, in competition with other national states, seek to strengthen their national power. Italy and Germany had been forged by unification into new nations with newly developed national loyalties. Japan had emerged from centuries of seclusion to become a self-conscious national state. Eastern Europe was seething with national aspirations of subject peoples. And in the United States, a civil war had determined beyond further argument that a federation of states had evolved into a nation proud of its new strength. In Europe national rivalries had led to alliances and counter-alliances. Rival groups of nations were formed for mutual protection. Occasionally one nation became too ambitious and the others combined to redress the balance. But, once Napoleon's imperial ambitions were disposed of, peoples bound together by cultural, economic, and political ties remained relatively peaceful through the nineteenth century

so long as they faced each other from behind clearly defined
boundaries as nations. Indeed, in the mid-nineteenth century
an anti-imperialist reaction was strong and, in some European powers, dominant.

Now, however, new forces were arousing in these nations
ambitions to expand their political and economic, perhaps
too their cultural, control beyond their national boundaries
as far as their energies and opportunities permitted. A struggle began among newly industrialized nations for the power
and prestige that would come from dominating distant parts
of the world. Earlier, European nations had overflowed their
boundaries and established colonies of their own people in
distant waste places of the world, notably in the Western
Hemisphere and the Pacific. Some of those colonies had
asserted their independence and become national states. A
few examples of the old colonialism still survived under
British rule in Canada, Australia, and New Zealand, and
America had absorbed into itself colony after colony of this
older type in adjacent areas until there was no more con-
tiguous land to colonize. The new imperialism was, however,
of a different order, based on industrial rivalry, on conflicting,
economic nationalisms inflated to world proportions, and on
intellectual ferment that produced exciting new ideas like the
teachings of Herbert Spencer.

The world's sparsely inhabited areas that could support
Western Europeans had been claimed. The new empires consisted of subject peoples with their own cultures, religions,
laws, languages, and customs, often living in great conges-
tion. One day the new imperialism would stimulate the
nationalist aspirations of these subject peoples into far-reaching revolts against imperialistic rule, but at the turn of the
century when America had to make her decision the rival
imperial powers were vigorously intensifying their rivalries
and their chauvinisms in distant parts of the already crowded
imperial world. They were competing for markets, for the

right to exploit resources of thickly settled backward populations, too weak to resist them. They were seeking influence that would grant special privileges, or were actually seizing territory so that they might preserve order, collect taxes, grab natural resources, employ cheap labor not available at home, make speculative profits, and exclude rival powers. Basically they were striving to build up might and prestige in what, above all, was a struggle for world power. The possibilities of conflict in distant places over imperial possessions far exceeded the dangers of conflict between rival nationalisms living side by side, each within its own borders. Britain and Holland and France had made their entries upon the imperial stage earlier than most and were eager to retain the leading rôles they had won and to extend their power and influence. Newer nations like Germany and Italy sought to emulate the older empires. Thickly populated Japan had to move overseas if she was to expand at all. At the end of the century she was unhappy and somewhat outraged because European nations that had forced her to give up imperial gains of a victorious war over China were now moving in to appropriate to themselves the very things they had forced her to yield. And Russia and the United States had gradually extended themselves to the limits of their natural boundaries and would have to move into foreign parts if they expanded further.[1]

It was at this juncture that Theodore Roosevelt and the United States simultaneously came of age. America had to choose what course she would pursue. The alternatives were not entirely clear, and the people of America never really consciously decided what they wanted to do. Yet as the obvious trend toward becoming an imperial power in real or potential conflict with other empires emerged, many Americans foresaw dangers and opposed steps that were leading us into imperialism. Anti-imperialist sentiment was powerful but ineffective, lacking as it did a positive and appealing program. Cleveland as President blocked the ambitions of expansionists. Former President Harrison, by 1900, was opposed to imperialism as sponsored by many of his fellow-Republicans in the campaign of that year.[2] William Jennings Bryan tried to organize an effective political opposition, but, in part because he insisted upon confusing the cheap-money issue with anti-imperialism and partly because he was Bryan, he was defeated and with him perhaps the best chance to dam the tide of American imperialism. Conservative Republican Senator John C. Spooner of Wisconsin wrote, as we went to war with Spain over Cuba, " I dread war, and, looking beyond to-morrow, I dread what is to follow war. . . . I fear Cuba having been rescued from Spain, may more than once demand rescue from the Cubans." [3] Charles J. Bonaparte, later a member of Roosevelt's Cabinet, assured a Danish friend in 1902 that nobody but a few " Jingoes " wanted more island possessions. " The acquisition of the Phillipines [*sic*]," he said, " has cost us a great deal of money; and any benefits which have resulted from it to this country, are, as yet, imperceptible to the naked eye." [4]

Tom Reed, popular and powerful Speaker of the House of Representatives, broke with his best friends in the Republican party and lost his chance for the Presidency in 1897, partly because from conviction he opposed the imperialism of his Republican friends. Carl Schurz, Moorfield Storey, Charles Francis Adams, Jr., and a host of men deeply concerned with domestic reform felt that arbitrary rule over other peoples not only violated democratic principles of self-government but endangered democracy and freedom at home.[5] Indeed Storey felt Roosevelt as President " left an indelible stain on the honor of my country." " His course," wrote Storey, " is fraught with the very gravest danger to human liberty." He was taking the country downward on a course that could be retraced " only at a very great cost to all." [6] Intellectuals, too, like President Eliot, Professor

Charles Eliot Norton, and Roosevelt's old professor at Harvard, the philosopher William James, spoke out vigorously against imperialism.[7] Many in the business community, cautious, conservative, and conscious of dangers in so sharp a break with the past, opposed the trend of events and the new foreign policy. Indeed, business leaders and bankers among Henry Cabot Lodge's constituents kept him busy answering their protests, calming their fears, and arguing with them over his imperialist activities.[8] Henry Lee Higginson, the Boston financier, disputed vigorously with Lodge over what he and Roosevelt were doing.[9] And Andrew Carnegie helped finance the anti-imperialists.[10] Thoughtful men, publicists and economists, there were who analyzed the proposals and arguments of the imperialists and sounded warning. Thus James Bryce, recognized British authority on America, warned America of the dangers of expansionism.[11] Thus, too, in America Paul S. Reinsch, later to be Wilson's minister to China, published in 1900 in this country a critical book entitled *World Politics*, and in England John A. Hobson's *Imperialism* appeared in 1902.

The anti-imperialists argued that the modern sort of colony greatly increased the cost of national defense and administration without proportionately enhancing overseas trade and domestic prosperity. They pointed out that what profits empire did bring benefited only a few businessmen directly involved and the officials who won lucrative jobs administering the colonies, while the greatly increased cost of armed services and administration was borne by all the people. They maintained that political control or preponderant influence was not necessary to profitable trade, that trade was often more important with other nations than with a nation's own colonies.[12]

In addition, the anti-imperialists warned that imperialism threatened democracy. They called attention to the incongruity of democratic political principles at home and undemocratic rule over the other peoples abroad. Bryce did not believe that "a democratic government intended to be worked by educated men of the best European stock, whose ancestors have enjoyed freedom and been accustomed to self-government for centuries," could rule this new type of possession satisfactorily. In Cuba or Hawaii, Bryce warned, the United States would either have to set up "among an inferior and dissimilar population its own democratic institutions or so far depart from all its traditions as to attempt to govern that population and its own citizens abroad by despotic methods." Either alternative would involve "danger to its new subjects and injury" to the United States.[13] Anti-imperialist writers cautioned that overseas power would tend toward greater centralization and hence power for government at home and toward power, too, for certain special interests favored by government in extending controls overseas. Prophetically the anti-imperialists predicted that progressive-minded groups in their preoccupation with national glory and power abroad would neglect the regulation of home affairs, and social betterment and improvement of politics would suffer. Men busied with overseas concerns would even lose interest in maintaining liberty at home.[14]

One by one the anti-imperialists denied the advantages claimed for imperialism. By a grim analysis of the realities of imperial rule Hobson rejected the scientific argument, "survival of the fittest," the "spread of civilization" theory, and the religious and humanitarian defenses of imperialism.[15] Prophetically, too, the anti-imperialists foretold that imperial rule would be short-lived, for it would arouse nationalism and aspirations for self-government among subject peoples, who would one day rise and throw the foreign rulers out.[16] No stable balance of power was possible among rival imperialisms as it had been among nations, these opponents of imperialism felt. The alternatives, predicted Reinsch, were gradual federation into a world community or unrestricted competition with the final preponderance of one state that would overpower and absorb all others.[17]

" Is humanity the helpless victim of historical forces, or can it consciously modify and control its destiny? " asked Reinsch. " World politics," he warned, " appear to be entering a stage where grim, silent, passionate forces will hurry humanity along, like leaves in a torrent." " Conscious purpose and reasoned action " seemed to Reinsch to be proving " but a small factor in the workings of ' destiny.' " " But," he asked, " as the human will and intellect has tamed the fierce powers of the lightning and the storm, can it not master . . . the tumultuous energies that are now stirring its own deeper nature and breaking forth into the battle cry of action, conquest, expansion, glory, and might? " Could not the publicist analyze the nature of these forces and " point out the dangers that follow in their train "? [18]

It was the answer to these questions that Theodore Roosevelt was helping provide by his very active participation in the formulation of American foreign policy in the nineties. It is the answers to these questions and Roosevelt's part in determining them that I want now to pursue. Roosevelt and his friends symbolized for America these new forces in the world, and their attitudes portended the future and help explain how and why America entered into the struggle for world power that has led much of the world to disaster and is not yet ended.

Alone Roosevelt could have accomplished little. But, as a member of a group of men strategically placed to make themselves felt, he became a leader of the movement to win for America her place in the world. Among these articulate men Henry Cabot Lodge, with a new Ph.D., had been a young instructor at Harvard when Theodore was an undergraduate, but they had become friends only in the presidential campaign of 1884. By 1889 Lodge had gone to Congress and Roosevelt was Civil Service Commissioner. Henry

Adams, whom Roosevelt knew at Harvard, had now built a house in Lafayette Square where Roosevelt and his friends dropped in to run the world over cups of Adams tea. Henry's brother Brooks came often to Washington and moved in the Roosevelt-Lodge inner circle. In 1889 he had married Nannie Lodge's sister.[19]

In March, 1890, the Roosevelts and the Kiplings became acquainted in Washington. Mrs. Roosevelt found Kipling precisely what she had expected, but her husband, who had expected much, was disappointed.[20] Strangely, in view of their later mutual admiration, Roosevelt at first reacted unpleasantly to Rudyard Kipling. This was partly because he and Mrs. Roosevelt found the Kipling manners bad, but partly because of Kipling's offensive contempt for America. In 1892 Roosevelt hoped it was true that Kipling had been barred from the Players Club. " There is no earthly reason he should not call New York a pig trough," Roosevelt conceded; " but there is also no reason why he should be allowed to associate with the pigs." Roosevelt feared Kipling was a cad.[21] He found Kipling lacking in breeding and his wife " dreadful " and in 1892 he struck out at Kipling in an article in the *Cosmopolitan.*[22] But he did like Kipling's writings and considered him a " genius." [a] [23] By 1895 he could enjoy sparring with Kipling [b] and take a fall out of him now and then. " I have come round to your way of looking at Kipling," he wrote Brander Matthews. It now seemed preposterous to mind what Kipling said about America. Roosevelt had come to regard him as " a pleasant little man, bright, nervous, voluble," still " rather underbred." [24] Kipling on his part ad-

[a] In 1890, 1893, and 1895, he was admiringly calling the attention of Brander Matthews and in 1892 that of Spring Rice to stories and poems by Kipling. In 1897 he suggested John Hay read " a fine, strong poem " of Kipling and told Hay how good *Captains Courageous* was. In 1899 he sent Lodge an advance copy of a Kipling poem that was " poor poetry, but good sense from the expansionist standpoint."

[b] Now he had him to dinner with Hay and Rockhill.

mired Roosevelt and advised Roosevelt to give up politics
and become a colonial administrator since as such he would
have a great future. Kipling felt Roosevelt was a bigger man
than his people understood or, at this time, knew how to
use.[25]

Among Roosevelt's imperialistic intimates, too, in Washington, was professional diplomat William W. Rockhill, expert on Far Eastern affairs, who served as Chief Clerk, Third
Assistant, and finally as Assistant Secretary of State between
1893 and 1897.[26] In Washington Roosevelt came to know
William E. Chandler, who, as Secretary of the Navy under
Chester A. Arthur, had fathered the modern navy and was
now old guard senator from New Hampshire. Another asso-
ciate was Senator William P. Frye of Maine, who shared
Chandler's views. Among Roosevelt's close friends were
Benjamin F. Tracy, Harrison's Secretary of the Navy,
Charles H. Davis, Lodge's brother-in-law, then commander
in the Navy and chief of naval intelligence, and retired
Admiral Stephen B. Luce, a strong supporter of the Mahan
point of view.[27] In 1887, while himself giving a lecture on the
War of 1812, Roosevelt met Alfred T. Mahan at the Naval
War College where Mahan was stationed as instructor. In
1890 and again in 1893 Roosevelt reviewed in the *Atlantic
Monthly*, in 1894 in the *Political Science Quarterly*, and in
1897 in the *New York Sun* Mahan's books on sea power,
which he praised in highest terms.[28] By 1890 Lodge, Roosevelt, and Mahan had begun exchanging views. In 1890
Roosevelt, Lodge, Luce, and Davis combined to try to save
Mahan from assignment to sea duty so that he could continue full-time his propaganda for expansion. " Oh what
idiots we have had to deal with," Roosevelt exploded to
Mahan when the Navy Department insisted upon sending
him to sea.

During the first half of the second Cleveland administration Roosevelt, as Civil Service Commissioner, stayed on in

Washington and was a vigorous member of a group critical of Cleveland; and, even after he became Police Commissioner in New York, he kept in touch with Lodge, Rockhill, Hay, and the Adamses. He corresponded with them, entertained them at dinners in his sister's home in New York, and saw them on visits to the Lodges in Washington. Eliminated from the diplomatic service by the Democratic President, Henry White in 1893 joined the group and his views delighted Roosevelt.[29] In 1895 Richard Olney became Cleveland's Secretary of State and Rockhill was promoted to be Assistant Secretary, both of them already adopted into the Roosevelt circle. " In spite of your Democratic politics," he wrote Rockhill, " I *have* to be proud of Olney and yourself." [30]

Chandler and Frye, and eventually Lodge and several others of Roosevelt's friends, were powerful members of the Senate, and Lodge, Mahan, and Roosevelt reached an élite following with books and essays. Mahan lectured to naval officers and published articles for the general public and supplied other jingoes with arguments so phrased as to catch popular attention. Charles A. Dana of the *New York Sun* was a powerful aid. Two secretaries of State, a secretary of the Navy, an assistant secretary of State, and an assistant secretary of the Navy were strategically placed to help. Collectively these men were a potent influence in giving American participation in world affairs a nationalist and imperialist cast.

What was it that led Roosevelt and his friends to urge an expansionist rôle upon us? A number of fundamental preconceptions can be identified, along with a host of associated ideas. First, the imperialists were strong nationalists and were impelled by national pride. " We're a gr-reat people," said Mr. Dooley with the Roosevelt sort of nationalist in mind. " We ar-re that. An' th' best iv it is, we know we ar-re." [31] Roosevelt was determined that we should put the

interests and honor of the United States above those of
other nations. He wanted therefore to drive every European
power " off this continent." " I am not hostile," he explained,
" to any European power in the abstract. I am simply
American first and last, and therefore hostile to any power
which wrongs us." [32] When his Catholic friend Maria Storer
wrote him that the Pope was angry with Archbishop Ireland
for not stopping the War with Spain, Roosevelt replied ve-
hemently: " I would resent as an impertinence any European,
whether Pope, Kaiser, Czar or President, daring to be angry
with an American because of his action or nonaction as regards any question between America and an outside nation.
. . . If any man, clerical or lay, Bishop, Archbishop, priest,
or civilian, was in any way guilty of treasonable practices
with Spain during our war, he should be shot or hung. . . .
But I cannot . . . recognize for a single moment the right of
any European to so much as think that there is need of
defense or excuse in such a case." [33] It was his tense nationalism that led him at home to attack Jefferson Davis as a
traitor as late as 1885.[34] His nationalism also explains his
contempt for Thomas Jefferson, his attacks on Jefferson's
" cowardly infamy." It explains, too, his charge of " tortuous
intrigues against Washington " that thwarted his " wishes
. . . in regard to Genêt " and of complicity in French intrigues against our Western lands. Such contempt did he
have for a man who allowed the country to remain militarily
weak and tried to solve international problems by other
methods than by superior force that he could never be fair
to Jefferson. Besides, Jefferson did not uphold what Roosevelt considered the national honor and that prevented Roosevelt's being proud of his country under Jefferson.[35] Roosevelt's initial antagonism to Kipling, too, as has been noted,
was created chiefly by Kipling's affronts to his national pride
by outspoken contempt for America.[36] James Bryce laid
the imperialism of American expansionists to a sort of pride.

He found the objections in 1897 to American acquisition of Cuba or Hawaii so obvious that he was forced to conclude that such expansionists as Roosevelt were motivated by " the notion that it is a fine thing for a great country to have vast territories, and to see marked as her own, on the map of the world, dominions beyond her natural borders." [37] Expansion to a " masterful " people is " not a matter of regret," Roosevelt insisted, " but of pride." [38]

Second, Roosevelt was convinced, as are many nationalists in most countries, that his country would never act unjustly or wrongly. Hence, whatever position America took was right. American expansion became part of a crusade for the right. Consequently, whoever at home or abroad opposed American expansion was morally derelict. In Roosevelt's case this moral purpose was unusually strong. Carl Schurz said: Roosevelt's conviction that the honor of the country demands his continuance in office leads him to twist facts in a manner that we would have to call " disingenuous, did we not think that he believes them to be true." He seems to have the impression, Schurz declared, " that everything apt to promote his chances [of reëlection] is good and every adverse influence wicked, and that, therefore, those who decide to vote against him—about one-half the voters of the United States, more or less—are unpatriotic citizens and bad Americans." [39] Thus his and Lodge's quarrel with political opponents in Massachusetts in 1905 became a matter of ethical principles and anyone that opposed him and Lodge showed " a lack of moral sense." [40] Thus, in his disagreements with the Senate, senators that vigorously opposed him were " demagogues " or " crooks." [41] Carl Schurz, when he opposed imperialism, became in Roosevelt's eyes a " prattling foreigner " and Roosevelt would not read what he shrieked or prattled.[42] " What is wrong when done by others is right when it is done by him or his friends," Harry Thurston Peck declared in analyzing his administration as he left the White House.[43] He not only told the people but believed himself in 1912 that we were at Armageddon and that he and his friends were "battling for the Lord." He charged his old and once trusted friends, Elihu Root and William H. Taft, with theft and violation of public morals. " Roosevelt is as sincere as he is intemperate," wrote George W. Smalley, a British journalist who had followed his career for two decades. " Let us admit, and regret, that he honestly believes it impossible to differ from him honestly." [44] Similarly, in international affairs he could not imagine a situation where there could be any justification in opposing America. He wished to make America so strong that, whatever she did, no one would dare oppose the " right " by trying to thwart her. " Peace," he said, " comes not to the coward or to the timid, but to him who will do no wrong and is too strong to allow others to wrong him." [45] In short, Roosevelt believed only in " just wars," but any war America fought would be " just." The war with Spain he pronounced " the most absolutely righteous foreign war " of the nineteenth century.[46] So morality, America's idea of international morality, became an important element in the foreign policy of the Roosevelt expansionists. Their effective advocacy greatly strengthened in our diplomacy the force of moral conviction with which many Americans tend to face public issues. They accustomed many admirers to believing American policies always moral and opponents' aims immoral in international affairs, however reprehensible American actions might occasionally seem to non-Americans.

Third, Roosevelt shared with other imperialists a sense of Anglo-Saxon superiority to peoples over whom we were extending our rule and also superiority to some of those with whose imperialism we would compete. Roosevelt's sense of superiority was not the usual sort of racism preached by the more extreme leaders of his own day, still less the brand found on the Pacific Coast of the United States or in the

American South, or yet in Nazi Germany. Roosevelt had studied under John W. Burgess at Columbia and this may have introduced him to a belief in the special ability of Anglo-Saxons to rule backward peoples. But his attitudes toward race were not peculiar to Burgess and Columbia; there were many others that believed in Anglo-Saxonism. In the nineties he, like others then and now, used the term " race " loosely. Sometimes he used it to describe the peoples of Europe and America and Semitic West Asia as one race and Orientals or Africans as another. Sometimes he considered Anglo-Saxons, Germans, and Russians as distinct races, at other times Anglo-Saxons and Germans as together constituting a race.* Again it was " the English speaking race." Sometimes he spoke as if the English and Americans constituted separate races. In his Romanes Lecture at Oxford in 1910 he defined " the so-called white race " as " the group of peoples living in Europe, who undoubtedly have a certain kinship of blood, who profess the Christian religion, and trace back their culture to Greece and Rome." [48] In 1896 he quarreled with much of the book but expressed enthusiasm for the portion of Gustave Le Bon's *Les premières civilisations* in which Le Bon described the superior qualities of an Anglo-American " race " that was destined to rule the world.[49] In whatever form Roosevelt used the term, the " race " to which he belonged was superior to others and he took pride in his group. Preoccupied with the question, he asked the *North American Review* in 1895 to let him review a new edition of Benjamin Kidd's *Social Evolution,* which he pronounced crude, dogmatic, and superficial but suggestive and worth pondering, though its conclusions

---

* " Racial affinity," protested Reinsch, a leading critic of Rooseveltian theories, "would not be sufficiently strong to insure continued political unity, if any powerful material interest should arise to separate the . . . nations. Race is scarcely a sufficient bond for the unity of a single national state, much less for an international alliance of many such states." [47]

were usually wrong.[50] In 1907 he raised the question whether
"there really *is* an ' Aryan ' race," "Aryan speech, yes;
Aryan race—well, I am *very* doubtful." [51] In 1911, still intrigued with race concepts, he reviewed Houston S. Chamberlain's *Foundations of the Nineteenth Century* critically
and dubbed much of the book " bedlamite passion and non-
sanity." He quarreled with Chamberlain's loose use of " Teuton " and " Aryan." He found it ridiculous for Chamberlain
to postulate Aryan, or better still, Teutonic blood for everyone he admired: David and Paul from the Bible, for instance,
whom he made Aryans, and Dante and Leonardo da Vinci
whom Chamberlain made Teutons. Chamberlain was a
" fantastic extremist." His " hatreds cover a wide gamut,"
Roosevelt explained. " They include Jews, Darwinists,
the Roman Catholic Church, the people of Southern Europe,
Peruvians, Semites and an odd variety of literary men and
historians." Roosevelt found " the extremist whose doctrines
are based upon foolish hatred . . . even more unlovely than
an extremist whose doctrines are based upon foolish benevolence." He found Chamberlain, however, " in brilliant lapses
into sanity " capable of " noble thought " and a " lofty
manner "; yet he disagreed with most of Chamberlain's
views.[52] Actually, to Roosevelt and many of his contemporaries " race " was no more than a loose term for any given
group, distinguished by its color, language, degree of industrial development, or national culture, to be used as the
situation demanded.

In reviewing Pearson's *National Life and Character* in
1894 he accepted the concept of white superiority and spoke
even of the Chinese with their ancient culture as an inferior
race. He was concerned about the well-being of the white
race. He admitted he had once taken " the educated view of
the Chinese question," but he had come to see that the
Chinese had to be kept out of America because " his presence
would be ruinous to the white race." [53] He came to feel that

even the Japanese, whom he admired, could not be admitted to this country.[54] In 1897 he told James Bryce that we ought to take Hawaii " in the interests of the White race." [55] Democracy, he thought, had justified itself by keeping " for the white race the best portions of the new world's surface." In 1894 he justified Chinese exclusion by the comment: " Democracy, with the clear instinct of race selfishness, saw the race foe, and kept out the dangerous alien." " Democracy, with much clearness of vision, has seen that his presence is ruinous to the white race," Roosevelt explained.[56] In 1908 he wrote Arthur Balfour of the necessity of keeping the white man in America and Australia " out of home contact " with Orientals.[57] At Oxford in 1910 he declared that the period of supremacy of the white race had seen an "unexampled spread of civilized mankind over the world," an " unexampled advance of man's dominion over nature," and " a literary and artistic activity to be matched in but one previous epoch." [58]

Yet he was unlike many racists in that he laid these differences of " race " to acquired characteristics and to the effect of geographic environment. In the common parlance of his day, he talked of Latin Americans contemptuously as Dagoes, but his contempt was not for their Latin origin. It was provoked by the weakness and inability of these particular Latins to rule themselves effectively. Again like most Americans, he felt superior to Filipinos and Chinese. One of his strongest words of contumely was to dub a weak incompetent a Chinese. He talked of the Chinese as a backward race. Yet, though they were of the same color and were ethnically similar to the Chinese, he felt as much admiration for the Japanese who were strong and efficient as he felt contempt for the weakness and inefficiency of the Chinese. Japan, he pointed out, though " in blood and in culture " as " remote as possible " from " our ancestral descent," and though " keeping most of what was strongest in her ancient

character and traditions, has assimilated with curious com-
pleteness most of the characteristics that have given power
and leadership to the West." [59] " What wonderful people the
Japanese are," he wrote Spring Rice in 1905. " They are
quite as remarkable industrially as in warfare. . . . I believe
that Japan will take its place as a great civilized power of a
formidable type." [60]

Roosevelt saw no chance of the white man's overthrowing
the darker races in the tropics, permanently holding them
under control, or materially changing the culture of China or
India; but he had no fear these other peoples could overwhelm the whites in their own habitat in the temperate zone.
And he did not share the fear of a " yellow peril " that
haunted Mahan, the Kaiser, and others of his contemporaries. The Chinese he felt might push southward and drive
Western Europeans out of Indo-China, Indonesia, and Ma-
laya in the tropics where Europeans could not thrive, but he
thought to the north of China where the environment was
propitious the Russians would not merely hold their own but
would expand into Northern China. [61] In so far as he feared
the Japanese he feared them not because of their race but for
the same reasons he feared Germans and Russians—because
they were an economically powerful, militarily effective rival
power.

Again unlike many promoters of racism of his day he did
not regard the " backward people " as permanently or inherently inferior. Those that regarded Asiatics as inherently
inferior he reminded of our own past. " As for their having
a yellow skin," he recalled, " if we go back two thousand
years we will find that to the Greek and Roman the most
dreaded and yet in a sense the most despised barbarian was
the white-skinned, blue-eyed and red or yellow-haired barbarian of the North—the men from whom you and I in a
large part derive our blood. It could not seem possible to
the Greek or Roman . . . that this northern barbarian should

ever become part of the civilized world. . . . The racial
difference seemed too great." [62] He doubted whether China
would soon become a modern nation as Japan had. He
believed it would be a matter of a thousand years before
Africans could develop high forms of civilization or become
dangerous to the white race. Like many contemporaries, he
believed in the doctrine of progress widely subscribed to in
his America. Yet unlike many other Americans he did not
limit the possibility of progress to white men but expected
Negroes, Filipinos, and Chinese ultimately to develop, too,
however slowly. Even if they did rise more rapidly than he
anticipated, he still would not fear them, for, while they were
backward, they were too impotent to be a threat, and, he
pointed out, " if any one of the tropical races ever does reach
a pitch of industrial and military prosperity which makes it
a menace to European and American countries, it will almost
necessarily mean that this nation has itself become civilized
in the process; and we shall then simply be dealing with
another civilized nation of non-aryan blood . . . without any
thought of their being ethnically distinct." [63]

Finally, in Roosevelt's race attitudes there was no element
of contempt for an individual member of a race who had
attained qualities superior to other members of a backward
people. So thoroughly imbued was he with what he considered the American quality of individualism, such respect
did he have for the sacredness of the individual personality
that he judged separate men as individual human beings, not
as members of a class, a race, or a nation. So any particular
Negro, Chinese, or Filipino who displayed qualities he admired was to him an admirable person and an equal. When
he spoke of national groups, or races, or peoples he spoke in
general and classed each as a group in a category superior
or inferior to other groups. Individuals, though, he judged
as individuals. In 1894 and 1895 he opposed pressures put
on the Civil Service Commission by the American Protective

Association.[64] He congratulated Senator George F. Hoar on
his attack on the A.P.A. " If I could be of the least assistance
to you in your battle with the A.P.A., I will esteem it a favor
to have you call upon me. I will write or speak at any time or
any place you think best. . . . It is the fight of all others I
should care to be in." [65] If men " act as Americans," he told
a Boston audience, " it is an outrage to discriminate against
them in any way on account of creed or race." [66] " The
A.P.A. business is thoroughly despicable," he wrote a postal
employee in 1894. " To me," he declared, " the question of
doing away with all race and religious bigotry in this country
. . . is the most important of all." [67] He publicly attacked
the A.P.A. in an article in the *Forum* of 1894.[68] This fight
against racial and religious bigotry he continued in the police
commission.[69] All his life he prided himself on holding no bias
in personal relations and on making no distinction of race,
creed, color, or national origin in judging a man's worth.

Yet Roosevelt and his friends did firmly believe that the
spread of English-speaking people meant attainment of world
peace and the spread of civilization, and this belief dominated his views on foreign policy. " The object lesson " of
expansion is, he declared, " that peace must be brought about
in the world's waste spaces. . . . Peace cannot be had until
the civilized nations have expanded in some shape over the
barbarous nations." This " means the co-operation of the
civilized peoples of the earth to that end, whatever the cost
or time." [70] In 1897 he wrote Bryce that " England would be
doing her duty as a civilized nation if she overthrew the
Mahdists and opened up the Sudan." [71] England's rule in
India and Egypt had of course benefited England, but it had
benefited Egypt and India still more, and " most of all, it . . .
[had] advanced the cause of civilization." [72] " It is to the
interest of civilization," Roosevelt wrote Henry White, " that
the English speaking race should be dominant in South

Africa, exactly as it is . . . that the United States . . . should be dominant in the Western Hemisphere." [73]

This superior civilization that Roosevelt associated with English-speaking people is a little hard to define from his speeches and writings. In it, however, was a strong mixture of manly virtues, of industrial development, of power to defend oneself effectively; in it, too, were an ability to provide orderly government, an inherited set of political institutions superior to those of anyone else, and respect for free individuals, and for the various freedoms won through the centuries by Western Europeans. Roosevelt had studied at Harvard and Columbia in a day when scholars were tracing our institutions back of Magna Carta into the forests of Germany. He always understood how long it had taken to attain the English-speaking civilization and he profoundly respected the heritage. Its preservation and extension was in his mind the greatest attainable good, even if it had to be extended by force.

For " backward people " Theodore Roosevelt had no particular concern when they stood in the way of " civilization." In 1915 he justified his having ignored the wishes of the Colombians, who owned the territory where he wished to build a canal, by explaining that the Colombians were not a superior but an inferior people. Sensitive lest our action toward Colombia be compared in 1915 to Germany's violation of the rights of Belgium, he explained that " the Belgians were as ' superior ' as the Germans," whereas " to talk of Colombia as a responsible Power to be dealt with as we would deal with Holland or Belgium or Switzerland or Denmark is a mere absurdity." " The analogy " of Colombians, he insisted, " is with a group of Sicilian or Calabrian bandits. . . . You could no more make an agreement with the Colombian rulers than you could nail currant jelly to the wall." " The Canal," he explained, " was for the benefit of the entire world. Should the blackmailing greed of the Bogotá ring

stand in the way of civilization? . . . I determined that I
would do what ought to be done without regard to them." [74]

Yet Roosevelt was not unmindful of " backward " peoples
when they did not stand in the way of the extension of civilization. Indeed, much of our imperialist activity he justified
upon the ground of serving the " backward " peoples. He
shared the conviction of many Americans of his day that the
superior white man must bear the burden of civilizing colonial peoples of the world, if necessary against the will of those
peoples. " A nation's first duty is within its own borders," he
conceded, but " it is not thereby absolved from facing its
duties in the world as a whole; and if it refuses to do so, it
merely forfeits its right to struggle for a place among the
peoples that shape the destiny of mankind." It is cowardly
for us to shrink from solving the problems of the West Indies
and the Philippines, " for solved they must be, if not by us,
then by some stronger and more manful race." [75] " It is our
duty toward the people living in barbarism to see that they
are freed from their chains," he told Minnesotans a fortnight
before he became President, " and we can free them only by
destroying barbarism itself. . . . Exactly as it is the duty of a
civilized power scrupulously to respect the rights of weaker
civilized powers . . . so it is its duty to put down savagery
and barbarism." He recognized that since human instruments were imperfect, this meant occasional injustice. " Let
us," he urged, " instantly condemn and rectify such wrong
when it occurs. . . . But shame, thrice shame to us, if we are
so foolish as to make such occasional wrong-doing an excuse
for failing to perform a great and righteous task," for
" throughout all history, the advance of civilization has been
of incalculable benefit to mankind, and those through whom
it has advanced deserve the highest honor." [76]

Closely tied to his pride in America and his sense of her
moral rectitude and her superiority to others was a special
brand of national honor. Roosevelt, when his pride was

aroused or his will crossed, sometimes just reacted, as many adults do, like a child determined to have his own way and to resort to fisticuffs if thwarted. This tendency developed into a kind of national honor that made one's standing as a strong nation depend upon making other weaker nations understand that they could not defy the wishes of the great power. " Some time soon I shall have to spank some little brigand of a South American republic," he told his brother-in-law in 1905.[77] Our integrity as a world power demanded similarly that we make the Chinese understand by force if necessary not only that they could not stage a Boxer Rebellion and take the lives of foreigners whom they did not wish in their country, but that they could no more be permitted to put pressure on a great power through the legitimate and effective method of boycotting the great power's goods. Roosevelt's definition of national honor not only required that we must prevent the taking of American lives or seizing of American property in a small Latin American country, but that we could not permit the " Dagoes " of Colombia to question our building a canal on our terms where we wanted to build it through their territory. Roosevelt's excited outbursts over the refusal of Colombian senators to ratify the canal treaty we had dictated were akin to the behavior of the recognized leader of a group of small boys whom some smaller boy had successfully defied. " He is still mentally in the *Sturm und Drang* period of early adolescence," William James wrote in 1900.[78] In short, Roosevelt's and his friends' interpretation of the " national honor " required that they should permit no nation to prevent their doing what they wanted to do. Naturally, the corollary of militarism could not be avoided. America would never start a war if she could have what she wanted without it. But if she could not get what she wanted and do as she pleased without war, then she must fight, for it would be dishonorable to let any nation or group of nations tell America what she could or could not do.

Actually Roosevelt was confused about the whole problem of war and peace. He and his associates came close to seeking war for its own sake. Ignorant of modern war, Roosevelt romanticized war, and fighting in the Spanish War was not of a sort to dispel the romanticism. Like many young men tamed by civilization into law-abiding but adventureless living, he needed an outlet for the pent-up primordial man in him and found it in fighting and killing, vicariously or directly, in hunting or in war. Indeed he had a thoroughly good time in war when war came. He would have hesitated to proclaim openly that he liked war. Yet there was something dull and effeminate about peace. A civilized tradition drew him back from open advocacy of war. Yet personally he gloried in war, was thrilled by military history, and placed warlike qualities high in his scale of values. Without consciously desiring it, he thought a little war now and then stimulated admirable qualities in men. Certainly preparation for war did.

Though he valued the blessings of peace, he craved the excitements of war. He therefore sought a big navy because it would prevent war, but also because it was such fun to have a big navy. In the sense of power that ordering ships about gave him he found exhilaration and perhaps compensation for unfulfilled yearnings of a sickly boy whose boyish urges had been unsatisfied. Boylike he wanted many contradictory and mutually exclusive satisfactions and the logical qualities of mind necessary to perceive the contradictions in his desires had not been part of his intellectual training. In 1885 a college chum had written, " He would like above all things to go to war with some one. He has just walked out of the hotel with a rifle over his shoulder. . . . He . . . wants to be killing something all the time." [79] " Frankly I don't know that I should be sorry to see a bit of a spar with

Germany," he confided to Spring Rice in 1889. " The burn-
ing of New York and a few other sea coast cities would be a
good object lesson in the need of an adequate system of coast
defenses," he explained, " and I think it would have a good
effect on our large German population to force them to an
ostentatiously patriotic display of anger against Germany." [80]
In 1892 he was eager to fight in the invasion of Chile and
John Hay wrote Henry Adams how disgusted Theodore and
Brooks Adams were "because Harrison had not declared
war." " For two nickels he would declare war himself—shut
up the Civil Service Commission and wage it sole." [81] When
he and Lodge wrote a volume of *Hero Stories for Young
Americans*, the *Critic* pointed out that " all but three or four "
of their heroes " were shedders of blood and wearers of the
sword." [82] The *New York Evening Post* suggested in 1896
that Roosevelt's " value to the community would be greatly
increased if somehow he could somewhere have his fill of
fighting." " No man of Mr. Roosevelt's bellicose tempera-
ment," the *Post* felt, " is qualified to give advice about war
who has not seen war." [83] In reviewing Mahan's book in
1897 Roosevelt praised the " noble passage " in which Mahan
deplored as " ominous for the future of the race " the " tendency, vociferous at present, which refuses to recognize in the
profession of arms, in war, that something which inspired "
poets and heroes, " that something which has made the
soldier to all ages the type of heroism and self-denial." [84] " If
it wasn't wrong I should say that personally I would rather
welcome a foreign war," Roosevelt wrote privately in 1896.
Again, " It is very difficult for me not to wish a war with
Spain, for such a war would result at once in getting a proper
Navy." [85] In 1897 he declared, " In strict confidence, . . .
I should welcome almost any war, for I think this country
needs one." [86] He " gushes over war," protested William
James, " as the ideal condition of human society, for the
manly strenuousness which it involves, and treats peace as

a condition of blubberlike and swollen ignobility, fit only for huckstering weaklings, dwelling in gray twilight and heedless of the higher life. . . . One foe is as good as another, for aught he tells us." [87]

The Roosevelt-Lodge expansionists who took the American people into an imperialist struggle for world power were not primarily concerned with American economic interests around the world. Nor did they attempt to justify expansion chiefly on economic grounds. Where they were interested in economic matters it was because economic advantages won converts to imperialist policies or enhanced the prestige of the country. Economic factors *were* important in imperialism and were to become important in American expansionist foreign policy of the twentieth century. But the primary concern of Roosevelt and his fellow-expansionists was power and prestige and the naval strength that would bring power and prestige.[88] They gloried in the thought of American greatness and power that their expansionist policies would create. " I wish to see the United States the dominant power on the Pacific Ocean," Roosevelt wrote in 1900. " Our people are neither cravens nor weaklings and we face the future high of heart and confident of soul eager to do the great work of a great world power." [89]

To take our place in the world we must have a great Navy, but again defense was not the chief purpose of the Navy, in spite of the fact that the big navy enthusiasts urged a larger Navy as a preserver of peace and as a defense of the country and its honor. " If we build and maintain an adequate navy and let it be understood that . . . we are perfectly ready and willing to fight for our rights, then," Roosevelt believed, " the chances of war will become infinitesimal." [90] The Navy had, however, in Theodore's mind, a positive purpose. As early as 1894 he had pointed out that it was British naval supremacy that had won America and Australia for the English-speaking people and won South Africa for the English, perhaps even had saved South Africa from rule by blacks.[91] The Navy was an instrument of national policies that could not be carried out without it. " I have a horror of bluster," Roosevelt confided to John Hay, " which does not result in fight; it is both weak and undignified." [92] He wanted us to act upon the old frontier principles, he told Lodge; " don't bluster, don't flourish your revolver and never draw unless you intend to shoot." [93] He desired " to make all foreign powers understand that when we have adopted a line of policy we have adopted it definitely, and with the intention of backing it up with deeds as well as words." [94]

Roosevelt, then, would have us maintain the instruments of great imperial power. We must have warships equal in numbers with " the greatness of our people." If we had a large Navy and did go to war, he urged, we would " emerge from any war immeasurably the gainer in honor and renown." [95] He hoped this country would " take the position to which it is entitled among the nations of the earth." [96] " If," he warned, " we announce in the beginning that we don't class ourselves among the really great peoples who are willing to fight for their greatness, that we intend to remain defenseless, . . . we doubtless can remain at peace," but " it will not be the kind of peace which tends to exalt the national name, or make the individual citizen self-respecting." [97]

It was essential that our national policies be determined and engineered by men who possessed and valued fighting qualities. In 1886 in his *Thomas H. Benton* Roosevelt had written of the lawlessness and violence of the frontier: " This ruffianism was really not a whit worse in its effects on the national character than . . . the ' universal peace ' and ' non-resistance ' developments in the Northeastern States; in fact, it was more healthy. . . . A Quaker may be quite as undesirable a citizen as a duelist. No man who is not willing to bear arms and to fight for his rights . . . should be entitled to the privilege of living in a free community." [98] Roosevelt did not want our position as a nation determined by "the man of mere wealth, to whom the stock market is everything, and whose short-sighted vision is bounded by the horizon of a material prosperity." Nor did he wish it decided by "the anaemic man of culture whose education has been so one-sided as to develop cultivation and refinement at the expense of the virile qualities." Nor yet by "the good quiet soul, with many indispensible civic virtues, who is decent and re-spectable, but who is incapable of those generous and lofty thoughts which make a nation rise above the level of the commonplace." [99] He was disturbed by the number of men in the nation "who either lack the robust patriotism common to most Americans, or else who have lost the proud masterful instincts which have always been part of the character of any really great race." [100] "There is no place in the world," he warned, "for nations who have become enervated by soft and easy life, or who have lost their fibre of vigorous hardi-ness and manliness." [101] "All the great masterful races have been fighting races," he told the Naval War College, "and the minute that a race loses the hard fighting virtues, then . . . no matter how skilled in commerce and finance, in science or art, it has lost its proud right to stand as the equal of the best." [102] "No triumph of peace," he proclaimed, "is quite so great as the supreme triumphs of war." [103]

For the moment or for the long run Roosevelt, Lodge, Mahan, and their friends considered overseas empire the climax of their program. Cuba they at first hoped to win without fighting if we could become so strong that Spain would not dare object to our encouraging revolution in the Spanish islands. They also wanted Puerto Rico. Roosevelt, along with Lodge and White, tried to get the government to acquire the Danish West Indies.[104] "I believe we should build the Nicaraguan canal at once," he wrote Mahan in May, 1897.[105] He even hoped to take Canada or at least to force Britain to relinquish control of it.[106] He criticized

Cleveland for not seizing it.[107] Farther afield he wanted Hawaii and Samoa. When the Philippines entered his dreams is not clear.

Aims and desires, however, could not immediately be realized in spite of the strength of the imperialists' stock of ideas and the vigor of their expression. Much of the 1890's Roosevelt spent in Washington where he and his friends concerned themselves deeply with schemes for expansion and for impressing the world with our power. Harrison's handling of the seal fisheries in the Bering Sea distressed him.[108] The failure there Roosevelt laid to " our overanxiety for a peaceful settlement, and consequent willingness to yield what we ought not to have yielded." Had we followed the advice of Secretary of the Navy Tracy, " there would have been no war, the seals would now have been alive," he wrote in 1895, " and there would have been no danger of the extinction of the greatest industry of the North Pacific." [109] " Great Britain's conduct about the seals is infamous," he protested to Lodge. " We should at once take her action as a proof that she has abrogated the treaty and should . . . seize all Canadian sealers as pirates." [110]

On the whole, however, he was enthusiastic about the Harrison foreign policy. Harrison had stood up to Germany in regard to Samoa and forced the mighty Bismarck to share a protectorate over that island kingdom with us. He had made progress, Roosevelt hoped, toward a Nicaraguan canal. Given a little more time, he would have annexed Hawaii where his agents had helped organize a revolution and protected the revolutionists with our marines, and then arranged a treaty of annexation.[111] Publicly Roosevelt praised Harrison's handling of relations with Italy when a mob in New Orleans lynched some Italians. " Even here," Roosevelt pointed out in the *Independent*, " we made it perfectly clear that we acted . . . because of our sense of justice, and not through fear of any possible consequences." " Here Americans were the aggressors," and we were "prompt to offer satisfaction." [112] Privately, however, he wrote his sister that he personally thought the lynching " rather a good thing, and said so," at dinner at the Camerons' with "various dago diplomats . . . all much wrought up by the lynching." [113]

A Chilean difficulty Harrison had handled in a manner to make Roosevelt's breast swell with pride.[114] During Harrison's administration occurred one of those episodes that arise where great powers are protecting their citizens in "backward" countries. Harrison acted in a manner that won the high praise of Roosevelt and his friends and provided a model in their eyes and in the eyes of "backward people" like the Chileans for future action by the United States. Let Roosevelt tell the story: "One of the revolutions, so deplorably common in the South American States, broke out in Chile. . . . While the Presidential [Balmacedist] party was still in power, . . . [Minister Egan] was forced to extend the asylum of his legation to certain members of the Revolutionary party." "So when the Revolutionists were successful he protected in the same manner various Balmacedist officials from the cruelty of their foes. The Revolutionists . . . set spies all around [the American Legation] . . . and harassed the Minister and the other American inmates in many different ways." "Mr. Egan in his conduct toward the two parties behaved with entire impartiality, and showed himself to be actuated . . . solely by a desire to uphold the honor of the American flag." "The *Itata*, a ship belonging to the insurgent party, . . . came to one of our ports, as was alleged by competent authority, with the purpose of violating the neutrality laws." Therefore, "it became our duty to seize her. . . . A United States officer was put in charge; but she made her escape, ran off with the officer," whom she later put ashore, and carried with her a cargo of American arms. An American warship followed and back in Chile forced the new Revolutionary government to return the Chilean ship to us. In the meantime a war of words was fought. Finally, sailors went ashore in Santiago from an American ship, " behaved in a perfectly proper and ordered manner," but " were assailed by an organized mob. Several of the men were killed and others mishandled with . . . inhuman and revolting brutality; and the police in many cases rendered active or passive assistance to the rioters. The most careful investigation has shown conclusively that the American sailors committed no act of disorder, and that the attack was wanton and unprovoked "—caused only by hatred of the American uniform. The Chilean foreign minister replied with " a grossly offensive and impertinent open circular " to Harrison's " perfectly temperate " statements. The Legation was put under what Roosevelt felt amounted to siege. On January 21, 1891, Harrison sent an ultimatum demanding apology and redress. On January 25 he " very properly " sent a message to Congress " practically announcing," to use Roosevelt's words, " that unless his demands were complied with immediately and fully by Chile there would be a war." Preparations for war were made. " This timely display of firmness . . . produced a change of heart in our opponents." The " offensive circular " was withdrawn and ultimately $75,000 reparation was paid for the deaths of our sailors.[a][116] So Roosevelt described an episode that led Hay to write Henry Adams: " We have been awfully near a fight."[b][118]

It is the assumptions of Roosevelt and his friends that are interesting. Our national honor was involved and " for us to have yielded would have been an intolerable national disgrace and humiliation." Yet it seems never to have occurred to Roosevelt that the Chileans might have national pride, too, and might not enjoy " national disgrace and humiliation." He apparently could not comprehend that a nation

---

[a] Lodge described the episode in equally anti-Chilean terms.[115]
[b] Lodge, too, thought war was inevitable.[117]

too weak for him to respect might consider it an affront to
national pride for great powers to keep warships in a smaller
nation's harbors to overawe a government that resented the
activity of foreign business men. Roosevelt recognized the
economic factor involved but blamed rival British business
men for stirring up trouble. He did not reveal that while the
British interests were tied up with the revolutionists, our
own rival business interests were closely tied to the legiti-
matist group, so that our sheltering their leaders may with
some justice have looked to the Chilean revolutionists like
an unfriendly act. Nor does Roosevelt reveal that our minister Patrick Egan had come recently from Ireland and may
have had personal reasons for feeling no friendship for the
group backed by Britain.* Again it never occurred to Roosevelt that there could be any justice in a backward country's
objecting to its resources' being exploited for foreign profit
by foreigners who did not treat natives as equals but as backward people. Since our honor was involved, it was incredible
to Roosevelt that our cause might not have been wholly
righteous and our actions entirely proper or that the Chileans
could have acted other than outrageously in opposing us.
Statements of the Chilean government were " impertinent,"
ours calm and fair, though they included an ultimatum and
threat of war. Roosevelt felt we had behaved " with a strict
impartiality, with dignity, and moderation." Lodge, too, was
convinced we had shown the utmost forbearance. Roosevelt
accepted as completely unbiased enquiries into our sailors'
conduct by our own naval authorities. They found the action
of the Chileans " a wanton, unprovoked and deliberate piece
of brutality." Our diplomatic agents' report found every
accusation of " wrong to Chile . . . absolutely groundless."
The statements of Chilean authorities Roosevelt found universally untrue. Statements of American newspapers that

* Boston financial leader Henry L. Higginson suspected Egan of trying to
foment war, and Lodge tried to reassure him about Egan's peaceful purposes.[11⁰]

disagreed with official interpretations of facts were falsehoods, the editors "violent factional opponents" of the
national well-being. Roosevelt therefore saw no need of
further investigation of facts. Yet the revolutionists' ship,
the *Itata*, on which we had put an officer and which we had
pursued to Chile and forcibly brought back to America without permitting it to land its arms, our own court later ruled
had obtained its arms legitimately. A suggestion of arbitration of our difficulties with Chile would have questioned our
complete righteousness and would have implied that Chile
might have some case against us, and would therefore in
Roosevelt's mind have been an affront to our "national
honor." Roosevelt recognized widespread feeling in Chile
hostile to foreigners and especially to Americans, but he emphasized this feeling only as proof of the iniquity of Chileans.
His was not a state of mind to seek the causes of such anti-
Americanism and to question whether, had he been a Chilean,
he would have considered it justified. Basic to his approach
was his attitude toward Chileans and other "backward"
people. Almost certainly he would not have dealt this way
with a "civilized" country even though small, such for
instance as Belgium or Switzerland. But with people like
Chileans and Colombians one did not deal as with civilized
people.[120]

The foreign policy of Cleveland and his first Secretary of
State, Walter Q. Gresham, was a source of humiliation and
frustration to the Roosevelt-Lodge jingoes. Roosevelt did
not wish to play the rôle of a bully, but Cleveland had come
near playing in Roosevelt's eyes "the part of a coward."
Cleveland's "tame submission to insult" he deprecated. The
Democrats had adopted a "thoroughly improper and un-
American tone in foreign affairs." "Honorable peace is always desirable, but under no circumstances," Roosevelt lectured the Democrats, "should we permit ourselves to be
defrauded of our just rights by any fear of war. No amount

of material prosperity can atone for lack of national self-respect; and in no way can national self-respect be easier lost than through a peace obtained or preserved unworthily, whether through cowardice or through sluggish indifference." [121]

In May, 1894, Roosevelt wrote his sister what a misfortune it was that we had not gone on with the Navy and built an interoceanic canal.[122] He was worried lest Cleveland and Gresham abandon Samoa.[123] They had " made a most horrible failure " in China.[124] Roosevelt and Lodge were apparently aroused by an article in *Harper's Weekly* titled " American Helplessness in China." During the Sino-Japanese War two Japanese students charged by the Chinese with being spies found safety along with fifteen hundred other Japanese refugees in the American consulate in Shanghai. The Chinese minister in Washington protested and persuaded Gresham that the two students were spies and asked that they be handed over to the Chinese authorities. In consultation with Charles Denby, Jr., our well-informed chargé in China, and upon promise of the Chinese minister that they would have a fair trial under Chinese law, Gresham ordered that they be surrendered to the Chinese. After trial Chinese fashion, they were executed. The Chinese were accused of brutally torturing them into confessions. Gresham insisted that under international law he had acted properly and the Japanese almost certainly were spies. But Roosevelt's national honor was touched by this yielding to pressure, especially from the weak Chinese. Furthermore, the right of foreign-born residents of China to remain immune to Chinese law and be tried in foreign courts under their own foreign law was involved. Gresham's " brutal stupidity and cowardice " Roosevelt insisted called for " the most decided and prompt action." He thought Gresham should be impeached. But in any case, he wrote Lodge, " there is a great chance for you at once on Monday, to demand all the papers for the Senate." Lodge did so in a resolution of December 3 and on January 15 a full report with all the papers was transmitted.[125]

On Hawaii, too, the jingoes denounced Cleveland's action in withdrawing from the Senate the treaty of annexation Harrison's officers had negotiated. " I . . . feel very strong about . . . Hawaii," Roosevelt wrote six weeks after Cleveland became President in 1893. " I am a bit of a believer in the manifest destiny doctrine. . . . I don't want to see our flag hauled down where it has been hauled up." [126] Hawaii should be annexed immediately. " It was a crime against the United States," Roosevelt proclaimed, " it was a crime against white civilization, not to annex it " in 1893. " The delay did damage that is perhaps irreparable; for it meant that at the critical period of the island's growth the influx of population consisted, not of white Americans, but of low-caste laborers drawn from the yellow races." [127] The Republican expansionists did what they could. " I had half a dozen Congressmen and Senators, who thought right on . . . Hawaii, to dinner," Roosevelt wrote his sister in 1894. In the campaign of 1896 the Republicans made the most of Democratic failure in Hawaii.[128]

For Thomas F. Bayard, Cleveland's ambassador to Britain, Roosevelt felt particular contempt. It was largely Bayard's misunderstanding of British diplomacy, Roosevelt felt, and his failure to keep the British aware of American thinking about their handling of Venezuela that obliged Cleveland and Olney to speak plainly in what amounted to a threat of war.[129] An abler man would have made it clear how strongly Americans felt about the Monroe Doctrine and would have persuaded Salisbury to reconsider his blunt message refusing to arbitrate. Roosevelt understood that even the English " despise . . . [Bayard] for not being more of an American." [130] " A little resolute, clearsighted firmness, and upholding of the American cause, by him, at the right time, would have averted all the subsequent trouble," Roosevelt later told his sister.[181] To Henry White he wrote, "Bayard seems to me to be rapidly becoming a prize fool." [182] Roosevelt's sister, who was hostess to Bayard's secretary of legation, Rosy Roosevelt, confided to Theodore that Rosy had long been " uneasy over Bayard's inability to understand Salisbury." [183] In exchange Theodore divulged to his sister at Bayard's own embassy that Secretary of State Olney did not " overmuch admire Bayard." [184] A year later he wrote that " Olney and everybody at Washington feel utter contempt for Bayard." [185] And White reported that the British Government had " sized up " the position of Bayard " with respect to his own government." [186] Roosevelt explained to his sister in London how, during the ten months of important negotiations, Henry White, the displaced Republican that had preceded and was to replace Rosy Roosevelt, had been used by a Democratic administration to carry on delicate negotiations that the Democratic ambassador and secretary of legation in London could not be trusted with.[187] Indeed, in July, 1896, White went to London unofficially and talked plainly to the Prime Minister and other members of the British Government and found them not opposed to settlement.[188]

Roosevelt, Lodge, and the others were unhappy even under Olney's secretaryship that we did not intervene in Cuba,[189] but a quarrel with England over her position in Latin America soon overshadowed their concern over Spain in Cuba.

Cleveland's and Olney's intervention in 1895 in the boundary dispute between Venezuela and Britain's territory of Guiana delighted the jingoes. The story is a familiar one. Olney sent a sharp note to Britain warning her that our fiat was law in the Western Hemisphere and that we regarded her settling a boundary dispute with an American country through her superior force as a violation of the Monroe Doctrine. Olney insisted that she arbitrate. Olney's truculence and Salisbury's own failure to understand the feeling that could be aroused in America over the Monroe Doctrine led Salisbury to delay responding and then to reply sharply with a refusal. Cleveland sent a message to Congress requesting authority to appoint a commission to determine the just boundary and threatened war if Britain refused to accept the commission's finding. At that point Britain, eager for friendship with the United States, backed down and agreed to arbitrate.

Again it is Roosevelt's part in this episode that interests us. He and his friends talked the Venezuelan matter over thoroughly. In June, 1895, six months before President Cleveland took action, Lodge published an article attacking Britain's position.[140] " I have just read your article," Roosevelt wrote on June 5, " the most convincing showing of what England has done; if only our people will heed it! " [141] Henry White, too, was delighted. The article will be, wrote White, " an ' eye-opener ' not only to many in this country but also in England where the action of the Foreign Office in respect to Venezuela, is practically unknown; and certainly not understood." [142] Lodge urged Roosevelt to try to make Smalley, Washington correspondent of the *London Times*, understand American sentiment so that he could warn his British readers. Roosevelt spoke to Smalley in August " as plainly as mortal can " and cautioned him that general sentiment was hostile to England and strongly behind the Monroe Doctrine, but Smalley retorted that no one of high standing felt that way. " He does not meet the men who share our views," Roosevelt told Lodge, and so Smalley kept telling the British that there was no general interest in the Monroe Doctrine, that only a few jingoes talked about Venezuela.[143] Lodge, who in October was traveling in France, was " on pins and needles to get home." " If we allow England to invade Venezuela nominally for reparation . . . really for territory our supremacy in the Americas is over," he wrote Roosevelt. " I am worried and angry beyond words. . . . England is

simply playing this administration for what she can get." [144]
On his way home he talked to his British friend, Arthur
Balfour, about Venezuela. [145] In November Roosevelt was insisting that we "inform Great Britain, with equal firmness
and courtesy . . . that the United States cannot tolerate the
aggrandizement of a European power on American soil." [146]
When Congress convened, Lodge introduced a strong resolution on Venezuela that " delighted " Roosevelt, who promised
to talk to Smalley of the *Times* again. [147] By December 18
Lodge could assure his mother that " the temper here is firm
and excellent." " I first alone in the wilderness cried out
about Venezuela last June and was called a Jingo for my
pains," he wrote, but " Jingoes are plenty enough now. . . .
The President is a late convert but this message written by
Olney is right and good." " Outside of the moneyed interests
in New York and Boston," he wrote Henry White, " the
American people, like Congress and the press, are solidly
behind the President in defense of the Monroe Doctrine." [148]
Banker Henry L. Higginson disliked this jingoism. " If the
case had been stated in gentler, quieter language," he protested, " if we had stated our case firmly and made no
threats, or suggestions of threats, of any name or nature,—
having stated our wishes emphatically . . . , but in gentle
language and allowed the matter to rest there, there would
have been no suggestion of a war." " You have misconceived
the wishes and thoughts of the community of men who think
and feel rightly and carefully upon their duties as citizens,"
Higginson warned Lodge. " Such action . . . seems to all the
world very hasty and uncalled for." [149]

In letters to constituents Lodge explained his and Roosevelt's views. " It is not a question of territory but of a
principle." [150] " If England's title is good, we have no wish
to disturb it." But " if England can set up a territorial claim
and then refuse to arbitrate about it, there is nothing to
prevent her taking any amount of territory." [151] " If Great

Britain can extend her territory in South America without remonstrance from us, every other European power can do the same and in a short time you will see South America parcelled out as Africa has been. We should then find ourselves with great powers to the South of us and we should be forced to become at once a nation with a powerful army and navy with difficulties and dangers surrounding us." [152] The Nicaraguan canal, too, was involved.[153] Trying to calm the fears of Henry Higginson, that we would get into war, Lodge wrote this Boston banker friend of his and Roosevelt's, " I do not think there is any danger of . . . war unless England insists on forcing it upon us.ᵃ " Hesitation or vacillation or the refusal to support the President would have done more to involve us not in one war but in many than any other course." [154] " England mistakes civility and good nature for weakness," Lodge wrote a constituent. " Now that she understands the American feeling, I think you will find she will respect the American position." [155]

Meantime Lodge's friend Roosevelt was " pleased with the President's or rather with Olney's message " and with the " remarkable vindication " of Lodge's attitude of the spring before. " Let the fight come if it must," he wrote Lodge; " I do'n't care whether our sea coast cities are bombarded or not; ᵇ we would take Canada." [156] " Such a war we would deplore," he declared in an article, " but . . . much more for England's sake than for our own, for . . . the mere fact that Canada would inevitably be rent from England in the end

---

ᵃ Higginson unconvinced replied: " I agree . . . that there is little danger of war with Great Britain; but I heard unfortunately just the same thing said about the quarrel between the North and the South, that there would be no war, so people went on and provoked . . . Firmness . . . is one thing; well chosen language is quite another."

ᵇ Roosevelt's civil service reform friends deplored his war talk. " It seemed to me most injudicious and unfortunate," wrote Herbert Welsh to Carl Schurz, " that a man of his influence and position should talk of war with Great Britain, in what I could not but feel was a very juvenile fashion."

would make the outcome an English disaster." [157] Indeed, to
his brother-in-law, who was American naval attaché in London, he wrote, " It seems to me that if England were wise
she would fight now; we could'n't get at Canada until May,
and meanwhile she could play havoc with our coast cities and
shipping." Actually, he was already looking forward to getting into a war as a soldier. " I earnestly hope our government do'n't back down," he wrote. " If there is a muss I
shall try to have a hand in it myself! They'll have to employ
a lot of men just as green as I am even for the conquest of
Canada." [158]

In spite of his assurance that " the bulk of the American
people will I think surely stand behind the man who boldly
and without flinching takes the American view," [159] Roosevelt was worried lest the people weaken. He blamed the
American correspondents of the British press, particularly
Smalley, for " misrepresenting the tone of American
thought." [160] Smalley was " contemptible beyond words." So
was the " anglo-maniac " American press. The editors of the
Evening Post and the *World* it would give him " pleasure to
have . . . put in prison the minute hostilities began." [161] " The
antics of the bankers, brokers and anglomaniacs generally "
were " humiliating to a degree." " Our peace at any price
men, if they only knew it," he declared, " are rendering war
likely, because they will encourage England to persist; in the
long run this means a fight. Personally I rather hope the
fight will come soon. The clamor of the peace faction has
convinced me that this country needs a war." [162]

He was particularly disturbed by a stand of certain Harvard professors against war. " I am more indignant than I
can say," he wrote Lodge. " I wish to at least do what I can
to save Harvard from degredation." So he wrote " a smash-
ing letter " to the *Harvard Crimson* " saying a word for
Patriotism and Americanism." [163] Lodge, who read it in advance, liked the letter and so Roosevelt sent it, and he in

turn praised Lodge's speeches.[164] Roosevelt was delighted when his letter " drew blood." Lodge judged it a great success. The *Boston Herald* attacked Roosevelt. Albert Bushnell Hart, his classmate and now a professor of history at Harvard, wrote " a raving letter . . . the kind of anger which showed shame underneath." [165] The *Harvard Graduates Magazine* assailed him " with the ineffective bitterness proper to beings whose cult is nonvirility." [166] Roosevelt professed amusement " at the seething fury " of " educated Boston." [167]

The fact remained that conservative business men were deeply disturbed over the Venezuelan episode and its threat of war with Britain. From New York Roosevelt wrote of " the cowardice, stupidity and selfishness of the great majority of the people I meet here." [168] To one business constituent who praised him Lodge wrote with feeling: " When so many persons are writing me from State Street as if I were guilty of some heinous offense for sustaining the rights of my country, . . . and threatening me with personal and party defeat for doing so, it is very agreeable to have such a letter as yours." Lodge's letters indicated that men in Boston financial circles opposed the " get tough " attitude toward Britain or actually regarded the Monroe Doctrine " as a most infamous thing." [169] " In Boston and some of the other money centres " there was " panic." [170] To one moneyed constituent Lodge wrote, " You speak of the feeling of the men who have a stake in the country. When it comes to a difficulty with a foreign nation, all American citizens have a stake in the country and the stake of the working men and the mass of the people who would have to stand behind the guns if there was trouble is just as great as that of anyone else." These ordinary people Lodge insisted were behind him and Roosevelt and the President.[171] In March, 1896, Roosevelt could hardly " restrain his indignation " over the " cowardice " of some members of his own party who ought to have

supported "Americanism." He was "disgusted," for instance, with Republican leaders Hale, Hoar, and Reed.[172]

In December and January, 1895-1896, Congress discussed
the Monroe Doctrine and adopted a resolution redefining it.
Again there were protests from the financial and business
circles of Lodge's constituency.[173] Roosevelt wrote his sister
on February 2 that he favored refraining from further action
for the present. But, he added, " if Salisbury obstinately refuses to yield, I see no alternative but to fight." [174] By February 11 he was persuaded England had learned her lesson
and "hereafter European nations will recognize that the
Monroe Doctrine is a living entity." [175] Roosevelt wrote congratulating Cleveland who replied: "It has taken a little
time and strength for the good people to understand our
position . . . but as usual they are ' coming around.' " [176] In
March, 1896, Roosevelt closed the episode so far as he was
concerned by publishing in the *Bachelor of Arts* an article
that he told his sister " made rather a hit," in which he fully
expounded his views on the Monroe Doctrine and defended
our action against England.[177]

Thus by the time the anti-imperialist Cleveland left office,
and two years before the Spanish War awoke most Americans to our new rôle, Roosevelt, Lodge, and their coterie had
formulated an imperialist philosophy for America, had map-
ped out a program, and had marshaled their forces. America
had with their hearty support successfully stood up as a great
power to a great power at risk of war. The stage was set to
win us a place in the sun of world power, if the jingoes could
ever win control of the government.

chapter **II**

ROOSEVELT *and America's Plunge into World Power*

Republican victory gave this group of strategically placed expansionists their chance in 1897 to apply the principles they had long espoused. A few men in powerful positions were able to plunge the nation into an imperialist career that it never explicitly decided to follow. Each worked to promote the other for high position. Lodge promoted John Hay for the secretaryship of State. He journeyed besides to Canton, Ohio, to appeal personally to President-elect McKinley for Henry White's appointment as secretary of Legation in London and for Roosevelt's as assistant secretary of the Navy.[1] "I am afraid he is too pugnacious. . . . I want peace and I am told that your friend Theodore is always getting into rows with everybody," McKinley protested to Maria Storer.[2] "Give him a chance," Mrs. Storer pleaded, "to prove that he can be peaceful."[3] Judge William H. Taft, a new member of the group, pleaded Roosevelt's cause with McKinley. "The truth is, Will, Roosevelt is always in such a state of mind," McKinley told Taft.[4] But Roosevelt was appointed Assistant Secretary of the Navy; White went to London as Secretary, and Hay as Ambassador.

In his new office Roosevelt set out to build up the Navy and to win powerful people in the Administration and in Congress to large naval appropriations. He wrote articles and made speeches urging a great navy.[5] As soon as he took office, he and Mahan began coöperating. "To no one else excepting Lodge do I talk like this," he once wrote Mahan.[6] "This letter," he warned Mahan, "must be strictly private," for "I speak to you with the greatest freedom."[7] One letter, at least, Mahan assured him he had read and burned.[8] Roosevelt urged Mahan to write him often and promised, "All I can do towards pressing your ideas into effect will be done."[9] Mahan supplied arguments. Theodore reported confidentially the shifting state of mind of their common chief, John Long, Secretary of the Navy.[10] In June, 1897, he urged Mahan to write Long.[11] In August he called Lodge's attention to "a really noble article" of Mahan's in *Harper's Monthly*.[12] He argued his views with McKinley at the White House and with powerful Mark Hanna.[13] Discouraged, he wrote in August to the British naval authority, William Laird Clowes, "The bulk of our people are curiously ignorant of military and naval matters, and full of an ignorant self-confidence, which is, I hope, the only quality they share with the Chinese."[14] Thrilled by watching fleet manoeuvers in September, he wrote Chairman Charles A. Boutelle of the House Naval Affairs Committee, "Oh, Lord! if only the people who are ignorant about our Navy could see those great warships in all their majesty and beauty, and could realize how . . . well fitted" they are "to uphold the honor of America!"[15] Again discouraged he wrote his German friend Speck von Sternburg in January, 1898, "It is very difficult to make this nation wake up. Individually the people are very different from the Chinese, . . . but nationally our policy is almost as foolish." "I sometimes question," he confided to this servant of the Kaiser, "whether anything but a great military disaster will ever make us feel our responsibilities and our possible dangers." [16]

In appealing for a larger navy Theodore always emphasized his desire for peace. "We must prepare for war in order to preserve peace," he told a New York yacht club. "I hope we will ratify the [arbitration] treaty [with England] and build ten new battleships." "There may be a time," he admitted, "in eight or ten thousand years, when there will be no need to prepare for war; but until then, we need try to secure peace with a sword girt at our side." [17] In June, 1897, he admonished Mahan in dealing with Long to "make the plea that this is a measure of peace and not of war." [18] "Again and again," he himself declared, "we have owed peace to the fact that we were prepared for war." [19] "If any man is base enough to wish that we keep peace on conditions so contemptible that it will not be worth while to kick us, let him understand that that is not the way to keep peace." [20]

Lodge, Roosevelt, and Mahan, in constant consultation, worked on Secretary of State Sherman and President Mc-Kinley to get them to seize Hawaii, and Roosevelt prepared a memorandum for Long to use in Cabinet meeting. "If only we had some good man in the place of John Sherman as Secretary of State there would not be a hitch," Roosevelt wrote Mahan. [21] "Do nothing unrighteous; but as regards the [political] problem [involved in annexation], take the islands first," Mahan prodded Roosevelt in May, 1897, "and solve afterwards." [22] Finally, Lodge, Roosevelt, Assistant Secretary of State William R. Day, and others persuaded McKinley over Sherman's head. On June 16 an annexation treaty was signed. Sherman himself, ignorant of the treaty negotiations, had assured the Japanese minister that no treaty was being negotiated, and so when the treaty was announced Japan protested. [23] Roosevelt answered Japan's protest in a speech in which he declared: "The United States is not in a position which requires her to ask Japan or any other foreign Power what territory it shall or shall not acquire."[24] Even the Republican *New York Tribune* suggested that he "leave to the Department of State the declaration of . . . foreign policy," which "is not the business of the Assistant Secretary of the Navy."[25] Long reprimanded him severely for this speech,[26] but Lodge felt: "You were all right in what you said."[27] So too, to Roosevelt's surprise, did McKinley, who thought "it was only the headlines that were wrong."[28] Roosevelt wrote an article in *Gunton's Magazine* pleading for ratification.[29] He, Lodge, and others made speeches and worked on doubtful senators.[30] Roosevelt, Lodge, Mahan, and White were "sick" when they thought how easily the Harrison Treaty could have been ratified in 1893.[31] On March 17 the Treaty was laid finally aside and the annexationists won Hawaii only in 1898 and then by joint resolution.[32] By that time, however, Roosevelt was busy fighting a war against Spain.

Hawaii seemed important to Mahan, Lodge, and Roosevelt for several reasons. Commercially Hawaii was necessary to insure us "a share in the vast trade and commerce of the Pacific." Second, "The people . . . who have civilized and developed those islands are Americans. . . . We have not . . . any right to leave them to be engulfed by an Asiatic immigration," Lodge contended. Ignoring the presence of more Orientals than whites, Lodge argued on democratic grounds that "a majority of whites and natives, who alone have a right to speak, seek annexation."[33] Similarly disregarding the huge Oriental population Roosevelt pronounced the native Hawaiians unable to govern, and the whites therefore entitled to rule the islands.[34] Besides, if we did not take Hawaii, Japan, Germany, or Britain would.[35] Annexation would advance civilization, said Roosevelt, and taking the islands was the only policy compatible with our interests.[36] "We did not create the Hawaiian Islands," Roosevelt told New York Republicans in February, 1898; "they already exist. We merely have to face the alternative of taking them ourselves and making them the outpost for the protection of the Pacific Coast or else of seeing them taken by any powerful nation with which we are at war, and at once transformed into the most dangerous possible base of operations against our Pacific cities. We cannot help Hawaii's being either a strong defense to us or a perpetual menace. We can only decide whether we will now take the islands when offered to us as a gift, or by force try to conquer them from the first powerful nation with which we may become embroiled." [37]

Our interest in Samoa was chiefly strategic. At the time we acquired American Samoa, Secretary of State Hay wrote, " Our interests in the Archipelago were very meagre, always excepting our interest in Pago Pago, which was of the most vital importance. It is the finest harbor in the Pacific and absolutely indispensable to us." [38]

Roosevelt originally wanted to drive Spain out of Cuba by a show of force short of war. In 1895 Lodge conferred with Prime Minister Antonio Cánovas del Castillo of Spain about Cuba.[39] Throughout 1896 Lodge and Roosevelt sought intervention, not to annex Cuba, but to win her independence.[40] In close accord with Theodore in these matters Lodge conferred in 1896 with the Committee of Cuban Patriots; he served on the Senate sub-committee on Cuba; he went to see Cleveland to urge him to act; he supported Senate resolutions in favor of Cuban independence; he formulated a principle on intervention in Cuba strikingly similar to Roosevelt's later corollary to the Monroe Doctrine.[41] In regard to Cuba as in regard to Venezuela, business men protested over the risk of war involved in these policies.[42]

As Assistant Secretary of the Navy Roosevelt had given up action short of war and was doing all in his power to promote war with Spain over Cuba.[43] "I am a quietly rampant 'Cuba Libre' man," Roosevelt wrote his sister in January, 1897.[44] He invited key senators to the Metropolitan Club with a special envoy just back from Cuba.[45] By March, 1898, he was writing Mahan, "I can hardly see how we can avoid intervening in Cuba if we are to retain our self-respect as a nation."[46] "We have been derelict in not interfering," he wrote Bryce on March 31.[47] To his classmate, Bob Bacon, now a J. P. Morgan partner and one day to be his Secretary of State, he wrote on April 8: "I am perfectly willing to follow the policy of intervening without recognizing independence, although I think it a mistake; for I should be very doubtful about annexing Cuba in any event, and should most emphatically oppose it unless the Cubans wished it. . . . I don't want it to seem that we are engaged merely in a land-grabbing war."[48] Roosevelt and his friends believed the sinking of the *Maine* an act of treachery by the Spaniards that should be avenged by war, and he was distressed when he found the country was not sufficiently aroused to go to war over it.

Roosevelt's motives in Cuba were again not economic, but humanitarian and strategic. He denounced "the limited mental horizon" of opponents and "the craven fear and brutal selfishness of the mere money-getters" that opposed war with Spain.[49] When he found business men opposed to war even after the *Maine* was sunk, he lamented to his friend Bacon, "We here in Washington have grown to feel that almost every man connected with the big business interests of the country is anxious to court any infamy if only peace can be obtained and the business situation be not disturbed." "All the people of means, all the people to whom one had been accustomed to look up as the leaders, or should-be leaders, in civic matters," he protested, "seem to show . . . callous indifference to the honor of the country."[50] "We should decline longer to allow this hideous welter of misery at our doorsteps," he urged Root.[51] "Let us treat the whole question as an entirety," he urged, "and put Spain out of the western hemisphere."[52]

Since he could not persuade the Administration of which he was part to go to war, the best Roosevelt could do was to prepare the Navy for war in case McKinley changed his mind. "If we drift into the war butt end foremost, and go at it higgledy-piggledy fashion," he protested, "we shall meet with occasional difficulties." [53] But he was determined that all the preparations in his power should be made to reduce those difficulties to a minimum. He tried to keep naval vessels in good condition and so disposed as to be most useful if war came.[54] He opposed laying up vessels.[55] Orders were issued that concentrated our ships.[56] He hoped to manoeuver a head-on sea fight and urged his German friend Speck to come to observe "the pretty fight" it would be.[57] He discussed war plans with naval officers,[58] tried to prevent taking ships out of service, and even sought to buy more.[59] When on February 25, 1898, Secretary Long went home early intending to take a day's rest and Roosevelt became Acting Secretary for three or four hours, he made the most of his opportunity.[60] He sent a momentous cable to George Dewey.[a] [61] He issued instructions to the European and South Atlantic squadrons where to rendezvous, if war broke out.[62] He ordered commanders all over the world to keep their ships filled with the best possible coal.[63] He bought all the coal he could buy in the Far East.[64] He sent a "strictly confidential" letter to the New York adjutant general urging him to make plans for supplying men in case of war.[65] In short, Long found next morning that Roosevelt "in his precipitate way" had "come very near causing more of an explosion than happened to the *Maine*." In his diary Long described those few hours: "He immediately began to launch peremptory orders: distributing ships; ordering ammunition, which there is no means to move, to places where there is no means to store it; sending for Captain Barker to come on

---

[a] Roosevelt later told that Lodge came in just as he was preparing this order.

about the guns of the Vesuvius . . . , sending messages to Congress for immediate legislation, authorizing the enlistment of an unlimited number of seamen; and ordering guns from the Navy Yard at Washington to New York." Indeed, Long recorded, "He has gone at things like a bull in a china shop." [66] Long abandoned his day's vacation and returned to the office early next morning and never left Roosevelt in charge again even for part of a day.[67] Long, Speaker Reed, Chairmen Charles A. Boutelle and Eugene Hale of the naval committees of Congress were distressed by Roosevelt's precipitateness.[68] Long concluded that the serious illness of Mrs. Roosevelt and young Ted had "accentuated . . . his natural nervousness" so much that he was "hardly fit to be entrusted with the responsibility of the Department at this critical time." [69]

Long's error lay in ascribing Roosevelt's action to impulsiveness. The orders were deliberate acts that Roosevelt and his friends had discussed for months but had been unable to accomplish.[*] Long's absence gave Roosevelt the chance to carry out carefully-laid and well-matured plans to prepare better for war than he had been able to persuade his associates to do when he was not in command.

Apparently the concurrently developing problem of the Philippines was not part of a well-thought-out Far Eastern policy. None of the expansionists seems to have coveted the islands until Mahan found need for them as he planned naval strategy of the hoped-for war with Spain.[71] Then in September, 1897, Roosevelt wrote Lodge, "Our Asiatic squadron should blockade, and if possible take, Manilla [sic]." [72] From then on Roosevelt worked to have the Asiatic squadron in shape for that purpose, and in March he persuaded Long to order the Baltimore to Asia.[73] When a commander was

---

[*] "Throughout this period," Roosevelt testified, "I was in the closest touch with Senator Lodge, and either consulted him about or notified him of all the moves I was taking." [70]

needed for the Asiatic squadron, Roosevelt, with his eye on war and the Philippines, was determined to have a fighting man who would act with daring.[74] Over the heads of senior officers and against political opposition Roosevelt manoeuvered Dewey's appointment.[75] When Dewey found insufficient coal and could not get any through normal channels, Roosevelt cut through red tape and navy routine and had coal sent him.[76] Then among his momentous activities of February 25 Roosevelt cabled Dewey instructions of far-reaching consequences: " Order the squadron except *Monocacy* to Hong Kong. Keep full of coal. In the event of declaration war Spain, your duty will be to see that the Spanish squadron does not leave the Asiatic coast, and then offensive operations in Philippine Islands." Dewey's talks with Roosevent in Washington had made it clear what Roosevelt wanted. Now he had authorization.[77] Long was upset, but as Lodge put it, " The deed was done. The wise word of readiness had been spoken and was not recalled." [78] The Assistant Secretary had seized the opportunity given by Long's absence to insure our grabbing the Philippines without a decision to do so by either Congress or the President, or least of all the people. Thus was important history made not by economic forces or democratic decisions but through the grasping of chance authority by a man with daring and a program.

Then Roosevelt set about buying ships where possible, laying in supplies, getting appropriations for ammunition, seeing when he could that the best commanders were assigned to the right ships.[79] In the end the Navy was better equipped than the Army. Long gave credit to the professional personnel.[80] But in 1910 Taft testified: " If it had not been for Theodore Roosevelt we would never have been in a position to declare war, for it was he and only he who got from Congress sufficient ammunition to back any bluff we might make with actual play." [a][82]

_____

[a] Roosevelt himself, Admiral Robley D. Evans, Vice-President Hobart, General

The War brought us Cuba, Puerto Rico, and the Philippines; during the war period we cleared our title to part of Samoa and picked up Hawaii, Guam, and Wake Island. Roosevelt felt the war had decided much for our destiny and had been of incalculable benefit to the country. Now all Americans could be proud in the knowledge that America stood as one of the great powers of the world.[83] Mrs. Roosevelt wrote Senator Lodge in 1900 that as she steamed into Havana Harbor and saw the stars and stripes floating above Morro Castle she felt a thrill of pride that she feared Senator Hoar * would not approve of.[84]

Roosevelt was fully aware of the "extremely perplexing problems" that Bryce had warned him America would face in trying to apply her political experience to the rule of these new types of territory. As governor, Roosevelt continued active about overseas expansion and the government of the backward peoples we had acquired. On July 1, 1899, he wrote Hay a letter that he invited Hay to show the President. In it he urged the necessity of appointing the most competent men available to rule "with a proper mixture of firmness, courtesy and tact"—Major General Leonard Wood over Cuba and Major General Francis V. Greene in the Philippines. "About Hawaii," Roosevelt told Hay, "I know nothing. The men in whom I have most confidence tell me that the condition in Porto Rico is very bad and that the people are really regretting the ending of Spanish rule. In Porto Rico there can be no revolt, but this does not render it less incumbent on us to give it the best type of government." "I am uneasy," Roosevelt confided, "at the way things seem be going both in the Philippines and in Cuba, and also at the mutterings of discontent . . . which can be heard here and

Leonard Wood, and the *New York Evening Post* also credited Roosevelt's "strong will and earnest recommendations" with much of this better preparation.[81]

* George F. Hoar, one of the leading anti-imperialists.

there[a] throughout the country even now. A series of disasters at the very beginning of our colonial policy would shake this administration, and therefore our party, and might produce the most serious and far-reaching effects upon the nation as a whole, for if some political cataclysm was the result, it might mean the definite abandonment of the course upon which we have embarked—the only course I think fit for a really great nation."[86] In December, 1899, Governor Roosevelt wrote his British friend Spring Rice, "What I should really most like to do would be to be Governor-General of the Philippines, but I do not suppose I could leave New York, and in any event, it would not occur to the President to appoint me."[87]

The question as to whether to continue on this expansionist course became an important issue in the campaign of 1900, and Roosevelt was the vice-presidential candidate. He campaigned widely. He even made an extensive trip through the mountain states. Between September 9 and October 6 he traveled 12,870 miles west of Detroit, made 290 speeches, and was estimated to have addressed 600,000 people.[88] Everywhere Roosevelt stressed the expansionist issue, but it bulked particularly large west of Chicago where it was impolitic to discuss Eastern Republican views on the money issue.[b]

Part of his time Roosevelt had to spend answering attacks of the Democrats that it was feared would be damaging. His opponents had scrutinized his record and he had to defend

[a] Even Roosevelt's friend Henry Adams wrote, "I fully share with [Senator] Hoar the alarm and horror of seeing poor weak McKinley, in gaiety, . . . plunge into an inevitable war to conquer the Philippines, contrary to every profession or so-called principle of our lives and history. I turn green in bed at midnight if I think of the horror of a year's warfare in the Philippines . . . where . . . we must slaughter a million or two of foolish Malays in order to give them the comforts of flannel petticoats and electric railways."[85]

[b] The Western press commented on "the marked omission from all his speeches of any reference to the money question." As late as 1902 he wanted to keep the "anti-imperialist issue to the fore in the congressional campaigns, for if it is made the main issue we can certainly beat the Democrats out of their boots."[89]

his own past. For instance, in 1886 in his life of *Thomas H. Benton*, before he knew Mahan or had become interested in expansion, he had described Manifest Destiny of the mid-century as an "idea . . . that it was our manifest destiny to swallow up the land of all adjoining nations who were too weak to withstand us." It was "a theory," Roosevelt had written, "that forthwith obtained immense popularity among all statesmen of easy international morality." [90] That was a hard one to explain away when the Democrats asked how his proposed expansionism differed from Manifest Destiny. He never satisfactorily answered the question, but fell back upon the argument that the Republicans were now doing just what Democratic presidents Jefferson and Jackson had done, so that Democrats were in no position to criticize. [91] He had also in his *Benton* criticized European nations for warring over "thickly settled districts which, if conquered, will for centuries remain alien and hostile to the conquerors." "We, wiser in our generation," he had boasted, "have seized the waste solitudes that lay near us. . . . Of course no one would wish to see . . . any . . . settled communities, now added to our domain by force; we want no unwilling citizens to enter our Union." [92] This, too, was hard to answer, and the best he could do was to throw back the argument to the Democrats that "the Philippine Islands were acquired under . . . McKinley by treaty and purchase exactly as the Louisiana territory was acquired by Jefferson." In Louisiana, he said, "the great majority of the inhabitants . . . were bitterly opposed to the transfer," but Jefferson never took any vote "as to whether they were willing that their territory should be annexed." [93] Roosevelt, of course, despised Jefferson but he argued that Democrats, who admired him, had no ground for criticizing Republicans for doing what Jefferson had done.

In a Quaker community at Plainfield, Indiana, he tried to extricate himself from his earlier denunciation of Quakers as people who had no right to be citizens. Now he praised "the social and industrial virtue" of Quakers that entitled them "to the respect of all people"; he assured his audience that without the Friends "we would never have been able to make the Republic what it is and should be." He praised the Quakers for standing by McKinley and exerting "their influence toward international arbitration . . . at the Hague." "It is not possible as yet," he told his Quaker audience in an understatement of his usual views, "to settle all difficulties peaceably by arbitration, but in every case we should avoid appeals to arms where possible." In answer to Quaker criticism the man who had for a year frantically promoted the Spanish War declared, "We believe in being slow to enter upon war, but having entered upon it we believe in seeing it through. We believe we have a right to appeal to all lovers of peace to stand by us in the Philippines," for to give them up would be to "turn them over to bloody chaos and anarchy." [94]

The charge of militarism must have worried the Republicans, for Roosevelt recurred to it time after time in order to answer it.[95] Again and again he delivered eulogies of the brave deeds of our soldiers and whipped up pride in those deeds. "The Chinese Boxer, his hands red with the blood of the slaughtered women and children, . . . has flinched as he heard the drumming guns . . . of Chaffee . . . leading his little army across the flooded rice fields." "The Manilla [*sic*] bandit has had cause to fear the flag as he lurked in ambush to shoot our men." The Spanish soldiers "had cause to dread the flag as they saw the great battleships ploughing to and fro through the seas of the Gulf" or "listened to the thunder of Dewey's canon, that waked the world, that bid [*sic*] the older nations know that the young giant of the West had come to his glorious prime." But who else need fear our soldiers? The charge of militarism was "the most shadowy ghost that ever was raised to frighten political children." Bryan's charge was "what he either knows, or ought to know, to be an absolute slander." Bryan "asks us to dishonor the flag."[96] More than once Roosevelt waved the bloody shirt by recalling that the Democrats had charged the "patient, kindly Lincoln" and "the million men in blue" with militarism and had accused Lincoln of wanting to become emperor.[97] The anti-imperialists Roosevelt branded as "the political heirs and assigns" of the copperheads of the Civil War.[98] In Detroit he asked men in uniform in the audience to stand up and then, after the cheering died down, provoked more cheering by exclaiming: "Behold your tyrants!"[99]

Roosevelt and the Republicans had to meet attacks on them as imperialists.[a] That Americans were imperialists Lodge and Roosevelt publicly denied.[b] "The simple truth is," Roosevelt wrote in his letter of acceptance, "there is nothing even remotely resembling 'imperialism' . . . involved in the present development of that policy of expansion which has been part of the history of America from the day she became a nation. The words mean absolutely nothing as applied to our present policy in the Philippines."[102] "There is not an imperialist in the country that I have yet met," he told a Utah audience.[103]

Much of the campaign, indeed, was a positive appeal to make us a world power through "expansion" that campaign speakers insisted was not "imperialism."[c] The denial that

[a] After the election Henry Higginson, the Boston banker, warned that the Republicans must remodel their foreign policy and let the Philippines and Cuba "manage their own affairs well or ill," or they would "go out of power next time." "If a good and able democrat of high character had been put up" in 1900, Higginson wrote, McKinley would have been defeated on the imperialist issue.[100]

[b] Yet privately to his friend Clowes, the British naval expert, he called the spirit he admired "the imperialist instinct" and expressed disheartenment over the lack of it Americans exhibited.[101]

[c] Lodge, for instance, declared, "I do not think there is any such thing as 'imperialism,' but I am clearly of the opinion that there is such a thing as

we were like foreign nations "imperialistic" and the insistence that we were rather carrying forward an old American tradition were useful, both because they quieted fears of people about a new departure and because they made possible the marshaling of national pride in a glorious past. Jefferson's acquisition of Louisiana, Jackson's exploits against the Seminoles, Custer's against the Sioux, and American victories over the dictatorship of Santa Anna in the Mexican War were all brought forward to arouse national pride in support of American expansion into the Philippines.[105] The thing "we look back to with the greatest pride," Roosevelt told the Mormons of Utah, "is the fact that the wilderness here has been conquered by you men of the West. . . . To each generation is alloted its task. . . . Our fathers conquered the West but we are a feeble folk and we cannot hold the Philippines." "Base is the [anti-expansionist] counsel and base will be our people if they take that counsel," he told the men of Utah.[106]

Besides, our "national honor" was involved. "The question now," Roosevelt insisted, "is not whether we shall expand for we have already expanded—but whether we shall contract. The Philippines are now part of American territory. To surrender them would be to surrender American territory."[107] "From unimpeachable authority," he told a St. Louis audience, "we have heard . . . how the friendly natives who have trusted to our good faith are tortured for their friendliness to our flag, how their limbs are broken and their tongues torn out . . . because they have been friendly with us in this struggle. Now, shall we abandon them to such a fate as that? Never, while we keep faith."[108] Our duty encompassed Cuba, too, as well as the Philippines. "We cannot, in honor, refuse to do the duty left us" by the war, Roosevelt urged. "The blood of hundreds of thousands of

'expansion' and that the United States must control some distant dependencies."[104]

slaughtered Cubans" would "cry aloud in vain."[109] "We
have hoisted our flag," he told North Dakotans, "and it is
not fashioned of the stuff which can be quickly hauled
down."[110]

Roosevelt was convinced that expanding American rule
over the Philippines would extend civilization but he never
really defined what he meant by "civilization." The American flag was "to bring civilization into the waste places of
the earth."[111] Therefore anti-imperialists that opposed expansion were opposing the spread of civilization. In objecting to our establishing orderly government in the Philippines
by putting down rebellion they were continuing the bloodshed, Roosevelt charged, and were responsible for the cruelties of the warfare in the Philippines. The charges of Bryan
and his followers that "our gallant little army . . . in the
Philippines is an army of murderers and ravishers" are
"slanderous falsehoods" known to be slanderous falsehoods
when made.[112] We are fighting Filipinos, Roosevelt proclaimed, because they are killing our soldiers.[113] "Bryanist
democracy . . . is the most dangerous foe . . . of our soldiers
who are now facing death," Roosevelt declared. "The bullets that slay our men in Luzon are inspired by the de-
nouncers of America here."[114] The Filipino "will stop killing
our soldiers very soon after he becomes convinced that he
will receive no aid in the effort from the party of which
Mr. Bryan is the chief." Then, Roosevelt continued, "we are
going to civilize him and give him . . . peace, order, and
individual liberty."[115]

Roosevelt's normal capacity to convince himself that his
was the cause of righteousness was enhanced in this case by
the close relationship in his mind between foreign and domestic problems. He could believe the more easily that Bryan
and the Democrats were supporting "anarchy" in the Philippines because he was firmly convinced that Bryanism stood
for "anarchy, license, and mob violence" at home. "Bryan

seeks to sow seeds of malice and envy between Americans,"
Roosevelt warned. "He is a pupil of that most dangerous
political school . . . in which Marat and Robespierre were
the teachers." Bryan taught Americans "sullen hatred and
distrust of their fellows." At home Roosevelt warned against
"the devious way that leads to bitter class hatred, that leads
ultimately to class strife, . . . to loss of liberty." "If ever we
grow to substitute lawless mob violence for the orderly
liberty we enjoy under the law, . . . the rule of brute force
for the rule of the ballot, then we will indeed be in measur-
able distance of losing our liberty." [116] It was easy for a man
who was certain that his opponents represented these dangerous tendencies at home to become convinced that they
were promoting them in the Philippines. Consequently, "the
only danger of imperialism," Roosevelt proclaimed, "is if it
is invited as a reaction against anarchy. Anarchy is the
handmaiden of tyranny." [117] Hence tyranny and imperialism
would come to the Philippines only if Bryan succeeded in
creating chaos there that would lead to tyranny under natives or force outsiders to impose it to eliminate the chaos.

In part Roosevelt answered the charges about cruel treatment of Filipinos by countercharges concerning American
Negroes. During the campaign he repeatedly took Bryan
and the Democrats to task for insincerity in demanding self-
government for "Malay bandits" while they were conniving
at the "denial of the right of self-government to our fellow-
Americans of dusky color in North Carolina." [118] At Fort
Wayne in October Roosevelt answered Bryan's charge that
the Republican party was "concerned only with money and
ignored questions concerning human rights." "He has no
right to speak of those rights at all," Roosevelt retorted,
"until he is willing to denounce the wrong to the black man
in North Carolina, and with at least the fervor that he uses
in denouncing the wholly imaginary wrongs done to the brown
man in the Philippines." [119] Roosevelt told of the bravery of

Negroes he saw fighting in the Spanish War and suggested the Democrats devote some time to "the wrongs of the men on whose breasts may be seen the scars gained as they fought for the flag." [120] In insisting at St. Louis that the nation should not "shrink from its destiny," he urged that we should pursue it "in the spirit of true Americanism, that is not in the spirit that depends upon color, creed, or birthplace." [121]

Yet for darker people of the Philippines he repeatedly expressed contempt. They were "Tagal bandits," "Malay bandits," "Chinese halfbreeds." [122] He kept comparing the Chinese and Filipinos to the Sioux, the Comanche, and the Apache Indians. [123] He defended himself against attacks of Democrats, who sought to protect the natives' rights, by again citing Jefferson. Jefferson had seen no incongruity between the theory of "the consent of the governed" and "the establishment of a government on common sense grounds" in the new territory whose people he had pronounced "as yet [as] incapable of self government as China." [124] Why, then, should we apply our principles of self-government to Filipinos? Roosevelt expressed the common race superiority view of his day when he declared: "Peace has come through the last century to large sections of the earth because the civilized races have spread over the earth's dark places. It is a good thing for the world but "above all, . . . for the people of those countries . . . that France should be in Algiers, England in the Soudan and Russia in Turkestan." "Now what is our duty in the Philippines? It is a duty to govern those islands in the interest of the islanders, not less in accordance with our own honor and interest." [125] Yet he never introduced the idea of Beveridge and many other contemporaries that it was God who made the English-speaking peoples superior to others and had made darker peoples inferior. To have credited God with giving us peculiar fitness to rule over backward peoples would have ignored our long struggle upward to civilized beings. It would have implied a fixity of superiority and inferiority by Divine creation that was no part of Roosevelt's conception of race relations. Roosevelt believed in progress through struggle. He always credited English-speaking people with having developed their own superior institutions; he sounded constant warnings that it required striving and virility and willingness to sacrifice to preserve them. He believed that ultimately backward peoples could through the same effort over a similarly long period attain many of the same superior qualities.

Roosevelt had a genuine desire to give the Filipinos good government. He promised them liberty, but "liberty with order," "such liberty as throughout the dark ages of their history they have never known," such liberty as they could never have under the rule of their own nationalist leaders, but it was to be liberty "under the American flag." [126] "You cannot introduce to people in one stage of civilization the system which has been by slow degrees evolved by another people," Roosevelt warned. "Self-government is a difficult route. We have seen, during this century, too many cases where nations have sought to introduce just exactly the form of government we have, and have utterly failed, because, though they could introduce the name, they did not have the men to introduce the faith." [127] "The Cubans are being helped along the path to independence," Roosevelt declared, "as readily as her own citizens are content she should go." So, too, the Filipinos will be permitted gradual participation in their own government as fast as proves feasible. But the form of government is a mere matter of expediency. "If we have a right to establish a stable government," Roosevelt argued, "it necessarily follows that it is not only our right but our duty to support that government until the natives gradually grow fit to sustain it themselves. How else will it be stable? The minute we leave it, it ceases to be

stable." [128] "It must be remembered always," he cautioned,
"that governing these islands in the interest of the inhabitants may not necessarily be to govern them as the inhabitants at the moment prefer." [129]

What Roosevelt could never comprehend was the nationalist aspirations of the Filipinos. He wanted to give them
"civilization" and "liberty" as his father out of a sense of
noblesse oblige had given charity and moral precepts to the
poor of New York City. This desire was benevolent on his
part. Hence the Filipinos that opposed it were in his mind
opposing what was right; hence they were wicked. In consequence, he believed the worst of Emilio Aguinaldo and his
fellow-patriots. They were venal, corrupt; they were bandits,
traitors. In Roosevelt's eyes Filipino patriots were always
rebels and Filipinos that collaborated with Americans were
faithful. Our cruelty to Filipinos was justice; their justice
to traitors to their nationalist cause was "cruelty." Roosevelt was sincerely shocked that the Aguinaldo nationalists
should hate "their fellow countrymen who have had the
good sense and genuine patriotism to realize that the true
interests of the islands lay in the American government." To
compare Aguinaldo with George Washington Roosevelt
found preposterous. Roosevelt compared him instead to
Benedict Arnold. [130] The irony of it was that the group in
this country that were themselves most nationalistic could
not comprehend that "backward peoples" might develop
nationalist tendencies and might prefer liberty to efficient
government by a "superior race."* Roosevelt seems not to
have foreseen the possibility that the spread of civilization
through expansion of the rule of "superior races" over

---

* William James saw this. "We are now openly engaged," he protested, "in
crushing out the sacredest thing in this great human world—the attempt of a
people long enslaved to attain to the possession of itself, to organize its laws and
government, to be free to follow its internal destinies according to its own
ideals." [131]

" backward " ones might some day arouse nationalist aspirations that would threaten that civilization itself.

Economic factors were perforce coming to be important. The ardent expansionists had not themselves been motivated by the economic advantages of imperialism. Yet they were not unaware of the economic pressure groups that stood to gain by expansion. When therefore they came to sell expansion to the American people they gladly talked up its economic profitableness. It was not Roosevelt's forte to sell economic profits to the public. But as candidate he gladly accepted the help of those that did. At the Republican Convention where Roosevelt was nominated, Chauncey Depew, spokesman of big business, declared: " The American people now produce $2,000,000,000 worth more than they can consume, and we have met the emergency, and by the providence of God, by the statesmanship of William McKinley, and by the valor of Roosevelt and his associates, we have our market in Cuba, . . . in Puerto Rico, . . . in Hawaii, . . . in the Philippines, and we stand in the presence of 800,000,000 of people, with the Pacific as an American lake, and the American artisans producing better and cheaper goods than any country in the world. . . . Let production go on, . . . let the factories do their best, let labor be employed at the highest wages, because the world is ours, and we have conquered it by Republican principles." [132]

At a Carnegie Hall meeting to ratify Roosevelt's nomination, Depew justified our seizure of the Philippines. " The guns of Dewey in Manilla Bay," he explained, " were heard across Asia and Africa, they echoed through the palace at Peking and brought to the Oriental mind a new and potent force among western nations. We, in common with the countries of Europe are striving to enter the limitless markets of the east. . . . These people respect nothing but power." " I believe," he continued, " the Philippines will be enormous markets and sources of wealth, . . . but, beyond these con-

siderations, the part that they enabled us to play upon the
world's stage in this war of humanity" against the Boxers
in China and in improving our position "among the millions
of Asia compensate and justify their capture, the suppression
of the rebellion within their borders, and the holding of them
forever as territories of the United States."[133] Henry White
wrote Lodge from the London Embassy that events in China
were showing the wisdom of our acquisition of the Philippines.[134] And Roosevelt thought that we should keep the
flag flying over the Philippines because we must create a
market for American factories. "We are for expansion and
anything else that will tend to benefit the American laborer
and manufacturer," he declared.[135]

Lodge, White, and Roosevelt were all pleased over the way
our government had acted in the Boxer uprising. Lodge
wrote White that we would "inevitably act with England
and Japan," and possibly France, "to prevent the absorption
of China by Russia and keep the Empire open for our trade
and commerce."[136] White was glad we were acting in China
"as a great Power with our vast commercial interests
should."[137] Lodge regretted that the British were tied up
in the Boer War, for China he felt was ten thousand times
more important than South Africa.[138] White was delighted
that European nations now understood our position on China
and now were deeply interested as they would not have been
a short time ago in our intentions and policy in the Far
East.[139] Roosevelt felt McKinley deserved credit for all time
because of his promptness in joining the civilized powers in
China.[140]

In Roosevelt's own mind the desire to have us a great
power seemed to outweigh all other considerations. "I wish
to see the United States the dominant power on the shores
of the Pacific Ocean," he wrote in October, 1900.[141] If we did
not keep the Philippines some other power might take them
and with them the capacity to rival us in the Pacific.[142] He

sought reëlection of the Republicans "to declare in unmistakable terms . . . that we as little fear to face our duty in the far islands of the eastern seas as we fear to face our duties at home." [143] He asked reëlection of McKinley "because now at the dawn of a new century we wish this giant of the West, the greatest republic upon which the sun has ever shone, to start fair in the race of national greatness." [144]

Yet to fail to understand Roosevelt's concern for qualities of character is to misconceive the man. Throughout his activity to promote expansion ran the desire to develop qualities that he considered manly in a person and essential to greatness in a nation. Honesty, moral responsibility, courage, duty, willingness to struggle, liberty, being civilized were his ideals for himself and for a desirable citizen within a country. "Now, one moment upon what is greater than the material side?" he pleaded with a St. Louis audience. "It is a great thing to belong to a prosperous country, a country rich in mines, in factory, in farm, ranches and railroads. It is a greater thing to belong to a country that has for its background the memory of great deeds valiantly done, and woe to the country when a generation rises which . . . shrinks from doing the rough work of the world. . . . The man who counts . . . is not the man of mere refinement and ease loving pleasure. . . . It is the man who goes out into the world to struggle and stumble and get up again, and go on and try, and be beaten and try again, to face difficulties, and out of difficulties, trampling them under foot, to make his way to splendid ultimate triumph. So it is with the nation. . . . Thrice happy is the nation that has a great and glorious history, a history of glorious achievement for itself and the races of mankind. . . . Think of the peoples of Europe stumbling upward through the Dark Ages, doing much work in a wrong way, sometimes falling back, but ever coming forward again, forward, forward, until our great civilization, as we know it now, was developed at last out of the struggles

and failures and victories of millions of men who dared to do
the world's work." [145]

Actually Roosevelt was a premature rebel against the
dominance of the economic man of the nineteenth and early
twentieth century. He knew his Brooks Adams well. During
the campaign of 1900 he and his friend Lodge read Adams's
new book *America's Economic Supremacy* and Lodge sent
a copy of it to President McKinley. "It seems to me,"
Lodge told the President, "one of the most brilliant and
interesting discussions of present economic conditions and of
the policy of expansion." [146]

Roosevelt was himself concerned about the problem of the
future of civilization that intrigued his friend Brooks Adams.
Brooks he considered partly crazy, [147] but the sane part of
Brooks impressed him tremendously. He refused to accept
the pessimism of *The Law of Civilization and Decay.* He
would not admit that the advent of the capitalist meant an
inevitable decay of our society. Russia, Spain, and Morocco,
he pointed out, had almost entirely escaped capitalistic development. Spain had "exterminated the economic man in
the interest of the martial and emotional man," and yet, in
part because of this, artists and soldiers had sunk lower in
Spain than elsewhere. "There is a decrease of the martial
type found among savages and in the Middle Ages," Roosevelt admitted, "except as it still survives in the slums of
great cities." "But there remains," he insisted, "a martial
type infinitely more efficient than any that preceded it. . . .
There are branches of industry which call forth in those that
follow them more hardihood, manliness, and courage than
any industry of ancient times." "White men are more gentle and more honest than before, it cannot be said that they
are less brave; and they are certainly more efficient as
fighters." [148]

Yet he shared Brooks Adams's belief that *if* the economic
man conquered the military man, *if* the acquisitive man were
allowed to seize control and destroy through his greed the

creative forces of society, then civilization would be endangered. Roosevelt like Adams saw certain tendencies that did "constitute a standing menace not only to our prosperity but to our existence." He deplored the fact that the rich were getting richer, that there was absolutely, if not relatively, more poverty, and that the poor were huddling in immense masses in cities. "My own belief is," he wrote Spring Rice in 1899, "that we shall have to pay far more attention to . . . tremendous problems . . . of the relations of capital and labor . . . than to any question of expansion for the next fifty years, and this although I am an expansionist and believe that we can go on and take our place among the nations of the world." [149] "A certain softness of fibre in civilized nations" he admitted; and, "if it were to prove progressive," this "might mean the development of a cultured and refined people quite unable to hold its own in conflicts." He recognized and protested against a love of ease, a desire for profit at the expense of honor. He regretted a tendency to become fixed and lose flexibility. "Most ominous of all," was "a very pronounced tendency among the most highly civilized races, and among the most highly civilized portions of all races, to lose the power of multiplying, and even to decrease." [150] "There are grave signs of deterioration in the English speaking peoples here and there," he wrote his sister in December, 1899; "not merely in the evident lack of fighting edge in the British soldier, but in the diminishing birth rate . . . ; in the excessive urban growth; in the love of luxury, and the turning of sport into a craze of the upper classes." [151] He was still worrying about this problem of the survival of civilization in letters to Lord Balfour and Cecil Spring Rice in 1908.[152]

Yet he saw no need to yield to these tendencies nor to let the economic and slothful man overpower the creative and military man. Indeed, his whole life became a struggle to promote the heroic qualities in foreign policy and in his ideals for American youth. He saw no reason to permit Brooks

Adams's dire prophecy to come true. In his expansionism he had to use economic forces and the greed of his fellow-men. Material force could strengthen a nation, but material considerations remained to him merely means. Economic prosperity must be kept the servant of more important values. His ends were associated with the courage, the virility, the power, the greatness of his country.

Perhaps Brooks Adams himself in a letter to Lodge best sums up what Roosevelt was thinking as he entered the new century—and, coincidentally, the White House. "I most earnestly and honestly believe," wrote Adams, "that we are now in the great struggle for our national supremacy, which means our national existence. . . . We must now be masters or we must break down. We must become so organized that we can handle great concerns and vast forces cheaper and better than others. It is fate, it is destiny. I believe that, unsatisfactory in many ways as our present system is, the overthrow of McKinley, or even the failure to strengthen his administration, would be a blow to our national life." And then Adams added, "Feeling this I am happy at Roosevelt's nomination, for I conceive that he will strengthen the tendency toward activity. . . . I can't say I think the office of president of the Senate particularly adapted to him, but he has logically become the representative of a great principle—a question on which I feel very deeply." [153]

Roosevelt himself was serious with a sense of destiny. "The twentieth century looms before us big with the fate of many nations," Roosevelt prophesied as he peered into that new century. "If we stand idly by, if we seek merely swollen, slothful ease and ignoble peace, if we shrink from the hard contests where men must win at hazard of their lives and at the risk of all they hold dear, then the bolder and stronger peoples will pass us by, and will win for themselves the domination of the world. Let us therefore boldly face the life of strife." [154]

chapter **III**

ROOSEVELT *and the Cementing of*
an Anglo-American Entente

Six months before McKinley's assassination made
him President, Roosevelt wrote to his friend and confidant,
the British diplomat Cecil Spring Rice: " I think the twentieth century will still be the century of the men who speak
English."[1] To understand Roosevelt's views on foreign
policy it is essential to comprehend this belief of his in the
oneness of the American and British interest and his conviction that in combination the Americans and the British
could dominate the world—to the advantage of civilization.

To interpret Roosevelt and Lodge as unqualified Anglo-
phobes in the 1890's is to misunderstand them. To class
them together at all in this matter is mistaken, because Lodge
was always more suspicious of England than was Roosevelt.
Both men were simply intense American nationalists. Both
had contempt for the sort of American that chose to live in
England or that came to feel England was superior to his
own country. For this reason Roosevelt had from young
manhood disliked the expatriate Henry James and his books.
In 1884 he made a speech in Brooklyn in which he said James
was to other literary men as a poodle was to other dogs.[*][2]

_____

[*] " The poodle," explained the twenty-five-year-old Roosevelt, " had his hair

Roosevelt was always contemptuous of Americans that married European titled folk. He scorned importations of British sports as substitutes for American sports.[3] His and Lodge's Americanism was offended by the bigotry of Englishmen that neither knew nor wanted to know anything outside of England. It was Kipling's bigotry that made Roosevelt at first so dislike that fellow-imperialist. Roosevelt and Lodge delighted in stories at the expense of Englishmen ignorant of the rest of the world[a]—with whom they sometimes clashed.[4] The English *were* exasperatingly unaware of America in the 1890's. Even John Hay, widely known for his love of the British, wrote Lodge from London in 1894, " If it were not so offensive the ignorance of people over here about American politics would be very amusing. . . . I occasionally relieve my mind by saying something offensive in return. But it does not generally pay—they are too apt to take a kick for a compliment." [5]

These attitudes toward Britishers were a form of nationalism of the period before Roosevelt began to think of world politics. And in spite of his personal reactions to individuals, he and Lodge admired much about the British as a people. Both men also had close friends among the British ruling classes. Both felt that in our ideas and our interest we were closer to Britain than to any other power. Lodge joked about " twisting the lion's tail " and Roosevelt admitted in 1900

combed, and was somewhat ornamental, but never useful." So James " possessed . . . refinement and culture to see what was wrong, but . . . none of the robuster virtues that would enable . . . [him] to come out and do the right."

[a] Roosevelt's sharp tilt with Margot Asquith in 1910 sprang out of his old annoyance at English bigotry and ignorance about America. To Mrs. Asquith he wrote: " In your letter you say that ' there are some very nice Americans over here, but they are mostly idle and take their degree in society, that their kind of home life is not ' yours, but that ' they have always been kind ' to you personally. I quite agree with you as to some of the Americans of whom you speak, but I must add that they seem to me to be in entire intellectual and moral harmony with those among your countrymen and countrywomen with whom they like to associate."

that he had once been "rather anti-British." [6] But when they protested about Britain in the more serious field of foreign policy as they often did in the earlier 1890's, their protests were against British policies that conflicted with our interests, not expressions of a hostility to the British themselves.[7] With both men, protest against British policies that did conflict arose in part from a determination to force Britain to a realization of the importance of clearing up our differences so that our more fundamental mutual interests and common culture could be served to the fullest.

There was, however, in other quarters at the turn of the century a vigorous Anglophobia. Actually public opinion was divided. Much of it was friendly to the English; but the tradition of hostility to Britain was strong. Whatever leaders might decide, it would take years of amicable relations to overcome in one segment of opinion the hatred of England that frequently slowed the leaders in establishing an entente with Britain. After responsible leaders in both countries had gone far toward coöperation politicians and the press were conscious of the segment of public opinion still strongly Anglophobe. Responsible leaders had difficulty preventing the Republican Convention of 1900 from publicly urging the annexation of Canada. When Hay was trying to work out with Britain defense of the open door and the integrity of China he was impeded by a widespread Anglophobia. "Anything we should now do in China to take care of our imperilled interests," he cried out in despair, "would be set down to 'subservience to Great Britain.' . . . With England, Germany and Japan we might manage to save our skins, but such a proceeding would make all our fools throw fits in the market place—And the fools are numerous." "All I have ever done with England," wailed Hay, "is to have wrung great concessions out of her with no compensation, and yet these idiots say I am not an American, because I don't say 'to hell with the Queen' at every breath." [8]

The sharpness of the Venezuelan crisis of the '90's and the quick recovery of mutual respect illustrate, however, the fundamental soundness of the Anglo-American friendship that was developing. When the imbroglio occurred, close friends of Roosevelt and Lodge in England expressed dismay. Friends and foes of America alike were shocked when they were forced to realize the hostility toward Britain that existed. James Bryce, Moreton Frewen, economist and brother-in-law of Lady Randolph Churchill, Arthur Balfour, who would be Prime Minister while Roosevelt was President, all asked how America could feel so hostile to Britain.[9] "I confess myself astonished," Bryce wrote Roosevelt, "at . . . the apparent existence of ill will towards Britain in a large part of your population. What in the world is the reason?" "People here seem to have been taken utterly by surprise," Bryce continued. "Not one man out of ten in the House of Commons even knew there was such a thing as a Venezuelan question pending."[10]

This sudden realization of the American Government's willingness to go to war over something that was not of great importance to Britain shocked many British into new attitudes toward America. "The lesson taught Lord Salisbury," Roosevelt rejoiced, "is one which will not soon be forgotten by English statesmen."[11] Henry White was certain Lodge's article on Venezuela[a] had a marked effect in England.[12] "The plain speaking in the Venezuela question did infinite good here," Theodore's sister Bamie[b] reported from London.[13] Ten months later Lodge could announce: "Our relations with England have never been so cordial and friendly. Never has there been a time when there was less danger of trouble between the two countries."[14]

[a] "England, Venezuela, and the Monroe Doctrine," *North American Review*, CLX (June, 1895), 651-658.

[b] Anna Roosevelt Cowles, hostess to her fifth cousin, James Roosevelt Roosevelt, secretary at the American Embassy.

In giving assurance that nothing was farther from the people's minds than interfering with American rights in the New World, Bryce told Roosevelt significantly: "Our hands are more than sufficiently full elsewhere."[15] It was true, Britain's relations on the Continent were not going well. Isolated from both of the rival alliances that at this time had grown up, she was worried about the balance of power and about friendships for herself. In South Africa she was facing serious war with the Boers. At the height of Britain's dispute with America the Kaiser sent his telegram of January 3, 1896, to Boer President Paul Kruger congratulating him on the interception of England's Jameson raiders, which had struck a blow at British prestige. The very next day Prime Minister Salisbury, who had sent the provocative message to Cleveland, had a letter from his colonial secretary, Joseph Chamberlain, suggesting that the government should make "a serious effort to come to terms with America."[16] In February when Ambassador Thomas F. Bayard asked coöperation in determining the Venezuela boundary, the British granted it promptly, graciously, almost eagerly.[17] By March, in an article defending our stand on Venezuela, Roosevelt could show that Chamberlain had revealed himself blandly indifferent to the expressed view of his chief in the Government and had recognized the Monroe Doctrine and disavowed any thought of ignoring it. There were symptoms, Roosevelt pointed out, that even Salisbury was changing ground; "Balfour has gone still farther in the right direction," he exulted, "and the Liberal leaders farther still."[18] It was plain that the complications of international politics were making it easier for the British to see the value of American good will.

Roosevelt, Lodge, and Mahan, on their part, were friendly to Britain when her interests and ours did not clash. Mahan stressed the mutuality of Anglo-American interests. In November, 1894, he published an article on "The Possibilities of an Anglo-American Reunion." [19] Lodge in London in October, 1895, and John Hay and Henry White in the summer of 1896 talked over the critical Anglo-American relations with Balfour and other leaders of both parties.[20] " A war between the two great English speaking peoples," Lodge told Balfour, would be " a terrible calamity to civilization." [21] In October, 1895, Roosevelt, who had just left the Civil Service Commission in Washington to become Police Commissioner in New York City, told a Boston audience: "I have not the slightest feeling of hostility to England, only I want Americans to be Americans. There are many admirable traits in the British character, and one of them is the fact an Englishman stands up for England." [22] In his Venezuela article Roosevelt declared: "In general . . . [England's] success tells for the success of civilization, and we wish her well. But where her interests enlist her against the progress of civilization and in favor of the oppression of other nationalities who are struggling upward, our sympathies are immediately forfeited." [23]

Roosevelt and Lodge tried to explain America's position on Venezuela to their British friends. Roosevelt's similar letter to Bryce has vanished, but Lodge's long letter to Balfour explaining his and Roosevelt's position survives. " To you," Lodge explained, " the question in Venezuela involves some thousands of square miles of territory—nothing more. . . . For us there is at stake there a principle . . . vital to our safety and our peace." " I readily accept your statement that you do not desire to extend your possessions in the Americas," Lodge conceded. "But other nations are less scrupulous and if we submitted in silence to your taking territory with a strong hand in the name of a boundary dispute we could not oppose consistently any other nation doing the same. The earth hunger is very keen in these days. If it once began South America might easily suffer the fate of Africa and we should find ourselves . . . in constant danger of war." [24]

Lodge tried to clarify for Balfour, too, as Roosevelt did for Bryce, the causes of America's hostility toward England. Lodge charged the British with " a state of ignorance about the United States " that irritated America just as we have seen it irritated Lodge himself and Roosevelt. " Until very lately your newspapers gave less space to the United States than to Belgium or Holland. Surely this was not wise. Such information as you got in the newspapers was generally wrong ª and even now you are badly served." [25] Because of England's indifference to things American, much of her impression of the United States, Lodge and Roosevelt felt, came from Americans living abroad that knew little more about America than she did.ᵇ

Specifically Lodge complained to Balfour of England's attitude on several subjects important to the United States. One was Alaskan seals. " In two years," he declared, " those harmless and valuable animals will be extinct. We cannot see why you should have defended so far a set of adventurers chiefly Americans on such a pursuit under the Canadian flag." Lodge deplored, too, the sudden springing up of land claims in Alaska and the denunciation of the *modus vivendi* there. Britain's establishment of fortifications on Atlantic coast islands he called similarly unfortunate, for while the islands were unimportant the fortifications could have no

---

ª Among themselves, indeed, the Roosevelt-Lodge group constantly deplored four sources of misinformation in England about America: (1) the " Anglomaniac press " in America; (2) " selfish and timid men on this side of the water, who clamorously strive to misrepresent American, and to mislead English, public opinion "; (3) misinformed British correspondents in America like Smalley of the *London Times*; and (4) the class of Americans most frequently seen in England who, after a brief residence there, can not " speak except slightingly of their own home and people."

ᵇ Roosevelt's sister wrote of arguments at John Hay's dinner table in London with a group of this sort of expatriates that included Bret Harte, Mrs. Henry White, Henry James, John Sargent, and " Willie "—later Lord—Astor whom the group urged for the American ambassadorship—" all because the Prince of Wales had been stopping with Willie Astor for Sunday."

meaning except against us. Finally, and most serious, was England's standing alone in opposition to an international agreement on bi-metallism that would permit Eastern gold men and Western silver men to resolve their differences.[26] Britain's uncompromising attitude on silver, Lodge pointed out, made the whole South and West hostile to her as the cause of their own suffering and as the backer of Northeastern gold sentiment.[27] The bottom of the trouble in recent times, Lodge wrote Frewen, " is England's attitude on the money question and the way in which she has snubbed all our efforts to do anything for silver." [28]

" There is no nation on earth," Lodge argued with Balfour, " which England could so easily make her fast friend as the United States. Every consideration of sentiment and interest alike pointed to this as the right policy and it was moreover extremely simple." " Yet," Lodge protested, " from 1776 England's policy has been one of almost studied unfriendliness." " I know," he admitted, " that we have always had friends among English public men," from Chatham through Bright to yourself. " But these have been individuals." " The English statesman," he prodded Balfour, " who would . . . treat us as you speak of us and our relations to you in your speech, . . . would be astonished at the response which he would meet with—But we are very like our forefathers and our cousins in England, we are goodnatured but we dislike to be crowded." [29]

The British friends of America somehow felt it had been America and not England that had been hostile in Venezuela. " I daresay," Frewen replied to Lodge, " our statesmen are truculent, fierce and barbarous, and that the ' eagle ' is a bird with a soft and cooing note—it may be so; but apart from statescraft, I know that we as a Nation love you well." And he quoted Macaulay's speech about " that mighty Nation, whose veins are filled with our blood, whose minds are nourished by our literature, and upon whom is entailed the rich

inheritance of our civilization, our freedom, and our glory." [30]
" I am much puzzled," Balfour wrote Frewen in a letter
Frewen sent Lodge, " as to what Cabot Lodge means by
suggesting that English Governments ' seek to alienate the
United States.' This most assuredly has never been their intention." " Surely," he continued, " it is not mere national
prejudice which makes me think that . . . Salisbury's Des-
patch . . . compares favorably in point of *conciliatoriness*
with the document to which it was a reply." [31] Yet genuine
conciliation there was on both sides. Balfour made a speech
that warmed Lodge's heart. Olney, Cleveland's truculent
Secretary of State, in turn offered at this time to coöperate
with England in dealing with the Turks in Armenia and
Roosevelt approved the proposal.[32] Even before the Spanish
War, Olney spoke publicly about " the advantages of a joint
action between the U. S. and Gt. Britain ' for the betterment
of the human race.' " [33] And in 1899 Roosevelt wrote: " I
have been one of the people who have experienced a change
of heart. . . . I should not republish my Venezuela article
now. . . . Fundamentally I feel that all the English speaking
peoples come much nearer to one another in political and
social ideals, in their systems of government and of civic and
domestic morality, than any of them do to any other peoples.
I want to get along well with everybody . . . I wish them
well where they do not conflict with the English speaking
peoples, and I earnestly hope that there will not be the slightest rift come between the English speaking peoples themselves." [34]

During the crisis over Venezuela the British and American
governments had even discussed a general Anglo-American
arbitration treaty. Cleveland and Olney were enthusiastic
and on January 11, 1897, Olney and Ambassador Julian
Pauncefote signed a treaty whose terms were far broader and
more inclusive than those later agreed upon under Roosevelt
and Taft. Cleveland pushed the Treaty, but an outburst of

opposition in the Senate made a favorable vote impossible
before Cleveland left office. McKinley, however, also urged
his new Republican Senate to approve. After heated debate
ratification failed on May 5, 1897, by a 43-26 vote. Only
three more votes were needed for the necessary two-thirds.[35]
Rejection of the Treaty was disappointing to those seeking
Anglo-American coöperation.

The Roosevelt-Lodge-Mahan group's reaction to this
initial effort at closer friendship was interesting but confused.
Mahan never had confidence in arbitration; he always
stressed the importance of superior armed power in the settlement of disputes; yet he eagerly sought closer relations with
Britain.[36] Lodge's position was more difficult to determine.
Olney blamed him bitterly for helping kill the Treaty and
accused him of trying to harass England into accepting bi-
metallism.[37] Lodge did make a speech in the Senate vigorously attacking England.[38] On the other hand, Lodge professed to favor the Treaty and to be working for a favorable
report from committee and then for approval by the Senate.[39]
He insisted he believed in " the principle of arbitration and
the desirability of settling every question that can be properly settled in that way by peaceful means." But the Treaty
was " a very large and far reaching step, . . . the most important treaty . . . submitted to the country in many years."
Lodge sought time to study it. He wanted to be certain that
it was not so sweeping as to force us into abandoning the
Monroe Doctrine by submitting to arbitration cases that
arose under that Doctrine.[40] Olney assured Lodge that
neither he as American negotiator nor the British had any
idea of including Monroe Doctrine issues under the Treaty.
Lodge argued that if this were true then an amendment
specifically excluding them could give offense to no one and
should be included.[41] He opposed agreeing to arbitrate matters that, when they arose, no nation would actually arbitrate. To promise more than would be lived up to would

lead to throwing the whole Treaty aside and would retard the cause of arbitration.[42] Before long Lodge was arguing that the Treaty could not be approved at all without this fundamental amendment protecting the Monroe Doctrine.[43] After the defeat of the Treaty in May Lodge recorded in his diary that their talks with other senators had persuaded him and Chandler of the futility of attempting anything further.[44]

Roosevelt's view on the arbitration treaty is even harder to determine. When the Bering Sea arbitration went against the United States, he was upset. " It should teach us," he wrote in 1895, " to be exceedingly cautious about entering into any arbitration."[45] " I believe in arbitration and in peace," he told a New York yacht club, " but we would dearly purchase a hundred arbitration treaties if they lulled us into trusting to them alone to preserve peace. . . . I hope we will ratify the treaty and build ten new battleships."[46] To Henry White he wrote in March, " I am glad McKinley came out so strongly for the Arbitration Treaty."[47] Yet in June after the Treaty had been killed, he wrote to an Irish friend, " In its amended form I did not object to the arbitration treaty, although I confess I felt exceedingly lukewarm about it, and I should oppose it tooth and nail if it tended to make us rely less on our own strength and fighting force, or if it gave away any conceivable right." " I didn't take any interest in it really! " he added. " It is unimportant as amended."[48]

" Friends of the U. S. . . . are disheartened by the demonstrations in the Senate," Bryce wrote.[49] Yet the outpouring of certain sections of public opinion—church groups and intellectuals, for instance—in approval of the Treaty counteracted to some extent the strained feeling of Britain. Britain's eagerness for the Treaty, on the other hand, made evident her determination to cultivate American friendship.[50]

Seeking an additional chance to demonstrate policy changes determined as early as 1896, Britain found her opportunity in the Spanish War two years later. She maintained a technical neutrality that was unimpeachable, but her sympathies she made evident. And, where she could without violating her technical obligation as a neutral, she helped the American cause.[*] In Europe she opposed an effort to organize international support for Spain concerning Cuba. In the Far East she sold us ships and coal; Lord Cromer at Cairo enforced restrictions upon Spanish war vessels so as to delay their arriving to fight Dewey in the Philippines. Contrariwise, rules were interpreted in our favor at Hong Kong. Above all at Manila the British fleet coöperated with ours in such a way as to prevent German aggression if any was intended.[51] Hay reported as the war broke out that England was " the only European country whose sympathies are not openly against us." " The friendship and sympathy of this country . . . is beyond question," he wrote. " I find it wherever I go—not only in the press, but in private conversation." [52]

Americans grateful for this friendliness warmed to England as never before. Roosevelt's friend Owen Wister described how in the war " England saved us from Germany " and " every determining act of hers was as our friend." [53] To his friend the British military attaché, Arthur Lee, Roosevelt himself wrote, " I shall not forget, and I don't think our people will, England's attitude during the Spanish War, and we all know that it saved us from a chance of very serious foreign complications." [54] Lodge considered the friendly relations established with England one of the most important results of the war and he believed they would last.[55] " What but war," asked Mahan, could have " rent the veil which prevented the English-speaking communities from seeing eye to eye," or could have " revealed to each the face of a brother? " [56] Just before the Spanish War broke out Roose-

---

[*] Germans tried to deny this and persuade Americans that Britain had been hostile and Germans friendly.

velt expressed happiness at seeing " a gradual coming together of the two peoples." [57] In November following the war he wrote Spring Rice, " Isn't it nice to think how closely our two nations have come together this year? We must make every effort to see that they stay together." [58] To Spring Rice in August, 1899, he pointed out that indiscreet speeches of Canadian leaders contemplating war over the Alaskan boundary dispute would two years ago " have provoked frantic retaliatory denunciations . . . and action in the State legislatures and Congress, which really might have endangered the peace." Now the whole episode was dismissed for the most part " with the good-humored remark . . . that to talk of any rupture in . . . [Canadian-American] relations is mere nonsense." [59] " The great mass of Americans," Roosevelt explained to William Archer, a British essayist,"—those who know the least about England and foreign nations,— have been rather more stirred than we suppose to a kindliness for her; and in the second place, . . . in two or three generations, the great bulk of the descendants of the immigrants of non-English origin, become absolutely indistinguishable from other Americans and share their feelings exactly." [60] By 1900, then, Roosevelt was convinced that Americans had " a genuine friendly feeling towards England." [61] For himself he confessed: " The attitude of England in 1898 worked a complete revolution in my feelings and the attitude of the continent at that time opened my eyes to the other side of the question." [62] " All of this may not last," he admitted, " and it probably won't last in its present good shape, but I am greatly mistaken if we ever slide back into the old condition of bickering and angry distrust,* and there will always be at least a chance that in a great emergency, the nation of

---

* Yet in 1900 Roosevelt wrote Spring Rice sharply: " I am not an Anglomaniac any more than I am an Anglophobe. I do not believe in ' slopping over '; but I am keenly alive to the friendly countenance England gave us in 1898, and throughout the campaign I have made hearty acknowledgements of this."

the two which vitally needs it, may get more than moral aid from the other." [63]

On the British side, too, there were other indications of a new attitude in addition to the Government's official acts. Hay wrote from London in May, 1898, " The state of feeling here is the best I have ever known. . . . The Royal family, by habit and tradition, are most careful not to break the rules of strict neutrality, but even among them I find nothing but hearty kindness and . . . sympathy." Political leaders of both parties sought to outdo each other in sympathy.[64] " For the first time in my life I find the ' drawing room ' sentiment altogether with us. If we wanted it . . . we could have the practical assistance of the British Navy," Hay assured Lodge.[65] White found the British people in June " almost as much interested in ' the war ' . . . as our people are," and chafing at the delay in getting at the Spanish fleet.[66] Of Arthur Lee, the British military attaché with the American troops in Cuba, Roosevelt later wrote to Root: " No man of our own army took a greater interest in our success, felt a more sincere pride when we did well, or more genuine anxiety over our blunders and shortcomings." [67]

On receipt of a letter from Lodge suggesting how much it would help, Ambassador John Hay urged Colonial Secretary Chamberlain to show that the Opposition did not have a monopoly of friendliness for America. The result was Chamberlain's " startling speech " in May stating Britain's determination to cultivate America's friendship and suggesting " an Anglo-Saxon Alliance." Hay reported back to Lodge Chamberlain's delight over the reception of the speech in America.[68] White found Salisbury, the Prime Minister, deeply interested in America's attitude toward England. First Lord of the Treasury Arthur J. Balfour was " much elated at the turn Anglo-American relations have taken." He " repeated what he has often said before viz: that there is nothing which he has so much at heart as a perfect understanding between the two countries." [69]

Roosevelt and his friends had by now developed a full-blown foreign policy based on the belief that the British and Americans shared common interests. " Their interests are really fundamentally the same," Roosevelt wrote Arthur Lee in November, 1898, " and they are far more closely akin, not merely in blood, but in feeling and principle, than either is akin to any other people in the world."[70] They are " nearer to one another," he believed, " in political and social ideals, in their systems of government and of civic and domestic morality." [71] " The downfall of the British Empire," Roosevelt wrote at a moment when the Boer War was going badly for England, " I should regard as a calamity to the race, and especially to this country." [72] " If the British Empire suffer a serious disaster," he predicted in 1900, " I believe in five years it will mean a war between us and some one of the continental European military nations." [73] Roosevelt and the London *Spectator* were so convinced of the mutuality of our aims that they agreed in believing it was " really for England's interest that America should fortify the [Isthmian] canal." [74] " Probably her interest and our's," Roosevelt declared three months before he became President, " will run on rather parallel lines in the future." [75]

Before this new friendship could be finally consummated in a lasting entente, several remaining conflicts of national interest and international misunderstanding had to be resolved. One of these crises rose out of the Boer War. " There is no disguising the fact," Lodge wrote Henry White, " that sympathy here is overwhelmingly with the Boers. It could not be otherwise. They are making the most amazing fight for their firesides against overwhelming odds and that is enough for the average American." [76] Hay testified in June, 1900, " We had great trouble to prevent the Convention from declaring in favor of the Boers." [77]

Secretary of State John Hay was so passionately pro-British [78] that he could not understand friendliness for the

Boers except in terms of partisanship of some sort. He was therefore convinced that citizens who sought to be neutral or were pro-Boer must be Irish or German haters of England or Democrats trying to embarrass a Republican administration.[79] " I have the greatest admiration for the Boers' smartness," sneered Hay to Henry Adams in a letter in which he accused them of successfully running away from battle, " but it is their bravery that our idiotic public is snivelling over." [80] Hay spoke of " the present diseased state of the public mind," of the " mad-dog hatred of England prevalent among newspapers and politicians." He bitterly resented all criticism of himself for being hostile to the Boers and too friendly to England.[81] So much did he feel that England's cause was the American cause that, after the first British success, he greeted the Dutch minister with the news: " At last we have had a success," and then, somewhat embarrassed, had to admit that he meant the British success against the Boers.[82]

In contrast to this blind devotion of Hay to Britain, the Roosevelt-Lodge-White expansionists, less emotional in their approach, viewed the problem as more complex. America possessed no interests in South Africa to influence their stand. Had American expansionists been Anglophobe in their feelings, as they have been pictured, they could heartily have supported the Boers. Actually, however, they felt their interests coincided with those of England, while their human sympathies were with the Boers. Hence they suffered a serious conflict of loyalties. Initially, when trouble broke out, Roosevelt expressed admiration of the Boers.[83] Indeed, he was accused, probably unjustly, of being influenced to oppose England in Venezuela because of a " race sympathy " for the Boers that he did not dare avow openly.[84] There was no question of his sympathy. If only we had had a man like President Kruger in Buchanan's place in 1860, he admiringly assured the Holland Society of New York, we need not have fought a civil war.[85] In 1899 even Spring Rice, then at the

British Embassy in Teheran, confessed to his friend Theodore, " If I were not an Englishman I should certainly sympathize with the Boers—and we can't possibly complain of
people doing it." [86] When the War reached a critical stage,
Roosevelt was impressed at the way the Boers outfought the
British, and he admired good fighters. In April, 1901, he
confided to his son at Groton, " One cannot help admiring
the way the Boers have kept on in the face of the overwhelming material supremacy of the British Empire. It is as gallant a struggle as has ever been made." [87]

Besides, Roosevelt felt a certain contempt for the bungling
of the British. " What a wretched mess the invaders of the
Transvaal have made of it," he wrote his sister in January,
1896, at the time of the Jameson raid.[88] " I think that all of
England's troubles . . . now," he told White, " are due to her
having at first disregarded the rights of the Boers, and then
under the lead of Gladstone having made a cowardly retreat
before them." [89] " How old Kruger has whipped them,"
Lodge agreed with Roosevelt in 1896. " It was all a sordid
speculation of the money class,[*] reckless, dishonest and
feeble. This is a case which backs up Brook's [Adams's] conception of the economic type." [90] Roosevelt himself refrained
from public criticism of the British. In May, 1896, after he
had discussed " the Transvaal fiasco " with his friend the
German diplomat Speck von Sternburg, who was his house-
guest, and with Mahan, who came to dinner, he protested
to his sister, " Discreditable though the . . . [engagement]
was to the British I don't feel like saying anything, for I am
too heartily ashamed of Congress, which has blustered end-
lessly all winter and now refuses to build a decent navy." [91]

[*] Ex-President Harrison, too, agreed with Lodge's interpretation of sordid
economic motivation. " What a corrupting thing the lust for gold is! " he wrote
John Hay. " Gold . . . seems to me to have submerged the British sense of
justice. I think the fact that the British wash gold, and not the rather inconse-
quential fact that the Boers do not wash themselves, has brought on the war."

By 1900 the War was going badly for the British. Even
pro-British John Hay confided to Henry Adams: " The serious thing is the discovery now past doubt, that the British
have lost all skill in fighting, and the whole world knows it,
and is regulating itself accordingly." [92] The British, Lodge
reminded Roosevelt, " have been whipping hill tribes and
Dervishes so long that they have forgotten how white men
fight and underestimate their antagonist." [93] From England
White reported that the " mismanagement and disaster " had
" far exceeded the wildest imagination of anyone who gave
the subject consideration before . . . the war." [94] Roosevelt,
too, saw " grave signs of deterioration in the English speaking peoples," of which " the evident lack of fighting edge in
the British soldier " in the Transvaal was one.[95] Yet he refrained from " jumping on England " when she was down.[96]

Lodge found England inept, too, in her handling of world
opinion. In his discouragement he burst out to Henry White:
" What is worst . . . is not the unreadiness, the military
ignorance, the military blunders but the revelation of stupidity and incapacity in every direction from top to bottom.
Take one single instance; they seized American flour and
instead of paying for it next morning and saying how they
regretted it thus keeping it from the Boers and making it all
right with us they drag a discussion out over four weeks and
make no end of trouble here. Could anything be duller except to seize the ships of the one other friend, drag that out
over some weeks and thereby irritate the Germans and build
the German navy? " [97] Lodge felt it was England's " contempt for all the rest of the world which has been the root
of her misfortunes now as in 1776." He felt it explained, too,
" the pleasure the world feels over her misfortunes in South
Africa—' The pity of it.' " [98]

Roosevelt, torn between human sympathy and self-interest, tried to be fair. He listened to the Boer side of the story.
He talked at length, for instance, with Montague White, a

Transvaal advocate, and corresponded with him. Though he was not attracted to Montague White personally, he felt White made out a good case for the Boers. Roosevelt's own friend Frederick C. Selous, the British hunter of big game, was pro-Boer and Roosevelt wrote him to learn his reasons.[99] In April, 1901, Roosevelt confessed to Ted, Jr.: " What has gone on has shaken my conviction a good deal. The exposures about Chamberlain's family connections with the government in business matters, and about Chamberlain and Rhodes in their dealings with the Jameson raid, the domineering folly of Milner and the utter break down of the English army, make me feel that the English had no right whatever to go into this task as they did, for their capacity and the justice of their cause taken together did not warrant their position." [100]

In spite of all this, the Lodge-Roosevelt group successfully resisted their human sympathies and their sense of justice and turned their backs on the Boers. They maintained rigid technical neutrality,[101] but hoped Britain would win. " The trouble with the war," Roosevelt wrote his sister in 1900, " is not that both sides are wrong, but that from their different standpoints both sides are right." [102] To Albert Shaw Roosevelt expressed what was probably the heart of his feeling in forming a policy on the Boer War. " Of course I am friendly to England," he wrote. " Equally, of course, I am neither pro-Boer, nor pro-Briton; simply pro-American." [103] When one delegation seeking aid for the Boers pressed Roosevelt, he raised the question as to where the United States would stop if it once went into the business of interfering on behalf of oppressed groups for which it had sympathy. He pointed out that Americans felt the same interest in Danes under Germany and Finns under Russia as in the Boers.[104]

The real key to the expansionists' support of England, however, is found in a letter of Roosevelt to his friend Speck von Sternburg. " I have great sympathy for the Boers and great respect and liking for them," he wrote in 1899, " but I think they are battling on the wrong side in the fight for civilization and will have to go under." [105] The idea could not have been more simply stated. It was important that Anglo-Saxons rather than Dutch should dominate a temperate zone like South Africa. The position of English-speaking people in the world would be greatly weakened by " the race humiliation of a great catastrophe " in the Transvaal.[106]

After British rule was insured, Roosevelt was glad to help the Boers readjust themselves. He received money from Dutch in America and sent it through the State Department for the sufferers in South Africa. Among the contributions he thus forwarded was a check for three hundred fifty dollars that a Harvard undergraduate named Franklin Delano Roosevelt raised among his classmates.[107] After he became President he resisted an eloquent personal appeal of President Kruger that he intervene,[108] but he did appeal to his British friend, St. Loe Strachey, editor of the *Spectator*, for amnesty for the Boers.[109] In 1902 he expressed to the British unhappiness over their concentration camps.* [110] And in 1904 he read a book on the Boer war by vanquished Boer General Viljoen and then invited him to the White House for luncheon.[111]

In the end America's aiding Britain by standing aloof was the more appreciated in England because it was realized how strong was the sympathy for the Boers.[112] And Americans who had resented Britain's disdain of others felt that the near disaster she faced at the hands of the Boers had improved her attitudes. " The lesson administered to England was needed by her," Charles Eliot Norton wrote Frederic Harrison, " and if she learn it (and may she do so), you and I may live long enough to cherish once more our old pride in her, and renew our hopes for her." [113] " There can be no

---

* Hay on the other hand brushed aside the cruelty of concentration camps.

doubt," Henry White reported from London, "that this country is taking to heart the lesson so bitterly impressed upon her lately. The feeling of contempt for the rest of the world has for some time been diminishing under the pressure of events such as the crossing of her path in various directions by other powers." [114]

It was partly the feeling that England *had* learned her lesson that changed Roosevelt's attitude. He had once felt "we should be extremely careful," in order "to teach England her proper position." "England's failure in South Africa," he told George von L. Meyer, his future ambassador to Russia, "and our own success with Spain and the Philippines have been symptomatic of . . . changed conditions." "There is no danger to us from England now in any way." [115]

Besides the Boer War, another serious impediment to good Anglo-American relations was the old Clayton-Bulwer Treaty of 1850 that stood in the way of our building an Isthmian Canal. When we made that Treaty it was a greater gain to us than to Britain, but now Britain's right to build and fortify it jointly with us was a handicap to the domination of the Western Hemisphere that we felt in 1900 was our right. Britain, however, in her new mood of friendliness was ready to relinquish her rights and draw up a new treaty with us, abandoning her participation in construction and control of the canal. Sir Julian Pauncefote, who during his ten years in Washington had striven constantly for better relations between the two countries, had dropped a hint to Richard Olney while Olney was still Secretary of State that England would modify the Treaty.[116] Hay pursued this suggestion and in December, 1898, he and Pauncefote negotiated a treaty they hoped would be acceptable.[117] Hay, indeed, felt the British were being most generous. The Treaty had been drawn in general terms that Hay hoped would avoid acrimonious debate in the Senate, and, with his eye still on the Senate, Hay wrote Henry White in London urging him to make the British see the importance of promptly approving the Treaty without changes.[118] Hay and Pauncefote calculated without the jingoes if they counted on not arousing opposition in the Senate; and Britain, instead of signing quickly, let the Treaty get entangled with the unrelated subject of an Alaskan Boundary dispute on which even Hay felt the Canadians were unreasonable.[119] The Treaty therefore was held up a year.

In 1900 efforts to win the Treaty's acceptance were renewed. On January 15, Hay wrote to Ambassador Choate in England pointing out that a modus vivendi in Alaska had made the boundary issue less acute. Hay expressed hope that therefore the British would now agree to the canal treaty. " Nothing in the nature of a Clayton-Bulwer prohibition," Hay through Choate warned the British Government, " will finally prevent the building of the canal." The canal would benefit civilization and England as much as the United States, Hay argued. " It would be a deplorable result of all our labor and thought if . . . England should be made to appear in the attitude of attempting to veto a work of such world-wide importance; and the worst of all for international relations is that the veto would not be effective." [120] After some hesitation, on February 2, 1900, Britain authorized Pauncefote to sign and on February 5 the Treaty was submitted to the American Senate.[121] There it was immediately attacked for not conceding to America sufficient power over the canal.[122] On February 9, however, friends of the Treaty hoped the opposition had subsided, and White in London anticipated passage by the Senate without change.[123]

Then a bombshell exploded. On February 11 or 12 Frederick W. Holls invited to his country home near Yonkers, New York, David Jayne Hill, first assistant secretary of State, Albert Shaw, editor of the *Review of Reviews*, Nicholas Murray Butler, professor at Columbia University, and Roosevelt, then governor of New York.ᵃ After a long discussion Roosevelt, while the others looked on, wrote a statement for the press.[124] In Washington that Sunday evening Smalley of the *London Times* rushed over to John Hay's to tell Hay and Adams of Roosevelt's attack on the Treaty. " You can imagine to what extent the fat is in the fire! " chortled Henry Adams next morning. " Poor Cabot! What can he do? If Teddy . . . stabs Hay in the back, he has got to [go] on and tilt with the Major [McKinley] in the face. If Hay is beaten on his Treaty, he will resign; if he does not resign, he will certainly hamstring Teddy. Won't it be fun? " [125]

The essence of Roosevelt's pronouncement was his earnest hope that the Treaty would be rejected " unless amended so as to provide that the canal, when built, shall be wholly under the control of the United States, alike in peace and war." " This seems to me vital," the Governor of New York proclaimed, " no less from the stand point of our sea power than from the stand point of the Monroe Doctrine." [126] Privately to Mahan he wrote, " I do not see why we should dig the canal if we are not to fortify it so as to insure its being used for ourselves and against our foes in time of war." [127] To his navy brother-in-law, Will Cowles, he exploded, " What in the world has gotten into John Hay and McKinley? " [128] Angry with his chief subordinate, Hill, and hurt with his old friend Theodore, John Hay wrote what Roosevelt called " a pathetic letter " protesting Theodore's action.[129] " Cannot you leave a few things to the President and the Senate, who are charged with them by the Constitution? " was what Hay actually wrote Governor Roosevelt. " As to ' Sea Power ' and the Monroe Doctrine, we did not act without consulting the best living authorities. . . . Do you really think the Clayton-Bulwer Treaty preferable to the one now before the Senate? There is no third issue, except dishonor. Elkins and Pettigrew

---

ᵃ Butler in his memoirs thought Andrew D. White was there.

say ' Dishonor be damned.' I hardly think you will—Please do not answer this—but think about it a while." [130] Roosevelt, however, did answer it—in six days. " This step is one backward," Roosevelt responded to Hay, " and it may be fraught with very great mischief. You have been the greatest Secretary of State I have seen in my time, . . . but at this moment I can not, try as I may, see that you are right. . . . Oh how I wish you and the President would drop the treaty and push through a bill to build *and fortify* our own canal." In short, Roosevelt wanted merely to tear up the Clayton-Bulwer Treaty and build the canal in defiance of it. " I do not admit," he said, " the ' dead hand ' of the treaty-making power in the past."

Roosevelt's reasoning was interesting. First, the new Hay Treaty was wrong naval policy. Its provision forbidding fortification would have kept the canal open to all nations, even warships during war. Had the canal been built, under this rule our own *Oregon* could have reached Cuba quickly during the Spanish War, but Cervera's fleet, too, could have slipped through the canal to attack the California coast and Hawaii and to sail out to endanger Dewey in the Philippines. " If that canal is open to the warships of an enemy," Roosevelt warned, " it is a menace to us in time of war . . . an additional strategic point to be guarded by our fleet. . . . Unless . . . [it is] fortified it strengthens every nation whose fleet is larger than ours." [131] " I think that in the event of our having trouble with Germany or France it would be far better not to have the canal at all than to have it unfortified," Roosevelt wrote Spring Rice.[132]

Secondly, the clause of the Treaty inviting other powers to adhere and thereby accept joint responsibility threatened the Monroe Doctrine. " If," Roosevelt wrote Hay, " we invite foreign powers to a joint ownership, a joint guarantee, of what so vitally concerns us but a little way from our borders, how can we possibly object to similar joint action say in Southern Brazil or Argentina, where our interests are so much less evident? If Germany has the same right we have in the canal . . . why not in the partition of any part of Southern America? " [133] " The real ground " for the opposition of Roosevelt and Nicholas Murray Butler to the Canal Treaty was its providing " for an international guarantee of neutrality, thus giving European nations a right to come over here." [134]

In the Senate the fight against the Treaty was led by Roosevelt's friend Lodge and by Cushman K. Davis of Minnesota.[135] Roosevelt from Albany cheered Lodge and Davis lustily.[136] Roosevelt's and Lodge's friend White in England was dismayed.[137] So, too, was Hay. The Hepburn bill, which proposed to go ahead and build the canal anyway as Roosevelt urged, " directs you to act as if that treaty did not exist," Secretary Hay wrote McKinley, " that is, to repudiate and violate a solemn obligation to a friendly power, when that power is perfectly ready and willing to release us from it." [138] " When I sent in the Canal Convention," Hay declared, " I felt sure no one out of a mad house could fail to see that the advantages were all on our side. But I underrated the power of ignorance and spite, acting upon cowardice." [139] Hay later complained that Lodge and Davis had given him the heartiest assurances of anyone and had then changed position in fright over a few newspaper articles.[140] Lodge, on the other hand, felt affronted because neither he nor Davis nor other senators had seen a draft of the Treaty before it was signed. Lodge and Davis, initially friendly, turned against the Treaty in what Hay thought was mistaken fear that the Treaty would hurt the Republicans in the Presidential election.[141] Roosevelt's friend Arthur Lee in England wrote Roosevelt, " I am very disappointed in Lodge, because I believe him to be friendly to us at heart, but I am afraid his affection is not so strong as his fear of his constituents! " [142] Davis introduced an amendment to give us sole control of the canal, which he hoped would satisfy extremists without injuring the Treaty.[143] The matter was now put over until the following December when the elections would be safely past. Meantime McKinley and Ambassador Choate backed Hay and Roosevelt supported Lodge.[144]

In the end the Treaty passed with three amendments * and five votes to spare.[145] Lodge assured McKinley and Hay that without the amendments the Treaty could not have been ratified.[146] Hay firmly believed that Lodge had not played square and " our people " had not had any pluck. If Lodge and other administration leaders had vigorously supported the Treaty, Hay was convinced it would have been ratified without amendment.[147] When the amended Treaty was ratified, Lodge told Hay and McKinley, " Now the onus is on England. If she accepts well. If she out of infinite stupidity refuses then we can honorably go on abrogate the treaty and build the canal." [148] Hay on the other hand felt we had put ourselves in the wrong. " If Great Britain should now reject the Treaty," Hay wrote Choate, " the general opinion of mankind would justify her in it. If our Congress should then go forward and violently abrogate the Clayton-Bulwer Treaty . . . —which is to be apprehended—we shall be putting ourselves hopelessly in the wrong, and not . . . injuring England, except to the extent that the interruption of friendly relations will injure us both." [149]

Lodge agreed with Hay that, if England rejected the Senate amendments, Congress would defy the Treaty, but he hoped this fact would force England to accept the amendments. " The American people," he wrote Henry White, who would certainly show this letter to the leaders of the British Government, " mean to have the canal, and they mean to control it." " It would be ruinous " for England to make war

---

* One provided that the Clayton-Bulwer Treaty was " superceded "; a second gave the United States the right to defend the canal; a third provided that no other nations should adhere to the treaty.

on us. " As she is not prepared to go to war,* why is it not better that the canal should be built under the Hay-Paunce-fote Treaty with her assent to the amendments than to . . . force the United States to abrogate the treaty . . . ? " [150]

England's action in regard to modifying the Treaty was long in doubt and a matter of great concern to Americans friendly to her.[151] In March, 1901, Britain publicly rejected the Senate amendments.[152] British objection seems to have centered in the vagueness of the Davis amendment and in the " slap in the face " that the manner of the Senate action seemed to involve.[153] Roosevelt's friend Arthur Lee, just entering Parliament, expressed perhaps a common English feeling when he wrote Roosevelt, " Personally, I have no objection whatever to a mutual abrogation of the Clayton-Bulwer Treaty, and see no possible harm to us (or advantage to the U. S.!) in the Senate's amendments. . . . The Senate's amendments . . . were (to me) objectionable only in their gross disregard of international good manners." Lee's real objection to yielding, he explained to Roosevelt, was his question whether it would be " good policy for England to make any further concessions to that section of American feeling represented by the majority in the Senate? " " Would it not perhaps develop hatred into contempt," Lee queried, " and encourage the cry that England is afraid, and has no choice but to submit when America cracks the whip? " " I *do* think there may be real danger in too much complaisance. . . . I wish you would tell me (privately) what you think of this," he urged Roosevelt, " because . . . my maiden speech . . . may have to be on this subject, and I want to be sure of my ground and to have the best advice." [154]

---

* " That the English should undertake to go to war about the canal seems impossible," Lodge wrote Roosevelt, " although, I admit, they have done a good many impossible things lately." " If, however, there is any danger of that kind," he added, " now is the time to take the step [of abrogating the Treaty], for England is too exhausted by the African war to enter on any new struggle."

After rejection of the amendments by Britain, friends of an Anglo-American entente on both sides worked hard to persuade Britain to sign a new treaty that would include what the Senate demanded.[155] Actually, many men in Britain understood America's desire for complete control of the canal. Henry White felt that the British Government might have agreed to the amendments except for the weapon it would have put into the hands of the political opposition.[156] Lord Lansdowne's note explaining why Britain could not accept the amendments was so written as to make a good impression in America, after Hay had persuaded Pauncefote to withdraw one offensive paragraph.[157] By April a new treaty was drafted and under discussion.[158] The negotiations continued until fall.[159] The main task of our negotiators this time was, on the one hand, to persuade the British that, if they did not agree to a new treaty by December, Congress when it convened would act anyway; and, on the other, to persuade Britain that such terms as she agreed to would this time satisfy the Senate and save her another rebuff.[160] To accomplish this purpose, Lord Pauncefote went home for conference.[161] Henry White wished Roosevelt could have come over in January to talk concerning the treaty and " the feeling at home about the canal . . . to the many influential people " he would have met.[162] In June Lodge did go to England and dined privately with Lord and Lady Lansdowne the night after his arrival. He discussed the new treaty with Lansdowne, told him Congress would build the canal with or without a treaty, and described the absolute minimum the Senate would accept.* Then Lansdowne arranged for Lodge to lunch next day, again privately except for Arthur Lee,

---

* In March Lodge had confided to his friend Roosevelt: " If we cannot make a treaty with England which will pass the Senate . . . nothing in the world . . . will be able to stop the passage of the canal bill." He had " hoped against hope " for an " amicable " solution, " but," he concluded, " the stupidity of England seems to stand in the way of everything." [163]

with Balfour, the Prime Minister, to repeat what he had told Lansdowne. In September and October Lodge again stopped in London to discuss the treaty now about completed.[164] Hay playfully explained to Henry Adams, " We annexed . . . [Cabot] to the Embassy in London, so that if he kicks at the treaty this winter he will be kicking his own shins." [165] Indeed, this time Hay consulted senators about every detail.[166] In October through the patient work of Hay, Pauncefote, and Choate, the Treaty was approved; in November it was signed.[167] The American press was enthusiastic, indeed so pleased over our victory that Hay became fearful of the effect in England, particularly of certain leaks from senators.[168] " If we keep negotiations secret from leading senators," Hay complained, " we incur their ill-will and opposition. If we tell them confidentially what we are doing and thus secure their cooperation—their vanity leads them to blab everything to some newspaper, to show they are ' in it.' " [169] Nevertheless, this time the Treaty was ratified with little objection.

During the negotiations Roosevelt, as Vice-President, had made his views known in Britain. To Lodge he expressed his concern to get our way about the canal but not to injure our good relations with England. " I think," he exploded, " Lord Lansdowne's position is both mischievous and ridiculous," and then with his usual calm realism in the face of crisis he added, " but I also think we should be exceedingly cautious about embroiling ourselves with England, from whom we have not the least little particle of danger to fear in any way or shape." [170] To Arthur Lee, now in Parliament, he expressed his opinions freely. He assured Lee that the Senate's action in rejecting the first treaty had not been based on anti-English sentiment. He warned Lee, as he had warned Hay, that, since England had rejected its amendments to the new Treaty, the Senate would " now simply agree in abrogating the Clayton-Bulwer Treaty." " Most of the Senators," he explained, " sincerely dislike any loss of control . . . in the

Isthmus, and wish no continental European power to appear there. . . . They felt that the unamended treaty " gave other European powers " a certain right to qualified intervention in Central American affairs. To this they strenuously object; and so do I." [171] He denied that there was bad faith involved in rejection of a treaty. Indeed, he insisted that a nation must have the right to abrogate a treaty unilaterally for what the nation considers sufficient cause. He maintained that England had, in rejecting our amendments, behaved worse than we had in passing them. " It does not seem to me," he told Lee, " that the amendments gave any special ground for grievance to Great Britain; and very many men on this side, men who are entirely friendly to England, feel that the amendments represented the utmost possible in the way of concessions from us." [172] When the second Treaty was drawn up, Roosevelt was enthusiastic about the terms and, as soon as he became President, Roosevelt assumed an active rôle in pushing this second Treaty, but by then it had been practically completed.[173]

Britain, then, in this matter was coërced in part by the uncompromising attitude of Roosevelt and the Lodge-Roosevelt-Mahan expansionists. Twice she was forced to let us write our own terms for her expulsion from the Isthmian canal partnership to which our treaty obligations entitled her. Our expansionists were determined to have their own way and, under threat that we would take what we wanted anyway, in spite of resentment at our bad manners, Britain yielded everything as graciously as she could. Here was proof how much she did want American friendship.

Still another source of friction that had to be removed was the Alaska boundary dispute.[174] This controversy had dragged through the 1890's and was finally settled only after Roosevelt became President. A Joint High Commission had long considered the boundary disagreement without reaching a conclusion. Lodge had been agitated about the Canadian

position as early as 1896.[175] Canadian pressure upon Britain
about Alaska for a time delayed and appeared to threaten
solution of the Isthmian canal controversy. Finally Hay
agreed on October 20, 1899, to a protocol that gave the
Canadians temporary use of land at the head of the Lynn
Canal.*[176] When Roosevelt entered the White House, this
modus vivendi was still in force. It was the contention of
Lodge, Roosevelt, and other American expansionists that the
American claims were incontestable, that Canada had long
agreed to the boundary America claimed, and that the controversy was raised only when Canada made new and auda-
cious but unsupportable claims in order to share in the gold
that had recently been discovered.[177]

The essence of the argument over the Alaskan boundary is
found in an exchange of letters in April, 1901, between Roosevelt and Arthur Lee while Roosevelt was Vice-President and
Lee a member of Parliament. Lee did not doubt that the
United States was in the right, but he pointed out that
Canada thought she was right. England merely maintained,
Lee wrote, that " the Canadian contention should be seriously investigated by impartial judges." Lee recalled to
Roosevelt the Venezuela episode. " England thought she was
right," Lee reminded Roosevelt, " whilst Venezuela was
equally confident of the justness of *her* case. Whereupon the
U. S. intervenes (with some aggressiveness!) and *insists* that
England shall submit the whole dispute to arbitration. England agrees, and the consequent proceedings vindicate her
claims." " Now," Lee proceeded, " another boundary dispute
arises, with the U. S. as one of the parties concerned. England, mindful of the precedent of 1895-96 suggests arbitration. But the U. S. refuse—and say in effect ' oh-no—we

---

* The Lynn Canal was a narrow arm of the sea extending eighty miles into the
mountains. If the boundary were drawn so as to consider all of the Canal as sea
and hence American, Canadian gold fields would be cut off from the sea. If
Canada obtained any portion of the Canal, she would be able to ship her gold
out through a Canadian port at its head.

won't arbitrate about the boundary, because Canada " hasn't
a leg to stand upon." ' " Then Lee argued, " *If* the American
case is so overwhelmingly sound why not accept arbitration,
and so demonstrate the soundness of your claim before the
world? This would follow the precedent laid down by your-
selves and silence all comment. "Forget that you are an
American for a moment," Lee begged Roosevelt, " and put
yourself in our place and say if our view of the matter is not
natural and reasonable! I firmly believe that England is
always willing to go farther in the way of concession and
friendly service to the U. S. than to all other nations of the
earth combined, but it cannot be ' all give and no take,' and
your people should remember that we also are very proud
and very powerful! " [178] Roosevelt's friend St. Loe Strachey
wrote in much the same vein.[179]

To Lee Roosevelt replied, " My own horseback judgment
is . . . that we might as well let the modus vivendi be. By
this . . . we give you a bit of territory . . . to which you have
. . . no more right than we have to take part of Cornwall
or Kent. But so highly do I esteem the friendly relations
with Great Britain that I should be willing to make the sacrifice by merely continuing the modus vivendi." Roosevelt
was certain no treaty could be ratified that so nakedly gave
away American territory. But since the territory was of
small value the present arrangement could just ride. Roosevelt flatly refused to consider arbitration because " there are
cases where a nation has no business to arbitrate. . . . This
Canadian claim is . . . entirely modern. Twenty years ago
the Canadian maps showed the lines just as ours did." We
could no more arbitrate in Alaska than Britain could if we
suddenly claimed part of Nova Scotia. " You did not arbitrate the Transvaal matter," Roosevelt reminded Lee, " and
I do not very well see how you could." [180] " If we should
agree to arbitrate " in Alaska, Lodge argued, " there is nothing to prevent Spain setting up similar claims in Florida,

France in Louisiana, or Great Britain on the borders of New York and Vermont." [181]

The British were constantly under pressure from the Canadians to push Canada's claims. Hay and Pauncefote therefore carried on desultory conversations at long intervals made longer by an illness of Hay and by British sharing of the American Administration's eagerness not to complicate ratification of the Hay-Pauncefote Treaty. Neither side wanted to provoke American extremists into building a canal in defiance of treaty obligations.[182] Yet Hay stood firmly for his proposal of a new joint commission of six members, half American, half British, and Britain repeatedly voiced Canada's objections that such a commission of six could never come to a definitive settlement. Britain answered Hay's reiterated proposal of a mixed tribunal with arguments for arbitration that were hard to meet but that America flatly rejected. Here negotiations had deadlocked for years.[183]

Roosevelt initially felt that it was better not to stir the matter up. As late as January, 1902, he had personally instructed Ambassador Choate to "let sleeping dogs lie." [184] In March Hay heard that both England and Prime Minister Laurier of Canada were willing to yield everything if the United States would help them save face by submitting a limited question to " arbitration " by an equal number of English and Americans. Lodge opposed any further negotiation and reported Roosevelt in agreement with him. But Hay, " who," Lodge said, " has a passion for making arrangements with England," once more sounded England out and was once more rebuffed.[185]

In March, 1902, however, Roosevelt himself took control and precipitated action. Apparently the possibility that discovering gold in the disputed territory might bring serious trouble with Canada and hence with England determined Roosevelt's change of policy. Early in the month Roosevelt's old antagonist, Smalley of the *London Times*, went with Hay to see the President and warned that if gold were discovered there would be danger of bloodshed. " What shall we do then? " asked Smalley. " I know very well what I shall do," Roosevelt replied. " I shall send up engineers to run our line as we assert it and I shall send troops to guard and hold it." Smalley, " terribly disturbed," asked if that was not " very drastic," and Roosevelt assured him, " I mean it to be drastic." [186] On March 23 Lodge talked the matter over with the President who decided he would quietly send troops to the boundary, while Lodge was persuaded that his urging had brought the President to this action.[187] On the same day he talked to Lodge, Roosevelt requested Hay to send him the American plan for a tribunal and the private memorandum of Pauncefote containing the British suggestions. Hay told Roosevelt that in their last conversation Pauncefote had expressed willingness to urge his government to accept the American proposals.[188] Either that day or the next the President told Secretary of War Root that he wanted troops dispatched.[189] The next day Lodge and Hay dined at the White House. Hay like Smalley was " terribly disturbed " over the sending of troops and begged Roosevelt to do it " very quietly." [190] On March 27 an official order went to Root to move " additional troops . . . as quietly and unostentatiously as possible to Southern Alaska, so as to be able promptly to prevent any possible disturbance." [191] In May Roosevelt told a member of the British Embassy staff that he was " going to be ugly " over Alaska.[192] Repeatedly Americans, official and unofficial, made it clear to the British Government that America would never yield.[193]

Finally, in June Canadian Prime Minister Laurier and the Governor-General, Lord Minto, in London for the Coronation of Edward VII, reopened the boundary question. They confided to Henry White, who reported it to Hay, that they would be delighted to settle the issue if only America would let the Canadian leaders save face with their own people by winning an arbitration of the matter. Then, if the arbitration went against them, they could satisfy their people that they had done their best, and, if it went in their favor, they would yield the Lynn Canal to the United States but could then force Britain to give Canada compensation elsewhere for surrendering to America what America demanded.[194] Foreign Secretary Lansdowne now asked Ambassador Choate to talk to the Canadians. Choate was not in the Lodge-Roosevelt-White inner circle and apparently did not know of the conversations of his subordinate. In view of Roosevelt's parting instruction to him about " sleeping dogs," Choate felt compelled to cable Secretary Hay for instructions. Hay was ill and Roosevelt answered the Choate query. He had Assistant Secretary David J. Hill instruct the Ambassador to grant the interview to Minto and Laurier. But, he admonished, tell Choate bluntly that the President " thinks the Canadian claim has not a leg to stand on and that compromise is impossible." [195]

Worried lest trouble break out among " a rough population of miners of various nationalities," Laurier, in spite of the rebuff to Hay in March, now agreed to accept the American plan of a joint commission of six. He also agreed that if the American towns were awarded to Canada, Canada would permit America to keep them and seek compensation elsewhere. After long conversations Choate sent to Hay news of this willingness of the Canadians not to " hold out against your way of constituting the court . . . if the question to be arbitrated could be satisfactorily arranged." [196]

Roosevelt was unimpressed. He replied to Hay with a long argument from old maps about the validity of our position and concluded: " I think that the Canadian contention is an outrage pure and simple. . . . The fact that they have set up an outrageous and indefensible claim and in consequence are likely to be in hot water with their constituents when they back down, does not seem to me to give us any excuse for paying them money or territory. To pay them anything where they are entitled to nothing would . . . come dangerously near blackmail. I could not submit to any arbitration in the matter." Then he added, "I may be entirely willing to appoint three commissioners on our side to meet three commissioners on theirs and try to fix the line, but I should definitely instruct our three commissioners that they were not to yield any territory whatsoever, but were as a matter of course to insist upon our entire claim." [197]

Hay replied, somewhat hurt: "I regret to bother you with a matter which you seem to have already decided. . . . You did not quite understand my point of view, which is precisely the same as yours. . . . I do not think they have a leg to stand on, and I think any impartial court of jurists would so decide. At the same time, I recognize the danger of submitting such a matter to an ordinary arbitration, the besetting sin of which is to split the difference. My suggestion was . . . a tribunal of six, three on a side, a majority to decide. In this case it is impossible that we should lose, and not at all impossible that a majority should give a verdict in our favor." Hay then explained that Laurier's proposal was not that compensation should be given Canada if the Commission decided in our favor, but that if the decision went in Canada's favor, Canada would still let us retain what we wanted and seek compensation elsewhere.[198]

Roosevelt yielded to Hay's argument and permitted Choate to talk to Lansdowne, but gave warning that he would instruct our commissioners, if any were appointed, " in no case to yield any of our claim." He felt that our troops could keep the peace and added, " The Canadians have no right to make a claim based on the possible effect of their own wrong doing. . . . They now say that as they have got the false claim in, trouble may come if it is not acted on. I feel a good deal like telling them that if trouble comes it will be purely because of their own fault, and although it would be not pleasant for us it would be death for them." [199]

In the fall of 1902 when Sir Michael Herbert arrived as Ambassador the Alaskan boundary negotiations entered their final stage. In December Laurier was in Washington and conferred with Hay and Roosevelt. In January the Hay-Herbert Treaty was signed. It was more satisfactory than Canada had had reason to hope. The one drawback from Canada's point of view was the commission of six, three of them Americans, but the Treaty provided that the commissioners should be "impartial jurists of repute" and should "consider judicially the question submitted to them" and that each should take an oath that he would "impartially consider the arguments and evidence." [200] Henry White was delighted with the Treaty. "It saves Canada's face and will let her down easy," he wrote Lodge. "I fancy one or more British jurists will agree with ours, which will be not at all unwelcome here and if by chance they do not, no harm whatever will have been done and we shall remain where we are now with Canada powerless to do anything." [201] Hay argued this way with senators and assured them that no American would ever "give away our case" and that "the British know their case has little merit." [202] Even so the Treaty was withdrawn from the Senate and the word "arbitral" stricken out of the phrase "arbitral tribunal" before the Senate would ratify.[203] Roosevelt explained that the word had crept in by accident on the part of the copyist. "The question of an even or an uneven number has nothing to do with it," the President explained. "An arbitration is where some outside body decides a question at issue between two parties. To call a meeting between representatives of two parties in the endeavor to come to an agreement an 'arbitration' is in my idea a foolish misuse of words. . . . There is no 'proposition for an arbitration,' with an uneven or an even number of judges, or under any name, or upon any condition, which ever has received or ever will receive my sanction." [204]

"The Alaska Treaty went through beautifully—thanks to

your engineering," Hay wrote Roosevelt enthusiastically.[205]
Hay had worked on senators, too, and so had Lodge.[206] Ambassador Herbert told the Foreign Office that confirmation
of the Treaty was due to Lodge. To White, too, he wrote
" with enthusiasm " of Lodge's " invaluable " services.
" Lodge has worked like a galley slave," he reported.[207]

Engineering of the Treaty through the Senate had, however, involved a political manoeuver that was to cause criticism when it became publicly known. In consultation with
Lodge, Roosevelt had in advance secretly named the three
commissioners he would appoint under the Treaty and had
then let Lodge whisper confidentially to doubtful senators
who these commissioners would be: Lodge himself, Democratic expansionist Senator George Turner of Washington,
and Secretary of War Root. All were men with records of
vigorous insistence that we must not yield anything to the
Canadians. Turner swung the Democrats into line. Lodge
bought off the bitter opposition of Senator Henry M. Teller
of Colorado by confiding the secret to him. In consequence
the Treaty was ratified without opposition.[208] The British
and Canadians must have known that Roosevelt consented
to the Treaty only because of his conviction that the three
Americans, at least, would vote for the American position
as certainly the Canadians felt the Canadians would vote
for the Canadian position.[209] Since there were, besides the
three Americans, two Canadians and one Britisher, this
would leave the British member, Lord Alverstone, to decide
whether to prevent a settlement of issues by voting with the
Canadians to make a tie, or to resolve the dispute 4-2 in
America's favor by voting with the Americans. Canada could
not win. Both British and Canadians seemed to be unprepared, however, for Roosevelt's appointment not of " impartial jurists " who would vote for America, but of violent,
publicly-avowed partisans, none of them jurists at all.[210]
Roosevelt had first asked, in pursuit of the Treaty's pro-

visions, at least two justices of the Supreme Court to serve. It was only when the justices declined [a] and when Lodge persuaded him the Treaty would otherwise fail in the Senate that he picked the men who did not meet the terms of the Treaty. The Canadians were furious [b] and even the British most friendly to America were disappointed.[212] White reported embarrassment and dismay as well as surprise in London.[213] Arthur Lee, who felt the Canadians had no case, deeply regretted the American appointments.[214] Laurier wrote a dignified but unavailing protest to Hay against Lodge and Turner on the ground that, since they were not " impartial jurists," their appointment made it " extremely difficult to obtain and not a little humiliating to grant " assent of Parliament to the Treaty.[215]

Ambassador Herbert tried to analyze the situation for Lansdowne. Herbert, who liked America and was loved and respected by Roosevelt and his friends, declared himself " disgusted and disheartened." The appointments he found " more than unfortunate." " All my illusions are gone," he moaned, " in regard to men in whom I believed. Everything in this country is subservient to politics, and really an Ambassador in Washington needs more than an ordinary stock of patience." [216] Roosevelt told Herbert that the American case was so good that he consented to the Commission anyway only to afford England the means " to get out of the difficult position in which she has been placed by Canada." " In short," concluded Herbert, " he is obstinate and unreasonable." [217]

" The question is," Herbert wrote Lansdowne, " what is to be done? " " I realize," he conceded, " the impossible position in which the Laurier Government has been placed in Canada, and they have every right to complain of what has happened;

---

[a] Justice Edward D. White was one of those that refused.

[b] " Laurier kicks hard against Cabot," Henry Adams recorded. " He kicks also at Root and Turner, but I feel that Cabot is the real pill." [211]

but in spite of this, it would be useless and inadvisable for them to protest, and folly to break off as Laurier suggests, for the consequences would be too grave to contemplate." "I imagine," he concluded, "it will be more dignified and more politic to assume that the President has acted in good faith, and to appoint on our side the very best men we can get. To appoint three politicians on our side would be a mistake and a source of danger." [218] Lord Minto, then Governor-General of Canada, felt "the U. S. have behaved quite disgracefully" but advised his Government as Herbert did.[219]

Hay's public and private attitudes seem to have differed. Herbert described Hay as privately having no defense to make, and others have given the impression that Hay was not consulted and then felt outraged at the President's action. Lodge later testified that Hay protested against all three appointees but especially against Lodge.[220] Yet to Ambassador Choate Hay wrote, "The reasons which dictate these appointments you can at once see. Root is one of the ablest men in public life to-day, equally distinguished as a lawyer and statesman. Lodge is the President's most intimate friend in the Senate, and has been of very great use to us in getting the treaty ratified. Turner is one of the most important lawyers west of the Rocky Mountains, and represents a great body of opinion there which has always been more or less hostile to England, and his influence and standing will be most valuable in influencing the opinion of the northwestern states in favor of a just and amicable settlement with Canada." [221] Assuring Laurier that he personally had tried to persuade some of our highest judges to act, Hay then wrote the Canadian Prime Minister, "If by 'impartial,' you understand without opinion on the subject matter in question, I am afraid it would be impossible to find any one . . . to meet the requirement. We take it to mean learned in the law, of such character for probity and honor that they will give an impartial verdict." [222] This was the Secretary of

State speaking officially to his Ambassador and to the Canadians.

To his intimate friend Henry White, Choate's secretary of legation, Hay the man wrote with less reserve what he really thought: " I . . . can well appreciate the objections that our friends in London make to the composition of the tribunal, but the President thought it was impossible to get the treaty through the Senate without the earnest and devoted assistance of Lodge and Turner and of the groups which they represented." " I must say," he continued, " that we had an equal disappointment in the refusal of the Judges of the Supreme Court to serve. . . . It was only after they had positively declined on the grounds of etiquette and official dignity that the President invited Turner to act." Hay again defended Turner's appointment here privately as he had more officially to Choate. Root needed no defense. But of Lodge Hay wrote: " Of course, the presence of Lodge on the tribunal is, from many points of view, regrettable, and, as if the devil were inspiring him, he took occasion last week to make a speech in Boston, one-half of it filled with abuse of the Canadians and the other half with attacks on the State Department. He is a clever man and a man of a great deal of force in the Senate, but the infirmity of his mind and character is that he never sees but one subject at a time, and just at present it is the acceptability of his son-in-law to the voters of Gloucester." " Of course you know his very intimate relations with the President, which make it almost impossible that the President should deny him anything he has to give him, and he insisted upon this appointment on the tribunal." [223]

A long discussion ensued over arrangements for the meetings of the tribunal.[224] The details need not concern us. But the handling of one particular problem and the relations of Roosevelt, Choate, White, Hay, and Lodge to its handling and to each other reveal much. The British sought delay;

the Americans wanted to push matters through as fast as possible. All the evidence indicates that Choate and White were handling matters admirably. Then Nannie Lodge went to fashionable Newport and there ran into the British Ambassador, who said something or other about the Tribunal's not meeting until October. Nannie wrote Cabot, who was relaxing at his cabin on Nantucket Island. Cabot became excited and wrote Roosevelt that there was no reason whatever for this delay. He pointed out that if the Tribunal did not meet until October he and Root could not get back from London for the extra session of Congress in November and that they were needed there. He expressed his belief that it was important " on your account and on account of everything " that he and Root should stay on the Tribunal. But probably the British hoped by delay to get somebody " more amenable " in Lodge's and Root's place. Lodge therefore urged Roosevelt to threaten the British that if the Tribunal could not meet as planned early in September then it would have to be put off until the next summer. " I believe this would bring them to time. If we take a stiff tone I am sure it would," he prodded the President. " The English brother will always push you as far as you will let him," he taunted Roosevelt further.[225]

Under the spur of Cabot's irritation Roosevelt the same day dashed off to Cabot a note marked " personal " reiterating his reluctance " to let the negotiations go over until next summer or to have them delayed in any way." He had written Hay at once, he told Lodge, " that England must be kept right up to the mark." " The English behaved badly in Venezuela," he added, " despite the fact that we behaved with scrupulous impartiality during the Boer War. I don't intend that they shall do any shuffling now." [226] Stirred by Lodge's letter, Roosevelt told Hay that Lodge and Root had protested about the delays and that Lodge wanted to put the negotiation off until next year. " I don't want the thing pending during a presidential campaign," Roosevelt explained. Momentarily accepting Lodge's suspicion of their motives, he added, " Moreover if the English decline to come to an agreement this fall, under any pretense, I shall feel that it is simply due to bad faith,—that they have no sincere desire to settle the matter equitably." Then recalling a conversation Choate, Root, Hay, and Roosevelt had had on the portico of the White House while Choate was home on leave, but completely rejecting Lodge's proposals of threats and a " stiff tone," he proposed: " I hope Choate will gently convey to them the substance of our conversation . . . and will let them know that I shall probably, if they fail to come to an agreement, bring the matter to the attention of Congress and ask an appropriation so that we may run the line ourselves." " I do not want to make this as a threat and of course it may be that it would be inadvisable to do it; but my present feeling is that we would have to." [227]

Both Lodge and Hay answered promptly. Lodge now agreed with the President that to threaten to put the matter off a year was unwise because while the British would probably then come to terms we would be bluffing and Lodge, too, opposed threatening anything we did not intend to carry out. He took up, however, and strongly encouraged Roosevelt's idea of abandoning negotiations permanently if the British proposed delays. Then Lodge announced his intention of going over to England early and proposed that Roosevelt empower him to carry on private confidential negotiations with the British. " My instructions of course would have to come through the State Department, I suppose, but I want them dictated by you," Lodge continued. He warned that Harry White and Choate were " averse to taking an unyielding position." Hence he would rather work independently of them but he would see Lansdowne through Choate " if etiquette so requires." None the less, so that the Embassy could not interfere, he wanted to be " in the highest degree official and authoritative." [228]

Contrariwise, Hay replied patiently and soothingly to Roosevelt's watered down transmittal of Lodge's advice. "Choate is conducting the matter admirably in London," Hay wrote. "We are doing exactly what you suggest—resisting to the utmost bounds of courtesy or," he added significantly, "of equity, every attempt at delay. . . . You remember we crowded them out of two months they wanted, in the negotiation of the treaty." "I do not think they are acting in bad faith," Hay argued. "They are availing themselves of every possible pretext the treaty gives them of demanding more time to patch up their deplorably weak case. They see nothing but defeat before them, and they want to make as good a record of their fight as possible." Indeed, Hay told Roosevelt, "They are amazed at the strength of our case and the promptness with which it was made ready, and are trying to spar for wind." "I do not think any threats are at this time advisable or needful," he countered to Lodge's proposal. "We shall be as hard on them as is decent—perhaps rather more so." [229]

Impatient, Lodge wired Roosevelt a reiteration of his suspicions that the British wanted to "break off or wear out by delay." "Evidently they want trouble," he said. Assuming that Roosevelt was following his advice, he questioned whether he should go to England at all but also asked whether it was not better to go on to London anyway and "break off there." [230] Roosevelt was by now recovered from the influence of Lodge's letter trying to stir him up and had been reinforced in his own calmer judgment by the wisdom of Hay's advice and by letters from White and Choate in England. This time he replied to Lodge's telegram in a letter that must rather sharply have reversed the Senator's plans. The Alaska boundary, wrote Roosevelt, is "altogether too important a matter to take a snap judgment or to forfeit a single chance of bringing it to a successful conclusion. . . . There is not at present one single act which would justify so much as considering the breaking off of the negotiations." Choate's and White's able work in London had taken effect, Roosevelt now pointed out to Lodge, and the British, who had asked for delay, had none the less presented their case on the day appointed. " Choate writes that he thinks there may be a request for ten or fifteen days' extra time," the President told the impetuous Senator. " While on the one hand I should peremptorily decline to let the case go over until next summer, on the other hand I should feel that it would be an act of petulance and folly . . . to break off the negotiations if the British simply requested ten or fifteen days extra, or even a month. We should at once be putting ourselves in the wrong." Such a demand " could under no conceivable circumstances be taken as an evidence of bad faith." Meantime Roosevelt suggested to Lodge a personal conference at Oyster Bay.[231] This sobering letter brought from Lodge a reply accepting the President's view and trying to explain why he had ever proposed such a contrary policy.[232] Hay could now write of Lodge to his wife, " I think he is easier in his mind since Theodore has told him we are not surrendering everything to England." In the midst of all this, Hay had tried to resign because of attacks on the President over Hay, and the President had written him that he cared nothing for what " those swine " said, but found Hay an " immense help " and " a perpetual comfort and delight." [233]

When Lodge sailed for the conference he was not empowered to act independently of the Embassy but was told to ask Choate about policies Roosevelt had outlined to Choate six months before in Washington. He was not armed with the " official and authoritative " instruction he had desired but was given instead a letter that he could show privately stating the President's views. The letter Lodge did receive stressed the fact that the President must report success or failure to Congress when it convened. It stated his feeling that he had gone " very far " in his " endeavor to come to a friendly understanding with England." It repeated twice that the Tribunal represented " the last chance of coming to an agreement by the free act of both parties." [234] Thus Hay's calm judgment and Roosevelt's own good sense rejected Lodge's rough handling of England and preserved the good feeling that Roosevelt, Hay, and British leaders had in most cases labored together to build between the two countries.

In Roosevelt's instructions to the commissioners he told each of them: " You will of course impartially judge the questions that come before you for decision." But " the claim so roundly asserted by Mr. Laurier . . . is not in my judgment one of those which can properly be considered open to discussion.* . . . In the principle involved there will of course be no compromise." [235]

Now, besides, Roosevelt began to put pressures of a personal and informal sort upon the British government. Hay explained to White so that he could privately make it clear to the British leaders that " the whole machinery of the Tribunal is got up with the expectation on our part that the British Government would see in it the means of receding from an absolutely untenable position, by appointing on the tribunal a man of open mind, who would see the case as we shall present it and vote with our members." [236] In May Henry White had managed " a good talk " with Balfour to whom he could speak with " absolute freedom." White had also sought an opportunity to explain confidentially to Lord Alverstone " our view of the situation," in short, to explain to this key British member of the Tribunal " that we have consented to the arbitration in order to afford . . . [his] country a loophole to escape from an untenable position." [237]

Roosevelt used Oliver Wendell Holmes then in England

---

* Hay wrote White that Laurier's private messenger sent to Hay to protest the American appointments had confessed confidentially to Hay that " Sir Wilfred knows, and all of us know, that we have no case."

to further his ends. Toward the close of July a letter came from Holmes telling Roosevelt that Chamberlain had questioned " how you could with your known character send people whose minds were all made up and (pace Cabot) not strictly jurists." [238] The President immediately sent Holmes a letter stating his position on the appointment of commissioners and arguing the boundary issue. He invited Holmes to make the contents of this letter known " privately and unofficially " to Chamberlain. He clearly described the alternatives he faced and declared: " Nothing but my very earnest desire to get on well with England and my reluctance to come to a break " made me consent to the commission. " I wish to make one last effort to bring about an agreement," Roosevelt pleaded, " which will enable the people of both countries to say that the result represents the feeling of the representatives of both countries. . . . But if there is a disagreement I wish it distinctly understood . . . that in my message to Congress I shall take a position . . . which will render it necessary for Congress to give me the authority to run the line as we claim it, by our own people, without any further regard to the attitude of England and Canada. . . . That is the position I ought to take anyhow. I have not taken it because I wish to exhaust every effort to have the affair settled peacefully and with due regard to England's dignity." [239]

Meantime Lodge busied himself in England confidentially spreading the President's warning among British leaders. He talked with Choate and White, then with Balfour, Chamberlain, and Harcourt, and with Alverstone. He dined with Balfour at Chamberlain's and with Alverstone, the Ian Hamiltons, and the James Bryces at the American Embassy. Since Lansdowne was in Ireland with the King, Lodge sent him a long letter.[240] Then Lodge wrote Roosevelt, " There is no trouble at all with the English." " The fact is England cares nothing about the boundary," he elaborated to his daughter,

" but their fear of offending the Canadians is something inconceivable. That collection of bumptious provincials bullies them to any extent and they dare not say a word." To the President he predicted, " I do not think they will have the courage to decide against the Canadians, and the Canadians are so perfectly stupid . . . that they . . . fail . . . to see that a disagreement deprives them of their only chance to get out of the matter creditably and leaves the land in our possession." " The only thing I feel reasonably certain of," he reported, " is that England will not go to war with us." [241] " I shall make no threats," Roosevelt promised in reply, " and shall try to use language that will prevent trouble. But in some shape or way I shall have to say that the effort at an agreement is now at an end and that the whole territory in dispute is our own." [242]

When the Tribunal met in September Lodge and Root continued the informal pressure on Alverstone, whom Lodge found " intelligent, kindly, and agreeable." Choate had a dinner for all six commissioners and they talked to Alverstone there. The Tribunal sat for nearly seven weeks. During its sessions Root and Lodge persistently pressed America's case behind the scenes. Lodge and Root lunched with Strachey, editor of the *Spectator*; White weekended at Balfour's, and Lodge at Lord Alverstone's. Balfour anxiously sought them out, expressed concern, asked how things stood, and then advised Alverstone. Ultimately they saw the King.[243] Hay put pressure through arguments to White that might " indiscreetly percolate through to Balfour." [244] At the crucial moment just before the end Choate talked most urgently with Lansdowne, who talked to Balfour, and Choate was certain both Balfour and Lansdowne told Alverstone what they thought the necessities of the case were.[245] Alverstone himself early admitted that he felt Canada on the major issues had no case. He frequently consulted privately with the Americans. Finally, he made it clear that if the

Americans would go along with something that he could win for the Canadians he would side with them on the main issues. He indicated some minor matters where he felt the Canadians had a case. Lodge and Root sought instructions from Roosevelt, who was glad to yield some minor points to help the British save face with the Canadians.[246]

On this basis a decision was reached under a treaty that had called for a judicial determination by six " impartial jurists." Hay felt Alverstone was the " hero of the hour." " No American statesman," he said, " would have dared to give a decision on his honor and conscience directly against the claim of his own country." [247] But actually, as Hay must have known, Alverstone in deciding *against* the Canadians decided *for* his own country's policy of friendship with America. Roosevelt believed that if the American commissioners had been justices of our Supreme Court they would not have appealed to him and thus compromised to win a settlement but acting " purely judicially " would have denied the Canadians everything.[a] [249]

Roosevelt's rôle has been somewhat misrepresented.[250] The situation was a most delicate one. Hay had handled the problem under McKinley. After Roosevelt became President he and Hay coöperated admirably. Roosevelt exerted the pressure for settlement and Hay softened effects wherever he could. But their end was the same. Roosevelt's oft denounced threat to send troops in to take the territory if he did not get his way was perhaps the determining factor that led the great English jurist to throw his weight to the Americans. It seems, however, to have been the critical local situation on the boundary where a rough population had gathered on both sides that induced Roosevelt to change from his

---

[a] Holmes, who was supposed to have been one of the judges invited but unwilling to serve, wrote Roosevelt after the decision a letter that indicated he thought the Supreme Court justices might have decided more favorably to Canada than did the politically compelled English chief justice.[248]

policy expressed to Choate in January, 1902, that sleeping dogs should be allowed to lie, to the decision made in March, 1902, to send troops and hold them in readiness. Long before the Tribunal met and the threat was quietly used as an instrument of policy, Roosevelt had decided he must draw the line himself with the aid of American troops if this effort to do it through a mixed tribunal failed. In February, 1903, only a month after the treaty providing for the mixed tribunal had been agreed to, he had confided to the new German ambassador, his old friend Speck von Sternburg, that he would do just this.* [251]

Yet before it was used, the plan to employ troops to draw the line if amicable settlement failed was thoroughly discussed and sanctioned at a conference with Ambassador Choate, Secretary of State Hay, and Secretary of War Root early in June while Choate was home briefly for his son's wedding. On the portico of the White House the four men—three of them cautious by nature and two of them devoted friends of England—tried realistically to face what would have to be done if the Tribunal failed and the three conservative advisers apparently approved Roosevelt's plan to use troops.[252] In April pro-British John Hay had written, as we have seen, to warn the British that the Tribunal offered their last chance to back down gracefully without war.[253] The plan to use troops resulted not just from the desire of an impetuous President to bully or to have his own way; it grew in part at least out of a calm decision of cautious advisers, who feared growing frontier tension created by a lawless population might blow up into a dangerous international incident if " uncontrolled." [254]

Roosevelt and Hay directed the negotiations with great understanding of Britain's sensibilities and the pressures she was under. Judge Holmes wrote Roosevelt that he could not

---

* Into the margin of Speck's report on this the Kaiser wrote gleefully: " To your health! John Bull will also of course want this to happen."

exaggerate the satisfaction he felt over the settlement. He and White considered the solution " a personal triumph of yours." [255] The one serious blunder was the appointment of Lodge and Turner; that resulted in part from the hold of friendship Lodge had over the President, but in part from the refusal of the justices to serve and the problem of getting the Senate to agree to any settlement at all. Roosevelt's desire for a peaceful settlement and the accomplishment of that settlement both stemmed from his strong conviction, shared by British leaders, that Anglo-American friendship was of the utmost importance to both nations. " The temper of the politicians " in Washington made both Roosevelt and the British realize the importance of settling the question.[256] Strachey believed that both Roosevelt and Balfour would have counted their political lives failures if war had come between the two English-speaking nations.[257] Canada of course considered her interests sacrificed by Britain to Anglo-American friendship.[258] But on both sides of the ocean men shared Roosevelt's conviction that settlement of the Alaskan boundary removed the last obstacle to the agreement between the two peoples that had become the foundation of Roosevelt's foreign policy.[259]

These Anglo-American negotiations illustrate the extraordinary importance in this period of the kind of friendly contacts that existed between British and American public men. And Roosevelt's handling of these relations with England leaned heavily on his favorite method of dealing with foreign policy personally through intimate friends. His use of unofficial channels was peculiarly necessary in the case of England because the English refused to send after 1903 an ambassador whom Roosevelt trusted. In spite of his urging, they would not send one of his personal friends.

For a dozen years ending in 1903 Britain was remarkably served in Washington. Sir Julian Pauncefote, ambassador in Washington for nearly ten years, died early in Roosevelt's administration. Sir Michael Herbert, who succeeded him, died after about two years more. Though neither man had the personality or the physical stamina to play tennis with the President or to accompany him on his scrambles through streams and over cliffs as did the French and German ambassadors, both men belonged in other ways to the President's inner circle. He admired, liked, and trusted them, and they understood America and were in turn beloved by Americans that knew them. Sir Michael had been appointed at the suggestion of Lodge and Henry White.[260] When death removed Sir Michael, too, Roosevelt tried to name his successor. Indeed, he had already attempted through Lodge to get his friend Spring Rice sent over to a post under Herbert, while Herbert was ambassador, but the English had been obdurate.[261]

Now in 1903 Roosevelt wanted Spring Rice made ambassador in Herbert's place, but instead the British sent Sir Mortimer Durand, who stood high in the diplomatic hierarchy and had for twenty years wanted to go to America. Durand admired America and Roosevelt. White reported to Roosevelt: " He has a quiet almost shy—manner with a subdued voice and he speaks rather slowly and deliberately. At first he might be thought reticent but all this vanishes upon closer acquaintance and I am sure you will like him very much." [262] But Roosevelt did not like him. He never warmed up to him and would never deal through him. Sir Mortimer was estimable but simply not Roosevelt's kind. Lodge was commissioned in 1905 to talk with Lansdowne and the King about the President's dissatisfaction, in spite of the fact that Root, who succeeded Hay as Secretary of State, liked and admired Durand and got on well with him.[263] Durand was crushed at his failure where he so wanted to succeed.[264] But Roosevelt merely ignored him and kept trying to get him recalled. " Do not do anything to hurt Durand," Roosevelt instructed Lodge, " but . . . you might dwell upon the good qualities of Spring Rice." Lodge promised to "let fall some judicious observations about Springy which may do him good." [265] But they did him no good; nor did a long talk Lodge had with Balfour, to whom he told "exactly the truth about Durand." Lansdowne liked Durand, and Balfour could do nothing. Lodge did not succeed even in getting Springy sent over as first secretary under Durand.[266] Our own ambassador, Reid, tried in 1905 with no better success.[267] Roosevelt was persistent. When in 1906 Sir Edward Grey became Foreign Secretary, he tried again—this time with a personal letter that Ambassador Reid could show to both Grey and the King. He commissioned Reid to make it plain that Britain had not known of Roosevelt's activities so intimately as had France and Germany because Britain would not send over Spring Rice. By contrast, the President could be on quite confidential terms with Jusserand and Speck von Sternburg. Grey explained through Reid that for political reasons and because there was no place else for Durand, who would lose his pension if he were recalled, he could not accede to Roosevelt's wishes.[268] "Poor Durand!" Roosevelt exclaimed. "I would not for a good deal interfere with his . . . retiring on his pension, for he is a thoroughly well-meaning and upright soul; but I wish to Heaven they could send him on some mission of vital importance to Timbuctoo or Thibet or the Antarctic regions and give us a competent man in his place." [269] Later in 1906 Roosevelt was still trying through Arthur Lee, who took personal messages from him urging Durand's replacement with Spring Rice. He had Reid, too, try again. Now from both came the unwelcome news that Spring Rice could not be sent even if there were a change.[270] Then Roosevelt sought unsuccessfully to get Lee himself appointed.[271] Finally, in December, 1906, a change was made. The new ambassador, however, was neither Spring Rice nor Lee but Bryce, who was chosen after "more careful consideration than any cabinet ever gave a diplomatic appointment." [272]

Bryce seemed an excellent choice. He knew America and was well known here. He and Roosevelt had corresponded and entertained each other in England and America for twenty years. The Bryce appointment was widely acclaimed. Publicly Roosevelt was delighted. But Mrs. Roosevelt wrote Spring Rice how she had " pulled every known wire " to have him sent instead of the " worthy and dull old person " who was coming.[273] And Roosevelt wrote Lee that he was sure Bryce would do well and had peculiar strength in the eyes of the public, but Roosevelt himself would unquestionably have to communicate with the British Government from time to time through Lee rather than through the new ambassador.[274]

Why the British Government was so stubborn in refusing to let Roosevelt indulge his passion for personal diplomacy conducted through intimate friends in ambassadorial posts is difficult to understand; for the Kaiser, with equally good reasons for not doing so, had at a critical juncture called von Holleben home and sent Roosevelt's crony Speck von Sternburg in his place to a post Speck could never have won on his standing in the diplomatic service. By the same token, it is equally difficult to comprehend why a man that put such persistent pressure on the British Government to send an envoy in whom he had confidence should have sent as his ambassador to England a man like Whitelaw Reid through whom he would not carry on these same intimate negotiations.

This lack of confidence in official channels made the attainment of the objective of men on both sides difficult and drove diplomacy, as it were, underground. But it must be admitted that the intimacy of communication resulting from negotiation outside official channels was perhaps one reason for the ultimate success of Anglo-American relations. Under Ambassador Choate, Roosevelt had dealt with really delicate matters through Henry White, the secretary of legation, rather than through the Ambassador, and he had used Lodge,

Holmes, Lee, Spring Rice, and other friends for negotiation with Britain outside the American Embassy altogether. After Herbert's death and White's promotion to an ambassadorship in Rome in April, 1905, Roosevelt continued to depend on friends in difficult situations. Consequently, when negotiations over the Far East reached a delicate stage in December, 1904, the President sought an unofficial agent for communication with Britain. He wrote Henry White then visiting in London: " I wonder if you could arrange to have the Foreign Office send Spring Rice over here to see me for a week? . . . There is no one in the British Embassy here to whom I can talk freely, and I would like to have the people at the Foreign Office understand just my position in the Far East, and I would like to know what theirs is. . . . I do not know whether it is my fault or Sir Mortimer's, but our minds do not meet; and in any event I should be unwilling to speak with such freedom as I desire to any one in whom I had not such absolute trust as I have in Spring Rice." [275] Roosevelt kept the secret as he was surprisingly able to do in important matters. So did Spring Rice and White. Even Lodge and Hay did not know why Spring Rice came, though Speck von Sternburg either knew or shrewdly guessed.* White casually wrote Lodge that he might see Springy on a flying visit as Springy yearned to see his American friends.[276] It seemed wiser for Spring Rice not to make his mission too obvious by staying with Roosevelt at the White House. So White cabled Hay telling him when Spring Rice would arrive and asking Hay to cable whether he could stay with Henry Adams. Roosevelt helped keep the secret by forwarding the cable to the unsuspecting Secretary of State with the comment, " This is very interesting." [277] Spring Rice stayed a week, lunching, dining, and visiting at the Embassy, at the White House, and with Hay and Adams,

---

* The Japanese Minister was curious and made wild guesses as to the purpose of his visit.

and only he and Roosevelt knew that the President had sent
for him to come from St. Petersburg to Washington and back
on important confidential business.[278]

Similarly, in the fall of 1906 Roosevelt sent for Arthur Lee
to come from England to carry back all kinds of information
he wanted the British Government to have but would not
confide to the ambassador nor put on paper in a letter.
Roosevelt told Lee about his handling of "the Hague conference, the New Foundland fisheries, the seal fisheries, the
Chinese Customs, the Russo-Japanese peace negotiations, the
Algeciras negotiations and the Venezuela matter," and Lee
in his turn informed the British Government.[279] After a long
interview with the Foreign Secretary, Lee reported to Roosevelt: "Sir Edward was, naturally, immensely interested in
all I had to tell him, and is very grateful to you for sending
him so much new and important information—not only concerning the questions at issue . . . but particularly with regard
to the real truth about the Russo-Japanese Peace and the
Algeciras negotiations. . . . He, like nearly everyone else in
England, had entirely misunderstood the situation, and it has
been a work really worth doing to have set him and the government on the right track again." [280] Lee handled himself
so discreetly that no mention of his trip ever appeared in a
newspaper, and he was able to assure Roosevelt that only a
dozen people knew he had been in Washington * at all.[282]

Meanwhile Roosevelt joined with Edward VII, too, in
seeking through personal contacts of King and President to
bring the two nations closer. Even before Edward's acces-
sion, America had taken great pains to participate fully in
the celebration of Victoria's jubilee and her birthday, and the
British were delighted. Her death had given another opportunity for friendliness. Then on McKinley's death the new
King expressed personal grief that impressed Americans in
England as more than fulfilling a formal obligation, and,

---

* To Lee Roosevelt declared, "Your visit accomplished a very great deal." [281]

when Ambassador Choate called to express America's appreciation, the King grasped the opportunity to spend twenty minutes asking questions about Roosevelt. He asked that he have a photograph of the President and indicated that he knew much of Roosevelt's record and admired him.[283] Roosevelt replied through the Ambassador, sending his personal greetings and regards to the King and his assurance that he would do all he could " to preserve unbroken the friendly relations between the two countries." [284] Edward, with a desire for close personal association similar to Roosevelt's, would have played a stronger rôle had the British constitution and his Cabinet advisers permitted. So eager was he for friendly contacts that, although the Foreign Office protested that Americans might be offended at what they would construe as interference in American politics, the King on February 20, 1905, wrote an informal letter to Roosevelt congratulating him on his reëlection. In the original draft phrased by the King himself Edward wrote: " It is my dearest wish to do all in my power to promote cordial understanding between . . . [our peoples], based not on treaties and conventions but on mutual sympathy and cooperation in the realization of those principles which are our common inheritance." " You have shown," he told Roosevelt, " both in word and deed what is your conception of those principles." He wished Roosevelt could come while President to see " what a reception would be given to the President of the U. S. by the King of Great Britain and Ireland and his people." Since that was impossible Roosevelt must later come privately so that Edward could know him.* Then Edward sent a miniature of

---

* When his advisers got through with revising Edward's spontaneous friendly letter, the hope that Roosevelt would visit him was omitted and the following was substituted for what Edward wished to say: " You, Mr. President, and I have been called upon to superintend the destinies of the two great branches of the Anglo-Saxon race, and this fact should in my opinion alone suffice to bring us together. It has indeed often seemed strange to me that, being as I am on intimate terms with the rulers of Europe, I should not be in closer touch with

John Hampden, the seventeenth century Puritan leader, as a souvenir from " your sincere well-wisher." [285] Roosevelt cautioned Ambassador Durand that it was important in view of present relations with the Senate not to mention the miniature.[286] He then showed the King's " very pleasant letter " proudly to Hay, with the comment that he would answer the letter and pocket the miniature and say nothing to Congress about it. " If I submitted it to them," Roosevelt confided to Hay, " they would talk about a month, insult the King and myself and then decide by a vote of 50 to 9 that I should not have it." [287]

Roosevelt did not miss the opportunity to express his views about Anglo-American relations. To Edward he wrote: " I absolutely agree with you as to the importance, not merely to ourselves but to all the free peoples of the civilized world, of a constantly growing friendship and understanding between the English-speaking peoples. One of the gratifying things . . . during the last decade has been the growth in this feeling of goodwill. All I can do to foster it will be done. I need hardly add that, in order to foster it, we need judgment and moderation no less than the goodwill itself." " The larger interests of the two nations," the King was assured, " are the same; and the fundamental underlying traits of their characters are also the same." [288] The King had asked for one of Roosevelt's books. The President now sent his *Winning of the West* and the King was so delighted that he cabled to express his pleasure.[289]

During the summer of 1905, Edward used Sir Donald Mackenzie Wallace, on a visit to America, to express to Roosevelt the King's sympathy with Roosevelt's efforts to bring peace between Russia and Japan and to repeat the appeal of his earlier letter for an Anglo-American under-

the President of the United States. It would be agreeable to me and I think advantageous to both countries that this state of things should in future cease to exist."

standing, and Roosevelt again reiterated his views. "Both King Edward and myself have to teach our democracies to face the rest of the world," he commissioned Wallace to reply to the King.[290] On several other occasions Roosevelt and King Edward corresponded or sent personal messages to each other on this subject of Anglo-American coöperation.[291]

But on more explicit matters, too, they exchanged views. In March, 1905, Roosevelt wrote the King of the importance of Russia's making peace, obviously hoping the King might pass the word on to his nephew the Czar.[292] Also in March, wanting Britain's support against an international congress about the Russo-Japanese settlement, Roosevelt had John Hay write Balfour to remind him of the King's promise that Britain would go along with us.[293] Lodge, as has been seen, was used in that summer of 1905 to talk to the King about several matters on which Roosevelt wanted Britain's help.[294] In the summer, the King on hearing Hay was to be in England insisted on seeing him. To Hay the King talked about the efforts in certain quarters to break up Anglo-American friendship. When the President suggested that he try to influence the Czar to come to the peace conference that Roosevelt wished, Edward objected that his intervention would be futile because the Czar "had ceased to be a free agent." He "is the prisoner of his entourage," Edward explained. Through Hay the King predicted to Roosevelt that the Czar would face much more serious internal difficulties. And finally, the King urged Hay to persuade the President to have joint Anglo-American naval manoeuvers.[295] Roosevelt in turn gave the King his views on the fighting in the Russo-Japanese War.[296] Ambassador Reid was commissioned to show the King Roosevelt's "Russian correspondence," but when he did he found the King had already seen Roosevelt's letter to the Czar, presumably through the Czar. Again, Edward and Theodore exchanged views on the problem of immigration and competition of the "coloured races." Ed-

ward explained how peculiarly embarrassing this problem
was to him because of so many colored subjects in his empire,
but the King hoped the subject could be handled by friendly
negotiation, such as the Treaty the British had drawn up
with Japan. Roosevelt agreed that in this as in other matters
British and American interests were alike.[297]

Throughout Roosevelt's relations with Edward VII, the
monarch was suspicious of the Germans. Since Roosevelt
was also trying to attain his ends through the Kaiser, who
was in turn suspicious of the English and had much more
power than the King over foreign policy, Roosevelt had to
move discreetly.[298] The King and his Danish wife, for instance, expressed concern lest Germany get the Danish West
Indies.[299] Through one of the King's emissaries, Roosevelt
communicated his views on disarmament and the Hague
Conference to the King and promised that, though the
Kaiser would not like it, the President was going to back
England at that Conference.[300] In 1903 Hay apologized to
Roosevelt because the telegram he had sent on Roosevelt's
behalf to the King was " deficient in warmth." " But," Hay
explained, " you did not want to make it warmer than the
one to your great and good friend William." [301] When Hay
felt compelled by command of King Edward to visit the King
he and Roosevelt were embarrassed because Roosevelt had
promised the German Ambassador that if Hay did not visit
the Kaiser he would visit nobody.[302] Roosevelt tried in July,
1906, to have his views on the Algeciras Conference conveyed
through Reid to the King, but Edward, who was having
interviews with the Kaiser on this matter, avoided the interview, and in the end Roosevelt decided it was just as well
they had not confided in Edward on the matter.[303]

Indeed, in his dealings with Edward, Theodore was cautious. In an exchange between Reid and Roosevelt in 1905
is found perhaps the explanation of Roosevelt's unwillingness
to deal directly with the King more often. Donald C. Munro-

Ferguson, former member of Parliament, explained to Reid that though the King could not constitutionally meddle in foreign affairs, still this fact gave added advantage in the President's negotiating with Edward because the King and the President were alike in possessing no power to commit any one but themselves. Thus both King and President could speak freely. Lord Lansdowne, on the other hand, was reluctant to talk, Munro-Ferguson explained, because when he spoke he committed the British Empire in a way Roosevelt could not commit the American nation. Roosevelt was unenthusiastic about the implications of this reasoning. In consequence, he authorized Reid to speak on " occasions " to the King " incidentally," but admonished him to be very cautious about consulting Edward officially. Roosevelt reminded Reid of Palmerston's " stinging letter " to the Queen when she had attempted to negotiate directly with Germany through the Prince Consort. Roosevelt was also unimpressed with the English suggestion that he was the counterpart of the King because he could " only speak for the government with the proviso that the Senate does not disagree." Indeed, he protested, " I have been able to speak with much more boldness and decision than either Balfour or Lansdowne." [304] A year and a half later Roosevelt emphatically forbade Reid to show the King Roosevelt's correspondence with the Kaiser, " because if he happened to take offense at something the Kaiser had said, as he well might, it would bring me into trouble as violating the confidence of the Kaiser." " But," the President told Reid, " you should have the correspondence, so that, in case from the Kaiser's side the matter should get in twisted shape to the King, you would be able at once to set him right—even in that event, however, only after communicating with me." " I have had all kinds of queer confidences reposed in me," Roosevelt explained, " from the Kaiser down, but I have been careful not to repeat them because I felt it would be doing merely mischief." [305]

Perhaps the reluctance on both sides to have Reid nego-
tiate with the King arose in part from lack of confidence in
Reid as a go-between. In any case, in December, 1906, the
King sent for Arthur Lee, just back from personal conferences with the President, and Lee, with Roosevelt's authorization, gave Edward " a carefully edited account of the
German manoeuvers during the Algeciras and Russo-Japan
Peace negotiations," " bearing in mind, of course," he wrote
Roosevelt, " your word of caution as regards his relationship
with the Kaiser." Lee reported the King " deeply interested,
and much gratified to receive such authoritative and striking
proofs of the friendly feeling towards this country which has
animated you throughout." Then Lee added, " It is really
very fortunate that I should have had this opportunity of
blowing away the mist of misunderstanding and suspicion,
with regard to the true attitude of the U. S. Government and
yourself towards us." [306]

Back in the late nineties, as we have seen, even before the
last threat to Anglo-American friendship was removed, an
entente between the two countries was slowly developing.
At the First Hague Conference, for instance, the American
delegates consistently supported Britain.[307] The entente was
growing out of a sense of community of interest in various
parts of the world: the Western hemisphere, Eastern Asia
and the Pacific, and Europe. It was promoted by a common
concern for a united English-speaking domination of " backward areas " and for a joint maintenance of a world balance
of great powers. " Taking the constitution of the British Empire," Mahan wrote Roosevelt at the time of the Second
Hague Conference, " and the trade interests of the British
Islands, the United States has the certainty of a very high
order that the British Empire will stand substantially on the
same line of world privileges as ourselves; that its strength
will be our strength, and the weakening it injury to us." [308]

First the problem of control of the Western hemisphere

was solved. After the Venezuelan episode of 1895 Britain and America gradually and almost unconsciously worked out a mutual understanding that America was to dominate the Western hemisphere. As early as June, 1901, Roosevelt was annoyed at the " dullness of apprehension " of Englishmen, who had not seen that a vigorous speech he had made on the Monroe Doctrine was not aimed at them but at Germany. " As far as England is concerned," he wrote, " I do not care whether she subscribes to the Monroe Doctrine or not because she is the one power with which any quarrel on that doctrine would be absolutely certain to result to our immediate advantage." [309] British and Americans were later to disagree over American discrimination in regard to canal tolls in favor of American and against British coastwise shipping. Britain got herself entangled—and came to regret it—in joint intervention with Germany in Venezuela in 1902. A brief flurry was caused, too, by the discourtesy of a bigoted British official in Jamaica in 1907, but by this time both countries were so determined to be friends that they competed with each other in mutual forbearance concerning the episode. [310] For the most part, Britain acquiesced in American control in the Western world, and America guaranteed to the British fair commercial treatment as long as Britain was content to leave strategic control to America. It was an arrangement whose implementation came piecemeal over the years.

Roosevelt and his friends were not so worried over Britain's rôle in America as over that of other nations. They had made it clear that even their firm stand against Britain in Venezuela in 1895 had been taken not so much because they feared Britain as because they wanted to establish in regard to England, whom they did not fear, a principle that would keep France or some other power, especially Germany, from interfering. Similarly in objecting to joint guarantee of the canal provided in the first Hay-Pauncefote Treaty Roosevelt declared: " I am not afraid of England, but I do not

want to see Germany or France given a joint right with us
to interfere in Central America." [311] In Britain desire for
friendship with America was so great that fear of damaging
Anglo-American relations was an important factor in the
outburst in both the British press and Parliament against the
Government's use of force in Venezuela in 1902-1903.[312] At
the height of the Venezuelan episode Prime Minister Balfour
declared on December 18: " There is nothing nearer my heart
than to preserve the warmest and most friendly feelings
between this country and America, and I hope that the
people of the United States will see that nothing has been
done by us in Venezuela which can in the smallest way touch
their susceptibilities." [313] " None of us have any doubt of
the friendliness or of the absolute fairness either of the President or of our old friend Mr. Hay," Balfour wrote nine days
later at a time when Washington was putting pressure on
Britain. The British Government knew, he pointed out,
" that gusts of popular opinion sweep away well planned
structures of policy." " We wished," he explained, " to make
every allowance for all difficulties of the kind." [314]

Among the English, indeed, Henry White wrote, there was
no particular feeling about our enforcement of the Monroe
Doctrine against her. " They are rapidly realizing that its
assertion is really favorable to British interests," White explained, but " France and Germany are pretty sore about the
recent victory of the Monroe Doctrine." [315] Prime Minister
Balfour declared in 1902, " We have not the slightest objection (rather the reverse!) . . . to the Monroe Doctrine." He
went further. " These South American Republics are a great
trouble," he said, " and I wish the U. S. A. would take them
in hand." [316] The British had come to realize that when the
American Navy prevented Germany from endangering small
countries in the Western hemisphere or American possessions
there, it was also protecting British possessions against her
and was keeping small American nations open to British as

well as to American trade. America understood, too, that British power and British interest blocked aggression by other European states. Brooks Adams insisted in 1900 that " England is essential to the United States, in the face of enemies who fear and hate us, and who, but for her, would already have fleets upon our shores." [317] " If disaster came to the British Empire," Roosevelt warned Root in January, 1900, we might in a few years face " abandoning the Monroe Doctrine and submitting to the acquisition of American territory by some great European military power, or going to war." [318] And Lodge made a speech in the Senate in which he said Britain was helping maintain the Monroe Doctrine.[319] Our Government in turn helped the British get " rid of the incubus of the old Treaty of Managua " with Nicaragua; it assisted her in winning a more favorable agreement concerning the Mosquito Indians, though Hay and Pauncefote felt it necessary to keep the whole correspondence " private," " unofficial," and out of the record.[320] In 1902 Lord Lansdowne in his turn gave the British representative in Cuba instructions that in commercial negotiations he was not even to give an appearance of an attempt to thwart the policies of the United States.[321]

Britain's joining with Germany at all in 1902 might have strained American feelings, had our government not recognized that her object was different from Germany's. Actually hostility toward intervention was turned against Germany, not Britain. The American press and public, too, distinguished the British public's hostility to Germany from the British Government's alliance with Germany. Neither the American people nor many of its newspapers felt Britain had sinister motives. Indeed, both press and Government erroneously assumed she had been led into intervention.[*]

Britain, too, tried not to alienate America over Venezuela. Upon friendly warning from Henry White that American

---

[*] This episode will be treated in Lecture VI.

public opinion might be adversely affected, Balfour sent
orders forbidding the British commander to land troops or
open fire on anything Venezuelan. "It would be difficult to
exaggerate," White reported, "the extraordinary unpopularity of their agreement with Germany." [322] It was only
when Britain hesitated over signing the Venezuela protocol,
hoping still to get preferential treatment, that American
hostility threatened seriously. Then Sir Michael Herbert in
Washington cabled his government of a great change in
American feeling and of the danger that, if the alliance with
Germany continued, Anglo-American relations would be seriously imperiled. In consequence, Lansdowne immediately
yielded and signed the protocol. Throughout this controversy the American attitude was not so much annoyance
against the British as unhappiness over their joining with
Germany rather than with us. [323] The episode, White hoped,
had in the end rather helped Anglo-American relations by
making both peoples understand each other better and by
revealing to the British "the depth of German antagonism
to a good Anglo-American understanding." In his many
talks with the British leaders during this affair, White was
impressed that the British would make almost any sacrifice
rather than impair good relations with the United States. [324]

In pursuit of the idea of America's dominating the Western
hemisphere and Britain's controlling other parts of the world,
men early talked of exchanging British possessions in America for the Philippines. In 1899 Roosevelt declared privately,
"It would be the greatest possible good fortune if we could
hand the Philippines over to England, if she would leave this
continent. The relations between Canada and England always tend to bring friction between us and both of them." [325]
In August, 1898, Lodge proposed that we keep Manila or
perhaps all of Luzon but then trade all the rest of the Philippines to Britain in exchange for the Bahamas, Jamaica, and
the Danish West Indies, which Britain would be able to buy
anxious to have us take all the Philippines." [339]

from Denmark and then cede to us. " This would relieve us
of the burden of administering that great group in the East,
. . . and would leave us in the Phillipines [*sic*] associated with
a friendly power with whom we should be in entire accord." [326] Through the 1890's both Roosevelt and Lodge had
been eager to acquire Canada. And even after Roosevelt
became President they would still have been glad to see England leave the Western hemisphere entirely, abandoning
Canada in the process.[327] One reason Roosevelt did not fear
British violation of the Monroe Doctrine was that if trouble
came with England over it the United States would immediately take Canada and nothing England could gain* would
offset Canada.[328] On the other hand, Roosevelt and his fellow-expansionists had come to realize that taking Canada
would destroy the Anglo-American friendship they now
wanted; so they no longer seriously considered ousting England from that dominion.[329] As late as 1905, however, Lodge
urged Balfour not to be afraid to use a strong tone to keep
Canada in order since she could not leave Britain without
falling into our hands.[330] In any case, whatever Britain retained, she now recognized us as guardian of Anglo-American
interests in the Americas.

As part of the mutual arrangement that would leave the
Western hemisphere to us, Roosevelt spoke of a British Monroe Doctrine for South Africa and felt that Britain should
dominate that area of the world on behalf of English-speaking people and certainly ought to warn off others, like the
German Kaiser, as we did in America.[331] He looked forward
to that day when there would be a practically independent
English-speaking commonwealth south of the Zambesi.[332]
And in 1905 Lodge reported to Roosevelt: " Balfour . . . is
most anxious to have . . . the Panama Canal . . . built for he
feels that it will strengthen our position enormously and that

---

* " She could take the Philippines and Porto Rico," he told Lodge in 1901,
but " they would be a very poor offset for the loss of Canada."

with England at Suez and the U. S. at Panama we should hold the world in a pretty strong grip." [333] In like manner, Mahan's conception of Anglo-American unity stretched clear around the globe. The focal points were the Suez Canal and the projected canal in Central America. Together they would control the entrance to the Indian Ocean and the Pacific and hence easy access to the Far East. This joint control, Mahan argued, was not a matter of " British welfare " but of " our . . . community of interests." [334]

In her attitude toward American expansion into the Pacific, Britain promoted on her part this concept of Anglo-American coöperation. She wanted Americans to take Hawaii. She cheered them in their taking and keeping the Philippines.[335] Rudyard Kipling wrote Roosevelt in September, 1898: " Now go in and put all the weight of your influence into hanging on permanently to the whole Phillipines [sic]. America has gone and stuck a pickaxe into the foundations of a rotten house and she is morally bound to build the house over again from the foundations or have it fall about her ears." [336]

Britain's desire for American rule of the Philippines stemmed partly from fear that Germany might get the islands, but partly from hope that America's keeping them would bring her permanently into the Far East where Britain wanted her help.[337] Spring Rice spoke frankly to Lodge. " I think there can be no doubt," he said, " that there is an intention (and a natural one) to depose English civilization (I means yours as much and more than mine) from the Pacific. . . . We have the right and duty to defend what we most certainly have fairly won on the American, Australian and Chinese coasts. I don't believe that England, the island, is strong enough, or will remain comparatively strong enough to defend English civilization alone." [338] British Colonial Secretary Chamberlain told Lodge in September, 1898, that looking to future combinations in the Far East, he was " very

Indeed, Great Britain was delighted at American entry into imperialism. Nearly everyone in England " applauds your imperialistic new departure," James Bryce wrote Roosevelt in September, 1898.[340] Chamberlain congratulated Hay and Roosevelt in 1902 on the successful subduing of the Philippines. " This extension of American influence and dominion will work for the happiness of the native population," Chamberlain prophesied; and the " experience in the problems of government under such circumstances will help the American people to understand our world-work, and I hope to sympathize with it." [341]

In a world where rivalry and jealousy were leading to clashes of rival imperialisms that endangered world peace, a sense of common interest in the Far East was pulling Britain and America together. This was happening even before the Spanish War improved relations between Britain and America. This was because the expansionists in both countries saw in each other not enemies but allies. And the expansionists were the very ones that were strongly nationalist and might hence have been expected to promote ill feeling between the two nations.

American expansionists, for their part, became convinced that Eastern Asia and the Pacific were the areas into which American trade and power must extend. Lodge, for example, felt one of the most important results of the Spanish War was our entry into the Pacific and our gaining a foothold in the Far East.[342] Strongly as Lodge felt about the Alaskan boundary and the fishing rights of his Gloucester constituents, he considered that British and American common interests in the Far East were of infinitely greater consequence than all the Canadian differences.[343] " The Chinese question, which we are only just beginning to understand," he wrote in 1899, " is of infinitely more importance than the disposition we make of the Phillipines [*sic*] except in so far as a position in those islands gives us authority and standing in the East." [344] Britain, on the other hand, was already established with considerable influence in parts of China. Her policies were such that they did not exclude American trade, which the policies of certain other European powers seeking a foothold in China threatened to do. In fact, with other powers now entering into competition with her for control of China, Britain needed a powerful ally. On both sides, therefore, the advantage of Anglo-American coöperation in the Far East became evident before the Spanish War gave America the Philippines.

A year before the well-known " open door " talks, Roosevelt's friends, Lodge and White, were corresponding about the threat of a Russian and German partition of China and the possibility of an " Anglo-American alliance " in the Far East. On January 18, 1898, White reported British uneasiness about China. The English recognize, he wrote, " that China is no place in which to *take* territory with advantage." They do not " want any Chinese ports to be closed to the commerce of England and the rest of the world." White urged upon Lodge American support of England's open door policy. " I suppose," he said, " our country would view with favor and support morally, if not perhaps officially, England's efforts to prevent the closing of Chinese ports." [345] Lodge, who was seeing Roosevelt daily, replied, " If I had my way, I should be glad to have the United States say to England that we would stand by her in her declaration that the ports of China must be opened to all nations equally or to none and if England takes that attitude firmly I am in hopes this may come about, although our foreign policy is always more hap-hazard than I like to see it." Lodge hoped the British would not vacillate in their plans as the newspapers had predicted they would.[346] In March, 1898, White reported both Balfour and Chamberlain eager for Anglo-American coöperation in the Far East. Indeed, Balfour asked White whether America would join England in guaranteeing " the integrity " of Chinese territory. " I told him," White recounted to Lodge, " that I doubted it very much . . . but I thought it not unlikely that if the occasion should arise we might be disposed to make some sort of a declaration as to the maintenance of open ports in China." Balfour suggested that " if America and England were to join in such a declaration it would ' settle the question,' especially as Japan would probably concur." [347] This was a month before we entered the Spanish War that was supposed to have changed Roosevelt's and Lodge's opinion of Britain and to have won friendship for Britain in America. It was a year before Alfred Hippisley of the British Customs Service and William Rockhill, who was at this time out in Greece, had the talks that have been credited with first suggesting to us the possibility of a pronouncement about the open door and the integrity of China. Those thus early tentatively negotiating Anglo-American coöperation in an open door policy were intimate friends of Roosevelt, and one of them, Lodge, was talking everything over daily with Roosevelt.

Roosevelt and his friends, however, went even further. Throughout the period from the Spanish War until the end of Roosevelt's Presidency, they played with ideas very like an Anglo-American alliance and discussed them with British leaders like Chamberlain and Balfour.[348] The facts do not support Roosevelt's assurances to the violently anti-British Finley Peter Dunne, whose powerful pen he feared, that he was with Dunne " heart and soul, in laughing away such a folly as the ' Anglo-Saxon Alliance business.' " Roosevelt could join in the laughing only in so far as he talked about a formal technical treaty and could find amusement in rumors of something that did not exist. He could be amused only at the unreality of men without political sense enough to know that such an alliance was politically impossible. Actually, he never seriously considered an " alliance " with Britain, for he knew such a treaty could not pass the Senate and he was certain the American people would never in his day tolerate an out-and-out alliance with anyone.[349] He, too, was unwilling to sign away the nation's right to act as it pleased, and this fact restrained him from wishing a formal alliance were possible. Yet he was ready to enter into understandings with Britain that obtained the advantages of an alliance without being one. His friend Mahan thought no formal alliance was necessary. Mahan called instead for a " mutual understanding of common interests and common traditions." [350]

Roosevelt was busily fighting in the Spanish War when Joseph Chamberlain made his startling statement in May, 1898, that " even war itself would be cheaply purchased if, in a great and noble cause, the Stars and Stripes and the Union Jack should wave together over an Anglo-Saxon Alliance." [*] No record remains of what Roosevelt thought of the proposal, but the rest of Chamberlain's statement he would heartily have approved, namely, " that the closer, the more cordial, the fuller, and the more definite these arrangements [between Britain and America] are, with the consent of both parties the better it will be for both and for the world." [352] While they were both in office, Roosevelt and Chamberlain worked for this common end and each sought to build coöperatively a great English-speaking power in the world. When Chamberlain retired from public life Roosevelt pronounced him, " with the exception of Gladstone, . . . the ablest man in English politics " since Disraeli.[353]

Before Roosevelt's Presidency, discussion of a strong understanding with Britain was not confined to public statements by martial and race-conscious Chamberlain. In September, 1898, while the Chamberlains were visiting the Lodges at Nahant, Chamberlain and Lodge agreed about an " entente " and Chamberlain hoped some day we would

---

[*] In 1899 Roosevelt wrote Spring Rice, " Together . . . the two branches of the Anglo-Saxon race . . . can whip the world." [351]

come to an alliance.[354] In response to talk about an alliance even before Chamberlain's public proposal of one, Roosevelt had told White in March, 1898: " I don't believe we ought to have an alliance." [355] In September, 1899, Hay publicly denied that there was " a secret alliance with England," since Democratic charges that the Republicans had made one were hurting the Republicans politically. To White Hay explained, " The fact is a treaty of alliance is impossible. It could never get through the Senate." A " friendly understanding," yes. " But an alliance must remain in the present state of things, an unattainable dream." [356] In 1900 Hay again had to answer the charge that there was a secret alliance. " None exists," he replied categorically. " None has been suggested on either side. None is thought of." [357]

But even without the alliance, the foundations of British-American coöperation were well and truly laid. If Roosevelt or his Secretary of State or the usually well-informed Henry White in London knew in advance of the Anglo-Japanese alliance of 1902 there is no evidence of such knowledge. When he learned of it, however, Hay considered it a " renewed confirmation of the assurances " the two countries had given us concerning the independence and integrity of China.[358] Henry White assumed that Lodge would approve of the Treaty. White considered it " an excellent thing for the furtherance of our interests in the far east." " I always think it particularly satisfactory," White commented, " when other nations can be got to do our work or to contribute very materially towards it and this is . . . what the Treaty in question is likely to accomplish." [359]

On April 25, 1903, when we were trying to put pressure on Russia about Manchuria, Hay wrote to Roosevelt, " I am sure you will think it is out of the question that we should adopt any scheme of concerted action with England and Japan. Public opinion in this country would not support such a course, nor do I think it would be to our permanent advantage." [360] On May 13, Roosevelt responded to a query of Hay's with the advice that they say nothing at that time about Manchuria. "We are in no ' entangling alliance '; and things are settling down now anyhow," Roosevelt wrote Hay.[361] When the Russo-Japanese War broke out, however, Roosevelt and Hay sent notes to Russia and Japan and to the neutral powers insisting that they respect the integrity of China including Manchuria. Roosevelt's own views might have led him to feel that if Russia were joined by another power the United States ought to enter the war just as Britain would have been obligated to do, but there is no evidence anywhere to support his statement to Spring Rice on July 24, 1905, that he had warned France and Germany he would do this.[362] In December, 1904, however, the often well-informed Sidney Low published an article in England in which he predicted that " much more surprising things might happen than that the foundations should be laid of a League of Peace, based on a genuine and effective Anglo-Saxon Alliance, before it is time for . . . [Roosevelt] to quit the Executive Mansion." [363]

Then during the first half of 1905 Roosevelt took over the handling of his own foreign policy * and important events followed close one upon the other. This time the United States was kept informed and participated informally in discussions that brought about a renewal of the Anglo-Japanese agreement in modified form. Indeed, on January 1 Roosevelt told Hay he favored a suggested American " naval defense alliance with Japan." In May George Kennan then in Japan suggested an alliance in a letter that the historian Tyler Dennett thinks was prompted by Japanese Minister

* It was during the spring and early summer that Hay was ill and in Europe seeking health; he returned to Washington for a few days in June; then he went to his New Hampshire home exhausted, and on July 1 died. On June 12 the President wrote Mrs. Hay, " John . . . must rest for this summer. I shall handle the whole business of the State Department myself." [364]

Katsura, who Dennett thinks saw the reply. Roosevelt responded that he personally " entirely agreed " that an alliance with Japan was desirable, but that in view of the Senate's attitude toward treaties, he " might just as well strive for the moon as for such a policy." [365] This time, indeed, Roosevelt was shown a rough draft of the Anglo-Japanese treaty before it was signed and told both Japan and Britain,[a] in advance, that he " heartily approved of the treaty . . . and believed that it was advantageous to the peace of Asia, and therefore to the peace of the world." [366] It was during these negotiations that Roosevelt arranged Spring Rice's flying trip to Washington as a confidential emissary. Spring Rice was carefully briefed in England on the way over and stopped again on the way back to report to the King and Lansdowne. Though out of courtesy he talked with Hay, his real negotiations were with the President. He and Roosevelt were closeted for many hours. He brought from Lansdowne a promise that Britain would follow our lead in the Far East, " that we had only to let them know our programme . . . to have them support our position." Roosevelt made it clear to him that " an alliance was impossible; that the less said about an understanding the better; but that our interests in the Far East being identical, there ought to be no difficulty in parallel action, and in timely exchange of views." Back in England Spring Rice found Lansdowne much delighted over the President's desire to act with England. But the need for secrecy was well understood. " Every thinking man," Spring Rice reported, " is convinced of the absolute necessity for England of a good understanding with America—but they know, most of them—that they had better not say so. The King as much as anyone." King Edward was so delighted that, " rather against the wish of

[a] Through Jusserand Roosevelt told the French Government of his entire approval and Taft reiterated the approval in his talk with Japanese Prime Minister Katsura.

the Government, who were afraid it would embarrass "
Roosevelt, he wrote the President the personal letter we have
already seen the Government rewrite for him, and initially
he had even " wanted to say much more than he did." [367]
The next month, April, 1905, Prime Minister Balfour wrote
Lodge: " I agree with you in thinking that the interests of
the United States and of ourselves are absolutely identical
and that the more closely we can work together, the better
it will be for us and the world at large." [368] Roosevelt on
his part sent word to Ambassador Meyer in Rome that when
Meyer reached St. Petersburg Spring Rice would call on
him and talk over Rooseveltian policies with him. " He
knows just how I feel," Roosevelt told Meyer, " and you
can talk with him without any reserve. England's interest
is exactly ours as regards this Oriental complication, and is
likely to remain so. . . . It is important that without any
talk whatever being made of it, there should be a thorough
understanding between us and the English as to what is
happening." [369]

At the end of June Lodge, whom we have already seen
thus employed for other purposes, was sent to talk to the
Prime Minister and the Foreign Secretary, and Roosevelt
arranged for him to talk privately with the King. In London
he had a " full talk " with Balfour, and a long conference
with Lansdowne, in which he explained Roosevelt's views
and listened to Balfour's and Lansdowne's. Lodge reported
to Roosevelt that Lansdowne and Balfour both " expressed
the most absolute accord with our policy and position in the
East." Balfour assured Lodge that Britain's only desire was
to stand with us. Lansdowne " in confidence and for [Roose-
velt's] . . . information alone " told Lodge that the " new
treaty with Japan was proceeding well—that the main points
were the return of Manchuria to China and the complete
recognition of Japan's control of Corea which he said he
understood was what we approved." Balfour in turn under-

stood perfectly that we could not make a treaty of alliance with anyone. But Balfour and Lodge agreed that the two countries would keep each other " fully and confidentially informed " in regard both to " actions and wishes." [370]

Just a month later, on July 27, Secretary of War Taft was in Tokyo under instruction from Roosevelt holding " a long and confidential conversation " with Japanese Prime Minister Taro Katsura. Count Katsura, like Balfour, understood that the United States could not enter into a formal alliance, " but in view of our common interests he could not see why some good understanding or an alliance in practice if not in name should not be made." Taft explained that it was difficult for the President to enter even into an informal agreement without the consent of the Senate; but he assured the Japanese that " wherever occasion arose appropriate action of the Government of the United States, in conjunction with Japan and Great Britain for such purposes, could be counted on by them quite as confidently as if the United States were under treaty obligations." [371] Taft cabled the whole agreement to Roosevelt, who replied, " Your conversation with Count Katsura absolutely correct in every respect. Wish you would state to Katsura that I confirm every word you have said." [372] In the meantime the Anglo-Japanese Alliance, about which Roosevelt had been kept fully informed and the terms of which Ambassador Durand took to Oyster Bay in advance, was signed August 12.[373] What Roosevelt had done by personal diplomacy through Spring Rice, Taft, and Lodge, was to agree both in London and in Tokyo to join, as if we had signed a treaty, an alliance with Japan and England in which each party was committed to go to war in defense of the other if either was attacked by a third party, and in which, with Roosevelt's approval, previously independent Korea was handed over to Japan.

No record of the agreement was left in the State Department. Root was on vacation in Newfoundland and knew

nothing about this until later.[374] On October 4 a Japanese
newspaper, the *Kokumin*, learned of the conversation and
published news of a "Japanese Anglo-American alliance."
"We may be sure that when once England became our ally,"
said the Japanese journal, "America also became a party to
the agreement. . . . America is our ally though bound by no
formal treaty. We firmly believe that America, under the
leadership of the world statesman, President Roosevelt, will
deal with her Oriental problems in cooperation with Japan
and Great Britain." Lloyd Griscom, our ambassador in
Tokyo, cabled this newspaper story confidentially to Root,
who had now become Secretary of State.[375] But the rumor
was denied and the American people knew nothing of this
unofficial alliance with Great Britain and her ally, Japan,
until Tyler Dennett discovered the Taft-Roosevelt cables in
the Roosevelt papers in 1924.[376] In the summer of 1905, then,
under Roosevelt's temporary personal running of foreign
affairs, the entente with Britain that Roosevelt and his circle
had so long wanted but had not dared put into treaty form,
was sanctified by executive agreement, informal and secret,
but none the less significant.[377] That fall Roosevelt reiterated
his belief that "England and the United States, beyond any
other two powers, should be friendly." To Spring Rice he
renewed his oft-made promise, "What I can legitimately do
to increase this friendliness will be done."[378]

At the end of 1905 the friends in Britain, who had so long
run Anglo-American affairs in coöperation with Roosevelt,
Hay, White, and Lodge were turned out of office and a new
group of Liberals whose top leaders Roosevelt did not know
so well as he did the top British Conservatives came into
power. On December 5 Sir Henry Campbell-Bannerman replaced Arthur Balfour as Prime Minister and Edward Grey
took over the Foreign Office from Lord Lansdowne. Roosevelt had been pleasantly acquainted with Bryce, Morley,
and Trevelyan since his two honeymoons in England in the

1880's, but no record exists of any personal relations earlier or later between Roosevelt and the Liberal Prime Minister. And when Grey took office Roosevelt did not know him. Gradually, however, Grey and the American President developed a not close but friendly personal relationship.

On imperialism British Liberals were badly split. Campbell-Bannerman and some of the Liberal leaders were anti-imperialist. In February, 1905, Hippisley of "open door" fame had written his American friend Rockhill, "I fear a critical time is approaching when . . . the Liberals . . . come into power. They are 'little Englanders' and have no really Imperialistic policy; and it is only, I fear, straight speaking by America which will prevent them from committing some *betise*, such as throwing Japan into the arms of Germany and Russia by denouncing the existing alliance." [379] But Grey and another faction of Liberals in Britain like Progressives in America left their liberalism at home when they went overseas. Indeed, the Grey group held views about Anglo-American fitness to rule "backward peoples" that were often indistinguishable from the imperialism of Conservatives. It might have been more difficult to build the Anglo-American entente under the more impersonal relations of the two governments after 1906 than under the close personal friendships prior to the advent of Campbell-Bannerman and Grey. The entente, however, was established. And Liberals saw its value. The close coöperation that might have dominated the conferences had Lansdowne still been Foreign Secretary and Balfour Prime Minister was lacking at Algeciras and The Hague. None the less Grey gradually learned to understand Roosevelt and his aims.

One of the main purposes of the Anglo-American entente was promotion of an Anglo-American control of colonial areas.[a] This objective Roosevelt promoted privately as well

[a] As Paul Reinsch, a leading critic of Roosevelt, protested, "Much of the enthusiasm in favor of alliance must be identified with the spirit of desire for

as officially, out of office as well as during the Presidency. He sympathized as Chamberlain hoped he would, with England's " worldwork," as the British imperialist called it. Indeed, it was his sense of a common task of Britain and America in ruling " colonial peoples " with the ultimate purpose of civilizing them that provided the basis of Roosevelt's policy concerning Britain.* The common ideas on empire held by him and the British imperialists were a tie that drew the two countries together.

It was in justifying the methods of colonialism in the minds of humane men everywhere that race theories of superior and inferior people were most useful to imperialists. Thus in 1896 in his *Winning of the West* Roosevelt had stated important principles without which, in view of his realistic knowledge of the methods of colonialism, Roosevelt might have had difficulty in reconciling his imperialism with his own civilized background. In defense of the frontiersman's treatment of the American Indian he had expressed views that underlay his attitude toward imperial rule of " backward " peoples, whether in the Philippines, China, Africa, or India. How the whites won the land, he wrote, mattered little " so long as the land was won." " It was all important," he added, " that it should be won, for the benefit of civilization and in the interests of mankind. It is indeed a warped, perverse and silly morality which would forbid a course of conquest that has turned whole continents into the seats of mighty and flourishing civilized nations." Then he went on to explain that it is " idle to apply to savages the rules of international morality which obtain between stable and cultured communities." " Fortu-

exaggerated national aggrandizement, and may be ascribed to their belief that these two powers can without let or hindrance order the government of the world according to their own convenience." [380]

* " I entirely agree with you . . ." King Edward wrote Roosevelt, " and I look forward with confidence to the co-operation of the English-speaking races becoming the most powerful civilizing factor in the policy of the world." [381]

nately," he added, " the hard, energetic, practical men who do the rough pioneer work of civilization in barbarous lands, are not prone to false sentimentality." " The most ultimately righteous of all wars," he explained, " is a war with savages, though it is apt to be also the most terrible and inhuman. The rude, fierce settler who drives the savage from the land lays all civilized mankind under debt to him. American and Indian, Boer and Zulu, Cossack and Tartar, New Zealander and Maori,—in each case the victor, horrible though many of his deeds are, has laid deep the foundations for the future greatness of a mighty people." This is a " primeval warfare . . . where no pity is shown to non-combatants, where the weak are harried without ruth, and the vanquished mal-treated with merciless ferocity. A sad and evil feature . . . is that the whites, the representatives of civilization, speedily sink almost to the level of their barbarous foes. . . . There follow deeds of enormous, of incredible, of indescribable hor-ror." Yet he insisted this struggle was " vast and elemental in its consequence to the future of the world." It matters little, he declared, " whether Lorraine is part of Germany or of France, . . . but it is of incalculable importance that Amer-ica, Australia, and Siberia should pass out of the hands of their red, black, and yellow aboriginal owners, and become the heritage of the dominant world races." [332]

It was these beliefs that reconciled Roosevelt to all the cruelties of imperialism, and made him so exasperated when the " sentimentalist " criticized American cruelty in the Philippines, or that of the British in India, or the Dutch in South Africa. Roosevelt was a remarkably well-informed man. He knew as few men in America did the horrors of war in the Philippines, the outrages committed by foreign troops in China. Personal friends like Rockhill in China had de-scribed to him what civilized men did to the Chinese after the Boxer uprising. His humanity deplored brutality. But his sense of history told him that brutality accompanied struggles with "backward people," that morality did not apply here, and that in the end civilization would be advanced and white domination of the world established; and this was desirable for mankind, including the backward folk. So in a letter to Sydney Brooks, he applied the superior race theories discussed in an earlier lecture. "That you have committed faults," he wrote, "I have not the slightest doubt," but "English rule in India and Egypt, like the rule of France in Algiers or Russia in Turkestan means a great advance for humanity." [a] [383]

Hence, when imperialism was under criticism, but especially English-speaking imperialism, he came to its defense. He had long followed British rule in India closely. He had heard through Lodge and from Brooks himself what Brooks Adams thought of British rule in India. "No man knows" the English, Adams had written Lodge, "or anything really about them, till he has gone to India. I mean no man can see the under side of civilization until he gets underneath. India is underneath—and don't they bleed her. . . . We aren't in it, we are just children—both in squeezing and sanctimony." [384] Roosevelt had read with great interest long letters from Speck von Sternburg telling of the weaknesses and strengths of British rule in India when Speck was stationed there. [385] After dining at the White House with an officer of the British Army in India John Burroughs reported that Roosevelt knew more about India and England's relation to it than the officer did. [386] From Speck and others Roosevelt had formed a high opinion of Lord Curzon and his ideals for India and his efforts to build for India a prosperous future. [387] He coöperated with Britain when he could. For instance, in 1908 he sent confidentially to Lord Bryce a letter from Rockhill concerning the decline in power of the Dalai Lama that the British Government ought to see. [388]

Roosevelt's views, then, about India had developed out of

[a] See Lecture I for an analysis of this view.

long years of interest in British colonialism. In 1894 he had predicted if British rule were removed from India " famine and internecine war would again become chronic, and India would sink back to her former place." " The long continuance of British rule," he then believed, " undoubtedly weakens the warlike fibre of the natives, and makes the usurer rather than the soldier the dominant type." [389] In 1897 he had not liked the look of things in India. " The English position there is essentially false," he had written Spring Rice at that time, " unless they say they are there as masters who intend to rule justly, but who do not intend to have their rule questioned. If the English in India would suppress promptly any native newspaper that was seditious; arrest instantly any seditious agitator; put down the slightest outbreak ruthlessly; cease to protect usurers; and encourage the warlike races so long as they were absolutely devoted to British rule, I believe things would be more healthy than they are now." [390] Roosevelt believed, too, that India had done " an incalculable amount for the British character " just as ruling the Philippines would do for ours.[391] In September, 1908, he had written Ambassador Reid of the intricacy of " the problem of control of thickly peopled tropical regions by self-governing northern democracies." " The Indian Babu, who is educated in English methods," he wrote, " receives what in many ways is an exceedingly bad training. He is fitted by his education only to hold public office or to practice as a lawyer . . . under English control. But a limited proportion can hold public office, and the remainder including almost all the lawyers find the path of agitation against the government almost the only one open to them, and it is rendered congenial by the bitterness they feel because . . . the aspirations . . . their education has kindled . . . cannot be gratified." The Indian noble educated in England when he returns to India " has to suffer the well-nigh intolerable humiliation of discovering that he is not regarded as an Englishman but as an inferior, while his education has made him feel that the one thing to be desired is to be accepted by Englishmen as an equal." [392]

Roosevelt's views on the subject were put to a practical test when, late in 1908, serious unrest developed in India and uprisings threatened. Some American and British opinion was critical of British policies. Roosevelt, however, was sympathetic to the British rulers. " I am concerned about . . . the unrest in India," he wrote. " Are . . . the British authorities . . . confident they can hold down any revolt? " he asked Reid. To Sydney Brooks, editor of the British *Saturday Review*, he declared that British rule in India and Egypt meant " a great advance for humanity." " English rule in India," he insisted, " has been one of the mighty feats of civilization, one of the mighty feats to the credit of the white race during the past four centuries . . . of . . . expansion and dominance." Brooks and Bryce asked him to say this sort of thing publicly. He wrote Ambassador Reid and John Morley for material to support his views, which were essentially those of British imperialists. Reid sent arguments gathered from leaders of both parties. Morley wrote him and sent a recent address he had made. Roosevelt then chose a speech to Methodist missionaries on January 18, 1909, as the vehicle for his aid to British imperialists in India. The British press was delighted. Grey, Bryce, Lee all expressed gratitude. His old friend, Morley, in charge of the India Office, wrote to tell him how powerfully his " splendid vindication " had abated misgivings about India.[393]

Egypt, however, was the British colonial country that Roosevelt followed most closely. Even in the 1880's in London he had discussed it.[394] While he was governor he had met at dinner a fabulously wealthy Leigh Hunt, who had made a fortune in Korea and then had gone to the Sudan to build a huge irrigation project. In 1903 President Butler of Columbia heard Hunt speak on the Sudan and was so interested and impressed with " the largeness of his view and the great scope of his ideas " that he sent Hunt to Roosevelt at the White House.[395] With similar interest, Lodge and Roosevelt both followed Lord Cromer's rule in Egypt and admired him greatly. Roosevelt considered him " one of the greatest modern colonial administrators." In 1903 Roosevelt tried to get Cromer to come to Washington to talk about the problem of ruling Cuba and the Philippines.[396] In 1904 he wrote John Morley: " A man who has grappled, or is grappling, with Cuba, Panama and the Philippines, has a lively appreciation of the difficulties inevitably attendant upon getting into Egypt in the first place, and then upon the impossibility of getting out of it, in the second." [397] In 1908 the President read " Cromer's really great book " and was impressed with " the descriptions of the trouble caused in Egypt by some worthy statesmen and by some well-meaning but fatuous philanthropists." [398]

On his way out of Africa in March, 1910, Roosevelt toured Egypt, visited Khartoum, and talked to a number of British officials in Egypt, who deplored the fact that their government was unwilling to back them up in using a strong hand in Egypt.[399] Egypt was facing a crisis over the murder by nationalists of an Egyptian prime minister who had coöperated with the British. Roosevelt came to feel " contempt " for the " flabby " English attitude in Egypt.[400] From the Nile he wrote his sister, " I am greatly amused " that the English authorities " hail me as half ally, half teacher, and are wild to have me instruct the Egyptians here, and their own people at home, what the facts are." [401] Consequently he determined to use a lecture he had agreed to give at the new Egyptian National University to admonish both the anti-British nationalists in Egypt and the weak-kneed Government in England about affairs in Egypt. At an official dinner the night before, he told the British officials that he would have a " drumhead court martial " execute the Egyptian

murderer, and then tell superiors in England when they protested that he was already dead. When warned that he
would give offense if he mentioned the murder in his University address, he replied that he was willing to give up
speaking at all but that if he did speak he would " speak
frankly and openly " about a matter that struck " at the very
roots of law, order, and justice in Egypt." [402]

In his address in a hall filled with foreign officials and
Egyptian notables including the King, Roosevelt urged
Egyptians not to overdo literary education and turn out too
many professors and public officials for whom there was only
limited use, but to stress agricultural and industrial training.
Then quoting a proverb in the native Arabic to the delight of
the audience, he scolded the Egyptians for tolerating the
murder of their prime minister. " All good men, all the men
of every nation," he told them, " whose respect is worth
having, have been inexpressibly shocked by the recent assassination. . . . It is of no consequence whether . . . the crime
. . . be committed under the pretence of preserving order or
the pretence of obtaining liberty. It is equally abhorrent . . .
equally damaging to the very cause to which the assassin
professes to be devoted," namely, Egyptian nationalism.[403]
He left Egypt amidst mingled cheers and widespread popular
denunciations, but British officialdom gave him heartfelt
thanks.[404]

Roosevelt was not content with speaking in Egypt. The
King of Egypt had thanked him and urged him to repeat in
London what he had said in Egypt. In Britain as in Egypt
he consulted leaders in the Government. Before he spoke he
talked with Sir Edward Frey, the Cabinet minister responsible for Egypt, with Lord Cromer, with Liberal Foreign Secretary Sir Edward Grey, and with his old friend the former
Conservative Prime Minister, Lord Balfour, all of whom
approved heartily. He went over the speech word by word
with his friends Lee and Spring Rice. They approved. Lord

Cromer urged him to give the address as planned, and sent him his book on *Ancient and Modern Imperialism*. Cromer said it was imperative that England be told the facts by someone to whom England would listen and there was no one that would be listened to so readily as Roosevelt. Grey was " very anxious " that he should deliver the speech. Grey was uneasy at the course his party was taking about Egypt. His party associates were refusing to let him do what was necessary. " He wanted his hand forced." When Roosevelt was attacked for indiscretion, Grey defended him in Parliament, said Roosevelt had talked the matter over with him, and then added that he not only approved what Roosevelt was going to say but that he told Roosevelt he was rendering a great service by saying it. Balfour of the Opposition then joined Grey in defending the speech in the House of Commons.[405]

So at the Guildhall in London in one of his major public appearances in Europe Roosevelt took the British to task about their Egyptian policy.* " I have just spent nearly a year in Africa," he said. " I heartily respect the men whom I met there, settlers and military and civil officials. . . . Your men in Africa are doing a great work for your Empire, and they are also doing a great work for civilization. . . . The people at home, whether in Europe or America, who live softly, often fail fully to realize what is being done for them." He then told his audience the work civilized nations were doing conquering savage lands for civilization was benefiting mankind as a whole and all such civilized nations must stand together. " Independence and self-government in the hands of the Sudanese," he said, " proved to be much what independence and self-government would have been in a wolf pack." Now under British rule Uganda and the Sudan were making remarkable progress. " It would be a crime not to

---

* To the Kaiser, too, at King Edward's funeral he spoke critically of England's Egyptian policy.

go on with the work, a work which the inhabitants themselves are unable to perform, unless under firm and wise guidance." He spoke, he insisted, as a well-wisher of the British Empire who had deep concern for the future of civilization, as a democrat whose first thought was the welfare of the masses of mankind. " In Egypt," he told this distinguished British gathering, " you are not only the guardians of your own interests; you are also the guardians of the interests of civilization; and the present condition of affairs in Egypt is a grave menace to both your Empire and the entire civilized world. . . . Unfortunately it is necessary for all of us who have to do with uncivilized peoples, and especially with fanatical peoples, to remember that in such a situation as yours in Egypt weakness, timidity, and sentimentality may cause even more far-reaching harm than violence and injustice. . . . The attitude of the so-called Egyptian Nationalist Party in connection with this murder has shown that they were neither desirous nor capable of guaranteeing even the primary justice the failure to apply which makes self-government not merely an empty but a noxious farce. . . . When a people treats assassination as the corner-stone of self-government, it forfeits all right to be treated as worthy of self-government." Then he defined the alternatives. " Either you have the right to be in Egypt or you have not; either it is or it is not your duty to establish and keep order. If you feel that you have not the right to be in Egypt, if you do not wish to establish and to keep order there, why then, by all means get out of Egypt. . . . Some nation must govern Egypt. I hope and believe that you will decide that it is your duty to be that nation." [406]

Lord Charles Beresford, British Admiral, Lord George Curzon, former Viceroy of India, Field Marshall Viscount Horatio Kitchener, hero of Khartoum and former Commander-in-Chief in India, the poet Rudyard Kipling, Arthur Lee, Conservative member of Parliament, Earl Frederick

Roberts, former Commander-in-Chief in India, and Major-General Francis Wingate, Sirdar of the Egyptian Army and Governor-General of the Sudan, wrote enthusiastic letters of thanks, as was to be expected. " Roosevelt has come and gone and done our state great service," wrote Kipling. " Here you have one simple single-minded person, saying and doing, quite casually, things which ought to set the world flaming. . . . Take care of him. He's scarce and valuable." [407] So the imperialists in Britain and America were drawn closer together. But John Morley, Liberal statesman of an older order, had a deeper consciousness of the implications of the Roosevelt harangue. He wrote solemnly to Andrew Carnegie, " The guildhall speech was a grievous mistake, in spite of Grey being an accomplice. It gave powder and shot to our war men, and heaven knows they have plenty of ammunition already." [408]

In the midst of Roosevelt's most brilliant year of foreign-policy-making, the *Nation* commented: " In the President's passion for making the world altogether such as he is, he ignores one of the fixed elements of the problem. This is the obstinate preference of people that have tasted liberty and seen that it is good, for doing things in their own way. It may not suit us, but if it suits them, that means contentment, self-respect, freedom to develop along natural lines. Those are political blessings, all of which would be destroyed by such a forcible imposing of the will of a foreigner as President Roosevelt proposes. He is almost painfully conscious of his own benevolence, but he does not see that benevolence at the tip of a bayonet may be hateful." [409]

Roosevelt saw, it is true, with remarkable perspicacity many of the world's problems that his contemporaries missed; yet he seems never to have perceived the inevitability of a growing resentment of colonial peoples against imperial foreign rule even where it was benevolent. With all his prophetic insights, he never foresaw that one day this resentment would flare into a twentieth century type of nationalism that would threaten if not destroy the English-speaking, white man's dominance of the world that Roosevelt spent a lifetime trying to create. Whenever nationalist movements of people he considered " backward " appeared, he condemned them as examples of lawlessness and as proof that those people were not capable of ruling themselves but had to have civilization imposed upon them by the guns of superior nations. The qualities he most admired in people he considered civilized, he always condemned in " backward " people. He seems never to have comprehended that the more successfully Britain, America, and other civilized powers " civilized " their colonial peoples, the more certain became the overthrow of the world power he joined Britain in seeking to impose.

Two important results were accomplished by the attainment of the Anglo-American entente whose achievement we have traced at some length. First, British and American imperialists were joined together in an effort to dominate parts of the world they dubbed " backward." Their success was to have serious consequences for England and America, for the world, and for the colonial peoples, when the nationalism the Anglo-American policy helped stimulate should develop to the point where the colonial people could successfully activate their resentment of imperialist domination.

Second, Roosevelt and his friends had brought England and America together in an effort to preserve through united action an unstable balance among the nations he considered " civilized." Roosevelt and Britain did not always agree. Roosevelt at times found the British statesmen with whom he coöperated dull-witted, obtuse, lacking in vision.* He was

---

* The Kaiser quoted him as saying of Lansdowne, that he was " efficient in his way, and a good diplomatist, but [that] he runs between blinkers, has no broad views." On the Marquess of Londonderry, former Conservative cabinet member, William reported him to have commented, " This man has no more brains than

unhappy because Britain did not more effectively back his plans for Russo-Japanese peace by putting pressure on Japan as the Kaiser put pressure on the Czar. England worried about Roosevelt's reputed fondness for the Kaiser and was reluctant to go along with the President's plans for the Algeciras Conference. Yet in the end Roosevelt played England's game there and supported her at the Hague Conference the next year. The interplay of British and American interest in the Far East and Europe will be described later. From 1905, however, so long as Roosevelt was President we were committed to act with Britain and Japan in the Far East. The entente with Britain under Roosevelt was henceforth so close that it would have been surprising had he not felt we should enter World War I on Britain's side to preserve the dominance of the English-speaking people in the world. Roosevelt's entente was made possible in part by a growing feeling of kinship on the part of the two peoples. But that feeling was not strong enough for Roosevelt to dare tell the American people the commitments he had made as their President. The entente was in part the work of vigorous leaders inside the American government who were pursuing a policy they dared not take to the people. The important questions for the future were: To what extent could the idea of close coöperation be sold to the American people so that they could be told what their President had agreed to? And would succeeding administrations maintain and pursue Rooseveltian policies in regard to an Anglo-American entente?

those of a guinea pig, he was obtuse as a lamp post, I might as well have talked to the chair opposite us." [410]

chapter **IV**

ROOSEVELT *and China*

"Before I came to the Pacific Slope I was an expansionist," Theodore Roosevelt told a cheering audience in San Francisco in May, 1903, " and after having been here I fail to understand how any man . . . can be anything but an expansionist." He chose this his first trip to the West Coast to proclaim America's mission in the Far East. " In the century that is opening," he said, " the commerce and the command of the Pacific will be factors of incalculable moment in the world's history." [1]

" The seat of power," he warned, " ever shifts from land to land, from sea to sea." The Atlantic Ocean " became to the modern greater world what the Mediterranean had been to the lesser world of antiquity." " The empire that shifted from the Mediterranean," Roosevelt continued, " will in the lifetime of those now children bid fair to shift once more westward to the Pacific." For centuries the Pacific area had held little interest for Westerners. Now, however, Roosevelt observed, the situation has changed radically. " Japan, shaking off the lethargy of centuries, has taken her rank among civilized, modern powers." European powers were establishing themselves along the coast of Eastern Asia.

What, in this newly important Pacific area, was to be the " new " rôle of the United States? " Our mighty republic,"

Roosevelt explained, was now " a power of the first class in the Pacific." " The inevitable march of events," he insisted, " gave us control of the Philippine Islands at a time so opportune that it . . . [might] without irreverence be called Providential." Now, the " logic " of this divine push was being unfolded by human endeavor. A canal was soon to give ships on the Atlantic Coast easy access to the Pacific; a cable would connect America with the Far East. The number of steamships was increasing. America's participation in the Far East was not, then, a voluntary decision. " We have no choice as to whether or not we shall play a great part in the world," Roosevelt declared. " That has been determined for us by fate, by the march of events. We have to play that part." " All that we can decide is whether we shall play it well or ill."

Many problems confronted us in determining Far Eastern policy. One of the most important was our relations with China. China was in a state of decay and ferment. Throughout the Far East, the seeds of modern nationalism had already been planted. Japan had matured to world " status," and was recognized by the nations of the West as possessing influence in the Far East, whether for good or evil. The Western Powers, themselves, were anxiously jockeying for control, forming alliances one with the other, and using the Far East as an area where the intricacies of world politics could be unraveled—or further entangled. Here was an exciting task awaiting a President ambitious for world power. " I most earnestly hope that this work . . . [may] ever be of a peaceful character," Roosevelt said. " Let us speak courteously, deal fairly, and keep ourselves armed and ready. We must show to the strongest that we are able to maintain our rights." International respect and power in the Far East can be attained only by armed strength and the silent, or brazen, show of force, Roosevelt declared.[2] It was in this setting that his Far Eastern policy matured.

America's policies were developed, however, under the compulsion of significant domestic interests as well as outside conditions. American churches sought the Government's protection for their missionaries in Christianizing the Far East. Traders and manufacturers sought defense of their interests in China. Here they felt was a market, or, at least, a " potential " market that needed nurturing. North China and Manchuria specially concerned these business interests. Simultaneously the government was confronted by strategists like Alfred Mahan, to whom religious and economic considerations were only means to a more important end. These men believed the entire Far East, but especially the Yangtse Valley, crucial to America's growing rôle as an imperial power in the twentieth century. Mixed with these other factors, almost incongruously, was a deep-seated racial attitude of Americans anxious to eradicate the " yellow peril," who viewed the Far East largely in terms of actual and potential " racial " antagonism.

As an individual Roosevelt was in a position to determine important issues. As President he made the decisions—on matters, at least, where he was concerned enough to assume direct control. His views were affected, to be sure, by the domestic pressures, economic and religious, but he was himself primarily an international strategist with a peculiar *long-range* conception of the United States as a world power. " Our future history," he prophesied in 1905, " will be more determined by our position on the Pacific facing China than by our position on the Atlantic facing Europe." [3] John Hay shared this view of the future. " The diplomacy of McKinley and Roosevelt," Hay told an audience in Michigan in 1904, " has been directed principally to our present and future interests in the Pacific, on whose wide shores so much of the world's work is to be done." [4] The question is how wisely did Roosevelt and his friends choose among alternatives in the Far East. Did they play their parts " well or ill "? In 1912, a

friendly critic, reviewing the policy of the Roosevelt administration toward China, wryly observed: " The big stick [is],
of necessity, stronger than the olive branches of abstract
justice. . . . The American people have taken on the white
man's burden; they must pay the price of greatness." [5] In
1900 Paul Reinsch solemnly prognosticated: " The sudden-
ness with which the entire perspective of the political world
has been changed by recent developments in China is un-
precedented." [6]

America's rôle in China in Theodore Roosevelt's day provides an interesting case study both of the rivalries of great
powers there and of the implications of twentieth century
imperialism. It is important, however, to realize that the
struggle among the powers over China and America's relation
to this struggle were one aspect, but only one aspect, of a
world struggle for power that encompassed Europe, the
Americas, Africa, the Pacific, and other areas of Asia. The
form that America's part in the conflict in China would take
was determined by several factors. One was the ideology of
American expansionists considered in an earlier lecture. A
second was the urge of Western nations to win a place in
the imperial sun by winning a share in the Far East. A third
was the complex of rivalries and friendships among the big
powers into which this urge led them. And a fourth was the
condition of China at this time and the attitudes of Westerners toward China and the Chinese.

But why were the American expansionists concerned about
China at all? Why did America, whose tradition it was to
remain aloof from such contests, feel she must participate in
the struggle over China?

First, there was the American expansionists' desire to win
world power and world prestige. And the Far East, Brooks
Adams argued, was the central area of world conflict.
" Those who are excluded from the Eastern trade," Adams
insisted, " have already lagged behind in the race for life." [7]

To most of the Roosevelt-Lodge-Mahan group this motive of power was the dominating one. Secondly, there was the theory discussed in an earlier lecture of the spreading of civilization by advanced people to the " backward " peoples of the world. This principle was now to come to fruition.

It became evident that in China England needed allies. Specifically, she needed the United States. American expansionists were willing allies of Britain. " I cordially sympathize with England's attitude in China," Roosevelt told James Bryce in March, 1898, " and I am glad to say that there seems to be a gradual coming together of the two peoples." [8] Lodge, worried about the fate of English-speaking civilization in the Pacific, wrote Spring Rice: " I cannot but think that our appearance in that quarter of the globe will strengthen England, which of necessity, must always remain the great eastern power." [9] " Of all the nations we shall meet in the East," Alfred Mahan declared, " Great Britain is the one with which we have by far the most in common in the nature—not in the identity—of our interests there." [10] After Roosevelt had read Mahan's *Problem of Asia* in 1900, he wrote the author agreeing that America's and Britain's " cooperation and the effective use of sea power on behalf of civilization and progress which this cooperation would mean in the valley of the Yangtze Kiang, is of the utmost importance for the future of Asia, and therefore of the world." Roosevelt was unhappy that England had complicated matters by her stand on the canal and the Alaskan boundary, because " from the standpoint of world interests the questions are not nearly as important as what is happening in China." [11]

Roosevelt had been inclined at first to view all powers in terms of whether their interests conflicted with American interests and to consider as an enemy any nation that stood in the way of something wanted. " Nations may, and often must, have conflicting interests," he told Spring Rice in 1897,

" and in the present age patriotism stands a good deal ahead of cosmopolitanism." [12] Hence, since Japanese and German interests had conflicted here and there with American, he had opposed the ambitions of Japan and Germany.[13] Russian interests had not, on the other hand, stood in the path of American interests, and so Roosevelt had seen no ground for unfriendliness to Russia, and had defended her in arguments with Spring Rice, Mahan, and others more conscious of power conflicts in the world.[14]

Gradually, however, he, too, had come to possess a world view, and to see groupings of powers and qualitative differences among the great powers he encountered in the Far East. Even before two significant books by Brooks Adams and Mahan appeared, perhaps in part from reading earlier articles by the authors or talking with them, Roosevelt had changed his views sufficiently to write Speck von Sternburg in July, 1899, " The Pacific ought to be developed by the United States, England, and Germany working in harmony." [15]

Then in 1900 he read Adams's *America's Economic Supremacy* and Mahan's *Problem of Asia.* These books brought forcefully before him the qualitative differences between the civilizations the several powers promoted and confirmed him in the trend of thought revealed the year before. He came now better to understand the realities of the conflicts between combinations of great powers. The books impressed him greatly and persuaded him that, in the Far East, America's interest lay in coöperation, not only with England, but with Japan and Germany, and that the great obstacle to free access to trade and to the spread of Anglo-American power was Russia. During his Presidency, then, for reasons of power, of civilization, and of trade, he formulated his policy on the principle of coöperating in the Far East with Britain, Japan, and Germany to block the spread of Russian control.

Thirdly, there was also, of course, the economic motive for going into China. The Lodge-Roosevelt circle were all aware of its importance, though they were not primarily motivated by it. The American China Development Company, whose stock-holders were some of America's greatest men and financiers, had been organized in 1895 and had persistently put pressure on public men. Too, economic pressures were important, as is well known, in bringing the United States to the support of the open-door policy in 1899.[16] As early as January, 1898, while Lodge and White were considering with Balfour the possibility of America's joining Britain to enforce an open door in China, Lodge wrote White that " some of our large mercantile bodies are also beginning to move in the same direction." [17] Indeed, Lodge throughout these years was under pressure from constituents that wanted to sell the products of their textile mills in the China market.[18] White's reply to Lodge, a year before the official " open-door " discussions in Washington, sounded an economic warning: " If every European power is to claim commercial control over the entire province in which a Chinese seaport ceded to them is situated, I think our growing trade with China will be not a little hampered." [19] In 1899 Lodge defended our possession of the Philippines on the ground that those islands were the means of " maintaining our interest vigorously in China and seeing to it that that vast market is not closed to our trade and commerce." [20]

Roosevelt, too, though without Lodge's sensitiveness to textile interests, did recognize the importance of our commercial interests in the Far East. " If our trade relations with China are valuable," he wrote in 1898, " I should most unquestionably side with or against any European power out there purely with regard to our own interests." [21] In his *America's Economic Supremacy*, which had so strongly influenced Roosevelt, Adams had explained that as nations fell into debt, a great struggle developed for markets in which exports could be sold to cover the debt. "Eastern Asia," he observed, "now appears, without much doubt, to be the only district likely soon to be able to absorb any great increase of manufactures, and accordingly Eastern Asia is the prize for which all the energetic nations are grasping." "An effort at development in China," Adams had argued, "is inevitable." We must therefore face the question whether we "can safely allow that development to be wholly controlled by others." Adams had felt we must "control" the situation in the Far East. "Our geographical position, our wealth, and our energy," he had urged, "preëminently fit us to enter upon the development of Eastern Asia and to reduce it to part of our own economic system." The Chinese question was for America the great problem of the future, the problem from which there could be no escape. Unless the United States got a hold on Chinese markets, she herself might disintegrate. If she could win them, the United States would become a " greater seat of wealth and power than ever was England, Rome, or Constantinople." Adams had envisaged the day when the great interests of the United States would cover the Pacific, which it would hold " like an inland sea." [22] " As you so admirably put it," Roosevelt wrote Adams, " it is necessary for us to keep the road of trade to the east open. In order to insure our having terminals we must do our best to prevent the shutting to us of the Asian markets. In order to keep the roads to these terminals open we must see that they are managed primarily in the interest of . . . the commerce of the country." [23]

In spite, however, of the enthusiasm of the expansionists and their certainty that America would benefit by an imperialist policy in China there was not the popular support that their own enthusiasm seemed to warrant. "Public opinion is dull on the question of China," Roosevelt lamented in March, 1901.[24] In July, 1903, he was somewhat encouraged. " As yet public opinion is not so far awake that

I can go to the extent I would like to in the Manchurian business; but already I can go a great deal farther than would have been possible a few years ago, and I think the public is understanding the situation more and more all the time." [25] China herself was a factor of great importance in Far Eastern policy. She was facing two fundamental problems whose solution would determine her future. One was the need for reorganization of her government to meet modern conditions. Only through a more effective central government could she meet the threats to her territory and her resources posed by greedy powers that regarded her like other " backward people " as a fair prize of imperialism. Besides, even her decentralized weak form of government was made more inept by the corruption and inefficiency of a Manchu dynasty that seemed to be leading China to political breakdown and disintegration. The second problem was a " new spirit " that was growing among the Chinese people. Participants in the movement developed pride in China. They did so at just a moment when from Roosevelt's point of view that nation had little to justify pride because she could not protect herself from insults and injustice, from unreasonable demands of the Western powers, or even from being despoiled of her territory. The adherents of the new movement resented bitterly China's treatment at the hands of these Western powers. The example of a strong Japan encouraged this nationalist movement. Chinese anti-foreign sentiment and a government too weak to cope with it complicated China's problem in dealing with powers determined to protect their own interests and nationals in China if the Chinese Government did not. The weakness of its own government and the strength of the " new spirit " were both promoted by contact with the Westerners. And both were important determinants of the form Western imperialism took in China.

Roosevelt knew a good deal about China, its government, and what was going on internally. His interest was great, and close friends had long kept him informed. In the mid-nineties his friend Speck von Sternburg was military attaché at the German Embassy in Peking. " He is a mine of accurate teutonic information,' and with him I talk over to my heart's content the situation in China," Roosevelt wrote his sister.[27] With Brooks and Henry Adams Roosevelt often discussed China and both these men were students of China.[28] William W. Rockhill had learned to know China first-hand. He and Roosevelt often talked in Washington. Then in 1900 Rockhill was sent back to China and Roosevelt rejoiced, partly because Rockhill was an expert on China and partly because his intimacy with Rockhill would give Roosevelt a contact with the China situation of the personal sort he liked to employ. Perhaps because of the knowledge he did have of China, Roosevelt recognized the complications of the situation and the limitations of his own knowledge. " I felt as if a load were off my mind when it was announced that you were to go to China," he wrote Rockhill. " I shall be very grateful for any hints you can give me." [29] As President he depended heavily upon Rockhill for information and advice.

For China Roosevelt felt contempt. It was not, however, ignorance of China but his values that made him see in the Chinese with their rich culture only a " backward people." They lacked the qualities that to him spelled civilization, and the fighting qualities that he admired so tremendously in the Japanese. In 1903 he told Californians: " By her misfortunes . . . [China] has given us an object-lesson in the utter folly of attempting to exist as a nation at all, if at the same time both rich and defenseless." [30] Indeed, he pointed to the Chinese as a frightening warning for his own fellow-countrymen. If our country fell into the hands of " the futile sentimentalists of the international arbitration type," he once

---

* At one time " Speckie " wrote of the Sino-Japanese War that " All the war has done to this blessed country is to have increased the misery of the starving millions, and the vice and rascality among the governing classes." [26]

predicted to Lodge, we would then be reduced to the " timidity and inefficiency " of the Chinese and along with them would go " Chinese corruption." [31] Again: " The moneyed and semi-cultivated classes, especially of the Northeast," who are opposing appropriations for the Navy, " are doing their best to bring this country down to the Chinese level." * [32]

The Chinese lacked the cohesiveness, Roosevelt told the Hamilton Club in Chicago, to make them a warlike aggressive state. [33] When in 1894 Pearson in his *National Life and Character* held the Chinese up as a " menace " to the white race because of their high birth rate, Roosevelt protested that birth rate and population alone did not determine a " national character." The Chinese army could never wage a war of aggression against European peoples. " In China," he observed, " the military profession is looked down on." Only a European " leader " could direct the Chinese, and then only to repel an invasion. " Pekin could be taken at any time by a small trained army," he wrote six years before European and American troops fulfilled this prophecy. Indeed, China lacked central direction of any sort and was in reality only " an aggregate of provinces." In answer to fears of others that the Chinese might overwhelm the white race in Siberia, Roosevelt prophesied: " China will not menace Siberia until after undergoing some stupendous and undreamed-of internal revolution." Short of revolution, there was no danger that China would follow Japan's example and by becoming warlike and aggressive take its rank among civilized nations whom Roosevelt could respect. [34]

Shortly before Roosevelt became President the growing Chinese resentment toward the activity of foreign powers burst into flame in the " Boxer uprising." The Boxers were

---

* Another time, pressed for an explanation of Captain Mahan's inability to capture a popular audience in the United States, Roosevelt complained: " Individually the [American] people are very different from the Chinese, of course, but nationally our policy is almost as foolish."

local anti-foreign secret societies without leadership or national cohesion whom the Manchu dynasty, to serve its own interests, led into violence on a large scale. The movement was aimed at the Westerners' claim of special privileges for themselves and their assigning of the Chinese to inferior status. Ideologically the movement rejected Western ideas as well as Western interests and looked backward to a self-sufficient Chinese Empire based on traditional Chinese ideas. As is well known, it manifested itself in a series of anti-foreign outbreaks that culminated in June, 1900, in laying siege to the foreign legations in Peking to which all foreigners within reach of them had fled for safety. The great powers, realizing that not only the lives of their citizens but their prestige and power in China were at stake, sent in armies to raise the siege of their legations, rescue their citizens, and maintain their power in China by punishing the rioters.

That the Boxer movement was portentous for the future of foreigners in China American expansionists recognized. The final settlement of the Boxer question, Lodge wrote Brooks Adams, " is going to be the gravest and most difficult question which this or any other generation has confronted." [35] The Boxer protest, Mahan wrote, was a " reactionary movement " that aimed " at severing communication with the only possible source of real life ": the Western powers. America must " insist, in the general interest, by force, if need be, that China remain open to action by European and American processes of life and thought." " Can we," Mahan asked, " without responsibility to God and man decline our aid? " It would be a mistake, he warned, " to allow China to drift at the sport of circumstances." [36]

The violence in China gave the Republicans a ready-made campaign argument. It enabled them to claim that the Democrats, who were denouncing Republican efforts to win prestige for America overseas, would not have the will or the capacity to protect American citizens in China. To hand the country over to Bryan and "his gang" would be "a hideous misfortune," Lodge insisted, "for they have no foreign policy and understand no foreign questions." [37] Roosevelt excoriated the anti-imperialists for being "illogical," for they condemned America's Philippine policy and praised the intervention in China, whereas consistency, Roosevelt argued, obviously required that, if they were to oppose American policy in the Philippines, they should also condemn protecting American women and children in Peking. The alternative was to support our action in both instances.[38] The policy of the anti-imperialists, Roosevelt told a Chicago audience, would have left "wretched women and children [in the Philippines] to their awful fate," such as befell those in Peking. Their policy was "inhuman," "dastardly." [39] The peaceful non-expansionist character of China "invites aggression from without," Roosevelt told the voters, "and incites her own people to ferocious and hideous barbarism." [40]

The Boxer episode also justified, the expansionists thought, the acquisition of the Philippines. Chauncey Depew, corporation lawyer, soon to be United States senator, told a New York audience gathered to ratify the nomination of McKinley and Roosevelt how important the Islands were to the protection of American citizens, who were being massacred and tortured. "The American soldier and sailor arriving so speedily from our own territory," he argued, "is a demonstration which will advance our interests and procure for us a recognition which would be impossible otherwise in a half century of effort." [41]

Many felt that the fate of American business in China might be determined by the way the Boxers were handled. Roosevelt argued that the sending of troops into China was made legitimate by the need "to secure for our merchants, farmers, and wage-workers the benefits of the open market." [42]

The Boxer episode roused in England and America dormant suspicions of Russia.* Henry White in London thought that the Russians, unsuccessful in preventing the development of Anglo-American friendship, had stirred the trouble up so as " to strike . . . and round off what she wants . . . when England is occupied with the Boer War and we with our Presidential year and when Japan is not perhaps quite so ready to take up the cudgels to thwart Russia's projects as she may be a year or two hence." [44] At first Roosevelt deplored the hostility of many of his friends toward Russia. To be sure, she might be potentially dangerous in Manchuria, but the task of the moment was suppression of the anti-foreign movement in China. " I earnestly hope that the great powers will be able to act in concert," he told Spring Rice, " and once for all put China in a position where she has to behave." [45] " All of us Western fellows have been fools to let the Chinese movement gather such a head," he wrote Speck von Sternburg, " but I suppose such a folly is inevitable when half a dozen nations are interested and each is jealous or suspicious of one or more of the others." He told the Germans he hoped that at least Germany and the United States could act together in China.[46]

The need of joint action with Britain and Japan, too, was driven home by these suspicions of Russia, whether those suspicions were justified or not. " We shall inevitably act with England and Japan," Lodge predicted. " If we act properly together, we can prevent the absorption of China by Russia and keep the Empire open for our trade and commerce, which is all we want." [47]

As the Boxer trouble was settled, Roosevelt began to worry about Russian aims in Manchuria where most of American economic interests were centered. " If Russia begins slicing off Manchuria," his friend Speck wrote him, " the

* One well-informed American journalist believed, on the other hand, "the rumors [in America] about Russia's villainous rôle" were "largely British in origin." [48]

rest are *bound* to follow suit, and there we have the partition of China." [48] " I hope the powers do not get embroiled in a war in the interior of China," Roosevelt told him, for slicing up China would " be bad for everybody in the end." Danger of Russia's keeping Manchuria and excluding others from it, now swung Roosevelt forcibly over to an anti-Russian position. He turned to Japan as a bulwark against Russia. [49] He turned to Germany, too. When Germany and Britain formed a protective agreement for the Far East he wrote Sternburg, " I am sincerely glad of the Anglo-German agreement. As you know, I have a very strong hope that Germany, England and the United States will more and more be able to act together." [50] In his alarm over Russia's intentions in Manchuria, he entirely overlooked the fact that in approving the Anglo-German arrangement he was accepting a " separate " status for Manchuria, which was excluded from the " open door " provision in the agreement. [51]

Experience with the Boxers in China strengthened the belief of American expansionists that one had to deal with colonial or " backward " peoples with armed force and that military rule over them was justified by their inability to understand other methods. " Those people respect nothing but power," Chauncey Depew told a capacity audience in Carnegie Hall. [52] President McKinley deserved credit for the promptness with which he sent soldiers to rescue " the hunted Christians from the hands of a mob of unspeakably cruel barbarians," Roosevelt told a Chicago audience. [53] " The Boxers," he declared in St. Paul, " are the precise analogues and representatives of the Aguinaldian rebels." Like Filipino rebels the Chinese had to be brought under control, indirect this time, of superior nations. The Chinese could not be given the " ' liberty ' to butcher their neighbors," or to protect the Boxers " from the wrath of mankind." It apparently never occurred to Roosevelt that the aggression of Western imperialist powers was either a cause or a justification for the

Boxer uprising. The Boxers were, in Roosevelt's mind, a product of the deficiencies of Chinese character. The Chinese like the Filipinos had to be " lifted out of savagery " by the Western powers and the use of foreign troops was therefore necessary.[54]

The attitude of Roosevelt and his friends toward the behavior of the foreign troops in China is illuminating. They knew full well what the foreign troops had done in " revenge " and in sheer looting. One American writer in Peking published accounts in *Scribner's Magazine*, which Roosevelt read and called to Mahan's notice.[55] " Seized with a vertigo of indiscriminating vengeance," the correspondent asserted, " the powers are trifling with the peace of the world . . . [and] have carried war back to the Dark Ages, and will leave a taint in the moral atmosphere of the world for a generation to come." " Every town, every village, every peasant's hut in the path of the troops was first looted and then burned." " The Russian is brutal," this American observer who impressed Roosevelt insisted, but so were the rest of the powers.[56] " We have killed ten for one at least," Secretary of State Hay wrote to Secretary White of the Embassy in London; " we have looted and destroyed many millions of property." " The story," Hay observed in disgust, " is enough to sicken a Zulu." [57] What Hay and White knew Roosevelt certainly knew, and he must also have heard, either directly from his friend Rockhill or indirectly from Cabot Lodge, the contents of a letter Nannie Lodge received from our commissioner in China. In December Rockhill wrote:

> . . . From Taku to Peking the whole country is in a beautiful state of anarchy thanks to the presence of foreign troops sent there to restore order. The " disciplined armies of Europe " are everywhere conducting operations much as the Mongols must have done in the 13th century. Hardly a house remains from the seacoast to Peking which has not been looted of every moveable object it contained, and in half the cases the houses have been burned. Peking has

been pillaged in the most approved manner, and from the General down to the lowest camp follower, from the Ministers of the Powers to the last attaché, from the Bishops to the smallest missionary everyone has stolen, sacked, pillaged, blackmailed and generally disgraced themselves— and it is still going on. Yesterday my wife and I walked to the Observatory on the wall, the magnificent bronze instruments, some dating probably from the 13th century, were being taken to pieces by French and German soldiers to be sent to Paris and Berlin. These instruments had been left unharmed, untouched for seven centuries, but they could not escape the civilized westerners—French and Germans could bury the hatchet for once and rob in the most fraternal manner. Though General Chaffee has done and is doing all in his power to keep our good name clean, and our soldiers are said by the Chinese to be the best disciplined, still our men have committed many excesses— we are in such bad company. The other day I was telling Chaffee of the wounding of one of our men—probably by some other foreigner. He replied " I can take but little interest in the wounding of one of our men, when there are so many who should be shot."

Rockhill was more than disheartened. " I devoutly hope," he told Mrs. Lodge, " I shall never see China again. This visit to it has disgusted me so—Last night I was told that Waldersee had decided to have shot some of his soldiers who had gone a little far in looting. He should begin with his officers, with his own staff. This expedition will go down in history as the most disgraceful one of this century—and what breaks my heart is that we should be associated with it, that do what we may we must bear our share of the shame attached to the manner in which the military operations have been conducted." [58]

Roosevelt did not take so critical a view of the activity of the foreign troops as did Rockhill. The Russians, he told von Sternburg in mid-November 1900, were the " worst for plundering and murdering." The Americans, however, he argued, " never killed either women or children," although they " had a tendency to get drunk and to plunder." [59] By mid-March, however, when more accurate reports of what had transpired in China began to appear, Roosevelt himself reported to Captain Mahan that Generals Chaffee and Wilson, who had led the American contingent in China, were disgusted with the " awful outrages committed by many of the European troops . . . and the wanton so-called punitive expeditions . . . indeed the original misconduct of some of the foreigners." These outrages, Roosevelt told Mahan, made the two generals feel that the " count " was " against us rather than against the Chinese." " I wish you could see some of the reports of our officers as to the misconduct even of some of our missionaries," a disgusted Roosevelt told Mahan.[60]

Though Roosevelt was critical of some of the activities of the foreigners in China, and especially the troops, he seems never for a minute to have questioned the wisdom of sending the troops into China. To General Adna Chaffee, for example, who had commanded the American troops during the Boxer siege, Roosevelt wrote in early March of 1901: " We are all your debtors for what you have done in China—for everything, from the way you fought to the way you have done justice. . . ." [61] Privately he wrote to George Becker in July, 1901, that the suppression of the Boxers was essential. He admitted the problem was " infinitely complicated " and denounced " all our prize idiots from Mark Twain and Godkin down " because they " airily announced that both the problem and the solution were absolutely simple." " The Chinese outrages *had* to be stopped, and the Chinese ' bandits' punished. . . ." [62] In his famous " Home Market Club " speech in Boston on May 1, 1901, he insisted that the United States had " simply " done its part in " a bit of international police duty." Had the government not acted, it " would have been branded with infamy." Then, apparently forgetting what he had written both von Sternburg and Mahan some months earlier about atrocities, he told the Boston audience that American "gallantry was unstained by murder and cruelty." Forgetting, too, that the United States with his approval had agreed to the Anglo-German accord, which to all intents and purposes had separated Manchuria from China, he now proudly proclaimed that the United States, unlike other foreign powers, had refused to "yield to the clamor for mere revenge and [had] refused to take part in, or connive at, any effort to partition China." [63]

If Roosevelt forgot rather easily what Americans and other foreign troops did in China, the Chinese did not. They had seen representatives of the "civilized" nations loot, rape, murder, ravage in the name of Christianity and law and order. They had watched the "disciplined" troops of these civilized nations destroy their land. The Chinese were in Roosevelt's eyes contemptible because too weak to resist. But they did not forget.

When he returned to the national stage Roosevelt himself was confronted by the China issue. A few days before he became President, Speck von Sternburg wrote suggesting to him that "some strong power, or grouping of powers," ought to "establish a Monroe Doctrine for China." "You and Japan could easily do it," Speck wrote. "It's high time that the aims of certain wolves are checked in China. . . . Can't you proclaim a ' Roosevelt doctrine ' when your time comes in a few years? " [64] Before Roosevelt received this letter from India his time had come through McKinley's death. "I regard the Monroe Doctrine," the new President replied, " as being equivalent to the open door in South America. That is, I do not want the United States or any European power to get territorial possessions in South America but to let South America gradually develop on its own lines, with an open door to all outside nations." So he felt, too, about China. Roosevelt, however, perhaps with the Far East in mind, qualified the prohibitions of the Monroe Doctrine in such a way as to reserve to any state outside a right to " interfere with transitory intervention . . . when there was a row with some State in South America." [65]

" I wish that the same policy could be pursued in China," Roosevelt told his German friend. But he qualified the application of the Monroe Doctrine in the Far East in a manner that reveals the influence of Mahan and Adams and his own views on people not ready for self-government. Perhaps, too, there was a consciousness of the pressure of such groups as the American Asiatic Association. The principles of the Monroe Doctrine would work in China, he said, only " if the Chinese could be forced to behave themselves—not permitted to do anything atrocious, but not partitioned." [66] In Roosevelt's mind the Chinese were no more capable of self-government than the Filipinos.[67] Chinese ports must be " kept open to all comers," the President told Speck, and " the vexatious trade restrictions which prevent inter-Chinese trade in the interior " must be abolished.[68] In short, Chinese sovereignty would be tolerated as a convenient fiction that would prevent the powers from dividing China and excluding each other, but it could not be permitted to mean genuine independence for China. Use of force by the powers, short of taking actual territory, seemed to Roosevelt necessary in such a land as China.

In his first annual message the President sought to impress Congress with the importance of China. He discussed the various steps taken to preserve order and to increase trade with the vital untapped Chinese market. Portions of the message sounded as if he had rewritten passages from Brooks Adams's *America's Economic Supremacy.*[*] [70] " Owing to the rapid growth of our power and our interests on the Pacific," he told Congress, " whatever happens in China must

* Indeed, in September, in connection with another policy, he wrote Adams, " Before I finish my message, I would like to see you, for I intend (although in rather guarded phrase) to put in one or two ideas of your *Atlantic Monthly* article." [69]

be of the keenest national concern to us." " Our Government," he reported, " . . . has materially aided in bringing about an adjustment which tends to enhance the welfare of China and to lead to a more beneficial intercourse between the Empire and the modern world." We must leave " no effort untried," he said, " to work out the great policy of full and fair intercourse . . . on a footing of equal rights and advantages to all. We advocate . . . not merely the procurement of enlarged commercial opportunities on the coasts, but access to the interior by the waterways with which China has been so extraordinarily favored." In his stressing of this opening of China's interior he was helping provide the wealth and economic control that business interests were demanding, but he was also pursuing in " guarded phrase " the main tenet of Mahan's doctrine about China, the necessity of balancing for strategic reasons Russian power in Manchuria through Anglo-American-Japanese control of the Yangtse Valley. China had not been left much control. She has agreed, the President pointed out, " to revise the treaties of commerce and navigation and to take such other steps . . . as the foreign powers may decide to be needed." " We necessarily claim parity," he warned, "throughout the Empire for our trade and our citizens with those of all other powers." [71]

Before 1904 Roosevelt took surprisingly little active part in the handling of Far Eastern affairs. He and Hay agreed on policy. China was left weak after the punishment for the Boxer affair. The President was busy elsewhere. During the summer of 1903, however, he intervened in one episode that is important because it indicated his thinking concerning China. Some Chinese revolutionaries had been arrested, convicted of " violent incitements to insurrection," and sentenced by the mixed court in the foreign settlement of Shanghai. The Manchu Government protested that sedition by Chinese should be punished by the Chinese Government. The British and Americans refused to hand the men over.

Roosevelt heard of the episode and took a hand to urge the State Department not to yield. In this case, everyone was agreed on the guilt of the men. Roosevelt felt it important, however, to maintain the principle that our foreign court was independent of Chinese control and could refuse to hand over even Chinese criminals demanded for trial by the Chinese Government.[72] Roosevelt, who would have been the first to resent a suggestion that foreigners in our own country were not under our control, considered the Chinese " backward " people, and rules for " civilized towns " therefore did not apply in China.

During 1902 and 1903, too, trouble arose with Russia over Manchuria. Hay explained to the President that we recognized Russia's " exceptional position in Northern China," but were trying to gain a guarantee that no matter what happened eventually in Northern China the United States should not " be placed in any worse position than while the country was under the unquestioned domination of China." [73] Hay wrote the Russian minister insisting that " Russia should do nothing in Manchuria which would injure the commercial interests of the United States." [74] In April, 1902, the Russians and Chinese agreed upon terms for Russian withdrawal from Manchuria in three stages. In October Russia carried out the first stage. Then in April, 1903, she failed to continue the second stage of evacuation. Instead, she made new and sweeping demands upon China. Among other things, she insisted that China should open no new treaty ports in Manchuria and should permit no foreign consuls in Manchuria save Russians. " We have always recognized the exceptional position of Russia in relation to Manchuria," Hay declared. " We have only insisted upon that freedom of access and an opportunity for our commerce . . . guaranteed to us by the agreement of the whole civilized world, including Russia." When Hay protested to the Russians that American trade rights were being violated, both the Foreign Minister,

Count Lamsdorff, and Ambassador in Washington, Count Cassini, denied that any demands had been made.[75] Throughout the difficulty Hay had kept in close touch with the British and Japanese ministers,[76] and had stood up to the Russians as effectively as he could when they knew he could not use force but only persuasion. " I am sure you will think it is out of the question," he wrote Roosevelt on April 25, " that we should adopt any scheme of concerted action with England and Japan which would seem openly hostile to Russia. Public opinion . . . would not support such a course,' nor do I think it would be to our permanent advantage." [77]

Americans were divided over policy towards Russia. Albert Shaw, editor of the *Review of Reviews*, and Albert J. Beveridge, Republican senator, were both disturbed. " The whole Hay policy about Manchuria," Shaw wrote, " is ridiculous. . . . Hay is more English than the English themselves. . . . He has been trying to pull English and Japanese chestnuts out of the fire." Shaw was convinced that the United States should have " told Russia years ago that we would not misunderstand anything she might think it wise to do in Manchuria " and then Russia " would have entered into any kind of a trade treaty with us that we could have desired. . . . That would have given us our commercial advantages in Manchuria, and we should have been on the side of manifest destiny." So badly in Shaw's judgment had Hay mishandled the matter that the editor demanded a reorganization of the State Department as well as a change in our Manchurian policy. Beveridge agreed with Shaw and promised to discuss the matter with the President.[78] Lodge, on the other hand, was demanding " strong " action against the Russians. " I have been thinking a great deal about Manchuria," he wrote his friend Theodore. " Our trade there is assuming enormous

---

ᵃ " If our rights and our interests . . . were as clear as noonday," he wailed three days later, " we could never get a Treaty through the Senate . . . to check Russian aggression."

proportions." " There is more interest in this matter of trade than is generally realized," he wrote a President primarily concerned with strategic matters and hence with the Yangtse Valley more than with Manchuria. He told the President of letters he had received from cotton mill owners in Massachusetts demanding that the fleet be sent to Manchuria. Flour mills in the Northwest and cotton mills in the South, he reported, were making similar demands. The Senator had urged Hay to unite with England and Japan against Russian duplicity, but Hay had feared this would annoy the Irish and German voters. " To unite with England and Japan in a protest is not an entangling alliance," Lodge contended. " In any event, . . . we ought to take, whether alone or jointly, a pretty strong tone." [79]

Through all this discussion the President was making an extended tour of the West. In April Hay wrote Roosevelt in discouragement, " I take it for granted that Russia knows as well as we do that we will not fight over Manchuria, for the simple reason that we cannot." [80] He described his problem to Henry White, too. " If these Russians are convinced that we will not fight for Manchuria," he wrote, " and the Chinese are convinced they have nothing but good to expect from us and nothing but a beating from Russia, the open hand will not be so convincing to the poor devils of Chinks as the raised club." [81] Russian duplicity worried Hay, too. " Dealing with a government with whom mendacity is a science is an extremely difficult and delicate matter," he told the President.[82] He toyed with the idea of encouraging Japan to war on Russia. " It would require the very least encouragement on the part of the United States or England," he needled Roosevelt in the spring of 1903, " to induce Japan to seek a violent solution of the question." " If we gave them a wink " they would " fly at the throat of Russia in a moment." [83] On May 13, Roosevelt responded reassuringly about the Russian danger. " Things are settling down," he told Hay.[84]

Meantime Roosevelt wrote to his friends Lyman Abbott and Albert Shaw of his increasing annoyance with the Russians. " All we ask," he said, " is that our great and growing trade shall not be interrupted and that Russia shall keep its solemn promises " to evacuate Manchuria.[85] It was as much the manner of Russia's handling the situation as her actual refusal to open Manchuria up again that irritated the President. Russia told us she favored throwing open the ports in Manchuria to the United States, he pointed out, and then in Peking she refused to allow the Chinese to sign an agreement doing so. He accused the Russians of " extraordinary mendacity." In answer to the charge that he was working with the Japanese and the British, he exclaimed: Russia " seems to be ingeniously endeavoring to force us, not to take sides with Japan and England, but to acquiesce in their taking sides with us." [86] From Tacoma, Washington, he wrote praising Hay's " masterly " handling of the problem. " The bad feature of the situation from our standpoint," he wrote, " is that as yet it seems that we cannot fight to keep Manchuria open. I hate being in the position of seeming to bluster without backing it up." [87] On June 5, 1903, he returned to Washington and went over the whole matter with Hay. On June 18 Hay in a long interview talked sharply to Count Cassini, and accused Russia of bad faith, of violation of her promises, of " lack of goodwill " towards the United States. " Hay protested that his four years' effort to maintain friendship with Russia and settle the Manchurian problem " with Russia alone had failed. Hay now saw " no other course " open to him but to turn the whole matter over to the President and confess his failure. He hinted that it might now be necessary to call in the other powers to help.[88] That very day Cassini cabled his government a warning that the United States might be about to join the Anglo-Japanese entente.[89] In June, too, Hay talked with American Jews urging them publicly to protest massacres of Jews in Russia. He himself did protest privately in an interview with Cassini. After this Hay went to New Hampshire and on June 28 Roosevelt moved to Oyster Bay for the summer. Cassini then published a Russian manifesto concerning America's attitude toward the Jews in Russia. "Angered" over the "impertinent action" of the Russians the President instructed Hay to look up precedents for taking "summary action" against Russia.[90]

Finally, without consulting Hay who was in New Hampshire, Roosevelt acted. He ordered Francis Loomis, acting secretary of State, to issue an official statement in regard to Russia. Roosevelt used as an excuse for the statement a rumor that was circulating that Russia would be irritated if American Jews were allowed to use the State Department machinery to forward to the Russian Government a petition against Russian cruelty to Jews. "The State Department . . . will . . . not hesitate to give expression to the deep sympathy felt not only by the administration, but by all the American people for the unfortunate Jews," the Roosevelt-inspired document proclaimed. The statement to the press rebuked Russia for stating through the newspapers her position in regard to American handling of opposition to pogroms. The only proper mode of communicating between governments, Russia was reminded, was through official diplomatic channels. Then Roosevelt's statement reprimanded Russia for using devious methods in Manchuria to pursue a policy "certainly the reverse of friendly to the United States." Russia was bluntly accused of seeking to induce China to break "the plighted faith of all the powers as to the open door in Manchuria" and "to bar our people from access to the Manchurian trade."[91] "The petition came just at the right time," Roosevelt told Brooks Adams. "I had that interview given out about Russia because I thought it was time that she should understand that we were in earnest."[92]

Russia at this point backed down. She agreed to the open-

ing up of all the Manchurian ports save Harbin, which dominated the Chinese Eastern Railway that China had granted
her as a concession. She promised to withdraw all her troops
by October 8.[93] Hay immediately wired Roosevelt: " It
seems like a surrender; but they are a strange race, and you
may expect anything from them except straightforwardness."
" Permit me to observe," he added in a lighter mood, " that
your planet seems to be in good working order." [94] How
much the Russians were influenced by Roosevelt's statement,
how much by the fear that Britain or Japan might act, and
how much by Cassini's warning cannot be determined.

" I think the Russian business is in pretty fair shape,"
the President reported to Hay. " I don't intend to give way."
" I felt it was just as well to show our teeth," he told Hay;
" I am beginning to have scant patience with Adam Zâd." *
" And I wish in Manchuria, to go to the very limit I think
our people will stand." " I am year by year growing more
confident that this country would back me in going to an
extreme in the matter," he confided, and added eleven days
later, " If only we were sure neither France nor Germany
would join in, I should not in the least mind going to ' extremes ' with Russia." [95] It was apparently then the American people's lack of understanding of the importance of
markets and power in the Far East that pulled a man who
was a sensitive politician as well as a world statesman back
from serious thought of going to war with Russia.

The advantage gained in Russia's temporary backing down
in Manchuria was immediately pushed by the signing of a
commercial treaty with China guaranteeing that Manchurian
ports would be opened. Suspicious of Russia, America pushed
for speedy ratification. The Chinese, also fearing the Rus-

---

* " Make ye no truce with Adam-zad—the Bear that walks like a man,"
Kipling, who did not like the Russians, had sung in " The Truce of the Bear," a
little poem well known to Hay, Roosevelt, and their imperialist friends. The
poem was originally published in 1898 in *The Five Nations*.

sians might not keep their word, sought delays lest Russia resent their agreeing to open the ports and retaliate. Sufficient pressure was exerted on the Chinese, however, so that they agreed to sign the treaty on October 8, 1903, the day set for Russian withdrawal of the troops, whether Russia withdrew the troops or not. " I congratulate you with all my heart," Hay wrote the President when agreement was reached.[96]

How much this anti-Russian, pro-Japanese policy of the Roosevelt Administration encouraged Japan to make war on Russia is not known. Between Russia's backing down and the signing of the Chinese trade treaty, Horace Allen, long-time missionary in Korea and now minister to that country, spent an evening in heated debate with Roosevelt and his anti-Russian adviser Rockhill at the White House warning them that their attitude was thus encouraging Japan. We had erred, Allen told the President, in not seeking friendship with Russia. " Our present policy continued would undoubtedly lead Japan to count upon assistance from us which would lead her to adopt a too bellicose attitude toward Russia." " Whether we wished it or not," he warned, little realizing how much Roosevelt did want it, " we would simply be bound into more or less an alliance with England and Japan." Rockhill and Roosevelt vigorously defended their policy. Allen, discouraged, went home to confide to his diary, " I fear Rockhill is leading them to a precipice." [97] When a month later William C. Dix wrote Roosevelt to protest as Albert Shaw and Horace Allen had against a policy that played into England's and Japan's hands, the President sent the letter to Hay, who returned it with a memorandum attached that read: " Mr. Dix is evidently a member of that highly respected family, the common or barnyard Ass." [98]

In 1905 Roosevelt handled personally two important problems in China that more than anything else reveal his attitudes toward China, and that indicate how even at this period we were pursuing a policy that was ultimately to throw China into the arms of Russia.

The first episode, the story of the American China Development Company and Roosevelt's handling of its relations with China, throws interesting light on the nature of Rooseveltian imperialism in China.[99] In 1905 Hay was ill and then died. There followed an interregnum before Elihu Root returned to the Cabinet in Hay's place. Alvey A. Adee, long-time head of the Department's permanent bureaucracy, and Roosevelt's old friend Rockhill, then assistant secretary, handled routine business and lesser policy matters. But to a considerable extent, in policy forming, Roosevelt was his own acting secretary of State.

During the period following the Sino-Japanese War when China was weak and in need of economic reform, a group of American business leaders formed the American China Development Company. Its stockholders included former Vice-President Levi P. Morton, railroad organizer Edward H. Harriman, the presidents of the National City Bank of New York and the Chase National Bank, the head of the Carnegie Steel Company, and bankers Jacob Schiff and J. Pierpont Morgan.[100] The first request for permission to build a railroad into Hankow was rejected and the grant was given instead to a Belgian firm. Then in 1898 the company obtained the right to build between Hankow and Canton what promised to be one of the most important roads in China. Foreign competitors and the Chinese themselves successfully opposed other concessions the Americans sought for branch lines and mining rights. In 1900, however, a supplementary agreement was signed between the company and the Chinese Government. This contract provided that the railroad should be supervised by a board of two Chinese appointed by the Chinese director-general of railways and three foreigners named by the company. The company was to float forty million dollars' worth of bonds to construct 710 miles of main line, 130 miles of branch lines, and 78 miles of siding. Article 17 of the contract provided that the Americans should not transfer their rights " to other nations or people of other nationality." The French were building in the South and the Russians in the North and the Chinese were afraid this road might fall into their hands; the Chinese were less suspicious of Americans and they did not want the several parts of their railway system to be controlled by any one power.[101]

Almost immediately the company began to violate Article 17. Unbeknown to the Chinese, Belgian interests had bought into the company even before the agreement was signed. By 1901 Sheng Hsüan-huai, director-general of Chinese railways, was claiming that four thousand out of six thousand shares of stock had been transferred to non-Americans including Belgian King Leopold II and even American Minister Conger, after investigation, reported that it was " generally understood " that Europeans had purchased " the larger portion " of the stock. Besides, mismanagement, hostility of the local population, and conflict between the Chinese and non-Chinese directors prevented much accomplishment. After three years, on November 15, 1903, only ten and a half miles of road were completed and in use.[102] The Americans had persistently refused to divulge the identity of the stockholders, but the Chinese became aware, and the directors later admitted, that the company had passed into non-American hands. On this ground Chang Chih-tung, powerful viceroy at Hankow, and the governors of Hunan and Hupeh provinces, petitioned the Peking government in 1904 to cancel the company's concession. In due course notice of cancellation was given the American Government.[103] On December 23, 1904, indeed, the Chinese Ambassador to Washington, Sir Chentung Liang-Cheng, presented to Secretary Hay a formal revocation of the Canton-Hankow Railroad concession. He told Hay the Chinese " had stood it as long as they could, and now that control had passed evidently to the Belgians, they must declare the concession forfeited." [104]

The American Government stood ready to help when it could. Secretary Hay and Edwin Conger, minister to China, had assisted the company where possible. Hay now confessed to Rockhill that at this stage it would be extremely difficult to do anything at all.[105] On the appeal of one director, the State Department did put pressure on the Belgians to legalize the company by selling their stock to Americans. In January, 1905, Hay learned that King Leopold had sold twelve hundred shares to J. P. Morgan, who now became the leading spokesman of the company. This sale once more put a majority of the shares under American control and enabled the State Department to support the company's position. Now Hay cabled Minister Conger and Chargé John C. Coolidge in Peking to oppose revocation of the grant. " We cannot admit that such action can be taken in regard to a Company which we consider to be in good faith American," Hay explained.[106] Prince Ch'ing, chief grand councilor of the Emperor, reported to the American chargé that the whole matter, including the charges of the local people and their governors, was being investigated by Chang Chih-tung, the viceroy who had always been hostile to the road.[107] Early in March, 1905, the American shareholders were again urged to sell to European interests, but Morgan refused, " being firmly of the belief that the thing must be held American, the only possible alternative being that the Chinese should take the whole thing over." [108]

Roosevelt seems to have acquired his first knowledge of the problem when Hay talked the matter over with him during January, 1905. In spite of the company's violation of its agreement and in the face of incompetence so great that only twenty-eight miles of track had been built in five years, the President on January 26 wrote Hay, " I should be very sorry to abandon the project of building that road." [109]

Meantime Chargé Coolidge urged the Chinese Government to reconsider its action, but at the same time informed Hay and Roosevelt of the deep popular resentment against the company. The Imperial Government might reconsider revocation, if it were not afraid of arousing the hostility of the provinces, he reported on February 9.[110] Then for several months, under Hay's management, the American Government seems to have dropped the matter.

Between January and June Minister Chentung, and John W. Foster, attorney for the Chinese Government, on the one hand, and, on the other, Elihu Root and G. W. Ingraham, who spoke for the company, tried to come to some agreement. Foster on behalf of the Chinese offered to pay a reasonable sum to compensate the company for its efforts. Ingraham demanded $18,100,000.[111] "Reasonable compensation," Ingraham insisted, "would naturally be the profits that the American Company would receive if it were allowed . . . to complete its contract." "Certainly the Chinese government cannot consider that it is doing justice," he argued, "unless it is willing to place that Company in the same position that it would have been in if it had been allowed to complete its contract."[112] By June the Chinese had agreed to pay the stockholders a compromise indemnification of $6,750,000 for bonds and property.[113] Tentatively accepted by the directors, this proposal was to be presented to the stockholders at an August meeting.[114] The *New York Journal of Commerce* probably spoke realistically when it commented: "China has given the Development Company an extremely liberal price for twenty miles of railroad, the record of a batch of surveys, and a concession which, under any strict interpretation of its terms, the company has long ago forfeited."[115]

Early in June Roosevelt became interested. On June 1 King Leopold of Belgium wrote him a letter appealing for help. The titles, Leopold declared, were "complete and perfectly regular." The Chinese desire to exclude "whites" from "Chinese enterprise" was the real issue. The Belgians, who were accused of violating the contract by buying stock, had actually bought the stock " to serve civilization." " You know better than I, Mr. President," wrote Leopold, " how useless it is to have much discussion with the Chinese authorities, and that it is Christian not to permit them to forbid the Whites to bring well-being to their large, backward and unhappy population." If only Rockhill, the new minister, would tell the Chinese that the American Government had consented to the transfer of stocks to Morgan, the Chinese would back down.[116]

In July, a former Belgian minister to the United States was sent by Leopold to Paris to persuade Senator Lodge to go to Brussels for luncheon with Leopold. " He named six different days," Lodge explained to Roosevelt; " so there was no escape unless I flatly refused which I could not well do." Lodge and the King ᵃ discussed the wisdom of the company's selling. Leopold and other Belgians, who were large shareholders, were " very averse to selling " a property of such great value. Then the King explained that he had appealed to Morgan, but Morgan, said the King, felt " the amount was not for him serious enough to make him at his age enter on a struggle with the Chinese government." Besides, Morgan had pointed out, he had no assurance his government would back him up if he rejected the compromise offer. " I told the King," Lodge reported to the President, " that our government would not and could not advise American investors to hold or to sell property, but that we should not permit any government to withdraw a concession or violate the rights of American citizens and if our people wanted to hold on our government would certainly stand behind them." Tell the President of Morgan's position, Leopold urged, for Morgan

---

ᵃ " A shrewd, active able man of business," Lodge described him to Roosevelt, " —a cross between Jim Hill and Harriman, between the great organizer and promoter and the speculator . . . He is what we should call a ' worker ' and a ' hustler.' "

" would hold on " if he had assurance of government assistance.[117]

Though Lodge had professed to the King to know little but what he read in the newspapers, he wrote Roosevelt, " I think he is right . . . I think it would be a real misfortune to let go this great line of railway—a blow to our prestige and to our commerce in China which we want to foster in every way." If the Americans decided to hold on, " we could not allow the Chinese to wrest a concession from them." [118] With Lodge, Hay, Rockhill, King Leopold all urging Roosevelt to act, only Root favored settling and getting out, and Root had been the company's lawyer.[119]

The President now took the reins. He had deep concern not to let the contemptible Chinese push us around. So he sought out Morgan. Morgan was in Europe. Hence Roosevelt wrote him and quoted a long section of Lodge's letter. " Now, my dear Mr. Morgan, it is not my business to advise you what to do," said the President to America's leading financier. " I cannot expect you or any of our big business men to go into what they think will be to their disadvantage." Still, if Morgan was giving up the concession because he felt that the American Government would not support him, Roosevelt hoped he would reconsider. " The Government will stand by you," the President promised, " in every honorable way . . . to see that you suffer no wrong whatever from the Chinese or any other Power in this matter." " My interest of course is simply the interest of seeing American commercial interests prosper in the Orient," the President concluded.[a][121] Soon Francis Loomis [b] reported from London that Morgan was " now inclined to retain the property." The

---

[a] Roosevelt sent a copy of the letter to Root and told Lodge he had written both Morgan and Root. " I have not much hope in the matter," he reported to Lodge, " but I will do my best." [120]

[b] Loomis went to Europe in June as Special Ambassador to France to receive the remains of John Paul Jones. On July 2 he became Secretary of State ad interim after Hay's death.

" gist " of Roosevelt's letter had been cabled to him, and he promised to call on the President early in August. Loomis urged the President to have Rockhill report fully from China before Morgan called.[122]

The real issue in the minds of Roosevelt, Lodge, and State Department officials was America's prestige in the Far East. No one cared greatly about the company, which was wretchedly run and in ten years had accomplished little. But America's standing mattered greatly. The Chinese Government, in spite of the hostility of some local viceroys, would consider canceling the revocation of the concession, Rockhill explained, except for the way the company had been operated. Its violation of its contract, its extravagance, its mismanagement had made the Chinese wary of the company and had damaged America's reputation. None the less, talk of yielding the road to the Chinese " serves to intensify anti-American feeling and aids our competitors in these markets," Rockhill warned; " it has shaken belief in our business integrity." Assistant Secretary Loomis, Far Eastern expert Rockhill, and former Minister to China Edwin Conger agreed that selling the concession would deal " a blow to all our interests in China " and prevent Americans from getting any " new concessions for years to come." It would, indeed, " give American prestige a most fatal setback." Loomis urged the State Department to prohibit the sale. Rockhill advised that an arrangement be made with the Chinese by which work could begin under " good management " to redeem the reputation of American business methods.[123]

On August 7, J. Pierpont Morgan's yacht, the *Corsair*, steamed into Oyster Bay and Morgan and the President conferred for several hours. No official statement was given out, but the press was allowed to know that Morgan had agreed to hold the concession " if American interests in general in China would benefit thereby." The President felt, the *New York Herald* reported, " that the sale of the road would be a victory for the anti-American movement in China." [124] **The** day after Morgan's visit Chentung talked with Roosevelt and, though the President gave out no report, the Chinese Ambassador did. " China," he told the press, " wants to purchase the railroad and the concession, and has made an offer for it." The Chinese people are opposed to foreign control, he explained, and the Government wishes to meet their objections. Besides, Chentung commented dryly, " the road is 850 miles long on paper but only twenty-eight miles have been built." [125] From Peking, however, Rockhill reported contrariwise that, if certain revisions in the lease were made, the Foreign Office would leave the railway in American hands.[126] The President, irritated, now cabled Rockhill orders to clear up the discrepancy in the statements of the Foreign Office in Peking and the Minister in Washington. One of them was " guilty of gross prevarication," Roosevelt charged. Roosevelt authorized Rockhill to proceed on the basis of Morgan's decision that the company would agree to " reasonable " changes in the original contract and then go ahead and construct the road, if the Chinese still wanted it built. Roosevelt warned, however, that America would tolerate no " sharp practice " on the part of the Chinese that was detrimental to American interests.[127]

Rockhill at first replied that on August 12 the Foreign Office still disclaimed any intention to cancel the contract. On August 14, however, the Imperial Administration admitted having approved the efforts of the hostile viceroy, Chang Chih-tung, to regain control of the railway. It now confessed, too, that it had also granted the viceroy permission to coöperate for this purpose with Chengtung in Washington.[128] Roosevelt was annoyed, and also extremely busy with the Portsmouth Conference. His secretary, Barnes, in more diplomatic language than the President would have used, reported him " very dissatisfied with the action of the [Chinese] foreign office " and critical of Rockhill because of the Minister's earlier "complete misapprehension of the facts." "The President does not see how we can submit to such a blow," Barnes wrote Adee. "The Chinese government must be made to understand the gravity of the situation." [129] Adee in turn cabled the President's views to Rockhill. [130]

From Rockhill came the disquieting news that the June agreement between Chentung in Washington and the company had now been approved by the Emperor, and that Rockhill had entered a formal protest to no effect. [131] Besides, there had been rumors, which Rockhill had verified, that the British, with whom Roosevelt thought he had so happy an entente, were backing Chang Chih-tung in his efforts to buy out the concession. Rockhill reported the Germans, the French, and the Belgians also eager to help the Chinese pay the indemnity to the company. [132] The President is "puzzled," Assistant Secretary of State Adee cabled Rockhill. "He is inclined to think this Government must take a stand but would like to hear from you in full as to what you deem advisable in the matter." [133]

Rockhill's reply could not have made the President happy. The Chinese Government, the Minister explained, was not hostile to the United States, but the opposition to the company in Hunan and Hupeh provinces was so great that the Imperial Government did not dare oppose cancellation. Then Rockhill sounded solemn warning to Roosevelt. "It must be remembered," he cabled, "that throughout the whole of China at the present time there is a very strong feeling in favor of the Chinese regaining possession at the earliest possible dates of the railways building or built in their country, and a determination not to make concessions of any kind to foreign countries." The Chinese Government, Rockhill insisted, is too weak to do anything but yield to this pressure. True, this whole affair is a "serious blow to our interests," Rockhill conceded, but, "if the American China Development Company is willing to cancel its concession, I fail to see, . . . what the Legation can do." [134]

Roosevelt would not admit defeat, and so he turned once more to the company whose stockholders were to vote on the agreement on August 29. Again he wrote Morgan. " After some shillyshallying and many pleas of ignorance," he reported, " the Chinese Government is at last accepting responsibility for the action of the Viceroy [Chang Chih-tung] and Minister [Chentung] in agreeing to buy the company." " It seems to me that in the interest of American commerce in the Orient," he argued with Morgan, " it is of consequence for you not to give up your concession." " I am prepared to make a resolute stand and insist that this American Company be given its rights." " Can your company delay action for a few weeks longer? " he asked. " If so, I'll call a halt, in emphatic terms, to the Chinese Government." [135]

Preparatory to pursuing this strong policy when he should hear from Morgan, the President directed Adee to let Chentung know that we took " grave exception " to China's conduct, that we could not recognize China's right to act on the concession at all without the American Government's consent. He should therefore expect the proceedings to halt until the United States made its position known.[136]

But circumstances proved too much for Roosevelt. On August 27, Rockhill cabled Root, who had now become Secretary of State, that the Chinese would not yield. For Roosevelt's benefit he added, " Price paid company gives it great profit, nowise affects honor or interests of America." [137] The next day Chentung in Washington offered Roosevelt a compromise under which China would agree to give American bankers preference in floating certain Manchurian railroad loans. It was not, however, merely economic interests that concerned Roosevelt, and he refused the offer and reiterated his refusal to recognize any right of China to cancel the concession without his approval.[138] That same day the *Corsair* again visited Oyster Bay and Roosevelt made a final appeal to Morgan. Morgan refused to keep the company any longer. That night Roosevelt wrote Rockhill, "The Hankow Railway people have made up their minds that as the Chinese Government themselves have been acting with such duplicity and evidently intend to take away their franchises, the risk is too great for them to go on." [139] "They said that the price offered was large," he wrote Speck, "—probably much larger than they could get in the way of damages before any arbitral body—and if the Chinese would not allow the railroad to be built all they could hope for was damages." [140] "I cannot blame them," Roosevelt added significantly, "for I do not know enough about the situation to be able to guarantee" the Hankow railway people protection "in case trouble comes with China." [141] The morning after the Morgan conference the *New York Times* observed: "The matter has ceased to be a question of finance pure and simple, and has become a political problem of magnitude with several of the European powers now contending for spheres of influence in the Far East vitally concerned in its solution." [142]

Roosevelt accepted the inevitable most unhappily. To save face he announced to the press that the railroad would be sold, that Morgan had consulted the Administration and had wished to follow its wishes, but that the attitude of the Chinese Government left no other course open to the stockholders. [143] To Speck von Sternburg, however, he wrote confidentially, "I did my best to get Pierpont Morgan and the Hankow concession people to stand to their guns, but they would not do it." [144] In a long letter to Reid, he said nothing about the shortcomings of the company or its failure to build a railroad, but he blamed the original owners for selling out to the Belgians and he denounced the Chinese, who, he explained, "behaved in their usual manner." He also blamed himself for having left the earlier negotiations to Hay and the State Department. "If I had been in closer touch with the workings of the State Department I should have taken drastic action long ago, both against the American members of this corporation who had sold out to the Belgians, and against the Chinese government . . . I am sure I could have put the thing through." But even entering late as he did, he thought he could have succeeded if Morgan had stood firm. "I would [have] put the power of the government behind them," he told Reid, " so far as the executive was concerned, in every shape and way." [145]

Here, then, was dollar diplomacy in reverse. A badly run company had repeatedly violated its promises to China and, after five years, had built only 28 miles out of a promised 840. It had displayed to the Chinese the waste and incompetence of American corporate managers interested in financial manipulation rather than construction. The Chinese, disgusted with this particular company and hostile to all foreign railroad corporations, decided to cancel its concession. The company, having persuaded the Chinese to pay them one hundred percent profit on their investment and not primarily interested in railroad building anyway, wanted to get out. Business was not asking the Government to aid it, but the Government was begging business to help maintain the nation's prestige. Over the President's opposition, and even after his personal appeals to the great financier, Morgan and his associates insisted on getting out of a field where profits were not worth the trouble of dealing with the Chinese. In 1914 Rockhill, looking back on a lifetime of expertness on China, told the American Asiatic Association that the loss of this concession was the hardest blow the United States had ever suffered in China. [146]

The second and more serious problem Roosevelt had to handle in his relations with China was the boycott of American goods organized in 1905. The boycott grew out of resentment over American treatment of Chinese in China and in America. Roosevelt's attitudes toward the Chinese now took on new importance. So, too, did the memories of Westerners' behavior during the quelling of the Boxer uprising. American immigration policy became increasingly important, for the trouble in 1905 was precipitated by the immigration policy decision of 1904 and 1905. The motive force that led to the boycott, however, was provided by the new nationalist movement that was growing up in China.

The new nationalist spirit in China differed fundamentally from the Boxer movement. Both were anti-foreign. But the Boxers had opposed Western ideas; they had been traditionalists; the Manchu dynasty had used them to support its purposes. The new nationalists opposed Western domination of China, and Western treatment of Chinese as inferior, but they welcomed new ideas and looked to reform and modernization of China; they were anti-Manchu. Proud and defiant, they foresaw a great future for China. Chinese intellectuals, students, businessmen, and merchants joined in the movement. One of the leaders, Kang Yu-wei, was a Confucian scholar, and another, Sun Yat-sen, was Western trained and eager to westernize China.

The new nationalists resented with bitter hatred America's treatment of Chinese. They pointed out that illiterate Eastern European peasants were admitted to the United States without question, but that educated Chinese businessmen, scholars, and public officials eligible to enter even under the exclusion treaty, were subjected to abuse, insult, and a system of inspection that was corrupt and unfair. " They call it exclusion," Ch'ang Kiu Sing wrote in 1904, " but it is not exclusion; it is extermination." [147] Repeated outrages in the United States, based on an assumption of Chinese inferiority, stimulated the new spirit in China. In Boston, for instance, in 1903 the entire Chinese colony of several thousand persons was surrounded one evening by police and immigration officials, and Chinese that could not produce certificates of registration were arrested. Though only 45 proved to be potential deportees, 234 were held all night in two rooms so small that no one could lie down.[148] In 1904 official representatives of China, who had been invited to attend the Louisiana Purchase Exposition in St. Louis, were detained at San Francisco by immigration officials. They were held with immigrants on the end of the wharf in a building called " The Shed " that a student of Chinese immigration described as " unclean, at times overrun with vermin, and often inadequate to the numbers detained." Some of these " guests " of the United States were so indignant that they immediately returned to China; one contented himself with commenting that " The Americans are a race of pigs." [149]

The Chinese had resented our exclusion policy for decades. Helpless, however, to do anything about our policy, they had saved face as best they could by signing and then extending a treaty in which they agreed not to permit laborers to migrate and we agreed to permit non-laborers to enter but insisted they be registered.[150] Now the Chinese Exclusion Treaty, under which China had sanctioned exclusion, would expire and have to be renewed in December, 1904. This time the nationalist movement gave China more spunk in resisting.

Even before the Treaty expired in 1904, Chinese immigration had been discussed. In 1902 an immigration bill was heatedly debated. The Chinese minister, Mu Ting-fang, urged a revision of the laws in China's favor and he was particularly unhappy over the proposal to extend exclusion to the Philippines and Hawaii.[151] Californians and labor favored more stringent exclusion. Missionaries and business men urged moderation and, in any case, protection of intellectuals and merchants among the Chinese. Roosevelt's own views were what they had been since the late eighties. In the end he signed a compromise measure that reënacted the old exclusion laws and extended them to Hawaii and the Philippines.[152] The President himself favored exclusion of

laborers because " inferior " people should not be permitted
to " compete with our own workmen." " Cheap labor," he
warned, " means cheap citizenship." [153] On the other hand,
he wanted to cultivate friendly relations with students, intellectuals, and business men. He frequently expressed concern about the obstacles merchants and students met on
entering the country. He felt these obstacles did " serious
damage to our people," and he feared closing ports of entry
on the Canadian border to admissible Chinese would hurt
the expanding trade of New England cotton mills in China. [154]
" One of the greatest difficulties I have," he told his civil
service reform friend, Lucius Swift, comes from " keeping out
Chinamen that ought to be left in." [155] " We wish to enlarge
our trade with China; we wish to make even firmer our
intellectual hold on China," the President wrote Cortelyou. [156]
Roosevelt and Hay would have opened naturalization to non-
laborers, but, as Hay reminded the President, " Congress had
done its work so well that even Confucius could not become
an American—though he should seek it with prayers and
tears." [157]

Some Americans looked into the future of Chinese-Ameri-
can relations and were worried. Roosevelt and Hay were
among these. They seem to have realized that China was
maturing and that indiscriminate exclusion might have unfortunate repercussions. Mr. Justice Brewer of the Supreme
Court in a dissenting opinion sounded warning as prophetically as if he had seen in a vision events of the 1950's. " The
time has been," he said, " when many young men from China
came to our educational institutions to pursue their studies,
when her commerce sought our shores, and her people came
to build our railroads, and when China looked upon this
country as her best friend. If all this be reversed and the
most populous nation of earth becomes the great antagonist
of this republic, the careful student of history will recall the
words of Scripture, 'They have sown the wind and they

shall reap the whirlwind,' and for cause of such antagonism need look no further than the treatment accorded during the last twenty years by this country to the people of that nation." [158]

In 1904 it became obvious that agreement on renewal of the Treaty would be difficult. Congress would certainly pass an exclusion bill anyway. Roosevelt feared votes would be " lost on the slope " if something were not done to convince the West Coast that the President would " enforce the exclusion law, treaty or no treaty." So on April 5 the President, abandoning statesmanship for West Coast politics, announced at a cabinet meeting his intention of sending a message to Congress favoring an exclusion act. Congress needed little urging and speedily reënacted the exclusion legislation without reference to the Treaty.[159] Negotiations over the Treaty continued, however, through the year. Chinese Ambassador Chentung demanded drastic revision to guarantee fair and courteous treatment by American immigration officials and consuls. In October he presented a draft that Hay in the privacy of his diary called " a very strong paper; one which I could not conscientiously handle, as my convictions would be in his favor all the way through." [160] Unlike Hay, the new Secretary of Commerce, Victor Metcalf from California, opposed changing the Treaty. Even when Rockhill was sent to persuade him, Metcalf remained obdurate.[161] " There will be trouble on the 7th of December," Hay recorded in his diary, " unless we can sign a *modus vivendi.*" [162]

There *was* trouble but not immediately. The Chinese planned a boycott in the fall of 1904 and started raising funds to support it. They waited until the spring of 1905 apparently hoping that they might yet win modifications of American practices.ᵃ When in May no redress had been won,

* There were grievances in the Philippines as well as in the United States proper. Extension of the exclusion act to the Philippines had laid a burden on

steps were taken to organize a boycott. Boycotts had often been used in China,[164] but they had usually been local and limited to a single firm or group of foreign merchants. This one was general and spread to many Chinese ports, and it was aimed against a whole nation. Furthermore, this boycott represented more than economic retaliation. It embodied a proud and defiant new Chinese spirit. It was backed by the emotions aroused by victories of another Oriental people in the Russo-Japanese War and by the new nationalism in China. This new pride in China cut across social barriers, and even Chinese Christian students educated by Americans and other Westerners joined in the agitation.[165] Indeed, the boycott was the first major expression of Chinese nationalism. To support it was patriotic.

Boycott committees were formed to promote it. Chinese living in America supported the movement.[166] The leader in Shanghai was a wealthy merchant, Tseng Shao-ching, known to be philanthropic, active in the Red Cross, an enemy of foot-binding,* now an ardent nationalist. Formerly a great friend of the United States, he now worked up a feeling of hatred toward Americans.[167] The American consul in Shanghai reported to the State Department that he had a large following among " the literati, the student, and reforming class." [168] Some merchants joined the movement and some held back fearing loss of trade. So Tseng took matters into his own hands when the Chamber of Commerce did not wish to act, and himself telegraphed to other treaty ports and commercial guilds to notify them of the plan.[169] The boycott

merchants, particularly in the Canton area, who had long traded with or done business in those islands. Enforcement of the acts often caused them humiliation. Even in the United States it was the indignities to those not excluded even more than the exclusion of laborers that aroused anger.[163]

* Prior to the Revolution of 1911 the feet of Chinese girls were kept bound from babyhood to prevent their growing, since small feet that inhibited walking and hence usefulness were a symbol of social status and women's inferiority to men.

was to start July 20 and to extend to many areas. No Chinese was to purchase or use goods or machinery made in America, nor to use American ships for travel or shipping, nor to send children to American schools. No one would join American firms. Servants working for American families would leave their jobs.[170] Alarm among Americans spread rapidly. The American Association of China telegraphed home that a boycott would commence in August unless Chinese travelers, students, and merchants were granted " equitable treatment " under the pending treaty.[171] " The power of the guilds is very strong in China," warned the Association's president, James Jameson. " The feeling of the Chinese is very intense on this special subject.... Hampering of business even due to rumors of a boycott might cause much damage to commercial and other interests." Jameson also wrote the American consul in Shanghai expressing his fears and begging the consul to insure proper treatment to *bona fide* Chinese seeking entry into the United States.[172]

In America the Asiatic Association's president, John Foord, immediately warned Roosevelt of the consequences of a boycott for American trade in China, particularly for the cotton textile industry of New England. That industry, he pointed out, " has been saved from a period of destructive competition in the home market by the outlet which China has afforded for its surplus products." On his Association's behalf, Foord urged revision of the exclusion statutes and a satisfactory treaty.[173] Roosevelt immediately sent Foord's letter to Secretary of Commerce Metcalf with instructions to issue immigration officials " strictest orders " that " no kind of insolence against Chinese gentlemen will be permitted." " Undue harshness has been exercised," the President wrote. " Chinese coolies, that is Chinese laborers, must be and ought to be, kept out." But those entitled to entry must be shown " courtesy and consideration." " National interests " and " civilization " required this, he told Metcalf.[174] To Rockhill, just gone to China as the new Minister, he wrote, " I am trying in every way to make things easy for the Chinese here." [175]

In May the Chinese Ambassador also warned of the seriousness of the situation. " The Chinese people are in earnest," he declared. " Your exclusion act is humiliating. They would prefer to pay a huge indemnity or surrender a slice of territory rather than be insulted and menaced as they are by the attitude of the United States." [176]

By early June, 1905, the Chinese threat had again divided the country. The *San Francisco Chronicle* opposed any revision of the regulations. It saw a concerted attempt by Peking, Washington, and " Eastern trade centers " to flood the United States with Chinese hands " to compete with and degrade American labor." The workingmen's interests, the *Chronicle* warned, " cannot be subordinated to commercialism or sacrificed on its altar. . . . Congress will never dare to disregard the voice of American labor on this issue." [177]

On the other hand, business and commercial interests continued to seek reform of our treatment of the Chinese. On June 2 four Chinese students with a letter from American Ambassador Choate attesting their student status were detained in Boston on their way back to China from London. Several cotton manufacturers and cotton commission houses in Boston sent an immediate protest to the President. Action such as this, they declared, " is leading Chinese guilds to plan a boycott against American goods." " The cotton manufacturers in New England and the South . . . consider this action of our Government the most serious danger threatening their business." [178] Ten days after the Boston episode, a delegation from the American Asiatic Association presented to the President an address adopted the previous night signed by twenty-nine persons including seventeen representatives from Southern textile mills, and spokesmen for the United States Export Association, the Pennsylvania Steel Company, and the National Bank of Philadelphia.[179] Conditions in China, the delegation told the President, " threaten the continuance of a profitable and highly essential part of our commerce." To leave the exclusion laws and especially their administration as they are endangers " the industrial and commercial interests of the United States." A " new era of progress " is beginning in China, the delegation pointed out, but, because of its exclusion policy, " our country is being debarred . . . from either moral or material participation in that progress." [180]

To all protesters Roosevelt made his position clear. His policy was two-fold: to ease restriction against the exempt classes without yielding on the exclusion of laborers, but at the same time to take a strong stand with China against the boycott.[181] It was Congress, though, that they would have to persuade. " I am with you," he said, " without any qualifications whatever in any and every effort to expand the trade and promote the welfare of the industries which you represent." [182]

Even before the American Asiatic Association delegation visited him, the President took Secretary Metcalf to task about the " barbarous methods " of the Immigration Bureau. Metcalf had insisted the regulations did not need changing, but merely enforcing justly.[183] Now Roosevelt ordered that any official that acted unwisely toward a Chinese should either be dismissed or at least most severely reprimanded and " otherwise punished." [184] If no new law could be passed through Congress, at least the Immigration Bureau and the Consular Service could be cleansed by executive order. Roosevelt was especially critical of corruption in the handling of certificates of entry by the Consular Service in China. Perhaps a set of immigration officials could go to China to handle entry permits. " Can we not establish this rule ourselves, independently of action by Congress? " he asked Metcalf. " We are a civilized nation," he told the Secretary; " we are trying to teach the Chinese to be civilized. . . . We ought not to treat a Chinese representative in a way which we would not for a moment tolerate if applied by the Chinese to some of our representatives." [185] It should not be the Chinese that suffer because of corrupt officials. To allay Chinese resentment, he insisted that certificates of entry, once granted, however unwisely or fraudulently, were to be accepted.[186]

On June 15, 1905, Secretary of War Taft delivered a commencement address at Miami University in Ohio. " One of the greatest commercial prizes of the world," Taft asserted, " is the trade with the 400,000,000 Chinese. . . . Ought we to throw away the advantage which we have by reason of Chinese natural friendship for us and continue to enforce an unjustly severe law, and thus create in the Chinese mind a disposition to boycott American trade and drive our merchants from Chinese shores . . . ? " Taft upheld the exclusion of laborers, but condemned the position taken by " unreasonable and extremely popular leaders " on the West Coast. It was the duty of Congress and the Executive, he declared, to disregard these demands and to " insist on extending justice and courtesy to a people from whom we are deriving and are likely to derive such immense benefit in the way of international trade." [187] The *Chicago Tribune*, itself an administration paper, suggested that Taft spoke for the administration.[188] On the West Coast, however, Taft was criticized. Secretary Taft, the *San Francisco Chronicle* complained, had lent " the weight of his name " to " false " statements.[189]

The day after Taft's speech, Roosevelt instructed Metcalf to assist him in drawing up a circular of instructions that would end the corruption in the Customs and Immigration Service and " prevent the continuance of the very oppressive conduct of many of our officials toward Chinese gentlemen, merchants, travelers, students, and so forth." [190] Six days later, on June 24, the President issued a proclamation ordering a stricter observance of regulations in the administration of the exclusion laws. Unskilled and skilled Chinese labor was absolutely denied entry. Merchants, teachers, students, and travelers, as well as government officials, were to be shown " the widest and heartiest courtesy." All unnecessary inconvenience and annoyance toward these persons were to be " scrupulously avoided." " Any discourtesy shown to Chinese persons by any official of the Government will be cause for immediate dismissal." The President's order transferred the task of checking on the eligibility of a Chinese person for entrance into the country to the American officials issuing certificates in China, and these officials were instructed to work in coöperation with the Chinese government. Immigration officials in the United States were ordered to accept these certificates. The Chinese visitor, then, would *before* he left China be assured of entrance into the country. This would end many of the abuses that had taken place at ports of entry. " Our diplomatic and consular representatives," Roosevelt's order concluded, " are warned to perform this most important duty." [191] A few days later, anxious to allay the resentment that had developed in China, Roosevelt ordered Metcalf to avoid, if at all possible, sending back any Chinese that arrived with an invalid certificate. " Instead," the President blustered, " we will punish the United States official." [192]

The reception of Roosevelt's order was mixed. The *Chicago Tribune* called it the " most important administrative step in the solution of Chinese problems since the original exclusion act was passed." [193] On the West Coast, on the other hand, the Administration was regarded as " a victim of what is obviously a worked-up movement to break down the exclusion laws." [194] An Oakland, California, meeting of the Chinese, Japanese, and Korean Exclusion League passed resolutions condemning both Taft's speech and Roosevelt's action.[195]

Still others criticized the President because he had not gone far enough in justice to the Chinese. The Government's action was merely palliative, these critics protested. It did not solve the basic problem—the exclusion of the Chinese— as such. The Presidential order would have been more " worthy " had it been " brought about by some other motive than fear of deplenished pocketbooks." The *New York Evening Post* called the edict a " notable act of justice," but warned that China had " had a sudden awakening " and only free migration would end Chinese discontent.[196] Roosevelt had done well, but had he really allayed the boycott senti- ment, Richard Weightman of the *Chicago Tribune* asked.* Kang Yu Wei, the noted Confucian scholar in exile, who was visiting the United States, remarked, " The opinion of the Chinese within the empire is that not merely should more consideration be shown to what are known as the exempt classes, but that the non-exempt should be allowed some privileges also . . . The Chinese only want fair play . . . They say: ' We admit all Americans; why should we not insist that America should admit all physically fit Chinese? ' " [198]

In the meantime through May and June boycott sentiment in China was increasing. When Minister Rockhill arrived in Shanghai on May 20, the city walls were placarded with anti-American posters.[199] Rockhill and Consul Rodgers at- tempted to calm the native guilds united in the Shanghai Chamber of Commerce. Negotiations for a revised immigra- tion treaty were still going on in Washington, Rockhill told the merchants,[200] who then promised to cease talk of a boy- cott until the end of the treaty negotiations. " There the matter rested," Rodgers reported, " until the student class

* "Is it likely that the Chinese people will abate their resentment to any important extent," Weightman questioned, "because a few of their fellow creatures are held up and searched politely instead of being hustled and shaken down impolitely? " " We can hardly hope to placate the hostile sentiment by an apologetic application to the few of an affront intended for the entire people." [197]

took it up and began active work by correspondence and the press." [201] This student group dominated by Tseng Shaoching telegraphed requests for support to various cities and guilds throughout China and in the Chinese colonies in foreign countries including the United States. San Francisco Chinese raised funds early in July to assist the boycott.[202] The China Reform Association, a world-wide group of radical Chinese anxious to overthrow the Manchu dynasty, also subscribed to the plan and contributed money.[203] A Chinese merchant, Quan Yick Nam, hostile to the Chinese Reform Association, who knew the President well enough to send him Christmas presents each year, wrote telling the President how members of the Association were making pro-boycott speeches throughout the United States. He urged the President to stop them.[204] On July 3 the Chinese merchants in Singapore had voted unanimously to join the other Chinese of the Straits Settlements in the anti-American boycott.[205] In Canton representatives of twenty thousand Chinese met and backed the movement. The native Christians of Canton sent a petition to Roosevelt asking for treaty revision.[206] By July 7 the boycott was endorsed by gentry, merchants, and students and school teachers in twenty-five Chinese cities including Canton, Macao, Amoy, Foochow, Peking, Tientsin, and Chefoo.[207]

Roosevelt tried to force the Chinese Government to stop the boycott. In May he had instructed John Coolidge, the chargé in Peking, to urge the Foreign Office " to set its face against any policy of this character." [208] Soon after his arrival in China Rockhill, too, had officially protested to Prince Ch'ing. In mid-June Rockhill sent Ch'ing a hasty note, saying, " I am at a loss to understand why no sufficient action has been taken to put a stop to this foolish movement." [209] Ch'ing's response was significant. The Chinese government would try, he said, to prevent the agitation from spreading into a " general movement," but " the restrictions against Chinese entering America are too strong and American exclusion laws are extremely inconvenient to the Chinese." " If the restrictions can be lightened by your government," Prince Ch'ing suggested, " and a treaty drawn up in a friendly manner then this agitation will of its own accord die out." [210] This convinced Rockhill that the movement had official approval. Yüan Shih-k'ai, an energetic northern viceroy, who was on the make and hence the friend of the foreign powers, had taken " prompt and radical action " to suppress the boycott, but many officials seemed to be supporting the movement.[211] Some minor office-holders who opposed it hesitated to condemn it because the movement had popular support. The Manchu government shared this fear, especially since the discontent might be redirected against the corrupt dynasty rather than the Americans. Rockhill warned Hay that for the United States to force the Manchus to take hasty measures might result in revolution.[212] The native press and public opinion were " developing a national spirit in China," he wrote Roosevelt early in July. The nationalists " advocate on every subject, ' China for the Chinese.' " [213]

By July fear of a boycott had increased the pressure in the United States for a new more moderate treaty with China. William Wheelwright, president of the Chamber of Commerce of Portland, Oregon, commended Roosevelt for his June reforms, but asked that a number of Chinese laborers be admitted to the country. Otherwise, he cautioned, " it is easy to see that not only . . . trade will not continue to grow, but . . . there is danger of its complete cessation." [214] Non-business groups joined in the agitation. Booker T. Washington, for example, while praising Roosevelt's action, wished " it had happened before the Chinese boycott had been spoken of, or before our conscience had felt the value of Chinese dollars." [215]

Anti-Chinese opposition to the moderation of the President's policy continued, too. " If those countless millions of Asiatics are allowed to come to this country and are permitted to drink from the fountain without hindrance," a West Coast speaker told an Oakland meeting, " it means that our national existence is threatened." [216] The *San Francisco Chronicle* was convinced that the entire boycott plan had been " concocted " by the American Asiatic Association to permit the easy entrance of Chinese labor into the country.[217] Labor was aroused. A delegation of labor leaders, led by Samuel Gompers, visited the White House and protested against the entry of any Chinese labor at all. Roosevelt assured the group he foresaw no Chinese labor immigration to the United States. He was merely seeking to remedy the situation for Chinese that could legally enter.[218]

In China the leaders of the boycott movement went ahead with their plans to start the boycott on July 20. In the North where Yüan Shih-k'ai and others issued strong edicts calling for its suppression, the boycott made little headway, but throughout South and Central China agitation became more intense as the date approached. Literature, posters, and placards condemning the exclusion acts and calling for united support of the boycott were widely distributed. Cartoons showing the indignities to which immigration authorities subjected Chinese were drawn on posters and appeared in newspapers. The American colony in Canton recognized the danger and petitioned the President to frame a more liberal treaty.[219]

The boycott went peacefully into effect in the treaty ports throughout Southern China. Meetings were held. In Shanghai, on July 20, fifteen hundred persons gathered at the gates of the Wu Pên Girls' School. Representatives from all of Shanghai's leading guilds attended the meeting. " Some Americans have sneered at us," one patriotic citizen told the audience, " saying that there is nothing to fear because we Chinese never can unite. . . . We will show by precept and

example how fallacious an idea this is on the part of such
Americans." Everyone at the meeting voted to begin the
boycott immediately, and promised to refuse to buy from
Americans, though they were to sell whatever goods they had
on hand so that no Chinese would lose by the boycott.[220]
In Amoy a similar meeting was held. A committee of thirty-
six merchants agreed neither to buy from nor sell to Americans, nor to use their ships, to lease their premises, to attend
their churches and schools, nor to work for American merchants or missionaries. All schools having American teachers
were to dismiss them. Amoy's committee warned the unpatriotic that " their names will be published, their businesses
ruined, and any ceremony they might be engaged in will be
stopped in such manner as the committee may think fit." [221]

Placards now were posted in all the cities. In Shanghai
they were generally printed in large bold type on red paper.
The most common poster read: " In order positively to
retaliate against the American Treaty, you cannot buy or
sell American Goods. If you buy or sell American Goods you
are lower than a pig or dog." Others announced: " Determined Chinese do not buy American goods—those lacking
in determination wish to buy American goods—these are
truly ten thousand times over ' stinking turtles.' " " If I
smoke American Cigarettes," read another poster, " I am of
the species," and here a picture of a dog smoking a cigarette
labeled " Pinhead " followed. For those that refused to join
in the boycott special posters were drawn up. " America
prohibits Chinese laborers," read one of these, " thus oppress-
ing our brethren. This not only wounds our national pride,
but brings disgrace upon our people. . . . Even the women
students, determined to follow, rose up and decided positively not to use American goods. If you use American kero-
sene and ' Pin Head ' cigarettes you cannot bring about
united action. Foreigners will then not only slander and
make fun of us but our men will then become less than

women." [222] One placard circulated by Chinese students in Shanghai explained the full quality of Chinese resentment. It read:

Gentlemen, When America was discovered, it was a piece of wild land with only a small population who did not even know how to cultivate fields. It was on that account [that] Chinese were introduced into America and engaged as laborers in constructing roads, opening mines, and ploughing fields. When those enterprises were completed and America became rich, Americans began to treat Chinese cruelly and more cruelly than they treat their own oxen and horses. Now no Chinese are allowed to immigrate to America. Any man or woman of the student, farmer, laborer or merchant classes, on arrival in America, will be arrested by the American Inspectors and thrown as a prisoner into a small wooden house, which is dark and narrow and where he or she will be fumigated with sulphur being accused that he or she is infected with or brings plague from China. . . . Brethren, you have been told and are aware how Chinese are treated by Americans in America. Our anger can no longer be restrained and our hatred towards America endured. . . .[223]

Late in July many merchants realized the serious effects the boycott might have on their own trade and, in fear of economic disaster, began to call a halt. Then students and the intelligentsia took up the anti-American cry and dominated the movement. Incensed at the prospect of national humiliation, the students attacked not just administrative abuses, but the principle of exclusion itself. They condemned the exclusion of Chinese laborers as an insult. They urged the lower classes to join them. If the stevedore laborers are persuaded to take action and refuse to load or unload American ships, Consul Rodgers warned, "troubles of a grave character may arise since others of the laboring classes would hasten to express their sympathy and be easily persuaded to give an exhibition of what the labor of China can do in [an] anti-foreign movement." [224]

In spite of the defection of merchants in China, the boycott quickly spread to Chinese communities throughout the
Pacific area. In Portland, Oregon, the Chinese colony pledged
to raise $10,000 to aid the boycott.[225] The actual boycott
spread to Hawaii, the Philippine Islands, and Nagasaki and
Yokohama in Japan.[226] A mere threat had developed into a
great nationalist and patriotic movement. " The official publication of the Presidential message of June 25," the *London
Times* reported from Shanghai, ". . . has been without
effect." [227]

The boycott in operation brought an immediate response
from American firms. Even if the Chinese demands were
justified, a boycott could not be tolerated. Rumors circulated that the English, Germans, and Japanese had put the
idea of a boycott into Chinese minds to capture the American market.[228] New England cotton manufacturers protested
that the boycott would cost them twenty million dollars a
year.[229] The boycott, a representative of the Standard Oil
Company warned the State Department, " would be a grave
disaster to the petroleum industry of the United States." [230]
The reaction in China was more intense. Business men in
China, one consul reported, have " gone mad " and are acting like " regular wild Indians." [231] " While it is proceeding
quietly and without disturbance," Rodgers reported from
Shanghai, the boycott " is nevertheless effective to a considerable degree." [232] In Canton and in Amoy the property
of the Standard Oil Company was threatened. The company
was still selling oil in Canton but not the usual quantities.
Sale of American flour was also affected, and the trade of the
British-American Tobacco Company had fallen off fifty per
cent.[233] From Foochow came similar reports. The Chinese
agents of the Singer Sewing Company, the Standard Oil
Company, and the New York Life Insurance Company,
Consul Gracey reported, " have all been grossly abused, and
in cases threatened and in all intimidated." [234] The flour

trade in Canton was "nil"; the 500,000 bags usually sold over a similar period could not be placed. Standard Oil estimated its losses for a few weeks at $25,000. "Junks laden with American oil, covered by transit passes, which are at other times simply stamped at the *likin* stations, are now held for several hours," Consul Lay reported, "while the oil is examined and the cases punctured with holes."[235]

The American Government's answer to the boycott now actually functioning was vigorous. Consular officials put what pressure they could on local Chinese officials and viceroys to force them to condemn the movement. In Chefoo, for example, Consul John Fowler protested to H. E. Yang, governor of Shantung Province. Thousands of placards, he told the Government, were being sent from Tientsin and Shanghai. These placards were dangerous, for they "tended to excite the common people." Unchecked, Fowler warned, such agitation would "lead to open acts of violence with dire consequences." "Please issue stringent instructions," the Consul urged, "that all such be destroyed, and that the authors will be held responsible for all damages resulting directly or indirectly from same. . . . It is the duty of the Chinese government to protect American interests in China."[236]

While the consulates applied what pressure they could locally, Roosevelt, Rockhill, and the higher officials of the State Department worked on the Peking government. Roosevelt wrote weekly letters to Rockhill.[237] Roosevelt still moved cautiously, however, with a realization that since our own actions had provoked the boycott, public demands on China might only increase its intensity. On August 1, John E. Wilkie, chief of the Secret Service, returning from a trip to China, made a report on conditions there and warned that the English and Germans were helping create sentiment against the United States in China.[238] Roosevelt studied Wilkie's report forwarded to him by Secretary of the Treas-

ury Leslie Shaw. The " fundamental trouble," he wrote
Shaw, is that " we have behaved scandalously toward Chinamen in this country. Some of the outrages by mobs which
have resulted in the deaths of Chinamen were almost as bad
as anything that occurred at the hands of the Chinamen
themselves in the Boxer outbreak." The Germans and English may have taken advantage of the boycott, but the
boycott itself is " due to our own misdeeds and folly." [239]

Rockhill, too, was trying to move firmly but quietly, com-
bining protest about the boycott with an effort to alleviate
its causes. With conciliation in mind, he wrote the President
early in July recommending to him a proposal he and Hay
had discussed earlier for returning to China the Boxer indemnity.[240] Rockhill continued to urge the Foreign Office
in Peking to insist that provincial authorities suppress the
boycott.[241] Two days before the boycott officially began,
Rockhill instructed American consuls to explain to its sup-
porters that a treaty was still being negotiated; consuls
should make clear that the proposed boycott would hurt
only the " commercial interests " in the United States that
had always most " strongly opposed rigid exclusion." Tell
the restless and irritated Chinese, Rockhill admonished the
consuls, that their country will lose the sympathy of the
foreign government that has so far been most friendly to
China.[242]

When the boycott actually began Rockhill's patient tone
changed markedly. He then sharply demanded that the Imperial Government stop the boycott immediately. When the
Government replied that it had already instructed the provincial authorities to dissuade the people from anti-American
agitation, Rockhill protested that this was not enough. The
Foreign Minister promised him, then, that he would speak
with Prince Ch'ing about issuing an Imperial Edict.[243] The
Government feared, however, that any intercession on behalf
of the United States might turn the agitation from America

to China's own weak government. So it hedged and issued no edict. Actually, the Manchu Government feared about equally the ire of the Americans and that of the young nationalists. In mid-August Rockhill invoked the Treaty of Tientsin signed in 1858 during the Taiping Rebellion as ground for warning Prince Ch'ing that the American Government would hold the Chinese Government " directly responsible for any loss our interests have sustained or may hereafter have to bear through the manifest failure . . . of the Imperial Government to stop the present organized movement against us. . . ." Rockhill called for the punishment of Tseng Shao-ching. Negotiations for a new treaty, he told Prince Ch'ing, would remain suspended until the Imperial Government effectively stopped " the present unlawful attempt to interfere with our treaty rights." [244] Roosevelt, the *Chefoo Daily News* observed, " is turning on the screws and dealing with the silly movement in exactly the way it should be dealt with." [245]

Meanwhile by mid-August the boycott itself was petering out. What little strength it had had in the North was destroyed by strict enforcement of a ban against it. In South China, especially in Canton and Shanghai, the boycott continued, but largely in the face of a growing resistance of the merchants, who feared serious losses if it continued.[246] Where the agitation persisted, the movement was taken over and dominated by students and intellectuals.[247] Secret Service Chief Wilkie expected it to end shortly, " because," as he put it, " the Chinaman is too good a trader to long refuse to sell American goods because of sentiment." [248]

On August 26 Prince Ch'ing replied to the American demands. " This idea of a boycott of American goods," he told Rockhill, " came directly from the trades people " and the Government can assume no responsibility. The Imperial Government has ordered the provincial authorities to " take measures to put a stop to the trouble." What else can it do?

It cannot punish Tseng Shao-ching "for fear of exciting
still more trouble and disorder." "It is my opinion," Ch'ing
continued, "that the reason of all of this boycott affair lies
in the Coolie Immigration Treaty." Instead of issuing the
Imperial Edict Rockhill had demanded, Ch'ing called upon
America to sign a new and less harsh treaty. Then, "everybody will be pleased." [249] It was clear, Rockhill reported,
that many local officials were fighting the boycott,[250] but
Rockhill was irritated by Ch'ing's refusal to issue an Imperial Edict. Roosevelt, he told Ch'ing, had in June done
all he could to remove the grievances of Chinese students
and merchants. But "your government has allowed the agitation to continue to the great pecuniary loss of your own
people, as well as mine." The President Rockhill reported
as dissatisfied "at the inadequate means" used "to end this
hostility." Indeed, he doubted the friendliness of the Chinese Government toward the United States. The boycott,
Rockhill insisted, is "an unwarranted attempt of the ignorant
people to assume the functions of government and to meddle
with international relations. . . . It . . . is the duty of Imperial
Government to completely put a stop to this movement." [251]

In late August Roosevelt wrote Rockhill he was "very
much dissatisfied with the Chinese attitude." [252] "It is absolutely necessary for you to take a stiff tone with the Chinese
where they are clearly doing wrong," Roosevelt insisted. "I
. . . am taking a far stiffer tone with my own people than any
President has ever yet taken," but it is difficult to convince
Congress to "do the Chinese justice," when they act as they
do. "Unless I misread them entirely," Roosevelt explained
to Rockhill, the Chinese "despise weakness even more
than they prize justice, and we must make it evident both
that we intend to do what is right and that we do not intend
for a moment to suffer what is wrong." [253]

Reactions to the President's and Rockhill's handling of the
boycott were various. The American Asiatic Association and

its Chinese branch applauded the demands on the Imperial Government.[254] But the boycott leader, Tseng Shao-ching, was unimpressed. " Your Minister, Mr. Rockhill, has been moving our Government to suppress us," he said in a public statement, " but none of us are the same as we were three years ago." Addressing American merchants, Tseng observed: " Although you know the disease to be feverish you yet give heating medicine." [255]

In August an ominous note crept into discussions. " The apprehension for the future is greater than [the] losses sustained," Rockhill wrote on August 15. The boycott would set a " dangerous precedent if not broken." [256] Chinese student leaders were still bitterly denouncing the United States. So, too, were Chinese editors. " Men of the Orient and of the Occident constantly say, ' America is the good friend of China,' " said one editor. " Why, then are contempt and insult poured upon our people in America? " The movement was growing, too, into a broader revolt against " white " domination. Another editor cried out, " Europeans and Americans regard us as of inferior race, look upon us as a semi-civilized country, treat us as a barbarous people. It is because of this that my people . . . weep bitterly, not for a single day forgetting their grief." [257] Secret Service Chief Wilkie in describing the weakening of the boycott was still bothered by one fact: " Some of the radical Chinamen are going much farther than was at first contemplated," he reported.[258] American journals, too, began to comprehend what was happening. " It never will do to lose one's patience in dealing with China," the *Commercial and Financial Chronicle* declared. " We are inclined to call what is going on there, the Spirit of '76 in its birth-throes, applied to that Empire." [259] " Other nations will win from us the glory of leading China in her renaissance," the *Outlook* warned, " unless we heed the signs that reveal a new national spirit and a new sensitiveness in China." [260] A group of American merchants in Canton who petitioned Roosevelt for alleviation of restrictions on Chinese told him that this was important not just from the " business point of view " but because of other considerations as well. " The passion for reform has at last possessed the people and is now making rapid headway," said Canton's Americans. " We feel sure that China will advance more in the next generation than she has in the past one thousand years." The United States must be " headmaster " in the new movement. " We should cultivate the acquaintance and good-will of the students who are to be the moulders of the new China." [261]

Finally, on August 31, the Imperial Government issued the long demanded Imperial decree condemning the boycott and ordering provincial officials to stamp it out. The American Government had promised to reform the exclusion laws, the Chinese were told. The boycott could only endanger good relations between the United States and China. " If any ignorant persons seek to stir up strife by taking advantage of the present state of things, such must be immediately arrested and severely punished, so that trouble may be nipped in the bud." But then the Edict conciliated Chinese opinion and gave warning to Americans by proclaiming that feeling against the Americans is so unanimous that " none can guarantee that wicked and evil-disposed persons will not take advantage of the crisis to create disturbance against the public peace whereby the good order of the country might be endangered." [262] A few days later Ch'ing pointedly wrote Rockhill. The boycott, he said, has been banned and " the Chinese Government has great confidence that the President will certainly take some . . . further action later on." [263]

In the United States pressure was applied to Roosevelt to send Taft, then on a mission in the Far East, to Canton to settle the boycott. Taft, accompanied by the President's daughter, Alice, and several American dignitaries, was ostensibly on a " good will " tour. The group visited Hawaii, the

Philippines, and Japan. In Japan Taft had just arranged the secret Taft-Katsura Agreement handing over Korea to the Japanese. The viceroy in Canton had shown deep sympathy with the boycott movement and proved a stumbling block to the resumption of normal trade and it was hoped Taft could conciliate him. One advocate of a Taft visit to Canton was Senator George C. Perkins of California. " Canton is the backbone of the boycott," Perkins wrote the President. " Commercial organizations and Pacific coast merchants request you to appoint Secretary Taft a representative of the State Department. . . . With immediate authority they think he can stop the boycott, but it requires immediate action." [264] In a reply that was almost a rebuke, Roosevelt denied his request. " Everything that it is possible to do is being done now about the boycott, and will be done," the President told Perkins. Rockhill and American consuls in China are handling the problem, " and the National Government will go as far as it possibly can in backing them up." The West Coast merchants could best prevent the boycott, Roosevelt pointedly told this supporter of the anti-Chinese position in America, by helping the President secure " rational action by Congress." " I have the right," he told Senator Perkins, " to expect that the Pacific coast representatives will aid me in undoing the injustice in our treaties . . . which has probably been the whole, and certainly the main, cause of the present boycott." [265] A few days later, however, a representative of the British-American Tobacco Company telegraphed requesting that Taft be sent to Canton to " call officially on the viceroy . . . with a view to settling [the] boycott." [266] The same day the Standard Oil Company urged the President to let Taft try " to smooth out the situation and make better feeling " in the Canton area.[267]

That very day, September 2, the President, who had great confidence in Taft, cabled Taft to meet with the Viceroy and other high officials in the Canton area. Taft was instructed not to commit himself to any definite promises. " Make them realize," Roosevelt instructed him, " that we intend to do what is right and that we cannot submit to what is now being done by them." [268]

Taft planned his visit to Canton for September 3. In Hong Kong, however, his party was met by the Canton consul, Julius Lay, who warned that the city was in an uproar. The pro-boycott Viceroy had arranged a dinner for Taft, but was " ill " and did not plan to attend.[269] Posters and placards insulting the Taft mission were plastered throughout the city. The most conspicuous poster was considered a direct insult to Alice Roosevelt. An American woman was being carried in a sedan-chair by four turtles. The caption read: " Turtles carrying a beautiful woman." The turtle was to the Chinese the lowest of animal creation and the import of the poster was clear.* Chinese characters above the drawing read: " Shameful! Shameful! Shameful!! Americans (beautiful women) treat us as dogs. Now they are coming to visit our city to investigate whether or not our people are united. You fellows must not carry their chairs. If you do, you are like those pictured below." [271] It was considered unsafe for the President's daughter to go to Canton. So all the women in the party gave up the trip. Alice Roosevelt persuaded an officer of an American gunboat to take her to the Island of Shaneen in the river off Canton to the consulate where she had to content herself with a view of the city across the water, but where the American President's daughter was safe from more serious insult than an occasional coolie across the water shaking his fist.[272] Meanwhile Taft and some of the men journeyed to Canton to meet with American businessmen and Chinese officials.[273] During his stay in the city,

---

* In Chinese folklore the male turtle is unable to copulate and has to have a snake unite with the female turtle to produce his young. Hence a turtle is both impotent and a bastard. So was anyone who would carry a sedan chair for the American President's daughter.[270]

Taft was guarded by a battalion of the Viceroy's guards. In spite of the diminished effect of the boycott, there was no question of the intense bitterness toward Americans. Taft told the guests at the luncheon in his honor that the United States did not want one inch of the soil of China. The boycott he called an " unreasonable violation " of American treaty rights. He was glad, he said, that plans were being made to end it.[274]

During September and October relations with China seemed less critical. The boycott continued, but only sporadically in certain areas in South China.[275] Business groups continued to protest against it. Taft, however, on his return from the Far East, reported that the agitation was dying out. " Chinese merchants themselves are losing money," he said, " and their influence is not likely to further it." [276]

In October, after several Cabinet meetings at which Taft's mission and the Chinese exclusion laws were discussed, it was decided to pursue Roosevelt's old policy. The administration of the exclusion laws would be further improved in the spirit of Roosevelt's June directive.[277] Roosevelt would try to sell a more reasonable attitude to the people. On October 20, while on a tour of the Southern States, he made his first public pronouncement on the boycott and exclusion since his meeting with Gompers and the labor delegation early in July. " At present our market for cotton is largely in China," he told an Atlanta audience. " The boycott of our goods in China during the past year was especially injurious to the cotton manufacturers." The American Government had vigorously opposed the boycott. " We must insist firmly on our rights," he said, " and China must beware of persisting in a course of conduct to which we cannot honorably submit."

If America had rights, however, she also had duties. " We cannot expect China to do us justice unless we do China justice," he declared. The chief cause of the boycott, he insisted, was the unfair character of our exclusion acts. The

exclusion acts did not justify the boycott, but America had
fallen short in its " duty toward the people of China." The
President was determined that all Chinese except laborers
should be guaranteed " the same right of entry to this country and the same treatment while here as is guaranteed to
citizens of any other nation." Yet within the existing frame-
work full justice could not be done the Chinese. " I can do
a good deal, and will do a good deal, even without the action
of the Congress," he insisted. But a genuine remedy could
come only from Congress through a change in the law. " It
is short sighted indeed for us to permit foreign competitors
to drive us from the great markets of China," the President
protested.[278]

Characteristically, having appealed for fairness to the
Chinese, Roosevelt then felt he must at the same time stand
up firmly to China. So in planning his annual message to
Congress he incorporated a condemnation of the Chinese
Government for permitting the boycott to continue. " Not
only the Chinese people but the Chinese government have
behaved badly in connection with this boycott, and a boycott
is something to which we cannot submit," he wrote in the
first draft. On the advice of a friendly critic he finally de-
leted this passage. " I incline to think," Robert De Forest
wrote after reading the draft, " that even the Chinese people
who have behaved badly have not done half as much as we
should have done under like provocation." [279]

In China discontent continued. The Canton situation was
still unsatisfactory. The World Students' Chinese Federation, composed largely of Chinese youth that had studied in
America, sent a telegram to the Chinese Minister in Washington urging that it was nonsense to talk further about
altering the treaty and recommending that treaties with the
United States be abrogated.[280] In late October five American
missionaries were murdered at Lienchou in Kwantung Province. Actually the violence that resulted in the deaths de-

veloped out of purely local difficulties. The American consul reported that trouble over a Chinese temple and rivalries of Catholics and Protestants were factors.[281] None the less in the tense atmosphere the boycott had created, there was alarm lest this outbreak was the beginning of a vast anti-foreign movement. Rockhill feared that the anti-American movement was spreading to the interior of China where anti-American placards were being distributed. "It is very difficult to put a stop to," Rockhill warned Root on November 10.[282] On November 7 the American Association of China, a pressure group of American merchants, called upon the Administration to take more forceful action. These merchants, no longer urging conciliation, demanded that "pressure" be applied to the Peking Government to ban literature of "a seditious nature" and that no new treaty be negotiated in the face of the anti-American demonstrations, because "the Chinese would at once declare that they have compelled the United States to act justly, and that similar methods may well be employed in the future . . ."[283] The San Francisco Merchants' Exchange, too, pleaded that, if Roosevelt did not take "strong steps" to stop the boycott agitation, "American trade" would "be put back many years."[284]

Faced with the renewed seriousness of anti-American sentiment Roosevelt once again acted in his usual twofold manner. First he recommended to Congress some changes in the administration of the exclusion laws. Perhaps it would be wiser, he suggested to Congress, merely to define the excepted classes to include all Chinese laborers and then to permit all other Chinese to enter freely. These proposals the Asiatic Association found much too "vague."[285] At the same time Roosevelt turned to a solution he had long been restraining himself from using. On November 15 he ordered Charles Bonaparte, Secretary of the Navy, to "have as strong a naval force as possible concentrated on the Chinese shore." "The Chinese," he told Bonaparte, "are not showing a good spirit. We ought to be prepared for any contingency there." [286] Unable to halt the anti-American agitation through diplomatic channels, Roosevelt was now prepared to turn to the alternative—force. On December 23 Cal O'Laughlin, a *Chicago Tribune* correspondent who knew Roosevelt well, reported that the President wanted four battleships in Chinese waters besides the two cruisers already slated for use in the Far East. O'Laughlin said certain members of the General Board of the Navy opposed use of naval vessels in the Far East and wanted to call all battleships home, but that " the president believes the moral effect of their presence in the far east warrants their retention." [287]

In December the situation became worse. An American admiral in China was mobbed by a group of Chinese after he accidentally shot a Chinese woman while shooting at some birds.[288] General Leonard Wood from the Philippines warned the President: " The Chinese situation continues ugly. . . . Our consideration and courtesy seems to have been misinterpreted by the Chinese as a whole, who, I think, look upon us with a considerable degree of contempt." Of them Wood in turn was contemptuous. They have developed " no national spirit," Wood, unaware of the nature of what had been going on in China, told the President. It would be disastrous to admit any Chinese laborers to the country. " They have neither patriotism nor morals," Wood, voicing his race prejudice and revealing his ignorance of facts, continued. " We have enough national weakness and humiliation from the negro to avoid further trouble by the introduction of races with which we can never mingle." [289]

In Shanghai a conflict arose over the jurisdiction of the mixed court. The Chinese sought to gain more jurisdiction over the foreign settlement. Unsuccessful, they rioted on December 18, called a general strike, burned the municipal police station, and freed the prisoners. Twenty Chinese were killed and several Westerners injured. The foreign powers, including the United States, rushed ships and sailors to the scene to put down the angry rioting Chinese. Clearly a local issue, like the missionary murder in Lienchou, this event was widely ascribed to boycott sentiment.[290] " We have capped a long [?] period of failure to protect our citizens abroad with ships and guns," a friend wrote Lodge, " by establishing the fact that our consuls are powerless to protect them and our consulates are merely distributing points for the supply of victims for the Chinese." [291]

But Roosevelt had decided to teach the Chinese a lesson, and was now ready to remedy this situation. A large naval detachment was already on its way to the Far East. On December 23, the *Chicago Tribune's* Cal O'Laughlin reported that the War Department had besides directed two regiments of infantry and two batteries of field artillery to start by February 1 for the Philippines to prepare for probable trouble in China.[292] After a long cabinet meeting on January 2 Taft wired General Wood that reinforcements were being dispatched to the Philippines. " The troops at Manila," O'Laughlin calculated, " will be within fifty hours of Chinese territory." One foreign diplomat told O'Laughlin, " The United States has made the mistake of being too lenient with the Chinese and they have interpreted your policy as due entirely to weakness." [293] Five days after the dispatch of troops to Wood, the *Washington Post* reported on the authority of a " high official " that, if the situation in China did not " improve," additional troops would be sent to the Philippines. The mistake of 1900 of sending badly organized troops would not be repeated. This time, the *Post* declared, " only young and vigorous general officers will be on duty . . . for the prospective China expedition." The *Post* guessed Root and Taft were actually shipping troops chiefly to frighten the Chinese into submission. Chinese students, the *Post* lamented, " have returned home preaching the doctrine of ' Asia for Asiatics.' " They had to be shown that the United States stood ready to defend its "rights." [294]

The stories of troop shipment were founded in fact. Roosevelt was seriously planning armed force if the Chinese continued the boycott. On January 11, for example, he advised Taft that, in any possible operations against Canton, the War Department should "be absolutely certain that we provide amply in the way of an expeditionary force." He suggested that at least 15,000 men be sent immediately and 5000 follow within a month. "The Chinese Army," he warned Taft, "is far more formidable than it was five years ago. . . . We ought not to take any chances. We cannot afford a disaster." [295] Unable, then, to deal through a Manchu Government too weak to control anti-foreign sentiment, the Administration planned to set up its own "control." Probably the remedy was out of all proportion to the danger. Rockhill, at least, felt there would be no problem in the "near future." Still, the situation required "the most careful attention," he wrote the President. "China no longer requires to be pushed ahead, but rather to be restrained." She was "humiliated" by Japan's successes and her own "position of inferiority. . . . She wants to get out of it with a rush, and she may break her neck in the attempt, for so far as we can see, she has no broad, nor indeed, enlightened men to guide her." [296]

The American Government, then, offered the young Chinese nationalists in search of a new China not sympathy but a show of force. Critics of the use of force there were. The anti-administration *New York Evening Post*, for example, protested: "The absurd Chinese expedition is rapidly becoming a joke." "So great has been the Empire's progress in six years," that sheet declared, that Peking could not be taken with 250,000 men, much less 25,000 men. The Boxers, the *Post* warned, "were a rabble driven to desperation by two years of famine . . ." Today there is a "modernized

Chinese army." [297] Abettors of the use of force, however, were numerous and more vocal than the critics, and many of them made their view known to Roosevelt.

Rumors of a second Boxer uprising spread throughout the United States in January and February. Former Minister Edwin Conger urged that we " have our warships and troops ready, if only for the purpose of letting China know that we are watching her." [298] John A. T. Hull, chairman of the House Military Affairs Committee, noted that China was passing through a transition from an ancient to a modern civilization. " While that is going on," Hull warned, " every Government that has business relations with her must be ready to protect itself or else pull down its flag, leave the Pacific Ocean, and destroy its trade." [299] An American merchant accused William Jennings Bryan, then traveling in Asia, of stirring up the Chinese to renew the boycott.[300] Missionaries were vocal in their fear of an expected uprising. One of them blamed the entire anti-foreign movement on Morgan's sale of the Canton-Hankow Railroad to the Belgians.[301] Another religious leader, the Reverend S. H. Littell, proclaimed in an interview: " There should be more American warships in those waters. Men-of-war continually controlling the coast and running up the rivers every now and then would show the Chinese that we have our eyes on them. Only thus, I am convinced, will a big uprising be averted." [302] Richard Olney, Cleveland's Secretary of State, issued a statement supporting the President's action.[303] President D. M. Parry of the National Association of Manufacturers, told his directors that, if " recourse to arms to quell the disturbances " in China became necessary, it would be solely because of conditions that " organized labor " had created.[304] An American resident of Shanghai, home on a visit, urged the government to send " a dozen or a score of extra regiments in her own interests and in the interests of white humanity in general." " And let her use them," he pleaded. " Send also cruisers and gunboats to the Chinese coast and seize a port." [305]

The Roosevelt Administration needed little prodding. Taft and Root appeared before the Senate Committee on Appropriations to ask for $100,000 to house the Chinese expeditionary force in the Philippines.[306] To be prepared in case a campaign developed that would last through the year, winter clothing was collected for the troops that had been sent to the Philippines.[307] In Omaha, a force of men at the Army Quartermaster Depot was reported to be " at work day and night . . . loading cars . . . for immediate shipment to the Philippines." [308] An order for four million ball cartridges was placed at the Frankford Arsenal in Philadelphia.[309] Troops were held in readiness in the Philippines.[310] A gunboat, *El Cano*, was sent up the Yangtse River on a " cruise." The *Oregon*, a large battleship, loitered near Hong Kong and Canton. " Among other things," a prominent naval officer explained, " the old Oregon acts as a powerful deterrent; she sometimes does her best work just lying lazily around the ports of a bellicose country." [311] Taft told a Chicago audience: " The Eastern situation is problematical. China is now in a state of unrest. To many it seems that the conditions which prevail there are similar to those which preceded the Boxer Uprising." [312]

Roosevelt, in the meantime, was busy in Washington. In early February he was closeted in secret meetings with Taft, Root, and Admiral Dewey.[313] Rumors circulated among the Capital's foreign diplomats that Roosevelt was " preparing a grand international coup with China as the scene." Secretary Root, however, denied these reports and reaffirmed America's belief in the " open door." [314] Roosevelt, after playing his trump card—threat of military force—quickly subjected the Peking Government to new pressures to suppress all vestiges of the boycott movement and the nationalist spirit. The President would not send troops to the Chinese mainland, the *Washington Post* observed, until " there is clear evidence that the native government cannot or will not protect Americans or subjects of European nations." The President, O'Laughlin wrote, hoped that his actions would cause the Empress Dowager " immediately " to " adopt repressive measures " against the nationalist sentiment.[315]

Finally, on February 26, Roosevelt made a strong set of demands on the Chinese government. He insisted that " efficient measures be taken to prevent a renewal of the outrages of nineteen hundred." Those guilty of crime must now be punished. All sympathy with the anti-foreign movement must be " sternly dealt with." Provincial authorities, many of whom had been apathetic toward or sympathetic to the anti-American movement, were now to be punished if they failed " in their duty " to protect Americans. Finally, the boycott must be recognized as an unlawful combination in restraint of trade, and " effective steps " must be taken to " suppress inflamatory combinations in restraint of trade." Rockhill pressed Roosevelt's demands vigorously. Ch'ing replied to Rockhill that the masses of the people were still loyal in spite of the activity of revolutionists and " students of shallow learning " that sought to weaken the Manchu government by creating anti-foreign feeling among the Chinese. Ch'ing promised to meet Roosevelt's demands, and this time he did in so far as he was able. On March 6 an Edict was issued condemning anti-foreign sentiment and calling on students " to cultivate loyalty to the State." [316] In consequence, Roosevelt wrote Wood on April 2: " I do not believe there will be an expedition to China, but I wanted to be sure that if it was needed we would not be unprepared." [317]

Though most vocal groups in the United States supported the President's actions, there was interesting and thoughtful dissent. Critics felt that relations with China, especially with the " new China," had been damaged, perhaps beyond re-

pair. " The plain fact is that we have gone blindly ahead in
our dealings with the Chinese as if they had not the ordinary
attributes of human beings," the *New York Evening Post*
observed. " We thought that we could cut them and they
would not bleed, could wrong them and they would not
revenge. We are finding our mistake." [318] Some business
groups also recognized the dangers of Roosevelt's policy. John
Foord, executive secretary of the American Asiatic Association, condemned the military plans of the Administration
in no uncertain words. A military venture might threaten
already damaged trade relations. If the missionaries feared
the Chinese, Foord wrote contemptuously, " they should
promptly abandon their posts and come home." [319] An able
American consular official in Peking, a friend of the President
who was one day to be under secretary of State, also complained about Roosevelt's action. " In Washington, they
don't seem to understand how feeble the Chinese government is," William Phillips wrote to Joseph Choate; nor do
they realize that to " throw the entire responsibility of every
anti-foreign sentiment on the government makes it even
weaker than before . . . thus playing into the hands of the
anti-dynastic party and anti-foreign party." [320]

Fortunately, the anti-foreign agitation did not come to a
crisis in 1906. It was scattered and failed to gain the necessary mass support. When no " second Boxer Rebellion "
occurred, Roosevelt seems to have felt that his policy had
been effective. Others, however, viewed the President's response to Chinese nationalism more critically. The " frankness " with which the military plans were announced, the
Nation observed, " savors too much of ' shirt-sleeves diplomacy.' . . . The residents of China will see in our action a
determinedly hostile spirit, looking only for an excuse to
land an army and perpetrate again some of the horrible
crimes which thoroughly disgraced the so-called Christian
troops in 1900." " The attitude of our government, in brief,"

the *Nation* continued, "smacks of the same spirit which makes the average American look upon every Chinaman as an underfed and over-worked laundryman, to be kicked or stoned if the policeman's back is turned."[321]

Roosevelt's rôle in both the Canton-Hankow concession incident and the anti-American boycott was significant. He dominated the policy of his country in these crucial months, and made the key decisions. When Rockhill and the President disagreed, Roosevelt overruled Rockhill, as when, against his China expert's judgment, he adopted his "strong" policy and prepared to invade China.[322] Thus Roosevelt directly helped shape our twentieth century China policy. Did he shape it well?

The answer seems clear. Roosevelt was a victim of the limitations of his own views on colonialism. His trouble was not lack of information, but a point of view that made him incapable of seeing China in terms of the twentieth century world. In the Canton-Hankow concession he missed entirely the fact that the Chinese might desire to conduct their own industrial development. Rather, he viewed the railroad concession as did most international economic strategists in his day as an opening wedge into China to be used by a civilized power to pry open for exploitation the rich resources of a "backward" people. Roosevelt recognized the ineptness of the managers of the concession, and the questionable nature of their financial management. In the New York legislature he would have denounced their failure to provide a railroad for the people. But this time the people were colonials and our national interest and the prestige of a "civilized" nation were involved on the side of the company. America's national interest had to be "pushed" in China. The company's service to American "interest," and not the business practices of the company or its service or lack of service to the Chinese, was his primary concern.

In the struggle over the boycott, Roosevelt had a general

interest in solving the problem amicably and justly. To be sure, in the face of the realities of politics and labor relations, he had abandoned reluctantly his youthful idealistic opposition to exclusion of any Chinese. For many years he had been convinced of the need to exclude the Chinese in order to defend the "purity" of the American laboring classes. Still, this does not explain his lack of comprehension of the problem.

The trouble was that his solution was merely a palliative, and in the face of Chinese nationalism a palliative was not enough. The young Chinese nationalists were not interested in mere reform of the administration of exclusion laws. They challenged the entire premise upon which exclusion was based. Roosevelt politically could not and intellectually did not challenge that premise.

Roosevelt's failure to formulate a foreign policy that would have helped solve China's basic problems and that would have been in line with China's future rôle in world affairs resulted in part from the limitations of his own ideology and in part from the domestic political pressures under which he operated. His own values as a world statesman conflicted constantly with the self-interest of pressure groups at home. But, besides, the political pressure groups at home pushed and pulled him in opposite directions. West Coast prejudices and labor's demand for exclusion combined to prevent his alleviating Chinese grievances. Business in China for business reasons pushed hard for fairness and friendliness toward China. His action was in part the resultant of these two opposing American forces. Thus important foreign policy was affected by domestic politics, and Roosevelt's action was a compromise between what his statesmanship deemed desirable and what his political sense considered possible. When his limited reforms failed to ameliorate the antagonism that had developed, he became irritated at the affront to our prestige as a great power. Out of decency toward human beings he would try to win courteous treatment for " civilized " Chinese, but he could not brook defiance of our right as a powerful nation to do as we pleased, and China's weakness made her effectiveness in threatening our power the more galling. So he turned to the only alternative he understood—military force. Here, again, the action was premised on a long-standing conception of the Chinese " character." You could not deal with the Chinese, Roosevelt insisted, as you would with a civilized power. They had to be " led." To deal with them on equal terms was considered by them a sign of " weakness."

Roosevelt failed to comprehend the problem. China was undergoing significant developments in these years. The nationalist movement, both anti-foreign and anti-Manchu, was to overthrow the corrupt ruling caste in Roosevelt's own lifetime. Yet Roosevelt could not deal effectively with the young nationalist movement because his contempt for the weakness of China as a nation made him unable to realize that it was nationalism with which he had to cope. He worried lest, in case of overwhelming Japanese victory over Russia, the Chinese become " mere followers of Japan." Rockhill reassured him on this, but he missed the significance of Rockhill's reason for feeling certain this would not happen, namely, a new " national spirit in China " that would make her resist the preponderance of any one power and seek to control her own affairs.[323] Roosevelt's failure in China stemmed from his confusing this " new spirit " that was to shape much of twentieth-century history with the local uprisings that had characterized the Boxer groups earlier.

The alternative to supporting the new Chinese spirit was to prop up the old China regardless of its ineffectiveness and corrupt character as American governments have on occasion since then propped up in China corrupt governments repudiated by the Chinese people. Roosevelt, then, used the " big stick " formula to convince the Manchu bureaucracy that it had to maintain internal stability. His action was applauded by those that feared or did not understand what was transpiring in China. "If there is any trouble forboding," Gilbert Reid, president of the American Association of China, wrote, "the Central Government is not conniving, as in 1900, but is anxious to forestall it. . . . The only fear— and this is a reasonable one—is that the Government with its Manchu predominance will find itself too weak to hold in check or to safely direct the growing power of a popular and non-official independence." "Though ideas of popular sovereignty may at first glance stir our enthusiasms," spoke the nineteenth-century man in Reid, "we regard it as much safer for all governments to give support to the existing Chinese government . . ." [324] What the men whose advice Roosevelt followed did not comprehend was that the more they pressed the weak Manchu Government to try to do what it was impotent to do, the more evident they made its impotence and hence the nearer they brought the day of its overthrow by the very forces they feared.

Many, however, both Americans and Chinese, did understand the need for a more sympathetic approach to the new nationalism in China. "China is at a crisis," Wu Ting-fang, the former minister to the United States, warned the American people, "and is passing through a transition." [325] "The more the Chinese learn of Western science, Western methods, and all other things Western, the more discontented they become with conditions in China," Dr. T. W. Ayres, a missionary, explained in terms that were true by the 1950's of most Asians. The student classes, learning from Japan and the West, were seeking to strengthen Chinese society and replace the corrupt government with a more efficient, perhaps a republican system of rule. The anti-foreign movement, Ayres warned Americans, was "sweeping over the country like a tornado." It was basically, however, a means of removing the Manchu government. [326] "Chinese resentment against foreigners today is not the struggle of an expiring nation, wishing to die in peace, but of an awakening empire striving for larger recognition and more equal privileges among the nations of the earth," Methodist Bishop James W. Bashford explained. "Thus far the movement is a renaissance," he warned; "pray that it may not become a revolution." [327]

Roosevelt and his friends could not comprehend such a movement. Their minds were tuned to a set of values different from those implied in the rise of colonial nationalism. The boycott, Taft told an American audience in Shanghai in 1907, "has now become a closed incident, a past episode." [328] This was undoubtedly true, but, as the American consul in Canton warned, "Any broad and general deductions as to figures of imports and exports have nothing to do with the question of national feeling." [329] The block to Roosevelt's understanding was the inability he shared with many Americans of his day to associate qualities and aspirations of "superior" people with the Chinese. His persistence in regarding them, because of military weakness and industrial underdevelopment, as a "backward people" destroyed the effectiveness of his policy in the Far East, as it was one day to lead to failure there for his nation's policies. His habit of valuing an individual on his merits as a human being regardless of race or national culture enabled him to understand and share the indignation of educated Chinese over the treatment they received in America. But his contempt for a "backward" cultural group and his aristocratic view of labor combined to make it impossible for him to comprehend that Chinese laborers could also resent his attitude toward them or, more important, that Chinese intellectuals, through their newly aroused nationalist feeling, could resent his attitude toward a Chinese coolie.

The anti-American boycott in 1905 and 1906 was the first organized expression of modern Chinese nationalism. That it was directed against the United States was unfortunate but not accidental. The United States under Roosevelt's guidance seemed incapable of meeting the problem of a young and ebullient patriotism either to destroy it, or to become its friend. The remission of the Boxer Indemnity Fund, stimulated by the boycott agitation, was a mere gesture. The United States had no policy to meet the basic problem itself. Indeed, Roosevelt's policy repeatedly reiterated was to have outside powers in coöperation keep order in China and make the natives behave as he assumed the responsibility for doing in Latin America, and, in his mind, boycotting foreign nations, resenting their domination, or exhibiting nationalist aspirations was not behaving.

"The important question," the *San Francisco Chronicle* observed in early February, 1906, " is as to whether there has been aroused a real national spirit in China." " Whenever such a spirit exists, the people can do what they please in their own country, regardless of the rest of mankind." [330] This was precisely what Americans like Roosevelt feared. The boycott was an attempt to establish the right of Chinese to do what they pleased at home and abroad. The United States missed perhaps the greatest opportunity of its twentieth-century career when the premises of world power and imperialist ideology made it fail to become the friend and guide of the " new spirit " in China.

chapter **V**

ROOSEVELT *and the World Balance*

of Power: The Far East

In 1897 Theodore Roosevelt declared: "As our modern life goes on, ever accelerating in rapidity, and the nations are drawn closer together for good and for evil and this nation grows in comparison with friends and rivals, it is impossible to adhere to the policy of isolation. We cannot avoid responsibilities, and we must meet them in a noble or ignoble manner, by hiding our heads, hoping to escape them or shirk them, or by meeting them manfully, as our fathers did. We cannot avoid, as a nation, the fact that on the east and west we look across the waters at Europe and Asia." [1] Upon this concept of our relation to the world Roosevelt built his foreign policy as President. Thus decades ahead of most Americans he saw the interrelated world that events of the years after his death proved a reality. Forty years before Americans were willing to listen, he urged active participation in world decisions for which he felt we shared responsibility and whose consequences he felt we could not escape.

This theme recurred again and again in his speeches and in his writing. In 1899, for example, he told Chicagoans, "We cannot sit huddled within our borders and avow ourselves

merely an assemblage of well-to-do hucksters, who care nothing for what happens beyond." [2] Toward the end of his public career, as earlier, Roosevelt sought to arouse the American
people to assume their responsibilities in the world. " We are
as naturally insular," he wrote Henry White a year before he
left the Presidency, " as ever the English were in the old days
when compared with the rest of Europe. The same feeling
that made England believe that it did not have to take part
in any European concert . . . makes this country feel that it
can be a law for itself. . . . As yet our people do not fully
realize the modern interdependence in financial and business
relations." " There will be an awakening," he predicted, " but
it will be gradual."[3]

In the earlier nineties, as we have seen, Roosevelt had
been preoccupied with theories of the spread of civilization
through the expansion of control by " superior races " over
" backward " areas. Under the simpler approach of those
days, two principles had governed his judgment of acts on
the international scene. First, the spread of any more advanced people over a region occupied by a less advanced
population benefited mankind, though expansion of English-
speaking culture was the most desirable. Hence he had
sought increased power in the world for America. Second,
his own nation's interests must be defended wherever they
clashed with those of another state. He had welcomed rather
indiscriminately the expansion of Britain, France, Germany,
Italy, Russia, or Japan, except where the expansion of one
of them had clashed with American desire for territory or
markets or world prestige. Unfriendliness toward one of the
Western powers had usually grown in that earlier period out
of clashes like the ones with Britain over seal fishing in the
Pacific or trade in Chile or the contest with Germany for
control of the superb harbor of Pago Pago in Samoa.

Then between the middle nineties and his years as President Roosevelt's conception of relationships between world

powers matured. Little by little his picture of the world grew more complex. He began to differentiate the great powers qualitatively. It came to matter which power expanded. He discovered that great powers clashed with each other as well as with colonial peoples, and that sometimes the clashes between great powers were about the colonial peoples. He learned that the same power whose expansion in Hawaii or the Caribbean would threaten American interests might share common interests with America in the Orient. Great power relationships went another step in his conceptions and began to evolve into rival alliances of great powers. He commenced to realize that the struggle for supremacy in Eastern Asia was closely related, sometimes in a complicated and baffling fashion, to a struggle for dominance in Europe, and that both of these component struggles were parts of a world struggle that encompassed much besides either Europe or the Far East. In terms of this newly acquired world view, America's friendships among nations and the friendships and enmities of friends of America among nations took on significance. In short, Roosevelt came to comprehend the discouraging but basic fact that, if America was to become a world power among imperial rivals as he wished her to do, she must enter a game in which, through complicated moves and countermoves, each nation was trying to increase its own power but was determined that no other power or group of powers should attain sufficient strength to threaten it and its friends.

In formulating his ideas Roosevelt was greatly influenced by discussions with his friends, who were also interested in the intricacies of world power. He and they exchanged letters and several of them wrote articles and books, whose ideas they all then debated. In 1900, about the time Roosevelt was evolving his more mature picture of international rivalries, two of his close friends published books into which they gathered recent articles they had written. One such volume was Brooks Adams's *America's Economic Supremacy* and the other Alfred Mahan's *The Problem of Asia*.

Adams's book presented an analysis that closely resembled the one Roosevelt acted upon as President. A major premise was the importance to America of a world balance of power. Britain had been supreme for a century but was now " wearing down," Adams wrote. With her collapse the world " equilibrium " was disturbed. All the continental powers gained by the new imbalance, but Russia was the special beneficiary of instability. The conflict of the future was going to be between a declining England and a rising Russia.[4] America would have to enter the world conflict to redress the balance, for " the risk of isolation promises to be more serious than the risk of an alliance." " Economic exigencies seem likely to constrain Englishmen and Americans to combine for their own safety," Adams believed. " Should an Anglo-Saxon coalition be made, and succeed, it would alter profoundly the equilibrium of the world." [5] A triumph of Germany or Russia was a danger " both real and near." Adams thought that Germany with her advanced economy was the more immediate threat, but that from the long-range view Russia was the primary menace, because of her great land mass stretching into both Europe and the heart of Asia, and her policy of excluding everyone else from any area she controlled.[6]

A second tenet of Adams was the decisive importance of China in the world picture. " On the decision of the fate of China," he prophesied, " may, perhaps, hinge the economic supremacy of the next century." [7] Since England was a decaying empire, the main responsibility in China would fall to the United States. " America must more or less completely assume the place once held by England, for the United States could hardly contemplate with equanimity the successful organization of a hostile, industrial system on the shores of the Pacific, based on Chinese labour, nourished

by European capital, and supplied by the inexhaustible resources of the valley of the Ho-hang-ho." The Russians,
Adams admitted, " were ignorant, uninventive, indolent, and
improvident." Their Empire was bulky and unwieldy, and
could be " integrated " only by social revolution. Yet in
spite of her weaknesses, Russia's expansionist tendencies
made it likely that she would ultimately absorb North China.[8]

In this setting Adams sought world power for America for
its own sake. " If the President is ably advised and well
supported," he wrote his friend Lodge about their mutual
friend, who had just entered the White House, ". . . I see no
reason why the present administration should not go down
as the turning point in our history—As the moment when
we won the great prize." " I do deeply believe," he prognosticated hopefully, " that we may dominate the world, as
no nation has dominated it in recent times. . . . For the first
time in my life I feel that for us is the earth and the fulness
thereof." [9]

Mahan's book, too, presented a picture of world rivalries
dominated by fear of Russian expansion. Like Adams,
Mahan considered China the focal point of the struggle.
Mahan, however, pictured a " no man's land " open to
foreign imperial influences extending clear across Asia between the thirtieth and fortieth parallels of latitude and
including Persia, India, and the Yangtse Valley. The great
imperial battle of the twentieth century, Mahan predicted,
would be fought over this area and would be a struggle
between Britain to the South and Russia to the North.[10]
The contest was really one between sea power and land
power. Control of the seas, as Mahan had always maintained, meant control " of merchandise in transit, the incre-
ment from which constitutes the material prosperity of
nations." Hence Russia, the great land power, was pushing
south because of an irresistible search for " extensive maritime regions." [11] Russia, as Spring Rice was also always

telling Roosevelt, would attack through Persia and China. The struggle would come when Russia began attacking the already established sea powers. " Hence ensues solidarity of interest between Germany, Great Britain, Japan, and the United States, which bids fair to be more than momentary, because conditions seem relatively permanent." [12]

The world conflict in Asia Mahan defined as a " racial " one, between Teuton * and Slav. " The Teuton . . . possesses the sea, from which the Slav is almost debarred," he explained, but the Slav is superior in land power, particularly in Asia. [14] When faced with the threat of Russian expansion, the four sea powers, America, Britain, Germany, and Japan, " would be found following a common line of action." [15] Russia could not be shut off entirely from the sea and so Mahan would permit her Manchuria and the Maritime provinces but would stop her there and hold the Yangtse Valley for the sea powers. The navigable Yangtse, he contended, " is their necessary line of access into the land, and the nucleus essential to the local spread of their influence." [16] Repeating what Roosevelt had said some years earlier, Mahan explained that the Asiatic " races " would either remain impotent into an " indeterminate " future or would fall under external leadership. [17] Whoever " controlled " China would then determine her future. Influence established on the Yangtse, which flowed out from the heart of China, possessed " the advantages of the interior position, and of open and constant communication, through the river, with its base—the sea." Here Mahan favored an " open door " for competing commercial powers, but he had no conception of a free and independent China. [18] The Yangtse

* Unlike Adams, who distrusted her, Mahan included Japan among the stabilizing sea powers. Since Japan did not fit into his picture of racial affinities and distinctions, Mahan had to explain her alliance with the Anglo-Saxons on the basis of " expediency, resting upon the fact that, land and sea power being for the time in opposition, her place is with the latter." [13]

Valley, Mahan believed, " is the decisive field where commerce, the energizer of material civilization, can work to greatest advantage." Control of it by the sea powers, he argued, would keep China free from foreign domination, notably by the Russians, but keep her under the wing of " legitimate " foreign " influence." [19] Mahan did not make clear what he considered the difference between " domination " when exercised by the Russians, and " legitimate influence " imposed by the " sea powers."

During his Presidency views strikingly similar to those expounded in the Mahan and Adams volumes were expressed by Roosevelt. He had always been deeply influenced by Mahan, but his feelings about Adams had been mixed. When Roosevelt reviewed *The Law of Civilization and Decay* in 1897, he had been impressed with parts of the Adams analysis and had quarreled seriously with other parts, particularly its pessimism,[20] but had later written Spring Rice confiding that he would have criticized " much more brutally " except that he really thought Adams's " mind . . . a little unhinged " and, besides, he was " very fond of all the family." [21] Yet in some particulars Adams had influenced him for many years. In any case, *America's Economic Supremacy* stated in Adams's inimitable form theories that supported and justified practical analyses of world politics that Roosevelt himself had been working out and Roosevelt was impressed by it.* Both Mahan and Adams regarded Roosevelt, too, with the admiration that a writer of theories feels for the man of action, who carries them out. Probably the influence was complementary and not all onesided. In any case, the concepts on which Roosevelt based his plans for action in the Far East are strangely like what Adams and Mahan wrote.

Actually, Roosevelt's attitude toward the several great

* So, too, was Lodge.[22]

powers changed as the years progressed. Britain and China
have already been discussed. France, it may be said in passing, was less important in the Far East than the others
because usually less active in things that concerned Roosevelt than were the others. In Eastern Asia Roosevelt was
usually hostile to France, in Europe friendly. Part of his
friendliness in Europe stemmed from his personal friendship
with Ambassador Jusserand and part from France's growing closeness in Europe to Britain. America's contacts with
Russia were, on the other hand, more important in the Far
East than in Europe. From the mid-nineties to the Russo-
Japanese War, Roosevelt's judgment of Russia was practically reversed as her interests and ours clashed in Eastern
Asia.

Initially he had not felt hostile toward Russia. American
relations with her had been traditionally friendly. To Charles
A. Moore, president of the American Protective Tariff
League, Roosevelt wrote in 1898: "Russia, and Russia
alone, of European powers, has been uniformly friendly to
us in the past," though "I have no question that this friendliness came almost solely from self-interest." [23] In the nineties her interests and ours did not seem to conflict. Indeed,
Russia was serving the purposes of "civilization" by blocking the spread of "backward peoples" in Asia. "The Russians," Roosevelt observed in 1894, "are not democratic
at all, but the State is very powerful with them; and therefore they keep the Chinese out of their Siberian provinces." [24]
In 1896 and 1897 Roosevelt and his British friend Spring
Rice used to argue about Russia. Spring Rice felt that
Russia imperiled the British Empire in Persia, India, and
China. If the Russians could develop a North Chinese army,
he warned Roosevelt in July, 1896, they would be a "pretty
big power—such a power as the world has never seen. They
are quite conscious of it and mean to wait." [25] Roosevelt
admitted that if Russia "ever does take possession of North-

ern China and drill the Northern Chinese to serve as her Army, she will indeed be a formidable power." He refused, however, to be worried. " Even if in the dim future Russia should take India and become the preponderant power in Asia, England would merely be injured in one great dependency." [26] Australia, for instance, peopled by whites, Roosevelt deemed much more important than India.

In 1897 Spring Rice was again trying to persuade his friend. " The Russians," he wrote, " amuse me and frighten me. . . . They watch the fruits of civilization growing, intending when they are ripe, to come and take them. . . . They despise all of us, but none perhaps so much as the Americans, who have, they say, the faults of the old world without its *agréments*. . . . Do you believe that the Russians are the hope of an effete world? Anyhow, *they* do." [27] Roosevelt conceded that the Russians were a serious problem—" if not for our generation, at least to the generations which will succeed us." [a] But for the moment, he replied, " Russia and the United States are friendly." He refused to be afraid of them and the United States had something to teach them. " I look upon them," Roosevelt explained, " as a people to whom we can give points, and a beating; a people with a great future, as we have; but a people with poisons working in it, as other poisons, of a similar character on the whole, work in us." Then he confessed, " Sometimes I do feel inclined to believe that the Russian is the one man with enough barbarous blood in him to be the hope of a world that is growing effete. But I think that this thought comes only when I am unreasonably dispirited." " I still think," he added, " that though the people of the English-speaking races may have to divide the future with the Slav, yet they will get rather more than their fair share." [28] Through 1898 and 1899 he defended Russia as being an agent of civilization.[29]

[a] Roosevelt conceded that the two countries had " nothing whatever in common "; and the Russians did despise America as " effete."

Then about 1900 came a change: Russian interests were now challenging in the Far East Anglo-American interests that Roosevelt had by this time persuaded himself were the interests of "civilizaton." Hence Russian expansion, which had once seemed desirable, no longer meant extending control of a superior over a backward race, but had become an obstacle to the "push" of another civilizing power. Whether Roosevelt was dominated more by a concept of superiority of English-speaking to Russian culture or by national self-interest, Russia none the less had to be stopped. In 1901, too, he was worried because England seemed certain " in the long run to lose ground relatively to Russia in Asia." [30]

The shift of view came gradually. In August, 1900, Roosevelt was talking of " a check on Russia." [31] At this time he was wavering. As late as July, 1901, he again said, " I feel that an immense boon to humanity has been conferred by . . . Russia when she expanded over Turkestan, and for the matter of that, over Manchuria. It was a hard task but a task for the immeasurable benefit of civilization, and above all, for the benefit of the provinces taken." Yet now he qualified his enthusiasm for Russian expansion. " I should not regard it at all for the advantage of mankind," he wrote, " to have one civilized power expand at the cost of another. I am glad to see Russia expand in Asia. I am very sorry to see her expand over Finland. I should regret to see Germany take Switzerland or Holland or Denmark, but I should hail with delight Germany getting control of Asia Minor." [32] Yet he still felt that China, an uncivilized power, " would be benefited by Russia's advance." " I look at the matter from a rather visionary standpoint," he admitted, " and it may be that if I knew more of the trade needs between China or Asia generally and our Pacific slope, I might alter my views." [33]

By 1902 and 1903 Roosevelt's attitude toward Russia in

the Far East had undergone a complete reversal. Now he crossed swords with her over her failure to withdraw her troops from Manchuria as she had promised and to maintain an " open door " in that province. By February, 1904, just before the Russo-Japanese War began, the President was writing Spring Rice, " I have a strong liking and respect " for the Russians; " but unless they change in some marked way they contain the chance of menace to the higher life of the world." " Our people have become suspicious of Russia and I personally share this view." [34]

Roosevelt was remarkably well informed about Russia's internal problems, the weakness of her government, the distress of her people, the revolutionary forces at work there.[35] Spring Rice wrote Mrs. Roosevelt long, often indiscreet letters from the British Embassy in St. Petersburg; [36] and later his own ambassador, George Meyer, in European Russia and a young State Department official, Willard Straight, in Asiatic Russia kept the President informed.[37] Russia's internal affairs Roosevelt believed were crucial to her future power. " There is much about the Russians which I admire," he wrote a year before the revolution of 1905, " and I believe in the future of the Slavs if they can only take the right turn. But I do not believe in the future of any race *while it is under a crushing despotism....*" [a] [38]

More than once through the early part of his Presidency Roosevelt spoke of the possibility of war against Russia. " I think," he speculated in 1901, " that if no outside powers interfered Japan could at the moment give Russia a stiff fight in the far East, for I do not believe her line of communication across Siberia is as yet in sufficiently good order to enable her to use effectively her enormous mass." " Undoubtedly the future is hers," he conceded, " unless she mars it from within. But it is the future and not the present." [39] " Probably our

---

[a] " People who feel as we do," he told Spring Rice, " would be happier today living in Japan than living in Russia."

interests are not at the moment so great as to make it possible for us to be drawn into war with them," he wrote Spring Rice in February, 1904; " I shall certainly not fight unless we have ample reasons, and *unless I can show our people that we have such cause.*" But, he added, " Remote though the chance is, it does exist, if the Russians push us improperly and too evidently." [40] In July, 1904, he asked the Navy for a plan of action, " in case it became necessary for our Asiatic squadron to bottle up the Vladivostok Russian squadron." " I do not anticipate the slightest trouble," he explained, " but in view of Russia's attitude toward neutral vessels carrying what she is pleased to call contraband, I want to be prepared for emergencies." [41] " My own inclination is to notify them immediately that we will not stand [their seizing another ship] . . . and to move our Asiatic squadron northward," the President wrote his Secretary of State. " Of course I would put our statement in polite language, but very firmly, . . . and with the intention of having our squadron bottle up the Vladivostok fleet." [42]

In regard to Japan, Roosevelt's feelings shifted in just the opposite direction. Even in the nineties he had admired the Japanese, but they had seemed to threaten American expansion into Hawaii. When Japan sent a warship to Hawaii while our expansionists were trying to get McKinley to annex it, Roosevelt warned the President of the weakness of our fleet in comparison with the " efficient fighting navy " of Japan.[43] In April, 1897, he was so worried over Japan that he wanted to annex Hawaii at once. " I am fully alive to the danger from Japan," he wrote Mahan, " and I know that it is idle to rely on any sentimental good will toward us." [44] Japan, he felt, is " holding off in the Hawaiian matter to see if she won't have a chance to jump in and smash us." [45] When, with a justified feeling that John Sherman as Secretary of State had not spoken truthfully to her about our plans, Japan protested our signing the annexation treaty,

Roosevelt made it clear in a public speech that what we did in Hawaii was none of her business.[46] In June, 1897, he discussed what we would do in case of war with Japan. " The determining factor," he suggested, " would be the control of the sea, and not the presence of troops in Hawaii. . . . I think our objective should be the Japanese fleet." [47] In September he warned his superior, the Secretary of the Navy, that " Japan is steadily becoming a great naval power in the Pacific, where her fleet already surpasses ours in strength. . . . Our Pacific fleet should constantly be kept above that of Japan." [48]

Throughout his career Roosevelt was torn between an admiration for Japan's efficiency and fighting qualities and a fear of her strength if war should be provoked by hot-heads in her country or ours. In the years 1900 to 1905, however, his admiration greatly overpowered his fears and his policy was one of friendship. This was in part because, after Japan had accepted our acquisition of Hawaii, she was no longer a threat to our ambitions and partly because Roosevelt became convinced she was a powerful ally in support of our interests in the Far East. As his sense of the Russian menace increased, his feeling that Japan's blocking of Russia was important made him, for a time at least, as friendly to Japan as to Britain. He was now willing for Japan to dominate parts of the Far East because he believed Japan was serving American interests there.

During the Boxer uprising, Roosevelt had learned all he could about the comparative effectiveness of the troops of the several nations and had concluded that the French and Italians were the poorest and the Japanese perhaps the best both in discipline and in fighting qualities. " Our own troops out in China write grudgingly that they think the Japs did better than any of the allied forces," he told Spring Rice.[49] " What natural fighters they are," he exclaimed to his German friend, Speck von Sternburg.[50] But between 1898 and

1900 Roosevelt's tone about the Japanese military strength had changed from respect for the ability of an enemy to delighted admiration of a friend. " Japan . . . will be as formidable an industrial competitor as, for instance, Germany," he wrote admiringly in 1905. " In a dozen years . . . she will be the leading industrial nation of the Pacific." " She is as formidable from the industrial as from the military standpoint. She is a great civilized nation; though her civilization is in some important respects not like ours. There are some things she can teach us, and some things she can learn from us." [51]

Early in June, 1904, at Oyster Bay Roosevelt entertained for luncheon Japanese Ambassador Takahira and Baron Kaneko, an influential Japanese graduated from Harvard through whom the President later negotiated the calling of the Portsmouth Conference. Their conversation illumines the President's thought during this period. He told the Japanese that he believed they had a great future. But he warned them frankly of the chief danger they confronted: " Japan might get the ' big head ' and enter into a general career of insolence and aggression." Prophetically he cautioned them that if they followed this course " such a career would undoubtedly be temporarily very unpleasant to the rest of the world, but that it would in the end be still more unpleasant for Japan." " I added," he recorded afterward, " that though I felt there was a possibility of this happening, I did not think it probable." " I most earnestly hoped," he told them, " that Japan would simply take her place from now on among the great civilized nations." He then conceded to his Japanese guests that Japan had " a paramount interest in what surrounds the Yellow Sea, just as the United States has a paramount interest in what surrounds the Caribbean." He hoped the Japanese in exercising this paramount interest would show " no more desire for conquest of the weak than we had shown ourselves to have in the case of Cuba, and no more desire for a truculent attitude toward the strong than we had shown toward the English and French West Indies." His Japanese visitors agreed with him and promised him there was no " danger of Japan's becoming intoxicated with the victory, because . . . the upper and influential class would not let " this happen, and " would show . . . caution and decision." Takahira and Kaneko assured Roosevelt that " all talk of Japan's even thinking of the Philippines was nonsense," and Roosevelt conceded to them that he knew this was true.[52]

He told them he " hoped to see China kept together, and would gladly welcome any part played by Japan which would tend to bring China forward along the road which Japan [had] trod." " Unless everybody was mistaken in the Chinese character," he predicted for his Japanese guests, " they would have their hands full." They grinned and said they " were quite aware of the difficulty they were going to have even in Korea and were satisfied with that job." The President and his guests talked, too, about the future of Manchuria. The Japanese made it clear that they hoped to drive the Russians entirely out of that province. They would like to turn it back to China if they thought China could control it. They and Roosevelt agreed that the ideal solution would be to maintain the autonomy of Manchuria under a guarantee of the great powers.[53]

The Japanese used the occasion to protest with much feeling against " the talk about the Yellow Terror " and the habit of classing people possessed of an old civilization like theirs as " barbarians." They pointed out that in the thirteenth century they were a civilized nation dreading the Yellow Terror of the Mongolians just as Europeans did. Roosevelt soothed their pride by explaining that some of his ancestors had been in the tenth century part of a " White Terror " of the Northmen that " represented everything hideous and abhorrent and unspeakably dreadful to the

people of Ireland, England, and France." Just as Americans
"had outgrown the position of being part of a White Terror,"
he told them, he thought "such a civilization as they had
developed entitled them to laugh at the accusation of being
part of the Yellow Terror." [54]

When on February 8, 1904, the Japanese employed a tactic
that closely resembled a similar attack at Pearl Harbor in
1941, and began the Russo-Japanese War with an unan-
nounced assault upon the Russian Navy while negotiations
were going on, Roosevelt and his friends did not call the
attack "a stab in the back." They were, on the contrary,
jubilant in admiration of a friend who was serving our purposes in the Orient.[a] In the spirit that characterized both
of them, Elihu Root, by then one of the President's most
trusted advisers, wrote from New York, "Was not the way
the Japs began the fight bully? Some people in the United
States might well learn the lesson that mere bigness does
not take the place of perfect preparation and readiness for
instant action." [56] "What nonsense it is to speak of the
Chinese and the Japanese as of the same race!" Roosevelt
exploded to Hay in admiration of the victorious Japanese.
"They are of the same race only in the sense that a Levan-
tine Greek is of the same race with Lord Milner." [b][57] Hay
recorded in his diary on June 27 that "the President talked
with great unreserve" to German Ambassador Sternburg
"about the Russian Army and Navy and the comparative
attainments of the Japanese." [58] "My feeling is . . . about
the Japanese Nation that they are a wonderful and civilized
people," Roosevelt declared in 1905, "who . . . are entitled to
stand on an absolute equality with all the other peoples of
the civilized world. In art, in many forms of science, in mili-

---

[a] In this they voiced an overwhelming sentiment of Americans.[55]

[b] Lord Milner had consolidated British interests into the Union of South
Africa after the Boer War and had thus won Roosevelt's admiration as an
empire builder.

tary matters and industrial matters they have a position which entitles them to the hearty respect of every other nation." "There are bad Japanese, of course, just as there are bad Americans," he explained, but, he added, "I should hang my head in shame if I were capable of discriminating against a Japanese general or admiral, statesman, philanthropist or artist, because he and I have different shades of skin." [59] "The Japs interest me and I like them." [60] "The Japanese I am inclined to welcome as a valuable factor in the civilization of the future," he wrote the historian, George Otto Trevelyan. "But it is not to be expected that they should be free from prejudice against and distrust of the white race." [61]

During the Russo-Japanese War Roosevelt weighed frequently the relative dangers of a victorious Japan and a victorious Russia. He recognized the danger in either one. In 1903, Leigh Hunt, who had large concessions in Korea, talked over the Far Eastern situation as a guest at the White House,* and gave Roosevelt detailed arguments as to why Japan would win a war against Russia. "Russia is an old-fashioned engine, clumsy, weighty, and hard to manage," Hunt insisted, "while Japan is a modern, compact, and up-to-date machine." "Whatever may be said of Japan's commercial integrity, it must be admitted," Hunt argued, "that in government expenditures she is honest, while Russia is hopelessly dishonest." Besides, "the Japanese are the most dashing fighters in the world." Roosevelt considered Hunt right. [62]

Yet, while he did not become pro-Russian, Roosevelt saw danger in too powerful a Japan. "If the Japanese win out, not only the Slav, but all of us will have to reckon with a great new force in eastern Asia," he wrote Spring Rice soon after the outbreak of war. No one, he said, wants Japan

* Roosevelt invited Hunt to the White House again in May, 1904, and in June, 1905.

firmly established in China. "The victory will make Japan by itself a formidable power in the Orient because all the other powers having interests there will have divided interests, divided cares, double burdens, whereas Japan will have but one care, one interest, one burden." "If, moreover," he added, "Japan seriously starts in to reorganize China and makes any headway, there will result a real shifting of the center of equilibrium as far as the white races are concerned."

He reassured himself, however, with the hope that Japan would lead both herself and China into the circle of "great civilized powers." [63] From Britain came further reassurance. When Spring Rice came in January, 1905, to confer with Roosevelt, he brought verbal advice from Prime Minister Arthur Balfour himself not to worry about the Japanese. "I am completely skeptical about the 'Yellow Peril,'" Balfour told Spring Rice as he departed for America. "The idea of Japan heading an Eastern crusade on Western civilization seems to me altogether chimerical. . . . Even if . . . any Japanese statesman, present or future, could meditate so wild a project, . . . Japan is never likely to have a Navy sufficient to meet the fleets of the Christian world, who could therefore always cut her off from free communication with the mainland of Asia." [64]

Still, Roosevelt's hope was that neither power would become predominant. He did not wish Japan too strong. "I am perfectly aware," he wrote again in June, that if the Japanese "win out it may possibly mean a struggle between them and us in the future; but I hope not and believe not." [65] On the other hand, "to judge from the Russians' attitude at present," he wrote Hay, "if they were victorious they would be so intolerable as to force us to take action." [66] "If Russia wins she will organize northern China against us. . . . Therefore, on the score of mere national self-interest, we would not be justified in balancing the certainty of immediate damage against the possibility of future damage." [67] Besides, Roosevelt believed, " Whether Russia wins or Japan wins the victor will in the long run only yield either to England or to the United States substantially the respect which England or the United States is enabled to exact by power actual or potential." [68] At one time he even speculated hopefully, " It may be that the two powers will fight until both are fairly well exhausted, and that then peace will come on terms which will not mean the creation of either a yellow peril or a Slav peril." [69]

Fifteen months before the Portsmouth Conference Roosevelt talked at length with Speck von Sternburg about his aims for Eastern Asia and sought through Speck to commit the Kaiser. On May 9, 1904, he outlined to Speck his ideas of suitable terms of peace. The strength of the two powers should be kept as nearly equal as possible. A serious weakening of Russia in the Far East he did not wish. Contested geographic areas must be left as they were before the fighting. Japan could have Korea but must guarantee protection for American concessions there. Japan must not be permitted to establish herself in China. America would recognize Russian predominance in Manchuria, but Russia must give up Port Arthur as a fortified base and must permit freedom of trade in Manchuria. In August, through Speck, he renewed his proposals to the Kaiser. This time, in place of Russian control, he envisaged rule of Manchuria by a Chinese Viceroy appointed by Germany (not England) under a neutrality guaranteed by the Great Powers jointly. " The Japs," Roosevelt argued with Speck, " were not threatening any legitimate German interest in Shantung." If the Japanese succeeded this time " there must not be another coalition of powers to deprive them of the results." Roosevelt suggested to the Kaiser that the danger of violation of Chinese neutrality would become acute only in case Russia suffered a severe defeat. Japan, the President felt, would not break her

word about Chinese neutrality and thus provoke a coalition
against her. Roosevelt asked Speck whether Germany would
agree to the terms he outlined and Speck thought she would.
Von Bülow took the matter up directly with the Kaiser and
both he and the Foreign Office reported that " Mr. Roosevelt is sincere and that no hostile intention to us underlies
his proposal." Hence Roosevelt should be supported by
Germany.[70] Again in December, 1904, the President had a
" serious and necessary " talk with Speck. He tried to impress upon Speck that " it was equally to the advantage of
Germany and America that Japan should succeed, but not
too overwhelmingly—that Manchuria should be restored to
the Chinese, with the open door—but that there should [be]
sufficient strength left on both sides to guarantee fair treatment to other nations." [71]

His concern to preserve the balance of power in Asia combined with his feeling that a war between " civilized " nations
was detrimental to civilization itself to make Roosevelt seek
to maintain peace between Japan and Russia. Indeed,
months before war broke out, he and Secretary Hay had
foreseen the impending conflict. As early as September 3,
1903, Hay had written Roosevelt of talking with Japanese
Ambassador Takahira and finding him disturbed over " Russian aggression in Korea." Takahira had felt Japan might
have to act. " I thought proper not to leave him with any
illusions," Secretary Hay had reported to the President,
" and so told him plainly that we could not take part in
any use of force in that region, unless our own interests were
directly involved." " And it was a hard thing to say," Hay
had added. " I believe those little people will fight," * he
told Roosevelt, " if they are crowded too far." [73]

Roosevelt hoped war might be averted. On January 4,
1904, at his request, Hay, who was pro-Japanese, talked to

* Ambassador Meyer in Rome believed they would, too.[72]

French Ambassador Jusserand, who sympathized with Russia. Roosevelt " earnestly . . . desired . . . some honorable peaceful solution," and Jusserand was persuaded to cable his government about the possibility of mediation. The President desired peace " in the interest of both parties and of the civilized world," Jusserand was to tell his Government. The next evening the President and Secretary of War Root stopped at Hay's house to discuss the matter further. But neither Russia nor Japan would listen.[74] Roosevelt finally decided early in February that " to try to secure what we know to be impossible at this time would merely do damage " ; and Hay agreed.[75]

In Washington and the several capitals of Europe efforts were made to commit both Russia and Japan to guaranteeing the neutrality of China including Manchuria if war should come.* In January, 1904, Britain, for instance, was pressing Russia for guarantees about Manchuria in case Russia annexed it, and Germany was urging Roosevelt to take a stand against division of China with approval of a coalition of powers.[77] On January 11 Hay got from both the Japanese and the Russian ambassadors private assurances that their governments would respect Chinese neutrality.[78] In February the Kaiser proposed that Roosevelt take the initiative in persuading the powers jointly to demand that China's neutrality be maintained. Roosevelt first suggested that the Secretary include in the note insistence on " the integrity of China," and then, on February 8, he approved Hay's draft of a note on Chinese neutrality.[79] This was the very day Japan attacked and destroyed the Russian fleet, and on February 10 Roosevelt issued the circular demanding that the powers respect the integrity and neutrality of China.[80]

---

* Japan is inviting us " to take a position that might lead to embarrassments in the future," Assistant Secretary of State Loomis warned in December, 1903. " I do not see," Loomis protested, " that we are called upon to admit that the fate of Manchuria is to be determined solely by Japan and Russia." [76]

Hay had deliberately used language that was somewhat vague and now with varying enthusiasm and limitations the powers accepted. Japan concurred on condition that Russia should also agree. Russia consented with some reservation, and suggested further consultation of the powers, which Roosevelt and Hay forestalled " by accepting at once and finally the answer of Russia as responsive to our note." [81] Throughout the remainder of the War Roosevelt and Hay watched jealously and protested all violations or threats of violation of Chinese territory by anyone.[82]

The Kaiser warned that France was planning to mediate in order to get Chinese territory for herself, and Roosevelt was fearful that peace brought about by a concert of powers might eventuate in the partition of China among them. Hence the President had Hay send on January 13, 1905, a circular letter to American representatives abroad cautioning against schemes of neutral powers to use the peace negotiations to gain parts of China for themselves. The powers were asked to agree once more to a " self denying " declaration concerning China, and Hay and Roosevelt exerted pressure behind the scenes to win acceptance.[83]

While he feared intervention by the neutral powers, Roosevelt had never lost sight of the possibility that Japan and Russia might form a Russo-Japanese alliance to divide northern China and Manchuria and exclude all other powers. On December 27 he wrote Spring Rice, " It is always possible that Japan and Russia may come to terms of agreement, as . . . Count Ito . . . wished them to do." [84] In March from St. Petersburg Spring Rice wrote of a plan for such an alliance to divide Northern China between them and mutually guarantee each other's spheres of influence. The alternative for Japan was an alliance with England to protect the status quo, the open door, and the integrity of China. America would not join such an alliance and the Japanese feared there was some question whether Britain would. Hence a

Russo-Japanese alliance might appeal to Japan.[85] Yet Roosevelt wrote Meyer in February, 1905: " I do not believe that Japan has the slightest intention of making an alliance with Russia." * [86]

The President realized that European powers were using the Far Eastern situation to jockey for advantage in the uneasy European balance of power. In Eastern Asia European powers had conflicting interests. Britain's concerns differed, for example, from those of her European ally France, for in Asia Britain was an ally of Japan then at war with France's European ally, Russia. Britain contended she could not offer mediation unless Japan wished it. She felt both Japan and Russia would resent even moral suasion about terms of peace. So Britain persistently refused to offer mediation.[87] France's sympathies were with Russia and Jusserand pleaded Russia's cause in Washington. Indeed, France was heavily involved in Russian success through loans and investments. Yet French financiers were not certain enough of Russian success to be eager to finance the war; as Russian defeats made Russian weakness clear, France became increasingly concerned to have Russia make peace without further disaster.[88] Germany was torn between a desire to preserve a balance of power and the open door in the Far East and her concern to woo Russia in Europe away from France and Britain. In Europe the Kaiser was torn between a fear of Russia that made him wish Russia weakened and sympathy for a fellow-autocrat, especially one he believed he could dominate and use. In the fall of 1904, indeed, von Bülow and the Kaiser were secretly drawing up a treaty of alliance between Czar and Kaiser that would wean Russia from France. Whether Russia defeated the Japanese or exhausted her own resources to become less of a threat in

---

* Only " if the Russians beat her," he insisted, " and . . . America and England separately or together will give her no help, she may conclude that she has to make what terms she could with Russia."

Europe, Germany would gain. At first, then, the Kaiser seems to have encouraged the Czar to continue the war. By 1905 the Czar had rejected the alliance with the Kaiser, but now Nicholas was being threatened by democratic revolution that alarmed the Kaiser, and that could be put down only by stopping the war. After the defeat of Russia's second fleet in May, the Kaiser became eager for peace. Besides, Germany feared France and Britain might engineer joint action by several powers to make a settlement disadvantageous to Germany.[89] Hence Germany turned to Roosevelt.

Roosevelt's eagerness to end the war made him ready from the first to act as mediator. He or Hay talked at length and repeatedly to Ambassadors Liang, Takahira, Cassini, Sternburg, and Jusserand. The rivalries of European powers complicated the problem of mediation, and Roosevelt and Hay continually studied these rivalries as the key to peace in the Far East.[90] Late in May, 1904, neither side would accept anybody's intervention.[91] Roosevelt and Hay persisted, however, and throughout 1904 used every opportunity to press their good offices.[92] Yet " Cassini throws a pink fit," Hay reported in November, " at any reference to peace." His government persistently declined to consider ending the war.[93] Japan, too, opposed mediation, because it " would enure to the advantage of Russia, through fruitless delays." [94]

During the early months of 1905 Roosevelt continued his efforts.[95] Rumors were circulating that various European powers or combinations of powers were about to mediate.[96] One story reported Japan weary of the war and Britain and France ready to back collective mediation, but Germany determined to support Russia in opposing it.[*][97] The President became more and more convinced that direct negotiation between the two belligerents would bring a peace better for the world than would a congress of rival powers each

* Actually von Bülow believed at this time that Germany did not need to take a position at all.

distrustful of the other and each seeking its own advantage. On March 29 Roosevelt asked Lodge to write urging Prime Minister Balfour to oppose an " international congress." The King and Lansdowne had said they " would go with us in all these matters," but the President thought it wise for Lodge to write them holding them to the American position.[98] On March 30, 1905, Roosevelt told Hay jestingly, " The Kaiser has had another fit and is now convinced that France is trying to engineer a congress of the nations, in which Germany will be left out. What a jumpy creature he is, anyhow! " Yet Roosevelt added firmly, " I am against having a Congress * to settle the peace terms." [101] This opposition of Roosevelt to peace through a congress of powers arose not from a desire to protect German interests, nor entirely from concern about China's integrity nor American business interests, but partly from concern about Japan whose friendship Roosevelt considered important to American strategy. As early as May, 1904, he told Hay, " We could hardly afford to allow a combination of R. G. & F. to step in and deprive Japan of the results of this war." [102]

So Roosevelt actively pressed the warring powers themselves to stop fighting and negotiate.[103] Rumors frequently circulated that the President was going to intervene,[104] and he received frequent suggestions that he ought.[105] Whatever he did, he was determined not to take any public stand until he was in private persuaded that both powers would respond favorably.[106]

Even before the war, in January, 1904, he began setting up machinery through which he might bring the belligerents together. For this he drew on his excellent personal connections.[107] He used Speck von Sternburg to get the Kaiser

---

* Germany vigorously opposed such a congress because she felt France and England would dominate it. Japan distrusted a congress of powers but also distrusted Germany.[99] England gave assurance that she, too, was opposed to group intervention.[100]

to put pressure on his cousin the Czar. His own ambassador, Charlemagne Tower in Berlin, he ignored.[108] Jusserand, too, employed the French Foreign Office when Roosevelt needed it to bring pressure upon France's ally, Russia.[109] With Japanese Ambassador Kotoro Takahira and Baron Kentaro Kaneko the President worked harmoniously. Takahira he had come to trust. Baron Kaneko, a private citizen of Japan who advised his Government on financial matters, had been at Harvard with Roosevelt and between them a friendship had developed through the years. Leaving his own ambassador in Tokyo, Lloyd Griscom, as uninformed as the Russians left Cassini, the President conducted his own business with the Japanese in Washington.[110] He worked with the British through his personal friend Cecil Spring Rice, and it was in January when he was first seriously planning mediation that he had Spring Rice come over confidentially from St. Petersburg to lay plans for coöperation with Britain and for putting pressure on Russia. Yet Spring Rice was suspicious of both Russia and Germany and kept sounding warnings, and after all when he was in St. Petersburg he gave more aid in dealing with Russia than in influencing Britain.[111] Roosevelt also used Lodge, who was in Europe during the crucial summer, as a confidential agent with the British.[112] From the British, however, he received little help. Japan confided little in them and at one stage asked Roosevelt to sound out her allies the British for her. Britain in turn was less willing to help influence her ally, Japan, than France and Germany were to help with the Czar; and Lansdowne, as Foreign Secretary, was critical of Roosevelt's whole mediation venture.[113]

Communicating with Russia posed Roosevelt's most difficult problem. Count Cassini, the Russian ambassador, Roosevelt considered untruthful and tricky. He was in addition afraid to transmit unpleasant communications to his Government. When early in June Roosevelt tried to communicate with the Czar through him, he gave highly secret information to the press so that the President had to rebuke him. Besides, he was often left uninformed as to what his own Government was doing, so that Roosevelt frequently heard what was happening in St. Petersburg before Cassini did. On more than one occasion Cassini in Washington denied the truth of what Meyer had cabled that Foreign Secretary Lamsdorff or the Czar had said in St. Petersburg. In such cases Roosevelt had to cable to St. Petersburg for confirmation to convince Russia's own ambassador.[114]

Hence Roosevelt in the end had to deal with Russia through St. Petersburg. To this end he moved Robert S. McCormick, whom he considered politically important but incompetent, from St. Petersburg to Paris, in order to send to Russia George von Lengerke Meyer, through whom he could conduct delicate confidential negotiations.[115] To Meyer he sent a personal letter of instruction that Hay found " of singular directness and indiscretion." " Few Ambassadors have ever gone to their posts," Hay remarked, " with a letter so full of the mind of their ruler." [116] Besides, Roosevelt arranged for Meyer and Spring Rice, both in his confidence, to collaborate.[117] Spring Rice reported to Roosevelt: " Meyer is come and is very much liked. He seems to have a very level head and will not be got at by the Grand Dukes." [118] Then, too, the Czar, with whom Meyer was to negotiate found Meyer " charming." Nicholas reported him " a fascinating talker and personality " with whom one could arrive at an " understanding." [119] On the way to Russia Meyer had stopped in Paris to talk with Foreign Minister Delcassé, and in Berlin to confer with von Bülow and the Kaiser.[*][120]

In the negotiations with Russia the Kaiser and the German Minister in Washington both assisted Roosevelt. From the first Speck von Sternburg helped keep Roosevelt in-

---

[*] The Kaiser, too, liked Meyer, and facilitated Meyer's work.

formed of European happenings and rumors. In January he warned that France wanted to get part of China.[121] In February he reported that the British Ambassador in St. Petersburg had argued with Foreign Minister Lamsdorff that making peace would benefit Russia. Lamsdorff agreed, said Speck, and so too did Russian Ambassador Benckendorff in London. But Speck added that his own Government felt these peace views had been expressed without the Czar's knowledge.[122] In March he informed the President that the German Ambassador in Russia found " in highest quarters . . . no inclination to make peace," and had sent word that " the whole army in the field demands the continuation of the war." [123] In Washington Sternburg labored with Cassini to make him see the futility of Russia's continuing the war.[124] Yet at the beginning of April the Kaiser told Roosevelt neither side would make peace. Russia would consider an indemnity a deep national humiliation, a ' caudinic joke.' " [125] Then after the second Russian naval disaster and the rise of revolt at home, the Kaiser became desperate to save the Czar from his folly by persuading him to end the war.[126] Again Speck von Sternburg put pressure on Cassini, who now admitted that Russia's cause was hopeless. Speck persuaded him to talk with Roosevelt.[127] Throughout the June crisis the German Ambassador continued this remarkable and close coöperation with Roosevelt.[128] On June 3 William himself sent word that he was " ready to silently support any efforts " the President might make " in the interest of peace." [129] When the peace conference was agreed upon Roosevelt instructed Speck with a chuckle: " If you see His Majesty tell him (but only for his own ear) that in Meyer's last audience with the Czar the latter commented upon the fact that whenever Meyer made a visit to him, simultaneously there came a cable from the German Emperor. . . . I think this may amuse the Emperor." [130]

In spite of the help of France and Germany, Roosevelt

and Hay found Russia most difficult. " Neither the Czar nor the Russian Government nor the Russian people are willing to face the facts as they are," the President wrote Lodge. " They are hopeless creatures with whom to deal. They are utterly insincere and treacherous; they have no conception of the truth, . . . and no regard for others, . . . no knowledge of their own strength or weakness." [131] " Every time the Russians get a kick from the Japanese," wrote an exasperated John Hay, " they turn and swear at us." [132] " Did you ever know anything more pitiable than the condition of the Russian despotism in this year of grace? " the President asked Hay in April, 1905. " The Czar is a preposterous little creature as the absolute autocrat of 150,000,000 people. He has been unable to make war, and he is now unable to make peace." [133]

Roosevelt early pleaded with Russia to make peace. Both through Cassini in Washington and through Delcassé in France he told the Russian Government immediately after their loss of Port Arthur that they ought to stop. Then after the defeat at Mukden on March 10 he warned her that if she did not make peace before further Japanese successes the terms would " certainly be worse for her." [134] At the end of March he again urged upon Cassini that " it was eminently to Russia's interest to make peace," that " each delay if the delay meant another Japanese victory, would mean an increase in the onerousness of the terms." [135] " I am entirely sincere," he insisted, " when I tell them that I act as I do because I think it in the interest of Russia." [136] To the end Cassini in Washington denied that Russia would consider terms of peace short of complete Russian victory.[137]

The question was: could either side without losing face initiate peace discussions? As early as February it was rumored that Japan would talk peace whenever she had assurance that Russia would, and even out of Russia came an occasional peace rumor.[138] In February, too, Durand told

Hay that Foreign Minister Komura had assured the British Ambassador in Tokyo that a peace feeler from Russia would "meet with a frank and cordial response." [139] In the end Baron Komura approached Roosevelt through Ambassador Takahira and the President's old friend, Kentaro Kaneko. As early as March these men began conferring in secret directly with the President. A confidential cable of March 14 from Baron Komura handed over to Hay referred to these secret talks and gave assurance that the matter would be kept confidential. "Absolute secrecy best can be maintained," said Komura, "by using for the future the same direct means of communication as has been so successfully employed in the past." [140]

Japan from the first made clear what she was fighting for. Above all she wanted a guarantee she could depend upon in regard to her rights in Manchuria. She did not care whether it was a bilateral agreement with Russia or a guarantee by all the powers. But protection she was determined to have.[141] Three days after the war began the Japanese assured Hay that "they did not intend to make any selfish use of their victory, if Providence continued to favor them." Takahira "with his strange smile" told Hay, "there need be no fear of the Yellow Peril," and Hay replied that he had "never lost sleep over it." [142] To Roosevelt and Hay, however, the Japanese did express fears about the attitude of European powers toward further Japanese successes and toward the peace settlement.[143] Before the battle of Mukden the Japanese had talked over their war aims with Roosevelt, and he had agreed that they were reasonable. At that time they were satisfied to control Korea, to succeed to Russia's rights at Port Arthur, and to have the rest of Manchuria restored to China. When, however, they came to him after victory in that battle and insisted they must add an indemnity to their earlier demands, the President "refused to commit himself on that." Roosevelt and Hay continually counseled moderation.

Roosevelt strongly urged the Japanese to make peace on the terms they had considered before Mukden. A few extra months of war, he told them, would eat up any indemnity they could win.[144]

The Japanese, however, stood firm and added new demands. They " are evidently quite anxious for peace," Taft summed up their position, " but they are also determined in their desire for peace not to lose the fruits of a successful war, and in this they are entirely right." Roosevelt thought them right in seeking security. He considered their demands for indemnity and new territory, in view of their successes, not unreasonable but extremely unwise.[145]

Encouraged by his talks with the Japanese, the President turned again to Russia. On April 12 he sent Meyer to make a personal appeal on his behalf to the Czar. Meyer proffered the President's good offices, but had to talk in the presence of the Czarina, who wished to continue the war and was believed to have attended the conference deliberately to prevent the Czar's yielding. In any case, the Czar made no comment but changed the subject after hearing the President's plea.[146] Even with naval disasters at sea and incompetence and bankruptcy at home and revolution threatening, the Czar would not yield.[147] Hence " the folly of the Russians, who refused to face facts," blocked Roosevelt's April efforts.[148]

On April 3 Roosevelt went to hunt bear in Colorado and left Taft authorized to act for him. During his absence, the Japanese continued their secret talks with Taft, who kept in close touch with Roosevelt.[149] Both the Japanese and Kaiser William now cabled Roosevelt on April 5 of a French effort to mediate by getting the Japanese to agree in advance to moderate terms. The Japanese refused to negotiate other than directly with Russia. From the Colorado wilds the President wired backing them in this stand.[150] Then on April 25 Taft sent the President a cable from Foreign

Minister Komura saying Japan " would be highly gratified "
if the President " has any views of which he is willing or feels
at liberty to give them benefit in regard to the steps to be
taken . . . by Japan to pave the way for . . . [direct] negotiation." [151] This telegram seemed so important that Roosevelt wired he would come home a week early from his bear
hunting to handle negotiations himself.*

At this point Takahira broke out of his rôle as formal
representative of his Government and pleaded with Roosevelt as friend to friend to use his influence with Japan. His
Government really wanted to end the war before a second
naval battle so that Russia could get out with honor, he
confided, but there was a war party that wanted to continue
the war to get indemnity and territory. Takahira felt that
in driving Russia from Manchuria and getting the Manchurian railroad and Port Arthur Japan had gained all she
originally wanted. Insisting upon indemnity, Takahira
feared, would prolong the war, weaken Japan, and perhaps
consume all the indemnity as well. Roosevelt had great influence in Japan. If he would only express his views on the
wisdom of " peace without indemnity or territory," pleaded
Takahira, " he would greatly strengthen the peace party." [153]
Pending his arrival in Washington the President instructed
Taft to sound out the Japanese about Taft's seeing Cassini
to tell him Roosevelt believed he and Takahira should have
" an absolutely frank talk . . . without any intermediary at
all." " There should be no reservations on either side. . . .
I cannot help feeling that they can make an honorable
peace," the President wired.[154] The Japanese, however, felt
talking with Cassini was futile. Instead they promised to
propose a Japanese counter-plan.[155]

Until May, then, Roosevelt's efforts had proved unavail-

---

* " Poor Theodore," Hay wrote Henry Adams; " fancy him breaking camp a
week too soon and careering back to Washington with mild Dutch reformed
profanity and the gnashing of white teeth." [152]

ing. "Takahira and . . . the . . . Foreign Office agreed with my position," Roosevelt confided to Lodge, " but the war party, including the army and the navy, insisted upon an indemnity and cession of territory, and rather than accept such terms the Russians preferred to have another try with Rojestvensky's fleet." [156] In any case, said Roosevelt, " I cannot trust the word of those at the head [of the Russian Government] . . . and . . . it was impossible to get a straightforward answer at all, and so there is nothing to do but let them work out their own fates " or at least await the result of the impending naval battle.[157]

On May 27 and 28 the Japanese encountered and destroyed the Russian fleet and Roosevelt immediately renewed his efforts to end the war.[158] The Japanese this time were also eager for peace.* On May 31 Foreign Minister Komura cabled to get Roosevelt, " in view [of] the changed situation resulting from the recent naval battle . . . , directly and entirely of his own motion and initiative to invite the two belligerents to come together for the purpose of direct negotiation." " The Japanese Government will leave it to him to determine the course of procedure," Komura promised, but " the Japanese Government have no intention by the present communication to approach Russia either directly or indirectly on the subject of peace."[160] The President urged a peace conference upon Cassini, but the Russian " answered by his usual rigmarole . . . that Russia was fighting the battles of the white race, . . . that Russia was too great to admit defeat." This time Roosevelt talked " pretty emphatically " to him and made him promise to transmit Roosevelt's views to his Government.[161] On June 6, however, Cassini turned up with an instruction from his Foreign

---

* The Kaiser had long suspected Japan of trying to get someone, a concert of powers, the Anglo-French entente, even the Chinese, to " mediate in favour of Japan for peace "—because, he told the Czar, " Japan is nearing the limits of its strength in men and money." [159]

Office that Russia wanted neither peace nor mediation, but that Russia would be pleased if Roosevelt would urge moderation upon Japan and would ascertain what Japan's terms were. Until Japan's terms were made known, Russia would not negotiate and she would never consent to conditions injurious to Russia.[162] Roosevelt insisted he had already urged moderation, but he refused to approach Japan about terms. Instead he let Cal O'Laughlin, a newspaper correspondent whom Cassini used to communicate with the President, tell Cassini why he could not.[163]

Now the negotiations shifted back to St. Petersburg. Meyer reported the popular outcry against defeat so strong that even the bureaucracy was shaken.[164] On June 5 Roosevelt cabled Meyer secret instructions * to see the Czar at once to tell him that outsiders " including all of Russia's most ardent friends " consider " the present contest . . . absolutely hopeless," and to convey Roosevelt's personal advice that Russia consent to direct negotiations with Japan. " I will try to get Japan's consent," Roosevelt promised, " acting simply on my own initiative, and not saying that Russia has consented . . . ; all the proceedings so far to be strictly secret. Then I will openly ask each power to agree to the meeting." [165] The Kaiser, alarmed over the revolutionary threat to his cousin's throne, fearful that revolution might spread, and persuaded by Speck and Roosevelt, wrote on June 3 a letter that arrived just before Meyer's interview urging Nicholas to accede to Roosevelt's request. And the German Ambassador sought out the Czar to give similar advice and to point out that America had greater influence in Japan than any European power. William cabled Roosevelt confident that the Czar would now yield.[166] On June 7 Meyer presented the President's message in an hour's private audience, which he obtained promptly on the Czarina's birth-

* He sent a copy, however, to Speck, Jusserand, and the British chargé.

day only by making the request a personal appeal from the President. Meyer pointed out the hopelessness of winning, the unpopularity of the war with the Russian people, and the threat of revolution at home. He recognized how hard " it was in adversity to make a decision contrary to one's pride and ambition." Yet, if he accepted Roosevelt's plan, Meyer pleaded, Nicholas " would have the consolation . . . of saving possibly hundreds of thousands of lives and doing . . . what was best for his people . . . , and at the same time winning the respect of the world." The Czar finally agreed, provided Japan's consent was obtained before the Czar's was made public * and provided the conference should meet without intermediaries.[168]

At last public action could be taken. On June 8 President Roosevelt officially, though still secretly, urged both warring governments " to open direct negotiations . . . , not only for their own sakes, but in the interest of the whole civilized world." [169] On June 10 the President was able, knowing in advance the answers, to extend both powers a public invitation to a conference.[170] This, Meyer noted in his diary, " is a great victory for the President, who has brought this about by his own initiative," while " the press and the diplomats " were " very skeptical about it all." [171] The Kaiser was delighted at the outcome.[172] Even the skeptical British, who had refused to help, now praised Roosevelt. In London both the *Post* and the *Times* spoke of him with admiration. " Mr. Roosevelt's success has amazed everybody," the *Post* declared. " He has displayed . . . great tact, great foresight, and finesse really extraordinary. Alone—absolutely without assistance or advice—he met every situation as it arose,

* Without breaking faith with the Czar by telling that the Czar had yielded, Meyer informed the German and British ambassadors of the interview and confided that the Czar had talked freely with him. Meyer felt he owed it to the Kaiser to send him word, and Sternburg in Washington, he suggested, might be able to supply more details.[167]

shaped events to suit his purpose, and showed remarkable
patience, caution, and moderation." "As a diplomatist," the
British paper concluded, "Mr. Roosevelt is now entitled to
take high rank." [173]

Roosevelt, Takahira, Meyer, and Sternburg in Washington
and Lodge, who was told in detail on June 16, kept their
secret so well that for years no one knew of the secret
Roosevelt-Takahira-Komura conferences in which the Japanese asked Roosevelt to extricate them from the war and
admitted to him that their resources and their manpower
were in danger of exhaustion if the fighting continued.
Neither the Russian Ambassador in Washington nor the
American Ambassador in Germany knew what was going on.[a]
Neither the British nor the American Ambassador in Tokyo,
each pursuing his own effort to bring about peace, was given
a hint of what was transpiring.[174] So well was the secret kept
that the British Government itself was ignorant of Roosevelt's activities.[b] Indeed, after the secret negotiations had
borne fruit in an agreement that Roosevelt at the request of
the Japanese would try to win Russia to a peace conference,
British Foreign Secretary Lansdowne wrote privately, "I
am . . . very apprehensive as to the effect . . . upon Russian
and Japanese opinion by ill-advised and premature attempts
to bring about peace negotiations." "Between ourselves,"
continued Lansdowne whom his Japanese allies had not
taken into their confidence, "I suspect that Roosevelt has
been overanxious . . . , and, as usual, there has been a good
deal of indiscretion as to his sayings and doings, with the
result that the Japanese are thoroughly suspicious." "No

---

[a] Hay was told on June 19 on his way from Europe to New Hampshire
where he died a few days later.

[b] Roosevelt laughed with Lodge over the "rather comic turn" that the well-
kept secret gave "to some of the English criticisms to the effect that my move
is really in the interest of Russia . . . and that Japan is behaving rather
magnanimously in going into . . . [the Conference]." [175]

one," he continued in his ignorance of what was going on, "could perform such a task better or more tactfully if the conditions were favourable [than our King], but the pear is not ripe." [176]

Details had still to be worked out. Only with great difficulty did Roosevelt obtain agreement on a place of meeting. Russia wanted Paris, Japan Chefoo. Roosevelt urged The Hague or Geneva, but Russia raised objection and Japan refused. They both wished Washington, which Roosevelt desired to avoid. To attain a solution, he yielded. Then, after Washington was announced, Russia demanded The Hague. Roosevelt declined to go back and ask Japan to reconsider. After endless wrangling Russia yielded, though ultimately the meeting was moved to Portsmouth, New Hampshire. Russia delayed and quibbled over the range and powers its delegates should have. The Court clique, the Grand Dukes, and most of the Czar's ministers opposed making peace; they were suspicious of America and jealous of independent action by the Czar. They did all they could to block the Czar's moves for peace. In conference after conference and letter after letter Roosevelt patiently ironed out these difficulties.[177] Meyer felt the Czar wanted to end the war, but he found Foreign Secretary Lamsdorff " tricky and not absolutely reliable." He encountered great difficulty getting to talk directly with the Czar. He sometimes had to get word privately to the Czar * that he had a communication from Roosevelt in order to be certain the Czar saw the letter or knew he wanted an audience.[178] Actually Russian leaders were divided whether they should go to the conference or continue fighting. Meyer cabled that popular discontent had grown and that revolution was a " serious possibility." Martial disasters and revolution did soften Russian resistance to peace. Yet in the end Roosevelt had to send

* He finally succeeded through an intimate friend of the Czar in getting to Nicholas a protest over Lamsdorff's attitude.

Meyer again to the Czar to persuade him that Russia should for her own good speedily come to terms. He had also to rebuke Japan for hanging back and quibbling.[179] More haggling took place over the date of meeting and over what delegates would be mutually satisfactory. Again Roosevelt had to interpose.[180] He tried, too, to get agreement on an armistice pending peace negotiations. But the Japanese, distrusting Russia's intentions and hoping to improve their own chances of a more favorable peace, refused and conquered their first actual Russian territory.[181]

" Oh Lord! I have been growing nearly mad in the effort to get Russia and Japan together," Roosevelt exploded in his despair.[182] " The more I see of the Czar, the Kaiser, and the Mikado the better I am content with democracy, even if we have to include the American newspaper as one of its assets." [183] " Russia is so soddenly stupid . . . so corrupt, so treacherous and shifty, and so incompetent . . . and the Government is such an amorphous affair that they really do not know *what* they want." At times Roosevelt and Hay wondered " whether Russia would not rather save face by throwing the whole world into war and being beaten by a concert of powers than to suffer the humiliation of a defeat by Japan singly." [184] " Japan is . . . entirely selfish," he admitted, " though with a veneer of courtesy," but Japan has " infinitely more knowledge of what it wants and capacity to get it." [185] Finally, Roosevelt's patience paid off and the Conference met on August 9. The chief Russian delegates were Serge Witte and Baron Roman R. Rosen, who now succeeded Cassini as Ambassador in Washington. Japan was represented officially by Foreign Secretary Jutaro Komura and by Kotoro Takahira, the Japanese Minister, and unofficially by Baron Kentaro Kaneko, Roosevelt's friend, who served as confidential negotiator between the President and the Japanese delegates.

Though the conference was to meet without intermediaries, Roosevelt felt compelled to guide its deliberations so that it would not fail.[186] In mid-July before the other delegates arrived, Roosevelt invited Kaneko to spend the night at Oyster Bay. He had Takahira to luncheon one day and Rosen another. Thus he talked over informally with both sides plans for the approaching conference.[187] Both Takahira and Rosen went down again twice separately.[188] After Komura and Witte arrived, the President entertained Rosen and Witte and Takahira and Komura at luncheon, again on separate days.[189] Then the President introduced the opposing delegates to each other at a formal luncheon on the Presidential yacht *Mayflower*. Photographers and press were at hand to provide suitable publicity. Roosevelt handled all the delicate details with consummate tact. He offered, for instance, a toast to both emperors together that no one could refuse to drink and that raised no problem of toasting one emperor before the other. Similarly he served a buffet stand-up luncheon to avoid difficulties of protocol [a] in seating these precedence-conscious men at table.[190]

The President's intervention for the most part, however, took the form of pressure on Russia to yield to Japan's demands, for he remained strongly pro-Japanese [b] and found it difficult to see reason in Russia's position.[192] As the Conference met Roosevelt still felt he must convince the Russians that they had been beaten. "Witte, and above all the Czar, . . . must understand definitely that this war is a failure and that peace must be made with the Japanese as victors," he declared. "They cannot . . . prevent peace coming on terms which will show that the Russians have suffered a severe defeat. If they refuse to acknowledge that they have

---

[a] At the beginning of the Conference he had to iron out various disputes over procedure.

[b] Two days before war began, he had confidentially told the German Ambassador, " The sympathies of the United States are entirely on Japan's side, but we will maintain the strictest neutrality." [191]

met with a severe defeat and to make peace accordingly, they will only succeed in changing severe defeat into irremediable disaster." [193] Roosevelt at first backed Japan in her demand for an indemnity, which he thought reasonable and which in any case he had been unable to persuade Japan not to demand.[194] On the other hand, the Czar counted on Roosevelt to " reduce some of the exorbitant demands which the Japanese will be making to reasonable proportions." [a][195] When Roosevelt talked with Witte soon after his arrival he was disturbed by Witte's intransigence over an indemnity and told him that if he maintained his position the Conference would break up.[196] On August 16, when the Russians still remained adamant, he exploded to his sister, " The Russian idiots are perfectly capable of refusing to make peace at all." [197]

Witte refused even to discuss an indemnity and stood ready to break up the Conference if Japan insisted upon one. Meyer insisted that for peace Witte would do everything possible under instructions from the Czar, but Witte himself agreed with the Czar's instructions barring an indemnity. Indeed, he had accepted his appointment as delegate only because it was understood Russia would stand firm against an indemnity.[198] Roosevelt heard from Paris, however, that, though Witte would be unmovable about an " indemnity," he " would consider paying at least a part of Japan's expenses in the war." The President hastened to pass what he had heard from Paris on to Kaneko and to " suggest . . . that great care be used about the word indemnity and that if possible it be avoided." [199] Kaneko replied that he had learned from a friend close to the Russian Embassy that all

---

[a] Immediately after agreeing to the Conference, the Czar appealed to the Kaiser to get the President to have the Japanese peace terms submitted to him for examination. " In case they really should be exorbitant, and too humiliating," William suggested in transmitting this request to Roosevelt, " you could have them held back."

the secretaries there admitted Russia ought to pay the war expenses of Japan. Kaneko and Komura privately assured Roosevelt that they must insist on payment whatever it was called. " Without the payment of the cost of the war . . . ," Kaneko wrote, " we can hardly manage our national finance and economy after the war." [200] During the Conference American bankers conferred with Witte and Kaneko, and pro-Japanese Americans hoped that willingness of these bankers to lend money to Russia if she made peace but not to finance her if she continued the war would lead her to concede what the Japanese demanded.[201]

In Serge Witte Roosevelt and the Japanese were dealing with a remarkable man. He had opposed policies that led his country to war with Japan and had felt Japan and Russia should be friends. The Czar and his advisers were hostile to him and appointed him only after trying unsuccessfully to persuade two far less capable men to become delegates. While Witte was negotiating, the Czar and Foreign Office kept plaguing him with cables of instruction that hampered rather than helped.[202] Nicholas expected failure and was willing to blame Witte for the failure he expected, but he wanted negotiations conducted in such a way that Japan and not Russia would appear responsible for the failure.[203] Witte had to combat, too, the well-known pro-Japanese sympathies of the American people, the American press, and the American President.[204] Witte felt his " relations with President Roosevelt were not particularly harmonious or cordial." He later publicly described Roosevelt and his advisers as " ignorant " of " international politics generally, and European political matters in particular." Some American leaders he found " naive." [205] At the opening of the Conference the Czar told Meyer, however, that Witte was tremendously impressed with the President. And near the end of it Witte and Rosen wrote a friend in Europe, " When one speaks with President Roosevelt he charms through the ele-

vation of his thoughts and through that transparent philosophy which permeates his judgment." [206] The press reported
Roosevelt on his part as calling Witte a " splendid fellow." [207]
To Rockhill, on the contrary, Roosevelt wrote, " The Russian Government jumps from side to side . . . ; their representatives give me the worst impression; they are tricky
and inefficient." [208] To Spring Rice he confided: " Witte impressed me much while he was here, but by no means altogether pleasantly. He spoke with astonishing freedom of
the hopeless character of the Russian despotism. . . . I
thought this pretty frank. . . . He also commented on the
brutality of the treatment of political suspects with contempt
and indignation. . . . In short, he impressed me with being
entirely alive to the need of radical reform in Russia and all
the more fitted to do good work because he was not a doctri-
naire. But he also impressed me with being very much more
concerned for his own welfare than for the welfare of his
nation,* and as being utterly cynical, untruthful and un-
scrupulous." The Russian Government and the public, however, were allowed to believe that Witte had produced a most
favorable impression on Roosevelt.[209] Yet Witte was more
amenable to suggestion and more truthful than the untrustworthy Cassini with whom Roosevelt had dealt so long, and
Witte actually displayed an integrity and wisdom that
Roosevelt had not previously encountered in high officials of
Russia.

As a diplomat Witte was astute. In a difficult situation
he handled himself ably and got what Russia wanted. He
proved himself shrewd in coping with the Japanese, in culti-
vating American sentiment originally hostile to Russia, and
in persuading his own difficult Government to be more rea-

* Witte has been generally regarded as comprehending Russia's needs and as
showing great courage and devotion to country in working for them in the
knowledge that to do so would antagonize the Court clique, which would
destroy him.

sonable and less stupid.[210] He knew Japan well. He admired Count Ito, leader of those Japanese that wanted friendship with Russia. Eager as he was for peace for his own country, he sagaciously estimated that, though Japanese like Russians were torn between a war party and a peace party, still the Japanese Government was desperately eager for peace.[211] As the Conference progressed his skilful handling turned the sympathies of newsmen against the Japanese and to the Russians. With the journals American public opinion also shifted.[212] To his own Government Witte gave the advice on which final success for Russia was based. On August 13, for instance, he cabled Count Lamsdorff, the Foreign Secretary, that the Russians could win at the Conference or in subsequent war only if they followed three rules: " 1. We must so act as to be able, with clear conscience, to publish all the documents and submit the whole matter to the judgment of humanity . . . ; 2. We must let Japan have all those gains which she has obtained owing to her good luck in this war and which do not injure either the dignity of Russia . . . or the feelings of the Russian heart; 3. We must be fair in our estimate of the situation, inasmuch as fairness is practicable in such cases." [213]

After several days of peaceful discussion the Conference faced a crisis on August 13. Assuming she was victor, Japan had presented formal demands.[214] At Roosevelt's suggestion the less important of them were first discussed and these were adjusted. Hopes rose and fell.[215] Ultimately the Conference reached Japan's demands for indemnity and for cession to her of Saghalin Island, part of which she had captured since she had agreed to confer with Russia. Witte and Rosen were under strict instruction not to yield on these issues and they did stand firm. The Japanese felt they must win at least this much or their war party would force a continuance of hostilities.[216] Finally on August 18 the impasse was reached when neither side would back down on indemnity or Saghalin. A breakup of the Conference seemed certain.[217]

Roosevelt had already argued with the Japanese and had persuaded them to yield on minor matters.[218] Now he decided he must intervene on the major problems. On August 15 Oscar Straus had suggested that he invite the plenipotentiaries to Oyster Bay. You can urge them " out of deference to you and for the peace of the world " to make " mutual concessions," Straus had suggested. " In the event a break practically comes such an invitation will keep the conference alive," Straus had argued, " until your sentiments will have awakened the respective countries to the gravity of their responsibilities in renewed war." " I shall try to act along those very lines," the President had replied on August 16.[219] On the same day he had written his sister, " I wish to Heaven I could make these peace conferences meet under my immediate supervision, or else turn the matter over to me." [220] So on August 18, when the crisis was reached, Roosevelt sent word to Witte requesting that Rosen or some one in authority among the Russian delegates visit him at Oyster Bay immediately.[221]

In the meantime several persons had been active behind the scenes. On August 17 Witte had cabled Lamsdorff that a decisive session would occur the following Monday or Tuesday. " If neither side yields," he had warned, " we shall have to break off the negotiations." " In view of the infinite importance of the matter," he had pleaded, " it is necessary, it seems to me, to gauge the situation again and to take an immediate decision." " I have not the slightest doubt," Witte had warned, " but that a continuation of the war will be the greatest disaster for Russia." [222] On August 17 and 18, too, Sternburg had sent messages from the Kaiser that Roosevelt dubbed " brand new pipe dreams from my constant correspondent." In them William warned that France was preparing to call for joint action of the powers to bring peace. He hoped Roosevelt would use his influence with both powers to prevent this and offered to aid in dealing with Russia if asked.[223] On August 18 and 20 Meyer had cabled from St. Petersburg that the Czar had been annoyed at the Japanese demand for limitation of Russia's Pacific fleet and had said " peace for Russia was impossible if Japan held to her demands of an indemnity or the cession of territory." [224] On August 17 Komura had wired Kaneko to take to the President at Oyster Bay a " new proposition " the Japanese wished to make. On August 18 Kaneko and Roosevelt discussed it, and, at Komura's request * transmitted through Kaneko, Roosevelt telegraphed the invitation for Rosen to come to Oyster Bay.[226] Then on his return from this Oyster Bay talk Kaneko found in New York City a telegram from Komura telling of an important conversation with Witte. " To-day the Russian Envoy proposed a compromise in regard to Saghalin," said Komura's telegram, which Kaneko sent on to Roosevelt; " therefore you are requested to ask the President to wait for the outcome of this Compromise before he takes a decisive step. Moreover the Compromise is to be kept in a strict secrecy. . . ." But it was too late to withhold the request that Rosen come to Oyster Bay.[227] So at Portsmouth the Conference recessed while Rosen made the trip. In spite of the " strict secrecy," rumor of a Russian proposal of compromise did come to the ears of newspaperman Cal O'Laughlin, who sent it on to the President, who had already learned the secrets from the Japanese.[228]

Rosen traveled southward on August 19. The New York Limited made an unscheduled stop at New Rochelle whence the *Sylph* took Rosen across the Sound directly to Oyster Bay. He spent an hour with the President.[229] The *Washington Post* reported Rosen " brusque " as he went in and " wreathed in smiles " when he emerged. Though Roosevelt and Rosen both were silent, guesses that successful compro-

---

* Again the secret was well kept. Takahira innocently asked newsmen whether Roosevelt " had sent for Rosen or whether he had gone of his own volition." [225]

mise had been reached circulated after the talk, and Roosevelt began to be praised for breaking the deadlock.[230]

The President now played his trump card. He transferred negotiations to St. Petersburg.[231] There Meyer had been reporting gloomily that the war party had gained the ascendancy and that even the reformers had decided their reforms would stand a better chance if the war continued.[232] Meyer had cabled, too, that Russia would never pay an indemnity nor yield territory.[233] So Roosevelt persuaded the Japanese to make some concessions and then on August 21 cabled the Czar a direct appeal.* The Japanese, Roosevelt told Nicholas, had "abandoned their demands for the interned ships and the limitation of the Russian naval power in the Pacific," and had agreed "to restore the Northern half of Saghalin ᵇ to Russia" if Russia would pay "a substantial sum for this surrender of territory . . . and for the return of Russian prisoners." [234] "It seems to me," he appealed to the Czar, "that if peace can be obtained substantially on these terms it will be both just and honorable, and that it would be a dreadful calamity to have the war continued when peace can thus be obtained." "No one can foretell the result of the continuance of the war," he admitted, "and I have no doubt that it is to Japan's advantage to conclude peace." "But . . . it is infinitely more to the advantage of Russia," he told Nicholas. "If peace is not made now . . . it may well be that, though the financial strain upon Japan would be severe, yet . . . Russia would be shorn of [her] east Siberian provinces." [235] To strengthen his entreaty the President got the Kaiser to telegraph the Czar urging acceptance of these terms; he urged Jusserand to get the French Government, too, to put pressure on Russia.[236] Less hopefully he appealed also to Britain to persuade Japan to be reasonable.[237]

---

* To be courteous, he transmitted the cable through Witte; to be certain it reached Nicholas he sent it also through Meyer.

ᵇ As to the loss of half of Saghalin he pointed out that without a navy Russia could not retake it and the northern half would adequately protect Vladivostok.

On Sunday and Monday, August 20 and 21, everyone waited anxiously. The principals remained silent. The press engaged in excited speculations. Roosevelt hoped that success at last was at hand based on his compromise terms. Finally the answer came. The Czar resolutely rejected Roosevelt's arguments presented in his own forceful language by cable and in a two-hour interview by Meyer and supported in a telegram from the Kaiser. Nicholas refused to give indemnity or territory. Indeed, he instructed Witte to break off the negotiations " because of the intractibility of the Japanese as regards . . . indemnities." [238]

Witte now showed himself the ablest statesman of them all. With the concessions concerning the fleet, the interned ships, and the northern part of Saghalin won from the Japanese by President Roosevelt, he shrewdly estimated the rôle of public opinion and suggested to his Government the terms on which peace was finally made. On August 21 he cabled: " I believe that . . . peace-loving public opinion will recognize that Russia was right in refusing to pay a war indemnity, but it will not side with us on the subject of Saghalin, for facts are stronger than arguments. Consequently, if we wish the failure of the Conference to be laid to Japan, we must not refuse to cede Saghalin, after having also refused to indemnify Japan." Then he warned further: " If it is our desire that in the future America and Europe side with us, we must take Roosevelt's opinion into consideration." [239] To Roosevelt Witte wrote on August 22 even before hearing from the Czar. " These proposals [that you have urged upon the Czar] . . . mean in reality under cover of another form, a payment to Japan. . . . To this Russia will not consent as she can not admit herself to be vanquished." * Then he charged: " Japan evidently . . . is . . . willing to prolong the

* On receipt of this statement Roosevelt exploded: " The Chinese or Byzantine folly " of the Russians makes " it all I can do not to tell them some straightforward truths in uncomplimentary language."

shedding of blood . . . to secure at any price a considerable
sum of money." [240] This argument he rightly guessed would
have popular appeal and on it he took his stand.

Roosevelt became worried about public opinion and, in
letters of August 22 and 23 to Kaneko, warned Japan that
by continuing the war to gain a money payment she was
alienating public opinion.[a] Besides, Japan would gain nothing. Russia would refuse to pay; and the "sentiment of the
civilized world . . . [would] back her in refusing to pay."
Then the war would continue. Japan would spend millions
of dollars more, spill an immense amount of blood, gain all
Siberia, which she did not want, and get no money at all
from Russia. "Every interest of civilization and humanity
forbids the continuance of this war merely for a large indemnity," he urged.[242] He then appealed to the British to
help impress this fact upon Japan.[243] He requested that his
views be cabled to the Japanese Government. "I became
rather doubtful whether they were telling the Mikado's Government just what I had been saying to them," he explained,
"and I concluded to put it in writing." On Wednesday,
August 23, as he was writing the second letter to Kaneko,
the Conference deadlocked and adjourned until Saturday to
give time for consultation with home governments.[244]

Roosevelt now became frantic.[b] On Wednesday he wrote
to Witte reiterating his arguments for paying a reasonable
indemnity and to Kaneko pleading with Japan not to continue the war for the sake of indemnity.[c] Through both

[a] On one of these days he received a letter from his friend Lodge declaring,
"If . . . [Japan] renews the fighting merely to get money she will not get the
money and she will turn sympathy from her in this country and elsewhere very
rapidly." [241]

[b] "I am having my hair turned gray . . . dealing with the . . . peace negotiators," he wrote Kermit at this point. "The Japanese ask too much, but the
Russians are ten times worse than the Japs because they are so stupid and won't
tell the truth."

[c] Yet after the peace was agreed to Roosevelt privately expressed the belief

Witte and Meyer, he also sent a second appeal to the Czar and instructed Meyer to see Nicholas again. He contended with Witte and the Czar that paying for the support of troops and for territory was not an indemnity, and he promised he would see that the Japanese accepted his terms if Russia would.[246]

All parties now worked feverishly behind the scenes. Kaneko and Komura cabled to the Japanese Government Roosevelt's letters to Kaneko.[247] Meyer went again to see the Czar, who this time following Witte's advice conceded that, since the lower half of Saghalin had been only temporarily Russian, he could yield that part without loss of honor. Still, he would pay no indemnity for the traditional half. In conversation the Czar agreed to the Japanese position on all the other points at issue and concentrated on his insistence that he should have half of Saghalin and pay no indemnity. There is some reason to believe the Czar yielded on these other matters only because it seemed so certain the Japanese would not retreat on the two major issues that the Czar's agreement on the lesser ones was consequently unimportant. Meyer went home and put the Czar's remarks into writing and obtained the Czar's approval for his statement of the new terms as the Czar had stated them in friendly talk with Meyer. Thus Meyer turned what the Czar meant as an ultimatum into terms of peace from which, when the Japanese gave way on indemnity and half of Saghalin, the Czar could not retreat.[248] This time Witte, too, replied to Roosevelt. He reiterated his objection to payment for half of Saghalin, but he threw out the suggestion that he might consider the Japanese sincere in their desire for peace and might therefore consent to their keeping the lower half of Saghalin if they proposed handing back the upper half with-

that Japan gave up too much " when they returned the northern half of Saghalin, which I am confident I could have obtained for them—or at least which I think I could have made Russia redeem for a small sum of money." [245]

out any money payment for it.[249] At the same time came four other wires: one from Kaneko quoting instructions Komura had had from Japan not to concede anything further, another from Meyer with a still briefer and still firm " no " from the Czar, a third from the Kaiser quoting a telegram from the Czar, and a fourth from Jusserand in Paris. Both the Kaiser and Jusserand made it clear to Roosevelt that Russia would pay no indemnity. William promised to appeal once more to the Czar but felt the outcome would depend upon Japan. Jusserand held out hope that, if the indemnity were waived, Russia might consent to divide Saghalin.[250] The Conference seemed about to fail and on Friday, August 25, Roosevelt sent a third desperate plea to the Czar.[251] Meyer cabled back immediately that Foreign Secretary Lamsdorff was certain the Czar would not change his mind, and on Saturday Meyer transmitted the Czar's refusal to make further concessions.[252]

On Saturday, August 26, when the Conference reconvened, gloom prevailed.* The press had been predicting failure unless Japan backed down. " The vital question of . . . peace or war . . . depends . . . mainly on the amount of influence President Roosevelt can bring to bear upon the two belligerents," the *New York Sun* announced.[254] Witte, however, consented once more to postpone abandonment of the Conference. Still in hopeless deadlock the delegates agreed to recess until Monday, and ultimately Tuesday, August 29, to give Takahira opportunity to hear from his Government. Witte warned, however, that this would be the final session. He even gave orders to pack, and asked the hotel for his bill. Both Russian and Japanese delegates informed Roosevelt that peace could not be agreed upon.[255]

The President, still unwilling to admit defeat, spent Satur-

---

* On this day James Stillman, president of the National City Bank of New York, wrote to tell Roosevelt he was confident New York bankers would float Russian bonds " issued as a foundation for permanent peace " to pay an indemnity. Frank Vanderlip, vice-president of the National City Bank, also conferred with Witte on this subject.[253]

day and Sunday exerting what further pressure he could. To the Japanese he made it clear that the Conference would end unless they yielded, and Witte had already told the Japanese this.[256] On Sunday at Komura's request Roosevelt again appealed to Kaiser William to persuade the Czar to accept the principle of money payment and leave it to an arbitral board to determine the amount, and William telegraphed Nicholas accordingly.[257] The President made a last appeal to Jusserand, too.[258] Two more cables from Meyer on Sunday and Monday made it clear, however, that Russia would not budge. Meyer warned that the war party had been strengthened by the indemnity issue.[259]

As Tuesday's final session approached the President was privately denouncing the unreasonableness of the Russians; he was preparing to break the news of failure to the press in such a way as to show that failure was " Russia's fault." [260] Witte was preparing to leave Portsmouth. Indeed, he was under orders from the Czar to " finish the negotiations and come home at once." It was in the face of these orders that he risked attending one more session of the Conference. The Japanese desperately wanted peace, and had now carefully weighed the realities Roosevelt had made clear to them. Just before the Conference reconvened Witte cabled his Government, " I am almost certain that they will yield." [261] And yield they did under instruction from the Japanese Emperor to abandon the effort to obtain indemnity. Peace terms were quickly agreed upon on August 30.[262]

Roosevelt acknowledged help he had received, especially from Germany and France.[263] Through personal pressure on the Czar the Kaiser had helped.* Roosevelt could not see " why excepting on disinterested grounds the German Emperor should want Russia and Japan to make peace." [265] But,

---

* Actually the Kaiser's personal meeting with the Czar in July had contrariwise started false rumors that Germany was going to back Russia in continuing the war.[264]

whatever his motive, " the Kaiser has behaved admirably,"
Roosevelt wrote Spring Rice, " and has really helped me." [a] [267]
To the Emperor of Japan the President sent his " earnest
congratulations upon the wisdom and magnanimity he and
the Japanese people have displayed." [268] For France's help [b]
also Roosevelt expressed gratitude. [270] Meyer's endeavors in
St. Petersburg, too, particularly his persuading the Czar to
accept the loss of the southern half of Saghalin, the President
considered crucial. [271]

Grateful though Roosevelt was to those on the outside
who had helped, he had none the less found the envoys and
the nations behind them exasperating. " Dealing with senators is at times excellent training for the temper," he confided
to his friend the French Ambassador; " but upon my word
dealing with these peace envoys has been an even tougher
job. To be polite and sympathetic and patient in explaining
for the hundredth time something perfectly obvious, when
what I really want to do is to give utterance to whoops of
rage and jump up and knock their heads together—well, all
I can hope is that self-repression will be ultimately helpful
for my character." " When they drive me too nearly mad,"
he wrote Jusserand, " I take refuge in Maspero and study the
treaty between Rameses II and the Hittites, comparing it
with Rameses' preposterous boastings over his previous victories, and feel that after all we are not so far behind the

---

[a] Spring Rice with his usual suspicion of the Kaiser was convinced that his
telegrams to the Czar had had no " practical effect." David Jayne Hill, Minister
to Holland, accused the Kaiser of " using every secret means of fanning the
flames of war." In his *Memoirs* the Kaiser spoke of " the Peace . . . brought
about by me in conjunction with President Roosevelt." [266]

[b] Speck von Sternburg, however, who usually reflected conversations with
Roosevelt, cabled home at the time: " Had Delcassé remained at the helm, it
would scarcely have been possible for the President to have mediated the Russo-
Japanese peace." And later the President himself told the historian Rhodes of
" Delcassé's underhand game," how he " wanted the negotiations to fail so that
England and France might step in and bring the two warring nations together." [269]

people who lived a few thousand years ago as I am sometimes tempted to think." [272]

Britain's refusal to coöperate by using her influence with Japan irked Roosevelt. The President repeatedly sought to persuade Britain to help.[273] Her Government disclaimed any desire to have bloodshed prolonged. At least, she wanted peace when peace could be established on a desirable basis satisfactory to both belligerents.[274] Yet Britain persistently refused to give any advice to Japan.[275] In June, indeed, King Edward suggested confidentially to Ambassador Reid that it might be desirable to have the war continue until Japan conquered Vladivostok. Then, said the King, Japan could magnanimously give it back to Russia and this would " ease the final settlements." [276] " It seems to be simply childish," Roosevelt exploded, " to *talk* of their being ' magnanimous ' and ' giving it back '—for the excellent reason that it would *be* childish to spend the necessary blood and treasure . . . of ' being magnanimous and giving it back.' " The President found it hard to believe " the British seriously think that the Japanese intend to . . . give it back." " It would be better for England," he argued, " to have peace come with Russia face to face with Japan in east Siberia . . . [as] a guarantee against any Russian move toward India or Persia." Roosevelt came to believe that Britain wanted the war to continue until both Russia and Japan were exhausted.[277] Yet he was also convinced that, whether by intent or not, the renewal of the Anglo-Japanese alliance " was a powerful factor in inducing Japan to be wise and reasonable." [278]

Roosevelt was generally credited * with bringing peace.[279] Henry White doubted whether a single Foreign Office in Europe thought up to the very last that he would be success-

---

* People as different as Irving Cobb and Joseph Pulitzer of the usually hostile *World*, Emile J. Dillon, financial adviser to the Russian delegation, Maxim Kovalevsky, Russian international lawyer and editor of *Vestnik Europy*, British Conservative Arthur Lee, French Premier Rouvier, and Senators Lodge of Massachusetts and Nelson of Minnesota joined in the acclaim.

ful.[281] " Your personal energetic efforts . . . brought the
peace," the Czar cabled. " My country will gratefully recognize the great part you have played." [282] " The great success
[was] due to your untiring efforts," the Kaiser told him.
" The whole of mankind must unite and will do so in thanking you for the great boon you have given it." [283] British
Ambassador Durand and German Ambassador von Sternburg, to both of whom he sent the crucial cables, felt that
except for his efforts the war would have continued.[284] Komura said it was " owing to your earnest and unceasing efforts
and the magnanimity of His Majesty the Emperor of Japan
[that] peace . . . [was] assured." [285] Emperor Mutsuhito
thanked him for his " disinterested and unremitting efforts "
and " the distinguished part " he had played in establishing
peace.[286] The British, too, now belatedly praised Roosevelt.[287] Spring Rice, who had observed the negotiations from
the British Embassy in St. Petersburg, was convinced that
it was " the direct influence of the President here and the
language of the American Ambassador in his two interviews "
that had brought Russia to a settlement. " It seems to me,"
he concluded, " and to all of us here, that the peace is directly
and solely due to the President's personal intervention." [288]

It was apparently the personal appeal of the President [b]
to the Emperor through Baron Kaneko that persuaded the
Japanese Government.[289] Even Lansdowne grudgingly admitted that the letters to Kaneko " did have the desired
effect, or at any rate that they were a most potent factor in
determining the Japs to give way." [290] Kaiser " Willy " wrote
to Czar " Nicky," " Roosevelt . . . has made nearly superhuman efforts to induce Japan to give way. He has really

[a] King Edward was among those who was certain there would be no peace
because Japan would never give up the indemnity, and Lodge believed there
would have to be another great battle first.[280]
    [b] " Without your warm sympathy for our country and your perfect confidence
in me," Kaneko later told Roosevelt, " I could never have done as much as
I did."

done a great work for your country and the whole world." [291] Baron Kaneko, who knew most accurately what happened, broke the news of peace to Roosevelt exultingly: " Our Emperor has decided on the line of policy you suggested in your letters to me . . . transmitted by cable to our Government." " Your advice," Kaneko confided, " was very powerful and convincing, by which the peace of Asia was assured. Your name shall be remembered with the peace and prosperity of Asia." [292]

Success where failure had been predicted won Roosevelt enormous prestige at home and abroad. " Nothing you have done in your whole official career has appealed more strongly to human sympathies and understanding," wrote New York bank president James Stillman.[293] Even Senator Knute Nelson from supposedly " isolationist " Minnesota wrote imperialist Senator Albert J. Beveridge, " Wasn't that a grand move . . . in getting Japan and Russia together in a Peace Conference, and especially getting them to meet and hold it in this country. The very thought that a great power of the Orient and one of the great powers of Europe have to come here to America to settle their disputes is enough to make an old fellow like me swell up with more pride in our country than ever." [294] " The President's prestige throughout the world is beyond anything that he can imagine," White wrote Lodge from Rome.[295] " You probably don't realize the immense personal prestige and power which you exercise over here," Spring Rice agreed admiringly.[296] From St. Petersburg Meyer reported that an American could " have no idea what influence Roosevelt had in Europe and how he was looked up to and respected." [297] " At close range I see these things more vividly than at home and realize your position and that of the country more sharply than even you perhaps," Lodge in Europe at the time told the President. " I do not think either you or our own people realize the place you hold in public opinion here. . . . We are the strongest moral force—also physical—now extant, and the peace of the world rests largely with us." [298]

In spite of the acclaim he won, both belligerents whom he had extricated from costly war felt some bitterness toward Roosevelt. The day after peace was agreed upon Meyer reported that " the Russians are already beginning to say that, if they had only held out, they would have got the whole of Sakhalin." " The President . . . must not expect gratitude from the Russians," Meyer warned, " as they will say they would have won but for him." [299] Spring Rice quoted the Czar as protesting that he was " tricked into the peace." [*] " If I had only known that the Japanese were willing to yield on the indemnity," he reportedly remarked, " I should never have consented to give half of Saghalin." [302] This Roosevelt proclaimed " a poor piece of silly bluster." " As a matter of fact," he declared, " I think that through Meyer we could have gotten a small payment." [303]

In Japan anti-American rioting broke out. The Japanese Government knew it had made an unpopular peace. The consequences of disappointing the war party and the populace were sidestepped by making Roosevelt a scapegoat. The Government that had asked Roosevelt to do what he did permitted rioting and demonstration against America, for it did not dare tell a victory-mad people it had put Japan where continuing the war would have meant disaster.[304] Roosevelt became so unhappy over the Japanese people's attitude toward him that he wrote Kaneko, " It seems to me that it would be well for the Japanese to point out, or at least lay stress on, the enormous amount they have won." [305] Roosevelt could not understand why " the Japanese states-

---

[*] Admiral Charles S. Sperry of the United States Navy agreed. "I have now in my files," he said, " a letter from our Naval attaché in Tokyo who names the official in the Foreign Office who told him the Japanese envoys had *orders* to make peace before they left Tokyo, with or without either indemnity or territory." [300] General Wood felt " Russia quit just when she was in the position to do her best work." [301]

men, usually so astute, permitted their people to think they had to get a large indemnity." " If they had in the beginning blown their trumpets over the immense amount they were getting," he wrote Sternburg, " . . . Corea . . . Manchuria . . . Port Arthur and Dalny . . . how they had won a triumph which since the days of Napoleon has only been paralleled by Germany in 1870—I think they could have made their people feel proud instead of humiliated." [306] To his British friend Strachey the President wrote, " The only difficulty came from their having, as I think unwisely, allowed the Japanese people . . . to indulge in utterly extravagant anticipations as to what could be obtained until they really thought they could get as much as if their armies occupied Moscow." [307]

Actually, Roosevelt as well as the Japanese had suffered defeat in the final terms. In a real sense the great accomplishment was Witte's, for the terms adopted were those he had proposed to the Czar on August 20 and the Czar had formulated in Meyer's audience with him on August 23.[308] Roosevelt until the very end had tried to win indemnity for the Japanese. During the whole Conference he had continued through Kaneko the confidential relations with them that they had originally employed to get him to call the Conference without letting the world know they had asked it. Some of the things he did as impartial mediator he did at the request of the Japanese. Besides, Kaneko saw and approved every cable sent the Czar before it was sent.[309] So well, however, did Roosevelt and his Japanese friends keep secrets that, though it was known he was pro-Japanese, no one guessed the extent of his secret coöperation with them. " I am amused to see the way in which the Japanese kept silent," he wrote his daughter Alice. " Whenever I wrote a letter to the Czar the Russians were sure to divulge it, almost always in twisted form, but the outside world never had so much as a hint of any letter I sent the Japanese.

The Russians became very angry with me . . . because they thought I was only writing to them." [*] [310] At the end Roosevelt felt compelled to abandon the Japanese and accept the Russian position. The President was brought to this shift by two factors. Witte's skilful handling of the press and public opinion persuaded him that Japan had lost favor and that breaking up the Conference over a demand for money would do her irreparable damage in American and world opinion and he wished to spare her that.[311] At the same time, when he became convinced that Russia would not pay indemnity, he saw that, unless Japan yielded, the Conference would break up and this failure he wished to prevent probably both because it would have serious consequences for the world and because it would damage the prestige of the man who had called the Conference.[312] Russia's success on the indemnity did not, however, endear her to him. " Bad as the Chinese are," he wrote Rockhill at the height of their boycott of American goods, " no human beings, black, yellow, or white, could be quite as untruthful, as insincere, as arrogant—in short as untrustworthy in every way—as the Russians under their present system. I was pro-Japanese before, but after my experience with the peace commissioners I am far stronger pro-Japanese than ever." [313]

In spite of the unpopularity of the Treaty with the Japanese people and his own efforts to get Russia to pay a small sum, Roosevelt was convinced that he had done what was best for the Japanese themselves in persuading them to abandon an indemnity.[314] " I should not have made a bluff that I did not expect to make good, and I would not have . . . [asked] an indemnity which was sure to be refused, and thereby . . . [give] the Russians the simulacrum of a diplomatic victory," Roosevelt wrote Spring Rice. " But the Russians are such a preposterous people . . . and lying and

---

[*] To disabuse them Roosevelt gave Witte copies of his letters to the Japanese to show the Czar. And, he records, " they made amends in good shape."

bluffing and breaking faith are so ingrained in them, that it may well be they would not have given up the south half of Saghalin if the Japanese had not made the bluff they did about the indemnity." [315] When pro-Japanese George Kennan published an article criticizing Roosevelt for not postponing intervention until Japan had won more victories, Roosevelt wrote defending himself and then withheld the letter as too indiscreet to send. In it the President not only explained that Japan had asked him to make peace on just the terms finally adopted, but he explained why. " The head men of many villages and country communities in Japan were notifying the government that they could not spare any more of their young men," Roosevelt explained: " that if more of their young men were drawn for the army the rice fields would have to be partially abandoned and a partial famine would ensue, and that moreover the little savings of their people had all been exhausted." Japan asked him to make peace, he declared, because " to go on with the war meant such an enormous loss, such an enormous cost to her, that she could not afford to incur it." [316] The next year Kennan told the President that from " the higher officials of the government and the army he found out [after he wrote his article] that Japan was being bled white, and that peace was necessary." [317]

Critics there were in America that felt Roosevelt's intervention had been unfortunate. Mark Twain believed he had irreparably set back the revolution in Russia so necessary, Twain thought, to Russia's " liberation from its age-long chains." [318] Roosevelt was censured even for aiding French bankers by letting Russia, who owed them money, " go scot free " of indemnity.[319] Frank Cobb of the *New York World* held that an " indemnity would have been of incalculable benefit as a deterrent of possible wars in the future." [320] Many friends of the Japanese * insisted they had not received " all

---

* George Kennan was one of these, but he later changed his mind.[321]

their victories entitled them to." [322] Those who feared Japan, on the other hand, deplored settling Japan's war with Russia as one of the big mistakes of Roosevelt's career.[a] John Hays Hammond, engineer and international business man, and the President's close friend, General Leonard Wood, were of this group. "Japan was broke financially," the General argued. "Her long thin line of troops in Manchuria couldn't be maintained much longer." "A peace of exhaustion," Wood felt, "would have prevented Japan's becoming a great power and hence a menace to others in Europe." [324] Roosevelt's old law professor, John W. Burgess, called the Peace of Portsmouth "one of the most disastrous things that has ever occurred to the peace of the world." "I was in Europe . . . and came into contact with the Foreign Ministers of several of the European states," Burgess testified, "and I found the opinion unanimous among them that the lodgment of Japan in Northern Asia was bound to result in driving half Asiatic Russia back upon Europe, to the ruin of European civilization and indirectly to the injury of North America." [325] "Japan's path from Mukden . . . and Portsmouth led directly to . . . Pearl Harbor," wrote one student of this period forty years later during World War II, and in the light of subsequent events historians with hindsight have often expressed this view.[326]

Roosevelt's motives for undertaking the rôle of peacemaker are interesting. He had a double purpose. First he wished to stop war between civilized powers that was bad for the world and second he hoped to maintain the rights of all nations in the Far East by stabilizing the balance of power there. To accomplish these purposes Roosevelt had to argue with both sides. Had Russia made peace earlier the balance

[a] "Of course," said Paul Reinsch, "there are many things in Russian affairs against which we must always protest; but it would be a calamity if Russia, by constant and malign misrepresentation of her motives, should be driven into complete hostility to all western social and political ideals." [323]

would not have been so seriously threatened.* But if she had insisted on further fighting and lost eastern Siberia there might have been no counterweight left to balance Japan at all. " I had hoped she would make up her mind that she would have to make concessions in order to obtain peace because her military position was now hopeless," Roosevelt explained. " I should be sorry," he wrote Lodge, " to see Russia driven completely off the Pacific coast, . . . and yet something like this will surely happen if she refuses to make peace. Moreover, she will put it out of the power of anyone to help her in the future if she now stands with Chinese folly upon her dignity and fancied strength." " In this crisis," he insisted, " the interest of Russia is the interest of the entire world." " To continue the war " meant for Russia from this point on, " humanly speaking . . . to go from disaster to disaster." [328] He did not like Russia, but he did not want her driven out of East Asia or so weakened that she could not check Japan.[329]

With the balance of power in mind, he argued with Japan, too. After great victories Japan had " a right to ask a good deal," he admitted. Yet he urged Japan to moderate her demands. " If . . . [the Japanese] made such terms that Russia would prefer to fight for another year," he conceded, " they would without doubt get all Eastern Siberia." " But, . . . " he reasoned with them, " it would be an utterly valueless possession to them, while they would make of Russia an enemy whose hostility would endure as long as the nation herself existed." " To achieve this result," he pleaded, " at the cost of an additional year of loss of blood and money and consequent strain upon Japanese resources seems to me to be wholly useless." And there was always the chance that Japan would exhaust herself in this useless war, or that on

* Jusserand agreed with Roosevelt about this.[327]

the other hand a large indemnity might enable her to become too strong a rival naval power.[*] [330]

By stopping the war and bringing peace on the terms agreed upon at Portsmouth, President Roosevelt hoped he had opened the trade of Manchuria to American and other merchants and had so stabilized the Far Eastern balance as to guarantee peace. It was, in short, a balance that Roosevelt sought. "While Russia's triumph would have been a blow to civilization," he summarized his position to Lodge, " her destruction as an eastern Asiatic power would also in my opinion be unfortunate. It is best that she should be left face to face with Japan so that each may have a moderative action on the other." [331]

Roosevelt's attitude toward Korea, too, illustrated both his conception of Japan's rôle as a bulwark against Russia and his concern with strategic rather than economic considerations where the two conflicted. In the same letter in 1900 in which he deplored the possibility of the powers' " slicing up " China after the Boxer rebellion, he confided to his friend Speck von Sternburg, then on the staff of the German Embassy in Washington, that he would " like to see Japan have Korea." " She will be a check upon Russia," Roosevelt wrote, " and she deserves it for what she has done." Again in May, 1904, he told Speck to tell the Kaiser that so far as America was concerned Japan could have Korea.[332]

During Roosevelt's first four years as President, Korea was torn by a gigantic struggle between Japan and Russia for power in that small and backward kingdom.[333] Our Minister

---

[*] "I can fully understand, and sympathize with, the disappointment of the Japanese at not securing any money indemnity," wrote Arthur Lee to Roosevelt, " but from a purely cold-blooded international standpoint I think this is a matter for discreet rejoicing. I can't think that it would be to the advantage of either England or the United States to have Japan (whose head may be suffering from a little excusable swelling) equipped with ' millions to burn ' on a fresh fleet of battleships."

in Korea was Horace N. Allen, who had gone out as a missionary and had then become our first Minister to Korea, and in both capacities had shown an aptitude for intrigue. As Minister he was working in still another rôle, that of agent of American business interests in Korea, pleading their cause with the Government he represented.[334] Allen deplored Roosevelt's unwillingness to take " strong measures " with the Koreans.[335] The picture of imperialism at its crudest that Allen's voluminous correspondence paints explains a great deal in subsequent attitudes of Oriental peoples toward the " white man " and his culture. Japan's imitation of " Western civilization " that made Roosevelt so admire the Japanese was also described in Allen's letters with a stark realism about Japanese ruthlessness and brutality toward Koreans[*] that left little to be admired.[336] The Korean Government was extravagant, corrupt, cruel, untrustworthy, and hopelessly weak. But the Korean people Allen found better than their government. " The Korean people," he wrote Secretary of State Hay, " are a docile, good-natured, patient and hard working race. They differ from the Chinese in being able to take on our ways rather easily. Koreans have become naturalized American citizens and are a credit to us." " They seem able to absorb ideas of liberty and equality very readily." [337]

Besides the two great military powers, business men of Japan, Russia, Germany, France, Britain, and the United States were in Korea grabbing all the resources of the coun-

---

[*] It has been charged that the elder George Kennan influenced Roosevelt in his Korean policy. Kennan's writings Minister Allen considered " venomous." Kennan " went to Korea on a picnic provided by the Japanese," Allen charged, " and wrote some of the silliest nonsense imaginable. This was so severely criticized that he returned in a year to make good and he certainly did so. It disgusted all Americans in Korea . . . and made us ashamed of him as an American." Kennan's " hatred for the Russians," Allen protested, " seemed to cause him to take up the Japanese with such ardor that he could tolerate nothing that seemed antagonistic to them and he certainly can write."

try they could lay hands on, each group scheming to increase
its influence at the expense of its rivals. American business in
a rich but backward region far from the restraints of " civilization " was playing for big stakes. Collbran and Bostwick
was one of the large public utility, banking, contracting, and
mining firms of North China. Another important operator
was one Leigh Hunt who had made a fortune and lost it
again in the panic of 1893 and then made another in Korean
mines. Hunt had gone on from Korea to open more mines
in South Africa and to build irrigation projects in the
Sudan.[338] Hunt knew Boss Platt in New York and other
senators like Allison and Dolliver of Iowa.[339] He was an acquaintance of Roosevelt's friends, essayist Brander Matthews and President Nicholas Murray Butler of Columbia,
who sent him to Roosevelt. Roosevelt invited him to stay
at the White House in June, 1903, found him interesting, and
had him again at the White House in 1904 and 1905. Brander Matthews called him " a true idealist who happens also
to be a man of affairs." Hunt's mines in Korea were reputed
to be the largest anywhere in Asia.[340]

The American business group and the American Minister,
Allen, tried hard to make Roosevelt see the need for protection of these vast interests against Japanese as well as
Russian interference and against British competition.[a] Both
the British and the Japanese, Allen reported, had " assumed
a stronger attitude here in Korea [b] . . . since the Anglo- Japanese alliance." [342] " The English are not acting nicely to us
here," Allen complained, " though I have helped them greatly
in the past. They hate to see the Yankee leading in the large
commercial developments here." [343]

[a] Yet both Hunt and Congressman Jacob Sloat Fassett, who was in business
with Hunt, though originally friendly, came to distrust Allen, and Allen blamed
them for his dismissal. Allen did not always have good relations with Collbran
and Bostwick, either, though he often rendered them services.[341]
[b] Allen had warned against this and had predicted Japan would be a more
ruthless competitor than Russia.

Allen himself was hostile to Japan, which he feared might take over Korea some day and shut everyone else out. Hence he became increasingly distressed as Roosevelt made it more and more obvious that he was going to let Japan take control, as he probably had determined from the first to do. In 1902 Roosevelt told Allen to talk matters over with Rockhill who was handling Korean affairs for him. When he came to realize the Administration's friendliness to Japan, Allen sought to persuade Baron Komura that Japan's best policy would be to favor the advance of American as opposed to other non-Japanese interests in Korea.[344] When in 1902 Rear Admiral Frederick Rodgers visited Korea to make surveys for a naval base, Allen was eager to have the base built because " the Koreans seem to think that America does not count and they may treat us as they please with no fear of their conduct being brought home to them." [345]

Allen wrote of the keen competition between the Japanese and the Russians. But Japan was gradually getting the upper hand. In 1902 the Minister declared, " Russia seems to have so much on her hands that she is now apparently willing to let Korea pretty much alone. . . . The Japanese, however, are careful not to do anything to precipitate trouble with Russia." The Japanese, he reported, have the most influence in Korea and seem able to get more in the way of advantages than do the Russians. " The Japanese scheme is to build railways " and colonize Japanese " in most of the large cities in the interior." They seem, he warned, " to be getting pretty complete control of the trade of the country, while Russia is making no forward move." [346] Through the shifting scenes, Allen found it easier for American business men to get on with the Russians who sometimes worked with them than with the Japanese who persistently wished to push them out. In Manchuria Russia in control built railroads that made trade possible and controlled bandits, who made trade impossible when the Russian troops were re-

moved. Indeed in the end Allen felt he was removed for
being pro-Russian, a charge he vigorously denied.[347] " The
Koreans," he reported, " dislike the Japanese . . . for their
high handed methods and seem to be generally hoping that
the Russians will come down and relieve them." [348]

On September 30, 1903, Allen, home on leave, had the
momentous discussion at the White House referred to in the
last lecture. He argued with Roosevelt and Rockhill, who
was by then back in Washington acting unofficially as adviser on Far Eastern affairs. Allen attempted to persuade
the President that his anti-Russian policy discussed earlier
was a mistake. It would be wiser, Allen said, to let Russia
occupy Manchuria and maintain an open door for us. Russia
had opened up a great commercial field in Manchuria; she
had policed an area that without policing was useless and
that had never been safe for trade until Russia took over.
She was building railroads and roads. And seventy-five per
cent of the trade was coming to us. Besides, Russia would
never voluntarily vacate Manchuria any more than we would
Hawaii. No, Allen argued, the President's policy was not
serving American interests but was making America the
cats-paw of Britain and Japan. Roosevelt's policy would
prompt Japan to expect our backing and would " lead her
to adopt a too bellicose attitude toward Russia." Then " we
would simply be forced into more or less of an alliance with
England and Japan." Roosevelt and Rockhill denied that
this result could follow their policy, and said they had assurances from Japan that she would not expect our support.
But Allen countered by pointing out that Hayashi, Japanese
representative in Seoul, had for a year been boasting that
" the United States and England were friends and both were
very strong friends of Japan and that the United States
was almost the same as in the Japan-English Alliance."

Roosevelt asked Allen who he thought would win in case
of war between Japan and Russia. Allen admitted that

Japan would be victorious on the sea and possibly on the land. Roosevelt asked why then he wanted to back the nation that would lose the war. Because, replied the Minister, Russia " wanted us to have all the trade we could handle," and " Japan . . . would make us increasing trouble until we might have to cross swords with her." The argument became heated. Roosevelt was furious. To make matters worse, Allen on the way back to Korea gave out an interview defending his position and criticizing the President.* [349]

When Allen reached Korea he realized that he was beaten, and that, with his government's backing, Japan was eventually to take over Korea. He found the Korean Government deteriorated still further until it was incapable of preserving order in its capital and Allen had to get a guard to protect his house. He found the Emperor, as he put it, " playing with dancing girls like Nero fiddling while Rome burned." He seems to have despaired and tried to make the best of a policy he still thought unwise. " These people," he wrote Rockhill in January, 1904, " cannot govern themselves. They must have an over-lord as they have had for all time. When it was not China, it was Russia or Japan, and as soon as they came out from one they made such an awful mess of things as to oblige someone else to take charge of them." " Let Japan have Korea outright," he now urged Rockhill, " if she can get it." " She will have to take charge of everything here. We will be protected in our vested rights and if we get no more troublesome concessions it will be as well, for the people will be in good condition for the development of large commercial interests." He had come to feel

* His friend James R. Morse warned Allen that his reported utterances after the interview had angered the President, who was much more friendly to Japan than to Russia, and that Allen might be recalled. Allen denied that it was in Korea that he had favored Russia over Japan. It was only in Manchuria, he insisted. He also denied talking to the press, but explained that a personal friend with whom he had conversed confidentially had talked indiscreetly to the press.

about Japan in Korea as he had always felt about Russia in Manchuria. He was not " opposed to any civilized race taking over the management of these kindly asiatics for the good of the people and the suppression of the oppressive officials, the establishment of order and the development of commerce." But the United States " will make a great mistake," he wrote Rockhill who was advising Roosevelt, " if it tries to have Japan simply continue this fiction of independence. Let the thing be plainly understood and Japan will then be able to prepare herself against any future absorption from the north." [350] " There is little we can really do for . . . [the Koreans]," he admitted in May, 1904. " Official corruption has become so bad of late years that it was only a question of time until someone should be obliged to step in and put things to rights." [351]

Yet Allen was not happy over Roosevelt's solution. " I am working along in great harmony with the Japanese," he wrote in March, 1904. He felt, though, that they would be " very angry " whenever American firms made favorable " deals." " The Japanese . . . think that Korea is theirs and will dislike to see Americans come off ahead in any commercial matters." [352] Willard Straight, American vice-consul-general in Seoul, was as unhappy over Roosevelt's policy as Allen.[353] That same month Sloat Fassett, large American mine owner and congressman, called on Hay at the State Department to get protection for his mines.[354] In May Allen wrote, " Our dear cousins, the British, camp right on our trail and never lose a chance to do us an injury if they can. How they do love us. The Japanese want the whole country for themselves and have no use for us, and with their British allies to egg them on you can see that this is a place that requires wakeful hours and constant work of an annoying kind. The Japanese show up well from the U. S. A. but when you have to combat them commercially, it is quite another thing." [355] After the great Japanese naval victory of May,

1905, Allen wrote in alarm, " It is going to be very hard for the Japanese Government to restrain its people and already we are feeling the effect over here where they look with great disfavor upon the holdings and successes of Americans. They are already trying to put the screws on American concessionaires." [356]

From the American Legation in Tokyo, too, Roosevelt had warning of the way the Japanese might oppress the Koreans. When Japan was about to take the foreign relations of Korea into her own hands, Lloyd Griscom, Minister to Japan, wrote Roosevelt, " I think we ought to throw our whole moral weight onto the scales to prevent the Japanese from abusing the Koreans. As conquerors the Japanese civilians are very different from the disciplined Japanese Army. The Koreans don't deserve much good treatment but we should try to prevent the Japanese from going too far." [357] Roosevelt replied, " I am inclined to think that it is all right for Japan to take the foreign relations of Korea in her hands, but I shall speak most earnestly along the lines of your letter to Takahira." [358]

Roosevelt ever since 1900 had been convinced that Korea could not govern itself, that the United States must not undertake responsibility for it, and that it would be better for everybody if Japan took Korea over and governed it efficiently, preserving law and order as the Koreans never could. The overall scheme for Anglo-Japanese-American control of as much of Eastern Asia as possible to balance Russian strength there seemed to him much more important than American interests in Korea. In any case, he hoped Japan would maintain an open door there. Hence, business interests protested in vain. [359] Hay talked over Japan's control of Korea with the Chinese minister in February. [360] Allen, who had opposed what Roosevelt had determined to do, was recalled in May.[*] Lodge learned in London in June that we

[*] The decision to recall him had been made several months earlier. In Febru-

had approved "Japan's control of Corea."[362] Though the
American Embassy in Tokyo did not know of this agreement ten weeks later,[363] Roosevelt had instructed Taft in
July to agree to "Japanese suzereignty over Corea to the
extent that Corea enter into no foreign treaties without the
consent of Japan."[364]

In November, 1905, then, with American approval, Japan
took over Korea, and the United States was the first nation
to recognize this destruction of Korean freedom, which she
was by solemn treaty obligated to guarantee. "The Japs
have got what they have been planning for these many
moons," wrote a member of the American firm of Collbran
and Bostwick, "and it is clear that Roosevelt played into
their hands when he posed as the great peacemaker of the
20th century."[365] The Emperor sent frantic pleas for help to
Hay and after Hay's death to Root, and to Roosevelt,
reminding them of America's repeated protestations of interest in Korean independence.[366] The State Department
declined to see Homer B. Hulbert, whom the Emperor sent
to Washington to plead his cause. Roosevelt justified his
refusal to receive the Emperor's letter because the Emperor
asked that it be kept secret especially from the Japanese, and
because a few days before Roosevelt received the Emperor's
letter the Emperor himself had signed a protocol with Japan
accepting a Japanese protectorate. Eugene A. Elliott, director of Collbran and Bostwick, reported to his employer, however, that the treaty between Japan and Korea was "a
gigantic fraud." The Emperor had tried to get someone to
intercede with Roosevelt to insist upon a joint protectorate
held by America, England, France, and Germany. A protectorate was necessary, Elliott believed. "But," Elliott explained to the owner of his firm, the Koreans "have long ago

ary Hay told Roosevelt of appeals of Koreans to leave Allen in Korea, and added
jocosely, "I have given . . . no encouragement, knowing the marble heart to
which they are appealing."[361]

made up their minds, and correctly too, that no justice will be received by them as long as they are entirely in the hands of the Japs alone." [367] On August 4, 1905, Roosevelt did receive at Oyster Bay two Korean envoys with a petition that he tender "the good office of the United States" in the preservation of "the integrity of their country." The President received them cordially and read their memorial but told them that they would have to present it officially through their legation. The younger of the two envoys was interestingly one Syngman Rhee, then a student at George Washington University. [368] Two years later Roosevelt wrote Secretary of State Root that he felt they should "positively decline to see" another Korean mission. [369]

"Why," asked Allen, "should these eight millions of people be so forgotten by the nation that stood sponsor at their birth into the family of nations." [370] To Hay Roosevelt gave part of the answer. "We can not possibly interfere for the Koreans against Japan," the President said, for "they could not strike one blow in their own defense." [371] "It was out of the question to suppose," he later elaborated, "that any other nation, with no interest of its own at stake, would do for the Koreans what they were utterly unable to do for themselves." [372] But the major part of the answer to Allen's question lay in Roosevelt's picture of a balance in the Far East in which Japan would control Korea and have major influence in Manchuria and the Anglo-Americans would dominate the Yangtse Valley, all as an offset to Russia, and everywhere the door would be kept open for the trade of all. For the sake of this world balance that would prevent any one nation from dominating, Roosevelt was ready to sacrifice both the Koreans and American business interests in Korea.

Roosevelt's friendliness for Japan was not shaken even when, after the Russo-Japanese War, the anti-American rioting against the peace terms broke out in Japan in Sep-

tember, 1905. His faith was justified a few days after the
rioting by a cable from Minister Lloyd Griscom reporting:
" Your popularity with the Japanese people has for the past
few months been increasing with great rapidity. . . . Whatever feeling of annoyance there is in Japan now towards us
is very slight and a few months will see the end of it." [373] Just
after the anti-foreign rioting, Roosevelt wrote a British
friend, " All I can do to help . . . [Japan] will be done. It
may be that we shall have trouble with her, and the attacks
by the Tokio mob on foreigners and Christians have an
ominous side. . . . But for all that and in spite of my realization that she may show herself at times as unpleasant a
neighbor as all European and American powers have at times
shown themselves to be, I yet admire and believe in the
Japanese and feel that their advent into the circle of great
civilized powers is a good thing." [374]

Still, Roosevelt was not unmindful of the possibility of
future danger in Japan. Shortly after the Portsmouth Conference met, he expressed privately to Lodge his own view
about the effect of victory upon the Japanese. " That Japan
will have her head turned to some extent I do not in the
least doubt, and I see clear symptoms of it in many ways.
We should certainly as a nation have ours turned if we had
performed such feats as the Japanese have. . . . I have no
doubt that some Japanese . . . will behave badly to foreigners," he confided to Lodge. " They cannot behave worse
than the State of California, through its Legislature, is now
behaving toward the Japanese." But Roosevelt was not
worried. " Most certainly the Japanese soldiers and sailors
have shown themselves to be terrible foes," he wrote. " There
can be none more dangerous in all the world. But our own
navy, ship for ship, is I believe at least as efficient as
theirs." [375]

Indeed, Roosevelt's solution for any possible danger was
two-fold. " I hope," he wrote, " that we can persuade our

people on the one hand to act in a spirit of generous justice and genuine courtesy toward Japan, and on the other hand to keep the navy respectable in numbers and more than respectable in the efficiency of its units.* If we act thus we need not fear the Japanese." [376] It was, after all, as we have seen, a balance of powers in the Far East that was the goal of his policy there.

In the years after the War Roosevelt watched Japan with interest and frequently speculated on what her future portended for America. In December, 1905, his intimate friend, General Leonard Wood, wrote Roosevelt that unless we kept a strong navy and fortified Hawaii, Japan might seize Hawaii and thereby cut off the Philippines.[377] Roosevelt replied that Wood was right about fortifying Hawaii and keeping the Navy strong, but added, " I do not for a moment agree, however, that Japan has any immediate intention of moving against us in the Philippines. Her eyes for some time to come will be directed toward Korea and southern Manchuria." " If she attacked us and met disaster," the President explained to General Wood, " she would lose everything she has gained in the war with Russia; and if she attacked us and won, she would make this republic her envenomed and resolute foe for all time, and would without question speedily lose the alliance with Great Britain and see a coalition between Russia, the United States, and very possibly Germany and France to destroy her in the Far East." [378] Eleven months later, in a letter to Sir Edward Grey, Roosevelt deliberated on Japan's use of her growing military strength. " I have no question myself," he told Grey, " that Russia keeps steadily in mind her intention to try another throw with Japan for supremacy in easternmost Asia." Revolution in Russia might prevent this. " But if Russia remains a

---

* His ideal was "the position of the just man armed." " We can hold our own . . . only if . . . we do the exact reverse of what the demagogues on the one hand and the mugwumps on the other would like to have us do."

united empire, then I believe Japan will need to keep herself formidable unless she expects to be overwhelmed in Manchuria." " I am inclined to think," he declared, " that Japan knows this and that this is one of the reasons which have actuated her in continuing to prepare for war." " But it is also possible," he admitted, " that she has designs upon some other power—Germany or America, for instance." " Again," Roosevelt conjectured, " it is quite possible she has no designs on any power but is simply bent upon achieving and maintaining a commanding position in the Western Pacific and East Asia." [379]

It has often been said that Roosevelt came to fear Japan in the last years of his administration and to regret his rôle in the Portsmouth Conference. There is no evidence of such a change in attitude. Indeed, former Assistant Secretary of State Loomis felt that " the sending of the fleet disabused . . . [the President's] mind of such fears as he had had." After an official visit to Japan in 1908 Loomis reported to Roosevelt that Japan had no thought of world domination, that the Emperor was " a great man," and that Japan was controlled by " level-headed, sane men." [380] True, Roosevelt was deeply concerned because he had not been able to persuade his fellow-countrymen to regard the Japanese with the respect he felt for them.* He knew better than most Americans the bitterness with which proud Japanese listened to insults and watched mistreatment of their countrymen by people who considered them inferiors.[382] In March, 1905, he wrote John A. T. Hull, Republican chairman of the House Military Affairs Committee, demanding that Hull repudiate an alleged interview about Japan. " Many of our own people," he told Hull, " grow suspicious of the Japanese be-

* One Japanese newspaper suggested that Roosevelt was pleased rather than surprised at the strong expression of the Japanese because he might be able to use it to accomplish his ends in dealing with California in regard to the Japanese.[381]

cause an occasional Japanese official is reported to use language such as this which you . . . are reported as using." " The proper way for us to behave as regards foreign affairs is to scrupulously pay proper courtesy to all foreign nations, and neither to wrong them nor talk about them in ways which will make them think we are hostile or intend to wrong them." [383] In October, 1906, he warned Senator Hale of Maine, " I do not think that . . . [Japan] wishes war as such, and I doubt if she would go to war now; but I am very sure that if sufficiently irritated and humiliated by us she will get to accept us instead of Russia as the national enemy whom she will ultimately have to fight; and under such circumstances her concentration and continuity of purpose, and the exceedingly formidable character of her army and navy, make it necessary to reckon very seriously with her." [384] " I am utterly disgusted," he exploded to Lodge. " The feeling of the Pacific Coast people . . . is as foolish as if conceived by the mind of a Hottentot." With " careless insolence " they wish " grossly to insult the Japanese . . . and at the same time . . . be given advantages in Oriental markets." " With besotted folly," the President complained, the West Coast people " are indifferent to building up the navy while provoking this formidable new power—a power jealous, sensitive and warlike, and which if irritated could at once take both the Philippines and Hawaii from us if she obtained the upper hand on the seas." [385]

Though he had given up the idea he once had held that the Japanese could be allowed freely to enter America, still he was determined to bring about their exclusion in a manner that would alleviate their bitterness and avoid offense to their pride. This was why " the idiots of the California Legislature " incensed him. " The California Legislature would have had an entire right to protest as emphatically as possible against the admission of Japanese laborers," he wrote George Kennan in 1905, " for their very frugality, abstemi-

ousness and clannishness make them formidable to our
laboring class. . . . But I . . . feel humiliated by the foolish
offensiveness of the resolution they passed." [386] Roosevelt
managed to hold off the Pacific slope "idiots" and handle
the problem his way. In 1907 he negotiated the Gentlemen's
Agreement.[387] This fulfilled a long-cherished hope. It was
the complement of the trip of the fleet around the world.
The agreement "is a knock-out for the mischief makers on
both sides of the Atlantic—and I may add on both sides of
the Pacific," he wrote Arthur Lee.[388] Even while he was
sending the fleet around the world to impress Japan with
our strength he instructed former Assistant Secretary of
State Loomis [a] personally to persuade the Japanese of our
friendliness in sending it.[389] Near the end of his administration he noted proudly, "My policy of constant friendliness
and courtesy toward Japan, *coupled with sending the fleet
around the world*, has borne good results!" [390] This was not
the remark of a man frightened about Japan. It was a statement of gratification over the fulfillment of the very policy
he had laid down for relations with victorious Japan as he
brought the peace conference together at Japan's request
in 1905.[391]

It was in 1907 that Roosevelt sent the fleet around the
world. Unquestionably a main object was to impress Japan
with our power so that she would not be tempted to make
trouble.[b] But it must be remembered that this was only one
of the objectives. The President also wanted to give the

---

[a] Loomis was in Japan as United States High Commissioner to a world exposition that was to have been held there.

[b] In 1911 Roosevelt wrote George O. Trevelyan that he had sent the fleet
because he had "become uncomfortably conscious of a very, very slight under-
tone of veiled truculence" in Japanese communications to us and because he
was convinced that the Japanese war party and even his British friends believed
that the Japanese could beat America and thought that Roosevelt, too, believed
it. "I thought it a good thing that the Japanese should know," he told German
Admiral von Tirpitz, "that there were fleets of the white races which were
totally different from the fleet of poor Rodjestvensky." [392]

people an object lesson that would win support for speeding up the completion of the Panama Canal. The fleet by stopping in various Latin American ports followed up Root's good will tour there. Furthermore, the voyage stimulated American pride in the navy and therefore increased sentiment for a large navy, and Roosevelt carefully chose to accompany the fleet journalists that would best stimulate interest in it. Watching this manifestation of America's power and seeing the world standing in awe of it was, too, an exciting experience for the President.* Then, besides, the cruise provided the navy much needed practice. " I have not the slightest doubt," the President confided to Root, " that unexpected defects will appear in coaling, repairing and the like; but it is highly important that we should remedy these defects at a time when they can be remedied, and not in a time of war." When objection was raised that sending the whole fleet to the Pacific endangered the fleet and laid Eastern cities open to attack, Roosevelt replied a little heatedly, " The fleet is not now going to the Pacific as a war measure; but if there is the slightest doubt of the expediency of sending it there for military reasons, then it becomes imperative that it be sent there in peace and not in war—unless we are prepared definitely to take the ground that we never intend to send it to the Pacific at all, in which case . . . we should abandon every position of ours in the Pacific Ocean that is not coterminous with our own territory." [394]

Japan met the sending of the fleet with assurances of her peaceful intentions and publicly expressed confidence that America did not intend the fleet to threaten her.[b] [396] She

---

* At a reception, for instance, in Berlin in 1910 he was lionized by German naval officials, who admired the man that had accomplished a feat they had considered impossible. They told Lawrence Abbott, who was with him, that his " achievement was a stroke of genius." [393]

[b] Joseph Pulitzer and his *New York World*, however, did charge the President

cordially urged Roosevelt to send the navy to Japan so that she could express her friendship and admiration for America.[397] Roosevelt shared none of the fears of some of his countrymen that the Japanese would use this opportunity to attack the fleet,[a] though he took every precaution to have the fleet well prepared if trouble did arise.[b] His chief worry arose from the possibility of an incident created by some fanatical individual. " There is always the chance," he explained, " of some desperado doing something that will have very bad effects." " If you give the enlisted men leave while at Tokio," the President instructed Rear Admiral C. S. Sperry, ". . . be careful to choose only those upon whom you can absolutely depend. There must be no suspicion of insolence or rudeness on our part." " Aside from the loss of a ship," the President warned, " I had far rather that we were insulted than that we insult anybody. . . . I firmly believe that the Japanese Government will use every effort to see that the highest consideration and courtesy are accorded to our people, and you of course will do everything in your power to show the utmost consideration and courtesy to the Japanese." [399]

How the sending of the fleet around the world affected Japanese policy has never been satisfactorily determined. No incident of the sort Roosevelt thought possible occurred.

with bullying Japan, encouraging the anti-Japanese mobs on the West Coast, and risking war.[395]

[a] The Kaiser believed the Japanese " not *yet* ready with their fleet, and therefore not inclined to fight with America at this stage."

[b] On June 27 Secretary of the Navy Victor Metcalf, Postmaster-General George Meyer, Captain Richard Wainwright of the Navy General Board, and Lieutenant Colonel Wm. W. Wotherspoon, president of the Army War College, met with Roosevelt at Oyster Bay and arrangements for coaling and supplying the fleet were made; plans for war, which Roosevelt felt certain would not occur, were made; preparations were projected for fortifying a base at Subic Bay in the Philippines, and while the fleet was sailing around the world a decision was made to transfer the base to Manila Bay, which was more defensible from the land.[398]

Temporarily at least the enthusiastic welcome Japan gave the navy increased the friendliness of the two nations. The Japanese press was universally cordial.[400] Cal O'Laughlin of the *Chicago Tribune* reported, " The fleet made a vivid and far reaching impression. It caused the Japanese to realize the formidable power of the United States, as nothing else possibly could have done." [401] " In France, England and Germany the best information is that we shall have war with Japan and that we shall be beaten," the President reported to Root in July, 1907.* His own judgment was perhaps not so much a commentary on Japan as a lifelong conviction about international relations even with friendly powers. " The only thing that will prevent war," he insisted, " is the Japanese feeling that we shall not be beaten, and this feeling we can only excite by keeping and making our navy efficient in the highest degree." [403] Roosevelt always felt that impressing Japan with our power had been one of the most effective acts of his administration.ᵇ " The sending of the fleet to the Pacific stopped the Japanese talk of war," he boasted.[404]

Yet it is not certain that Roosevelt's much lauded sending of the fleet did not worsen rather than improve the ultimate chances of peace with Japan. It seems not without significance that it was during this same year that Japan joined her enemy Russia to destroy the balance of power Roosevelt had hoped his intervention in the Russo-Japanese War had established. There is some reason to believe that while the Japanese were at this time friendly toward us, while they professed not to believe the Navy trip could possibly be intended as a threat against them, and while they smiled and

---

* In 1910 von Tirpitz told Roosevelt in Berlin that he and the British had both felt Roosevelt would fail in sending the fleet around the world because Japan would use this opportunity to attack it.[402]

ᵇ The Kaiser and Admiral von Tirpitz believed the sending of the fleet did more for peace in the Orient than anything that could have happened.

fêted our sailors, the fleet's trip actually implanted in the Japanese a grim determination not again to be caught where they could be overawed by superior power.* In Japan a great struggle was taking place that was to continue until the attack on Pearl Harbor concluded it—the contest of militarists, big-navy men, and other anti-American forces against civilian, pro-American elements that admired Western culture and institutions. On the outcome of this battle for control of Japan hung far-reaching consequences for the future. Much that Roosevelt did for better treatment of Japanese in America strengthened the civilized pro-Western group. There is reason to believe that, on the contrary, his sending the fleet to the Pacific and to Japan added greatly to the strength of the Japanese navalists and helped get appropriations for battleships in Japan as well as in America.[406]

Several factors ultimately defeated Roosevelt's balance of power and open door aims in the Far East. One was the rise of nationalism in China and China's determination to control her own destinies. A second was the combination of Japan and Russia to divide Northern China between them, instead of balancing each other to everyone else's advantage. Even before Roosevelt left office, the balance of Japan against Russia, which he thought he had secured at Portsmouth and on which he counted to keep Asia open, was destroyed. In 1907 these two powers made a secret treaty in which the two balanced rivals combined to divide Korea, Manchuria, and Mongolia between them as spheres in which each nation had " special interests " and from which each hoped to exclude everyone else. They did, however, again become rivals. And, in 1910, in spite of the fact that they formed a new pact in that year, Roosevelt still believed

---

* Assistant Secretary of State Loomis testified that after the fleet sailed, Roosevelt had misgivings whether he should have sent it or not, whether doing so would do more harm than good. But Loomis reported him pleased in the end with having sent it.[405]

Japan and Russia preparing for future conflict and still hoped to protect the interests of other powers by maintaining the balance between them.[407] Third, Roosevelt did not foresee that Japanese businessmen would not be content to share areas Japan controlled with Americans, and that American businessmen would not easily give up rich potentialities of trade and exploitation. He failed to envisage the international bitterness that would grow out of business rivalries. Fourth, Roosevelt's own government was soon to reverse his policy. Younger diplomats in his service, like Willard Straight, Francis M. Huntington Wilson, and his youthful friend Billy Phillips had long been critical of the pro-Japanese policy of their superiors under Roosevelt. When he left the Presidency, his own authority on Far Eastern affairs, William W. Rockhill, was removed from the scene and sent by Taft in May, 1909, from Peking to St. Petersburg. The younger, more aggressive men, less friendly to Japan, rose to power and under his and Root's successors reversed his policy of friendliness and began to use the power of government to contest the Japanese domination that Roosevelt had helped create.[408] Fifth, aided in part by American policies unfriendly to Japan that Roosevelt would have deplored and in part by the support Roosevelt himself gave these militarists in sending his powerful fleet to Asia, Japanese militarists grew in power * and ultimately supplanted with America's aid the pro-American Japanese, who

---

* Huntington Wilson, of the pro-Russian group in the State Department, who disapproved the President's policy anyway, thought Roosevelt's siding with Japan in the Russo-Japanese War was the basic error. Looking backward from World War II against Japan he wrote in 1945: " I don't think we then realized the enormity of Japanese insincerity. It is conceivable that Marquis Ito and our civilian friends in the government, and even some of the military Elder Statesmen, intended a decent measure of justice and fair play. But immediately after the war with Russia the arrogance of the military became manifest . . . . Following the victory over Russia, the ascendancy of the military . . . was restored." [409]

had controlled Japan in Roosevelt's day. Thus Roosevelt's
Japanese policy failed and his balance of power program collapsed in the Far East. Perhaps no peace based on maintaining a delicate balance of power could have succeeded, but
in any case Roosevelt's carefully cultivated balance in the
Far East scarcely outlasted his Presidency. Sixth, blinded
by his concept of the Chinese as a backward people, he
utterly failed to comprehend or take into account the rise of
an independent and assertive China to a rôle of major importance in the twentieth century. China was therefore not
permitted to attend the Portsmouth Conference or have the
voice she sought [410] in Roosevelt's decision about the Far
East. A sharing of responsibilities and decisions in the Far
East with the representatives of the " new spirit " in China
might have made a vast difference in China, in the Far East,
and in the world.

chapter **VI**

ROOSEVELT *and the World Balance of Power: Europe*

Roosevelt's concern about America's relation to a world balance of power led him to an interest in Europe, too. Just as he had early discovered that Far Eastern problems could not be solved without an understanding that they were a part of world problems, so he discovered that the world balance of power was seriously affected by what happened in Europe. He early realized, in short, that the same rival imperial powers faced each other in Asia and in Europe and that an imbalance either place might seriously affect America.[a] Some of the powers, indeed, he knew faced each other clear across the two continents of Eurasia. In recognition of this he wrote Speck in 1901, " I wonder if the presence of Russia and Germany face to face, and with their commercial frontiers overlapping alike in Asia Minor and

[a] Germany, also interested in the Far Eastern balance of power as part of the European balance, feared Japan and Britain in combination would overthrow it and regarded Germany and America as the counterbalance. The round-the-world cruise of the American Navy " knocks all the calculations of the British and the Japanese on the head," the Kaiser rejoiced. " The British must, *nolens volens*, again send a strong squadron to the East, which they imagined to be secure under Japanese protection, that must weaken them in Europe against us." [1]

in China, will have any effect upon future affairs! " [2] Roosevelt and his friends were as concerned as they were about
Russia's power in the Far East, partly because of their consciousness that Russia was an uncertain element in the *European* balance of power. What a power she would be in
Europe, Spring Rice ruminated in a letter to Roosevelt, if
she would " arm large bodies of semi-civilized people " !
Then she would become a " menace to the world," indeed,
because she could turn the whole mass of Asia against
Europe.[3]

Throughout his Presidency Roosevelt thought in terms
of the possibility of a war that might become a general world
war if the world balance were not maintained. He was concerned about all the smaller rivalries between two powers
that might start such a general war. When Spring Rice wrote
him that he could " keep the peace of Europe," he replied
that he did not want to become " an international ' Meddlesome Mattie.' " But, he promised, " if at any time I see
where I can thus help I shall most certainly try to help . . .
keep the peace of Europe." [4] In his consciousness of the
possibility of world war and of America's involvement in it,
and hence of America's concern to help avoid it, he was unusual in an America that was for the most part innocent of
the danger of war and certain that a war in Europe or Asia
would not concern us if it did come.

Roosevelt sought in three ways to avoid the outbreak of
such a general war. He constantly advocated building a
powerful navy; he promoted arbitration and participated in
the Hague Conference; and he pulled wires behind the scenes
in Europe trying to bring the nations closer together and to
remove distrust and threats of war. His navy views are well
known. It is important here only to emphasize the fact that
he wanted a navy not simply as a protection for America,
but as a means of making his and America's voice effective
when he spoke for peace in the world—or for our " national

interest " in the international struggle for power. Concerning the first Hague Conference, for instance, in 1899, he had told Maria Storer, " Something was done for peace at the Hague last year, but our influence was due to the fact that we came in as a strong man and not as a weakling." [5] When he had persuaded Germany and Britain to agree to arbitrate their dispute with Venezuela in 1903, he still felt, " Important though it is that we should get the Hague Tribunal to act in this case, where it can properly act, it is very much more important that we have a first-class navy and an efficient, though small army. No Hague Court will save us if we come short in these respects." [6]

Roosevelt's part in the second Hague Conference reveals much of his own attitude toward international action and much, too, of the difficulty in attaining peace by international action. To bodies like the Interparliamentary Union he had spoken enthusiastically about the Hague meetings. In 1904 at the request of the Union he called a second conference, which he talked about convening at The Hague, but the Russo-Japanese War made the time seem inopportune. So in a second note to the powers he announced his intention of calling one when the time seemed right.[7] In 1905, much more interested in having the conference a success than in getting acclaim by summoning it, he graciously stepped out of the way in the Czar's favor. The Russians made it clear that the Czar wanted to sponsor the conference.[*] [8] Anyway, " It gives us a freer hand in every way to have the Czar make the movement," Roosevelt told Root.[9] " I would have aroused many jealousies," he explained to Carl Schurz, and " there would be a feeling that I was posing too much as a professional peacemaker." [10] At one stage the President

---

[*] " Kings and such-like are fundamentally just as funny as American politicians," Roosevelt quipped. " Odell's anxiety that he and not Platt should receive the credit of certain presidential appointments . . . is not a bit more amusing than the attitude of the Czar about the Hague Conference."

wrote Andrew Carnegie, " I sometimes wish that we did not
have the ironclad custom which forbids a President ever to
go abroad. If I could meet the Kaiser and the responsible
authorities of France and England, I think I could be of help
in this Hague Conference business." [11]

As the Conference approached, Roosevelt did all he could
in talks with the French and the British to prepare the way
for accomplishment. He and his friends were agreed that
France, England, and the United States could and should
work together for common ends, and constant behind-the-
scenes negotiations were carried on to insure this coöperation.[12] Germany and Russia, both suspicious of the Conference, stood ready to block effective action. But Carnegie,
who had talked with the German ruler, felt the Kaiser could
be brought to support peace projects. Roosevelt also hoped
that he might influence William. In any case, he was willing
to try.[13]

The President was somewhat embarrassed by the activities
of the professional " peace men." Carnegie, for example, self-
appointed, busily wrote to and talked with the leaders in
England and with Roosevelt and the Kaiser about what the
Conference should do. Too, he brought William T. Stead,
British peace advocate, to this country to talk with Roosevelt about the Conference. Optimistically Carnegie reported
that both Britain and Germany would support reduction of
armaments.[14] At one stage Carnegie, to whom the British
leaders talked with more freedom than did Roosevelt, repeated to Speck what the British had said and complained
bitterly of the Kaiser's hostility to America and to peace.
Speck cabled home the conversation and Roosevelt received
what he called " a somewhat lurid telegram from William "
in consequence.[15] Peace advocates like Carl Schurz and
Andrew Carnegie constantly pressed the President to go
farther than he was willing to go. Indeed, he took pains to
have no " peace men " on his delegation at the " peace con-

ference." [16] He had of course to be polite, but he was frequently exasperated by their point of view.[17] His own views he made constantly clear. " I have the heartiest scorn," he wrote his British friend St. Loe Strachey, " for those . . . peace-at-any-price . . . people . . . who, whether from folly, from selfishness, from short-sightedness, or from sheer cowardice, rail at the manly virtues and fail to understand that righteousness is to be put before peace even when, as sometimes happens, righteousness means war." [18] When President Eliot wrote making proposals he thought impracticable, Roosevelt replied, " In The Hague my chief trouble will come from the fantastic visionaries who are crazy to do the impossible. Just at present the United States Navy is an infinitely more potent factor for peace than all the peace societies of every kind and sort, . . . At The Hague I think we can make some real progress, but only on condition of our not trying to go too far." [19]

One of the few accomplishments of the Conference was in part an American contribution. The American Government had insisted that the Hispanic American nations be invited to this second Hague Conference. In accepting the Russian agenda, America had reserved the right to introduce at the Conference the problem of recovering debts from small nations. Almost all Hispanic American countries participated. With the support of their delegates, General Horace Porter of the American delegation sponsored and the Conference adopted the doctrine of Luis M. Drago, foreign minister of Argentina, that no nation should use force in collecting from another country debts due its nationals. By international agreement, then, small nations were provided the protection that had concerned Roosevelt ever since his clash with Germany over forcible collection of debts in Venezuela in 1902-1903 had shown him the dangers in a practice he had previously accepted.[20]

The Americans tried, too, to obtain the establishment of

an international court that would function better than the
panel of names set up at the first Hague Conference in 1899.
The chief American delegate, Joseph Choate, was instructed
to seek " to increase the effectiveness of the system [of arbi-
tration] so that nations may more readily have recourse to
it voluntarily." America wanted this time a " permanent
and continuous court " to decide legal matters. Secretary of
State Root hoped that the judges of this new court would be
" dominated solely by jurisprudence " and would remain
" unaffected by national and diplomatic considerations."
Roosevelt thought the proposal " excellent." The Conference
supported the principle, but could not agree upon a method
of choosing judges. So in the end this plan came to nothing
practical.[21]

Roosevelt favored limitation of armaments, though not
reduction of armaments, and certainly not disarmament.*
Jaurès, the French Socialist, who favored limitation of armaments, praised him as the prime mover of the Conference.
The opponents of the Conference, however, attacked him as
insincere in claiming to want limitation of armaments. As
proof they pointed to his imperialism of 1898 and his campaign speeches of 1900 and 1904.[23] Yet he did sincerely wish
to limit armaments. His position did not require great self-
sacrifice, for he had written Richard Bartholdt in 1905 that
he thought if we would replace worn-out units in the navy
with " thoroughly efficient ones " we would not need any
increase in order to be thoroughly protected. With these
replacements accomplished, he told Bartholdt, " I think
without exposing ourselves to even the appearance of inconsistency we shall now be in shape to ask for the stoppage of
the increase of armament." [24] Indeed, even Mahan had proposed to him in December, 1904: " It has occurred to me, as
an agreement tending to lessen the expense of armaments,

---

* This subject was not on the agenda proposed by Russia, but the United
States reserved the right to introduce it.[22]

that nations might agree on a limitation of the tonnage of single ships." [25]

Roosevelt sought to line up the various powers behind such a reduction of expenditures on armaments. He had Ambassador White sound out the King of Italy on an international agreement that would prevent any increase. The King replied by proposing that the nations agree not to alter or improve the weapons of their armies, but he and White agreed that even to make this proposal would bring an outcry from arms manufacturers all over the world and that the Kaiser would never consent to have his Krupp works limited in their output. [26] The President then had White ask if the King thought it possible " to agree hereafter not to build any ships of more than a certain size." [27]

France and Russia opposed discussion of reduction of armaments, and French opposition affected British support. Sir Edward Grey thought the French Government was afraid to have limitation discussed because the French people would then demand genuine reduction in armament costs. [28] The Russians were determined to oppose considering armament limitation. But Russia dreaded to give offense by leading the opposition. Hence she sought through negotiation to keep the matter off the agenda. To this end Professor Fedor de Martens, a Russian privy councilor who had been a delegate to the earlier Hague Conference, too, was sent to the various capitals of Europe for private talks. [29]

Roosevelt tried to persuade the British Government to join him in demanding a limitation in armaments. In September, 1906, he used his friend George O. Trevelyan as a means of pleading with the British. " I recognize," the President wrote, " the great difficulty of coming to an agreement as to their limitations; but it does seem to me that it would be possible to come to some agreement as to the size of ships." Roosevelt urged the British to agree to limit the size of battleships to fifteen thousand tons. " I do not believe

that it would result in any more battleships . . . than if the
limit were not agreed to," Roosevelt argued, " and the result
would be a great diminution in expense." Trevelyan heartily
agreed with him.[30] To Sir Edward Grey Roosevelt wrote in
October, 1906, at length and with frankness. " As for the
matter of disarmament," he declared, " it is again difficult
for us in America to help you much, because we over here
have only a corporal's guard of an army; and relatively to our
wealth, population, and extent of territory, a navy smaller
than that of Germany or France. . . . Our people as a whole
are proud of their navy and wish to see it kept up to a good
point of efficiency." " The matter is of course far more vital
to you than to us," Roosevelt admitted, " and I wouldn't
venture to give you too much advice." Still, he pleaded with
Sir Edward for limitation. " I have hoped," he argued, " that
we could limit the size of ships and am not yet convinced that
this is impossible; but the new big ships are unquestionably
so much more efficient than the comparatively small ships
even of the most recent date as to make it evident that your
own people, as well as some others, will be extremely reluctant to go into any such movement unless they are sure that
it will not result to their own disadvantage; and the practical
difficulties in the way may be enormous. If we can· get an
agreement by the various nations that no more than a certain
number of ships, agreed upon between them, will be built by
any one, that might accomplish something." [31] In September,
too, Henry White had written his friend Secretary of War
Richard Haldane pleading the cause of the President's armaments proposals.[32] George Meyer went to London in February and Henry White in March to talk with Sir Edward
and other members of the British Government, but in vain.[33]
At the end of February Roosevelt himself again pleaded with
Grey. " I do not think," he contended, " that the limitation
of armaments will have any very great effect upon diminishing the likelihood of war, tho it may have a little. The chief

thing would be the relief of the strain upon the budgets of the different nations; and this is a very desirable end, for which I shall do whatever is in my power." [34]

Roosevelt was painfully aware of the obstacles that impeded even limitation. " When we come to the navy," he wrote Sir Edward, " there are great practical difficulties to be faced. If Russia rebuilds her fleet—and I do not see how she can be forbidden to do so—Japan may very well desire to build hers so as to keep ahead of Russia, and that would create a very strong feeling in the minds of the people here that we should continue building. Germany, I suppose, will feel that any proposal to stop building fleets now is really aimed at her." " I have felt," Roosevelt explained, " that the most practical way to secure a limitation in the increase of naval expenditures was to agree that no ship should be built beyond a certain size—say fifteen thousand tons." " But neither your people nor Germany would consider this," the President chided the British Foreign Secretary, " and the building of the Dreadnought inaugurated a new race in the matter of size. Japan entered the lists, and it was then impossible for us to refrain from following, and I suppose Germany will be bound in the end herself to try to emulate or surpass your ships." [35] Roosevelt also transmitted his proposals to King Edward through Count Gleichen.[36]

Germany proved difficult indeed on the matter of armaments. Meyer stopped in Berlin to talk with Charlemagne Tower, the American Ambassador there, and with the Kaiser and other German officials. Both Meyer and Tower agreed that Germany would do everything to block consideration of armaments. Even optimistic Carnegie was disappointed in his friend the Kaiser.[37] " I tried to show Von Bülow how matters stood," Carnegie wrote Roosevelt, " and urged him to take the lead and let Britain drag behind, which would very soon stir the [British Liberal] party in the Commons and the Press." [38] In spite of Carnegie, Germany continued to refuse to discuss limitation of armaments. Early in May, 1907, Chancellor von Bülow made a speech in the Reichstag in which he announced this refusal to the world.[39]

Henry White described an hour's confidential conversation he had had with Prince Hugo von Radolin, the German Ambassador in Paris, that probably partly explains why the Kaiser was in this instance so uncoöperative with his friend Roosevelt. White took the German Ambassador to task for Germany's position. " I said," White reported, " that I came as a friend of his, without authority or inspiration from my government; that I feared by opposing, as I had good reason to believe, and endeavoring to influence Russian Government to oppose, the raising at the Conference of certain questions which nearly all other first-class powers wish to discuss, German Government would find itself in the same position of isolation as last year and incur besides the obloquy of rapidly increasing lovers of peace everywhere, including Germany." Then unofficially as his private opinion, the German Ambassador explained, " The Emperor is in a very difficult position, as the military and imperialist parties firmly believe that England's sole reason for raising the disarmament question is to compel Germany to disarm in order to attack her when weakened and to reduce her to impotence; . . . the Emperor is very much blamed for having yielded at Algeciras instead of fighting, and if he were to agree to discuss the disarmament question and find himself, as Germany must in the event of serious proposals to disarm being adopted at the Conference, not only in a minority there but in Germany also on that subject, there is no telling to what extremes the party aforesaid might resort; possibly even change of form of government, all of which very desirable to avoid." [40]

When Roosevelt first approached him, the Kaiser replied indignantly that he was not blocking disarmament, that the British were telling " foul and filthy lies . . . to sow distrust between us two." The Kaiser insisted that King Edward had told him he was opposed to the Conference altogether and considered it a " humbug." The King thought it useless, William reported, " as nobody would, in case of need, feel bound by its decisions." Indeed, Edward considered it " even . . . dangerous," since " it was to be feared that instead of harmony more friction would be the result." [41] The British, in their turn, accused the Kaiser of objecting to discussing disarmament. John Morley, for instance, wrote, " The Kaiser is the difficulty. He is moving heaven and earth against the whole thing, and makes no secret of it that if the topic of disarmament is raised, his men will walk out. I see from his letter that T. R. is quite well aware of this." [42] So the Kaiser blamed Edward, and the British blamed the Kaiser, and both refused in the end to consider disarmament.[43]

Actually, England's position was equivocal. When he heard what the Kaiser had said of Edward's views, Ambassador Reid reported on May 1, 1907: " The King himself used strikingly similar expressions in a conversation with me one morning on the esplanade at Biarritz." [44] Ambassador Meyer on a visit to England in February had given the same report of the King's views.[45] In July, 1907, Edward told Reid confidentially that he " looked upon ' C.-B.'s ' demonstration * in favor of limitation of armaments, both in speech and newspaper article, as not well considered and likely to do harm." [46] On the other hand, Campbell-Bannerman, the Prime Minister, had vigorously supported reduction of armaments. His Cabinet, however, was divided. " Liberal Party is with Prime Minister Chancellor. Morley, Birrell Haldane but Grey and Asquith are very offish," Carnegie reported to Roosevelt. " Anti-Germanism at the root of it." [47] American Admiral Charles S. Sperry was unfavorably impressed by Britain's preparation for the Hague Conference. " Three fourths of

* Sir Henry Campbell-Bannerman, leader of the Liberal Party, had succeeded Conservative Arthur J. Balfour as Prime Minister on December 5, 1905.

the Russian programme bears on maritime war," he wrote, "and yet the naval delegates have only been appointed" at the end of April. "The Prime Minister's utterances on the subject of the limitation of armaments," Sperry continued, "are beneath contempt: They are models of disingenuous pettifogging." [48]

Sir Edward's position was difficult to understand, but he seems to have wanted limitation of armaments discussed to satisfy the British electorate but not discussed too seriously or acted upon. He admitted to Roosevelt that if Britain and Germany "were to agree to stop new construction for a few years or to agree to limit it the whole of the rest of Europe and perhaps the world would feel the relief" and probably "would all stop building." [49] Grey could not face his constituency unless the subject was introduced. Yet he was not willing to do anything that would limit British naval supremacy. Nor would he let his delegates introduce the subject at the Conference. He wanted the United States to propose armament limitation. Then Britain would second America's proposition. But if America was not to introduce it, he wished to be forewarned; for "it will be a poor lame conference," he wrote Roosevelt, "if the Powers all meet there and shirk the question." [50]

Roosevelt, too, seemed to wish the subject considered, but seemed to feel accomplishment was too unlikely to make pushing the issue worthwhile. "My present feeling is the same as yours," Roosevelt conceded to Grey, "namely, that there should be a discussion of, or at least a proposal to discuss, at the Hague, the question of excessive expenditure in armaments; but Germany's extreme reluctance to have the question raised causes me some doubts as to what course is advisable, for we shan't get much good result from The Hague if we go there with one of the great powers (Germany) and perhaps another (Russia) thoroly angered and suspicious, and anxious, therefore, to find some good excuse for preventing the accomplishment of anything even as regards other features of the program." [51] " I think there is a general feeling also that in view of the marvelous ability certain nations have of concealing what they are doing, we would have no real idea whether or not they were keeping down their armaments even in the event of an agreement to do so." [52]

Perhaps, too, Roosevelt was hesitant because he was no longer dealing with a Conservative Government in England that he knew and trusted or because close advisers warned him that Britain, too, would finally oppose him on armaments. His friend St. Loe Strachey, a Conservative editor, sounded warning. " I am I confess a little anxious," he wrote Roosevelt, " as to whether our Government may not do something foolish at the Hague Conference." [53] And Mahan, on whom he depended heavily for advice in such matters, wrote the President, " It must be obvious to you that the present prepossession of the public mind in most countries is such that the question of war itself, and of questions incidental to war, are in danger of being misjudged and ' rushed.' " [54]

In the end Roosevelt decided not to risk defeat by supporting a cause that was to be hopeless if Russia, France, and Germany opposed it and Britain wished only to appear to support while really scuttling it. So Choate was instructed: " If any European power proposes consideration of the subject, you will vote in favor of consideration and do everything you properly can to promote it." But if no European power made such a proposal Choate was not to ask the Conference to consider it. [55] " Ever since I found out," Roosevelt told Secretary of State Root, " that the English government would not consent to a reduction in the size of ships and would insist, quite properly, upon maintaining its own great naval superiority, I felt that its attitude in favor of limitation of armaments as regards other nations would be treated as merely hypocritical and would cause damage and not good." [56] "Of course," Root replied with blunt realism, "the armament question will be shelved. It can't be that Sir Edward Grey expected to do any more than satisfy English public opinion. His action doesn't square with any other view." [57] "It is pitiable," Carnegie protested to his friend John Morley, "that the only real peace loving party the Liberal party now in power should belie its professions so completely. . . . We had a great man in Pauncefote. . . . Now you have a delegation of doubters, small & narrow & without soul." [58] Roosevelt, more of a realist, had not hoped for too much, and hence was not so disappointed.

In preparing for the Hague Conference, Roosevelt also, in pursuit of America's traditional policy, planned to support a declaration granting private property at sea immunity from capture in wartime. Again the British, with the aid of other major powers, opposed the American point of view; and, in spite of the support of the smaller nations, Roosevelt had to back down and decide not to press the issue. [59] This time Henry White, now American Ambassador to France, opposed Roosevelt's position and so, too, did Mahan. "Maritime transportation, and commercial movement which is what so-called 'private property' really amounts to, is now one of . . . [Germany's] great interests, and is steadily growing," Mahan wrote Roosevelt. "Great Britain and the British Navy, lie right across Germany's carrying trade with the whole world. Exempt it, and you remove the strongest hook in the jaw of Germany that the English-speaking people have—a principal gage for peace." [60] Perhaps Roosevelt himself had been partially persuaded by Mahan, for when opposition arose, he wrote Ambassador Reid, "I hold to our traditional American view, but in rather tepid fashion." [61] Indeed, when he learned that Choate as delegate was expecting to urge our point of view in the face of opposition, he was disturbed. Reid, however, after talking with Choate assured the President, " [Choate] . . . certainly sees now that with so many strong nations against it, there's no good in doing any more than merely what is necessary to preserve on the record our historic attitude." [62]

Roosevelt strongly favored working out an agreement to arbitrate such disputes as lent themselves to settlement by arbitration.[63] As early as 1905 he proposed a general arbitration treaty by international agreement and hoped it would be adopted at a new Hague conference. He thought that collection of debts was one matter that nations should agree to arbitrate.[64] To Sir Edward Grey again the President stated his position in a private letter: " Personally I think that the strengthening of the Hague Court is of more consequence than disarmament. Every effort should be made to extend the number of possible international disputes which are to be subjected to arbitration, and above all to make it easier to secure effective arbitration." Roosevelt's position, however, was a cautious one. " Even here, . . ." he warned, " we can accomplish anything at all only by not trying to accomplish too much. I fear quite as much the amiable but irrational enthusiasts for an impossible progress in peace as I do those who desire that no real progress shall be made in the matter." [65]

While Roosevelt did not want to try to go too far, still the kind of treaty his Senate had insisted upon seemed to him silly to negotiate. " I am myself embarrassed," he wrote Grey, " owing to the peculiar constitution of our Government and the great difficulty of getting the Senate to allow the President anything like a free hand in such matters; while of course it does not represent any real advance for me or anyone else to sign a general arbitration treaty which itself merely expresses a ' pious opinion ' that there ought hereafter to be arbitration treaties whenever both parties think they are adviseable—and this was precisely the opinion that most even of my own good friends in the Senate took

as regards the last batch of arbitration treaties which I sent
them." "All that I can say," he concluded, "is that I will
do my best to get this Government to agree to any feasible
scheme which will tend to minimize the chances for war
occurring without previous efforts to secure mediation or
arbitration." [66]

Compulsory arbitration of legal disputes was considered.
Though Roosevelt had failed to get bilateral arbitration
treaties through the Senate, he had Choate now seek at The
Hague a general arbitration agreement. Choate was instructed to support "obligatory arbitration as broad in scope
as now appears to be practicable." "There is very great reluctance on the part of these fighting nations to bind themselves to anything," Choate reported. But on July 17, 1907,
he was still hoping that his proposal would "command a
large support." Germany, however, and seven other European states voted against compulsory arbitration even of
legal disputes. The best, therefore, the Conference could do
was to improve the procedures under the old Hague Court
of Arbitration of 1899 that everyone agreed was not serving
the purpose hoped for it. [67]

When the Conference had finally met, Mr. Dooley summarized its achievement with pertinent comments: "All th'
Powers sint dillygates an' a g-reat manny if th' weaknesses
did too," said Mr. Dooley. "They have been devotin' all
their time since to makin' war impossible in th' future. Th'
meetin' was opened with an acrimonyous debate over a resolution offered be a dillygate fr'm Paryguay callin' f'r im-
meejit disarmamint. . . . This was carrid be a very heavy
majority. Among those that voted in favor iv it were: Paryguay, Uryguay, Switzerland, Chiny, Bilgium, an' San
Marino. Opposed were England, France, Rooshya, Germany,
Italy, Austhree, Japan, an' the United States." "This was
regarded be all present as a happy auggry. Th' convintion
thin discussed a risolution offered be th' Turkish dillygate

abolishin' war altogether. This also was carrid, on'y England, France, Rooshya, Germany, Italy, Austhree, Japan, an' th' United States votin' no. This made th' way f'r th' discussion iv th' larger question iv how future wars shud be conducted in th' best inthrests iv peace." [68]

Disappointment in the Conference was widespread.[69] Those that could found consolation in the fact that the world was better off at the end of the Conference than it had been at the end of the first conference eight years earlier or in the fact that there was agreement to hold a third conference.[70] Henry White felt the experience of meeting together week after week had brought better understanding.[71] But the great British historian of the period, George P. Gooch, was later to write: " The second Peace Conference at the Hague . . . was a waste of time, energy and money, for the limitation of armaments was ruled out." [72] Much had been expected of Roosevelt's leadership.[73] For some reason, he did not exert the influence upon this Conference that he exercised at Portsmouth and at Algeciras. There were those who felt that had he assumed the dominant rôle the Conference would not have failed.[74] Perhaps he really had no heart in reducing arms and agreeing to arbitration.* Mahan may have left a clue to Roosevelt's thinking, too, when he warned the President, " With a Conservative Government . . . [in Britain] we might afford to be persistent in our old national policy, feeling safe that it would not be accepted, but would go over to another conference; with the present you will on military questions be playing with fire." [76] Perhaps, on the other hand, Roosevelt correctly analyzed the task as hope-

---

* The President's friend Lodge wrote Henry White how " delighted " he was that Choate was going to the Hague Conference, which was unimportant, because then White could get to the important Morocco Conference. Roosevelt and Root showed how little they expected when they told their delegates: " The immediate results of such a conference must always be limited to a small part of the field which the more sanguine have hoped to see covered." [75]

less and, as often in domestic policy, avoided leading to defeat by not leading in this case at all.

In spite of the lack of spectacular accomplishment, the Conference and planning for it brought out discussion that enlightened the story of Roosevelt's developing ideas. For example, we can follow in the discussions of these middle years of his Presidency his views on war. First, his more youthful exuberance about war was toned down. "I have grown to feel an increasing horror for pointless, and of course still more for unjust, war," he wrote St. Loe Strachey in 1905. A continuance of the Russo-Japanese war "was of course utterly pointless and meant hideous slaughter of gallant men to no purpose aside from the waste and exhaustion of the peoples involved." [77] "I have no sympathy," he wrote Trevelyan in 1906, "with those who would lightly undergo the chance of war in a spirit of mere frivolity, or of mere truculence, and I hate to see the budgets of civilized nations burdened with constantly increasing cost because they vie with one another in the matter of armaments." [78]

At the same time, he despised men who opposed "just" wars, and in the distinction between just and unjust conflicts is found the key to his views while President. This distinction he emphasized over and over. "I have no sympathy," he told Trevelyan, "with those who fear to fight in a just cause, and who are not willing to prepare . . . [to] fight effectively." [79] To Carnegie, too, he wrote, that justice is greater than peace, that really civilized nations will ask peace in the name of justice and not from any weakness.[80] "Unjust war is dreadful," he wrote peace advocate Carl Schurz; "a just war may be the highest duty." [81]

Roosevelt gradually evolved the view that war between civilized nations was tragic for civilization and should be averted, but that war of "civilized" nations against "barbarous" ones was the means of preserving civilization. "It is eminently wise and proper," he wrote Whitelaw Reid in

1906, " that we should take real steps in advance toward the policy of minimizing the chances of war amongst civilized people, of multiplying the methods and chances of honorably avoiding war in the event of controversy; but we must not grow sentimental and commit some Jefferson-Bryan-like piece of idiotic folly such as would be entailed if the free people that have free governments put themselves at a hopeless disadvantage compared with military despotisms and military barbarisms." [82] England and America, of course, as the most " civilized " nations had to keep themselves strong.[83] " I should bitterly regret seeing England or America left at the mercy of any great military despotism," he explained to Trevelyan, " or unable to check any military barbarism." [84] He agreed whole-heartedly with his British friend Strachey who wrote him, " If the English speaking world were to go ' peace at any price ' mad, the result would be that we should be ultimately dominated by autocracies. Men of the type of Napoleon I would spring on the backs of the people and ride them at will." [85] " The hopeless and hideous bloodshed and wickedness of Algiers and Turkestan were stopped," Roosevelt explained to Carl Schurz, " and only could be stopped, when civilized nations in the shape of Russia and France took possession of them. The same was true of Burma and the Malay states, as well as Egypt, with regard to England. Peace has come only as the sequel to the armed interference of a civilized power which, relatively to its opponent, was a just and beneficient power." [86] " If China became civilized like Japan," he conceded to Henry White, " if the Turkish Empire were abolished, and all of uncivilized Asia and Africa held by England or France or Russia or Germany, then I believe we should be within sight of a time when a genuine international agreement could be made by which armies and navies could be reduced so as to meet merely the needs of internal and international police work." [87] Here was the Roosevelt of the nineties expounding in more sophisticated terms the " superior race " theory of that decade. The difficulty was that as he freely admitted, " It is not easy to see how we can by international agreement state exactly which power ceases to be free and civilized and which comes near the line of barbarism or despotism." [88]

What Roosevelt dreamed of was a world in which imperial powers would live at peace with one another and coöperate to control colonial peoples—by war if necessary. What he failed to see was that in the real world imperial rivalries made this coöperation impossible, and that in this real world Japan, England, France, Russia, or Germany, his " civilized powers,"—and even the United States—could be as serious threats to each other and to world peace as the " backward " peoples. Besides, when America's national interest, functioning within " civilized power " rivalries, was challenged, Roosevelt could then easily persuade himself that the opponent was barbarous. Otherwise why would anyone war against a civilized power like England or America? Thus Roosevelt could justify any war that America felt she needed to fight. So he considered Russia and Japan civilized when they were fighting China, but when he thought in terms of their fighting England or America they became barbarous. When in World War I he felt America must fight Germany, he had persuaded himself it was not Germany the civilized nation that he had once admired whom we were fighting, but the land of the " Huns."

As part of his effort to prevent the war he dreaded among civilized nations, Roosevelt called the Portsmouth Conference, already discussed, and personally intervened in Europe at the Algeciras Conference in 1905-1906. The story of this latter conference itself is well known, but Roosevelt's rôle in it is much less understood,[89] and this conference, too, throws much light on Roosevelt's conception of America's rôle in the world and his conception of the problems she faced.

The background is important to an understanding of the Algeciras Conference and Roosevelt's relation to it. In 1901 Spain was worried about French encroachments in Morocco; she suspected France had English backing in her activities. Hence she appealed to Britain not to let France disturb the *status quo*, but Britain denied that she had assured France of a free hand there.[90] During the first years of Roosevelt's Presidency, however, France and England were coming to an agreement to support each other diplomatically and were hoping through France to tie Russia to the Anglo-French interests and thus isolate Germany.[91] In the meantime, Germany, alarmed but craving power, was seeking a Russo-German alliance. She hoped she might either alienate Russia from France or perhaps even draw France into a Russo-German combination.[92] Roosevelt received frequent testimony that England and Germany feared and distrusted each other.[93] In France the Foreign Minister, Theophile Delcassé, also alarmed, built his policy upon hostility to Germany, and upon keeping Britain and Germany from being friends.[94] In treaties signed April 8, 1904, Britain and France made a deal advantageous to both of them, by which the British agreed to French control of Morocco in exchange for French acquiescence in British control of Egypt. The British knew they were " asking for a good deal " and expected that Germany would object. British statesmen speculated on what Germany would demand in payment for not pressing her objections.[95] Spain was won over by concessions to her in Western Morocco.[96] Not only was Delcassé trying to encircle Germany; he was strengthening Germany's conviction concerning his hostility to her by failing to notify her of his agreements with Spain and Britain.[97]

Delcassé, on the one hand, and, on the other, the Kaiser, his chancellor Bernhard von Bülow, and that man of mystery Friedrich von Holstein, who was formulating German policy from behind the scenes, were all ambitious, and eager for power. Which was the more aggressive and dangerous to the peace of the world is a question. But Germany was the stronger.[98] At a critical moment Russia became absorbed in her disastrous war with Japan in the Far East, and in her weakened position temporarily ceased to be capable of providing strong support for French ambitions.[99] Those forming German policy believed England would not actually join a continental war in support of France.[100] Delcassé in France, willing to gamble on war [a] to gain power for his nation, was convinced Germany was bluffing and would not fight.[b] More cautious, however, the French Premier, Pierre Rouvier, was unwilling to risk war.[c] Under pressure from Germany, he forced his anti-German foreign minister to resign on June 6, 1905, hoping thereby to satisfy Germany, prevent war, and avoid a conference.[104] All realized they were playing with the possibility of a general war. Each was trying to put his alliances in order so that he could prevent such a war by being too strong for his enemies to attack. So the European nations manoeuvered for power and bluffed each other. Thus grew rivalries and tensions that were ultimately to plunge the world into destructive world war.[105]

Germany finally determined that Morocco was the place for her to take a stand against extension of French power. The European balance might in Morocco be tipped against Germany. And Germany might be excluded, if not from trade, certainly from the economic exploitation of Moroccan resources.[106] Perhaps more important, France and Germany were competing for enhanced national prestige. Besides, von

---

[a] White reported to Roosevelt " on authority which can hardly be questioned " that Germany had told France that if France marched troops into Morocco, German troops would invade France.[101]

[b] Convinced, too, were Senator Lodge then in Paris and Ambassador White in Italy.[102]

[c] After the crisis was safely passed English diplomatists and many on the Continent insisted they knew Germany was bluffing and would not risk a war. But at the time people were generally seriously worried.[103]

Bülow believed the French did not want war and certainly would not fight over Morocco.[107] Hence this might be a chance to make her lose face. Germany debated, but rejected, various aggressive moves against French power in Morocco. She did, however, encourage the Sultan in opposition to French rule.[108] Finally, on March 31, 1905, under insistence from Holstein and von Bülow, a reluctant Kaiser on a visit to Tangier made a belligerent speech outlined for him by von Bülow. So doubtful was the Kaiser of the wisdom of this procedure that he pleaded roughness of the sea to avoid landing at all, but, when Holstein and von Bülow insisted, he proceeded to speak vigorously. In terms that alarmed Europe, but particularly France, he made it clear that he regarded Morocco as an independent power and not as a French dependency. Germany wanted no territory, he said, but would insist upon her rights.[109] Even Delcassé's dismissal in June did not ease the tension.

Early in 1905 Germany had begun insisting that the Moroccan question must be decided by an international conference of powers in which Germany should have a part. France claimed the sole right to control the police in Morocco. Germany charged that France would use the police to shut out German commerce. Germany proclaimed her determination to maintain the principle of the " open door " in Morocco as she had joined the United States in maintaining it in the Far East.[110] She stood strongly against dividing Morocco into spheres of influence even when it became clear she could have obtained one herself.[111]

It was under these circumstances that Roosevelt, then directing his own foreign policy, decided to assume the rôle of conciliator. The United States on her part had little interest in Morocco.* But von Bülow and Holstein conceived

---

* The United States had, however, acknowledged that little interest by signing the Treaty of Madrid in 1880. She was, in consequence, one of the powers with treaty rights in Morocco.

the idea of appealing to Roosevelt through the President's good friend, their ambassador in Washington, Speck von Sternburg.[112] On January 20 the German chargé in Washington reported that Roosevelt had told him at a White House dinner that he was carrying on " a very interesting correspondence " with the German Ambassador.[113] In the Kaiser's name von Bülow on February 25 sent a long dispatch to Speck, which Speck talked over with Roosevelt on March 6. Von Bülow sought Roosevelt's support for the principle of the " open door " in Morocco and pointed out that Franco-Spanish control would exclude all seafaring and commercial nations and dominate the passage to the Near and Far East. Germany, von Bülow insisted, had no territorial ambitions. She was merely trying to prevent France from altering the commercial situation to everyone's disadvantage.* Though England would prefer not to be asked to participate in a protest over Morocco, still many Englishmen, the German Chancellor told Roosevelt, were fearful of loss of trade in Morocco, wished to maintain the " open door," and would privately welcome a curbing of France. Von Bülow hoped Roosevelt would join Germany in encouraging the Sultan to demand an international conference.[115] If America and Germany would protest separately but simultaneously, the Moroccan question could probably be settled satisfactorily by peaceful means.[116] On March 7 Roosevelt told John Hay of his talk with Speck and of von Bülow's proposals. " I have never heard of such indiscretion and of such implicit reliance upon our discretion," Hay confided to his diary. " By giving England and France the least hint of

* In 1914 von Bülow admitted what was probably the determining motive of Germany. Delcassé, he wrote, hoped to " deal our prestige in the world a severe blow. . . . Our dignity and our newly-won position in international politics were at stake." So, too, were " our sense of honor and pride." " If once we suffered ourselves to be trampled on with impunity, this first attempt to treat us badly would soon have been followed by a second and a third." [114]

what he has said to us in the last few weeks we could make very serious trouble." [117]

Roosevelt authorized Speck to explain the President's position to the Kaiser. He valued the Kaiser's communication highly. He explained, however, what great difficulty he had with Congress on foreign policy. He had finally made Congress understand and support his Far Eastern policy, though two years earlier that would have been "absolutely unthinkable." But he was still having trouble over his Caribbean and South American program. "Should I now engage myself in Morocco, a land which is here entirely unknown," he asked Speck to explain to the Kaiser, "I would expose myself to the bitterest attacks." "Should I approve the convening of the Notables and raise hopes in the Sultan," Roosevelt explained, "then I would have to be prepared for further steps. I take, however, in foreign policy no step at all, if I am not certain that eventually I can carry out my intentions with force." None the less, he promised, "I will instruct my minister in Morocco to put himself into close coöperation with his German colleague." [118]

In transmitting the President's reply Speck reported that the President this time was much more interested in Morocco than he had been earlier.[119] On March 26 von Bülow exulted to the Kaiser that it would certainly be of special interest to the American Minister Gummere to learn from home that "your Majesty has sent greetings to the President and has drawn a parallel between maintaining the open door in China and in Morocco." [120] Von Bülow, Speck, and the Kaiser might have been taken aback, however, if they had read the guarded instruction Roosevelt actually sent Gummere in fulfillment of the promise to Speck. "Of course I am anxious that you should keep on the most friendly terms with the French," he wrote his representative in Morocco, "but I should be obliged if you would also be careful to keep in touch with the German Minister, telling him that I have

requested you to do so. I should like you to work with him
so far as you can do so without causing friction with France."
" Of course," Roosevelt added, " I hope you will also get on
well with the English and all other representatives of foreign
governments." [121]

Germany continued to urge Roosevelt to act. It was during the early stages of the negotiation that the President
went off hunting in Colorado far from mail and telegrams.
The European situation seemed so important that he kept
in close touch with Taft, the acting president. When on
April 5, 1905, Speck again pressed his point with Taft, Taft
wrote Roosevelt.[122] On April 13 through Speck the Kaiser
told Roosevelt that Italy believed France would " continue
her aggressive policy " only if she felt sure England would
back her up by force. William believed England's attitude
would depend on Roosevelt's and begged Roosevelt to urge
England to refuse to support France.[123] On April 17 Gummere sent word from Morocco that the German minister had
informed him Germany would back the Sultan in resisting
France and that Germany wanted American financiers to join
Germany in helping the Sultan meet payments on his French
loan. Roosevelt replied that the American Government
never interfered about loans but let financiers decide such
matters. He instructed Gummere in Morocco " not to commit us in any way but to be friendly with both French and
Germans." [124] To Speck he expressed regret that he was off
on a hunt, " for," he said, " I hardly know how to arrange
out here what the Emperor requests." He repeated his
unwillingness to be diverted from his own plans in Santo
Domingo, Venezuela, and Panama, and again told Speck,
" I dislike taking a position . . . unless I fully intend to back
it up, and our interests in Morocco are not sufficiently great
to make me feel justified in entangling our Government."
Then instead of refraining he reminded Speck how cordially
he was working with William in China and the Japanese··

Russian War, and instructed Speck to "take this letter at once to Secretary Taft, . . . tell him exactly how far you want us to go in sounding the British Government." "Meanwhile," he promised, " I shall write him, . . . and shall suggest his finding out from Sir Mortimer [the British Ambassador] what the British Government's views in the matter are." [125]

Roosevelt's promised instruction to Taft began jocularly with the comment: "The Kaiser's pipe dream this week takes the form of Morocco." But then the President went on to say seriously, " I do not care to take sides between France and Germany in the matter. At the same time if I can find out what Germany wants I shall be glad to oblige her if possible, and I am sincerely anxious to bring about a better state of feeling between England and Germany." " I do not wish to suggest anything whatever as to England's attitude in Morocco," he continued. " But if we can find out that attitude with propriety and inform the Kaiser of it, I shall be glad to do so." " If Sir Mortimer, or O'Byrne, (or whatever the First secretary's name is), is in any rational mood and you think the nice but somewhat fat-witted British intellect will stand it, . . . tell them . . . what . . . I write." " But," he added, " I have to leave a large discretion in your hands . . . , for if we find that it will make the English suspicious— that is, will make them think we are acting as decoy ducks for Germany—why we shall have to drop the business. Fortunately, you and I play the diplomatic game exactly alike, and I should advise your being absolutely frank with both Speck and the British people." " Remember, however," Roosevelt cautioned, "that both parties are very suspicious." [126] Two days after Roosevelt wrote these letters from the Colorado wilderness, the British Foreign Secretary, Lansdowne, on a rumor that Germany would demand a Moorish port, asked France to confer with England in such case, and promised Delcassé all support possible in Morocco against the " unreasonable " German stand.[127]

Taft did talk to Sir Mortimer. He refrained from urging
Britain to consult with the other treaty powers before taking
a stand on the French proposals concerning Morocco. He
did, however, convey Roosevelt's request for information.
Sir Mortimer argued bitterly that Britain had reason to distrust Germany, who opposed and attacked her at every turn.
Yet he promised he would report to his government Roosevelt's desire to know its attitude and would try to get a reply
before he departed for his leave in England.[128] The reply was
a statement that England did not intend to attack Germany
but was not afraid of Germany. Foreign Secretary Lansdowne reiterated Britain's distrust of " the vagaries of the
German Emperor " and her determination to leave to France
a free hand in Morocco. Taft and Roosevelt passed this
British statement on for Speck to cable to the Kaiser.[129]

Throughout April, May, and June, 1905, the Kaiser and
Chancellor von Bülow, through Speck, kept urging Roosevelt
to put pressure on England to withdraw her support from
French policy in Morocco. Speck reminded Roosevelt that
America had participated in a Moroccan conference twenty-
five years earlier. The Anglo-French agreement had presumably guaranteed the *status quo*, but France had violated
it, he argued. Hence, Speck urged Roosevelt to argue with
the British that Britain's backing France made it appear that
Britain, too, was trying to deprive other powers of the right
to an open door. A new conference, therefore, Germany
reasoned with the President, was the only foreseeable, peaceful means of maintaining the open door in Morocco. If the
President did not intervene to persuade England and France
to hold a general conference on Morocco, then Germany
would be left only the alternative of war with France or a
weighing of such proposals as France might make to avoid a
conflict.[130] On May 6 Henry White reported to Roosevelt
from Rome that the Kaiser had tried to get Italy and Spain
to support him against France, but had failed.[131]

It was really England that was holding up the conference, Speck contended. She was using the Moroccan question to oppose Germany in the Far East. There were several French newspapers that indicated a willingness to participate in a conference, while journals close to the British Government were strongly opposed. The French attitude would ultimately depend upon what the British Cabinet decided. Both France and Britain would drop their opposition, Speck pleaded with the President, if only Roosevelt dropped a hint to London and Paris that he favored a conference. By persuading France and England, the Kaiser told Roosevelt, he would render another great service to the peace of the world.[132] On May 13 Speck was able to report to his Government that Roosevelt had talked to the departing British ambassador * and through him had expressed to the King and Foreign Secretary Lansdowne an emphatic wish for an improvement in relations between Britain and Germany. The President also arranged for his new ambassador in London, Whitelaw Reid, to talk with Lansdowne and the King about Morocco and world politics in general, and Roosevelt promised to report to Speck the result of these negotiations.[134] Roosevelt's friend Lodge, too, was instructed to confer with the King and Lansdowne and with Prime Minister Balfour.[135] Hay talked with Delcassé in Paris, but, though he was Secretary of State, he was not informed as to what Roosevelt was doing, and Hay would have opposed it had he known.[136]

On June 3, 1905, Roosevelt himself discussed Morocco with his intimate friend, French Ambassador Jules Jusserand, and told him the German Emperor was certain the American

---

* Roosevelt gave up all effort to deal with England through Durand, who seemed to have "a brain of about eight-guinea-pig power." "Why, under Heaven the English keep him here," the President protested, "I do not know! If they do not care for an Ambassador, then abolish the embassy; but it is useless to have a worthy creature of mutton-suet consistency like the good Sir Mortimer."[133]

President could overcome French objections to a conference. Roosevelt expressed a strong desire to see war avoided and urged Jusserand to report this desire for peace to the French Government.* The President said he would tell the German Ambassador that he had talked with Jusserand as he had been urged to do. Then he asked Jusserand to assure his own government privately that America would not participate in a conference. " I have not yet had any invitation," he explained, " and I should not want to give the appearance of saying no in advance, solely to be disagreeable to Germany." He asked that this intimate conversation be kept completely confidential, particularly that it should not appear eventually in some " yellow book." [138]

In the meantime, throughout April and May, as tension increased, France had in her turn tried to commit England. Foreign Secretary Lansdowne refused to give a commitment of military support. He even avoided a definite commitment to consult specifically about a Moroccan crisis. Instead he gave France a general promise of willingness to enter into " full and confidential " discussion not just after an act of unprovoked aggression of Germany but " in anticipation of any complications to be apprehended." Actually, Lansdowne later said he supposed this promise of May, 1905, was the origin of the offensive-defensive alliance between France and Britain.[139]

As the Germans kept telling Roosevelt, England was urging France not to agree to a conference. And Britain herself declined the Sultan's invitation to confer.[140] Indeed, England's suspicions of Germany made her determined not to participate. " I am afraid that we can hardly regard this Tangier ebullition as an isolated incident," wrote Foreign

---

* Roosevelt later testified that Jusserand was greatly concerned lest there be a war. Jusserand " sympathized absolutely with the general French indignation with Germany but felt that it was better to yield so far as the conference was concerned, if it could be done honorably, rather than have a war." [137]

Secretary Lansdowne. "We shall . . . find that the Kaiser avails himself of every opportunity to put spokes in our wheels. . . . My impression is that the German Government have really no cause for complaint either of us or the French." [141] After talking with his friends in the British Cabinet and dining with Lansdowne, Lodge wrote Roosevelt in June: " The Kaiser's interview with the Czar has filled all Europe with suspicion. No one has any idea what he said or what mischief he may have done." Then Lodge concluded, " I confess I share the suspicion—He is thoroughly dangerous and even now is getting concessions out of Morocco— under commercial guise." Then, hoping to appeal to a vulnerable spot in Roosevelt's thinking, Lodge added, " just as he has done in the W.[est] I.[ndies] with that island which we ought to watch." [142]

Early in June, 1905, a crisis was reached. The Sultan of Morocco invited the powers to a conference. On the fifth, Ambassador Reid cabled Roosevelt that the British Foreign Secretary had expressed alarm over the proposal of a conference, which he considered merely a scheme of Germany to embarrass France. Lansdowne wanted to know Roosevelt's opinion.[143] On June 6 Roosevelt cabled Reid that he had told both Speck and Jusserand he would join in no conference unless France acquiesced. That very day Premier Rouvier forced Delcassé out of the Cabinet and instituted a more conciliatory policy toward Germany.[144] Delcassé's resignation was generally regarded as a German victory, though Britain still hoped to forestall a conference.[145] Germany urged Roosevelt to use the crisis to persuade Britain and France to joint action.[146]

Delcassé's fall alarmed those already afraid of Germany, but at the same time opened the way for conciliation. Britain was disturbed lest the triumph of Germany in forcing Delcassé's fall tempt her to action that might lead to war. Britain realized that she had lost as an ally the most pro-

British and anti-German member of the French Government. Rumors flew about London that the Anglo-French entente was dissolving.[147] Germany became convinced, on the other hand, that Britain had now offered France an offensive-defensive alliance.[148] Germany became bolder in her insistence that she would back the Moroccan sultan against the French. Rouvier, now wavering, was eager to settle the whole issue peaceably.[149]

It was at this time that Roosevelt decided intervention on his part might succeed. He now saw the French, British, and German ambassadors. He promised the Germans he would exert his full influence for a conference and pleaded for moderation on the Kaiser's part. Britain he urged not to put any difficulties in the way of a conference if France would agree to one.[150] With Jusserand he spoke frankly.[a] " I know your government will consider that I am meddling in its affairs," he conceded, " but since the Moroccan question threatens a war between Germany and France that would destroy world peace, I feel justified." On June 16 he urged Jusserand to point out to his Government that France could only lose in a war with Germany, that it would be England who would win. " It would cause me anguish," he told Jusserand, " if any misfortune overtook France." [b] So he begged France to accept a conference. Even large concessions could wisely be made, he argued, if the crisis could be dissipated.[152] Two days later, on June 18, Roosevelt again pressed conciliation on Jusserand. The President, urging realism in meeting

[a] " If . . . I had not been able to treat you with the absolute frankness and confidence that I did," Roosevelt later told Jusserand, " no good result could possibly have been obtained; and this frankness and confidence were rendered possible only because of the certainty that you would do and advise what was wisest to be done and advised, and that you would treat all that was said and done between us two as a gentleman of the highest honor treats what is said and done in the intimate personal relations of life." [151]

[b] " I desired to do anything I legitimately could for France," he later admitted; " because I like France, and I thought her in this instance to be in the right."

a crisis, pleaded, " You know what I think of humiliating oneself in the face of a threat. None the less, these are concessions that can with honor be made to avert a conflict, and . . . I should not hesitate." Then he shrewdly suggested: " What is needed is to give some satisfaction to the immeasurable vanity of William II and it would be wise to help him save face if thereby one can avert a war." [153] The French attitude, apparently influenced by the Presidential suggestion, became immediately conciliatory.[154]

Five days after the earlier conference Roosevelt again talked with Jusserand. Afterward Jusserand reported to the French Foreign Office: " Examining . . . the means by which he might help us in avoiding war, the very idea of which struck him with horror, the President has concluded that the only chance to do what might be useful, would be perhaps to flatter this excessive vanity of William II to which he attributes, in large measure, the present difficulties." [155] Roosevelt then dictated in Jusserand's presence a message to Sternburg for the Kaiser. He told the Kaiser the French Government had unofficially informed him that it had withdrawn its opposition to the conference. It seemed usual, Roosevelt said, that a program of the conference be drawn up in advance and he suggested France and Germany get together to do this. Roosevelt then turned on all the flattery he could command. He credited the Kaiser with the suggestion through which he had won the French to the conference idea. " Let me congratulate the Emperor most warmly," Roosevelt wrote, " on his great diplomatic success. . . . I had not believed that the Emperor would be able to secure this [French] assent. . . . I consider such peaceful solution as vitally necessary to the welfare of the world . . . , and in view of its having been secured by the Emperor's success . . . , I wish again to express my hearty congratuation. It is a diplomatic triumph of the first magnitude." [156] On receipt of the report of this conversation, the French

Government agreed to the conference.[157] Germany on her part had already agreed to meet with the French to decide in advance upon the agenda if and when France agreed to come to a conference at all.[158]

The Germans were taken aback when the note they received from the French said they considered such a conference would be " dangerous if it were not preceded by an understanding and useless if it were." [159] Germany protested that the conference itself must decide the issue, and that Germany could not betray the Sultan by ignoring him while deciding matters in preliminary talks with France.[160]

But Roosevelt persevered.[161] Again praising the Kaiser he wrote Speck * on June 25, " As you know . . . I finally determined to present the case to the French Government only because I wished to do anything I properly could do which the Emperor asked, and of course also because I felt the extreme importance of doing everything possible to maintain the peace of the world. . . . I am not merely a sincere admirer and well-wisher of Germany, but also of His Majesty. I feel that he stands as the leader among the sovereigns of to-day who have their faces set toward the future, and that it is not only of the utmost importance for his own people but of the utmost importance for all mankind that his power and leadership for good should be unimpaired." " I say with all possible emphasis," Roosevelt wrote, " that I regard this yielding by France, this concession by her which she had said she could not make . . . , as representing a genuine triumph for the Emperor's diplomacy; so that if the result is now accepted it will be not merely honorable for

---

* It was only because Speck was an " excellent " man that Roosevelt was able to accomplish such delicate negotiations. Speck was concerned about outbreak of war. "Loyal though Speck was to his Government," Roosevelt explained, " down in his heart the honest, brave little gentleman did not really believe Germany was acting as she should act." [162]

Germany but a triumph." Then he sounded a solemn warning that apparently estopped Germany from further bickering or threatening. " I feel," he continued, " that now, having obtained what he asks, it would be most unfortunate even to seem to raise questions about minor details, . . . [for] if under such circumstances the dreadful calamity of war should happen, I fear that his high and honorable fame might be clouded." [163]

Roosevelt made it clear to the French that his desire was to prevent a war and not to serve German interest. Then while Rouvier, under pressure from Delcassé's friends, still hesitated, Speck on June 28 transmitted to Roosevelt a promise of the Kaiser. " In case during the coming conference differences of opinion should arise between France and Germany," Speck promised on William's behalf, " he, in every case, will be ready to back up the decision which you should consider to be the most fair and the most practical." " In doing this," Speck explained, " he wants to prove that the assistance which you have rendered to Germany has been rendered in the interest of peace alone, and without any selfish motives." [164] The President immediately wired Jusserand of the Kaiser's promise.[165] Knowledge of the Kaiser's promise overcame the doubts and fears of the French. Roosevelt and the few to whom he confided them kept his secrets well. He told Lodge, Taft, and Root the rôle he had played, but did not tell his anti-German Secretary of State, Hay, who would have disapproved. His ambassadors in Paris and Berlin were not informed. Nor did he tell his friend Henry White, then his ambassador in Rome, who was intimate with British officialdom. He divulged the secret to his ambassador in London, Whitelaw Reid, only ten months later.[166] Both the French Premier and the German Kaiser, who knew what he had done, and their ambassadors in Washington credited Roosevelt with breaking the deadlock and preventing possible war,[a] and both sides in the struggle expressed gratitude for his service to world peace.[168]

Though there were still difficulties between France and Germany [b] that Roosevelt helped straighten out,[169] the agenda was agreed upon in advance and the conference ultimately met on January 16, 1906, at Algeciras in southern Spain.[170] Henry White went as an official American delegate.[171] Once it was determined the conference should meet, many British leaders seemed glad that America was to participate, " since certainly the others concerned would be sure to regard the United States as entirely disinterested and accord great weight to its position and opinions." [172] Meantime Germany's insistence on the conference greatly strengthened at a critical moment the Franco-English understanding and Rouvier at the conference felt more secure and less willing to yield than he had felt the summer before.[173]

Roosevelt's participation led to vigorous discussion at home. Senator Bacon of Georgia introduced a resolution into the Senate objecting to participation in the Moroccan negotiations because it had been " the settled policy of this Government since its foundation to abstain from taking part in such political controversies between European nations." Even Secretary of State Root felt our interests were not sufficient to justify our taking a leading part.[174] Senator Spooner of Wisconsin, Senator Lodge,[c] and others defended

[a] No supporting evidence has been found for Bunau-Varilla's claim that he persuaded Senator Lodge and Assistant Secretary of State Francis B. Loomis that war was inevitable unless the United States would let it be known that she would come to France's defense if war came. Bunau-Varilla related that on his suggestion they gave the French Premier assurance concerning this. Lodge and Loomis *were*, however, in Paris at this time. Lodge did urge Roosevelt for political and economic reasons to support the Anglo-French entente in negotiations. And on July 8, upon Loomis's urging, Lodge did send Roosevelt a long telegram the contents of which remain unknown.[167]

[b] On November 8, the Kaiser appealed to the Czar to help him.

[c] Lodge insisted that it was in conformity with America's policy to use our " moral influence . . . to prevent war." America " will be drawn into no

the President's action and the opposition was overcome.[175] Lodge's friend and constituent, the powerful Boston banker, Henry Higginson, who had opposed imperial expansion, now hoped that if Germany attacked France we would join England in supporting France. But he hoped we would take a firm stand " before there is any row " because, he wrote Lodge, " I cannot believe that the German Emperor would attempt to do anything if England, France and we . . . would remonstrate seriously against a warlike attitude."[176]

Roosevelt himself felt the conference important,[a] because it could prevent a Franco-German war. "We have no interest in the matter," he wrote former Ambassador Choate, " save the interest of trying to keep matters on an even keel in Europe." " My sympathies have at bottom been with France and I suppose will continue so." Yet " while I want to stand by France, I want at the same time to strive to keep on fairly good terms with Germany."[178] To White he added, " I want . . . if possible to prevent a rupture between Germany and France."[179]

Through the latter part of the negotiations that preceded the conference Root and Roosevelt worked more closely together than the President had been able to work with the always anti-German John Hay. Indeed, Roosevelt told Speck that Root had seen more clearly than he from the beginning the importance of working with Germany. Much of the detail Root handled. At the critical points, however, Roosevelt made the decisions and did the negotiating.[180]

White's instructions were sent by Root, but represented his and the President's common judgment. Concerning France, White was instructed, " You may find . . . that

alliances . . . and into no wars by connection with any European Power. Yet . . . she will not hesitate to use her moral influence to prevent wars . . . in any portion of the globe where her efforts can rightfully be exercised."

[a] So, too, did Foreign Secretary Grey in England, who believed that if the Morocco conference failed " a state of general uneasiness would continue through Europe."[177]

France has legitimate interests by reason of her proximity to Morocco, . . . which ought to be specially safe-guarded. If . . . so, we do not wish to oppose a provision for the protection of those interests. We do not, however, wish to become the advocate of these special interests." White was not to support any special claims of Germany, since there was no " just ground on which she could make such a claim." " While we are friendly to Germany, and wish to remain so," White was admonished, " we regard as a favorable condition for the peace of the world, and, therefore, for the best interests of the United States, the continued entente cordiale between France and England, and we do not wish to contribute towards any estrangement between those two countries." In general, aside from France's special claims, " we stand equally with all other countries," the instructions proclaimed, " for the most unrestricted trade,—the open door, and for a policy which will create and foster civilization and trade within the open door." [181]

As the Algeciras Conference convened in January, 1906, both sides tried to convince the American President. There were still those that felt Germany would be truculent and might still attack France.[182] Speck von Sternburg pleaded the German cause with Roosevelt. He tried to persuade him that, in objecting to French control of the Morocco police, Germany was only defending the open door for all nations, since control of the police would give France control of trade and economic life as well.[183] Both France and Russia, on the other hand, told Roosevelt that France was only trying to create " a moral atmosphere making it impossible for the military part of Germany . . . to precipitate war." Russia hoped Roosevelt would exercise " moral influence " with both France and Germany.[184] Russia herself unsuccessfully sought to restrain Germany at Algeciras.[185]

At the Conference the controversy was in reality a contest for prestige and power between France and Germany centering in control of the Moroccan police and a Moroccan bank.[186] Germany sought to force joint control. Through Speck, Chancellor von Bülow tried to persuade Roosevelt to support the German position and on January 28 Speck proposed to Roosevelt a German compromise between French control that " the conference will not accept " and an international police that " is likewise . . . undesirable." Speck proposed that the Sultan be entrusted with organizing the police, that he be allowed funds for this purpose, and that international control be established over both the funds and the carrying out of the whole plan. Speck hoped Roosevelt would advise France to present this plan, which would meet with sympathy.[187]

The United States was quietly playing for conciliation, but hoped not to have to assume a leading rôle. As late as February 1 Roosevelt wrote George Meyer in Russia, " I do not know that I can do anything if the circumstance becomes strained . . . , and of course I want to keep out of it if I possibly can." [188] On February 8 when Speck assured Root that Austria and perhaps Italy would back Germany's proposal for organization of the police, Root replied that he must talk the matter over with Roosevelt and that, since the United States had the least interest of all the powers in the Conference, she must take no position that would not accomplish a definite result rather than merely stir up discussion. And Root asked significantly what position Britain took.[189] Meantime Henry White reported, " My head fairly turns with the details of private talks every day with both German delegates . . . , the French man and his very able expert . . . the British and Italian; besides occasionally the Russian and Austrian." White pleaded lack of authority to join either France or Germany officially, but tried to persuade the French and the Germans to agree before public opinion in their two countries became aroused. He found both the Germans and the French difficult and the

French unrealistically legalistic besides.[190] After four weeks White reported little progress, but was still hopeful. "It is difficult," he wrote, " to bring people to agree when both want to obtain all that they came here to get which is necessarily impossible." On February 12 he feared "the President's good offices may have to be invoked." "But," he explained, " I am reserving that appeal as a last resource." [191] White wrote home how "patent . . . the advantage " had been " of our being free from entangling alliances—not to be confounded with taking our part in every important Council of Great Powers." Though she has the same interest as America in neutrality, "Italy . . . is debarred by the triple alliance on the one hand and her arrangements with France on the other from saying a word." " England's hands are tied as to giving France advice," he continued, "by her ' entente.' " " We," on the other hand, " are free to take an impartial view and say what we like in private to either France or Germany when asked—a privilege I have not failed to use with perfect frankness." [192]

By mid-February, 1906, a serious deadlock threatened failure at Algeciras and well-informed men feared failure would result in German aggression and perhaps general war. In Britain Foreign Secretary Grey had serious talks with the German Ambassador and confided to a doleful memorandum his fear that Germany would make war on France and Britain would have to go to war to support France.[193] Ambassador Meyer reported Russia alarmed.[194] Indeed, the Czar was reported to be considering personal intervention with William. Germany was seeking means of saving face as she saw the neutral powers going over to the French side.[195] Roosevelt's friend Spring Rice was fearful lest Germany irritate the French public into forcing its government to attack Germany.[196] Meyer, too, reported that Germany was taking advantage of Russia's weakness to force France's hand, but Meyer was more optimistic* because he felt no country would undertake the expense of conducting modern war.[198] France, however, was nervous.[199] Roosevelt had held aloof and left White to manage things.

At this point, however, on February 19 the President replied to the latest plea of Speck for support of Germany's position with a suggestion that the President lay before the Conference a compromise based on Germany's January 28 proposal to the President. The President said he had been keeping this German plan in mind. He felt that now was the opportune time to introduce it, but " that to be effective it should now be somewhat more specific in regard to the nature of the international control." The President would propose therefore a four-fold solution: (1) He would entrust the policing in all ports to the Sultan with Moorish men and officers. (2) He would supply the funds for the police through an international bank in which the stock would be alloted equally to all the powers " except for some small preference claimed by France," which Roosevelt considered " immaterial." (3) He would entrust " instruction, discipline, pay and assisting in management and control . . . to French and Spanish officers . . . to be appointed by the Sultan " from names suggested by France and Spain, and he would oblige " the senior French and Spanish instructing officers [to] report annually to . . . Morocco, and to . . . Italy, the [other] Mediterranean Power, which shall have the right of inspection and verification, and [the right] to demand further reports in behalf of . . . the powers." Finally, (4) he would require " that full assurances be given by France and Spain . . . for the open door, both as to trade, equal treatment and opportunity in competition for public works and concessions." Roosevelt assured Speck through Root that this draft had been " carefully framed . . . so as

---

* Lodge, too, felt " it would be so criminal to bring on a war " that he could not believe the Conference would fail.[197]

to . . . make concessions from the French position as easy
as possible." Roosevelt felt his proposal conserved " the
principle of the open door without unduly recognizing the
claims which rest[ed] upon proximity and preponderance of
trade interests." Roosevelt assured William the proposal was
" fair " and hoped William would accept it.[200]

This brought a prompt reply. Indeed, Chancellor von
Bülow penned a notation at the top of Speck's dispatch that
in view of Roosevelt's " good intentions " a " prompt answer " was demanded and obviously " a very friendly "
one.[201] William himself replied. He expressed gratitude for
Roosevelt's offer of mediation and special appreciation for
the fact that Roosevelt would " act as mediator only in
agreement with " the Kaiser. Germany accepted completely
points 1, 2, and 4. Point 3, the Emperor objected, was essentially the plan France had been demanding. Under it the
Sultan, William insisted, would not be free to choose officers;
they would in reality be named and controlled by France
and Spain, who would thus dominate the police. The Kaiser
proposed instead that the Sultan be permitted a free choice
of officers among other nations or among the nations that
owned shares in the bank. If this principle was adopted the
Kaiser would then be willing to make concessions. If France
feared that Germany might gain control, Germany would be
willing to require that the Sultan choose officers from at least
four powers and, if France preferred, in equal numbers. Germany would also be willing to have the Sultan acknowledge
special rights of France in Tangier and perhaps some other
port by appointing there only French officers. If Roosevelt
would accept these modifications Germany would gladly
negotiate on the basis of the President's thus amended
proposal.[202]

During the next week, the first in March, the reports were
discouraging. " Things do not look as well as they should
in Algeciras," Roosevelt wrote his ambassador in London on

March 1. The President had even heard reports that German authorities believed, with Russia out, they could defeat France and England and successfully occupy the British Isles.[203] Austria, discouraged, offered Berlin her friendly offices.[204] Russia was worried and America urged the Czar to intervene with the Kaiser.[205] Germany's representative at Algeciras had to wire his government that all powers but Austria were lined up against Germany.[206] Yet both France and Germany were immovable. French Ambassador Louis-Maurice Bompard in St. Petersburg told Ambassador Meyer that as fast as France made concessions Germany would make new demands. " The whole trouble," he insisted, " was that the Emperor of Germany had personally taken such a prominent part . . . that his *amour propre* was at stake and everything depended upon him personally." [207] On March 7 Joseph-Marie von Radowitz, the chief German delegate, wired home that Sir Arthur Nicolson, chief British delegate, insisted the Conference break up by Saturday night. Radowitz advised his government that to hold the Conference together Germany must permit sufficient agreement on the bank and police to make a final agreement possible.[208] Russia at this point suggested that Roosevelt mediate. " All the world respects him," Count Aleksandr von Benckendorff told the American Ambassador, " and it is well known the German Emperor admires him." [209]

On March 7 Roosevelt did intervene. He cabled the Kaiser on whose emotions and vanity he knew so well how to play. He had given, he said, serious thought to William's suggestion for modifying the President's proposals. " I cannot bring myself," he told the Kaiser, " to feel that I ought to ask France to make further concessions than the arrangement suggested in . . . [Root's] letter would require." " I would gladly drop the subject in which our traditional policy of abstention from the political affairs of Europe forbids the United States to take sides," he assured the Kaiser. But

.

" the events which led to the Conference . . . forbid me to
omit any effort within my power to promote a settlement of
differences." He reminded the Kaiser that at Germany's
request he had urged France to consent to a conference and
had assured her of his belief that a " most fair and most
practical " decision would be reached. He then quoted the
Kaiser's promise made in Speck's letter of June 28 that the
Kaiser would support at the Conference whatever Roosevelt thought fair and practical. " I feel bound to state to
Your Majesty," Roosevelt now wrote, " that I think the
arrangement indicated . . . is a reasonable one, and most
earnestly urge Your Majesty to accept it." In this arrangement, he insisted, " Germany will have accomplished the
declared object for her intervention in . . . Morocco. . . . I
feel such arrangement would be in very fact the evidence
of the triumph of German diplomacy." Then he admonished
William: " If the conference should fail because of Germany's
insisting upon pressing France beyond the measure of concession described in this proposed arrangement, the general
opinion of Europe and America would be unfavorable, and
Germany would lose that increase of credit and moral power
that the making of this arrangement would secure to her,
and might be held responsible, probably far beyond the
limits of reason, for all the evils that may come in the train
of a disturbed condition of affairs in Europe." " I most
sincerely hope," he concluded, " that Your Majesty may take
this view and throw upon France the responsibility for rejecting, if it is to be rejected, the suggested arrangement." [210]

Though it was not known until the German Foreign Office
papers were published twenty years later, this demand of
Roosevelt that the Kaiser keep his promise to follow the
President's advice at the Conference created embarrassment
within the German Government. Von Bülow cabled Speck a
reprimand on March 12. The Chancellor said he had com-

pared his own instruction ᵃ to Speck with Speck's transmission of it to Roosevelt. " You have in a twofold direction exceeded the instruction transmitted to you.ᵇ First you were in my telegram empowered only to promise that *I* would urge upon His Majesty any proposal of the President, while you have promised unqualified acceptance of this *in the name of His Majesty himself*. Further through the phrase ' during the coming conference ' you have given your word about any differences arising between us and France during the *Conference*, while I had in mind only the then forthcoming special discussion between us and France." " In view of this assurance His Majesty can hardly consider a disavowal now that the President has offered his proposal on the basis of this demand," von Bülow explained.

There is no doubt that Speck, in his eagerness to bring together the two governments to which he was devoted, had exceeded his instructions in transforming a promise of von Bülow to advise into a commitment of the Kaiser to act. On the other hand, it is equally clear that Speck was justified in interpreting von Bülow's language to apply to the Conference as well as the preliminaries. It seems obvious that von Bülow, elated because he thought he had won Roosevelt to serving Germany's purposes, had made a promise that, with Roosevelt now supporting France's position at the Conference, it was embarrassing to have made. Von Bülow therefore tried to slip out of this part of his blunder by shifting

---

ᵃ Von Bülow's cable of June 27, 1905, had said: " If after the resulting acceptance of the conference by France we shall be negotiating and in the process shall run upon differences of opinion, I (von Bülow) shall at all times be ready to urge upon his Majesty the Kaiser those decisions that the President shall recommend as practical and fair." ²¹¹

ᵇ Actually Speck if he remembered the ungiven promise he had transmitted should have had warning in a cable of January in which Bülow restated his position as willingness to follow every American wish that served Germany's purpose of American support for an international police in Morocco and an " open door " and a guarantee of equality for all nations in Morocco.²¹²

it unjustly to Speck's shoulders. In any case von Bülow and the Kaiser now faced the unhappy alternative of keeping a promise the Kaiser at least had never made or publicly repudiating Roosevelt's friend Speck and thereby offending Roosevelt. They chose to keep the promise Speck had no authority to make. But they urged Speck to press with all the influence he had an Austrian plan proposed as a substitute for Roosevelt's.[213]

The Kaiser therefore replied most politely to Roosevelt, thanking him for his " repeated kind endeavors." " I am gladly willing to take your advice as a basis of an understanding. . . . In principle I consented to . . . your proposition." Then, however, the Kaiser tried to persuade Roosevelt that the plan Austria had presented, to which the Kaiser said all the powers including the British had agreed, was the best basis for a settlement. " This proposal," he told Roosevelt, " almost covers yours." " A satisfactory end of the conference would be secured," William urged, " if you, Mr. President, would likewise give your consent to that . . . acceptable development of your proposal."[214] Germany's " giving way beyond the Austrian proposals," Speck added, " would gravely endanger the open door. The opposition lies with the mighty french banking interests which are aiming at a monopolization of the resources of Morocco."[215]

Roosevelt, however, sympathizing with France and convinced that the French had yielded as far as it was desirable to yield to Germany, told the Kaiser he considered the Austrian proposal " absurd." " It favors the very ideas the conference has been trying to eliminate," he protested, " namely partition and spheres of influence. Placing Spanish and French officers in the same ports gives according to my view a safer guarantee than placing them separately in single ports. This has distinctly the flavor of a French, a Spanish and a Dutch or Swiss sphere of influence." He also objected to the Austrian plan of inspection as productive of friction.

" The proposal I suggested," he concluded, " is the better and safer and the only one I can support." Speck tried to argue with Roosevelt, but the President stood firm. If Germany would agree to his better proposal, he would urge it upon France.[216]

When Speck's March 14 report of his conversation with the President reached Germany, von Bülow cabled back arguments for him to present to Roosevelt in support of the Austro-Hungarian plan rather than Roosevelt's. Von Bülow protested that in Speck's previous proposals to the President the main point had " remained unnoticed." Therefore rather heatedly von Bülow told Speck that if the President insisted upon his own mediation proposal, the Chancellor would be forced either to disavow the explanations made in the name of the Emperor in Speck's letter of June 28, 1905, or else would have to acquiesce in the knowledge that, at this moment when Austro-Hungary, Italy, Russia, and Spain were working on the French in Germany's favor, the American President had taken the side opposed to Germany.[217]

On receipt of this cable Speck went immediately to Roosevelt on March 16 to present von Bülow's arguments. This time Roosevelt argued no further. Instead he firmly expressed the hope that the Conference would speedily reach an agreement that would guarantee the peace. He told Speck he was beginning to believe Germany was not unwilling to have a war with France.[218] Speck assured him that the Kaiser's desire at Algeciras was to insure the peace. Then the President remarked that among his advisers and in Congress the view was being strengthened that Germany was seeking, through its obstructionist tactics, to humble France. People see this in the speeches of the Kaiser, too. France would submit to no more public humiliation. The conviction about Germany's purpose, which was more and more becoming the view of the American people, was making the President's rôle as mediator increasingly difficult. He was under constant pressure from senators to abstain from further participation at Algeciras and to recall the American delegates. The President had reports from Algeciras that Germany's exaggerated demands were creating distrust among the other powers, too. Austria and Russia had already urged him to advise Germany to mitigate her demands that they said went beyond the open door. The President had firmly declined to do this. But the people here distrusted the Austrian plan because they felt it was inspired by Germany and that Germany herself hoped under it to get a sphere of influence and a Mediterranean port.[219]

This time Speck added his plea to the President's. " I, too, have found public opinion turning against Germany," he reported. " I am reproached over His Majesty's speeches, which are regarded as warlike in flavor and meant to humiliate France." " Newspapers here," he pointed out, " daily receive provocative telegrams from Paris and London. So far it is only the more sensational and poorer papers . . . that criticize His Majesty's speeches and make them responsible for friction at the conference." But the feeling is growing. " Many feel that the Conference is dealing with European matters with which the constitution does not permit America to concern itself." " The French Ambassador has a strong hold on the President and influential leaders," Speck warned, " and his words fall on fruitful soil." And " the President wants me to make it plain to His Majesty how disagreeable it would be for him to assume the rôle of mediator lest the world regard him a ' busy boy [Stänker].' " [220] On March 17 Secretary Root delivered to Speck a written statement of the President's objections * already orally stated and, on March 18, Speck cabled them to Germany.[221]

---

* " France has yielded to this view of international right," Root wrote, " to the extent of offering to become jointly with Spain, the mandatory of all the powers. . . . It was further proposed that an officer of a third power, acting in behalf of all the powers, should have the right of general inspection. . . .

Meantime Roosevelt had one more conference with Speck. Again he opposed the Austrian proposal. It would plant the seeds of future trouble. Spheres of influence would degenerate into possessions. Besides, he could not understand how the powers could support a proposition whose acceptance by France he doubted. He had not the slightest purpose at this stage to frustrate the Austrian proposal with still a newer plan. He preferred to stand on the original proposal. Then he issued a threat designed to bring Germany to terms. In case the Conference collapsed, he warned, he would feel compelled to publish the correspondence between himself and " certain powers " in order to make it clear what rôle the United States had played.* In reporting to his government Speck said he had appealed to Root, but Root had told him the United States would have to abstain from the Austrian proposals. The President, too, Speck added, had spoken again of the " exaggerated demands " of Germany. He had spoken " very emphatically " and in " very clear language." " Confidentially I learned today," Speck cabled, " that the Secretary of State labeled Germany's conduct at the Conference as paltry and unworthy a great power." In short, Speck warned his government, " Germany has entirely lost its originally strong position at Algeciras and is in danger of losing the confidence of the world." [223]

With two mandates jointly charged, no individual claim of possession or control was likely to grow up. . . . The Austrian proposal . . . seems to us to provide for a potential partition of the territory. The immediate effect can only be the creation of three separate spheres of influence. . . . We . . . consider that the distribution of ports to separate single powers is wrong in principle and destructive of the declared purpose of both Germany and the United States. If we had sufficient interest in Morocco to make it worth our while, we should seriously object, on our own account. . . . We have not however any such substantial interest. . . . Our chief wish is to be of service in promoting a peaceable settlement of the controversy which brought the Conference together."

* Roosevelt himself believed this the " vital feature of what I did." " While I was most suave and pleasant with the Emperor," Roosevelt wrote, " yet when it became necessary at the end I stood him on his head with great decision." [222]

The success of Roosevelt's handling of Germany became immediately evident.* Speck's cable shocked Berlin into immediate capitulation. The next day von Bülow cabled his "astonishment" that Americans should think Germany was seeking special advantages. How could they believe that to attain her end Germany would not shrink from a war with France. Germany, Speck was to assure the President, sought neither special advantage nor war. The Kaiser had never thought of war over Morocco, which the German people would not understand. We had no object, Speck was to insist, except to guarantee equality of economic rights, and we urged the Conference because we thought this the suitable way to obtain this purpose peacefully. Germany favors the American position and renounces all propositions that threaten the main German-American principles. "In looking back over the various important results of German-American coöperation during the past two years—localizing of war, guarding international order, and finally restoration of peace —it seems to me," von Bülow concluded, "the preservation of the confidence that has existed between Berlin and Washington and the immediate removal of all misunderstandings is more important than the whole Moroccan affair." [225] The next day Root in superb understatement cabled the American Ambassador in Berlin, who had had no part in these negotiations: "We have had a pretty active exchange of correspondence and interviews with the German Ambassador here recently over Moroccan affairs. The indications are now that the matter will end satisfactorily." [226]

When firmness, unpleasant charges, blunt talk, and even a threat to publish confidential correspondence had seemed necessary, Roosevelt had employed them, but now that he had won his point he set out to help the Kaiser save face. In short he turned to flattery. "Communicate to His

---

* In Paris Le Temps gave Roosevelt credit at the time for the proposal on which success of the Conference was founded.[224]

Majesty the Kaiser," he urged Speck, " my sincerest felicitation on this epochmaking political success at Algeciras. The policy of His Majesty on the Morocco question has been masterly from beginning to end. The Kaiser has accomplished at the Conference, what he wanted to accomplish, and the world must acknowledge deep thanks to him for the result." Speck assured the Kaiser on his part that if this did not seem to accord with the facts, still Speck was certain that these words of the President came completely from the heart. The President said further that he wanted to proclaim to the world in an unmistakable manner how highly America appreciated the unselfish and masterly policy of His Majesty. He then asked Speck to advise him on the best way to make his gratitude known.[227]

Roosevelt himself did not want to sponsor his own proposal. So he instructed our chief delegate, Henry White, to get Austria to introduce it.[228] A few more days were required to iron out differences. On March 23 Speck told Roosevelt that Spain was objecting to the newest proposal, and the President promised he would protest emphatically against the resistance of England, France, and Spain. Speck, indeed, reported him particularly sharp in his criticism of England for backing France in making difficulty. Then Roosevelt cabled White that he cared nothing about specific administrative arrangements so long as France and Spain accepted joint responsibility for all ports and the inspector was responsible to all the powers.[229] In this final stage White and the neutral Italians played an active rôle in persuading France to agree to a compromise.* The proposals concerning the exact authority and the obligations of the police inspector responsible to all the powers were presented by White.[231]

When the Conference ended both France and Germany were grateful to Roosevelt. The French Foreign Minister

---

* England had urged France to acquiesce in the compromise, but because of her commitments to France had had to yield when France stood firm.[230]

thanked the President for the support he had lent. " We are happy," he wrote, " to acknowledge how much his personal activity contributed to facilitating the final settlement." [232] Von Bülow in a Reichstag speech proclaimed the " great service . . . to the peace of the world " America had rendered at Algeciras, for he believed if the Conference had failed relations between France and Germany would have been broken off and this " would have introduced a disturbing and threatening element into the politics of all nations." [233] To his brother he wrote: " We have avoided a war in which . . . we should have risked much, could lose a great deal, but gain little." [234]

Roosevelt, however, agreed with his chief delegate at the Conference in a " not very exalted opinion of either French or German diplomacy as exhibited at the Conference." Both French and Germans showed " a want of frankness and an indisposition to say exactly what they were driving at." " Jusserand, who is a trump, toward the end became very much disgusted with the evident furtiveness and lack of frankness of the French in handling their case," the President told White. " Until the Conference met," Roosevelt testified when it was over, " I felt that France was behaving better than Germany, but toward the end it seemed to me that neither one was straightforward." [235] Yet an individual Frenchman, Jusserand, the President believed was " the man most instrumental " in arranging for an international conference " compatible with France's honor and dignity " and such an international conference Roosevelt felt had been the only way of avoiding war. [236]

In later years Roosevelt came to feel that Germany failed to gain her ends and that her prestige, originally great, suffered from her insistence upon the Conference and her failure there to gain her ends. How Germany could have made the mistake of insisting on the Conference he could not understand, von Eckardstein reported him as saying in 1910, for during its progress " German prestige had fallen sharply in all countries." [288]

In a long letter to Roosevelt, Henry White congratulated him on a " solution . . . satisfactory to both sides," which was, he pointed out, " with the exception of a Swiss instead of an Italian Inspector, exactly the proposal you made." " On the one hand," White pointed out, " all that Germany legitimately claimed in behalf of all the Powers in the way of equality of economic rights &c. has been granted and, on the other, France's special position has been recognized while she has been stopped from taking practical possession of the country which was, I think, her eventual intention." White hoped that better Anglo-German relations, too, would grow out of the Conference. " The critics in the Senate of your policy in causing the U. S. to be represented at the Conference at all," White wrote the President, " must now admit that it is possible for us to take an important part in a European assemblage . . . and to fully assert our right to equality of rights commercial and economical . . . and yet in nowise to take sides in any of the political questions." " There were

---

[a] Even at the time von Bülow had had to defend himself against attacks of Pan-Germans. He admitted to his brother that " on a number of minor points we might have obtained even more if His Majesty had not turned nervous toward the end." But he felt Germany had gained its main objectives, had caused the fall of her " most dangerous opponent," and had avoided a war. Hermann von Eckardstein, long German chargé in London, had, on the other hand, opposed German policy in demanding a conference. He blamed Fritz von Holstein's power behind the scenes for what he considered a fatal policy. At the critical moment in June 1905 he had written von Holstein himself: " I have done all possible . . . to induce Premier Rouvier to accept the plan for a conference so categorically promoted by the Imperial Government. . . But . . . my heart was not in my efforts in this direction. What good for Germany could come out of such a conference is to me unintelligible. I fear that Your Excellency and the Chancellor err greatly in expecting we will come out of a conference as victor. . . . At such a conference England and France would not be isolated, but we and no one except ourselves, would emerge the defeated nation. Not only that. At such a conference nothing else can result but that we will let our isolation be attested officially before the whole world, and that the ring of the coalition forming against us will be closed and sealed." [287]

many occasions . . . ," he declared, " on which my influence, privately exercised, with both French and German Delegates, has brought about pacific terminations to crises which seemed on the point of becoming acute." " The knowledge at Paris . . . ," White wrote, " that you were exercising your influence with the German Emperor prevented the French from acceding—as they were advised privately by their friends to do —to . . . the ' Austrian proposal,' . . . and thereby gave time for your opinion . . . to bear fruit and eventually to cause the Germans to give way. . . . So . . . I consider—and I think their Delegates do—that the French owe the whole eight ports on which they have laid such particular stress, to your good offices." " When I tell you," White wrote Lodge, " that the German Ambassador said to me immediately after the Conference met that Germany would break up the Conference rather than consent to France alone—or France & Spain alone—being in charge of the Police, you can realize how much the German mind became modified." " The conclusion reached . . . has afforded great relief," White reported, " in circles susceptible to the effects of war scares." [239]

Roosevelt himself was convinced that the Conference had prevented a war that in June, 1905, was " imminent." He felt that this war " if it had begun would probably have extended through a considerable part of the world." [240] When White finally heard the inside story of Roosevelt's activities [a] he

---

[a] The first full account of Roosevelt's part in the Conference was contained in a long letter he wrote on April 28, 1906, to Whitelaw Reid, of which he sent copies to White and Meyer. Bishop depended upon this letter in 1920 and accepted its story uncritically. Eugene Anderson, interested in the Conference from the point of view of European history, largely ignored Roosevelt and American sources, as European historians often do. Sir Edward Grey refused to accept or reject the Roosevelt version until he saw documents, but acknowledged that " it was not upon us or with us that his influence was exercised." [241] With certain American historians it has been fashionable to disparage Roosevelt and question the veracity of his accounts of events in which he participated. Latané dubs Roosevelt's letter to Reid " a highly self-conscious document, written not for . . . Reid but for posterity." Bailey, Jessup, Latané, Pringle, and Rippy

wrote in admiration, " The . . . story . . . is a wonderful piece of diplomacy of a very high order and when one thinks that he claims no credit for it and has allowed the credit for the outcome of Algeciras to go to any nation disposed to claim it one has an even greater admiration for his magnanimity and ability than before." [244] Sir Edward Grey, too, in England felt the participation of the United States and the influence of President Roosevelt were important.[245]

In 1908 a new crisis seemed likely to develop between France and Germany over Morocco. By October White, now Ambassador to France, reported: " The Morocco business . . . [is] better . . . as far as trouble between France & Germany is concerned." " But popular feeling in England," he wrote Lodge who was in constant touch with the President, " seems pretty hostile against Germany and is I imagine fairly reciprocated. The possibility of a German invasion is quite seriously considered in England and in many localities I am told they are drilling locally so as to be ready, much as was the case at the Napoleonic period." [246] This new crisis led Roosevelt to exclaim to Jusserand, " I wish to Heaven, not

directly or by innuendo suggest that the account was of course distorted to serve Roosevelt's purposes. Pringle even says that Roosevelt did not follow the Conference's activities. These charges seem to have been made without using the sources to check the President's accuracy.[242] It is interesting, therefore, that a checking of the sources shows Roosevelt an amazingly accurate reporter in this instance. In contrast to American historians who disparage, the English historian George Gooch, who had used European source materials extensively, credited Roosevelt with greater importance than did the American writers. Among Americans Bemis, who considered his policy " perilous . . . risky business, . . . from which the United States had nothing to gain," none the less like Gooch credited him with an important part in settling the crisis. Bemis spoke of his " successful rôle as a world statesman." " If one could justify President Roosevelt's diplomatic interference at all," Bemis concludes, " one would recognize the skill and adroitness with which he brought the powers to a peaceful compromise." And Allan Nevins, who used the Henry White papers, declared: " It was evident from the outset that the American rôle in the conference would be of the first importance. . . . Three nations . . . looked with anxious eyes upon the course which Roosevelt would take at the Conference." [248]

in your interest but in the interest of civilized mankind, that
France could take all Morocco under her exclusive charge." [247]
Yet the United States agreed in October to the Franco-
Spanish recognition of a new sultan, and, in January, 1909,
just before Roosevelt left office, he agreed to a great powers'
approval of a renewal by the new sultan of the Franco-
Spanish mandate in Morocco.[248]

Wherever the question of balance of power arose or the
maintenance of the peace of the world was being considered,
whether in Europe or in Asia, in the South Pacific or in
Africa, Germany and her attitudes were important. Indeed, as America under Roosevelt took her place among
world powers, her relations with Germany became crucial for
the future.

Toward Germany Roosevelt had mixed feelings that somewhat fluctuated with events.[249] He had lived and studied in
Germany as a boy. His love of the martial prevented Germany's militarism from offending him as it did some Americans. Indeed, he greatly admired German military leaders
and empire builders. Frederick the Great, Kaiser William I,
Bismarck, Helmuth von Moltke, and Albrecht von Roon
were heroes to him.[250] Besides, where they did not conflict
with American interests, he understood and sympathized
with Germany's imperial ambitions. " I am by no means sure
that I heartily respect the little Kaiser," wrote Assistant
Secretary of the Navy Roosevelt at a time when Germany's
territorial ambitions were alarming much of the world, " but
in his colonial plans I think he is entirely right from the
standpoint of the German race." " If I were a German,"
Roosevelt told his British friend Spring Rice, " I should want
the German race to expand. I should be glad to see it begin
to expand in the only two places left for the ethnic, as distinguished from the political expansion of the European
peoples; that is, in South Africa and temperate South
America. Therefore, as a German I should be delighted to

upset the English in South Africa, and to defy the Americans and their Monroe Doctrine in South America. . . . . International law, and above all inter-racial law, are still in a fluid condition, and two nations with violently conflicting interests may each be entirely right from its own standpoint." [251] While he was Vice-President, Roosevelt sent word to the Kaiser that he was " anxious to keep on friendly relations with Germany—indeed I might say peculiarly anxious, for I have a hearty and genuine liking for the Germans both individually and as a nation." [252] In 1907 he wrote: " I am glad to say that during the last five years there has been in America a steady growth of good will towards Germany." [253]

Some of Roosevelt's most intimate friends, on the other hand, were obsessed with what William L. Langer aptly calls " the almost pathological suspicion of Germany which was prevalent in American political and diplomatic circles." [254] Spring Rice poured into Roosevelt's ear hysterical warnings about Germany and the Kaiser. As Langer put it, he " fanned the flames of American suspicion of Germany." [255] So also did St. Loe Strachey, Henry White, Brooks Adams, and Captain Kimball of the Navy.[256] Lodge, too, was strongly anti-German. So also was John Hay. On July 27, 1898, Hay, then Ambassador to Great Britain, had written Lodge: " I have been under great obligations the last few months to Spring Rice, who knows Germany as few men do. . . . The jealousy and animosity felt towards us in Germany . . . can hardly be exaggerated. . . . The Vaterland is all on fire with greed, and terror of us. They want the Philippines, the Carolines, and Samoas—they want to get into our markets and keep us out of theirs. . . . I do not think they want to fight. . . . But they want by pressure, by threats, & by sulking and wheedling in turn to get something out of us and Spain. There is to the German mind, something monstrous in the thought that a war should take place anywhere

and they not profit by it." [257] The author of these sentiments was soon to be Roosevelt's Secretary of State. At the
end of his Presidency Roosevelt testified that Hay was so
pro-British that he "could not be trusted where England
was concerned," and that, "on the other hand, he was foolishly distrustful of the Germans." [258] In view of the hysteria
of his close friends, Roosevelt's calm judgments about Germany and the Kaiser, his intimacy with Speck von Sternburg, and his desire to work with Germany when to do so
served American ends become remarkable.

Roosevelt and Lodge, influenced by Brooks Adams as well
as by Mahan, were aware that economic forces helped develop international rivalries, and they thought of Germany
in part in terms of them. Though Lodge did not believe
Germany would attack us if we had "a strong and well
equipped navy," still he conceded to Roosevelt that "there
is a fundamental danger which arises from our rapid growth
economically." "We are putting terrible pressure on Europe,"
he wrote Roosevelt, "and this situation may produce war
at any time. The economic forces will not be the ostensible
cause of trouble, but they will be the real cause, and no one
can tell where the break will come." [259] In discussing European threats to America in 1901, Roosevelt declared, "The
chance of our having any hostile military complication with
any foreign power is very small. But that there will come a
strain, a jar, here and there, from commercial and agricultural—that is, from industrial—competition, is almost inevitable." [260] It was his comprehension of the importance to
Germany of this trade element in her Latin American policy
that led Roosevelt three months before he became President
to assure German Consul-General Karl Bünz that he "did
not want any exclusive trade privileges as against Germany
. . . save as they might come legitimately by reciprocity
treaties." [261] "I regard the Monroe Doctrine as being equivalent to the open door in South America," he wrote Speck

von Sternburg a month after he entered the White House.
" I . . . want the United States . . . to let South America
gradually develop on its own lines." [262] He assured Bünz that
he was " delighted to see South America kept open commercially to Germany and to the United States on an equal
footing." He went surprisingly even further. " If a big Ger-
man-speaking community in a South American state could
not stand mis-government, and set up for itself," he told the
German Consul, " there would be in that fact by itself nothing to which I should object." [a] I would have differentiated
our keen interest in the Caribbean from a slighter concern
about nations farther south, he told Whitelaw Reid, had I
not been afraid that " if I said anything of the kind, it would
be accepted abroad as an invitation to make aggression on
the part or parts of America, in which I said we had less
interest." [264]

On occasion Roosevelt foresaw a possibility that economic
factors might lead not only Germany but all of Western
Europe to make war on the United States. His appeal in
his first message to Congress for reciprocity agreements was
inspired in part by an article of Brooks Adams on " Reciprocity or the Alternative." In this essay Adams warned
that as the balance of trade shifted more and more against
Europe in America's favor, Europe would face financial ruin
and might make war on the United States unless by a wise
reciprocity policy we helped encourage the sale of European
products. " Before I finish my message," the new President

---

[a] Actually Mahan, concerned chiefly about strategic matters, held "that we
should not undertake to keep Europe out of South America below the Caribbean
Sea, that Northern South America and Central America are enough for us to
protect." Lodge, who felt trouble with Germany, if it came, would come
"through some attempt in South America, probably Brazil," disagreed with
Mahan. "I do not agree with this view at all," he pleaded with Roosevelt,
"and yet I see the difficulties of enforcing the Monroe Doctrine in Southern
Brazil, for example, and in getting our people to understand the importance of
doing so." [263]

wrote Adams, "I would like to see you, for I intend (although in rather guarded phrase) to put in one or two ideas of your *Atlantic Monthly* article." And so in guarded phrase, indeed, but to the extent of six paragraphs he pleaded for reciprocity treaties, since "the phenomenal growth of our export trade emphasizes the urgency of the need . . . for a liberal policy in dealing with foreign nations." "The customers to whom we dispose of our surplus products," he warned Congress, "in the long run directly or indirectly, purchase those surplus products by giving us something in return." [265]

Ultimately, however, in spite of his understanding of economic forces on the international scene, Roosevelt did not wish to depend upon the removal of economic conflict, but rather upon military might. Strategic matters therefore outweighed economic in his dealings with Germany. "Modern Germany is alert, aggressive, military and industrial," he told Oscar Straus in 1906. "It thinks it is a match for England and France combined in war. . . . It respects the United States only in so far as it believes that our navy is efficient and that if sufficiently wronged or insulted we would fight." "Now I like and respect Germany," he concluded, "but I am not blind to the fact that Germany does not reciprocate this feeling. I want us to do everything we can to stay on good terms with Germany, but I would be a fool if I were blind to the fact that Germany will not stay in with us if we betray weakness." [266]

In spite of his friendliness toward her and admiration of many things about her, Roosevelt was conscious that Germany's imperial ambitions did conflict with our interests in various parts of the world—in Latin America, in Hawaii, in the Philippines, in Samoa. In 1889 he had looked with favor on a war with Germany.[267] "I entirely agree with you," he later wrote Captain McCalla in August, 1897, "that Germany is the Power with which we may very possibly have ultimately to come into hostile contact."[268] His secret instructions to Dewey to take Manila aimed partly at forestalling German seizure of the Philippines. "The only power which may be a menace to us in anything like the immediate future is Germany," he declared privately in March and again in April, 1901.[269] "Some friends of mine who have been at the German field maneuvers last year," he wrote Lodge, "were greatly impressed with the evident intention of the German military classes to take a fall out of us when the opportunity offers." * He was troubled because "the Germans regard our failure to go forward in building up the navy this year as a sign that our spasm of preparation, as they think it, has come to an end; that we shall sink back, so that in a few years they will be in a position to take some step in the West Indies or South America which will make us either put up or shut up on the Monroe Doctrine." "They are counting upon their ability to trounce us," he was convinced. Roosevelt even worried a little lest Germany and Britain combine against us if we abrogated the Clayton-Bulwer Treaty. "Of course such a combination would be one of the utmost folly for England," he conceded, "because she is certain to have her paws burned, while the nuts would go to Germany. But the last two years have shown that British statesmen are capable of committing the wildest follies."[271] In Venezuela he watched Germany carefully and stood up to her tactfully but firmly in 1902 and 1903.

Roosevelt's rôle in the controversy over Venezuelan claims has been widely debated.[272] Indeed, it remains one of the most baffling puzzles of recent American historiography. Upon its solution hangs Roosevelt's reputation for veracity. As one of the most important examples of Rooseveltian

---

* Lodge, usually more anti-German than he, was not at this time alarmed. "I have myself very grave doubts as to their undertaking to attack us," he replied. "It would be a pretty dangerous undertaking." "But," he conceded, "the German Emperor has moments when he is wild enough to do anything."[270]

personal diplomacy it is important to an understanding of
Roosevelt's foreign policy. Hence we must abandon narrative and enter upon an examination into this historiographi-
cal problem. Roosevelt himself later recounted how he threatened the Kaiser with Dewey's fleet to make him arbitrate his
claims against Venezuela, and to force him to abandon hope,
if he ever had any, of acquiring American territory.[273]

The background facts run as follows. In 1902 Germany,
Britain, and Italy joined in the use of naval power to force
Venezuela to pay debts and claims accumulated during local
civil war in 1898-1900.[274] Rumors that Germany had designs
on territory in Latin America had periodically troubled the
United States. On his return from Germany to his Washington post in November, 1901, for instance, Ambassador von
Holleben denied rumors that the Kaiser had ambitions in
America. Such reports were mere inventions of the enemies
of German-American friendship, the Ambassador insisted.[275]
Concerning the Venezuelan dispute, Germany, eager not to
offend the United States, notified her in December, 1901,
that Germany might have to use coërcive measures to collect money due her citizens,[a] but she gave assurance that she
had "no purpose or intention to make even the smallest
acquisition of territory."[277] Hay drafted a reply in the
President's name that disclaimed any objection to forceful
collection of claims provided no territory was acquired. This
response quoted what the President had already said in his
annual message of December 3, 1901: "We do not guarantee
any State against punishment, . . . provided that punishment
does not take the form of the acquisition of territory by any

---

[a] On November 11, 1902, Britain gave the United States notice that she
might have to use force, but did not accompany the notice with the disavowal
of intent to obtain territory. Hay in replying conditioned his acquiescence with
a proviso "that no acquisition of territory was contemplated." It was not,
however, until the height of the crisis that Lansdowne on December 16 and
Balfour on December 17 made the disavowal that Germany had made from the
beginning.[276]

non-American power." [a] [279] Joint intervention was probably first proposed by Britain rather than Germany. [b] [280] Britain was taking strong measures on her own initiative, and was more uncompromising than Germany. It is certain that she was not led into the venture by Germany, as Roosevelt later believed. In any case, by November, 1902, the two nations had agreed to act jointly. [281] They sent several ultimata, the last on December 7. After some debate as to the best measures, they seized or sank Venezuelan gunboats on December 9, landed troops at La Guayra on the tenth, and bombarded Puerto Cabello on the thirteenth. On the sixteenth they were joined by Italy. [282] Then, through the United States, Venezuela urged arbitration, and Germany and Britain agreed to it in principle, but with reservations. They invited Roosevelt to act as arbiter. [283] Roosevelt was tempted, hesitated, was urged by Hay and others not to accept, and finally declined. He refused partly in order to resuscitate the dying Hague Tribunal by trying to send it an important dispute to settle. He urged the powers to take their arbitration to the Hague. [284] Roosevelt's unwillingness to become arbiter led to several weeks of further argument over who should arbitrate, over the precedence of classes of claims, and over rules. Meantime, on December 20 Britain and Germany established a formal blockade pending detailed agreements. [285] During this later phase Germany again twice bombarded Venezuelan territory. [286] Finally on February 19 the blockade was lifted and by May a series of protocols

[a] In December, 1905, France notified Roosevelt that she might have to use force against Venezuela and Roosevelt replied as he had earlier to Germany and Britain that he had no desire to protect the Southern republics from the consequences of their own torts. He trusted France, but did not want to establish a troublesome precedent for the future, and so he asked Jusserand to write giving a pledge that there would be no permanent occupation of territory or customs houses. [278]

[b] William insisted that Lord Lansdowne had proposed it to him while he was visiting in Britain.

had been signed agreeing upon mixed claims commissions and ultimate Hague arbitration of certain disputed points.[287] This is the simple outline of events.

The presence of foreign ships blockading and then bombarding the ports of a Caribbean country caused great excitement. In spite of Roosevelt's and Hay's formal approval of the action, and notwithstanding the fact that Dictator Castro of Venezuela had obviously misbehaved and had clearly shown himself irresponsible, the American press and American political leaders cried out in alarm. So, too, did the British press and British leaders over a partnership with Germany that was none too popular in Britain and that was now arousing hostility in America where Britain wished friendship. Because of the firm entente that was developing with Great Britain, she was on the whole exonerated from evil intent and the onus of American opinion fell on Germany, increasingly so after she alone bombarded again in January.[288] Roosevelt later explained, " I had not the least fear of England and knew that there was no danger from England. . . . I also knew that English public opinion was already very hostile to the action of the English Government." [289]

That Germany had any designs on Venezuelan territory seems doubtful. In the light of events from 1914 to 1945, many American historians have, however, persuaded themselves of the evil intent of Germany in her earlier relations with America.[a] On the other hand, William Langer, one of

[a] Typical of these are Alfred Vagts and Samuel F. Bemis.[290] Such historians can easily find foolish statements of the Kaiser or the militarists of Germany that support their thesis. The evidence, though, proves no more than that Germany, like her rivals and like the United States itself, had leaders that were imperialists and militarists as well as leaders that were not. One of the favorite quotations is from the instruction to Prince Henry as he started on a " good will " tour to America. In this von Bülow told Henry that Germany above all wanted peace and friendship with the United States in the Western hemisphere and advised him to deny as " absurd fancy " stories of German

the leading American historians of Germany, found little basis for these "pathological suspicions" of Germany, and Howard Hill, who most carefully studied the question from the American side, found "no evidence" of German intent to seize Venezuelan territory.[292] Just as historians with confidential writings of the actors before them widely differ as to Germany's intentions, so, too, did contemporaries disagree in their judgments of Germany. Roosevelt rejected the dim view some of his close friends took. Still, there was no harm, he felt, in making certain that, if Germany had designs on Venezuela or other American territory, she be made to realize their futility.

Even more controversial has been the rôle Roosevelt himself played in bringing the nations to arbitrate. At the time, the secret of whatever he did was kept so well that no one suspected he was doing more than to encourage arbitration, to refuse to act as arbiter himself, and to help persuade the disputants to use the Hague Tribunal instead. Then in 1916 as an appendix to a new printing of his *John Hay*, William R. Thayer published a long letter from Roosevelt written August 21, 1916, that told a startling story. The ex-President recounted how he threatened to make war on Germany, prepared his fleet for action, and sent a personal ultimatum to the Kaiser that forced him to submit his claims to arbitration, and to abandon his plans to acquire territory:

> I speedily became convinced that Germany was the . . . really formidable party, in the transaction. . . . I became convinced that England would not back Germany in the event of a clash over the matter between Germany and the United States, but would remain neutral. . . . I also became convinced that Germany intended to seize some

interest in influence or territory there, but cautioned this rather pathetically pompous and inept younger brother of the Kaiser not to give such "an ironical rejection" the air of a formal declaration. This word "ironical" is proof sufficient to Bemis of the "insincerity of German professions." [291]

Venezuelan harbor and turn it into a strongly fortified
place of arms, on the model of Kiaochow, with a view to
exercising some measure of control over the future Isthmian Canal, and over South American affairs generally.
. . . Germany declined to agree to arbitrate . . . and declined
to say that she would not take possession of Venezuelan
territory, merely saying that such possession would be
" temporary "—which might mean anything. I finally
decided that no useful purpose would be served by further
delay, and I took action accordingly. I assembled our
battle fleet, under Admiral Dewey, near Porto Rico, for
" maneuvres," with instructions that the fleet should be
kept in hand and in fighting trim, and should be ready to
sail at an hour's notice. . . . I saw the [German] Ambassador, and explained that in view of the presence of the
German squadron on the Venezuelan coast I could not
permit longer delay in answering my request for an arbitration, and that I could not acquiesce in any seizure of
Venezuelan territory. The Ambassador responded that his
Government could not agree to arbitrate, and that there
was no intention to take " permanent " possession of Venezuelan territory. I answered that Kiaochow was not a
" permanent " possession of Germany's—that . . . I did
not intend to have another Kiaochow, held by similar
tenure, on the approach to the Isthmian Canal. The Ambassador repeated that his Government would not agree to
arbitrate. I then asked him to inform his Government that
if no notification for arbitration came during the next ten
days I would be obliged to order Dewey to take his fleet
to the Venezuelan coast and see that the German forces
did not take possession of any territory. He expressed very
grave concern and asked me if I realized the serious consequences that would follow such action; consequences so
serious to both countries that he dreaded to give them a
name. I answered that I had thoroughly counted the cost
before I decided on the step, and asked him to look at the
map, as a glance would show him that there was no spot
in the world where Germany in the event of conflict with
the United States would be at a greater disadvantage than
in the Caribbean sea. A week later the Ambassador came
to see me, talked pleasantly on several subjects, and rose

to go. I asked him if he had any answer to make from his Government to my request, and when he said no, I informed him that in such event it was useless to wait as long as I had intended, and that Dewey would be ordered to sail twenty four hours in advance of the time I had set. He expressed deep apprehension, and said that his Government would not arbitrate. However, less than twenty four hours before the time I had appointed for calling the order to Dewey, the Ambassador notified me that His Imperial Majesty the German Emperor had directed him to request me to undertake arbitration myself.[293]

The Roosevelt story published by Thayer led to disputes,[294] but it was not until Howard C. Hill in 1927 published his *Roosevelt and the Caribbean* that a careful historian made a thorough study based on adequate sources including both Roosevelt's own papers and the German Foreign Office documents. Hill concluded that the Roosevelt account was inaccurate. He sought to explain the inaccuracies. Roosevelt's memory, he suspected, suffered from the fact that he had not written an account of the event until fourteen years after its occurrence. The President might have confused the incidents of January and February with those of the preceding December—the question of arbitration with " the problem aroused . . . by the German bombardment of Fort San Carlos." He perhaps in retrospect confused " conversations with Holleben with those he had with Sternburg." Hill suspected Roosevelt's narrative was " colored by an active imagination, enlarging upon the substratum of facts . . . recalled more or less dimly after a lapse of many years." " Was the coloring of the account," Hill asked, " due in part to the intense hostility Roosevelt felt toward Germany during the world-war when he first wrote the story? "[295]

Subsequently, historians have debated the issue and taken sides. Henry F. Pringle and J. Fred Rippy accepted the Hill findings but inclined with Hill to believe that there was an episode that, though later exaggerated in Roosevelt's mind,

provided some basis for the story. Pringle, for instance,
found evidence that Hill had missed. " There is no possible
doubt that he dramatized and heightened the part he
played," wrote Pringle. Yet " official documents can fall
short of the truth just as a too dramatic memory can go
beyond it." So Pringle insisted Roosevelt did talk on this
subject with German representatives. But Pringle believed
that " exactly what occurred " would, in all probability,
never be known.[296] Alfred Vagts and Dexter Perkins have
both disparaged Roosevelt. Perkins rejected even the moderate Rippy and Pringle positions and labeled the whole story
a " legend," an " utterly inaccurate reminiscence," an " inaccurate and untrustworthy " bit of " 1916 romancing." The
whole story " must, alas, be regarded," says Perkins, " as
one of the least attractive examples of his extraordinary ego-
tism, and of his vivid and sometimes uncontrolled imagination." Roosevelt, Perkins insists, was not concerned in this
instance about the threat to the Monroe Doctrine and was
willing to acquiesce in what Germany was doing. In actu-
ality it was an aroused public opinion expressed in the press
and in Congress, says Perkins, that compelled him to come
along and forced Germany to arbitrate.[297]

In spite of Pringle's findings and the facts, the impression
has spread that Roosevelt fabricated the entire incident
under the influence of anti-German World War hate. Even
careful historians have repeated the insistence of the more
extreme disparagers of Roosevelt that there is no evidence
anywhere of a Rooseveltian warning to the Kaiser. " Scholars
have . . . discredited the sensational account," says Bailey.[298]
This " debunking " of one of Roosevelt's proudest accomplishments, more perhaps than any other one factor, has
become the basis for a growing conviction, professional and
popular, that Roosevelt was something of a fraud, that he
invented happenings or doctored stories of his part in historic
events to enhance his own reputation.

A careful reëxamination of the facts is now necessary. The truth, it appears, is nearer to Roosevelt's version than to that of special pleaders against him like Perkins.

In the first place, Roosevelt did not need a wave of public opinion to force him to protect the Monroe Doctrine. There was no question in his mind that the United States must prevent the acquisition of territory or even a protectorate by an outside power in the Western Hemisphere. He and Lodge had long been concerned about Germany in Venezuela. From London in 1900 Henry White reported to Roosevelt's friend Lodge a rumor that Germany had obtained or was trying to obtain a coaling station there.[299] In 1901, during the early stages of the debt controversy, a report that the German ship *Vineta* was taking soundings there led to the rumor that Germany intended to seize Margarita Island off the coast of Venezuela. Hay instructed American Chargé Jackson in Berlin to inquire about German intentions. He was " discreetly and informally but decisively " to warn Germany that acquiring such an island would be " a source of concern " to the United States and might embarrass the " cordial and frank relations " of the two nations.[300] At the formal opening of the Pan-American exposition in Buffalo, Lodge and Roosevelt both sounded warning to other nations not to violate the Monroe Doctrine. In his speech on May 20, 1901, Roosevelt coupled a reassurance to Latin American nations that the United States would not use the Doctrine for its own aggrandizement with insistence that we would " not submit to territorial aggrandizement on this continent by any Old World power." * Then he and Lodge watched the British

---

* Perkins, unmindful of the fact that Roosevelt, in office and out, had long been important as a leader of American expansionists, was unable " to repress amusement at the authoritarian tone in which this mere Vice-President expressed himself." Yet Perkins completely forgot this " amusing " warning of the Vice-President and even Perkins's own earlier admission that Roosevelt was " by no means indifferent to the maintenance of the principles of 1823 " when he later in the same book tried to prove that Roosevelt was unconcerned about Germany's threat to the Monroe Doctrine.

and German papers for their reaction. German, Russian, and British papers carried news stories and editorials on the speeches. The *Glasgow Herald* and Smalley in the *London Times* attacked both men, and Roosevelt dubbed Smalley a " copper-riveted idiot " for failure to see that the speeches were aimed not at Britain but at Germany. He and Lodge were gratified, however, that the speeches had " created a sensation " and had roused all the discussion they both had hoped for.[301]

Soon after his Buffalo speech Roosevelt talked at length with Consul-General Karl Bünz who was about to return to Germany and wanted to convey Roosevelt's views to the Kaiser. Roosevelt made it clear that he had no " desire to see the United States itself gain any territory in South America," but he warned that he would do everything in his power " to have the United States take the attitude that no European nation, Germany or any other, should gain a foot of soil in any shape or way in South America, or establish a protectorate under any disguise over any South American country." [302] In July and again in October, 1901, Roosevelt wrote Speck von Sternburg in similar terms and assured him that both the German Ambassador and the German Consul-General " understand my views and assure me that they sympathize with me." [303] When he was urging a bigger navy in 1900 he wrote privately to his Navy-Captain brother-in-law: " if we do not build a big fleet then we shall have . . . a disastrous war against say Germany. . . . If Germany seizes South Brazil and puts a couple of hundred thousand men there, we of course could not touch her at all unless we could whip her fleet, and after we whipped her fleet, if she had retained mastery of the sea long enough to get her men down there, it would be a desperate task to develop an army capable of putting them out." [304] Hay with the approval of Roosevelt and Lodge persuaded Secretary of the Navy Long to send a warship to the Venezuelan port of La Guayra, which Hay and Lodge considered " the most important point in the world just now for a powerful ship of the American navy." " With great difficulty and much urging," Lodge reported to Roosevelt on June 17, 1901, " we have succeeded in getting Long to send the ' Mayflower,' which seems very insufficient but still . . . is something." [305] In September, 1901, at the Minnesota State Fair, and again after Congress adjourned both in 1902 and in 1903 Roosevelt made speeches that he meant as warnings to Europe in which he insisted that the Monroe Doctrine must be respected. [306] When in March, 1903, Speck proposed that America take the initiative in having " the great powers collectively stand back of some syndicate which should take possession of the finances of Venezuela," Roosevelt objected strenuously. " I told him," the President recounted, " that at first blush my judgment was very strongly that our people would view with the utmost displeasure any such proposal, because . . . it would not only tend to produce complication among the guaranteeing powers but would pave the way for reducing Venezuela to a condition like that of Egypt," and that the Monroe Doctrine meant " of course that no European power should gain *control* of any American republic." [307]

Second, critics like Perkins completely overlook the duality of Roosevelt's belief in both the Monroe Doctrine and the mission of civilized Western powers to spread civilization to backward peoples. The Monroe Doctrine had to be enforced, but a civilized power like Germany of course had the right to use strong measures when necessary to civilize a backward people like the Venezuelans. Venezuela under the Castro dictatorship was one of the least trustworthy and most irresponsible of nations.[a] Indeed, with Venezuela ob-

[a] In 1905 Roosevelt himself was still having serious trouble with Castro. He sent a representative down to try to work matters out and exercised great restraint not to send a military force. In 1906 he asked the General Staff for a plan of campaign against Venezuela in sufficient strength " to minimize the

viously in mind, Roosevelt wrote German diplomat Speck
von Sternburg, "If any South American state misbehaves
towards any European country, let the European country
spank it." [309] To feel that Roosevelt's willingness to let Germany deal strongly with Venezuela is proof that he was not
enforcing the Monroe Doctrine [310] is to misunderstand Roosevelt's views on the relations of "advanced" and "barbarous" peoples. What he was doing in Venezuela was to
balance two conflicting beliefs. His willingness to have Germany intervene by force provided she did not try to acquire
territory was genuine. His determination that she should
not use this as a pretext to get a foothold in America was
equally clear from beginning to end. His later corollary,
voiced in regard to Santo Domingo, was his resolution of the
conflict of principles into a workable compromise. The Doctrine, as he put it, could not be used "as a warrant for

chance of effective resistance." In 1907 he was again inclined to interfere
forcibly to make Venezuela pay up, but he waited to see whether Congress
would back him and decided it would not. "Some day," he wrote, "I fear we
shall have to spank Venezuela." In 1908 he felt we really must take action.
"We have suffered a great deal of wrongdoing at the hands of Venezuela," he
wrote Root. He favored sending a transport, landing Marines, and seizing a
customs house. Root agreed with all the President's charges against Venezuela.
"I have had to hold myself with both hands to keep from acting under the
influence of irritation," Root replied. "Nevertheless, my sober judgment always
has been that the circumstances were not such that the people . . . would
sustain the Administration in making war or in asking for authority to make
war." Hence Root persuaded Roosevelt to pass the matter without recommenda-
tion to the Senate for advice. The Senate refused to get excited. In August,
1908, Roosevelt exclaimed, "How I wish I could get the American people to
take the least interest in Castro." "It is literally true," he wailed to French
Ambassador Jusserand, "that if I started to deal with him as he deserves, the
enormous majority of my countrymen would be so absolutely amazed and so
out of sympathy with me as if I undertook personally to run down and chastise
some small street urchin who yelled some epithet of derision at me while I
was driving." But in the end, Root prevailed and by December, 1908, in spite
of "pressure to bulldoze Venezuela," the policy to which Root had won Roosevelt, after years of suppressing exasperation, had brought settlement through
"friendly consideration and moral suasion." [308]

letting any of these republics remain as small bandit-nests," but, on the other hand, a nation like Germany would not have to intervene to insure justice and preserve order.[311]

Third, to cite Roosevelt's public speeches and statements to Germany after the danger was removed and Germany had acquiesced and the Monroe Doctrine was safe as testimony about what had occurred during the crisis is again to fail to comprehend Roosevelt. In this as in his dealings with the Kaiser over Morocco and many another battle of Roosevelt's career, he was concerned with substance, not with personal prestige. He understood the importance of face-saving. When he had won his point he was perfectly happy to help his opponent save face and often went out of his way to praise an opponent for action the opponent would not have taken except under pressure Roosevelt had skilfully exerted. Hence the Hay memorandum (never sent),[312] the conversation with Roosevelt [a] that Hugo Münsterberg reported on January 23, 1903, to the German Foreign Office,[313] Roosevelt's conversations with his old friend Speck von Sternburg,[314] and his public address at Chicago on April 3, 1903,[315] all of which Perkins cites as proofs that Roosevelt could never have sent an ultimatum, are not necessarily any more than pleasant gestures meant to help Germany save face after Roosevelt had forced her to retreat. The assumption that these documents are to be taken as serious evidence against an ultimatum overlooks a persistent Roosevelt characteristic. When necessary he dealt firmly with the Kaiser and then removed the hurt to imperial pride through flattery.

The argument that absence of records disproves the ultimatum story indicates unfamiliarity with the degree to which

[a] Here Roosevelt, hoping for common action of the three great civilized peoples—Germans, English, and Americans—is saying that while these three coöperate to control backward people the Monroe Doctrine is not so rigid as to bar such coöperation. To take the statement about the Monroe Doctrine out of context of Roosevelt's principle of rule of the world by the civilized nations is to misinterpret him.

Roosevelt engaged in direct personal negotiations outside the State Department. The great error of most of the doubters in this matter is their assumption that an " ultimatum " from Roosevelt implied blustering and unpleasantness. When Roosevelt was delivering an ultimatum he could combine firmness with the utmost pleasantness. He could present such an ultimatum to people that were his good friends, as he did to the British leaders in regard to the Alaska boundary, and could do it without interrupting the friendship and without bellowing defiantly from the housetops. Such ultimata, indeed, required the utmost secrecy and the greatest tact to avoid humiliating the friendly recipients or making them lose face.

Fourth, arguments based upon the inaccuracy of details in the 1916 version of the story break down in the face of the Thayer-Roosevelt correspondence of 1916. In July, 1915, Thayer, who already knew of the supposed ultimatum, began trying to persuade Roosevelt to give details. Roosevelt was reluctant. Only after thirteen months of urging did he commit the story to paper and grant Thayer permission to use it. On August 8, 1915, he corrected the manuscript of Thayer's revised *John Hay*, but it was not until August 21 a year later that he consented to write a letter describing what had happened; he wrote it then chiefly because of the attacks upon the veracity of Thayer's story * printed without Roosevelt's own authentication.[318] When he did write, he frankly admitted that his memory of details might be faulty after so many years. He tried hard to verify his story. Only Secre-

---

* Roosevelt in 1915-1916 did hate Germans, but in the Roosevelt-Thayer correspondence about Venezuela the virulence is in Thayer's letters, not Roosevelt's.[316] Roosevelt himself explained his decision to release the hitherto carefully guarded story because " our native Americans . . . need to have their self respect restored by knowing that under proper leadership they can stand up against the Germans (and Japanese!); and because . . . the decent German Americans . . . need to visualize the fact that in order to be good Americans . . . . they may have to take a strong anti-German stand." [317]

tary of the Navy Moody, Secretary of State Hay, Admiral Dewey, and possibly Dewey's chief of staff " knew about the order for the fleet to be ready to sail at an hour's notice." [319] " I did not consult Hay or anyone else . . . any more than I consulted him about the Panama business until I had acted," Roosevelt wrote Thayer, " for councils of war don't fight. Of course, . . . Dewey never knew there was any thought of sending . . . [an order to attack]; and Hay did not know the details—indeed he said he thought he had better not know them." " When I told . . . [the story] to you," Roosevelt explained to Thayer, " I did not suppose that there could be any corroboration." " I took no notes, as far as I can remember, of what I did; at that moment I was trying to achieve results, and never thought of the historical record." [320]

When, however, the story recounted by Roosevelt to Thayer for the 1915 edition was disputed, unexpected corroboration came from two sources. A former neighbor of Roosevelt, Adolph W. Callisen, wrote privately to a friend in Buffalo telling of his interest in the Thayer narrative because from Karl Bünz, the German Consul-General in New York, he had had a confidential account of a conversation between Bünz and von Holleben. Von Holleben's testimony, thus recorded, confirmed the Roosevelt story. The Callisen letter was sent Roosevelt, who then summoned his one-time friend to Oyster Bay. On May 7 Callisen read and authenticated the Roosevelt copy of his letter as " absolutely accurate." Roosevelt then obtained Callisen's permission to quote his letter, which he " had not intended for publication." [321] The other corroborative testimony came from Admiral George Dewey. When the mobilization of Dewey's fleet was questioned, Henry A. Wise Wood wrote Dewey about it and received a reply of May 23, 1916, in which Dewey confirmed the part of Roosevelt's story that concerned his fleet's actions. [322]

Discrediting of the Roosevelt account has depended

heavily on discrepancies of dates, particularly in the lapse of time between a possible ultimatum and Germany's agreement to arbitration. On this matter of dates, too, Roosevelt was cautious. On August 8 he struck out of Thayer's account " the statement as to the days of the week," " for it is possible I am mistaken as to these." Thayer urged him, " Give exact dates—if you can." Under this prodding Roosevelt reluctantly named ten days as the time limit of his ultimatum, but two days later he concluded, " Perhaps it would be safer for me, when I correct the proof, to say ' a certain number of days' or ' a few days,' " and he also expressed uncertainty whether the Holleben reply came " on the evening before instead of the morning before, the afternoon I had indicated as that on which I would notify Dewey to sail." " I had no means of getting the exact dates," he persisted almost plaintively. Thayer, still determined to have him specify a detail that he was uncertain of, looked up in contemporary newspapers the dates of the various December events and assured him that " ten days " would fit. Roosevelt, however, replied, " I am inclined to think . . . that I gave Holleben exactly ten days leeway . . . but as I cannot be absolutely certain whether I said he should have ten days or a fortnight, the statement should be made a little elastic as I have left it." [323]

Fifth, the oft-repeated claim that Roosevelt invented the tale because of his hatred of Germany during World War I is exploded by the discovery of earlier versions of the episode told at a time when Roosevelt was friendly to both Germany and the Kaiser. As early as 1904 Senator Orville Platt of Connecticut had heard of Roosevelt's part in attaining a settlement. On September 27 Platt wrote George G. Hill, Washington correspondent of the *New York Tribune*, deploring the fact that people did not know that in the Venezuela crisis " the President guarded efficiently the Monroe Doctrine, avoiding complications with Germany which might have been serious even to the point of war." An article on Roosevelt's rôle would " refute this crazy charge that he is a man who wants to get us into war," Platt believed.[324] Undoubtedly a few of Roosevelt's intimates knew the story and as in other confidential matters kept the secret well. Roosevelt's first reference to the matter in writing was not during war with Germany in 1916, but in 1905, less than three years after the event. On November 1, 1905, he wrote Spring Rice: " I have more than once been greatly exasperated with the Kaiser myself. When I first came to the Presidency I was inclined to think that the Germans had serious designs upon South America. But I think I succeeded in impressing on the Kaiser, quietly and unofficially, and with equal courtesy and emphasis, that the violation of the Monroe Doctrine by territorial aggrandizement on his part around the Caribbean meant war, not ultimately but immediately and without any delay." [325] Then on June 27, 1906, he wrote Whitelaw Reid more fully.* By 1906 he was already blaming Germany more than England. " The English, again with their usual stupidity, permitted themselves to be roped in as an appendage to Germany in the blockade of Venezuela," he wrote Reid. " I finally told the German Ambassador," he confided, " that in my opinion the Kaiser ought to know that unless an agreement for arbitration was reached, American public opinion would soon be at a point where I would have to move Dewey's ships which were then in the West Indies, south, to observe matters along Venezuela; and that I would have to let it be known publicly that . . . I would have to object even to temporary possession of Venezuelan soil by Germany, unless such possession was strictly limited to say three or four days or a week." This brought the Kaiser to terms, Roosevelt told Reid, but, " I suppose we shall never make public the fact of the vital

---

* He again referred to this episode in a letter of December 4, 1908.

step," he added.[326] On August 14, 1906, he recalled to Henry White: " On one occasion (that of Venezuela) [I] have had to make a display of force and to convince . . . [the Kaiser] definitely that I would use the force if necessary." This story, told to an intimate friend four years after the event, has the ring of authenticity. " I saw the German Ambassador privately myself," the President confided to White; " told him to tell the Kaiser that I had put Dewey in charge of our fleet to maneuver in West Indian waters; that the world at large should know this merely as a maneuver, and we should strive in every way to appear simply as cooperating with the Germans; but that I regretted to say that the popular feeling was such that I should be obliged to interfere, by force if necessary, if the Germans took any action which looked like the acquisition of territory." " This was not in any way intended as a threat," Roosevelt had assured the Kaiser, " but as the position . . . which the American people would demand." He wanted the Kaiser to understand the American position " before the two nations drifted into such a position that trouble might come." To White Roosevelt commented, " I do not know whether it was a case of post hoc or propter hoc." " But," he concluded, " immediately afterwards the Kaiser made to me the proposition that I should arbitrate myself, which I finally got him to modify so that it was sent to the Hague." Then Roosevelt admonished White that he must not tell anybody but George Meyer what the President had just revealed to him about the Kaiser, for, he quoted Carlyle, " the Kaiser . . . is ' gey ill ' to live with, on occasions." [327] Oscar Davis, a journalist friend of the President, recounts that Roosevelt told him the tale on August 7, 1908, but since Davis did not publish his version until after the 1916 discussions of the episode, Davis's testimony lacks the value of contemporaneity.[328] In March, 1909, Roosevelt talked for four hours aboard the *Hamburg* on his way to Africa to E. Alexander Powell and told him the story in detail. This 1909 account was immediately recorded by Powell in a letter to his wife, which is available.[329] The latest of these accounts was given five years before the beginning of the War that presumably inspired in Roosevelt the hate that prompted him to invent this story.

Enough of what happened is known to establish the fact that Roosevelt in friendly fashion, softened by references to the pressure of public opinion and professions of personal esteem, sent messages to the Kaiser that Roosevelt always believed led him to arbitration. What, then, were the series of actions that can be established?

The use of force in Venezuela aroused criticism in both Britain and the United States. On December 8, the day before Britain and Germany seized and sank ships, Henry White in London warned Lansdowne that American public opinion was unfriendly.[330] On December 9, the day on which Venezuelan ships were seized and sunk, Venezuela, who had refused to arbitrate, informally proposed arbitration.[331] On December 11, the day after Britain had landed forces on Venezuelan soil, Venezuela made a formal proposal of arbitration.[332] On December 12 Hay forwarded this request without comment to Britain and Germany and the same day Britain felt it wise to assure the United States that she had no desire for territory.[333] On December 12, too, von Bülow informed the Kaiser of the hostility of the British press toward Germany and of British reports that the American press was hostile. He told William that the sinking of the ships had provoked the anti-German feeling.[334] On December 13 Germany bombarded Puerto Cabello and Ambassador Metternich bluntly warned Berlin of the criticism provoked in the press of various countries by what was regarded as undue German harshness in sinking Venezuelan ships. That day, too, von Holleben cabled from Washington warning of the hostility of the American press.[335] The next day, December 14, Germany decided to accept arbitration in principle so that Britain would not win more favor than she with America.[336]

By December 15 criticism of the venture was troubling the British Government. On that day White reported the " whole Venezuelan matter, especially British acting with Germans, unpopular " in England.[337] The same day Metternich described Lansdowne as deeply concerned not to offend America. King Edward, he said, was unhappy over the whole Venezuelan engagement.[338] On December 15, too, the Government's Venezuelan venture was sharply criticized in a House of Commons debate and Germany and Britain were both vigorously attacked in the United States Senate.[339] That same day Speck wrote Roosevelt from Berlin: " The Venezuelan crisis is causing considerable stir here. Castro's departure seems to me a bit high handed. . . . Letting blood though would be a nasty thing, nowadays it so easily might lead to more." [340]

December 16 saw the climax of the first phase of the dispute. On that date Hay repeated Venezuela's proposal for arbitration and this time urged its acceptance.[341] On the same day von Holleben from New York again cabled to describe the hostility of American papers and the alarm in German-American and English-American financial circles. He transmitted the views of Latin American merchants that German trade would be injured and passed on the rumor that Britain might desert Germany and join the United States. Finally, he recommended considering the acceptance of the principle of arbitration * for the sake of the impression this would make on America.[342] In London that day Lord Lansdowne spoke to German Ambassador Metternich of the British Cabinet's concern to withdraw from Venezuela by accepting arbitration if a good opportunity offered. Lans-

---

* Von Bülow made a marginal comment on this dispatch that " His Majesty does not want under any circumstances to take a step further than Britain takes, or to take any step without Britain."

downe was alarmed about Parliament and about " signs that in the United States a storm of public opinion was rising against which the Government there would be helpless." Lord Lansdowne wished Germany and Britain therefore to agree on replies whose substance would be similar. Metternich warned that the British Government was too weak to stand up against protests at home and in America and hence he advised his government to join with Britain in getting out of Venezuela with honor if that could be done. On the fateful December 16, finally, the British Cabinet agreed to an arbitration or joint commission for limited purposes at least and Lansdowne assured the Commons that Britain would not take territory or land more troops.[343]

On December 17 Hay's urgent proposal of arbitration was delivered in both London and Berlin, and Lansdowne received that morning a cable from Sir Michael Herbert describing growing irritation in the American Congress and regret on the part of Britain's American friends that Britain was acting with Germany. The same day Prime Minister Balfour announced in the House of Commons that the British " never had any intention of landing troops in Venezuela or of occupying territory, even though that occupation might only be of a temporary character." That day, too, Henry White was notified informally of Britain's agreement to arbitrate. And in Berlin von Bülow sent instructions to Metternich to promise Lansdowne full coöperation in dispelling criticism of their joint action. Bülow urged Lansdowne to join him in seizing the initiative from Washington and making a proposal of arbitration before America abandoned its rôle as messenger for an active diplomatic rôle. Bülow proposed joint action before America should insist upon a program that would have strong support. Germany, indeed, hoped Roosevelt would act as arbiter.[344] On December 18 von Quadt found Hay friendly and determined that America should not intervene, but worried over the growing excitement in Congress and the nation and hence eager for a settlement.[345] On December 18 Britain and on December 19 Germany officially accepted arbitration in principle, though on December 20 they proclaimed an official blockade pending settlement of details.[346] This was the period when Roosevelt presumably delivered his ultimatum to the Kaiser.

What was Roosevelt himself doing? First, he was holding the fleet in readiness for action. From the days when he was Assistant Secretary of the Navy, Roosevelt and the Navy had been interested in defense of the Caribbean. It was with this in mind that he tried in January, 1902, to buy the Virgin Islands. Only three days after the German Government informed him that to collect debts it might have to occupy Venezuelan territory temporarily, Roosevelt issued an executive order on December 17, 1901, transferring Culebra, off the coast of Puerto Rico, to the Navy Department so that a base could be established there " in case of sudden war." [347] The Navy in January, 1902, sent Commander John E. Pillsbury to investigate German naval activities off Venezuela. In January, too, Congress was asked for money to finance a fleet mobilization at Culebra. In February the State Department sought information through its consuls about landing places and roads in Venezuela. In May the Navy became alarmed again over the activities of another German vessel. In the early summer a naval board inspected places where the Germans might land. Landing possibilities for Americans, too, were secretly explored, and plans drawn for the defense of the Venezuelan coast. In June a great mobilization of the fleet in the Caribbean was announced. In June, too, Roosevelt wrote Dewey and in July Secretary Moody informed the fleet that the President was deeply interested in the success of the manoeuvers. In November the fleet gathered at Culebra. Dewey consented to command during the mobilization and on November 18 received his orders. He was instructed to hold the fleet ready to move at a moment's notice. His fleet comprised " fifty ships including every battleship and every torpedo boat that we had." On December 8, the day after the final Anglo-German ultimata, Dewey took command. At the same time a naval attaché was stationed in Caracas, capital of Venezuela, to explore roads and to consult about defense of the country.[348] Because of the crisis, Admiral Henry C. Taylor cabled December 14 for confirmation of his instructions to scatter the fleet during the holidays. On December 18, the day after fright over American opinion had brought both Germany and Britain separately to decide to conciliate America by agreeing to arbitrate, Taylor received instructions to divide the squadron as planned.[349]

Several bits of contemporary evidence indicate that the fleet was being used to back up foreign policy concerning Germany and that by the end of December the objective had been won. Just before Christmas Captain William S. Cowles. then acting chief of the Office of Naval Intelligence, guardedly wrote Rear Admiral Taylor in the Caribbean that " the presence of the fleet " in the Caribbean, " concentrated and organized for work, was probably a convenience to the administration in discussing the Venezuelan situation." [350] Cowles was the President's brother-in-law and always in close touch with him. On January 3, Dewey entered in his journal the comment, " The work laid out so long ago and with such care . . . is now ended and successfully accomplished. . . . When one considers the technical success . . . and the effect on foreign powers, particularly at the present moment of the demonstration against Venezuela, of so powerful and mobile a fleet in the Caribbean, it can only be considered as a work redounding immensely to our naval and national prestige." [351] Some months later Secretary Moody declared in a speech, " This country was never upon the borders of a greater peril than at the time of the Venezuela difficulty. . . . We had a battle fleet within reaching distance." [352] In March, 1903, Admiral Dewey had to be called to the White House and reprimanded because he had told newspaper men he saw in the manoeuvers " an object lesson to the Kaiser, more than to any other person." [353] When four years later Roosevelt wrote him the ultimatum story, Henry White replied, " What you write of your action in respect to the Emperor . . . is especially interesting to me as I was in charge at London during the whole of that episode and always suspected that you had given that Potentate a warning which no doubt saved the situation as other similar warnings given privately have settled other incidents known to me without wounding any national susceptibilities or causing any friction." [354]

Besides manoeuvering the fleet for foreign policy purposes, Roosevelt had been making periodic pronouncements insisting that no European power could be allowed to acquire American territory. Certainly his warnings in conversation with Consul-General Bünz in June and in letters to Speck von Sternburg in July and October were transmitted to the German Government. In October, 1901, and November, 1902, Speck came briefly to America and stayed with Roosevelt, and on his return to Germany was questioned both times about Roosevelt's views on South America. He was known to be one of the President's most trusted friends, and it is now known that he was on occasion used by the President as a confidential agent.[355]

As the crisis approached, Roosevelt and Hay used every possible means to settle the controversy peacefully without actually officially intervening. On December 5, four days before the attack on Venezuelan ships, Hay cabled Chargé H. Percival Dodge in Berlin and Henry White in London that the President would be glad if an arrangement could be made that " might obviate the necessity of any exhibition of force on the part of Germany and Great Britain." [356] On December 8, the day on which German and British representatives withdrew from Venezuela and the day before the naval engagement, White had a long confidential talk with Prime Minister Balfour, in which he expressed anxiety over the Venezuelan situation and pleaded with Balfour " not [to] allow his government to be led by Germany into doing anything to exacerbate our public opinion." White saw Balfour again later in the week, again on December 15, and then every day, occasionally twice a day, during the weeks preceding and following Christmas.[357] White believed that it was partly because of these talks that Balfour persuaded the Cabinet to let him announce publicly on December 11 what they had intended to keep secret, namely, their decision not to land troops on Venezuelan soil.[358]

Dates of talks of von Holleben and his chargé von Quadt with Roosevelt and Hay are important but difficult to ascertain. Von Holleben did have an interview at the White House December 8. This was the day after Britain and Germany had delivered their ultimata to Venezuela. It was the very day on which White sounded warning to the British Government and on which Dewey took command of the fleet Roosevelt had concentrated in the Caribbean to meet possible trouble. An " ultimatum " could well have been delivered that day.* On December 13, the day after Hay sent his informal proposal of arbitration, von Holleben cabled the first of his two known warnings about public opinion. On December 16, the day before Hay's more urgent appeal, von Holleben's second warning was sent and this time he recommended considering the acceptance of arbitration, which already had been decided upon unbeknown to von Holleben

---

* The official records show only one appointment for Holleben, but White House records were always incomplete on callers. Actually the Appointment Book shows an appointment for both December 6 and December 8, but indicates that the earlier one was canceled. Roosevelt's secretary, William Loeb, long afterward remembered two calls, two or three days apart, and testified that Roosevelt had talked sharply to von Holleben.

and not publicly announced for another three days.[359] On
December 18, 20, and 29 von Quadt had talks with Hay
and reported them to his government. Hay was friendly and
assured von Quadt of his friendliness toward Germany, but
on December 18, the day following Hay's urgent appeal and
the day before the agreement to arbitrate was announced,
Hay warned him and he warned his government that if
Germany did not soon agree to arbitrate Congress might
adopt a resolution instructing the President to enforce the
Monroe Doctrine against her.[360] On December 29, on the
same day when von Quadt was reporting that Hay had no
distrust of Germany, Sir Michael Herbert cabled his government that " the outburst in this country against Germany
has been truly remarkable, and suspicion of the German
Emperor's designs in the Caribbean Sea is shared by the
Administration, the press, and the public alike." Sir Michael
ventured the guess that the irritation was in part spontaneous but was in part stimulated by the Navy. " It will continue to be fostered," he predicted, " by the naval authorities
. . . who wish to increase the navy, and by the powerful ship-
building firms of Cramp in the East and Scott in the West,
who want more orders for ships." [361]

A fact whose importance has been overlooked by everyone, defenders and depreciators of Roosevelt alike, was a
conversation that took place in Berlin two days after Roosevelt probably made whatever threat he did make to von
Holleben. On December 10, the day after the sinking of
the ships, when the newspapers of various countries were full
of criticism of Germany's action, Speck von Sternburg, home
on leave from India, was summoned to give the German
Government his impressions of his recent visit to Roosevelt.
" Nothing could have pleased me more," Speck wrote Roosevelt, " because it gave me a chance to tell them the truth.
I've told them every bit of it and have used rather plain
talk. When I left here a month ago found them comfortably

basking in the illusions of the great visit [of Prince Henry to the United States]." "Fear I've knocked them down rather roughly," he confided to his friend the American President, "but should consider myself a cowardly weakling if I had let things stand as they were." [362]

One other factor seems important. Through these years Germany was trying desperately to go "hand in hand" with America, to win and keep her friendship.[363] She was aware of American sensitiveness over the Monroe Doctrine. She did everything she could to avoid trouble about it. She was more conciliatory toward Venezuela before the intervention than Britain had been. She sought and thought she had American approval for each step she took. Had she foreseen what the American reaction was going to be, she would almost certainly have refrained from the venture entirely.[364] Ambassador von Holleben, however, and Chargé von Quadt had given the Kaiser and his Chancellor no hint of unfavorable reaction. On the contrary they had transmitted repeated assurances of American friendliness.[a][366] Then on December 10 came the burst of hostility toward Germany in America, and on that same day Roosevelt's friend Speck, direct from long talks with the President, administered to the German Government the shock of a true picture of American sentiment and the failure of German diplomacy. Events now proved Speck's information acquired before trouble broke out correct. In that interview Speck gained sufficient impression of the distress his frankness had created to write Roosevelt, "I feel absolutely confident that a radical change must take place in Mass. Ave." He even speculated on his own chances of appointment.[b][367] On January 9 Roosevelt was notified confidentially by cable that his friend Speck

---

[a] So, too, of course had Sir Michael Herbert to the British Government.[365]

[b] "As regards the Emperor feel I'm alright," he wrote Roosevelt, "but the rest never loved me very much on account of what they call my 'English proclivities.'"

would be appointed ambassador, and would sail January 20. The President cabled immediately what "great pleasure" Speck's coming afforded him. On January 10 public announcement was suddenly made of von Holleben's recall on the ground of ill health ᵃ of which he had shown no sign, and on January 31 Roosevelt's intimate friend, the new ambassador, arrived in Washington. He had been hastily appointed as he was about to return to a consulate in India. Roosevelt had long wanted Speck brought back to Washington in some capacity, but Germany had refused to send him, perhaps because he was too pro-American. Certainly his status in the diplomatic service did not warrant making him ambassador.[368] The sudden recall ᵇ of one of the top men in the service before time for his retirement and the sending of an obscure person in his stead seem to indicate that the Kaiser had been seriously jolted in his relations with Roosevelt and was now willing to take drastic measures to create closer ties with the man and the country he had hoped were his friends.[369]

Only the principle of arbitration, however, had been agreed upon in December, 1902, and settlement of details proved difficult.[370] While haggling over specific terms and priority claims proceeded, the armed intervention continued. A second time men began to wonder if Germany intended to stay in Venezuela. Roosevelt and Hay worked behind the scenes to bring about an agreement that would end the in-

---

ᵃ The Foreign Office made no reference to the causes for the change beyond the statement that Holleben was ill and the Emperor had granted him leave of absence. Yet the *Review of Reviews* recorded that he was "enjoying his usual excellent health."

ᵇ When von Holleben's warning of December 13 about the hostility of the American press had arrived, the Kaiser had recorded his irritation with von Holleben by writing into the margin that it was von Holleben's business as ambassador to quiet the American press. As early as June, 1900, Secretary of State Hay had written confidentially, "Holleben is absolutely without initiative and in mortal terror of the Kaiser."

tervention. Early in January Henry White had several interviews with Foreign Secretary Lansdowne trying to persuade him to a speedy raising of the blockade.[371] On January 17 White urged Hay to continue pressure on both countries. " I cannot imagine, and have not yet succeeded in ascertaining, what ever possessed this government to go in with Germany," he declared. " If the whole matter is not settled before Parliament meets, . . . they will have a pretty time of it."[372] White continued to press the British. Roosevelt later told Lodge confidentially that White's " work . . . had been simply invaluable, and that he had learned more about Berlin through . . . [White] than he had from Berlin itself."[373]

German action once more precipitated a crisis. On January 14 a German ship fired on the fort of Puerto Cabello and on January 18 three German ships, without consultation with the British, bombarded Fort San Carlos. They insisted they fired only after the forts had fired on them. There was a new outburst of anti-German feeling in both England and America. King Edward was reported eager to end the intervention.[374] Von Quadt called on Hay to express renewed surprise at American public feeling and Hay urged lifting of the blockade " especially as the interests damaged by further delay were rather German and English than Venezuelan."[375] To his government von Quadt cabled, " I hear indirectly that Secretary Hay expressed himself very bitterly concerning our action. . . . At no time . . . had feeling against us been so heated as now."[376] By January 22 Britain and Germany had come to an understanding on the terms they would jointly require of Venezuela before they raised the blockade.[377] J. Pierpont Morgan, who was " irritated and angry," was urged to " take hold of the situation " as " he would satisfy Germany and England better than anybody else."[378] The British public, too, was aroused. On January 23 both Britain and Germany felt compelled to pacify public opinion by promising to return the Venezuelan boats they still held.[379]

On January 27 Britain privately begged Germany to facilitate a settlement by reducing her cash demands and warned that refusal to do so would increase anti-German feeling in England and perhaps endanger the friendly relations of the two countries. The next day King Edward himself talked to Metternich. Germany, disturbed, acquiesced.[380]

On January 30 a new crisis was reached. Germany and Britain had demanded preferential treatment for some of their claims. In lieu of paying claims, Venezuela finally offered thirty per cent of the customs receipts for one month.[381] Roosevelt, who had tried to keep in the background, now became insistent upon immediate settlement. " The feeling against Germany is intense here for the moment," Sir Michael Herbert wrote his Government from Washington on January 30, " and after the bombardment I was very nervous as to what was going to happen, for complications with Germany meant trouble for us." " You may possibly think me too anxious to arrive at an agreement," he told Lansdowne, " but my business is to think first of all of our relations with the U. S." " In my opinion," he urged, " it is better to let the claimants and bondholders wait a few years than to embarrass the Administration here, which is so friendly to us, and alienate good feelings towards England." [382] " Herbert rushes—or rather shuffles, about—desperately trying to straighten things out, and worried half thread-bare," wrote Henry Adams. But Adams himself was worried. " All is chaos," he wrote Mrs. Cameron. " The Germans are trying our patience very badly indeed, but unless the Kaiser really means trouble, he will soon stop. My own real uneasiness is that he may not be sane. . . . In a dynamite magazine lunatics are dangerous. We are sitting on a safety valve anyway, and for once we know it, all of us." Roosevelt troubled him, too. " Our Emperor is more irrepressible than ever," Adams wrote. " He . . . sits in the midst of a score of politicians and reporters describing his preparations for war with Germany." [383]

It was at this moment that the President's friend "Speckie" arrived as emergency ambassador from Germany. In September, 1901, he had written, "As to South America I always have upheld that the Monroe Doctrine was a blessing to civilization as regards its power as a *peace maker.*" [384] On January 15, too, in Berlin when his appointment was announced, Speck made a statement friendly to the Monroe Doctrine that was quoted in America.[385] Just off the boat he gave an interview in which he assured America that William II understood America's feeling about the Monroe Doctrine and would as soon try to colonize the moon as to violate its terms.[386] Speck came with detailed verbal instructions.

On his arrival in Washington on January 31 the special ambassador was immediately summoned to Roosevelt, who talked frankly with him. The President urged a settlement " as soon as possible since the negotiations were beginning to irritate public opinion in lively fashion both here and in Europe." Roosevelt made it clear that France was coöperating with the President and that the small powers would certainly come along. Sir Michael told Speck that Bowen, the American minister in Caracas whom Venezuela had appointed to act for her, was openly influencing the press in favor of Venezuela.[387] That day Sir Michael cabled Lord Lansdowne, " The German minister . . . informs me that the President told him this morning that he earnestly hoped that a prompt settlement . . . would be arrived at as public opinion in this country was growing more and more irritated." [388] On February 3, after a talk with Roosevelt that lasted a half hour or more, Speck cabled home again telling his government that " the little sympathy " that Germany still had had in the United States she had sacrificed. The Latin American states, too, were swinging to the side of the United States. The German Ambassador told of secret orders Dewey's fleet had received to stand ready for action. The

President was eager to have the blockade terminated. And Speck urged acceptance of the Venezuelan proposal.[389]

Now negotiations to settle the problem of preferential claims proceeded feverishly in Berlin, London, and Washington. On January 30 Lansdowne and Metternich had agreed that they " were riding for a fall " if they asked Roosevelt to arbitrate. But a week later they were forced by public opinion and the urging of Ambassadors Herbert and von Sternburg in Washington to do just that; again the President refused; again agreement was reached to go to the Hague Tribunal.[390]

At the end of the first week in February, 1903, public opinion was still aroused. On February 3 Lodge wrote White in London, " People have distinguished between English and German feeling and there has been up to today no sentiment against England. . . . But the news . . . in regard to England's insisting on the preferential . . . will do great harm I fear. . . . The English *Government* appears to be no more friendly than that of Germany. Why the Government should run contrary to the feeling in their own country and take the very great risk of arousing bitter feelings here is something hard to understand." [391] On February 4 Metternich again warned of the growing sympathy in England for the Venezuelans. The Royal Family as well as the press were opposed to further coöperation with Germany. " When Parliament convenes on the seventeenth," he predicted, " the situation may become dangerous for the Government, if sharper opposition has developed in the United States by that time. . . . If Roosevelt should lose patience, should give way to the yellow press, and should for example demand a raising of the blockade, then the English Government would speedily fall." " It cannot stand," Metternich insisted, " against the American fetish when combined with the dislike of Germany." " A new ministry," he pointed out, " which had defeated the opposing government because of its cooperation with Germany would create a serious danger for official German-English relations." [392] On February 7 Herbert cabled Lansdowne from Washington that opinion had turned against Britain. "The time has almost come, in American opinion," he warned, "for us to make the choice between the friendship of the United States and that of Germany." [393]

The same day a cable from White indicated a hitch in the negotiations. Roosevelt was troubled. It was at this time he asked about the strength of the Caribbean fleet and got a reply from his brother-in-law, Captain Cowles, comparing American and German ships there. [394] On February 9 he sent word to White to tell Lansdowne how "ardently" he desired a settlement, and White told Lansdowne Roosevelt felt it was the German demands that were holding up a settlement. On February 11 German Ambassador Metternich passed this word on to his government, which immediately called in the American Ambassador to assure him that it was most eager to settle all difficulties. [395] As a result of all this pressure from public opinion and from Roosevelt, Britain and Germany were brought to sign on February 13 a protocol lifting the blockade and agreeing to refer the problem of preferential claims to The Hague. [396]

On the very day when the protocol was signed Roosevelt, on a horseback ride, described to his friend Speck the American side of an exciting episode. The whole story was not repeated because President, Ambassador, and Kaiser presumably knew many of the details.* But Roosevelt did tell his friend, who reported the remarks to his government: "The sinking of the Venezuelan ships and the bombardment of the forts during the negotiations immediately aroused sympathy for Venezuela here and created a critical situation.

---

* This conversation comes from the very report home of which Perkins used another portion to show that relations were so friendly that Roosevelt could not have delivered an ultimatum.

The German warships of the blockade would have seen in the fleet of Admiral Dewey their approaching opponents; [a] Dewey's people in turn would have considered the German ships their next object of attack. [b] It had become high time to bring an end to these conditions. Now German ships were involved; in six weeks, however, it could possibly have been British ones." [397] This conversation, ignored or explained away by Roosevelt's critics, fits exactly into either of two hypotheses. A pleasant but firm warning could have been delivered to Germany at the time of von Holleben's talk with Roosevelt on December 8 and Speck's conversation with the Kaiser on December 10. This "warning" could have led to the change of German policy and to the recall of the Ambassador whose ineptness had put Germany in this position. The other possibility is that the President was referring on the horseback ride to recent conversations with Speck, which, reported by Speck, had brought his government to agree this second time to arbitration, thereby preventing a serious crisis. And this fragmentary description was recorded not thirteen years later in 1916 during war with Germany but on February 13, 1903, two months after the first event and only days after the second, while memories were still vivid.

Now that his point was made, arbitration agreed to, and the threat to American territory removed, Roosevelt as was his wont coupled compliments with his firmness. The peaceful settlement had created the best possible impression concerning Germany, he assured Speck on the same horseback ride. The President was " in the highest degree pleased." He hoped Germany would see that the best way to improve relations with South America was for Germany to develop her influence peacefully, for example, through Germans living in Brazil where she " already had so strong a foothold." Still, Speck warned his government, " I feel that the President

---

[a] " They would not have dreamed of it," the Kaiser wrote in the margin.
[b] " Very foolish of them," ejaculated the Kaiser.

does not absolutely trust Germany's assurances in regard to the Monroe Doctrine." "I took the opportunity," he reported, "to assure him emphatically that Germany did not think of land acquisition in South or Central America." [398]

"Sternburg has had a terrible time," Hay confided to Henry White after the episode had closed, "first in inducing his Foreign Office to allow him to make peace, and secondly in fighting a boycott in his own embassy." "I never heard of anything so extraordinary," Hay continued. "His counsellor, Quadt, and his second secretary, Ritter, refused to recognize him or his wife, socially or officially, on the ground of his inferior social standing. He has had them both recalled." Hay had heard that von Bülow, too, was unfriendly. "But," he concluded, "the President is his Dutzbruder, and the Emperor seems inclined to keep him, as a *persona gratissima.*" [399] Actually, when Speck reported on his horseback conversation with Roosevelt, the Kaiser inserted a marginal note on the dispatch: "How good it is if the German representative of His Majesty can ride out with the President.—W. Approved." [400] In the end, however, Roosevelt and Hay had finally to put pressure on the German Government to get Speck his ambassadorship. "When Baron Sternburg came here . . . , our Embassy in Berlin was informed that it was the intention of the Emperor to name him Ambassador," Hay wrote American Ambassador Tower in Berlin on April 28, 1903. "This appointment has not yet been made, and the result is a considerable embarrassment to the Baron and to his colleagues." Tower was not to take any official stand on the matter, but he was instructed to let the Foreign Secretary know "that the Baron is greatly liked here, is a personal and intimate friend of the President, and that we should all be glad if it seemed proper to the Royal Imperial Government to accredit him as Ambassador." [401] When his ambassadorial appointment finally came through, Roosevelt helped by breaking precedents in receiving him officially at

Oyster Bay in July. Perhaps to help Speck's standing with his German superiors, the President broke another precedent by keeping the newly accredited Ambassador as his guest for the night and then spending the afternoon target shooting, tramping in the woods, and riding horseback with him.[402]

In conclusion it becomes clear from the foregoing analysis that Germany had no territorial ambitions in Latin America at this time, that she was in any case most eager not to offend America, that she was misled about American attitudes by the ineptitude of von Quadt and von Holleben, that, when she acquired correct information, she was strongly influenced by American and British opinion, and that she would have been thus influenced had the Roosevelt Administration taken no action. It becomes equally certain, however, that she was warned by the Administration and did heed the warning. Our analysis further reveals three times when an urgent warning was actually delivered to Germany: through von Holleben after his December 8 conversation in dispatches of December 13 and 16 and perhaps in an earlier one not recorded, through Speck's conversations with Roosevelt reported in Berlin on December 10, and between January 30 and February 3 through Speck in Washington. Roosevelt's *post facto* naming of a specific time limit was the result of importuning by Thayer, and the implication that the " ultimatum " was violent and unpleasant is partly an addition of the war years not present in the earlier accounts and partly a false assumption of historians. Whatever warning was given was firm and backed by force, but it was a pleasant warning to a friend. It was delivered in such a manner as to avoid hurting German pride and it was accompanied by flattery of the Kaiser ministered with characteristic Rooseveltian concern to help Germany save face once the President's objective was obtained. It would have been in character for Roosevelt to transmit such a friendly admonition so unofficially and secretly that no record of it should remain.

It is also possible that he had in mind one of the three conversations of which records do survive, or that, as the years
passed, he confused all three. But it seems certain that the
substance of the story was not an invention of war years and
that only the color and tone were heightened in the account
recorded in 1916.[403]

It also seems certain that the episode effectively impressed
the Monroe Doctrine, not only upon Germany, but upon
Britain and other European nations, and upon the American
public.[404] The episode also confirms Roosevelt's pronouncement, like Voltaire's predication of God, that " if the Monroe
Doctrine did not already exist, it would be necessary forthwith to create it," and that it " is not a matter of law at all,
[but] a matter of policy." [405] Out of this experience, too, grew
Roosevelt's determination to formulate the corollary to the
Monroe Doctrine subsequently applied to Santo Domingo.

When our interests did not clash with hers as they had
seemed to do in Venezuela, at The Hague, and at Algeciras,
Roosevelt coöperated with Germany. " I . . . [am] anxious
to keep on friendly terms with Germany," he told Consul-
General Bünz in 1901. " Indeed I might say peculiarly
anxious, for I have a hearty and genuine liking for the Germans both individually and as a nation." [406] " It is a good
thing," wrote the President late in 1905, " to have softened
down the spirit of bitterness that was certainly rife in both
countries four years ago." [407] He came to feel the Venezuelan
unpleasantness had actually improved this relationship. Indeed, in 1905 he wrote: " The Kaiser has always been as nice
as possible to me since [the Venezuelan episode] and has
helped me in every way, and my relations with him and
relations of the two countries have been, I am happy to say,
growing more close and friendly." [408] The Kaiser on his part
did everything he could to cultivate the friendship of America and its President.* For example, when they were negoti-

---

* His sending his brother Henry to America, his presenting Roosevelt and

ating the secret agreement of 1905, William warned Czar Nicholas, " It is very essential that America should not feel threatened by our agreement." [410] Roosevelt's personal relations with William II were, indeed, among the most interesting of his associations.

Kaiser and President alike enjoyed handling various matters that mutually concerned them by personal negotiations. Thus, as we have seen, they coöperated in regard to the Portsmouth and Algeciras conferences. Thus, too, they both played rôles, this time opposing ones, in the Venezuela dispute.

In the Far East, where Roosevelt felt our interests and Germany's coincided, William and Roosevelt worked together. Speck von Sternburg, who while Roosevelt was President was to do much of the negotiating between President and Kaiser, had often talked over with his American friend their mutual concern about China. Even as counselor and first secretary at the German Embassy in Washington from 1897 to 1900, he recalled, " I had . . . strongly sympathized with Secretary Hay's Chinese policy and had done my best to convince my Gov't that it was the *only* course to follow in China." [411] But the Kaiser himself did not have to be persuaded by Speck. He wished, as he put it, " to go hand in hand " with Roosevelt in China. He expressed great sympathy," Roosevelt testified, " with our views of the open door in China." At the end of February, 1902, carefully omitting North China, the Kaiser proposed in a personal

America with gifts, his asking Alice Roosevelt to christen a ship, his inviting official and unofficial Americans to be his guests were all rather obvious efforts in this direction. So, too, were more important actions like his efforts to coöperate with Roosevelt in China and his backing down on a policy close to his heart in Morocco rather than offend Roosevelt by disgracing his friend Ambassador von Sternburg. Even the inscrutable power behind the throne Friedrich von Holstein supported the policy of coöperating with Roosevelt. Von Bülow looking back attributed the better relations to the Kaiser's desire for friendship with America, his " understanding and appreciation of the United States," and his personal friendship with Roosevelt. [409]

message to the President " that we should invite the powers
to guarantee an open door in the Yangtse Valley." He promised Roosevelt that Germany would immediately give the
proposal her support.[412] Hay, who was in Roosevelt's phrase
" vigorous always with Germany," drew up a " sharp note."
The President rewrote it, toned it down, expressed appreciation of the Emperor's proposal, but then made it clear that
" our policy was to have the open door for *all* China & if
Germany would propose to the Powers a guarantee for that
we would join in & back it up & give it *our* support." Roosevelt later told the story to Root and added, " It is a good
thing to give Germany all credit for making the suggestion.
As a matter of fact, in this instance Germany behaved better
than any other power, for in England Lansdowne drove us
half crazy with thick-headed inquiries and requests about
our making more specific exactly what it was highly inex-
pedient to make specific at all." [413]

In 1904 Roosevelt in turn sought through Speck to influence William. He told Speck he wanted to keep in touch
with the Kaiser. Then he outlined what he would like to see
result from the war in the Far East. He asked Speck to
find out what the Kaiser thought best. Speck dutifully
cabled to His Majesty the President's desire to " go hand in
hand " with Germany in Eastern Asia, and the President's
questions and proposals. In transmitting them, Chancellor
von Bülow appended his gratuitous suggestion that William
should take into account " that the President is a great
admirer of Your Majesty and would like to rule the world
hand in hand with Your Majesty, as he certainly conceives
himself to be the American pendant to Your Majesty." [414]

In December and January of 1904-1905, again, Roosevelt
and the Kaiser carried on personal negotiations through
Speck and von Bülow concerning the problem of the powers
in China. Speck, who was home on leave, explained that the
President would stand firmly for the open door and the in-

tegrity of China. William was " delighted." Roosevelt, however, made it clear that he would not act in opposition to
Japan, whose increasing strength he did not fear and whose
friendship he wished to win. He did, however, distrust
Russia and was unwilling, he told the Kaiser, to hand over
China, Manchuria, or Korea to the Russians. Von Bülow
advised William: " Naturally we cannot put ourselves into
opposition to Russia in order to fall in with the Asiatic policy
of America. Nevertheless, we must manage to give a reply
to Roosevelt which will not endanger the gradual development of the friendly relations between Germany and America." [415] Two days later he suggested that William " dwell
more on the danger of a Quadruple Alliance (England,
France, Russia, and Japan) than on that of a Yellow
Peril." [416] " The Americans will be more ready to believe in
the former danger," von Bülow suggested, " as it is nearer
to them. . . . Japan, as the fourth member of an alliance
with three European powers, is more dangerous than if she
stands alone with China. The latter contingency is that
which Roosevelt foreshadows when he says it would not be
difficult to deal with Japan." [417] Ultimately William had
Speck cable Roosevelt: The Emperor " is highly gratified to
hear that you firmly adhere to the policy of the Open Door
and uphold the actual integrity of China." " Close observation of events," Speck reported, " has firmly convinced him
that a powerful coalition, headed by France, is under formation directed against the integrity of China and the Open
Door. The aim of this coalition is to convince the belligerents
that peace without compensation to the neutral powers is
impossible." Then through Speck William made a proposal
to Roosevelt. " The formation of this coalition, the Emperor
firmly believes, can be frustrated by the following move,"
Speck cabled. " You should ask all powers having interests
in the Far East including the minor ones whether they are
prepared to give a pledge not to demand any compensation

for themselves in any shape of territory or other compensation in China or elsewhere for any services rendered to the belligerents in the making of peace or for any other reason." [418] Roosevelt immediately summoned Hay and they concluded " that it would be best to take advantage of the Kaiser's proposition, 1st to nail the matter with him and 2nd to ascertain the views of the other powers." Hay then went home and drafted the notes, which were sent out on January 13, 1905.[419] Throughout that spring Roosevelt and William continued to correspond about Chinese neutrality, which they endeavored to protect not only to serve German and American interests, but for the preservation of world peace.[420]

In July, 1905, the Kaiser again sent word to Roosevelt that France and England were going to seek compensation in territory in the Far East for helping Russia and Japan settle their war. Roosevelt was skeptical, but he politely replied that he would not stand for this if it were attempted.[421]

With the open door still in mind, William rejoiced in 1907 over Roosevelt's sending of the fleet around the world. Unlike Roosevelt, William considered Britain and Japan and their alliance a threat to the open door. " The Japanese naturally want China for themselves," he wrote his Chancellor on December 30, 1907, " but they also want to get rid of all the whites in Asia." " The largest fleet under a *single command* in the world, will prevent the others," the Kaiser rejoiced, " from attempts at partition to the prejudice of ourselves and America." [422]

On other matters, too, William and Theodore coöperated through the personal diplomacy that each liked. In November, 1904, Roosevelt got Speck to wire the Kaiser proposing a treaty of arbitration and received the prompt reply: " Delighted. Do it immediately." [423] In 1908 the President himself appealed directly to the Kaiser to accept the modified arbitration treaty of that year. " I freely admit," Roosevelt

wrote, " that . . . in the form in which the treaty now is . . .
it is not as effective as I could wish. Nevertheless good would
result from the expression of good-will implied in the
treaty." [424] In 1905 the President had Meyer go from St.
Petersburg to Berlin ostensibly on private business but
actually to get himself invited to talk with William. Roosevelt wanted him to discover whether the report of the King
of Italy that there was an agreement between Germany and
Russia was correct. Meyer encouraged the Emperor to talk
at length about Russia; he committed William to full support of the neutrality and integrity of China; and he transmitted personally Roosevelt's hope that President and Kaiser
could coöperate on Far Eastern policy. [425]

Roosevelt, however, did not always treat the Kaiser's communications seriously. To John Hay Roosevelt wrote in
April, 1905, " The Kaiser has become a monomaniac about
getting into communication with me every time he drinks
thre pen 'orth of conspiracy against his life and power; but
as has been so often the case for the last year, he is at the
moment playing our game—or, as I should more politely put
it, his interests and ours, together with those of humanity in
general, are identical." [426] The Kaiser was obsessed with the
" Yellow Peril." Roosevelt laughed off as " pipe dreams " [*]
the Kaiser's periodic warnings that Japan was about to
attack the United States. [428] In August, 1905, for instance,
he wrote Jusserand then in Paris, " I have received a couple
of brand new pipe dreams from my constant correspondent.
I'll tell you about them next month." [429]

Emperor and President frequently exchanged cordial let-

---

[*] The Kaiser's most indiscreet letters were sent off without his advisers' knowledge. On one occasion when the Kaiser wrote such an indiscreet epistle to " his
friend " Roosevelt about the " yellow peril," passing on to him " news " that
his Chancellor found " rather fantastic," von Bülow learned of the letter only
after it had been sent but persuaded the Kaiser it was unwise to put such a
letter into anyone's hands. Hence this letter was extracted from the courier's
pouch in New York and never reached Roosevelt. [427]

ters or cablegrams. After the Kaiser had personally sought to persuade the Czar to be reasonable in making peace, the Kaiser cabled Roosevelt congratulations on his success and the President wired William thanks for his help. To William the President said in 1907, " I have entire confidence in your genuine friendliness to my country. . . . Primarily owing to your attitude, the relations of the two countries have been placed on an excellent footing." [430] More impressive, however, is a confidential letter to Spring Rice in which the President wrote on September 1, 1905, " In my letters to you I have sometimes spoken sharply of the Kaiser. I want to say now that in these peace negotiations he has acted like a trump. He has done everything he could to make the Czar yield and has backed me up in every way, and I thoroughly appreciate how he has behaved." [431] In 1907, Roosevelt sent Taft for a personal conference with William. " No distrust will be sown between Germany and America by any gossip," he assured William in 1907; " I sincerely believe that the growth of good feeling . . . is steady and permanent." [432] In 1908 William and Roosevelt personally corresponded about working out tariff difficulties between them.[433] In 1908, too, Roosevelt thanked William for his " constant friendliness toward the United States." " I attributed the constantly growing feeling of good-will between the two nations," Roosevelt told William, " more to your own influence than to anything else." " It has been a very real pleasure to me to be able so often to cooperate with you and to second your efforts," Roosevelt wrote.[434]

The President's British friends were perpetually worried lest Roosevelt get on too well with the Kaiser.[435] " The heavy witted creatures," he exploded to Lodge, " do not understand that nothing would persuade me to follow the lead or enter into close alliance with a man who is so jumpy, so little capable of continuity of action, and therefore, so little capable of being loyal to his friends or steadfastly hostile to an enemy." [436] To quiet English fears, Roosevelt declared to Spring Rice in May, 1905, " Of course in a way I suppose it is natural that my English friends generally, from the King down, should think I was under the influence of the Kaiser, but you ought to know better, old man. There is much that I admire about the Kaiser and there is more that I admire about the German people. But the German people are too completely under his rule for me to be able to disassociate them from him, and he himself is altogether . . . too volatile in his policies, too lacking in the power of . . . sustained thought . . . for me to feel that he is in any way such a man as for instance Taft or Root. You might as well talk of my being under the influence of Bryan." " I wish the Kaiser well," Roosevelt explained. " I should never dream of counting on his friendship for this country. He respects us because he thinks that for a sufficient object and on our own terms we would fight, and that we have a pretty good navy with which to fight." [437] This worry about Roosevelt and the Kaiser so far as Sir Edward Grey was concerned seems to have been completely dispelled by the explanations of the Algeciras and Portsmouth conferences that Arthur Lee brought from Roosevelt in 1906. Sir Edward wrote the President after hearing them, " We *had* feared you might be an ally of the German Emperor there. But, in the event, I felt it was not so, even before I knew the story. If you ask why we feared, I should say your telegram to the German Emperor after the Portsmouth Peace had given an impression of a *parti pris* on the side of the Emperor. The explanation of that telegram has thrown a different and very amusing light upon it to me." [438]

One of the persistent problems of Roosevelt's personal international relations was the jealousy and fear of Germany and England for each other. The Kaiser frequently told Roosevelt of England's plotting war against Germany, and his British friends insisted Germany was planning to make war on Britain.* Their growing antagonism worried him.[440] He felt that this Anglo-German hostility endangered peace among civilized nations. Whenever possible he tried to quiet the fears of each about the other. Throughout his negotiations with Germany over preserving the open door in China, for instance, he had continually argued with the Kaiser that Britain was not scheming to get more territory in China.[441] In March, 1905, Lodge recorded in his diary a conversation he had while dining privately at the White House. Roosevelt told " how just before and at the time of the Dogger Bank incident England and Germany were on the brink of war—Both appealed to him—England wanted our fleet sent over first to show friendship and prevent war—German Emperor equally nervous and ' jumpy ' as President said—He made every exertion and calmed them down." Two years later, the President wrote his British-publisher friend Strachey: " Let me say . . . that in the war scare between Germany and England two years ago, some very foolish and irresponsible talk in England which was not official, but which the Germans accepted as official, undoubtedly influenced them . . . ; and I was almost as much surprised to find out how men like Durand lookt at affairs as I was to find out how the Germans lookt at them. Germany had no idea of making an attack, but was sure that England did intend to attack; and on the other hand, England had no idea of making an attack, and was sure that Germany intended to attack her. The result was that the blow came near being struck by one or the other simply from firm belief that the opponent intended to strike." [442]

In April, 1905, the President discussed Anglo-German relations in a letter to Hay. " The Kaiser," he explained, " sincerely believes that the English are planning to attack

---

* In December, 1904, for example, the British " were fully convinced . . . [the Kaiser] intended to make immediate war on them," Roosevelt reminded Spring Rice afterward.[439]

him and smash his fleet, and perhaps join with France in a war to the death against him. As a matter of fact the English harbor no such intentions, but are themselves in a condition of panic terror lest the Kaiser secretly intend to form an alliance against them with France or Russia, or both, to destroy their fleet and blot out the British Empire from the map! It is as funny a case as I have ever seen of mutual distrust and fear bringing two peoples to the verge of war." [443]

In May, 1905, the President wrote Spring Rice trying to persuade him that William was engaged in no " deep-laid plot " against England. " I very sincerely wish I could get England and Germany into friendly relations," pleaded Roosevelt. The Kaiser's " actions and words in reference to Russia and France during the last few months are in my judgment incompatible with any serious purpose on his part to get these two countries actively or passively to support him in the war with England." Had he been planning war on England, " he would never have mortally insulted France by his attitude about Morocco." " I do not for one moment believe," Roosevelt protested to Spring Rice, " that he had any long settled and well thought out plans of attack upon England, such as Bismarck developed, first as regards Austria, and then as regards France. . . . If the Kaiser ever causes trouble it will be from jumpiness and not because of long-thought-out and deliberate purpose." " He is more apt to be exasperating and unpleasant than a dangerous neighbor." [444] " I am obliged to say that as far as my own experience goes," he told Spring Rice, " I have heard just as wild talk . . . among Englishmen as among Germans." [445]

Roosevelt was convinced that neither Germany nor England wanted to make war on the other. " If England ever has trouble with Germany," he wrote prophetically in 1905, " I think it will come from some unreasoning panic which will inspire each to attack the other for fear of being attacked itself." [446] Whether anything can ever be done to reduce the feeling I cannot say," he lamented. " If I can do it I certainly will." [447]

William and Theodore were often compared. Many saw striking similarities * in them. [448] The Kaiser himself was proud to think he was like Roosevelt. [449] President Butler of Columbia, a friend of both, found them alike " in physical build, . . . the same strong stocky structure of bone and muscle, and the same well-tanned complexion from much exposure to the open air." " Their eyes were much alike, too, especially in the alert way in which they travelled about and the intent expression which they took on when deeply interested." [450] King Edward's friend Count Gleichen described them as " rather the same type of man," but judged Roosevelt " more open-minded and much less self-centered." [451] The Kaiser's " emphasis and energetic gesture vividly reminded " John Morley of Roosevelt. " Only the German is a good deal less solid in his vehemence," Morley told Bryce. [452] Colonel Edward House discovered in William " all the versatility of Roosevelt with something more of charm, something less of force." [453] Whitelaw Reid wrote that in London the two men were sometimes associated " because of the ebullient personality characteristic of both men." But Englishmen, Reid reported, noted an important difference: " They both talk unconventionally, but your President always makes good." [454] After his 1910 visit to William, Roosevelt himself declared: " In the fundamentals of domestic morality, and as regards all that side of religion which is moral, we agreed heartily; but there is a good deal of dogmatic theology which to him means much and to me is entirely meaningless. . . . There are many points in international morality where he and I were completely asunder. But at least we agreed in a cordial dislike of sham and pretence, and therefore in a cordial dislike of the kind of washy

---

* Perhaps most often commented upon was the capacity both men had to interest and charm people whom they met personally.

movement for international peace with which Carnegie's name has become so closely associated." [455]

William seems to have admired and trusted Roosevelt. In March, 1905, Meyer wrote Lodge of a talk with the Emperor about Roosevelt in which William's " admiration " seemed " absolutely genuine and sincere." [456] " The Kaiser," Roosevelt once wrote Spring Rice, ". . . has shown an astonishing willingness to put down in black and white what his feelings are. Evidently he regards me as a gentleman and feels . . . a confidence which is entirely justifiable." [457] It is revealing that after his secret meeting with the Czar at Björko in 1905, at which they agreed upon a treaty of alliance never ratified, William wrote Roosevelt a personal letter confiding details of the secret meeting and the purposes of the secret treaty. But von Bülow, trusting less than his master in Roosevelt's discretion, finally persuaded him not to send it. [458]

Roosevelt's private comments on the Kaiser are illuminating. They indicate a combination of clearsighted realism about William's foibles with personal feelings that range all the way from dislike to esteem. Often the comments voiced admiration. In 1899 Governor Roosevelt wrote his friend Speck, " The Kaiser . . . is far and away the greatest crowned head of the present day. He is a Monarch—a King in deed as well as in name, which some other Kings are not. He is a fit successor to the Ottos, the Henrys and the Fredericks of the past." As Vice-President, Roosevelt confided to Spring Rice that " The more I have heard of the Kaiser the more my respect for him has grown." [459] In 1907 he reiterated to Carnegie his high opinion. " He is a big man," the President declared, " and I have the heartiest admiration for him." In December, 1908, he wrote Ambassador Reid, " I really like, and in a way admire him." [460]

On the contrary, Roosevelt's comments were frequently critical, sometimes indiscreet. Thus from a hunting trip in

1905, Roosevelt wrote Taft, " I wish to Heaven our excellent friend, the Kaiser, was not so jumpy and did not have so many pipe dreams." " I wish he would not have brain storms," Roosevelt lamented.[461] Again, " I will write that letter to the Sultan," Roosevelt promised President Eliot of Harvard, " but I would rather not write to Emperor William. He is all the time asking me to do things. Sometimes I can do as he requests and sometimes I can not, but I do not want to put myself under obligations to him. I am sure you will sympathize with my feelings." [462] " I get exasperated with the Kaiser," Roosevelt exploded, " because of his sudden vagaries like . . . his speech about the yellow peril the other day, a speech worthy of any fool congressman; and I cannot . . . take too seriously a man whose policy is one of such violent and often wholly irrational zigzags. But I don't see why you should be afraid of him." [463]

An explanation of the friendliness that existed between Roosevelt and the Kaiser is perhaps contained in a rather shrewd analysis of the Emperor that Roosevelt sent White in 1906. Said the President: " I admire him, respect him, and like him. I think him a big man, and on the whole a good man; but I think his international and indeed his personal attitude one of intense egoism. I have always been most polite with him, have done my best to avoid our taking any attitude which could possibly give him legitimate offense, and have endeavored to show him that I was sincerely friendly to him and to Germany. Moreover, where I have forced him to give way I have been sedulously anxious to build a bridge of gold for him, and to give him the satisfaction of feeling that his dignity and reputation in the face of the world were safe. In other words, where I have had to take part of the kernel from him, I have been anxious that he should have all the shell possible, and have that shell painted any way he wished. At the same time I have had to speak with extreme emphasis to him on more than one occasion." [464]

Now and then Roosevelt helped the Kaiser when he was in personal trouble. When his Yellow Peril speech of 1905 caused savage criticism of him not only in Japan but among his own people, William cabled Speck and got Speck to persuade Roosevelt to pass on his version of the speech to Ambassador Takahira. He claimed the charge that he had ever referred to Japan as " the Yellow Peril " was " false and infamous." [a] [467] And though the Kaiser did not know it, the President threw his weight against the publication in the *New York Times* of an interview the Kaiser had given correspondent William B. Hale in 1908 so indiscreet that it would have created a storm in England and a crisis in his government that might have threatened his throne as a similar indiscretion actually did at the end of October.[b] Certainly added to the other episode this *Times* article might have had serious consequences. The American ambassador had been upset about the Kaiser's American interview. The Foreign Office " had a spasm " and took emergency steps to recall it before publication. Perhaps the *New York Times* would not have printed it anyway.[c] But the *Times* sent a

[a] Yet his chancellor, von Bülow, confirmed his saying it more than once.[465] And his American dentist told that he had boasted of coining the phrase.[466]

[b] This latter act of folly was an interview published in the *London Daily Telegraph* in which the Kaiser spoke of the anti-English feeling prevalent in Germany, claimed he had been a great supporter of England and had prevented Russia and France from "humbling England to the dust," boasted that he had drawn up the plan of campaign used against the Boers, and implied the German fleet was being built up for use against Japan.[468] " The Kaiser has come an awful cropper," Roosevelt wrote his son. " He has been a perfect fool, and the German people after standing his folly and bumptiousness for years finally exploded over something which was of course bad, but no worse than scores of similar things he had done before." [469]

[c] " The worst parts of it were struck out by Hale " and the rest printed in proof for the *Century Magazine*. The Foreign Office had this suppressed, too, Roosevelt felt not too wisely, for "now . . . everybody believes that it was full of all possible iniquity," whereas the President, who saw the proofs, felt the only unfortunate part that remained was " a very bitter attack on the Roman Catholics which would have caused trouble at home."

representative, Oscar K. Davis, to show it to the President and to ask his advice about publishing it. The President wrote both Arthur Lee and Elihu Root about it. " I earnestly urged that it be not done," he reported, " stating that it would undoubtedly create a general panic and would cause extraordinary bitterness between England and Germany." [470] For Root the President described the article:

The Kaiser had spent two hours talking to this unknown newspaper man in language which would invite an international explosion if made public. He stated among other things that he had arranged with the United States to back up China against Japan and thereby keep the equilibrium in the East, and that a Chinese statesman was at this moment on the way to Washington to arrange the details which he admitted had not yet been put into form. He exprest himself with intense bitterness about England and said that very shortly Germany would have to go to war with her, and that he believed the time had nearly come, and that England was a traitor to the white race, as had been shown by her alliance with Japan. With fine consistency he added that he was helping the Mohammedans in every way in giving them rifles and officers because he thought they would be a barrier against the yellow peril, about which he discoursed at length. He said that now everybody recognized that Russia had been fighting for the entire white race, but that she had fought very badly and that if German battalions had had to do the fighting, the Japanese would have been worsted. He stated that within a year or two we, the Americans, would certainly have to fight the Japanese; that he was glad we were preparing for it. He exprest himself most bitterly against the Catholics, and said that Archbishop Ireland was a Jesuit and in reality an enemy of the United States, and that he had fooled Taft at Rome, and added that he did not like Taft because he was under Catholic influence. He stated that Australia would welcome our fleet to show that she repudiated England's Japanese policy. [471]

This outburst of the Kaiser disturbed Roosevelt profoundly.* Confidentially he wrote Arthur Lee about it: " I have been persistently telling so many Englishmen that I thought their fears of Germany slightly absurd and did not believe that there was need of arming against Germany, I feel that perhaps it is incumbent upon me now to say that I am by no means as confident as I was in this position. . . . The Kaiser . . . displayed great bitterness toward England. . . . He spoke very bitterly of the King, saying that he and all those immediately around him were sunk in ignoble greed and lookt at life from a purely stock market standpoint, and that he and they hated me virulently because they had money invested in America and attributed the loss of value in their investments to my action. . . . As my advice to England of recent years has been in the direction of saying that there was nothing to apprehend from Germany, and as it is thru you that most of what I have said has been said (although not all of it) I feel that you ought to know these facts. They should be told to no one save to Balfour and Grey, and to them only on the understanding that they are to go no further." [473]

With far-reaching consequences, this episode seems to have destroyed Roosevelt's confidence, even the qualified kind his had always been, in the Kaiser.[b] To Lee he explained, " I admire his energy, his ability, his activity, and what I believe to be his sincere purpose to do all that he can for the greatness of his country. He is, however, very jumpy; . . . Now, I do not for a moment believe that the utterances of the Emperor indicated a settled purpose, but they did make me feel that he indulged in red dreams of glory now and then, and

----

* Von Bülow later recalled the Kaiser's " zealous striving " to " win the hearts " of his contemporaries and described the " kindness and simplicity " that made him " so humanly attractive." But von Bülow recalled, too, his lack of taste and judgment and his " sudden bursts of ill humour " that in the end succeeded in offending the people he sought to win.[472]

[b] His visit to the Kaiser in 1910 further disillusioned him.[474]

that if he was indiscreet enough to talk to a strange newspaper man in such fashion it would be barely possible that some time he would be indiscreet enough to act on impulse in a way that would jeopardize the peace." [475] Significant for the future was this distrust Roosevelt in the end came to feel for the Kaiser and hence for the German people who were " too closely under his rule " to be disassociated from him.

Underlying Roosevelt's concern about the world was a conviction that his country's interests could be protected only if no power became powerful enough to threaten the rights of other powers. The spread of civilization ultimately depended upon the freedom of those nations that were its guardians, above all others, Britain and the United States. Britain had always held aloof until the delicate balance of power was threatened and then had intervened. If Britain should ever prove inadequate to maintaining the balance, then, Roosevelt was convinced the United States, for the sake of her own interests would have to abandon her aloofness and interfere to restore the balance. In 1910 he told Hermann von Eckardstein, who had been German ambassador to the Court of St. James's at the time of the Moroccan crisis, that if German armies had overrun France " we in America would not have kept quiet." " I certainly would have found myself compelled to interfere," he testified. " As long as England succeeds in keeping ' the balance of power ' in Europe, not only in principle, but in reality, well and good; should she however for some reason or other fail in doing so, the United States would be obliged to step in at least temporarily, in order to restore the balance of power in Europe, never mind against which country or group of countries our efforts may have to be directed." " In fact," he concluded in 1910, " we ourselves are becoming, owing to our strength and geographical situation, more and more the balance of power of the whole world." [476]

Conclusion

What in conclusion can one say of Theodore Roosevelt's rôle in international relations?

It is clear that his comprehension of the problems was extraordinary, and his ability in dealing with them was superior to that of most presidents and secretaries of State. He perceived the growing interdependence of the world and the intricate involvement of America in that more closely-knit world. He comprehended, for instance, the rivalries of Britain and Germany and of Germany and France and the threat that both constituted to the peace of the world. He early grasped the importance of the Pacific and the Far East. In regard to many details of his universe, he had unusual understanding. Thus his characterizations of the Kaiser were uncannily perceptive. His comprehension of the importance of helping a rival to save face when discomfited and his ability to separate the non-essential from the important in international relations made him a skilled diplomatist. At his best, he could analyze problems and understand his opponents' motives with surprising perspicacity.

Many of his insights were prophetic. In reading his letters, one is startled by the number of times he foresaw the future and its problems. Russian revolution he prognosticated and often talked about, as early as the nineties; and, when the third revolution in twelve years put the Bolsheviki into power, he wrote an article that showed extraordinary understanding of its background, in which he tried to see that in some sense what had happened might under Russian conditions be good for Russia.[1]

Then, too, Roosevelt saw world events and policies in terms of power. He was intrigued with power, with the problems of power, and with rivalries for power. In this, too, he was prophetic. In his day many of those that were urging imperialist and expansionist policies were thinking in terms of economic factors and many opponents of imperialism were writing in terms of economic argument. A succeeding generation of historians and political scientists was to analyze the history of the foreign policy of Roosevelt's time with primary emphasis on economic motives and forces until the rise of the totalitarian dictatorships of Hitler and Stalin were to shock them into reëvaluations that brought recognition of the importance in human history of the urge to power. Charles Beard revised his economic interpretation to give the political man and the military man an important place beside the economic man. Indeed, in the end, he seems to have wondered whether the economic motivation that had dominated the making of history in the eighteenth and nineteenth centuries operated in the same manner in the mid-twentieth century world. In Hans Morgenthau and others at the mid-century a preoccupation with power politics and a world struggle for political and military power has replaced Reinsch's and Hobson's and, for that matter, Lenin's economic doctrine of imperialism expounded in the day when Roosevelt was acting an imperial rôle. Yet even in that day Roosevelt, like Bismarck before him but unlike many of his American contemporaries, thought more in terms of power than of economics, though he realized that the two were interrelated. This concern of Roosevelt with power relationships in international affairs was as noteworthy in his day as was his prevision of America's involvement in the world.

About the future of the British Empire, too, he showed prescience; he often talked about and deplored, though he did not want to face, the decline of British power. Many of the Roosevelt circle felt that England's power was doomed. "England is sad—to me very sad," Adams had written Lodge in 1900. "Like you I hope she may revive, but I admit my hope is faint. The current is flowing away from her." [2] "I do not apprehend any sudden or violent change," Adams continued, "but I fancy England will grow gradually more and more sluggish, until, at length, after our day, she will drop out of the strenuous competition of the new world which is forming." "What you tell me about England's decay," Roosevelt himself wrote Speck von Sternburg, "makes me feel rather sad, but it is in exact accord with my own observations and with what I hear from other sources." [3] "It certainly does seem to me that England is on the downgrade," he observed in 1901. "The English-speaking race shares with the Slav the future." [4] The structure of the British Empire, he lamented to another friend in the same year, is unwieldy. "She is so spread out that I think it will be very difficult to make a real and permanently workable imperial federation." [5] Yet for all his accurate prognostication of Britain's future he acted on his hopes about Britain rather than his sounder forebodings, and hence he miscalculated in his policies.

Roosevelt understood, as many people did not, the important effect of internal policies and domestic events upon the foreign policies of the various countries. Hence he was concerned about controlling China's internal affairs and thought the work of the missionaries there important because "it tends to avert revolutionary disturbances in China." [6] Hence, too, with the aid of Meyer and Spring Rice, he watched events in Russia as revolution threatened. He came to understand that Russia's foreign policy depended on whether Witte was in power or Kuropatkin and Bezobrazov and their palace clique gained control. And he learned always to qualify predictions about Russia's foreign policy with a question about internal disorder. His distrust of Germany's form of government and social structure contributed to his distrust of that country's foreign policy.

In spite of Roosevelt's vigorous talk, his reputation for brandishing the big stick, his determination to have a large navy so that he could support whatever policy he chose to pursue, and his undeserved reputation for making snap judgments, Roosevelt as President did not jump into international situations excitedly. He wished to be strong enough to take any action he might choose, but then, being strong, he chose his actions with caution. Contrary to the myth that has grown up about him, in international crises he was calm and careful in his decisions. He acted only after thought about all the consequences of action. Furthermore, he paid no heed to rumors and claims of the sort that were always exciting the Kaiser. " I am always being told," he wrote William, " of Japanese or German or English spies inspecting the most unlikely places—the Moro Castle at Havana, for instance, or some equally antiquated or indefensible fort; and now and then I learn of a high official in some West Indian island or South American republic who has been thrown into a fever by the (wholly imaginary) information that an agent of mine has been secretly inspecting his dominions." " I have no time to devote to thinking of fables of this kind," he protested; " I am far too much occupied with real affairs, both foreign and domestic. . . . No such tale . . . will ever cause me more than good-natured amusement." [7]

Furthermore, Roosevelt had one firm conviction that other nations and the government of his own country have often disregarded. He was unalterably opposed to bluffing, to making threats that he did not intend to back up. At times he took firm stands against other nations, but when he did he stood ready to make good with military force. One reason for his insistence upon a large navy was that he wished to be in a position to support with action any threat he felt it important to make in pursuing America's rôle as a world power. Speak courteously but firmly, and then stand ready to support your words in action was his formula. Confidential records today reveal questions about plans for military or naval action in cases where the public did not know any was contemplated because polite but firm words accomplished his purpose without his having to go to the public for support for the use of force. Roosevelt always believed that speaking softly sufficed because he carried a big stick, because it was known that *he* always stood ready to back words with deeds.

It was a short step from this determination not to take stands that could not be backed by force to a desire for sufficient power to be able to do as he pleased without restraint. Roosevelt admired the strong men of history, Frederick the Great, Napoleon, Bismarck, the elder von Moltke. At times he envied autocratic rulers their power. His strong conviction that he and his country acted from righteous motives made him oppose any international restraints upon his own power. His conviction that he could have handled his country's foreign policy more wisely had he not been restrained by selfish and weak-kneed elements in the population or in the Senate explains his often carrying out policies unbeknown to the public where he felt he could later win the public to support what he had done. His belief that he could handle foreign relations better by direct, secret personal relations with other rulers than through the normal channels of diplomatic negotiation prompted him to the bypassing of the State Department and to the personal diplomacy that characterized some of his most important foreign ventures. His aristocratic background, his established social status, his economic security gave him a freedom from social and political pressures that few presidents and secretaries of State have enjoyed, that in some respects resembled the freedom from restraint enjoyed for very different reasons by mid-twentieth-century totalitarian rulers at the head of one-party dictatorships.

In other hands his ability, his understanding of international problems, his interest in power, his desire to be strong enough to settle questions by might, his secret, highly personal handling of foreign affairs might have become dangerous to democracy and to the peace of the world. What was it that restrained Roosevelt and prevented his becoming dangerous? The democratic process with the chance to criticize government and to retire a leader from public office in the next election provides, of course, an important safeguard that is none the less somewhat offset by the President's power to put the country into war situations where the people would have to support the President however much they deplored his action. Roosevelt's own personal qualities, however, also prevented his use of power from becoming the threat the same power might have been in other hands. In part, Roosevelt was held back by a deep-seated concern about the well-being of his country, and in part by his cautious middle-of-the-road approach to all questions. Furthermore, to a considerable extent, it was the same American aristocratic background that gave him independence and freedom from ordinary social pressures that also restrained him. This background had given him a keen sense of the dignity of man and of the worth of the individual that was never acquired by the mid-century totalitarian rulers with the power he sometimes aspired to. His background, too, had given him a sense of social responsibility and above all an attitude of noblesse oblige that dominated him always. Too, he believed thoroughly in America and hence respected the American democratic tradition. And as part of that

democratic tradition he respected public opinion. Though
he was often frustrated by the inability or unwillingness of
the public to see things as he did, still he conceived his
rôle as a democratic head of state to be one of leading public
opinion where he could, and yielding where he could not
persuade until such time when able leadership like his would
be able to persuade. Even in his secret handling of foreign
affairs he sometimes refrained from actions he deemed wise,
such as formally joining the Anglo-Japanese Alliance, when
he felt he would not be able to carry public opinion with him
when he made his action known. His belief that progress
could be achieved by persuading people through democratic
processes was in itself part of the Western World's nineteenth-century democratic tradition and at the same time
an effective restraint upon the abuse of power.

Indeed, he believed that popular support was as necessary
as executive firmness and armed might. Roosevelt had no
intention of being left unable to support strong words in
foreign policy because the people would not back him. Better no strong words than strong words the people would not
stand behind. A foreign policy that the voters would not
approve in deeds was as bad as bluffing about something
the executive lacked the intention or the power to carry out.
Roosevelt never forgot that public opinion was important
to successful foreign policy. Hence he devoted much time
to creating public support for his policies. He was successful
in stimulating in many of the people pride in the new imperial rôle he envisaged for America. He prepared the way
for future comprehension of America's involvement in world
affairs. But it was difficult to carry public opinion with him
in support of the world rôle he felt America should play.
Just before the end of his Presidency he listed Caribbean
countries where he had interfered " for the immeasurable
betterment of the people." " I would have interfered . . .
[in several others]," he said, " simply in the interest of civil-

ization, if I could have waked up our people so that they would back a reasonable and intelligent foreign policy which should put a stop to crying disorders at our very doors." " Our prime necessity," he declared, " is that public opinion should be properly educated." [8] " This people of ours," he wrote on another occasion, " simply does not understand how things are outside our own boundaries. Of course I do not desire to act unless I can get the bulk of our people to understand the situation and to back up the action; and to do that I have got to get the facts vividly before them. . . . The worst of it is that the educated northeasterners are not merely blind, but often malevolently blind, to what goes on." [9]

In his more mature years, Roosevelt became troubled over the relation of democracy to empire. How a democracy was to rule colonial peoples under democratic machinery was a problem that worried him as he gained experience. The colonials he felt were not ready for democratic forms of government and so he believed rule by a great power benefited them. But could the imperial power itself maintain democracy at home and at the same time rule a colonial empire? " The problem of the control of thickly peopled tropical regions by self-governing northern democracies is very intricate," he wrote in 1908. " A legislative body, most of the members of which are elected by constituencies that in the nature of things can know nothing whatever of the totally different conditions of India, or the Philippines, or Egypt, or Cuba, does not offer the best material for making a success of such government." [*] [11] The weakness of British policy in Egypt and India that he deplored in 1910 he ascribed to this dilemma of democratic rule over empire. " I don't believe for a moment," he conceded, " that . . . the English attitude in Egypt is any worse than we would take, if at this time we had [as England does under the Liberals] what the *Evening*

---

[*] James Bryce had seen this problem in the 1890's and had sounded warning to American imperialists. [10]

Post desires, a mixture of mugwumps, ultra peace advocates and maudlin, hysterical sentimentalists, plus Bryanites to dominate our foreign affairs. But it certainly makes the English look flabby." [12] Because of this dilemma created by imperial rule through democratic parliaments, he came to have serious doubts about our keeping the Philippines that he had once worked so hard to get and keep. " The Philippines present . . . a very hard problem," he had concluded as early as 1907, " because we must consider it in connection with the country's needs and ideas also, and with what it is reasonable to expect as a permanent policy of this country with its alternating system of party control." " I am perfectly sure that the best thing for the Philippines would be to have a succession of Tafts administer them for the next century," he told a leading churchman, but he added, " I am not sure, either that under changing administrations we would get a succession of Tafts, nor yet that our people will patiently submit, as in my judgment they ought to, to doing an onerous duty for which they will get no thanks and no material reward; while from a military standpoint the Philippines form our heel of Achilles." [13]

In the end, for all his activity, his tremendous influence on foreign policy, his surprising insights and prophecies, Roosevelt failed in his most important objectives. He strove to create a stable world in which the great civilized nations would refrain from war upon one another. Yet in less than a decade after his much-heralded success at Portsmouth and his earnest efforts at Algeciras and The Hague, these " civilized " powers were at each other's throats in a gigantic struggle that was to destroy much of what he believed in and to prepare the way for a second world war that was to destroy much more. By balancing Russia against Japan in Manchuria and North China, without letting either one get strong enough to dominate, he believed he was creating a stable Far East open to the trade of all nations. Yet within three years of the Portsmouth Conference the two powers had combined to exclude all other imperial nations. He hoped he had created stability in China by preventing its partition and setting up large-power control over that nation. Yet during much of the next generation China was torn by internal strife and forty years after he left the White House China was to fall under domination by Russia that was to exclude all the powers except Russia. By building American naval power he planned to provide a safe future for his country, since no nation would dare attack her. Yet thirty years after his death, with military might such as his wildest dreams could not have pictured, and with a navy more powerful than any other, his country had suffered losses in battle as great as ever before in its history and was living armed to the teeth in dread of destruction of her cities in an atomic war. He thought he had prepared the way for a century of the " English-speaking " man, and yet by the middle of that century Britain had lost much of her empire and was struggling desperately for survival. By joining forces with British imperialism, he imagined he was assuring the orderly government of colonial areas that domination of the " civilized " imperial powers would create. By the mid-century, nationalism among colonial peoples had led to uprisings all over the world of a sort that military might and superior master races could not prevent or quell. America's tying herself to British imperialism had left her holding the bag and paying the price of liquidating, everywhere outside the Western Hemisphere, the imperialism Roosevelt had helped create. America was left fighting a costly rear-guard retreat in defense not only of British, but of Dutch and French empires in opposition to the aspirations for freedom that America would once have befriended. Instead of helping Britain maintain the balance of power in the *world* as Britain had more than once done on the Continent of Europe, the United States found itself the only remaining nation with power to stand up on one side of a balance that was precarious. Roosevelt's theory of saving democracy from autocracy by armed might had been strenuously pursued for forty years with the result that more and more of the free world had fallen under totalitarianism.

What had happened? Roosevelt and his friends had made several miscalculations. They had failed really to anticipate and take into account the rapid decline of Britain to whom they had tied America's fate, for while recognizing her decline and foreseeing Russia's growing power, they had still believed Britain's preëminence would last out the twentieth century. They had seen that, without becoming " civilized," people could not produce complicated weapons of modern warfare, but they had overlooked the fact that, without becoming civilized in their terms, colonial peoples spurred by nationalism could do great damage to the imperial powers Roosevelt counted on to control them. In underestimating the potentialities of China and failing to understand the aspirations of a New China, Roosevelt had inaugurated a Chinese policy disastrous for the future. That policy, continued by his successors, was ultimately to help lead China from initial friendliness toward America into communism in the hope that the New China would obtain from communism the aid and sympathy America and the Western powers had refused it. Roosevelt and his friends had failed to comprehend modern war and the potentialities of technology for destructiveness. They had not forecast the total nature of modern war. They had placed faith in a balance of power that could never be kept in balance. They had not divined that seeking safety through being more powerfully armed than rivals would only stimulate an armaments race in which no nation ever kept far enough ahead of its opponents to feel secure. They had refused to take seriously other methods than armed force in establishing international stability. In underestimating the destructiveness of modern war, they had overlooked the grim necessity of finding methods of organizing the world's will to peace so that there would be no war.

But could these factors have been foreseen? The answer is, of course, that many people did foretell them and did sound warning. There were Americans who felt that Roosevelt should have encouraged and befriended the forces of nationalism and freedom in China that instead he threatened to send an invading army to put down. Roosevelt himself saw dangers in China's developing modern techniques without accompanying changes in her values. " If the advantage to us is great of a China open to commerce," he warned, " the danger to us and to her is infinitely greater of a China enriched and strengthened by the material advantages we have to offer, but uncontrolled in the use of them by any clear understanding, much less any full acceptance, of the mental and moral forces which have generated and in large measure govern our political and social action." So far so good. What Roosevelt failed to see, in his contemptuous attitude toward the Chinese, was that neither America nor any other outside power could impose these moral and mental processes on China, but that she must come through her own development to new values in keeping with her own culture and history. There were those who saw that no stable situation in the Far East could come from a peace at Portsmouth drawn up for China by Russia and Japan. Such men felt that China should have been at the peace conference and that Roosevelt lost at Portsmouth a chance to protect China against both aggressors, and to win her friendship besides. In the field of colonialism, too, Bryce warned early that American institutions were " quite unsuited to the government of dependencies," where the population consisted of " elements utterly unequal and dissimilar." [14]

In 1907 Carnegie had protested against Roosevelt's easy justification of wars that were " righteous." " Disputants," warned Carnegie, " are both seeking ' Righteousness ' both feel themselves struggling for what is just." " Who is to decide? " he asked the President. " No one, according to you they must then go to war to decide not what is ' right ' but who is *strong*." [15]

Roosevelt's old professor of anatomy at Harvard, too, foresaw some of the effects of Rooseveltian policy. The year after the Spanish War, William James protested: " We gave the fighting instinct and the passion of mastery their outing . . . because we thought that . . . we could resume our permanent ideals and character when the fighting fit was done. We now see how we reckoned without our host. We see . . . what an absolute savage . . . the passion of military conquest always is, and how the only safeguard against the crimes to which it will infallibly drag the nation that gives way to it is to keep it chained forever. . . . First, the war fever; and then the pride which always refuses to back down when under fire. But these are passions that interfere with the reasonable settlement of any affair; . . . Our duty and our destiny call, and civilization must go on! Could there be a more damning indictment of that whole bloated idol termed ' modern civilization ' than this amounts to? Civilization is, then, the big, hollow, resounding, corrupting, sophisticating, confusing torrent of mere brutal momentum and irrationality that brings forth fruits like this! " [16] Unlike William James, Roosevelt and his friends assumed that economic power, the preservation of order, and military might constituted the test of civilization.

Whatever mistakes Roosevelt made that led to ultimate catastrophe for the policies he pursued, they were not merely his personal mistakes. They were the mistakes of a considerable segment of the American people that gloried in his temporary successes. One important element of his strength was that in so many respects, among them the urge for power and the sense of superiority over other people, Roosevelt merely symbolized and gave voice to widespread American attitudes.

Not only conservative Republicans, but Progressives were imperialists. Nor did Bryan and Wilson materially change the pattern of American expansionism when they succeeded Taft and Roosevelt. The men who had misgivings, of whom there were many, were not in the strategic positions of power.

So we return to the question with which we started. To what extent did Roosevelt and his fellow-expansionists and fellow-imperialists influence foreign policy? Concerned as they were, vigorous and active as they were in the key positions they occupied, were they able to direct foreign policy? Or was foreign policy determined by forces that would have sent America down the road of imperialism had these men never lived or had their high positions in government been occupied by men as much against as they were for expansion and empire? Were they conscious creators of America's world power or were they merely driven on into expansion by a sort of political atavism? [17] Or were Roosevelt and his friends perchance the catalysts that aided the operation of forces they did not create? Or was America's rôle determined for her by other nations whose policies she could not control but whose actions determined her own? To what extent did the leaders choose at all? One can perhaps only say that, strategically located as they were in positions of power and vigorous and able, they had as much influence on the course of events as men ever do and more than at many times or in many places men have succeeded in exerting.

Finally, to the extent that Roosevelt did choose, what was the effect of his choice between imperialism and its alternatives? One comes away from the study with admiration for Roosevelt's ability, his energy, and his devotion to his country's interests as he saw them, but with a sense of tragedy that his abilities were turned toward imperialism and an urge for power, which were to have consequences so serious for the future. Perhaps Roosevelt and his friends could not have led America along a different path. In so far, however, as they did influence America's course, they influenced it in a direction that by the mid-century was to bring her face to face with grave dangers. Roosevelt probably had as much ability and handled foreign policy as well as any other statesman of his day. The trouble lay not in his abilities, but in his values and in the setting in which he worked, whether from choice or from necessity.

Notes

INTRODUCTION

1. Henry Cabot Lodge to Anna Cabot Lodge, Feb. 28 [1892], Lodge MSS.

2. Irwin H. Hoover, *Forty-two Years in the White House*, 111.

3. John Hay, MS. Diary, June 25, 1904, Hay MSS.; TR to Acting Secretary of State, Sept. 2, 1904, Alvey A. Adee to TR, Sept. 7, 1904, TR to Dept. of State, Dec. 2, 1908, TR MSS.; Archie Butt to his mother Mrs. Lewis Butt, Dec. 2, 1908, *The Letters of Archie Butt*, Lawrence F. Abbott, ed., 212-214.

4. See, e. g., *St. Louis Globe Democrat*, Oct. 1, 1905, TR Scrapbooks. See also letters to Edward VII, Mutsuhito, Nicholas II, and William II.

5. Oscar K. Davis, *Released for Publication*, 141-144; George B. Cortelyou to J. Hay, March 31, 1902, TR MSS.

6. TR to J. Hay, Sept. 9, 1902, TR MSS.

7. See, e. g., J. Hay to TR, March 5, 1902, TR MSS.; George W. Smalley, *Anglo-American Memories*, 358.

8. TR to Department of State, Feb. 26 [?], 1908 (copy), Taft MSS.; TR to Kermit Roosevelt, March 4, 1908, TR MSS.; *Washington Star*, Jan. 6, 1903, TR Scrapbooks; Mark A. DeWolfe Howe, *James Ford Rhodes*, 172.

9. TR to J. Hay, Feb. 15, 1902, TR MSS.

10. Henry Adams to Elizabeth Cameron, Jan. 24, 1904, Henry Adams, *Letters, 1892-1918*, Worthington C. Ford, ed., 421; F. M. Huntington Wilson, *Memoirs of an Ex-Diplomat*, 164.

11. See, e. g., *Washington Post*, Aug. 9, 1905, TR Scrapbooks; letters from George von L. Meyer and Whitelaw Reid; Maurice F. Egan, *Recollections of a Happy Life*, 223.

12. See, e. g., G. von L. Meyer Diary, Nov. 13, 1905, July 11 and 25 and Aug. 27, 1906, and April 28, 1908, Mark A. DeWolfe Howe, *George von Lengerke Meyer: His Life and Public Services*, 221-222, 296, 301, 304-305, 389-390; Oscar

S. Straus, "A Night at the White House as a Guest of the President, Nov. 16, 1904," Straus MSS.; TR to Robert Bacon, Sept. 12, 1906, TR to Thomas J. O'Brien, July 11, 1907, TR to Elihu Root, Oct. 3, 1906, TR MSS.; TR to William H. Taft, Dec. 31, 1908, Taft MSS.; Lucius Swift to his wife, 1907, William D. Foulke, *Lucius Swift*, 78.

13. See, e. g., J. Hay to TR, March 5, 1902, TR MSS.; G. W. Smalley, *Anglo-American Memories*, 358.

14. A. M. Butt to Mrs. L. Butt, Dec. 2, 1908, *Letters of Archie Butt*, 212-214; *Washington Post*, March 1, 1902, TR Scrapbooks.

15. A. M. Butt to Mrs. L. Butt, Oct. 19, 1908, *Letters of Archie Butt*, 138-139.

16. TR to K. Roosevelt, Feb. 8, 1903, TR MSS.

17. A. M. Butt to Mrs. L. Butt, Sept. 30, 1908, *Letters of Archie Butt*, 106.

18. *Washington Times*, Jan. 29, 1905, TR Scrapbooks.

19. TR to George Otto Trevelyan, Oct. 1, 1911, and TR to Maurice Egan, May 9, 1910, TR MSS.

20. TR to Joseph H. Choate, March 3, 1902, TR to Prince Henry, May 10, 1902, TR to W. Reid, March 3, 1902, TR MSS.; H. Adams to E. Cameron, March 2, 1902, HA, *Letters*, 375.

21. G. von L. Meyer to TR, Jan. 20 and July 5, 1905, TR MSS.; GvonLM to H. C. Lodge, Feb. 14, 1906, Lodge MSS. See also A. A. Adee to Henry White, March 6, 1903, Hay MSS.; Lloyd C. Griscom, *Diplomatically Speaking*, 244-245.

22. E. Root to James Keith, April 9, 1903, Root MSS.

23. For a contradictory view that is not supported by the facts, see David F. Sinclair, "Monarchial Manner of the White House," *Harper's Weekly*, LII (June 13, 1908), 14-15.

CHAPTER I

1. For discussion of this imperialism see John A. Hobson, *Imperialism: A Study*, 3-27; Parker T. Moon, *Imperialism and World Politics*, 8-57; Paul S. Reinsch, *World Politics at the End of the Nineteenth Century as Influenced by the Oriental Situation*, 3-82, 223-224, 247-289, 309-320. Cf. Hans J. Morgenthau, *Politics among Nations: The Struggle for Power and Peace* (1948).

2. Edward P. Clark to Lucius B. Swift, March 3, 1900, Swift MSS.

3. John C. Spooner to Winfield Smith, April 9, 1898, Spooner MSS.

4. Charles J. Bonaparte to Count Adam G. C. de Moltke-Huitfeldt, Nov. 6, 1902, Bonaparte MSS.

5. Frederick W. Holls to TR, May 23, 1900, TR to Henry Cabot Lodge, July 30, 1902, TR MSS.; HCL to TR, Aug. 2, 1904, Charles F. Adams to HCL, Feb. 18, 1897, Lodge MSS.; Grenville M. Dodge to William B. Allison, April 30, 1902, Allison MSS.; Andrew Carnegie to John Hay, December. 27, 1898, Carnegie MSS.; Moorfield Storey to Carl Schurz, Nov. 11, 1895, CS to MS, Nov. 12, 1895, CS to CFA, June 15, 1902, CS to Mr. Ogden, May 26, 1904, Gamaliel Bradford

to CS, Oct. 7, 1904, Schurz MSS.; Richard H. Dana to L. B. Swift, Aug. 25, 1902, Swift MSS.; CS to Jacob G. Schurman, May 8, 1902, in CS, *Speeches, Correspondence, and Political Papers*, Frederick Bancroft, ed., VI, 288-290; MS to Edwin Burritt Smith, Oct. 29, 1902, Mark A. DeWolfe Howe, *Portrait of an Independent: Moorfield Storey, 1845-1929*, 230; CS, *Reminiscences*, III, 442. See also TR to Silas McBee, editor of the *Churchman*, Aug. 27, 1907, TR MSS.

6. M. Storey to R. H. Dana, Oct. 31, 1904, in M. A. DeW. Howe, *Storey*, 235.

7. Charles W. Eliot to TR, Nov. 9, 1900, TR to CWE, Nov. 14, 1900, TR MSS.; William James to Theodore Flournoy, June 17, 1898, WJ to the Editor, *Boston Evening Transcript*, March 1, 1899, WJ to the Editor, *Springfield Republican*, June 4, 1900, WJ, Address to the Anti-Imperialist League of Boston, in Ralph Barton Perry, *The Thought and Character of William James*, 245, 246; TR, Review of Brooks Adams's *The Law of Civilization and Decay* in the *Forum*, XXII (January, 1897), 584. See also TR to H. C. Lodge, Dec. 27, 1895, and Jan. 2, 10, 15, 16, and 19, 1896, HCL to TR, Jan. 11, 1896, Lodge MSS.

8. See, e. g., H. C. Lodge to William [W. Sturgis Bigelow], Dec. 22, 1896, HCL to [George P.] Gardner, Jan. 25, 1896, HCL to Henry Gaunt, Jan. 29, 1896, HCL to Curtis [Guild (?)], Dec. 31, 1896, HCL to Henry [L. Higginson], Jan. 20, 1896, HCL to [George H.] Lyman, March 17, 1896, HCL to [Francis (?)] Rawle, Jan. 21, 1896, HCL to [Royal] Robbins, Jan. 26, 1896, Lodge MSS.

9. See, e. g., H. L. Higginson to H. C. Lodge, Dec. 23, 1895, Feb. 19, 1898, and Nov. 12, 1900, HCL to HLH, Dec. 21, 1895, Jan. 20, 1896, and March 9, 1898, Lodge MSS.

10. G. M. Dodge to W. B. Allison, April 30, 1902, Allison MSS.; A. Carnegie to J. Hay, Dec. 27, 1898, Carnegie MSS.; C. Schurz to AC, Aug. 2, 1902, in CS, *Speeches, Correspondence*, VI, 292.

11. James Bryce, "The Policy of Annexation for America," *Forum*, XXIV (December, 1897), 385-395.

12. P. S. Reinsch, *World Politics*, 34-47, 310-326, 361-362; J. A. Hobson, *Imperialism*, 28-115, 356-360.

13. J. Bryce, *op. cit.*, 388, 391-392. P. S. Reinsch, *World Politics*, 18-20, 70-80, 210-212; J. A. Hobson, *Imperialism*, 113-124.

14. P. S. Reinsch, *World Politics*, 14-15, 78, 298-305, 327-355, 361-362; J. A. Hobson, *Imperialism*, 140-152, 360-361.

15. *Ibid.*, 223-327, 356-368.

16. P. S. Reinsch, *World Politics*, 185-195, 236-246; J. A. Hobson, *Imperialism*, 223-237.

17. P. S. Reinsch, *World Politics*, 6-9, 12-18, 23-26, 68-70, 205-216, 223-235, 253-257, 279-280, 289-297, 356-360; J. A. Hobson, *Imperialism*, 124-139, 328-355, 356-368.

18. P. S. Reinsch, *World Politics*, 79-80.

19. TR to Anna Roosevelt Cowles, April 7, 1895, and May 17, 1896, Cowles MSS.; TR to J. Hay, May 3, 1897, Hay MSS.; TR to H. C. Lodge, Nov. 5, 1896, W. S. Bigelow to HCL, Sept. 22, 1889, Lodge MSS.; TR to HCL, April 28, 1899, TR to JH, June 17, 1899, TR MSS.

20. Edith Kermit Roosevelt to [James] Brander Matthews, March 6 [1890], TR MSS.

21. TR to [J.] B. Matthews, May 31, 1892, TR MSS.

22. TR to [J.] B. Matthews, Dec. 6, 1892, TR MSS.; TR to A. R. Cowles, April 1, 1894, Cowles MSS.

23. TR to H. C. Lodge, July 31, 1890, Jan. 12, 1899, Lodge MSS.; TR to Cecil Spring Rice, May 3, 1892, TR to [J.] B. Matthews, June 6, 1893, April 3, June 29, and Dec. 9, 1894, and March 19, April 6, May 8, and Dec. 6, 1895, TR to John Fox, Jr., July 2, 1894, TR to J. Hay, Nov. 4, 1897, TR MSS.; TR to A. R. Cowles, April 7, 1895, Cowles MSS.

24. TR to [J.] B. Matthews, March 9 and 19 and April 6, 1895, TR MSS.; TR to A. R. Cowles, March 10 and April 7, 1895, Cowles MSS.; Rudyard Kipling, *Something of Myself: For My Friends Known and Unknown*, 131-133.

25. R. Kipling to TR, Sept. 23, 1898, TR MSS.; R. Kipling, *op. cit.*, 131-133.

26. TR to J. Hay, May 3, 1897, Hay MSS.

27. TR to A. R. Cowles, April 7, 1895, and May 17, 1896, Cowles MSS.

28. TR, Review of Alfred Thayer Mahan's *The Influence of Sea Power upon History* in the *Atlantic Monthly*, LXVI (October, 1890), 563-567; Review of *The Influence of Sea Power upon the French Revolution and Empire* in *ibid.*, LXXI (April, 1893), 556-559; Review of both books in the *Political Science Quarterly*, IX (March, 1894), 171; Review of ATM's *The Interest of America in Sea Power, Past and Future*, in the *New York Sun*, Dec. 26, 1897.

29. TR to Henry White, March 19, 1894, White MSS.

30. TR to William W. Rockhill, Feb. 12, 1896, TR MSS.

31. Finley Peter Dunne, " On War Preparations," *Mr. Dooley in Peace and in War*, 9.

32. TR to Francis C. Moore, Feb. 9, 1898, TR MSS. See also H. C. Lodge, " Our Blundering Foreign Policy," *Forum*, XIX (March, 1897), 16-17.

33. TR to Mrs. Bellamy Storer, May 18, 1900, TR MSS.

34. TR, " The President's Policy," *North American Review*, CXLI (October, 1885), 388-396.

35. TR, *The Winning of the West*, IV, 178.

36. TR to [J.] B. Matthews, May 31 and Dec. 6, 1892, March 9 and 19 and April 6, 1895, TR MSS.; TR to A. R. Cowles, April 1 [1894], Cowles MSS.

37. J. Bryce, " The Policy of Annexation for America," *Forum*, XXIV (December, 1897), 392. See also H. C. Lodge, " Our Blundering Foreign Policy," *Forum*, XIX (March, 1895), 16-17.

38. TR, " National Duties," Address at Minnesota State Fair, Sept. 2, 1901, in *The Strenuous Life: Essays and Addresses*, 291.

39. C. Schurz to James Pryor, September, 1904, CS, *Speeches, Correspondence*, VI, 397-399.

40. TR to Albert Shaw, Nov. 25, 1905, TR MSS.

41. *New York World*, Jan. 22, 1906, TR Scrapbooks.

42. TR to H. C. Lodge, Oct. 20, 1899, *Correspondence of TR and Henry Cabot Lodge, 1884-1918* (hereafter cited as *TR-HCL Correspondence*), I, 422.

43. Harry Thurston Peck, "President Roosevelt," *Bookman*, xxix (March, 1909), 29.

44. George W. Smalley, *Anglo-American Memories*, ii, 372.

45. *New York Sun*, Nov. 13, 1897. See also *ibid.*, Nov. 9, 1897, and *Marine Review*, Nov. 12, 1897, TR Scrapbooks.

46. TR, "Fellow-Feeling as a Political Factor," *Century Magazine*, lix (January, 1900), 466.

47. P. S. Reinsch, *World Politics*, 358-360.

48. TR, "Biological Analogies in History," Romanes Lecture for 1910, delivered at Oxford University, Oxford, England, June 7, 1910, *Literary Essays*, 93.

49. TR to H. C. Lodge, April 29, 1896, Lodge MSS.

50. TR to Gen. Lloyd Bryce, editor of the *North American Review*, May 4, 1895, TR MSS. TR, Review of Benjamin Kidd's *Social Evolution* in the *North American Review*, clxi (July, 1895), 94-109.

51. TR to [J.] B. Matthews, July 20, 1907, TR MSS.

52. TR, Review of Houston S. Chamberlain's *Foundations of the Nineteenth Century*, in the *Outlook*, xcviii (July 29, 1911), 728-731.

53. TR, Review of Charles H. Pearson's *National Life and Character: A Forecast*, in the *Sewanee Review*, ii (May, 1894), 365.

54. *Brooklyn Eagle*, Nov. 18, 1888, TR Scrapbooks. James Ford Rhodes, MS. notebook, quoted in Mark A. DeWolfe Howe, *James Ford Rhodes*, 170.

55. TR to J. Bryce, Sept. 10, 1897, TR MSS.

56. TR, Review of C. H. Pearson's *National Life and Character, loc. cit.*, 366.

57. TR to Arthur J. Balfour, March 5, 1908, TR MSS.

58. TR, "Biological Analogies in History," Romanes Lecture, *Literary Essays*, 93. See also TR, Review of C. H. Pearson's *National Life and Character, loc. cit.*, 354, 358-360.

59. TR, "Biological Analogies in History," Romanes Lecture, *Literary Essays*, 94.

60. TR to C. Spring Rice, June 16, 1905, TR MSS.

61. C. Spring Rice to TR, Aug. 9, 1900, TR MSS.; TR, Review of C. H. Pearson's *National Life and Character, loc. cit.*, 361, 362, 363, 365.

62. TR to Dr. David B. Schneder, June 19, 1905, TR MSS.

63. TR, Review of C. H. Pearson's *National Life and Character, loc. cit.*, 367.

64. TR to Washington Hesing, Chicago, June 6, 1894, TR to T. T. Hudson, Duluth, Minn., Oct. 12, 1894, TR to Bishop Keane, Catholic University, Washington, D. C., Oct. 15, 1894, TR to Irwin Mahon, Denver, Feb. 24, 1894, Civil Service Commission MSS.; TR to C. P. Connolly, Helena, Mont., April 11, 1894, TR MSS.; TR to H. C. Lodge, Oct. 8, 1894, Lodge MSS.; TR, "Phases of State Legislation," *Century*, xxix (January, 1885), 830. See also *New York Mail Express*, December, 1888, TR Scrapbooks.

65. TR to George F. Hoar, Aug. 15, 1895, in Frederick H. Gillett, *George Frisbie Hoar*, 192; *New York Sun*, Feb. 13, 1898, TR Scrapbooks; FHG, *op. cit.*, 193.

66. TR, Speech in Huntington Hall, Boston, *Boston Herald*, November, 1893, TR Scrapbooks.

67. TR to W. Hesing, June 6, 1894, Civil Service Commission MSS.

68. TR, "What 'Americanism' Means," *Forum*, XVII (April, 1894), 196-206.

69. See, e. g., TR to Alphonse Major, Jan. 29, 1896, TR to Andrew Powell, Nov. 9, 1898, TR MSS.; TR to a "Crank," *New York Sun*, December, 1896, TR Scrapbooks.

70. See, e. g., TR, Review of C. H. Pearson's *National Life and Character,* in the *Sewanee Review*, II (May, 1894), 358-360; Albert J. Beveridge, "Our Philippine Policy," *The Meaning of the Times*, 63, 84-85, 87; H. C. Lodge, "Our Blundering Foreign Policy," *Forum*, XIX (March, 1895), 17; *Wichita Daily Eagle,* July 5, 1900, TR Scrapbooks.

71. TR to J. Bryce, Sept. 10, 1897, TR to C. Spring Rice, Dec. 2, 1899, TR MSS.

72. TR, "The Strenuous Life," Speech before the Hamilton Club, Chicago, April 10, 1899, *The Strenuous Life*, 19. See also TR, "Expansion and Peace," *Independent*, LI (Dec. 21, 1899), 3403.

73. TR to H. White, March 20, 1896, White MSS.

74. TR to William R. Thayer, July 2, 1915, TR MSS.

75. TR, "The Strenuous Life," *The Strenuous Life*, 16-17.

76. TR, "National Duties," Address at the Minnesota State Fair, Sept. 2, 1901, *The Strenuous Life*, 293-294. See also A. J. Beveridge, "Our Philippine Policy," *The Meaning of the Times*, 84, 85, 87.

77. TR to Douglas Robinson, Aug. 31, 1905, TR MSS.

78. W. James to the Editor, *Springfield Republican*, June 4, 1900, quoted in R. B. Perry, *William James*, 246.

79. Charles G. Washburn to ———, Chicago, April, 1885, in George H. Haynes, *The Life of Charles G. Washburn*, 143-144.

80. TR to C. Spring Rice, April 14, 1889, TR MSS.

81. J. Hay to Henry Adams, Jan. 6, 1892, in JH, *Letters and Extracts from the Diaries of John Hay*, H. Adams, compiler, Clara Hay, ed. (hereafter cited as J. Hay, *Letters and Diary*), II, 235-236. See also H. C. Lodge to Anna Cabot Lodge, Feb. 2, 1896, C. Spring Rice to HCL, Sept. 3, 1893, Lodge MSS.; Joseph H. Choate to Carrie Choate, Jan. 25, 1896, Choate MSS.

82. *The Critic*, XXV (Nov. 23, 1895), 345. See also TR, *Address . . . before the Naval War College*, 8-9.

83. *New York Evening Post*, Jan. 14, 1896, TR Scrapbooks.

84. TR, Review of A. T. Mahan's *The Interest of America in Sea Power, Past and Future*, in the *New York Sun*, Dec. 26, 1897, TR Scrapbooks.

85. TR to A. R. Cowles, Jan. 19 and March 9, 1896, Cowles MSS. During a dinner at Lodge's, Roosevelt shocked Nicholas Murray Butler and Sir Spencer Walpole by his eulogies of war. Walpole turned to Reed and said, "We could not possibly talk of war in this lighthearted way. Tell me, what is the American idea of war?" Reed drawled out in reply: "The American idea of war is to take the farmer from his plow, and to return him to his plow—with a pension!"

NMB, *Across the Busy Years: Resolutions and Reflections*, I, 298-299. See also
C. Schurz, *Speeches, Correspondence*, v, 400.

86. TR to Francis V. Greene, Sept. 23, 1897, TR MSS.

87. W. James to the Editor, *Springfield Republican*, June 4, 1900, quoted in
R. B. Perry, *William James*, 246.

88. See, e. g., TR, Review of A. T. Mahan's *The Interest of America in Sea
Power*, in the *New York Sun*, Dec. 26, 1897, TR Scrapbooks.

89. TR to John Barrett, Oct. 29, 1900, TR MSS.

90. TR, " The Need of a Navy," December, 1897, TR MSS. (published in
Gunton's Magazine, XIV [January, 1898], 1-4).

91. TR, Review of A. T. Mahan's *The Influence of Sea Power upon History*
and *The Influence of Sea Power upon the French Revolution and Empire*, in the
Political Science Quarterly, IX (March, 1894), 171.

92. TR to J. Hay, Nov. 4, 1897, TR MSS. See also TR to H. White, March
20, 1896, White MSS.; TR, " The Need of a Navy," December, 1897, TR MSS.;
TR, " The Issues of 1896," *Century*, LI (November, 1895), 71-72; TR, " National
Duties," in *The Strenuous Life*, 288-289; Allan Nevins, *Henry White: Thirty
Years of American Diplomacy*, 119. •

93. TR to H. C. Lodge, March 27, 1901, TR MSS.

94. TR, " The Need of a Navy," December, 1897, TR MSS. See also TR,
Review of A. T. Mahan's *The Interest of America in Sea Power*, in the *New
York Sun*, Dec. 26, 1897, *Gloucester Times*, Feb. 10, 1898, *Gunton Institute
Bulletin*, Feb. 26, 1898, *Pittsburgh Post*, Jan. 19, 1898, TR Scrapbooks; TR,
" National Duties," in *The Strenuous Life*, 288-289; TR, *Address . . . before
the Naval War College*, 17-18, 19-20.

95. *New York Sun*, Feb. 13, 1898, TR Scrapbooks.

96. TR to John D. Long, Aug. 7, 1897, in unidentified clipping [Aug. 8, (?)],
1897, TR Scrapbooks. See also *New York Sun*, Aug. 10, 1897, *Marine Review*,
Aug. 12, 1897, [*Washington* (?)] *Post*, Aug. 21, 1897, TR Scrapbooks.

97. TR, " The Need of a Navy," December, 1897, TR MSS. See also TR to
J. D. Long, Feb. 18, 1898, TR MSS.; H. C. Lodge, " Our Blundering Foreign
Policy," *Forum*, XIX (March, 1895), 16-17.

98. TR, *Thomas H. Benton*, 33-34.

99. TR, " The Need of a Navy," December, 1897, TR MSS.

100. *Loc. cit.*

101. TR, Review of A. T. Mahan's *The Interest of America in Sea Power*,
in the *New York Sun*, Dec. 26, 1897, TR Scrapbooks. See also TR, *The
Strenuous Life*, 1.

102. TR, *Address . . . before the Naval War College*, 5. See also TR to J. D.
Long, Feb. 19, 1898, TR MSS.

103. TR, *Address . . . before the Naval War College*, 6.

104. H. C. Lodge to Mr. Appleton, Feb. 14, 1896, Lodge MSS.; HCL, " Our
Blundering Foreign Policy," *Forum*, XIX (March, 1895), 16-17.

105. TR to A. T. Mahan, May 3, 1897, TR MSS. See also H. C. Lodge,
" Our Blundering Foreign Policy," *Forum*, XIX (March, 1895), 16-17; Charles
A. Beard, *The Navy: Defense or Portent?* 56.

106. H. C. Lodge to Walter S. Brown, April 17, 1894, Lodge MSS.; *New York Sun*, June 3, 1897, TR Scrapbooks; HCL, " Our Blundering Foreign Policy," *Forum*, XIX (March, 1895), 16-17. See also unidentified clippings, TR Scrapbooks.

107. TR to Gen. James H. Wilson, July 12, 1899, TR MSS.; TR, " The Monroe Doctrine," *Bachelor of Arts*, II (March, 1896), 447; TR to Capt. William S. Cowles, Dec. 2, 1895, in ARC, ed., *Letters from Theodore Roosevelt to Anna Roosevelt Cowles, 1870-1918*, 166. See also C. A. Beard, *op. cit.*, 56.

108. TR to H. C. Lodge, June 19 and July 22, 1891, Lodge MSS.; TR, " The Issues of 1896," *Century*, LI (November, 1895), 72.

109. *Loc. cit.*; TR, Speech before the Republican Club of Massachusetts, Oct. 24, 1895, and TR, Review of A. T. Mahan's *The Interest of America in Sea Power*, in the *New York Sun*, Oct. 25, 1895, and Dec. 26, 1897, TR Scrapbooks.

110. TR to H. C. Lodge, May 21 and Aug. 27, 1895, Lodge MSS.; A. Nevins, *Henry White*, 70-71. See also TR to HCL, June 19, 1891, Lodge MSS.

111. TR to H. C. Lodge, July 27, 1892, Lodge MSS.; TR, " The Issues of 1896," *Century*, LI (November, 1895), 71-72; TR, Review of A. T. Mahan's *The Interest of America in Sea Power*, in the *New York Sun*, December 26, 1897, TR Scrapbooks.

112. TR, " The Foreign Policy of President Harrison," *Independent*, XLIV (Aug. 11, 1892), 1114.

113. TR to A. R. Cowles, March 21, 1891, Cowles MSS.

114. TR, " The Issues of 1896," *Century*, LI (November, 1895), 72. See also TR, Review of A. T. Mahan's *The Interest of America in Sea Power*, in the *New York Sun*, Dec. 26, 1897, TR Scrapbooks.

115. H. C. Lodge to Henry L. Higginson, Jan. 19, 1892, HCL to Arthur T. Lyman, Jan. 17 and 21, 1892, Lodge MSS.

116. TR, " The Foreign Policy of President Harrison," *Independent*, XLIV (Aug. 11, 1892), 1115; TR, " The Issues of 1896," *Century*, LI (November, 1895), 72; TR, Review of A. T. Mahan's *The Interest of America in Sea Power*, in the *New York Sun*, Dec. 26, 1897, TR Scrapbooks. See also *New York Sun*, Oct. 25, 1895.

117. H. C. Lodge to B. Adams, Jan. 21, 1892, HCL to H. L. Higginson, Jan. 19, 1892, HCL to A. T. Lyman, Jan. 17 and 21, 1892, Lodge MSS.

118. J. Hay to H. Adams, Jan. 6, 1892, JH, *Letters and Diary*, II, 235-236; TR to C. Spring Rice, Dec. 25, 1892, TR MSS.

119. H. C. Lodge to H. L. Higginson, Jan. 19, 1892, Lodge MSS. See also TR to C. Spring Rice, Dec. 25, 1892, TR MSS.

120. For a scholarly account of the Chilean episode see Henry Clay Evans, Jr., *Chile and Its Relations with the United States*, 135-154.

121. TR, " The Issues of 1896," *Century*, LI (November, 1895), 71-72.

122. TR to A. R. Cowles, May 20, 1894, Cowles MSS.; TR, " The Issues of 1896," *Century*, LI (November, 1895), 71-72. See also H. C. Lodge to Mr. Appleton, Feb. 14, 1896, Lodge MSS.

123. TR to A. R. Cowles, May 20, 1894, Cowles MSS.

124. TR to A. R. Cowles, Jan. 27, 1895, Cowles MSS. See also TR, Review of A. T. Mahan's *The Interest of America in Sea Power*, in the *New York Sun*, Dec. 26, 1897, TR Scrapbooks.

125. Julian Ralph, " Voyage to Asia's War Scenes," *Harper's Weekly*, xxxviii (Oct. 13, 1894), 975; " War Notes on Japan and China," *ibid.*, xxxviii (Nov. 10, 1894), 1076; " American Helplessness in China," *ibid.*, xxxviii (Dec. 1, 1894), 143; " Discussion," *ibid.*, xxxix (Jan. 26, 1895), 78; TR to H. C. Lodge, Dec. 1, 1894, Lodge MSS.; Dec. 3 and 5, 1894, and Jan. 15, 1895, *Congressional Record*, 53 Cong., 3 Sess., pp. 12, 39-41, and 967; HCL, " Our Blundering Foreign Policy," *Forum*, xix (March, 1895), 10-11.

126. TR [?] to James S. Clarkson, April 22, 1893, TR MSS. See also TR, " The Issues of 1896," *Century*, li (November, 1895), 72.

127. *Loc. cit.*; *New York Sun*, Oct. 25, 1895, TR Scrapbooks. See also TR to A. R. Cowles, May 20 and June 3, 1894, and Jan. 27, 1895, Cowles MSS.; H. C. Lodge to Mr. Appleton, Feb. 14, 1896, Lodge MSS.

128. TR to A. R. Cowles, Aug. 25, 1894, Cowles MSS.; TR, " The Issues of 1896," *Century*, li (November, 1895), 72.

129. TR to A. R. Cowles, Jan. 5, 1896, and Jan. 8, 1897, Cowles MSS. See also H. White to H. C. Lodge, July 2, 1896, Lodge MSS.

130. TR to H. C. Lodge, Aug. 27, 1895, Lodge MSS.; TR to A. R. Cowles, Feb. 21, 1897, Cowles MSS.; A. Nevins, *Henry White*, 119-120.

131. TR to A. R. Cowles, Feb. 21, 1897, Cowles MSS.

132. TR to H. White, quoted in A. Nevins, *Henry White*, 106. See also TR to H. C. Lodge, Aug. 22, 1895, Lodge MSS.; TR to J. Hay, May 3, 1897, Hay MSS.

133. TR to A. R. Cowles, Jan. 5, 1896, Cowles MSS.

134. TR to A. R. Cowles, Jan. 26, 1896, Cowles MSS.

135. TR to A. R. Cowles, Jan. 8, 1897, Cowles MSS.

136. H. White to H. C. Lodge, July 2, 1896, Lodge MSS.

137. TR to A. R. Cowles, Jan. 8, 1897, Cowles MSS.; A. Nevins, *Henry White*, 112-118.

138. H. White to H. C. Lodge, July 2, 1896, Lodge MSS.; TR to A. R. Cowles, March 30, 1896, TR to W. S. Cowles, April [5], 1896, Cowles MSS.; H. C. Lodge to Henry [L. Higginson], Dec. 31, 1896, Lodge MSS.

139. H. C. Lodge to William [W. Sturgis Bigelow (?)], Dec. 22, 1896, HCL to Curtis [Guild (?)], Dec. 31, 1896, HCL to Henry [L. Higginson], Dec. 21, 1896, Lodge MSS.; *New York Evening Post*, Jan. 4, 1895, TR Scrapbooks. See also *Rochester Herald*, April 25, 1895.

140. H. C. Lodge, " England, Venezuela, and the Monroe Doctrine," *North American Review*, clx (June, 1895), 651-658.

141. TR to H. C. Lodge, June 5, 1895, HCL to A. C. Lodge, Feb. 2, 1896, Lodge MSS.; Joseph H. Choate to Carrie Choate, Jan. 25, 1896, Choate MSS.

142. H. White to H. C. Lodge, June 2, 1895, Lodge MSS.; *Haverhill Gazette*, Oct. 20, 1897, TR Scrapbooks; N. M. Butler, *Across the Busy Years*, i, 288-289.

143. H. C. Lodge to TR, Aug. 10 and Sept. 12, 1895, TR MSS.; TR to HCL, Aug. 27, 1895, Lodge MSS.; A. R. Cowles, Jan. 19 and March 9, 1896, Cowles MSS. See also TR to H. White, March 20, 1896, White MSS.; C. Schurz, *Speeches, Correspondence,* v, 400-401.

144. H. C. Lodge to TR, Oct. 23 [1895], TR MSS.

145. TR to H. White, Nov. 27, 1895, TR MSS. See also TR to H. White, May 24, 1897, TR MSS.

146. TR, " The Issues of 1896," *Century,* LI (November, 1895), 71.

147. TR to H. C. Lodge, Dec. 6, 1895, Lodge MSS.; TR to Amos R. Wells, March 7, 1899, TR MSS. See also TR to H. White, March 20, 1896, White MSS.

148. H. C. Lodge to A. C. Lodge, Dec. 18, 1895, HCL to H. White, Jan. 10, 1896, Lodge MSS. See also HCL to Moreton Frewen, Jan. 9, 1896, HCL to [Stephen M.] Weld, Dec. 20, 1895, H. C. Lodge to H. White, Jan. 10, 1896, Lodge MSS.; A. Nevins, *Henry White,* 119-120; *TR-HCL Correspondence,* I, 208-209.

149. H. L. Higginson to H. C. Lodge, Dec. 23, 1895, Lodge MSS.

150. See, e. g., H. C. Lodge to Henry [L. Higginson], Dec. 21, 1895, HCL to [S. M.] Weld, Dec. 20, 1895, Lodge MSS.

151. H. C. Lodge to Frank L. Sanford, Dec. 20, 1895, Lodge MSS.

152. H. C. Lodge to Blackwell, Dec. 23, 1895, Lodge MSS. See also HCL to Arthur J. Balfour, Feb. 1, 1896, HCL to Henry Gaunt, Jan. 29, 1896, HCL to Edwin Ginn, Feb. 8, 1896, HCL to Albert Bushnell Hart, Jan. 18 and Feb. 4, 1896, HCL to Francis W. Hurd, Jan. 17, 1896, HCL to Mendenhall, Feb. 24, 1896, HCL to John C. Ropes, Feb. 1, 1896, HCL to F. L. Sanford, Dec. 20, 1895, Lodge MSS.; TR, " The Monroe Doctrine," *Bachelor of Arts,* II (March, 1896), 445-447.

153. H. C. Lodge to A. B. Hart, Jan. 18, 1896, Lodge MSS.; TR, " The Monroe Doctrine," *Bachelor of Arts,* II (March, 1896), 445-446. See also *ibid.,* 438; *TR-HCL Correspondence,* I, 210.

154. H. C. Lodge to Henry [L. Higginson (?)], Dec. 21, 1895, and Jan. 20, 1896, Lodge MSS. See also HCL to Appleton, Feb. 1, 1896, HCL to Blackwell, Dec. 23, 1895, HCL to Gardiner, Jan. 25, 1896, HCL to H. Gaunt, Jan. 29, 1896, HCL to E. Ginn, Feb. 6, 1896, HCL to A. B. Hart, Jan. 18 and Feb. 4, 1896, HLH to HCL, Dec. 23, 1895, HCL to F. L. Sanford, Dec. 20, 1895, HCL to [S. M.] Weld, Dec. 20, 1895, Lodge MSS.

155. H. C. Lodge to Hart, Feb. 4, 1896, Lodge MSS.

156. TR to H. C. Lodge, Dec. 20, 1895, Lodge MSS.; Herbert Welch to C. Schurz, Dec. 31, 1895, Schurz MSS.; TR to H. White, March 30, 1896, White MSS.

157. TR, " The Monroe Doctrine," *Bachelor of Arts,* II (March, 1896), 447.

158. TR to Will [S. Cowles], Dec. 22, 1895, Cowles MSS. See also TR to H. C. Lodge, Dec. 23, 1895, Lodge MSS.

159. TR to H. C. Lodge, Dec. 27, 1895. See also HCL to Gardiner, Jan. 25, 1896, Lodge MSS.

160. TR to H. C. Lodge, Dec. 27, 1895, Lodge MSS. See also TR to H.

White, March 20, 1896, White MSS.; TR, "The Monroe Doctrine," *Bachelor of Arts*, ɪɪ (March, 1896), 448.

161. TR to H. C. Lodge, Dec. 27, 1895, HCL to M. Frewen, Jan. 9, 1896, Lodge MSS.; TR to H. White, March 20 and 30, 1896, White MSS. See also A. Nevins, *Henry White*, 119.

162. TR to H. C. Lodge, Dec. 27, 1895, Lodge MSS.

163. TR to H. C. Lodge, Dec. 27, 1895, and Jan. 2, 1896, Lodge MSS. See also TR, "The Issues of 1896," *Century*, ʟɪ (November, 1895), 72.

164. TR to H. C. Lodge, Dec. 23, 1895, and Jan. 2, 1896, Lodge MSS.; TR to A. R. Cowles, Jan. 5, 1896, Cowles MSS.; TR to H. White, March 20, 1896, White MSS.

165. TR to H. C. Lodge, Jan. 10, 15, and 19, 1896, Lodge MSS.

166. TR to H. C. Lodge, Jan. 19, 1896, HCL to A. B. Hart, Jan. 18, 1896, Lodge MSS.

167. TR to H. C. Lodge, Jan. 16, 1896, Lodge MSS.

168. *Loc. cit.*; H. L. Higginson to HCL, Dec. 23, 1895, Lodge MSS.

169. H. C. Lodge to R. Robbins, Jan. 26, 1896, HCL to William [W. S. Bigelow], Dec. 22, 1896, Lodge MSS. See also HCL to H. Gaunt, Jan. 29, 1896, HCL to Curtis [Guild], Dec. 31, 1896, HCL to F. Rawle, Jan. 21, 1896, Lodge MSS.

170. H. C. Lodge to Gardiner, Jan. 25, 1896, HCL to A. C. Lodge, Jan. 26, 1896, Lodge MSS.

171. H. C. Lodge to Gardiner, Jan. 25, 1896, Lodge MSS. See also HCL to H. L. Higginson, Jan. 20, 1896, Lodge MSS.

172. TR to H. C. Lodge, March 13, 1896, Lodge MSS. See also TR to A. R. Cowles, Jan. 26, 1896, Cowles MSS.; HCL to Appleton, Feb. 1, 1896, Lodge MSS.

173. Dec. 30, 1895, *Cong. Record*, 54 Cong., 1 Sess., 413-420; H. L. Higginson to HCL, Dec. 23, 1895, HCL to Appleton, Feb. 1, 1896, HCL to W. H. Babb, March 23, 1896, HCL to Gardner, Jan. 25, 1896, HCL to H. Gaunt, Jan. 29, 1896, HCL to A. B. Hart, Feb. 4, 1896, HCL to HLH, Jan. 20, 1896, HCL to A. C. Lodge, Jan. 26, 1896, HCL to [George H.] Lyman, Jan. 18 and March 17, 1896, HCL to F. Rawle, Jan. 21, 1896, HCL to R. Robbins, Jan. 26, 1896, Lodge MSS.

174. TR to A. R. Cowles, Feb. 2, 1896, Cowles MSS.

175. TR to W. S. Cowles, Feb. 11, 1896, Cowles MSS. See TR, "The Monroe Doctrine," *Bachelor of Arts*, ɪɪ (March, 1896), 446.

176. Grover Cleveland to TR, March 26, 1896, TR MSS.

177. TR to A. R. Cowles, March 15, 1896, Cowles MSS.; TR to H. White, March 20, 1896, White MSS.; TR, "The Monroe Doctrine," *Bachelor of Arts*, ɪɪ (March, 1896), 436-454.

CHAPTER II

1. Henry Cabot Lodge to TR, Dec. 2, 1896, Lodge MSS.

2. Maria L. Storer, "How Theodore Roosevelt Was Appointed Assistant Secretary of the Navy: A Hitherto Unrelated Chapter of History," *Harper's Weekly*, LVI (June 1, 1912), 9. See also H. C. Lodge to TR, Dec. 2, 1896, TR MSS.; HCL to William B. McKinley, Nov. 9, 1896, WBMcK, Canton, to HCL, Nahant, Nov. 12, 1896, HCL to Anna Cabot Lodge, Dec. 1, 1896, and March 21, 1897, HCL to Bellamy Storer, Nov. 13 and Dec. 2, 1896, Lodge MSS.; *New York Sun*, Dec. 2, 1896, TR Scrapbooks.

3. M. L. Storer, *op. cit.*, 9. See also TR to MLS, Dec. 5, 1896, Poultney Bigelow MSS.; H. C. Lodge to TR, Dec. 2, 1896, TR MSS.; B. Storer to HCL, Nov. 10, 1896, HCL to BS, Nov. 13, 1896, Lodge MSS.

4. Archie Butt to Clara Butt, July 10, 1910, A. Butt, *Taft and Roosevelt: The Intimate Letters of Archie Butt, Military Aide*, II, 440-441.

5. See, e. g., TR to Paul V. Dana, Aug. 16, 1897, TR to W. B. McKinley, Aug. 30, 1897, TR MSS.; TR to H. C. Lodge, Aug. 17 and 26, 1897, HCL to TR, Aug. 19, 1897, Lodge MSS.; TR, *Address . . . before the Naval War College, Newport, R. I., June 2, 1897*; TR, *The Naval Policy of America as Outlined in Messages of the Presidents of the United States from the Beginning to the Present Day*; TR, "The Need of a Navy," TR MSS. (published in *Gunton's Magazine*, XIV [January, 1898], 1-4); Review of Alfred T. Mahan's *The Interest of America in Sea Power* in the *New York Sun*, Dec. 26, 1897; *Boston Journal*, Oct. 24, 1897, *Chicago Times Herald* (quoted in the *Fargo Forum and Daily Republican*, Sept. 8, 1897), *Chicago Tribune*, undated and Sept. 10, 1897, *Commercial Advertiser*, March 31, 1898, *Gloucester Daily Times*, Feb. 10, 1898, *Gunton Institute Bulletin*, Feb. 26, 1898, *Marine Journal*, Nov. 20, 1897, *Marine Review*, Nov. 12 and 18, 1897, [*New York* (?)] *Herald* [June (?)], 1897, *New York Marine Register*, Dec. 8, 1897, *New York Press*, Feb. 23, 1897, *New York Sun*, Feb. 10 and 23, June 3, July 31, Sept. 5 and 10, and Nov. 9 and 13, 1897, and Feb. 13, 1898, *New York World*, Feb. 23, 1897, *Pall Mall Gazette*, March 19, 1898, *Philadelphia Bulletin*, Nov. 10, 1897, [*Washington* (?)] *Post*, Aug. 21, 1897, TR Scrapbooks.

6. TR to Capt. Alfred T. Mahan, May 3, 1897, TR MSS.; William D. Puleston, *Mahan: The Life and Works of Captain Alfred Thayer Mahan, U. S. N.*, 185.

7. TR to A. T. Mahan, May 3, 1897, TR MSS.

8. W. D. Puleston, *Mahan*, 183.

9. TR to A. T. Mahan, May 17, 1897, TR MSS.

10. A. T. Mahan to TR, May 1, 1897, TR to ATM, May 3 and June 9, 1897, TR MSS.

11. TR to A. T. Mahan, June 9, 1897, TR MSS.

12. TR to H. C. Lodge, Aug. 26, 1897, Lodge MSS.

13. TR to H. C. Lodge, June 17, 1897, Lodge MSS.

14. TR to William L. Clowes, Aug. 3, 1897, TR MSS.

15. TR to Charles A. Boutelle, Sept. 16, 1897, TR MSS.

16. TR to Baron Hermann Speck von Sternburg, Belgrade, Jan. 17, 1898, TR MSS.

17. *New York Sun*, Feb. 10, 1897, TR Scrapbooks. See also *New York Press*, Feb. 23, 1897, *New York Sun*, Feb. 23, 1897, *New York World*, Feb. 23, 1897, TR Scrapbooks.

18. TR to A. T. Mahan, June 9, 1897, TR MSS.

19. TR, *Address . . . before the Naval War College*, 3, 4. See also *New York Sun*, Sept. 5, 1897, *Chicago Times Herald* (quoted in the *Fargo Forum and Daily Republican*, Sept. 8, 1897), *Chicago Tribune*, undated and Sept. 10, 1897, *Philadelphia Bulletin*, Nov. 10, 1897, "A Progressive Naval Policy," *Marine Journal*, Sept. 9, 1897, *New York Sun*, Sept. 10, 1897, TR Scrapbooks.

20. *New York Sun*, Nov. 13, 1897, TR Scrapbooks. See also *ibid.*, Nov. 9, 1897, *Marine Review*, Nov. 12, 1897, TR Scrapbooks.

21. TR to A. T. Mahan, May 3, 1897, TR MSS.

22. A. T. Mahan to TR, May 1, 1897, TR MSS.

23. Samuel F. Bemis, *A Diplomatic History of the United States*, 461; Lester B. Shippee and Royal B. Way, *William Rufus Day: Secretary of State April 28, 1898, to September 16, 1898* (*The American Secretaries of State and Their Diplomacy*, S. F. Bemis, ed., IX), 34.

24. Speech to the Ohio Naval Reserves, *New York Tribune*, July 27, 1897, TR Scrapbooks. See also TR to H. C. Lodge, Aug. 3, 1897, Lodge MSS.

25. *New York Tribune*, July 27, 1897, TR Scrapbooks.

26. TR to H. C. Lodge, Aug. 3, 1897, Lodge MSS.

27. H. C. Lodge to TR, Aug. 5, 1897, Lodge MSS.

28. TR to H. C. Lodge, Aug. 3 and Sept. 15, 1897, Lodge MSS.

29. TR, "The Need of a Navy," *Gunton's Magazine*, XIV (January, 1898), 1-4.

30. H. C. Lodge to Stephen O'Meara, Jan. 3, 1898, Lodge MSS. See also HCL to Justin Whitney, Jan. 5, 1898, Lodge MSS.

31. Henry White to H. C. Lodge, Jan. 18, 1898, HCL to HW, Jan. 31, 1898, Lodge MSS.; A. T. Mahan to TR, May 1, 1897, TR to James Bryce, March 31, 1898, TR MSS.

32. *New York Tribune*, March 17 and July 7 and 8, 1898; Edmund J. Carpenter, *America in Hawaii: A History of United States Influence in the Hawaiian Islands*, 244; L. B. Shippee and R. B. Way, *Day*, 40. S. F. Bemis, *A Diplomatic History*, 461; Joint Resolution to Provide for Annexing the Hawaiian Islands to the U. S., July 7, 1898, in *U. S. Statutes at Large*, 55 Cong., 2 Sess., vol. XXX (1897-1899), 750-751.

33. H. C. Lodge to Herbert Myrick, Jan. 10, 1898, Lodge MSS. See also HCL to S. O'Meara, Jan. 11, 1898, Lodge MSS.

34. TR, Review of A. T. Mahan's *The Interest of America in Sea Power* in the *New York Sun*, Dec. 26, 1897, TR Scrapbooks.

35. *New York Sun*, Feb. 13, 1898, TR Scrapbooks.

36. TR, Review of A. T. Mahan's *The Interest of America in Sea Power* in the *New York Sun*, Dec. 26, 1897, TR Scrapbooks.

37. *New York Sun*, Feb. 13, 1898, TR Scrapbooks.

38. John Hay to [Joseph H.] Choate, Nov. 13, 1899, Hay MSS.

39. H. C. Lodge to Edith Kermit Roosevelt, Oct. 23 [1895], TR MSS.; HCL to [Stephen M. (?)] Weld, Dec. 19, 1896, Lodge MSS.

40. TR to Anna R. Cowles, March 30, 1896, Cowles MSS.; H. C. Lodge to Henry [L. Higginson], Jan. 10 and Dec. 31, 1896, Lodge MSS.

41. A. R. Cowles to H. C. Lodge, March 1, 1896, HCL to Charles F. Adams, Jan. 22, 1897, CFA to HCL, Dec. 3, 1896, HCL to Moreton Frewen, March 11, 1896, HCL to Henry [L. Higginson], Dec. 21, 1896, HLH to HCL, March 8, 1898, HCL to A. C. Lodge, Jan. 13 and Dec. 26, 1896, and May 25, 1897, HCL to [George H.] Lyman, March 17, 1896, HCL to Pickman, March 12, 1896, HCL to [S. M.] Weld, Dec. 19, 1896, H. White, London, to HCL, July 2, 1896, Lodge MSS. See also HCL to HLH, March 9, 1898, Lodge MSS.

42. See, e. g., H. C. Lodge to Henry [L. Higginson], Dec. 21, 1896, HCL to William [W. Sturgis Bigelow], Dec. 22, 1896, Lodge MSS.

43. TR to Brooks Adams, March 21, 1898, TR to William B. Allison, June 18, 1897, TR to Robert Bacon, April 8, 1898, TR to W. S. Bigelow, March 29, 1898, TR to J. Bryce, March 31, 1898, TR to Capt. French E. Chadwick, Nov. 4, 1897, FEC to TR, March 24, 1898, TR to William E. Chandler, June 18 and Sept. 27, 1897, TR to Cushman K. Davis, June 18, 1897, TR to B. Harrison Diblee, Feb. 16, 1898, TR to Lt. George L. Dyer, London, Sept. 17, 1897, TR to William P. Frye, June 18, 1897, and March 31, 1898, TR to J. Hay, London, Nov. 4, 1897, TR to Dr. Henry Jackson, April 6, 1898, TR to Gen. Bradley T. Johnson, March 7, 1898, TR to Comdr. William W. Kimball, Nov. 19 and Dec. 17, 1897, TR to John D. Long, Feb. 10, 1898, TR to H. Speck von Sternburg, Belgrade, Jan. 17, 1898, TR to Lucius B. Swift, March 26, 1898, TR to H. White, London, April 30, 1897, TR MSS.; TR to H. C. Lodge, Aug. 3, 1897, HCL to Gen. William F. Draper, Dec. 20, 1897, Lodge MSS.; TR to A. T. Mahan, March 21, 1898, in Charles C. Taylor, *The Life of Admiral Mahan, Naval Philosopher*, 174; TR to H. White, March, 1898, in Allan Nevins, *Henry White: Thirty Years of American Diplomacy*, 132.

44. TR to A. R. Cowles, Jan. 2, 1897, Cowles MSS. See also TR to Robert Bacon, April 8, 1898, TR MSS.

45. TR to W. E. Chandler, C. K. Davis, W. P. Frye, and W. B. Allison, June 18, 1897, TR MSS.

46. TR to A. T. Mahan, March 21, 1898, in C. C. Taylor, *Mahan*, 174. See also TR to H. White, May 24, 1897, TR MSS.; H. C. Lodge to Henry [L. Higginson], March 4, 1898, Lodge MSS.

47. TR to J. Bryce, March 31, 1898, TR MSS. See also TR to W. P. Frye, March 31, 1898, TR MSS.

48. TR to R. Bacon, April 8, 1898, TR MSS. See also TR to H. Jackson, April 6, 1898, TR MSS.

49. TR to B. Adams, March 1, 1898, TR MSS. See also F. E. Chadwick to TR, March 24, 1898, TR MSS.; *Haverhill Gazette*, April 2, 1898, TR Scrapbooks.

50. TR to R. Bacon, April 5, 1898, TR MSS. See also TR to Capt. William S. Cowles, March 30, 1898, TR to William Tudor, April 5, 1898, TR to Gen. James H. Wilson, April 5, 1898, TR MSS.

51. TR to Elihu Root, April 5, 1898, TR MSS. See also TR to B. Adams, March 21, 1898, F. E. Chadwick to TR, March 24, 1898, TR MSS.; H. C. Lodge to Henry [L. Higginson], March 9, 1898, Lodge MSS.; *Haverhill Gazette*, April 2, 1898, TR Scrapbooks.

52. TR to R. Bacon, April 8, 1898, TR to H. Jackson, April 6, 1898, TR MSS.

53. TR to W. W. Kimball, Nov. 19, 1897, TR MSS.

54. TR to J. D. Long, April 26, 1897, TR MSS.

55. TR to W. B. McKinley, April 26, 1897, TR MSS.

56. TR to W. W. Kimball, Nov. 1 and 19, 1897, TR MSS.

57. TR to H. Speck von Sternburg, Belgrade, Jan. 17, 1898, TR MSS.

58. TR to Capt. Charles H. Davis, Jan. 17 and March 17, 1898, TR to Comdr. Robley D. Evans, Jan. 22 and March 16, 1898, TR to W. W. Kimball, Nov. 1 and 19, 1897, TR to H. C. Lodge, Sept. 15, 1897, TR MSS.; TR to A. T. Mahan, March 21, 1898, in C. C. Taylor, *Mahan*, 174; unidentified clipping [March 23 (?)], 1898, TR Scrapbooks; John D. Long, *The New American Navy*, I, 162; Ida M. Tarbell, *All in a Day's Work*, 190; W. D. Puleston, *Mahan*, 185.

59. TR to B. T. Johnson, March 7, 1898, TR to W. B. McKinley, April 26, 1897, H. White to TR, Feb. 26 and March 18, 1898, TR MSS.; TR to H. White, March, 1898, in A. Nevins, *Henry White*, 132; *Commercial Advertiser*, March 31, 1898, *New York Sun*, March 8, 1898, *Pall Mall Gazette*, March 19, 1898, unidentified clipping [March 23 (?)], 1898, TR Scrapbooks.

60. Feb. 26, 1898, *America of Yesterday as Reflected in the Journal of John Davis Long, Governor of Massachusetts, Secretary of the Navy*, Lawrence S. Mayo, ed. (hereafter cited as J. D. Long, *Journal*), 168, 169; Evan J. David, ed., *Leonard Wood on National Issues*, 135.

61. TR to George Dewey, Hong Kong, Feb. 25, 1898, TR MSS.; order to Commander-in-chief, Asiatic Station, Feb. 25, 1898, cited in Capt. Arent S. Crowninshield to H. C. Lodge, Sept. 24, 1898, Lodge MSS.; TR, *Autobiography* (Macmillan, 1916), 218-219; George Dewey, *Autobiography*, 179.

62. *Loc. cit.*

63. Orders to Commanders-in-chief, South Atlantic, Pacific, Asiatic, North Atlantic, and European Stations, Feb. 26, 1898, cited in A. S. Crowninshield to H. C. Lodge, Sept. 24, 1898, Lodge MSS.

64. E. J. David, ed., *Wood on National Issues*, 135.

65. TR to C. Whitney Tillinghast, II, Feb. 25, 1898, TR MSS.

66. Feb. 26, 1898, J. D. Long, *Journal*, 169, 170. See also *ibid.*, 168; David S. Barry, *Forty Years in Washington*, 255.

67. Feb. 26, 1898, J. D. Long, *Journal*, 169, 170. H. C. Lodge, "Theodore Roosevelt," *The Senate of the United States and Other Essays and Addresses, Historical and Literary*, 128, 129.

68. Unidentified clipping, Feb. 27, 1898, TR Scrapbooks.
69. Feb. 26, 1898, J. D. Long, *Journal*, 169, 170.
70. TR, *Autobiography*, 218.
71. Roosevelt first mentioned need of them in September, 1897. TR to H. C. Lodge, Sept. 21, 1897, J. Bryce to TR, Sept. 12, 1898, TR MSS. See also A. Whitney Griswold, *The Far Eastern Policy of the United States*, 11-13, 23-24, 24-25; Evelene Peters, *Roosevelt und der Kaiser*, 56, 60.
72. TR to H. C. Lodge, Sept. 21, 1897, TR to W. W. Kimball, Nov. 19, 1897, TR to J. D. Long, Jan. 14, 1898, TR MSS.
73. Orders to Commanders, *U. S. S. Mohigan* and *U. S. S. Baltimore*, March 3, 1898, cited in A. S. Crowninshield to H. C. Lodge, Sept. 24, 1898, Lodge MSS.
74. TR to W. W. Kimball, Nov. 19, 1897, TR MSS.; H. C. Lodge, " Theodore Roosevelt," *loc. cit.*, 128, 129; John J. Leary, Jr., *Talks with T. R. from the Diaries of John J. Leary, Jr.*, 13; Louis S. Young, *Life and Heroic Deeds of Admiral Dewey*, 97, 98; Carroll S. Alden, " George Dewey," *Dictionary of American Biography*, v, 270. See also A. W. Griswold, *Far Eastern Policy*, 11-13; Frederick Palmer, *With My Own Eyes*, 107.
75. TR to W. E. Chandler, Oct. 19, 1899, WEC to TR, Sept. 25 and Oct. 13, 1897, TR to Col. F. Dibble, Jan. 17, 1899, TR to J. Hay, July 1, 1899, TR MSS.; TR to WEC, Sept. 29, 1897, and Jan. 11, 1900, J. D. Long to WEC, Oct. 12, 1897, Chandler MSS.; G. Dewey, *Autobiography*, 167-169; J. J. Leary, Jr., *Talks with T. R.*, 13; TR, " Admiral Dewey," *McClure's Magazine*, XIII (October, 1899), 483, 487; L. S. Young, *Dewey*, 97, 98.
76. G. Dewey, *Autobiography*, 170-171; orders to Commanders, *U. S. S. Mohigan* and *U. S. S. Baltimore*, March 3, 1898, cited in A. S. Crowninshield to H. C. Lodge, Sept. 24, 1898, HCL to ASC, Sept. 26, 1898, Lodge MSS.; Willard H. Brownson, Guantanamo, to TR, July 31, 1898, Martin King to TR, July 14, 1899, TR MSS.; TR, " Admiral Dewey," *McClure's Magazine*, XIII (October, 1899), 490; F. Palmer, *With My Own Eyes*, 107; C. S. Alden, " George Dewey," *DAB*, v, 270.
77. TR to G. Dewey, Feb. 25, 1898, TR MSS.; order to Commander-in-chief, Asiatic Station, Feb. 25, 1898, cited in A. S. Crowninshield to H. C. Lodge, Sept. 24, 1898, HCL to ASC, Sept. 21 and 26, 1898, Lodge MSS.; HCL to TR, Sept. 21, 1898, TR MSS.; [*Philadelphia* (?)] *Enquirer*, March 3, 1898, TR Scrapbooks; TR, *Autobiography*, 218-219; G. Dewey, *Autobiography*, 179; E. J. David, ed., *Wood on National Issues*, 135; F. Palmer, *With My Own Eyes*, 107; Corinne Roosevelt Robinson, *My Brother Theodore Roosevelt*, 164.
78. H. C. Lodge, " Theodore Roosevelt," *loc. cit.*, 128, 129; TR, *Autobiography*, 218.
79. TR to F. E. Chadwick, Sept. 17, 1897, TR to W. E. Chandler, Sept. 27, 1897, TR to R. D. Evans, March 16, 1898, TR to B. T. Johnson, March 7, 1898, TR to W. W. Kimball, Nov. 19, 1897, TR to H. C. Lodge, Sept. 21, 1897, TR to J. D. Long, Sept. 20, 1897, TR to A. T. Mahan, May 3, 1897, TR to Corinne R. Robinson, March 16, 1898, TR MSS.; TR to A. R. Cowles, March 16 and April 1, 1898, Cowles MSS.; TR to D. Robinson, March 28, 1898, in

C. R. Robinson, *My Brother TR*, 161; C. H. Davis to HCL, March 29, 1898, Lodge MSS.; H. White, London, to TR, Feb. 26 and March 18, 1898, White MSS.; TR to HW, March, 1898, in A. Nevins, *Henry White*, 132; *Commercial Advertiser*, March 31, 1898, *New York Sun*, March 2 and 8, 1898, and unidentified clipping [March 23 (?)], 1898, *Pall Mall Gazette*, March 19, 1898, TR Scrapbooks; Arthur W. Dunn, *From Harrison to Harding*, I, 264; Charles R. Flint, *Memories of an Active Life*, 102-103, 105-106; J. Henry Harper, *I Remember*, 258, 259; Charles M. Remey, ed., *Life and Letters of Rear Admiral George Collier Remey, U. S. N., 1841-1928*, VIII, 812-814.

80. J. D. Long, *Journal*, 198; [*Philadelphia* (?)] *Enquirer*, March 3, 1898, *New York Post*, March 7, 1898, *New York Times*, March 7, 1898 (quoted in the *Savannah News*), *New York Herald*, Dec. 23, 1908, TR Scrapbooks; Chauncey M. Depew, "Speech . . . Presenting the Name of Colonel Theodore Roosevelt as Candidate for Governor, at the Republican State Convention at Saratoga, Sept. 27th, 1898," *Autumnal Speeches in 1898*, 12, 13; C. R. Flint, *Memories*, 102-103; A. W. Dunn, *From Harrison to Harding*, I, 262.

81. TR to A. T. Mahan, May 3, 1897, TR to P. V. Dana, April 18, 1898, TR MSS.; *New York Post*, March 7, 1898, TR Scrapbooks; E. J. David, ed., *Wood on National Issues*, 134-135; Robley D. Evans, *A Sailor's Log: Recollections of Forty Years of Naval Life*, 404; C. R. Flint, *Memories*, 102-103; C. R. Robinson, *My Brother TR*, 160, 161, 164.

82. A. Butt to Clara Butt, July 11, 1910, in A. W. Butt, *Taft and Roosevelt*, II, 441.

83. Oswald Garrison Villard, *Fighting Years*, 140. See also H. C. Lodge, MS. Diary, Jan. 12 [1902], HCL to H. White, Aug. 12, 1898, Lodge MSS.; HW to TR, Nov. 3, 1899, TR MSS.

84. E. K. Roosevelt to H. C. Lodge, March 10 [1900], Lodge MSS.

85. H. Adams to E. Cameron, Jan. 22, 1899, in HA, *Letters, 1892-1918*, Worthington C. Ford, ed., 208.

86. TR to J. Hay, July 1, 1899, TR MSS. See also TR to [J.] Brander Matthews, July 20, 1907, TR MSS.

87. TR to C. Spring Rice, Dec. 2, 1899, TR MSS.

88. *Anaconda Standard*, Sept. 16, 1900, *Chicago Times Herald*, Oct. 7, 1900, *Evansville News*, Oct. 12, 1900, *New York Times*, Aug. 28, 1900, *New York Tribune*, Oct. 10, 1900, TR Scrapbooks. The *New York Sun*, Nov. 3, 1900, said 18,000 miles and 600 speeches the last two months of the campaign. The *Rochester Democrat and Chronicle*, Nov. 3, 1900, estimated 21,209 miles, 567 towns and cities, 673 speeches, and 3,000,000 people. See also *Brooklyn Citizen*, Oct. 27, 1900, *Brooklyn Eagle*, Oct. 27, and Nov. 3, 1900, *Brooklyn Standard Union*, Oct. 26 and 27, 1900, *Commercial Advertiser*, Oct. 27, 1900, *New York Sun*, Oct. 26, 1900, *Troy Record*, Oct. 27, 1900, TR Scrapbooks.

89. *Colorado Victor Times*, Sept. 27, 1900, TR Scrapbooks; TR to H. C. Lodge, July 30, 1902, Lodge MSS.

90. TR, *Thomas H. Benton*, 36; *New York World*, Oct. 10, 1900, *Helena Daily Independent*, Sept. 18, 1900, TR Scrapbooks.

91. *Chicago Journal,* Sept. 8, 1900, *Helena Daily Independent,* Sept. 18, 1900, TR Scrapbooks.

92. TR, *Benton,* 235-236.

93. *Cincinnati Enquirer,* Oct. 13, 1900, *Helena Daily Independent,* Sept. 17, 1900, TR Scrapbooks.

94. *New York Times,* Oct. 13, 1900, *Cincinnati Enquirer,* Oct. 13, 1900, TR Scrapbooks. See also *Indianapolis Patriot Phalanx,* Sept. 20, 1900, TR Scrapbooks.

95. *Chicago Journal,* Sept. 8, 1900, *Cincinnati Enquirer,* Oct. 13, 1900, *Detroit Daily News,* Sept. 7, 1900, *Helena Daily Independent,* Sept. 17, 1900, *Kalamazoo Gazette,* Sept. 28, 1900, *New York Sun,* Sept. 6, 1900, *Omaha Bee,* Sept. 28, 1900, *Salt Lake City Tribune,* Sept. 20, 1900, *Wyoming Tribune,* Sept. 24, 1900, TR Scrapbooks.

96. *New York Tribune,* Oct. 27, 1900, TR Scrapbooks. See also *Brooklyn Daily Eagle,* Oct. 31, 1900, *Chicago Times-Herald,* Oct. 6, 1900, *Milwaukee Sentinel,* July 18, 1900, *New York Press,* Sept. 19 and Oct. 11, 1900, *New York Sun,* Sept. 11 and 18, 1900, *New York Times,* Aug. 6, 1900, *Omaha Bee,* July 18, 1900, *Rochester Democrat and Chronicle,* Nov. 1, 1900, *Syracuse Post Standard,* Oct. 27, 1900, *Troy Record,* Oct. 25, 1900, *Waterloo Daily Courier,* Oct. 5, 1900, TR Scrapbooks.

97. *Chicago Record,* Sept. 8, 1900, *Kansas City Journal,* Sept. 29, 1900, *New York Tribune,* Oct. 10, 1900, *Waterloo Daily Courier,* Oct. 5, 1900, TR Scrapbooks. See also *Denver Times,* Sept. 26, 1900, TR Scrapbooks.

98. *New York Tribune,* Oct. 10, 1900, *Waterloo Daily Courier,* Oct. 5, 1900. See also *Chicago Times-Herald,* Oct. 6, 1900, *Indianapolis Journal,* Oct. 12, 1900, *New York Times,* Oct. 23, 1900, *Omaha Daily Bee,* Oct. 6, 1900, *Oswego Times,* Oct. 26, 1900, *Syracuse Journal,* Oct. 26, 1900, TR Scrapbooks.

99. *Goshen Democrat,* Sept. 20, 1900. See also *Chicago Record,* Sept. 8, 1900, *Helena Daily Independent,* Sept. 17, 1900, TR Scrapbooks. See, too, his speech in Kansas City. *Kansas City Journal,* Sept. 29, 1900.

100. H. L. Higginson to H. C. Lodge, Nov. 12, 1900, Lodge MSS.

101. TR to W. L. Clowes, Jan. 14, 1898, TR MSS.

102. *Helena Daily Independent,* Sept. 17, 1900. See also *Brooklyn Daily Eagle,* Sept. 20, 1900, *Chicago Journal,* Sept. 8, 1900, *Detroit Evening News,* Sept. 7, 1900, *Kalamazoo Gazette,* Sept. 28, 1900, *New York Sun,* Sept. 6 and 20 and Oct. 12, 1900, *Omaha Bee,* Sept. 28, 1900, *Wyoming Tribune,* Sept. 24, 1900, TR Scrapbooks.

103. *Salt Lake City Daily Tribune,* Sept. 20, 1900. See also *Brooklyn Daily Eagle,* Sept. 20, 1900, *Detroit Evening News,* Sept. 7, 1900, TR Scrapbooks.

104. H. C. Lodge to James Ford Rhodes, Aug. 6, 1900, Lodge MSS.

105. See, e. g., *Brooklyn Daily Eagle,* Sept. 20, 1900, *Cincinnati Enquirer,* Oct. 13, 1900, *Detroit Evening News,* Sept. 7, 1900, *Salt Lake City Daily Tribune,* Sept. 20 and 22, 1900, *Waterloo Daily Courier,* Oct. 5, 1900, TR Scrapbooks.

106. *Salt Lake City Daily Tribune,* Sept. 20, 1900, TR Scrapbooks.

107. *Helena Daily Independent*, Sept. 17, 1900, *New York Sun*, Sept. 6, 1900, *New York Tribune*, Oct. 10, 1900, TR Scrapbooks.

108. *Denver Republican*, Sept. 20, 1900, *New York Times*, Oct. 23, 1900, *New York Tribune*, Oct. 10, 1900, *Oswego Times*, Oct. 26, 1900, *St. Louis Daily Journal*, Oct. 11, 1900, *Syracuse Journal*, Oct. 26, 1900, TR Scrapbooks.

109. *Wyoming Tribune*, Sept. 24, 1900, TR Scrapbooks. See also Albert J. Beveridge, "The March of the Flag," *The Meaning of the Times*, 49.

110. *Fargo Morning Call*, Sept. 15, 1900. See also *Cheyenne Leader*, Sept. 24, 1900, *New York Tribune*, Oct. 27, 1900, *Utica Herald Dispatch*, Oct. 25, 1900, TR Scrapbooks.

111. *Cheyenne Leader*, Sept. 24, 1900, *Wichita Daily Eagle*, July 5, 1900, TR Scrapbooks.

112. *Denver Republican*, Sept. 26, 1900, *Utica Herald Dispatch*, Oct. 25, 1900, TR Scrapbooks.

113. *Cincinnati Enquirer*, Oct. 13, 1900, TR Scrapbooks.

114. *Detroit Evening News*, Sept. 7, 1900, TR Scrapbooks.

115. *Cincinnati Enquirer*, Oct. 13, 1900, *Wyoming Tribune*, Sept. 24, 1900, TR Scrapbooks. See also A. J. Beveridge, *The Meaning of the Times*, 49.

116. *Omaha Bee*, Sept. 28, 1900, *Kalamazoo Gazette*, Sept. 28, 1900, *New York Sun*, Oct. 12, 1900, *New York Tribune*, Oct. 27, 1900, TR Scrapbooks. See also TR to Lyman Abbott, July 15, 1901, TR MSS.

117. *Omaha Bee*, Sept. 28, 1900, *Kalamazoo Gazette*, Sept. 28, 1900, *New York Sun*, Oct. 12, 1900, *New York Tribune*, Oct. 27, 1900, TR Scrapbooks. See also TR to L. Abbott, July 15, 1901, TR MSS.

118. *Newburgh Daily News*, Oct. 22, 1900, *Chicago Journal*, Sept. 8, 1900, *New York Tribune*, Oct. 10, 1900, unidentified clipping, Oct. 17, 1900, TR Scrapbooks.

119. *New York Tribune* [?], Oct. 10, 1900, TR Scrapbooks.

120. *Loc. cit.* See also *Denver Times*, Sept. 26, 1900, *New York Herald*, Oct. 16, 1900, TR Scrapbooks.

121. *New York Tribune*, Oct. 10, 1900, TR Scrapbooks.

122. *Chicago Journal*, Sept. 8, 1900, *Denver Republican*, Sept. 26, 1900, *New York Sun*, Sept. 6, 1900, *New York Tribune*, Oct. 10 and 27, 1900, *Waterloo Daily Courier*, Oct. 5, 1900, *Wyoming Tribune*, Sept. 24, 1900, TR Scrapbooks.

123. TR to W. Bayard Cutting, April 18, 1899, TR MSS.; *Chicago Journal*, Sept. 8, 1900, *Detroit Evening News*, Sept. 7, 1900, *Helena Daily Independent*, Sept. 17, 1900, *New York Sun*, Sept. 6, 1900, *Utica Observer*, Sept. 8, 1900, *Wyoming Tribune*, Sept. 24, 1900, TR Scrapbooks.

124. *Helena Daily Independent*, Sept. 17, 1900, *Chicago Record*, Sept. 8, 1900, *Denver Republican*, Sept. 26, 1900, TR Scrapbooks.

125. *New York Tribune*, Oct. 10, 1900, TR Scrapbooks. See also TR to Frederic R. Coudert, Jr., July 3, 1901, TR MSS.

126. *Waterloo Daily Courier*, Oct. 5, 1900. See also *Chicago Record*, Sept. 8, 1900, *Fargo Morning Call*, Sept. 15, 1900, *New York Tribune*, Oct. 27, 1900, TR Scrapbooks.

127. *Wyoming Tribune*, Sept. 24, 1900, TR Scrapbooks. See also A. J. Beveridge, *The Meaning of the Times*, 49.

128. *Helena Daily Independent*, Sept. 17, 1900, TR Scrapbooks. See also TR to L. Abbott, July 15, 1901, TR MSS.; *Chicago Record*, Sept. 8, 1900, TR Scrapbooks.

129. *Helena Daily Independent*, Sept. 17, 1900, TR Scrapbooks.

130. *Chicago Record*, Sept. 8, 1900, *Cincinnati Enquirer*, Oct. 13, 1900, *Denver Republican*, Sept. 26, 1900, *Fargo Morning Call*, Sept. 15, 1900, *Helena Daily Independent*, Sept. 17, 1900, *New York Tribune*, Oct. 10, 1900, *Utica Observer*, Sept. 8, 1900, *Wyoming Tribune*, Sept. 24, 1900, TR Scrapbooks.

131. William James to the *Boston Evening Transcript*, March 1, 1899, quoted in Ralph Barton Perry, *The Thought and Character of William James*, 245-246.

132. C. M. Depew, "Speech at the Republican National Convention," Philadelphia, June 17, 1900, *Speeches, November, 1896–April, 1902*, 42-43.

133. *Ibid.*, 51-52.

134. H. White to H. C. Lodge, June 25 and July 14, 1900, Lodge MSS.

135. *Kansas City Sunday Journal*, Sept. 30, 1900, TR Scrapbooks.

136. H. C. Lodge to H. White, June 29, 1900, Lodge MSS.

137. H. White to H. C. Lodge, June 25, 1900, Lodge MSS.

138. H. C. Lodge to H. White, June 29, 1900, Lodge MSS.

139. H. White to H. C. Lodge, July 14, 1900, Lodge MSS.

140. *Utica Observer*, Oct. 8, 1900, TR Scrapbooks.

141. TR to John Barrett, Oct. 29, 1900, TR MSS.

142. *Utica Herald Dispatch*, Oct. 25, 1900, *Wyoming Tribune*, Sept. 24, 1900, TR Scrapbooks.

143. *New York Sun*, Sept. 6, 1900, TR Scrapbooks.

144. *Fargo Morning Call*, Sept. 15, 1900, TR Scrapbooks. See also *Salt Lake City Tribune*, Sept. 20, 1900, TR Scrapbooks.

145. *New York Tribune*, Oct. 10, 1900, TR Scrapbooks.

146. H. C. Lodge to W. B. McKinley, Oct. 22, 1900, Lodge MSS.

147. TR to C. Spring Rice, May 29, 1897, TR MSS.

148. TR, Review of B. Adams's *The Law of Civilization and Decay* in the *Forum*, xxii (January, 1897), 587-588.

149. TR to C. Spring Rice, Aug. 11, 1899, TR MSS.

150. *Loc. cit.*; TR, Review of B. Adams's *The Law of Civilization and Decay* in *loc. cit.*, 578. See also TR to C. Spring Rice, Aug. 13, 1897, TR MSS.

151. TR to A. R. Cowles, Dec. 17, 1899, Cowles MSS.

152. TR to Arthur J. Balfour, March 5, 1908, TR to C. Spring Rice, July 21, 1908, TR MSS.

153. B. Adams to H. C. Lodge, June 26, 1900, Lodge MSS.

154. TR, "The Strenuous Life," Speech before the Hamilton Club, Chicago, April 10, 1899, *The Strenuous Life: Essays and Addresses*, 20.

CHAPTER III

1. TR to Cecil Spring Rice, March 16, 1901, TR MSS. See also TR to Edward VII, Feb. 12, 1908, in Sidney Lee, *Edward VII*, ii, 439; TR to CSR, May 29, 1897, TR MSS.

2. "Mr. Roosevelt's Creed," TR Speech at Brooklyn Young Republican Club meeting Oct. 18, 1884, in *New York Times*, Oct. 19, 1884, TR Scrapbooks. See also TR to [J.] Brander Matthews, Aug. 26, 1893, and June 29, 1894, TR MSS.

3. See, e. g., James Ford Rhodes, Memorandum of conversation with TR at dinner at the White House, Nov. 16, 1905, quoted in Mark A. DeWolfe Howe, *James Ford Rhodes*, 120-121; *Boston Evening Transcript*, July 29, 1884, TR Scrapbooks.

4. See, e. g., TR to Mrs. [Margot] Asquith, June 2, 1910, TR to [J.] B. Matthews, April 14, 1890, July 27, 1892, Dec. 31, 1893, Feb. 4 and 14 and Aug. 25, 1894, and March 9, 1895, TR to George von Lengerke Meyer, May 12, 1901, TR MSS.; TR to Henry Cabot Lodge, June 6, 1910, HCL to Anna Cabot Lodge, Feb. 3, 1895, Lodge MSS.

5. John Hay to H. C. Lodge, Aug. 30 [1894], Lodge MSS.

6. H. C. Lodge to A. C. Lodge, Feb. 3, 1895, Lodge MSS.; TR to Frederick C. Selous, Feb. 7, 1900, TR MSS. "Do you remember the tears of rage you and Cabot used to make me shed till the kindly influence of women had to be appealed to?" Spring Rice asked in 1900. C. Spring Rice to TR, Sept. 3, 1900, TR MSS.

7. TR to F. C. Selous, Feb. 7, 1900, TR MSS.; H. C. Lodge to A. C. Lodge, Feb. 3, 1895, Lodge MSS. See for another statement of this attitude, TR to Frederick W. Holls, July 4, 1903, TR MSS. During his Presidency it was only when he had to mollify someone like the vigorously anti-British Mr. Dooley or was stirred by thoughts of American expatriates in England that he could have said, "The average Englishman is not a being whom I find congenial or with whom I care to associate." Even then he qualified this by saying "For the English people I have a very sincere regard." TR to Finley Peter Dunne, Dec. 3, 1904, Dunne MSS.

8. J. Hay to John W. Foster, June 23, 1900, Hay MSS.

9. H. C. Lodge to [Moreton] Frewen, Jan. 17, 1896, HCL to [Arthur J.] Balfour, Feb. 1, 1896, Lodge MSS.

10. James Bryce to TR, Jan. 1, 1896, TR MSS.

11. TR, "The Monroe Doctrine," *Bachelor of Arts*, ii (March, 1896), 446.

12. Henry White to H. C. Lodge, June 2, 1895, Lodge MSS.

13. Anna Roosevelt Cowles to H. C. Lodge, May 30, 1896, Lodge MSS. See also HCL to Appleton, Feb. 1, 1896, HCL to Gardiner, Jan. 25, 1896, HCL to Henry Gaunt, Jan. 29, 1896, HCL to Hart, Feb. 4, 1896, HCL to Henry [L. Higginson], Jan. 20, 1896, HCL to [George H.] Lyman, March 17, 1896, Lodge MSS.

14. H. C. Lodge to William [W. Sturgis Bigelow], Dec. 22, 1896, Lodge MSS.

15. J. Bryce to TR, Jan. 1, 1896, TR MSS.

16. A. Whitney Griswold, *The Far Eastern Policy of the United States*, 37.

17. *British and Foreign State Papers*, LXXXVIII (1895-1896), 1242-1244; *Foreign Relations*, 1895, part 1, 576; 1896, 243-247.

18. TR, "The Monroe Doctrine," *Bachelor of Arts*, II (March, 1896), 438. H. C. Lodge to W. H. Babb, March 23, 1896, Lodge MSS. Lord Rosebury and Sir William Harcourt of the opposition, and the Queen's speech from the Throne gave further evidence of this. H. C. Lodge to W. H. Babb, March 23, 1896, Lodge MSS. See also H. White to HCL, Oct. 29, 1897 (?), Lodge MSS.

19. Alfred Thayer Mahan, "Possibilities of an Anglo-American Reunion," *North American Review*, CLIX (November, 1894), 551-563.

20. TR to H. White, Nov. 27, 1895, White MSS.; HW to H. C. Lodge, July 2, 1896, Lodge MSS.; J. Hay to R. Olney, July 31, 1896, in Tyler Dennett, *John Hay*, 175-176.

21. HCL to [A. J.] Balfour, Feb. 1, 1896, Lodge MSS. See also HCL to Francis W. Hurd, Jan. 17, 1896, Lodge MSS.

22. *New York Sun*, Oct. 25, 1895, TR Scrapbooks.

23. TR, "The Monroe Doctrine," *Bachelor of Arts*, II (March, 1896), 448.

24. H. C. Lodge to [A. J.] Balfour, Feb. 1, 1896, Lodge MSS.

25. *Loc. cit.*; TR to H. White, March 30, 1896, White MSS.; A. R. Cowles to H. C. Lodge, Feb. 5, 1896, HCL to M. Frewen, Jan. 9, 1896, Lodge MSS.; TR, "The Monroe Doctrine," *Bachelor of Arts*, II (March, 1896), 437-438, 448. See also HCL to W. H. Babb, March 23, 1896, TR to HCL, Dec. 27, 1895, and Jan. 16, 1896, Lodge MSS.

26. H. C. Lodge to [A. J.] Balfour, Feb. 1, 1896, HCL to TR, July 24, 1895, Lodge MSS. See also A. R. Cowles to HCL, Feb. 5 and May 30, 1896, Lodge MSS.; Oswald Garrison Villard, *Prophets True and False*, 261-262.

27. H. C. Lodge to [A. J.] Balfour, Feb. 1, 1896, Lodge MSS.

28. H. C. Lodge to [M.] Frewen, Jan. 17, 1896, Lodge MSS.; Bertha A. Reuter, *Anglo-American Relations*, 44-52. Higginson, his banker friend, did not agree with him. H. L. Higginson to HCL, Dec. 23, 1895, Lodge MSS.

29. H. C. Lodge to [A. J.] Balfour, Feb. 1, 1896, Lodge MSS. See also HCL to [M.] Frewen, Jan. 9 and 17, 1896, Lodge MSS.

30. M. Frewen to H. C. Lodge, Feb. 7, 1896, Lodge MSS.

31. A. J. Balfour to M. Frewen, Feb. 3, 1896, Lodge MSS.

32. H. C. Lodge to A. J. Balfour, Feb. 1, 1896, Lodge MSS.; TR, "The Monroe Doctrine," *Bachelor of Arts*, II (March, 1896), 447; A. W. Griswold, *Far Eastern Policy*, 37-38.

33. H. White to H. C. Lodge, March 5, 1898, Lodge MSS.

34. TR to William Archer, Aug. 31, 1899, TR MSS.

35. *Loc. cit.*; H. C. Lodge to Albert Matthews, Feb. 27, 1897, Lodge MSS.; B. A. Reuter, *Anglo-American Relations*, 52-55.

36. A. T. Mahan, "The Peace Conference and the Moral Aspects of War," *Lessons of the War with Spain and Other Articles*, 228-229; ATM, "The Hague

Conference and the Practical Aspect of War," *National Review*, XLIX (July, 1907), 699-700, 704 (reprinted in ATM, ed., *Some Neglected Aspects of War*, 82-84, 92-93); William D. Puleston, *The Life and Works of Alfred Thayer Mahan*, 319.

37. Henry James, *Richard Olney and His Public Service*, 149.

38. Dec. 30, 1895, *Congressional Record*, 54 Cong., 1 Sess., part 1, pp. 413-420; H. C. Lodge, *Speeches and Addresses, 1884-1909*, 197-241. See also HCL to A. B. Hart, Jan. 18, 1896, HCL to Rawle, Jan. 21, 1896, HCL to Robbins, Jan. 26, 1896, Lodge MSS.

39. H. C. Lodge to Curtis [Guild], Feb. 6, 1897, HCL to Dana, Feb. 6, 1897, HCL to William E. Dodge, Feb. 11, 1897, HCL to A. Matthews, Feb. 27, 1897, Lodge MSS.

40. H. C. Lodge to [Stephen (?)] O'Meara, Jan. 16 and 21, 1897, HCL to Curtis [Guild], Feb. 6, 1897, HCL to Dana, Feb. 6, 1897, Lodge MSS.

41. H. C. Lodge to [S. (?)] O'Meara, Jan. 16 and 21, 1897, Lodge MSS.

42. H. C. Lodge to Curtis [Guild], Feb. 6, 1897, Lodge MSS.

43. H. C. Lodge to W. E. Dodge, Feb. 11, 1897, HCL to A. Matthews, Feb. 27, 1897, Lodge MSS.

44. H. C. Lodge, MS. Diary, May 6 [1897], Lodge MSS.

45. TR, " The Issues of 1896," *Century*, LI (November, 1895), 72. See also Robert B. Mowat, *The Life of Lord Pauncefote*, 151-152.

46. *New York Sun*, Feb. 10, 1897, TR Scrapbooks. See also *New York Press*, Feb. 23, 1897, TR Scrapbooks.

47. TR to H. White, March 11, 1897, White MSS.

48. TR to Thomas St. John Gaffney, June 10, 1897, TR MSS.

49. J. Bryce to TR, Feb. 27, 1897, TR MSS.

50. R. B. Mowat, *Lord Pauncefote*, 151-152.

51. Sir Hiram S. Maxim to TR, Oct. 29, 1901, TR MSS.; Owen Wister, *The Pentecost of Calamity and a Straight Deal*, 201. For an example of the German point of view see Alfred H. K. L., Graf von Waldersee, *A Field Marshal's Memoirs*, 275.

52. J. Hay to H. C. Lodge, April 5, 1898, Lodge MSS. See also H. S. Maxim to TR, Oct. 29, 1901, TR MSS.; "Editorial," *Nation*, LXXVI (Feb. 5, 1903), 101.

53. O. Wister, *op. cit.*, 201.

54. TR to Arthur H. Lee, Nov. 25, 1898, TR MSS. See also H. C. Lodge to J. Hay, April 21, 1898, Lodge MSS.; TR to C. Spring Rice, Nov. 19, 1900, TR MSS.

55. H. C. Lodge to C. Spring Rice, Aug. 12, 1898, HCL to H. White, Aug. 12, 1898, Lodge MSS. Villard thinks Lodge changed his mind in the process of writing *The American Revolution*. O. G. Villard, *Prophets True and False*, 260-261.

56. A. T. Mahan, " The Peace Conference and the Moral Aspects of War," *Lessons of the War with Spain and Other Articles*, 230, 231, 232; J. Hay to [Joseph H.] Choate, Aug. 5, 1901, Hay MSS.

57. TR to J. Bryce, March 31, 1898, TR MSS.
58. TR to C. Spring Rice, Nov. 25, 1898, TR MSS. See also TR to A. H. Lee, Nov. 25, 1898, TR MSS.
59. TR to C. Spring Rice, Aug. 11, 1899, TR MSS. See also TR to H. White, Nov. 23, 1900, TR MSS.
60. TR to W. Archer, Aug. 31, 1899, TR MSS. See also TR to A. J. Sage, March 9, 1900, TR to C. Spring Rice, Aug. 11, 1899, TR MSS.
61. TR to A. J. Sage, March 9, 1900, Montague White to F. C. Selous, March 6, 1900, TR MSS.
62. TR to A. H. Lee, July 25, 1900, TR to F. C. Selous, Feb. 7, 1900, TR MSS.
63. TR to C. Spring Rice, Aug. 11, 1899, and November, 1900, TR MSS.
64. J. Hay to H. C. Lodge, May 25, 1898, Lodge MSS.
65. J. Hay to H. C. Lodge, April 5, 1898, Lodge MSS.
66. H. White to H. C. Lodge, June 3, 1898, Lodge MSS. See also C. Spring Rice to HCL, July 8, 1898, Lodge MSS.
67. TR to Elihu Root, Sept. 2, 1899, Root MSS.
68. J. Hay to H. C. Lodge, May 25, 1898, Lodge MSS. See also HCL, MS. Diary, Sept. 14 [1898], Lodge MSS.
69. H. White to H. C. Lodge, June 3, 1898, Lodge MSS. See also J. Bryce to TR, Sept. 12, 1898, TR MSS.
70. TR to A. H. Lee, Nov. 25, 1898, TR MSS.
71. TR to W. Archer, Aug. 31, 1899, TR MSS.
72. TR to A. R. Cowles, Dec. 17, 1899, Cowles MSS.
73. TR to A. H. Lee, Jan. 30, 1900, TR to E. Root, Jan. 29, 1900, TR MSS. See also TR to C. Spring Rice, Aug. 11, 1899, TR MSS.
74. TR to C. Spring Rice, March 2, 1900, TR MSS.
75. TR to H. C. Lodge, June 19, 1901, TR MSS. See also TR to A. T. Mahan, Feb. 14, 1900, TR MSS.; J. Hay to [H.] White, Sept. 24, 1899, Hay MSS.; ATM to HCL, Dec. 8, 1900, HCL to HW, Aug. 12, 1898, Lodge MSS.
76. H. C. Lodge to H. White, Jan. 27, 1900, White MSS.; Peter Vannlissinger to TR, Nov. 1, 1901, Bourke Cochran MSS. See also HW to HCL, Feb. 9, 1900, Lodge MSS.; M. White to F. C. Selous, March 6, 1900, TR MSS.
77. J. Hay to [J. W.] Foster, June 23, 1900, Hay MSS.
78. J. Hay to H. C. Lodge, May 25, 1898, Lodge MSS.; TR to HCL, Jan. 28, 1909, M. White to F. C. Selous, March 6, 1900, TR MSS.; JH to J. W. Griggs, Feb. 7, 1902, JH to Rev. Edward Everett Hale, Jan. 13, 1900, JH to Del [Hay], March 17, 1900, JH to HCL, Feb. 19, 1902, JH to James McMillan, June 3, 1900, JH to Stanford Newel, Dec. 3, 1900, JH to [H.] White, Sept. 24, 1899, Hay MSS.
79. J. Hay to J. H. Choate, Jan. 3, 1900, JH to J. W. Griggs, Feb. 7, 1902, JH to H. White, Sept. 24, 1899, Hay MSS.
80. J. Hay to [Henry] Adams, June 15, 1900, Hay MSS.; H. White to H. C. Lodge, Feb. 9, 1900, Lodge MSS.

81. J. Hay to Gen. [J. W.] Foster, June 23, 1900, J. Hay to J. McMillan, June 3, 1900, Hay MSS.

82. J. Hay to H. C. Lodge, Feb. 19, 1902, Hay MSS.

83. Memo supplied by Alfred Vagts to Tyler Dennett, in TD, *Hay*, 386. TR to H. White, March 30, 1896, White MSS.; TR to Baron Hermann Speck von Sternburg, Nov. 27, 1899, TR MSS.; TR to A. R. Cowles, Dec. 17, 1899, Cowles MSS.; H. C. Lodge to TR, Dec. 16, 1899, *Correspondence of TR and Henry Cabot Lodge, 1884-1917* (hereafter cited as *TR-HCL Correspondence*), I, 429; George W. Smalley, *Anglo-American Memories*, II, 347; Allan Nevins, *Henry White: Thirty Years of American Diplomacy*, 119.

84. TR to H. C. Lodge, Jan. 16, 1896, Lodge MSS.

85. *New York Sun*, Jan. 23, 1896, TR Scrapbooks.

86. C. Spring Rice to TR, Oct. 17, 1899, TR MSS.

87. TR to TR, Jr., April 9, 1901, TR MSS.; TR to C. Spring Rice, Dec. 2, 1899, in CSR, *Letters and Friendships of Sir Cecil Spring Rice*, Stephen Gwynn, ed., I, 305-306; TR to H. C. Lodge, Jan. 30, 1900, *TR-HCL Correspondence*, I, 444; H. White to HCL, Feb. 9, 1900, Lodge MSS.

88. TR to A. R. Cowles, Jan. 5, 1896, Cowles MSS. Lodge agreed. H. C. Lodge to TR, May 3, 1896, TR MSS. See also TR to HCL, May 2, 1896, Lodge MSS.

89. TR to H. White, March 30, 1896, White MSS.

90. H. C. Lodge to TR, May 3, 1896, TR MSS.; Benjamin Harrison to J. Hay, Jan. 22, 1900, Hay MSS.

91. TR to A. R. Cowles, May 3, 1896 (?), Cowles MSS.

92. J. Hay to [H.] Adams, June 15, 1900, Hay MSS.

93. H. C. Lodge to TR, Dec. 16, 1899, *TR-HCL Correspondence*, I, 429. Mahan, on the other hand, defended the British. A. T. Mahan to HCL, Dec. 8, 1900, Lodge MSS.

94. H. White to H. C. Lodge, Feb. 9, 1900, Lodge MSS.

95. TR to A. R. Cowles, Dec. 17, 1899, Cowles MSS.; TR to TR, Jr., April 9, 1901, TR MSS. Brooks Adams wrote in 1900: " Yes, England is sad—to me very sad. . . . I hope she may revive, but I admit my hope is faint. The current is flowing away from her. I do not apprehend any sudden or violent change, but I fancy England will grow gradually more and more sluggish, until, at length, after our day, she will drop out of the strenuous competition of the new world which is forming." B. Adams to H. C. Lodge, Oct. 14, 1900, Lodge MSS.

96. Roosevelt told Lodge he was " ashamed " of those Americans that " show the particularly mean attribute of jumping on England when she is down." TR to H. C. Lodge, Jan. 30, 1900, TR MSS.

97. H. C. Lodge to H. White, Jan. 27, 1900, White MSS. See also J. Hay to J. McMillan, July 3, 1900, Hay MSS.

98. H. C. Lodge to H. White, Jan. 27, 1900, White MSS.; HCL, MS. Diary, Feb. 4, 1900, Lodge MSS.; M. White to W. Bourke Cochran, Nov. 6, 1901, Cochran MSS.

99. TR to A. R. Cowles, Feb. 5, 1900, Cowles MSS.; TR to F. C. Selous, Feb. 7, 1900, TR MSS. See also TR to FCS, March 19, 1900, TR MSS.

100. TR to TR, Jr., April 9, 1901, TR MSS.

101. TR to H. C. Lodge, June 29, 1903, Lodge MSS.

102. TR to A. R. Cowles, Feb. 2, 1900, Cowles MSS.

103. TR to Albert Shaw, Oct. 9, 1901, TR MSS.

104. TR to Jacob Riis, April 16, 1901, TR MSS. See also " Editorial," *Nation*, LXXIII (Oct. 17, 1901), 291.

105. TR to H. Speck von Sternburg, Nov. 27, 1899, TR MSS.; " Editorial," *Nation*, LXXIII (Oct. 17, 1901), 291.

106. TR to A. R. Cowles, Dec. 17, 1899, Cowles MSS.; TR to H. White, March 30, 1896, White MSS. See also TR to TR, Jr., April 9, 1901, C. Spring Rice to TR, Oct. 17, 1899, TR to CSR, Dec. 2, 1899, and Jan. 27, 1900, TR MSS.; TR to ARC, Feb. 5, 1900, Cowles MSS.; HW to HCL, Feb. 9, 1900, Lodge MSS.; HCL to TR, Feb. 2, 1900, *TR-HCL Correspondence*, I, 446; TR to CSR, Dec. 2, 1899, CSR, *Letters*, I, 305-306.

107. S. Reeve Merritt to TR, June 2, 1902, TR MSS.

108. S. J. Paulus Kruger to TR, Feb. 12, 1902, TR MSS.; James Creelman to William Jennings Bryan, May 24, 1900, Bryan MSS.; H. White to J. Hay, Nov. 3, 1899, quoted in A. Nevins, *Henry White*, 219-220.

109. John St. Loe Strachey to TR, July 5, 1902, TR MSS.; Charles E. Norton to Frederic Harrison, Oct. 31, 1901, in CEN, *Letters*, Sara Norton and M. A. DeWolfe Howe, eds., II, 313-314.

110. Gerald Kitson to TR, March 18, 1902, TR MSS.; J. Hay to H. C. Lodge, Feb. 19, 1902, Hay MSS.

111. *Washington Post*, Feb. 3, 1904, TR Scrapbooks. See also TR to TR, Jr., April 9, 1901, TR MSS.

112. TR to TR, Jr., April 9, 1901, TR MSS.

113. C. E. Norton to F. Harrison, Oct. 31, 1901, in CEN, *Letters*, II, 313-314.

114. H. White to H. C. Lodge, Feb. 9, 1900, Lodge MSS.

115. TR to G. von L. Meyer, April 12, 1901, TR MSS.

116. J. Hay to [R.] Olney, Nov. 14, 1898, RO to JH, Nov. 15, 1898, Hay MSS.; H. White to H. C. Lodge, Dec. 14, 1900, Lodge MSS.; A. W. Griswold, *Far Eastern Policy*, 68-69.

117. J. Hay to Sir Julian [Pauncefote], Dec. 3, 1898, JH to [John T.] Morgan, Dec. 27, 1898, JH to J. H. Choate, Dec. 21, 1900, Hay MSS.; JH to H. White, Feb. 14, 1899, *Letters and Extracts from the Diary of John Hay*, Henry Adams, compiler, Clara S. Hay, ed., III, 141-143 (hereafter cited as J. Hay, *Letters and Diary*).

118. J. Hay to H. White, Jan. 13, 1899, Hay MSS.

119. H. C. Lodge, MS. Diary, Dec. 21, 1900, H. White to HCL, Feb. 9, 1900, Lodge MSS.; J. Hay to J. H. Choate, May 22, 1899, JH to [Cushman K.] Davis, Aug. 4, 1899, JH to J. St. Loe Strachey, June 13, 1899, JH to HW, Feb. 14, 1899, JHC to JH, Jan. 27, 1900, Hay MSS.; JH to HW, Feb. 21, 1899, JH, *Letters and Diary*, III, 145.

120. J. Hay to [J. H.] Choate, Jan. 15, 1900, Hay MSS.

121. J. H. Choate to J. Hay, Jan. 27 and Feb. 2 and 7, 1900, JH to JHC, Dec. 21, 1900, Hay MSS.; H. White to H. C. Lodge, Feb. 9, 1900, Lodge MSS.

122. J. Hay to J. H. Choate, Feb. 6, 1900, JH to [Whitelaw] Reid, Feb. 7, 1900, Hay MSS.; H. Adams to Elizabeth Cameron, Feb. 12, 1900, HA, *Letters, 1892-1918*, Worthington C. Ford, ed., 267. H. White to H. C. Lodge, Feb. 9, 1900, Lodge MSS. See also JH to JHC, Dec. 21, 1900, Hay MSS.

123. H. White to H. C. Lodge, Feb. 9, 1900, Lodge MSS. See also J. Hay to J. H. Choate, Dec. 21, 1900, Hay MSS.

124. TR, Memorandum after Conference with Nicholas Murray Butler, David Jayne Hill, F. W. Holls, and A. Shaw, Feb. 12, 1900, Yonkers, New York, TR MSS.; N. M. Butler, *Across the Busy Years*, I, 310.

125. H. Adams to E. Cameron, Feb. 12, 1900, HA, *Letters, 1892-1918*, 267.

126. TR, Memorandum after Yonkers Conference, Feb. 12, 1900, TR MSS.; Edward P. Mitchell, *Memories of an Editor*, 341-342. See also the *Nation*, LXX (Feb. 15, 1900), 120.

127. TR to A. T. Mahan, Feb. 14, 1900, TR MSS.

128. TR to Capt. William S. Cowles, Feb. 16, 1900, TR MSS.

129. TR to N. M. Butler, Feb. 15, 1900, TR to A. Shaw, Feb. 15, 1900, TR MSS.; NMB, *Across the Busy Years*, I, 310. See also A. Shaw, interview, 1920, TR to F. W. Holls, Feb. 15, 1900, TR MSS. The interviewing of people close to TR was done about 1920 by J. B. French, Hermann Hagedorn, and Marcus L. Hansen, who deposited their interview notes at Roosevelt House.

130. J. Hay to TR, Feb. 12, 1900, Hay MSS.

131. TR to J. Hay, Feb. 18, 1900, Hay MSS.; H. C. Lodge to H. White, Dec. 18, 1900, White MSS. See also TR to W. S. Cowles, Feb. 16 and 26, 1900, TR to A. Shaw, Feb. 15, 1900, AS to TR, Feb. 16, 1900, TR MSS.

132. TR to C. Spring Rice, March 2, 1900, TR MSS.

133. TR to J. Hay, Feb. 18, 1900, Hay MSS. See also TR to W. S. Cowles, Feb. 16 and 26, 1900, TR to A. Shaw, Feb. 15, 1900, TR to C. Spring Rice, March 2, 1900, TR MSS.

134. N. M. Butler to TR, Feb. 16, 1900, TR to W. S. Cowles, Feb. 26, 1900, TR MSS. See also A. Shaw to TR, Feb. 16, 1900, TR MSS.

135. H. C. Lodge, MS. Diary, Dec. 2 [1900], Lodge MSS.; HCL to H. White, Dec. 18, 1900, White MSS.

136. TR to H. C. Lodge, March 14, 1900, TR MSS. See also HCL to TR, March 10, 1900, TR MSS.

137. H. White to H. C. Lodge, March 24, 1900, Lodge MSS. So, too, was Ambassador Choate. J. H. Choate to J. Hay, Dec. 8, 1900, Hay MSS.

138. J. Hay to the President [William B. McKinley], Sept. 22, 1900, JH to J. H. Choate, Dec. 21, 1900, Hay MSS.

139. J. Hay to John J. McCook, April 22, 1900, J. Hay, *Letters and Diary*, III, 175-176; JH to J. H. Choate, Dec. 21, 1900, Hay MSS.; H. C. Lodge, MS. Diary, Dec. 21 [1900], Lodge MSS.; J. Hay to J. H. Choate, Dec. 21, 1900, quoted in T. Dennett, *Hay*, 414.

140. J. Hay to J. H. Choate, Aug. 5, 1901, Hay MSS.

141. H. C. Lodge, MS. Diary, Dec. 21 [1900], Lodge MSS.; J. Hay to Henry Watterson, Dec. 28, 1900, Hay MSS.; A. Shaw to Albert J. Beveridge, Dec. 15, 1900, Beveridge MSS.; C. K. Davis to the Editor, *Minneapolis Sunday Times*, Dec. 30, 1900, and JH to J. H. Choate, Dec. 21, 1900, quoted in T. Dennett, *Hay*, 414.

142. A. H. Lee to TR, Jan. 25, 1901, TR MSS. See also J. Hay to J. T. Morgan, Jan. 21, 1901, Hay MSS.; *Nation*, LXXII (March 14, 1901), 205.

143. H. C. Lodge, MS. Diary, Dec. 21 [1900], H. White to HCL, Dec. 14, 1900, Lodge MSS.; J. Hay to J. H. Choate, Dec. 21, 1900, Hay MSS.

144. H. C. Lodge, MS. Diary, Nov. 24 and Dec. 21 [1900], Lodge MSS.; J. Hay to H. Adams, Aug. 5, 1899, JH to J. H. Choate, Dec. 21, 1900, JHC to JH, Dec. 8, 1900, Hay MSS.; JHC to JH, Dec. 15, 1900, Choate MSS.; HCL to H. White, Dec. 18, 1900, White MSS.

145. H. C. Lodge to G. H. Lyman, Dec. 13, 1900, HCL to H. White, Dec. 20, 1900, Lodge MSS.

146. H. C. Lodge, MS. Diary, Nov. 24, and Dec. 2 and 21 [1900], Lodge MSS.; J. Hay to J. H. Choate, Dec. 21, 1900, Hay MSS.

147. J. Hay to [H.] White, Dec. 23, 1900, JH to H. Watterson, Dec. 28, 1900, Hay MSS.

148. H. C. Lodge, MS. Diary, Dec. 2 [1900] and March 27 [1901], Lodge MSS.; J. Hay to J. H. Choate, Dec. 21, 1900, Hay MSS.; HCL to H. White, Dec. 24, 1900, White MSS. See also JHC to JH, Feb. 6, 1901, Choate MSS.

149. J. Hay to J. H. Choate, Dec. 21, 1900, Hay MSS. Choate agreed. JHC to JH, Dec. 15, 1900, and Jan. 23 and Feb. 6, 1901, Choate MSS.

150. H. C. Lodge to H. White, Dec. 18, 1900, White MSS.; HCL to HW, Dec. 20, 1900, HCL to J. Hay, March 28 and April 2, 1901, JH to HCL, March 30, 1901, HCL, MS. Diary, Dec. 21, 1900, and March 14, 1901, Lodge MSS. See also HCL to HW, Dec. 24, 1900, White MSS.; HCL to TR, Feb. 14, 1904, TR MSS.

151. J. Hay to Alvey A. Adee, Feb. 21, 1901, JH to J. H. Choate, Jan. 11, 21, 22, and 25, 1901, JHC to JH, Feb. 1 and 29, 1901, JH to H. C. Lodge, Feb. 15, 1901, JH to J. T. Morgan, Jan. 21, 1901, Hay MSS.; JHC to JH, Jan. 23 and Feb. [?] 6 and 27, 1901, Choate MSS.; HCL, MS. Diary, March 27 [1901], H. White to HCL, Jan. 25, 1901, Lodge MSS.

152. H. C. Lodge, MS. Diary, March 12 [1901], H. White to HCL, March 13, 1901, Lodge MSS.; J. H. Choate to J. Hay, March 9, 1901, Choate MSS.; JH to JHC, March 13, 1901, Hay MSS.

153. H. White to H. C. Lodge, Jan. 25 and March 13, 1901, Lodge MSS.

154. A. H. Lee to TR, Jan. 25, 1901, TR MSS. See also J. Hay to J. H. Choate, Jan. 11, 1901, Hay MSS.

155. J. Hay to [J. T.] Morgan, March 13, 1901, JH to J. St. Loe Strachey, Jan. 30, 1901, Hay MSS.

156. J. Hay to H. White, Feb. 14, 1899, J. H. Choate to JH, March 13, 1901, Hay MSS.; HW to H. C. Lodge, March 13, 1901, Lodge MSS.

157. J. Hay to Lord Pauncefote, March 13, 1901, N. B. Scott to JH, March 28, 1901, JH to J. T. Morgan, April 2, 1901, H. D. Money to JH, April 3, 1901, Hay MSS.; J. H. Choate to JH, March 16 and 23, 1901, Choate MSS.

158. A. A. Adee to J. Hay, April 8, 1901, J. Hay to J. H. Choate, April 27, 1901, Hay MSS.; H. White to H. C. Lodge, May 31, 1901, HCL to George F. Hoar, June 7, 1901, Lodge MSS.

159. H. C. Lodge, MS. Diary, Sept. 30 and Oct. 1 [1901], H. White to HCL, Sept. 23, 1901, Lodge MSS.; J. Hay to [A. A.] Adee, Aug. 31 and Sept. 20, 1901, J. H. Choate to JH, July 24, Aug. 3, 16, and 20, Sept. 3, 13, 20, 25, and 27, and Oct. 2, 1901, JH to JHC, Aug. 5 and 26, 1901, George B. Cortelyou to JH, Aug. 28, 1901, D. J. Hill to JH, Sept. 27, 1901, JH to DJH, Sept. 28, 1901, JH to J. T. Morgan, Aug. 22, 1901, JH to the President [W. B. McKinley], Aug. 26, 1901, JH to Lord J. Pauncefote, Sept. 2, 1901, JP to JH, Aug. [?] 1901, Draft of Article IV, Hay-Pauncefote Treaty, No. 2 [August, 1901], Hay MSS.; JH to TR, Oct. 4, 1901, TR MSS.

160. J. H. Choate to J. Hay, July 24, Aug. 16, and Oct. 2, 1901, Hay MSS.; William B. Allison to James Wilson, Sept. 25, 1901, Allison MSS.

161. J. Hay to [A. A.] Adee, Aug. 31, 1901, J. H. Choate to JH, July 24, Aug. 3, 16, and 20, Sept. 20, 25, and 27, and Oct. 2, 1901, D. J. Hill to JH, Sept. 27, 1901, Lord J. Pauncefote to JH, Aug. [?], 1901, JH to JHC, Aug. 26 and Sept. 2, 1901, JH to JP, Sept. 2, 1901, JH to H. White, June 18, 1901, Hay MSS.

162. H. White to TR, Dec. 19, 1900, TR MSS.

163. H. C. Lodge to TR, March 30, 1901, TR MSS.

164. H. C. Lodge, MS. Diary, Sept. 28, 29, and 30 and Oct. 1 and 4 [1901], Lodge MSS.; J. Hay to TR, Oct. 4, 1901, TR MSS.; J. H. Choate to JH, July 24 and Oct. 2, 1901, Hay MSS.; Charles G. Washburn, "Memoir of Henry Cabot Lodge," *Massachusetts Historical Society Proceedings*, LVIII (April, 1925), 334, 335-337. See also JH to H. White, June 18, 1901, Hay MSS.

165. J. Hay to H. Adams, Oct. 13, 1901, JH, *Letters and Diary*, III, 238-239.

166. H. C. Lodge, MS. Diary, Sept. 28, 29, 30, and 31 and Oct. 1 [1901], Lodge MSS.; J. Hay to [J. H.] Choate, Aug. 5, 1901, JH to J. T. Morgan, Aug. 22, 1901, JHC to JH, Oct. 2, 1901, Hay MSS.; JH to H. Adams, Oct. 13, 1901, JH, *Letters and Diary*, III, 238-239.

167. J. H. Choate to J. Hay, Oct. 2, 1901, Hay MSS.

168. J. Hay to H. White, Oct. 14, 1901, JH, *Letters and Diary*, III, 240-241.

169. *Loc. cit.*

170. TR to H. C. Lodge, March 27, 1901, TR MSS.

171. TR to A. H. Lee, March 18, 1901, TR to H. C. Lodge, March 27, 1901, TR MSS.; HCL, MS. Diary, March 14 [1901], Lodge MSS.

172. TR to A. H. Lee, March 18, 1901, TR MSS.

173. J. Hay to [J. H.] Choate, Oct. 1, 1901, JH to Shelby M. Cullom, Dec. 12, 1901, Hay MSS.; JH to TR, Oct. 2 and 4, 1901, TR MSS.; JH to H. White, Oct. 1 and 14, 1901, JH, *Letters and Diary*, III, 233-235, 240-241. As the years passed Roosevelt forgot the part that Hay, Choate, and White had played and persuaded himself that he had got the satisfactory terms and pushed the treaty

through whereas it was actually practically completed when he became President. TR to H. C. Lodge, Jan. 28, 1909, Lodge MSS.

174. For an earlier treatment of this question see Thomas A. Bailey, "Theodore Roosevelt and the Alaska Boundary Settlement," *Canadian Historical Review*, xviii (June, 1937), 123-130. Hay claimed credit in letters that appeared in 1908 for a somewhat more dominant rôle than he played. Roosevelt, on the other hand, understates Hay's part in an account he wrote under the spur of irritation over Hay's version. TR to H. C. Lodge, Jan. 28, 1909. For a brief later account by Roosevelt see TR to John W. Foster, May 26 and June 5, 1911, TR MSS. Lodge wrote a long memorandum that overemphasizes Lodge's rôle, which was none the less great. Charles G. Washburn, "Memoir of Henry Cabot Lodge," *Massachusetts Historical Society Proceedings*, lviii (April, 1925), 338-342. His series of long contemporaneous letters written from London to his daughter Constance Lodge Gardner (July 28 and 30, Sept. 2, 3, 19, and 25, and Oct. 2, 5, and 11, 1903) are a rich source of information. The answer of a Canadian to Lodge's 1925 account points out supposed errors of Lodge and is useful. James White, "Henry Cabot Lodge and the Alaska Boundary Award," *Canadian Historical Review*, vi (December, 1925), 332-347.

175. H. C. Lodge to A. J. Balfour, Feb. 1, 1896, HCL to Mendenhall, Feb. 24, 1896, Lodge MSS.

176. J. Hay to [J. H.] Choate, Aug. 18, 1899, Hay MSS.; TR to H. C. Lodge, Jan. 28, 1909, Lodge MSS.; C. G. Washburn, "Memoir," *loc. cit.*, 339; T. Dennett, *Hay*, 350.

177. H. C. Lodge to Mendenhall, Feb. 24, 1896, HCL to H. White, Oct. 8, 1900, Lodge MSS.; C. G. Washburn, "Memoir," *loc. cit.*, 339.

178. A. H. Lee to TR, April 2, 1901, TR MSS.

179. J. St. Loe Strachey to TR, Aug. 18, 1902, TR MSS. See also John Buchan, *Lord Minto*, 173.

180. TR to A. H. Lee, April 24, 1901, TR MSS.

181. H. C. Lodge to Mendenhall, Feb. 24, 1896, Lodge MSS.; J. H. Choate to J. Hay, Oct. 2, 1901, Hay MSS.

182. *Loc. cit.*; H. C. Lodge to H. White, Oct. 8, 1900, Lodge MSS.

183. TR to N. M. Butler, June 3, 1901, TR MSS.; J. Hay to H. White, Jan. 3, Feb. 14, and May 16 and 29, 1899, JH to J. H. Choate, April 28, May 22, June 15, and Aug. 18, 1899, JHC to JH, May 12, 1899, JH to the President [W. B. McKinley], May 13, 1899, JH to H. D. Money, Dec. 16, 1902, JH to Lord Pauncefote, Nov. 29 [1899 (?)], JH to G. W. Smalley, June 1, 1899, JH to J. St. Loe Strachey, June 13, 1899, Lord Lansdowne to A. S. Raikes, Aug. 18, 1902, Hay MSS.; JHC to JH, July 19, 1902, Choate MSS.; JH to H. C. Lodge, Oct. 9, 1902, Lodge MSS.; TR to C. Spring Rice, Aug. 11, 1899, TR MSS.; JH to HW, Feb. 21, 1899, JH, *Letters and Diary*, iii, 145; T. Dennett, *Hay*, 230, 350; Oscar D. Skelton, *The Day of Sir Wilfred Laurier: A Chronicle of Our Own Time*, 211.

184. J. H. Choate to J. Hay, July 5 and 19, 1902, Choate MSS. See also H.

C. Lodge, MS. Diary, March 22 [1902], Lodge MSS.; TR to E. Root, Aug. 8, 1903, TR MSS.; T. Dennett, *Hay*, 350-351.

185. H. C. Lodge, MS. Diary, March 8 and 22 [1902], TR to HCL, Jan. 28, 1909, Lodge MSS.

186. H. C. Lodge, MS. Diary, March 8 [1902], Lodge MSS. Cf. T. Dennett, *Hay*, 350 ff. See also M. D. DeW. Howe, *Rhodes*, 121; O. D. Skelton, *Life and Letters of Laurier*, II, 146.

187. H. C. Lodge, MS. Diary, March 23 [1902], Lodge MSS.

188. J. Hay to TR, March 24, 1902, TR MSS.

189. H. C. Lodge, MS. Diary, March 24 [1902], Lodge MSS.

190. *Loc. cit.*

191. G. B. Cortelyou, TR's secretary, to E. Root, March 27, 1902, Root MSS.; Philip C. Jessup, *Elihu Root*, I, 390-392; Lord Newton [Thomas Wadehouse Legh, Baron], *Lord Lansdowne*, 263-264; C. G. Washburn, "Memoir of Henry Cabot Lodge," *Massachusetts Historical Society Proceedings*, LVIII (April, 1925), 339.

192. Lord Newton, *Lansdowne*, 263. See also H. Adams to E. Cameron, March 30, 1902, HA, *Letters, 1892-1918*, 382; TR to E. Root, Aug. 8, 1903, TR MSS.; M. A. DeW. Howe, *Rhodes*, 121.

193. See, e. g., TR to N. M. Butler, June 3, 1901, TR to J. St. Loe Strachey, July 18, 1902, TR MSS.; J. H. Choate to J. Hay, July 19, 1902, Lord Lansdowne to A. S. Raikes, Aug. 18, 1902, Hay MSS.; Andrew Carnegie to H. C. Lodge, Aug. 15, 1903, TR to HCL, Jan. 28, 1909, H. White to HCL, May 10, 1902, Lodge MSS.; A. Nevins, *Henry White*, 193; Lord Newton, *Lansdowne*, 263-264.

194. T. Dennett, *Hay*, 351-352; A. Nevins, *Henry White*, 192-193; J. Hay to TR, July 7, 1902, TR MSS. See also H. White to H. C. Lodge, June 27, 1902, Lodge MSS.

195. J. H. Choate to J. Hay, July 5, 1902, State Department Archives; JHC to JH, July 19, 1902, Choate MSS.; JH to [C. K.] Davis, Aug. 4, 1899, Hay MSS.; T. Dennett, *Hay*, 351-352. See also TR to H. C. Lodge, Jan. 28, 1909, Lodge MSS.

196. J. H. Choate to J. Hay, July 5 and 19, 1902, Choate MSS.

197. TR to J. Hay, July 10, 1902, TR to J. St. Loe Strachey, July 18, 1902, TR MSS.; C. G. Washburn, "Memoir," *loc. cit.*, 339. See also TR to H. C. Lodge, Jan. 28, 1909, Lodge MSS.

198. J. Hay to TR, July 14, 1902, TR MSS.; JH to H. D. Money, Dec. 16, 1902, Hay MSS.; T. Dennett, *Hay*, 353-354; P. Jessup, *Root*, I, 389-390.

199. TR to J. Hay, July 16, 1902, and Sept. 21, 1903, TR to E. Root, Aug. 8, 1903, TR to H. White, Sept. 26, 1903, TR MSS. See also TR to ER, Aug. 20, 1903, P. Jessup, *Root*, I, 397.

200. *Foreign Relations*, 1903, 488-493; John Charlton to J. Hay, Feb. 9, 1903, Hay MSS.; T. Dennett, *Hay*, 353-354; O. D. Skelton, *Life and Letters of Laurier*, II, 143-144.

201. H. White to H. C. Lodge, Jan. 28, 1903, Lodge MSS.

202. J. Hay to H. D. Money, Dec. 16, 1902, HDM to JH, Dec. 17, 1902, Hay MSS. See also Frederick W. Seward to JH, Feb. 2, 1903, Hay MSS.

203. T. Dennett, *Hay*, 226.

204. TR to F. W. Holls, Feb. 3, 1903, TR to David Starr Jordan, Feb. 4, 1903, FWH to TR, Feb. 5, 1903, TR MSS. See also TR to the Secretary of State [J. Hay], Jan. 14, 1903, TR MSS.; TR to H. C. Lodge, Jan. 28, 1909, Lodge MSS.; T. Dennett, *Hay*, 226.

205. J. Hay to TR, Feb. 11, 1903, TR MSS.

206. J. Hay to H. D. Money, Dec. 16, 1902, HDM to JH, Dec. 17, 1902, Hay MSS.; JH to H. C. Lodge, Feb. 11 [1903], HCL to JH, undated memorandum [*ca*. February, 1903], Lodge MSS.; C. G. Washburn, "Memoir," *loc. cit.*, 340.

207. H. White to H. C. Lodge, Feb. 24 and 28, 1903, Lodge MSS.

208. TR, Memorandum, Feb. 11, 1903, J. Hay to H. C. Lodge, Feb. 11 [1903], H. White to HCL, Feb. 24 and 28, 1903, HCL to JH, Memorandum, undated, Lodge MSS.; John C. Spooner to Thomas Burke, March 24, 1903, JCS to James J. Hill, March 26, 1903, Spooner MSS.; C. G. Washburn, *op. cit.*, 340.

209. See, e. g., O. D. Skelton, *Life and Letters of Laurier*, ii, 143-144.

210. H. C. Lodge to TR, Feb. 17, 1903, *TR-HCL Correspondence*, ii, 2.

211. H. Adams to E. Cameron, Feb. 15, 1903, H. Adams, *Letters, 1892-1918*, 399.

212. A. H. Lee to TR, Nov. 22, 1903, TR to AHL, Dec. 7, 1903, H. C. Lodge to TR, Feb. 14, 1909, TR MSS.; J. Hay to J. H. Choate, April 3, 1903, Choate MSS.; TR to HCL, Jan. 28, 1909, Lodge MSS.; H. White to JH, April 1, 1903, White MSS.; J. Buchan, *Lord Minto*, 173; O. D. Skelton, *Life and Letters of Laurier*, ii, 145; ODS, *The Day of Sir Wilfred Laurier*, 214; M. A. DeW. Howe, *Rhodes*, 121.

213. H. White to "Dear Chief" [J. Hay], April 1, 1903, White MSS. See also A. Maurice Low to JH, Aug. 9, 1903, Hay MSS.

214. A. H. Lee to TR, Nov. 22, 1903, TR MSS.

215. Sir Wilfred Laurier to J. Hay, Feb. 24, 1903, Hay MSS.

216. Sir Michael Herbert to Lord Lansdowne (Henry C. K. Petty-Fitzmaurice, Marquess), Feb. 21, 1903, Lord Newton, *Lansdowne*, 262-263.

217. *Loc. cit.*; O. D. Skelton, *Life and Letters of Laurier*, ii, 145.

218. Sir M. Herbert to Lord Lansdowne, Feb. 21, 1903, in Lord Newton, *Lansdowne*, 262-263.

219. Lord Minto (Gilbert J. Elliot, Earl), to Arthur Elliot, March 1, 1903, J. Buchan, *Lord Minto*, 171-172.

220. C. G. Washburn, "Memoir of Henry Cabot Lodge," *Massachusetts Historical Society Proceedings*, lviii (April, 1925), 340.

221. J. Hay to J. H. Choate, Feb. 17, 1903, Choate MSS.; Sir M. Herbert to Lord Lansdowne, Feb. 21, 1903, in Lord Newton, *Lansdowne*, 262-263.

222. J. Hay to Sir Wilfred [Laurier], March 27, 1903, Hay MSS.

223. J. Hay to H. White, April 10, 1903, White MSS.; JH to J. H. Choate, April 3, 1903, Choate MSS.

224. TR to H. C. Lodge, Aug. 6, 1903, HCL to TR, July 5, 1903, TR MSS.; TR to J. W. Foster, Aug. 5, 1903, Foster MSS.; J. Hay to J. H. Choate, April 3 and May 5, 1903, Choate MSS.; JHC to JH, April 25 and Aug. 14, 1903, Hay MSS.; H. White to HCL, May 30, 1903, HCL to HW, June 10, 1903, HCL to TR, June 23, 1903, Lodge MSS.; *Proceedings of the Alaska Boundary Tribunal* (*U. S. Senate Docs.*, 58 Cong., 2 Sess., doc. no. 162), vol. v, part 3, p. 63; JH to TR, July 2 [1903 (?)], T. Dennett, *Hay*, 359-360.

225. H. C. Lodge to TR, June 23, 1903, TR MSS.; HCL, London, to C. L. Gardner, July 28, 1905, Lodge MSS.

226. TR to H. C. Lodge, June 29, 1903, and Jan. 28, 1909, TR MSS.

227. TR to J. Hay, June 29, 1903, TR MSS.

228. H. C. Lodge to TR, July 1 and 5, 1903, TR MSS.

229. J. Hay to TR, July 2 [1903 (?)], T. Dennett, *Hay*, 359-360. See also JH to TR, Aug. 19, 1903, Hay MSS.

230. H. C. Lodge to TR, July 5, 1903, TR MSS.

231. TR to H. C. Lodge, July 8, 1903, Lodge MSS.

232. H. C. Lodge to TR, July 10, 1903, Lodge MSS.

233. J. Hay to [Clara Hay], July 14, 1903, Hay MSS.

234. TR to H. C. Lodge, July 16, 1903, HCL to C. L. Gardner, July 28, 1903, Lodge MSS.

235. TR to E. Root, H. C. Lodge, and George Turner, March 17, 1903, TR MSS.; ER to TR, March 28, 1903, in P. Jessup, *Root*, i, 395.

236. J. Hay to H. White, April 10, 1903, White MSS.

237. H. White to [J. Hay], May 13, 1903, White MSS.

238. Oliver Wendell Holmes to TR, July 14, 1903, TR MSS.

239. TR to O. W. Holmes, July 25, 1903, OWH to TR, Oct. 11, 1903, TR MSS.; TR to J. Hay, July 29, 1903, Hay MSS.; Lord Newton, *Lansdowne*, 263; Catherine D. Bowen, *Yankee from Olympus*, 363-364; M. A. DeW. Howe, *Rhodes*, 121. See also TR to H. C. Lodge, Jan. 28, 1909, Lodge MSS.

240. H. C. Lodge to TR, July 25, 1903, HCL to C. L. Gardner, July 28 and Sept. 2, 1903, Joseph Chamberlain to HCL, July 28, 1903, HCL to Lord Lansdowne, Aug. 1, 1903, and undated [ca. August, 1903], Lansdowne to HCL, Aug. 3, 1903, HCL to J. Hay, Sept. 30, 1903, Lodge MSS.

241. H. C. Lodge to TR, July 30 (?) and Aug. 20, 1903, HCL to C. L. Gardner, July 28, 1903, Lodge MSS.; HCL to TR, Aug. 30, 1903, TR MSS.

242. TR to H. C. Lodge, Aug. 16, 1903, TR to H. White, Sept. 26, 1903, TR MSS.; TR to HCL, Sept. 15, 1903, Lodge MSS.

243. H. C. Lodge to C. L. Gardner, Sept. 2, 3, 19, and 25 and Oct. 1, 5, and 11, 1903; HCL to TR, Sept. 5, 1903, HCL to J. Hay, Sept. 30, 1903, Lodge MSS.; HCL to TR, Sept. 29 and Oct. 12, 1903, TR to TR, Jr., Oct. 20, 1903, H. White to TR, Sept. 19, 1903, TR MSS.; JH to TR, Oct. 2, 1903, JH to J. H. Choate, Oct. 16, 1903, JH to Mrs. John Hay, Oct. 18, 19, and 20, 1903, Hay MSS.; JHC to JH, Oct. 15, 1903, HW to [JH], Oct. 20, 1903, White MSS.; *Washington Post*, Oct. 11, 1903, TR Scrapbooks; JHC to Mabel Choate, Oct. 19, 1903, in Edward S. Martin, *The Life of Joseph Hodges Choate*, ii, 235; C. G.

Washburn, "Memoir on Henry Cabot Lodge," *Massachusetts Historical Society Proceedings,* LVIII (April, 1925), 341-342.

244. J. Hay to TR, Sept. 25 [1903 (?)], in T. Dennett, *Hay,* 361; JH to TR, Sept. 15, 1903, Hay MSS.; H. White to JH, Oct. 20, 1903, White MSS.; A. Nevins, *Henry White,* 198. See also TR to H. C. Lodge, Jan. 28, 1909, Lodge MSS.

245. J. H. Choate to J. Hay, Oct. 20, 1903, Choate MSS.; JHC to JH, Oct. 21, 1903, Hay MSS.; M. A. DeW. Howe, *Rhodes,* 121.

246. TR to J. Hay, Sept. 15, 1903, TR to H. C. Lodge, Oct. 5, 1903, TR MSS.; HCL to TR, Sept. 24, 1903, Lodge MSS.; J. H. Choate to JH, Oct. 21, 1903, Hay MSS.; JHC to JH, Oct. 15, 1903, H. White to JH, Oct. 20, 1903, White MSS.; HW to JH, Sept. 19, 1903, in A. Nevins, *Henry White,* 197; C. G. Washburn, "Memoir," *loc. cit.,* 341-342; Lord Newton, *Lansdowne,* 265.

247. J. Hay to Mrs. J. Hay, Oct. 21, 1903, Hay MSS.; A. H. Lee to TR, Nov. 22, 1903, TR MSS. Alverstone always claimed his decision was strictly judicial. E. Root to Lord Alverstone [Richard Everard Webster, Viscount], Nov. 20, 1903, in P. Jessup, *Root,* I, 401.

248. O. W. Holmes to TR, Oct. 21, 1903, TR MSS.

249. TR to A. H. Lee, Dec. 7, 1903, TR MSS.

250. J. Hay to Mrs. J. Hay, Oct. 21, 1903, Hay MSS.; *Washington Star,* Oct. 21, 1903, TR Scrapbooks; O. D. Skelton, *The Day of Sir Wilfred Laurier,* 211. See also H. Adams to E. Cameron, Feb. 15, 1903, HA, *Letters, 1892-1918,* 399; T. Dennett, *Hay,* 359-360, 362; P. Jessup, *Root,* I, 396; A. Nevins, *Henry White,* 202; William R. Thayer, *Volleys from a Non-Combatant,* 112; Lord Newton, *Lansdowne,* 263-264.

251. J. Hay to TR, Sept. 25, 1903, TR MSS.; Nr. 5151, Der Gesandte in ausserordentlicher Mission in Washington Freiherr Speck von Sternburg an das Auswärtige Amt, den 19. Februar 1903, *Grosse Politik,* XVII, 292.

252. Roosevelt briefly described the conversation in a personal instruction to Lodge as a member of the Tribunal and suggested that he get Choate to tell him what was said. TR to HCL, July 16, 1903, in *TR-HCL Correspondence,* II, 39. Roosevelt also refers to the conversation in TR to J. Hay, June 29, 1903, TR MSS. Hay mentions it in JH to H. White, June 22, 1903, Hay MSS. Choate was home from London for a few days early in June for his son's wedding. On June 3 he had been in Washington in conference with the State Department, but Roosevelt was in Illinois. Roosevelt returned June 6, but Choate was in Albany that day at his son's wedding and spent the night in Stockbridge, Massachusetts. When Choate returned to Washington at 3:00 Sunday, June 7, Roosevelt, Root, and Hay were all in town. Choate stayed through Monday, June 8, and on that day Root arrived at the White House at 10:00 and stayed for luncheon. Choate sailed for England on Tuesday, June 9. Hence the portico conversation probably took place Monday, June 8. TR Appointment Book, TR MSS.; *New York Tribune,* June 8, 9, and 10, 1903; *Washington Post,* June 4, 5, 6, 7, and 8, 1903.

253. J. Hay to H. White, April 10, 1903, White MSS.; J. Hay to TR, Sept. 25, 1903, in T. Dennett, *Hay*, 361.
254. O. W. Holmes to TR, Oct. 21, 1903, TR MSS.
255. *Loc. cit.* See also H. C. Lodge to TR, Feb. 14, 1909, TR MSS.
256. Sir M. Herbert to Lord Lansdowne, Feb. 21, 1903, in Lord Newton, *Lansdowne*, 262-263.
257. J. St. Loe Strachey to TR, Aug. 18, 1902, TR MSS.
258. J. Hay to Mrs. Hay, Oct. 21, 1903, Hay MSS.; O. D. Skelton, *The Day of Sir Wilfred Laurier*, 216. See also H. Adams to E. Cameron, Feb. 15, 1903, HA, *Letters, 1892-1918*, 399; T. Dennett, *Hay*, 359-360, 362; P. Jessup, *Root*, I, 396; A. Nevins, *Henry White*, 202; W. R. Thayer, *Volleys from a Non-Combatant*, 112; Lord Newton, *Lansdowne*, 265.
259. H. C. Lodge to C. L. Gardner, Oct. 11, 1903, Lodge MSS.; O. W. Holmes to TR, Oct. 21, 1903, John Morley to TR, Jan. 2, 1904, TR to C. Spring Rice, Nov. 1, 1905, TR MSS.; George P. Gooch, *Before the War: Studies in Diplomacy*, I, 27-28. Because of this conviction that the settlement of this issue removed the last obstacle to complete trust between England and America Roosevelt was hereafter willing to agree with Britain, but with Britain alone, to arbitrate any dispute that arose. TR to C. Spring Rice, Nov. 1, 1905; TR to HCL, June 12, 1911, TR to A. H. Lee, June 27, 1911, TR to James Bryce, Nov. 19, 1918, TR MSS.
260. H. White to H. C. Lodge, Feb. 28, 1903, HCL to C. L. Gardner, Oct. 5, 1903, Lodge MSS.; C. G. Washburn, "Memoir," *loc. cit.*, 341; G. W. Smalley, *Anglo-American Memories*, II, 347-348.
261. H. C. Lodge to C. L. Gardner, Oct. 5, 1903, Lodge MSS.
262. H. White to TR, Nov. 17, 1903, TR MSS.
263. E. Root to J. H. Choate, Dec. 22, 1906, Root MSS.
264. J. Hay, MS. Diary, Jan. 30, 1905, Hay MSS.; W. Reid to TR, Nov. 27, 1906, TR MSS.
265. TR to H. C. Lodge, June 5, 1905, HCL to TR, June 10, 1905, TR MSS. See also Nr. 6288, Freiherr Speck von Sternburg an den Grafen von Bülow, den 10. Februar 1905, *Grosse Politik*, XIX-2, 572-573.
266. H. C. Lodge to TR, June 29, 1905, TR MSS.
267. TR to W. Reid, June 30, 1905, TR MSS.
268. TR to W. Reid, June 27, 1906, WR to TR, July 17 and Aug. 16, 1906, H. C. Lodge to TR, June 10, 1905, TR MSS.
269. TR to W. Reid, Aug. 27, 1906, TR MSS.
270. A. H. Lee to TR, Oct. 14, 1906, TR to AHL, Oct. 15 and Nov. 5, 1906, W. Reid to TR, Oct. 24, 1906, TR to WR, Nov. 6, 1906, TR MSS.; TR to H. C. Lodge, Nov. 27, 1906, Lodge MSS.
271. Earl [Albert H. G.] Grey to TR, Dec. 4, 1906, A. H. Lee to TR, Nov. 6 and 28, 1906, TR to W. Reid, Nov. 6, 1906, WR to TR, Nov. 27, 1906, TR MSS.
272. A. H. Lee to TR, Dec. 24, 1906, TR to AHL, Jan. 5, 1907, TR MSS.; H. White to H. C. Lodge, Dec. 24, 1906, Lodge MSS.; *New York World*, Feb. 1, 1907, *Washington Post*, Feb. 26, 1907, TR Scrapbooks.

273. Edith Kermit Roosevelt to C. Spring Rice, June 25, 1907, TR MSS.
274. TR to A. H. Lee, Jan. 5, 1907, TR MSS.
275. TR to H. White, Dec. 27, 1904, TR MSS.
276. H. White to H. C. Lodge, Jan. 11, 1905, Lodge MSS.; Nr. 6288, Freiherr
Speck von Sternburg an den Grafen von Bülow, den 10. Februar 1905, *Grosse
Politik,* xix-2, 572-573.
277. TR to H. White, Dec. 27, 1904, HW to TR, Jan. 7, 13, and 25, 1905,
TR to J. Hay, Jan. 13, 1905, TR MSS.
278. J. Hay, MS. Diary, Jan. 29 and 30 and Feb. 2, 3, and 4, 1905, Hay MSS.;
Nr. 6288, Freiherr Speck von Sternburg an den Grafen von Bülow, den 10.
Februar 1905, *Grosse Politik,* xix-2, 572, 573.
279. A. H. Lee to TR, Oct. 14 and Nov. 6, 1906, TR to AHL, Oct. 15, 1906,
TR MSS.
280. A. H. Lee to TR, Nov. 28, 1906, Sir Edward Grey to TR, Dec. 4, 1906,
TR MSS.
281. A. H. Lee to TR, Dec. 24, 1906, TR MSS.
282. TR to A. H. Lee, Jan. 5, 1907, TR MSS.
283. J. H. Choate to Mrs. Choate, Sept. 27, 1901, in E. S. Martin, *Choate,*
II, 204.
284. TR to J. H. Choate, Oct. 9, 1901, TR MSS.
285. Edward VII to TR, Feb. 20, 1905, in S. Lee, *Edward VII,* II, 429-430; Sir
George Arthur, *A Septuagenarian's Scrap Book,* 54-55; GA, *Not Worth Reading,*
167.
286. TR to M. Durand, undated in S. Lee, *Edward VII,* II, 432.
287. J. Hay, MS. Diary, March 3, 1905, Hay MSS.
288. TR to Edward VII, March 9, 1905, S. Lee, *Edward VII,* II, 432. See
also TR to H. C. Lodge, May 24, 1905, Lodge MSS.
289. Edward VII to TR, March 23, 1905, in S. Lee, *Edward VII,* II, 433.
290. Sir Donald M. Wallace to Lord Knollys, Aug. 9, in *ibid.,* 433-434.
291. J. Hay, MS. Diary, June 4, 1905, Hay MSS.; TR to H. C. Lodge, May
24, 1905, Lodge MSS.; W. Reid to TR, June 23, 1905, Nov. 6, 1906, and Jan.
12, 1907, TR MSS.; S. Lee, *Edward VII,* II, 434, 435, 440; Mark A. DeWolfe
Howe, *George von Lengerke Meyer: His Life and Public Services,* 350.
292. TR to Edward VII, March 9, 1905, S. Lee, *Edward VII,* II, 432-433.
293. H. C. Lodge, MS. Diary, March 29 [1905], Lodge MSS.
294. TR to H. C. Lodge, May 24, 1905, HCL to TR, May 8, 1905, H. White
to HCL, July 22 [1905], Lodge MSS.
295. J. Hay, MS. Diary, May 25 and June 4 and 5, 1905, Hay MSS.
296. TR to Edward VII, March, 1905, in S. Lee, *Edward VII,* II, 432, 436.
297. TR to Edward VII, Feb. 12, 1908, *ibid.,* 439, 440.
298. TR to W. Reid, Sept. 19, 1905, WR to TR, Sept. 2, 1905, TR MSS. See
also J. Hay to TR, July 11, 1903, Hay MSS.; Lord Newton, *Lansdowne,* 330.
299. H. White to J. Hay, April 7, 1903, in A. Nevins, *Henry White,* 207.
300. S. Lee, *Edward VII,* II, 437.
301. J. Hay to TR, July 13, 1903, W. Reid to TR, Oct. 2 and Nov. 11, 1905,
TR MSS.

302. J. Hay, MS. Diary, May 25, 1905, Hay MSS.

303. W. Reid to TR, July 17, Aug. 16, and Sept. 14, 1906, TR MSS.

304. TR to W. Reid, Sept. 19, 1905, WR to TR, Sept. 2, 1905, TR MSS. See also J. Hay to TR, July 11, 1903, Hay MSS.; Lord Newton, *Lansdowne*, 330.

305. TR to W. Reid, Jan. 14, 1907, TR MSS.

306. A. H. Lee to TR, Dec. 24, 1906, TR MSS.

307. TR to C. Spring Rice, Nov. 19, 1900, TR MSS.

308. A. T. Mahan to TR, Dec. (?), 1906, in Charles C. Taylor, *The Life of Admiral Mahan*, 146-147.

309. TR to H. C. Lodge, June 19, 1901, TR MSS.

310. See, e. g., John R. Carter, London, to TR, Jan. 25, 1907, TR to A. R. Cowles, Jan. 22, 1907, Cowles MSS.; Sir E. Grey, Feb. 28, 1907, TR to A. H. Lee, Feb. 12, 1907, TR to George Otto Trevelyan, Feb. 4, 1907, TR to the Department of State, Aug. 24, 1907, TR MSS.; TR to H. C. Lodge, Feb. 28, 1907, Lodge MSS. See also *Birmingham Post*, Jan. 18, 1907, *Florida Times Union*, Jan. 22, 1907, *London Times*, Jan. 21, 1907, *New York World*, Feb. 1, 1907, *Washington Herald*, Jan. 21, 1907, *Washington Post*, Feb. 2, 1907, TR Scrapbooks.

311. TR to W. S. Cowles, Feb. 26, 1900, TR MSS.

312. H. White to J. Hay, Dec. 31, 1902, in A. Nevins, *Henry White*, 211-212.

313. A. J. Balfour to A. Carnegie, Dec. 18, 1902, Carnegie MSS. See also AJB to AC, Dec. 27, 1902, in Burton J. Hendrick, *The Life of Andrew Carnegie*, II, 181.

314. *Loc. cit.*

315. H. White to H. C. Lodge, Jan. 5, 1897, Lodge MSS.

316. A. J. Balfour to A. Carnegie, Dec. 18, 1902, Carnegie MSS.

317. B. Adams, *America's Economic Supremacy*, 11.

318. TR to E. Root, Jan. 29, 1900, TR MSS.

319. H. White to H. C. Lodge, Jan. 20, 1903, Lodge MSS.

320. Sir J. Pauncefote to J. Hay, Nov. 5, 1901, Hay MSS.

321. J. H. Choate to J. Hay, Oct. 17 and 27, 1902, JH to Herbert Squiers, Oct. 18, 1902, Hay MSS.

322. H. White to H. C. Lodge, Jan. 20 and 28 and Feb. 24, 1903, Lodge MSS.; TR to Gen. James H. Wilson, July 12, 1899, TR MSS.; HCL to HW, Feb. 3, 1903, White MSS. See also " The New President of the United States," *Economist*, LIX (Sept. 21, 1901), 1394.

323. H. C. Lodge to H. White, Feb. 3, 1903, White MSS.; Sir M. Herbert to the Marquess of Lansdowne, Feb. 7, 1903, Lansdowne to MH, Feb. 9, 1903, in *British Documents on the Origins of the War*, G. P. Gooch and H. W. V. Temperley, eds., II, 172-173; Lord Newton, *Lansdowne*, 260-261.

324. H. White to H. C. Lodge, Jan. 20 and 28, 1903, Lodge MSS.

325. TR to J. H. Wilson, July 12, 1899, TR MSS.; H. White to H. C. Lodge, Jan. 20 and 28, 1903, Lodge MSS.; HCL to HW, Feb. 3, 1903, White MSS. See also " The New President of the United States," *Economist*, LIX (Sept. 21, 1901), 1394.

326. H. C. Lodge to William R. Day, Aug. 11, 1898, Lodge MSS.

327. H. C. Lodge to TR, June 29, 1905, TR MSS.

328. TR to G. von L. Meyer, April 12, 1901, TR to H. C. Lodge, June 19, 1901, TR MSS.

329. TR to H. C. Lodge, June 19, 1901, TR MSS.; Henry Demarest Lloyd to William T. Stead, Nov. 13, 1901, Lloyd MSS.

330. H. C. Lodge to TR, June 29, 1905, TR MSS.

331. TR, " The Monroe Doctrine," *Bachelor of Arts,* ii (March, 1890), 445-446.

332. TR, *American Ideals,* 240-244; TR to C. Spring Rice, March 16 and July 3, 1901, TR to J. St. Loe Strachey, Jan. 27, 1900, TR MSS. See also TR to C. Spring Rice, Dec. 2, 1899, CSR, *Letters,* i, 305-306.

333. H. C. Lodge to TR, June 29, 1905, TR MSS.

334. A. T. Mahan, *The Problem of Asia,* 179-181, 186-187.

335. H. C. Lodge, MS. Diary, Sept. 14 [1898], Lodge MSS.; A. W. Griswold, *Far Eastern Policy,* 19-20.

336. Rudyard Kipling to TR, Sept. 23, 1898, TR MSS.

337. H. White to H. C. Lodge, June 3 and July 27, 1898, C. Spring Rice to HCL, July 8, 1898, HCL, MS. Diary, Sept. 14 [1898], Lodge MSS.

338. C. Spring Rice to H. C. Lodge, July 8, 1898, Lodge MSS.

339. H. C. Lodge, MS. Diary, Sept. 14 [1898], H. White to HCL, June 3 and July 27, 1898, HCL to H. White, Jan. 7, 1899, Lodge MSS.; H. S. Maxim to TR, Oct. 29, 1901, TR MSS.; J. Chamberlain to J. Hay, July 5, 1902, Hay MSS.

340. J. Bryce to TR, Sept. 12, 1898, TR MSS.

341. J. Chamberlain to J. Hay, July 5, 1902, Hay MSS.

342. H. C. Lodge to H. White, Aug. 12, 1898, Lodge MSS. See also TR to C. Spring Rice, Nov. 1, 1905, TR MSS.

343. H. C. Lodge, MS. Diary, Sept. 14 [1898], Lodge MSS.

344. H. C. Lodge to Sears, Jan. 21, 1899, Lodge MSS.

345. H. White to H. C. Lodge, Jan. 18, 1898, Lodge MSS. See also A. W. Griswold, *Far Eastern Policy,* 44-47.

346. H. C. Lodge to H. White, Jan. 31, 1898, White MSS.

347. H. White to H. C. Lodge, March 5, 1898, Lodge MSS.

348. For a complete discussion of the proposed Anglo-American alliance, see Bertha A. Reuter, *Anglo-American Relations during the Spanish-American War,* chapter vii. See also A. J. Balfour to H. C. Lodge, April 11, 1905, Edward VII to TR, March, 1905, TR to Edward VII, Feb. 22, 1908, Edward VII to TR (?), 1908, cited in Lee, *Edward VII,* ii, 432, 439, 440; P. S. Reinsch, *World Politics,* 357-358.

349. TR to F. P. Dunne, Dec. 3, 1904, TR MSS.

350. A. T. Mahan, *The Problem of Asia,* 196.

351. TR to C. Spring Rice, Aug. 11, 1899, TR MSS.

352. T. Dennett, *Hay,* 219; Lionel M. Gelber, *The Rise of Anglo-American Friendship,* 25.

353. TR to H. White, Nov. 27, 1907, TR MSS.

354. H. C. Lodge, MS. Diary, Sept. 14 [1898], Lodge MSS.

355. TR to H. White, March 9, 1898, White MSS.

356. J. Hay to H. White, Sept. 24, 1899, Hay MSS.

357. J. Hay to J. McMillan, July 3, 1900, Hay MSS.

358. Department of State Memorandum, March 22, 1902, *Foreign Relations,* 1902, 931. See also P. S. Reinsch, *World Politics,* 357-358.

359. H. White to H. C. Lodge, Feb. 26, 1902, Lodge MSS.

360. J. Hay to TR, April 25, 1903, quoted in T. Dennett, *Hay,* 404.

361. TR to J. Hay, May 13, 1903, TR MSS.

362. J. Hay to Charlemagne Tower, Feb. 8, 1904, *Foreign Relations,* 1904, 309; J. Hay to Horace Porter, Feb. 8, 1904, *ibid.,* 301; TR to C. Spring Rice, July 24, 1905, TR MSS.; Alfred Vagts, *Deutschland und die Vereinigten Staaten in der Weltpolitik,* II, 1178-1179. Tyler Dennett accepted Roosevelt's statement to Spring Rice, but when Evelene Peters, author of *Roosevelt und der Kaiser* (Leipzig: Universitätsverlag von Robert Noska, 1936), wrote and asked him for evidence that Roosevelt did give the warning, Dennett had to reply, " This statement, of course, is no better than Roosevelt's word and memory. . . . I have never seen any supporting evidence of a textual character and should be very much surprised to find any." T. Dennett, *Roosevelt and the Russo-Japanese War,* 318-319; TD to EP, Dec. 19, 1934, E. Peters, *op. cit.,* 158-159. Dennett did conclude, however, that Roosevelt " had ranged the American Government as an unsigned member of the Anglo-Japanese Alliance." TD, *Roosevelt and the Russo-Japanese War,* 92. See also *ibid.,* 115, 118.

363. Sidney Low, " President Roosevelt's Opportunities," *Nineteenth Century and After,* LVI (December, 1904), 891.

364. TR to Mrs. J. [Clara] Hay, June 12, 1905, Hay MSS.

365. J. Hay, MS. Diary, Jan. 1, 1905, Hay MSS.; TR to George Kennan, May 6, 1905, A. H. Lee to TR, Sept. 10, 1905, TR to AHL, Sept. 21, 1905, TR to C. Spring Rice, Nov. 1, 1905, W. H. Taft to E. Root, July 29, 1905, TR MSS.; T. Dennett, " President Roosevelt's Secret Pact with Japan," *Current History,* XXI (October, 1924), 15-21. A. W. Griswold (*Far Eastern Policy,* 115) had obviously not explored manuscript records sufficiently when he said Roosevelt was not informed until August of the negotiating of the Anglo-Japanese treaty.

366. TR to A. H. Lee, Sept. 21, 1905, TR to C. Spring Rice, Nov. 1, 1905, TR MSS.

367. J. Hay, MS. Diary, Jan. 29 and 30 and Feb. 2, 1905, Hay MSS.; C. Spring Rice to E. K. Roosevelt, March 13, 1905, TR MSS.

368. A. J. Balfour to H. C. Lodge, April 11, 1905, Lodge MSS.

369. TR to G. von L. Meyer, Feb. 6, 1905, TR MSS. See also TR to C. Spring Rice, Dec. 27, 1904, TR MSS.

370. H. C. Lodge to TR, June 29, 1905, TR MSS.

371. W. H. Taft to E. Root, July 29, 1905, TR MSS.

372. TR to W. H. Taft, July 31, 1905, WHT to E. Root, July 29, 1905, TR MSS.

373. Sir H. Mortimer Durand to TR, Sept. 6, 1905, A. H. Lee to TR, Sept. 21,

1905, TR to W. Reid, Aug. 3 and Sept. 16, 1905, TR MSS. See also WR to TR, Sept. 2, 1905, TR MSS.

374. P. Jessup, *Root*, II, 5-6.

375. Lloyd Griscom to E. Root, Oct. 4, 1905, Taft MSS.

376. T. Dennett, "President Roosevelt's Secret Pact with Japan," *Current History*, XXI (October, 1924), 15-21.

377. See, e. g., T. Dennett, *Roosevelt and the Russo-Japanese War*, 317-318. See also *New York World*, Feb. 1, 1907, TR Scrapbooks.

378. TR to C. Spring Rice, Nov. 1, 1905, TR MSS.

379. Alfred E. Hippisley to William W. Rockhill, Feb. 19, 1905, Hay MSS.

380. P. S. Reinsch, *World Politics*, 357-358.

381. TR to Edward VII, Feb. 12, 1908, Edward VII to TR, March 5, 1908, TR to C. Spring Rice, Nov. 1, 1905, TR MSS.

382. TR, *The Winning of the West* (Statesman Edition), III, 128-130. See also his statement to the Methodists in Washington, Jan. 18, 1909, *Washington Post*, Jan. 19, 1909, TR Scrapbooks.

383. TR to Sydney Brooks, Nov. 20, 1908, TR MSS. See also TR to Carl Schurz, Sept. 8, 1905, TR MSS.; TR, Statement to the Methodists in Washington, Jan. 18, 1909, *Washington Post*, Jan. 19, 1909, TR Scrapbooks.

384. B. Adams to H. C. Lodge, April 3, 1896, Lodge MSS.; TR, "National Life and Character," *Sewanee Review*, II (May, 1894), 358-360.

385. H. Speck von Sternburg to TR, Sept. 1 and 12, Oct. 5 and 9, Nov. 8 and 21, and Dec. 1, 1901, and Jan. 26, March 30, April 18, and June 19, 1902, TR MSS.

386. John Burroughs, *Under the Maples*, 101.

387. H. Speck von Sternburg to TR, April 18, 1902, H. White to TR, Nov. 21, 1905, TR MSS.

388. TR to J. Bryce, Aug. 3, 1908, TR to W. W. Rockhill, Sept. 7, 1908, TR MSS.

389. TR, Review of Charles H. Pearson's *National Life and Character*, in the *Sewanee Review*, II (May, 1894), 365.

390. TR to C. Spring Rice, Aug. 13, 1897, TR MSS.

391. TR to C. Spring Rice, Dec. 2, 1899, in CSR, *Letters*, I, 306-307.

392. TR to W. Reid, London, Sept. 3, 1908, TR MSS.

393. TR to S. Brooks, Nov. 20 and Dec. 28, 1908, SB to TR, Nov. 11 and Dec. 12, 1908, and Feb. 13, 1909, TR to J. Bryce, Jan. 21, 1909, TR to Robert H. M. Ferguson, Jan. 17, 1909, TR to A. H. Lee, Feb. 7, 1909, J. Morley to TR, Jan. 8 and 22, 1909, TR to W. Reid, Nov. 27, 1908, and Jan. 6, 1909, TR MSS.; *Washington Post*, Jan. 19, 1909, *Washington Times*, Jan. 19, 1909, TR Scrapbooks; M. A. DeW. Howe, *Rhodes*, 180-182.

394. Frank Harris, *Contemporary Portraits*, IV, 266-268.

395. N. M. Butler to TR, June 2, 1903, TR MSS.

396. TR to Earl Cromer [Evelyn Baring], Jan. 15, 1903, TR to Silas McBee, Aug. 27, 1907, TR to Maj.-Gen. Francis Reginald Wingate, July 29, 1908, TR

MSS.; Charles Francis Adams to H. C. Lodge, April 27, 1906, HCL to CFA, May 1, 1906, Lodge MSS.

397. TR to J. Morley, Jan. 17, 1904, TR MSS.

398. TR to F. R. Wingate, July 29, 1908, TR MSS.

399. Oscar S. Straus, MS. Diary, March 19, 1910, Straus MSS.; TR to David Gray, Oct. 5, 1911, TR MSS.; Sir James Rennell Rodd, *Social and Diplomatic Memories, 1902-1919*, 120-121.

400. TR to H. White, April 2 [1910 (?)], White MSS.; Lawrence F. Abbott, *Impressions of TR*, 152-156.

401. TR to A. R. Cowles, March 19, 1910, Cowles MSS. See also TR to G. O. Trevelyan, Oct. 1, 1911, TR MSS.

402. O. S. Straus, MS. Diary, March 29, 1910, Straus MSS.; L. F. Abbott, *Impressions of TR*, 154-156.

403. TR, "Law and Order in Egypt: An Address before the National University in Cairo, March 28, 1910," *African and European Addresses*, L. F. Abbott, ed., 15-28; O. S. Straus, MS. Diary, March 28, 1910, Straus MSS.

404. TR to H. White, April 2 [1910 (?)], White MSS.; TR to H. C. Lodge, April 6, 1910, Lodge MSS.; Sheikh Ali Youssuf, "Egypt's Reply to Colonel Roosevelt," *North American Review*, cxci (June, 1910), 729-737; L. F. Abbott, *Impressions of TR*, 157.

405. TR to D. Gray, Oct. 5, 1911, A. H. Lee to TR, July 7, 1910, TR MSS.; E. Grey to J. Bryce, June 17, 1910, in G. M. Trevelyan, *Grey of Fallodon*, 160; "Conspiracy of Adulation," *Blackwood's Edinburgh Magazine*, clxxxviii (July, 1910), 140-141; L. F. Abbott, *Impressions of TR*, 157-159.

406. Edward Grey, *Twenty-five Years*, ii, 91-93; TR, "'British Rule in Africa': Address Delivered at the Guildhall, London, May 31, 1910," *African and European Addresses*, 157-172. See also his statement to the Methodists in Washington, *Washington Post*, Jan. 19, 1909, TR Scrapbooks.

407. R. Kipling to [J.] B. Matthews, June, 1910, enclosed in JBM to TR, June 21, 1910, TR to D. Gray, Oct. 5, 1911, A. H. Lee to TR, July 7, 1910, TR MSS.

408. J. Morley to A. Carnegie, June 19, 1910, Carnegie MSS. See also G. W. Smalley, *Anglo-American Memories*, ii, 367-368.

409. "The President's August Speechifying," *Nation*, lxxxi (Aug. 17, 1905), 134.

410. Nr. 10389, Wilhelm II an Theobald von Bethmann Hollweg (Eigenhändig), May 20, 1910, *Grosse Politik*, xxviii, 327.

CHAPTER IV

1. TR, "Address at Mechanics' Pavilion," San Francisco, May 13, 1903, in TR, *California Addresses*, 95.

2. *Ibid.*, 95-98.

3. TR to Benjamin Ide Wheeler, June 17, 1905, TR MSS.

4. John Hay, "An Address Delivered at Jackson, Michigan," July 6, 1904, in John Hay and Elihu Root, *The Republican Party: A Party Fit to Govern*, 15.

5. John O. P. Bland, *Recent Events and Policies in China*, 297-298.

6. Paul S. Reinsch, *World Politics at the End of the Nineteenth Century as Influenced by the Oriental Situation*, 85.

7. Brooks Adams, *America's Economic Supremacy*, 11-12.

8. TR to James Bryce, March 31, 1898, TR MSS.

9. Henry Cabot Lodge to Cecil Spring Rice, Aug. 12, 1898, *The Letters and Friendships of Cecil Spring Rice*, Stephen Gwenn, ed., I, 250, hereafter cited as C. Spring Rice, *Letters*. See also CSR to HCL, July 8, 1898, *ibid.*, 249.

10. Alfred T. Mahan, *The Problem of Asia*, 178, 181.

11. TR to Capt. A. T. Mahan, March 18, 1901, TR MSS.

12. TR to C. Spring Rice, Aug. 13, 1897, TR MSS.

13. See, e. g., TR to Capt. Caspar F. Goodrich, June 16, 1897, TR to John Davis Long, Sept. 30, 1897, TR to A. T. Mahan, May 3, 1897, TR to Capt. Bowman H. McCalla, Aug. 3, 1897, TR to William B. McKinley, April 22, 1897, TR MSS.

14. See, e. g., TR to Charles A. Moore, Feb. 14, 1898, TR to Francis Cruger Moore, Feb. 5, 1898, TR to C. Spring Rice, Aug. 5, 1896, and Aug. 13, 1897, TR MSS.

15. TR to Hermann Speck von Sternburg, July 12, 1899, TR MSS. See also TR, "Expansion and Peace," *Independent*, LI (Dec. 21, 1899), 3404.

16. Charles S. Campbell, Jr., *Special Business Interests and the Open Door Policy*, passim.

17. H. C. Lodge to Henry White, Jan. 31, 1898, Lodge MSS.

18. See, e. g., H. C. Lodge to Beal, Jan. 23, 1899, HCL to Sears, Jan. 21, 1899, Lodge MSS.

19. H. White to H. C. Lodge, March 5, 1898, Lodge MSS.

20. H. C. Lodge to Beal, Jan. 23, 1899, Lodge MSS.

21. TR to C. A. Moore, Feb. 14, 1898, TR MSS.

22. B. Adams, *America's Economic Supremacy*, 29, 43, 51, 221-222.

23. TR to B. Adams, July 18, 1903, TR MSS.

24. TR to A. T. Mahan, March 18, 1901, TR MSS.

25. TR to B. Adams, July 18, 1903, TR MSS.

26. H. Speck von Sternburg, Peking, to TR, July 30, 1895, TR MSS.

27. TR to Anna Roosevelt Cowles, April 26, 1896, Cowles MSS.

28. See, e. g., Henry Adams, Sydney, Australia, to H. C. Lodge, Aug. 4, 1891, Lodge MSS.

29. TR to William W. Rockhill, July 21, 1900, TR MSS. See also TR to WWR, Feb. 12, 1896, TR to Charles McCauley, March 9, 1899, TR MSS.

30. TR, "Address at Mechanics' Pavilion," San Francisco, May 13, 1903, in TR, *California Addresses*, 97. See also TR, "The Strenuous Life," in *The Strenuous Life*, 6.

31. TR to H. C. Lodge, April 29, 1896, TR MSS.

32. *Loc. cit.*; TR to H. Speck von Sternburg, Jan. 17, 1898, TR MSS.

33. TR, " The Strenuous Life," Speech before the Hamilton Club, Chicago, April 10, 1899, in *The Strenuous Life*, 6.

34. TR, " National Life and Character," *Sewanee Review*, II (May, 1894), 363-364.

35. H. C. Lodge to B. Adams, June 29, 1900, Lodge MSS. See also HCL to H. White, June 29, 1900, Lodge MSS.

36. A. T. Mahan, *The Problem of Asia*, 173-175.

37. H. C. Lodge to H. White, June 29, 1900, HCL to B. Adams, June 29, 1900, Lodge MSS.

38. *Nation*, LXXI (July 26, 1900), 61. The *Nation* saw no inconsistency in rejecting our Philippine policy and accepting our Chinese intervention.

39. *Utica Observer*, Oct. 8, 1900, TR Scrapbooks.

40. *Milwaukee Sentinel*, July 18, 1900. See also *Wichita Daily Eagle*, July 5, 1900, TR Scrapbooks.

41. Chauncey M. Depew, " At the Meeting at Carnegie Hall, June 26, 1900, to Ratify the Nomination of McKinley and Roosevelt," *Speeches, November 1896–April 1902*, 51-52.

42. *Milwaukee Sentinel*, July 18, 1900. See also C. M. Depew, *op. cit.*, 51-52.

43. Thomas F. Millard, " The Settlement in China," *Scribner's Magazine*, XXIX (March, 1901), 372.

44. H. White to H. C. Lodge, June 16, 1900, Lodge MSS. Lodge, on the other hand, denied this. HCL to HW, June 29, 1900, Lodge MSS.

45. TR to C. Spring Rice, July 20, 1900, TR MSS. See also *Milwaukee Sentinel*, July 18, 1900.

46. TR to H. Speck von Sternburg, July 20, 1900, TR MSS.

47. H. C. Lodge to H. White, June 29, 1900, Lodge MSS.

48. H. Speck von Sternburg to TR, Aug. 24, 1900, TR MSS.

49. TR to H. Speck von Sternburg, Aug. 28, 1900, TR MSS.

50. TR to H. Speck von Sternburg, Nov. 19, 1900, TR MSS.

51. Alfred L. P. Dennis, *Adventures in American Diplomacy*, 236-239.

52. C. M. Depew, " At the Meeting at Carnegie Hall June 26, 1900 . . . ," *Speeches, November 1896–April 1902*, 51.

53. *Utica Observer*, Oct. 8, 1900, TR Scrapbooks.

54. *Milwaukee Sentinel*, July 18, 1900.

55. TR to A. T. Mahan, March 18, 1901, TR MSS.; T. F. Millard, " A Comparison of the Armies in China," " Punishment and Revenge in China," and " The Settlement in China," *Scribner's Magazine*, XXIX (January-March, 1901), 77-87, 187-194, 370-377.

56. T. F. Millard, " A Comparison of the Armies in China " and " Punishment and Revenge in China," *Scribner's Magazine*, XXIX (January and February, 1901), 80, 86, 194.

57. J. Hay to H. White, Sept. 7, 1900, in Allan Nevins, *Henry White: Thirty Years of American Diplomacy*, 173.

58. W. W. Rockhill, Peking, to Nannie Lodge, Dec. 2, 1900, Lodge MSS.

59. TR to H. Speck von Sternburg, Nov. 19, 1900, TR MSS.

60. TR to A. T. Mahan, March 18, 1901, TR MSS.

61. TR to Gen. Adna Romanza Chaffee, March 14, 1901, TR MSS.

62. TR to George Ferdinand Becker, July 8, 1901, TR MSS. See also *Wichita Daily Eagle*, July 5, 1900, TR Scrapbooks.

63. TR, "Home Market Speech," Boston, *Boston Journal*, May 1, 1901, TR Scrapbooks.

64. H. Speck von Sternburg to TR, Sept. 1, 1901, TR MSS.

65. TR to H. Speck von Sternburg, Oct. 11, 1901, TR MSS.

66. *Loc. cit.*

67. *Helena Daily Independent*, Sept. 17, 1900, TR Scrapbooks.

68. TR to H. Speck von Sternburg, Oct. 11, 1901, TR MSS.

69. TR to B. Adams, Sept. 27, 1901, TR MSS. See also B. Adams, "Reciprocity or the Alternative," *Atlantic Monthly*, LXXXVIII (August, 1901), 145-155.

70. See B. Adams, *America's Economic Supremacy, passim*. See also William A. Williams, *American-Russian Relations*, 40-41; WAW, "Brooks Adams and American Expansion," *New England Quarterly*, XXV (June, 1952), 228-229.

71. James D. Richardson, *Messages and Papers of the Presidents*, XIV, 6677-6679.

72. See, e. g., TR to Francis B. Loomis, Aug. 26, 1903, TR MSS.; Alvey A. Adee to J. Hay, Aug. 22, 1903, Hay MSS.; AAA to Benjamin F. Barnes, Aug. 22, 1903, State Department Archives.

73. J. Hay to TR, May 1, 1902, Hay MSS.

74. J. Hay to Count Arthur Pavlovitch Cassini, Jan. 16, 1902, quoted in A. L. P. Dennis, *Adventures in American Diplomacy*, 377-381; W. W. Rockhill to J. Hay, Jan. 31 and Feb. 1, 1902, *ibid.*, 926-929; *ibid.*, 351-352; Edward Zabriskie, *American-Russian Rivalry in the Far East*, 78-79.

75. J. Hay to A. P. Cassini, June 21, 1903, enclosed in TR to A. Shaw, June 22, 1903, TR MSS. (also printed in A. L. P. Dennis, *op. cit.*, 380-381); Edwin Conger to J. Hay, April 23, 1903, JH to EC, April 25 and 29, 1903, *Foreign Relations*, 1903, 53-54; JH to Robert S. McCormick, April 25 and 29, 1903, *ibid.*, 708-710; JH to TR, April 25, 1903, and May 4 and 12, 1903, JH, Memorandum of a conversation with the Russian First Secretary of Legation, April 24, 1903, Hay MSS.; A. L. P. Dennis, *op. cit.*, 355-357; E. Zabriskie, *op. cit.*, 78, 81-82, 87.

76. See, e. g., J. Hay, Memorandum of a conversation with the British Ambassador, Sir Michael Herbert, May 4, 1903, Hay MSS.; *Washington Post*, May 9, 1903, TR Scrapbooks.

77. J. Hay to TR, April 25 and 28, 1903, Hay MSS.

78. Albert Shaw to Albert J. Beveridge, May 9, 1903, AJB to AS, May 12, 1903, Beveridge MSS.

79. H. C. Lodge to TR, May 21, 1903, TR MSS.

80. J. Hay to TR, April 28, 1903, Hay MSS.

81. J. Hay to H. White, May 22, 1903, Hay MSS.

82. J. Hay to TR, May 12, 1903, Hay MSS.

83. J. Hay to TR, April 28 and May 12, 1903, Hay MSS.

84. TR to J. Hay, May 13, 1903, TR MSS.

85. TR to A. Shaw, June 22, 1903, TR to Lyman Abbott, June 22, 1903, TR MSS.

86. *Loc. cit.*

87. TR to J. Hay, May 22, 1903, TR MSS.

88. J. Hay, Memorandum of a conversation with Ambassador A. P. Cassini, June 18, 1903, in A. P. L. Dennis, *Adventures in American Diplomacy*, 377-380; JH to TR, June 22 and 30, 1903, TR MSS.

89. E. Zabriskie, *American-Russian Rivalry in the Far East*, 93.

90. TR to J. Hay, July 1, 1903, TR MSS.; JH to TR, July 1, 1903, Hay MSS.

91. *New York Herald*, July 2, 1903, TR Scrapbooks; TR to F. B. Loomis, July 1, 1903, TR MSS.

92. TR to B. Adams, July 18, 1903, TR MSS.

93. E. Zabriskie, *op. cit.*, 95-97. See also J. Hay to TR, Aug. 14, 1903, TR MSS.

94. J. Hay to TR, July 14, 1903, JH, Memorandum, July 16, 1903, Hay MSS.

95. TR to J. Hay, July 18 and 29, 1903, TR MSS. See also TR to B. Adams, July 18, 1903, TR MSS.

96. E. Zabriskie, *American-Russian Rivalry*, 95-97; J. Hay to TR, Aug. 14, 1903, TR MSS.

97. Horace N. Allen, MS. Diary, Sept. 30, 1903, Allen MSS.

98. William C. Dix to TR, Oct. 26, 1903, memorandum attached, Hay MSS.

99. For a detailed picture of the early years of the American China Development Company see William R. Braisted, "The United States and the American China Development Company," *Far Eastern Quarterly*, XI (February, 1952), 147-165.

100. *Ibid.*, 148.

101. *Ibid.*, 148-153.

102. *Ibid.*, 153-155.

103. *Ibid.*, 155-158.

104. J. Hay, MS. Diary, Dec. 23, 1904, Hay MSS.

105. W. R. Braisted, *op. cit.*, 157-158.

106. *Loc. cit.*; J. Hay, MS. Diary, Jan. 4, 1905, F. B. Loomis to JH, Jan. 4, 1905, Hay MSS.; JH to John Gardner Coolidge, Jan. 26, 1905, TR MSS.; JGC to Prince Ch'ing, Jan. 9, 1905, transmitted in JGC to the Secretary of State, Jan. 25, 1905, JH to E. Conger, Jan. 6 and 26, 1905, State Department Archives.

107. Prince Ch'ing to J. G. Coolidge, Jan. 18, 1905, State Department Archives.

108. Charles A. Whittier to J. Hay, March 3, 1905, Hay MSS.

109. TR to J. Hay, Jan. 26, 1905, TR MSS.

110. J. G. Coolidge to J. Hay, Feb. 9, 1905, State Department Archives; W. R. Braisted, "The United States and the American China Development Company," *Far Eastern Quarterly*, XI (February, 1952), 159.

111. *Loc. cit.*

112. George W. Ingraham to John W. Foster, May 29, 1905, TR MSS.

113. W. R. Braisted, *op. cit.*, 159-160; W. W. Rockhill to E. Root, Aug. 17, 1905, TR MSS.

114. W. R. Braisted, *op. cit.*, 159-160.

115. *New York Journal of Commerce* quoted in "The China Development Company and the Open Door," *Journal of the American Asiatic Association*, v (August, 1905), 198. See also W. W. Rockhill to E. Root, Aug. 17, 1905, TR MSS.

116. King Leopold to TR, June 1, 1905, TR MSS.

117. H. C. Lodge to TR, July 6, 1905, TR MSS.

118. *Loc. cit.*

119. E. Root to C. W. Ingraham, July 8, 1905, Root MSS. In this letter Root disassociated himself from the settlement of the railway dispute. Should the matter come before me as Secretary of State, he wrote Ingraham, "I should have to ask the President to direct it personally."

120. TR to H. C. Lodge, July 18, 1905, TR MSS.

121. TR to J. Pierpont Morgan, July 18, 1905, TR MSS.

122. F. B. Loomis to TR, July 22, 1905, TR MSS.

123. *Loc. cit.*; W. W. Rockhill to the Secretary of State, July 25, 1905, enclosed in A. A. Adee to B. F. Barnes, TR's acting secretary, July 26, 1905, Rudolph Forster, TR's assistant secretary, to BFB, July 25, 1905, State Department Archives and TR MSS.; *New York Herald*, Aug. 7 and 30, 1905, TR Scrapbooks.

124. *New York Herald*, Aug. 8, 1905; *New York Tribune*, Aug. 8, 1905.

125. *San Francisco Chronicle*, Aug. 9, 1905; *New York Tribune*, Aug. 9, 1905; *New York World*, Aug. 9, 1905.

126. W. R. Braisted, "The United States and the American China Development Company," *Far Eastern Quarterly*, xi (February, 1952), 161.

127. TR to W. W. Rockhill, Aug. 8, 1905, WWR to the Secretary of State [E. Root], Aug. 9, 1905, Memo from WWR to the Chinese Foreign Office, Aug. 12, 1905, WWR to ER, Aug. 14, 1905, TR MSS.; Paul Varg, *Open Door Diplomat: The Life of W. W. Rockhill*, 74.

128. W. W. Rockhill, Memorandum left at the Chinese Foreign Office, Aug. 12, 1905, W. W. Rockhill to the Secretary of State, Aug. 14, 1905, Memorandum of a conversation at the Foreign Office, Aug. 13, 1905, between WWR and His Excellency, Na-t'ung, WWR to Prince Ch'ing, Aug. 16, 1905, TR MSS.

129. B. F. Barnes to A. A. Adee, Aug. 14, 1905, TR MSS.

130. A. A. Adee to W. W. Rockhill, Aug. 16, 1905, TR MSS.

131. W. R. Braisted, *op. cit.*, 163; W. W. Rockhill to Prince Ch'ing, Aug. 16, 1905, WWR to E. Root, Aug. 17, 1905, TR MSS.

132. W. R. Braisted, *op. cit.*, 162-163; W. W. Rockhill to E. Root [August, 1905 (?)] and Aug. 17, 1905, TR MSS.

133. A. A. Adee to W. W. Rockhill, Aug. 16, 1905, TR MSS.

134. W. W. Rockhill to the Secretary of State [E. Root], Aug. 17, 1905, TR MSS.

135. TR to J. P. Morgan, Aug. 17, 1905, TR MSS.

136. W. R. Braisted, *op. cit.*, 163.

137. W. W. Rockhill to E. Root, Aug. 27, 1905, State Department Archives.

138. W. R. Braisted, *op. cit.*, 164.

139. TR to W. W. Rockhill, Aug. 29, 1905, TR MSS.; for the development of later business interest in China see Charles Vevier, "The Open Door: An Idea in Action, 1906-1913," *Pacific Historical Review*, xxiv (February, 1955), 49-62; CV, *The United States and China, 1906-1913: A Study of Finance and Diplomacy.*

140. TR to H. Speck von Sternburg, Sept. 6, 1905, TR MSS.

141. TR to W. W. Rockhill, Aug. 29, 1905, TR MSS.

142. *New York Times*, Aug. 29, 1905, TR Scrapbooks.

143. *New York Herald*, Aug. 30, 1905, TR Scrapbooks.

144. TR to H. Speck von Sternburg, Sept. 6, 1905, TR MSS. See also TR to King Leopold, Aug. 31, 1905, TR MSS.

145. TR to Whitelaw Reid, Sept. 16, 1905, TR MSS.

146. P. Varg, *Rockhill*, 76.

147. Mary Coolidge, *Chinese Immigration*, 302.

148. *Ibid.*, 323.

149. *Ibid.*, 299-300.

150. Roy L. Garis, *Immigration Restriction*, 286-307; M. Coolidge, *Chinese Immigration, passim*; A. Whitney Griswold, *The Far Eastern Policy of the United States*, 338.

151. Wu Ting-fang to J. Hay, April 29, 1902, *Foreign Relations*, 1902, 213-214.

152. J. Hay, MS. Diary, April 8, 1904, Hay MSS. See also Orville H. Platt to TR, April 5, 1904, JH to TR, April 6, 1904, TR MSS.; M. Coolidge, *Chinese Immigration*, 251-252; R. L. Garis, *Immigration Restriction*, 304.

153. See, e. g., TR to George B. Cortelyou, Jan. 25, 1904, TR MSS.; TR, Reply to a Delegation of the American Asiatic Association, with a dispatch of the Washington correspondent of the *New York Evening Post*, June 15, 1905, reprinted in the *Journal of the American Asiatic Association*, v (July, 1905), 168-169.

154. See, e. g., *loc. cit.*; Terence V. Powderly to G. B. Cortelyou, TR's secretary, Dec. 11, 1901, TR MSS.

155. TR to Lucius B. Swift, Jan. 5, 1904, TR MSS.

156. TR to G. B. Cortelyou, Jan. 25, 1904, TR MSS. See also TR to GBC, Jan. 5, 1904, TR MSS.

157. J. Hay to TR, March 2, 1904, TR MSS.

158. *U. S.* v. *Sing Tuck or King Do and Thirty-one Others*, 194 *U. S.* 182.

159. J. Hay, MS. Diary, March 3 and April 4, 5, and 8, 1904, Hay MSS. See also O. H. Platt to TR, April 5, 1904, JH to TR, April 6, 1904, TR MSS.; M. Coolidge, *Chinese Immigration*, 251-252; R. L. Garis, *Immigration Restriction*, 304.

160. J. Hay, MS. Diary, Oct. 5, 1904, Hay MSS.

161. J. Hay, MS. Diary, Nov. 18 and 22, 1904, Hay MSS.

162. J. Hay, MS. Diary, Nov. 28 and 29, 1904, Hay MSS.

163. M. Coolidge, *Chinese Immigration.*

164. As late as 1904 a boycott was successfully instituted against two German firms in Hankow. *London Times,* July 3, 1905. For a full study of the use of the boycott technique in China see Charles Remer, *A Study of Chinese Boycotts.*

165. *Ibid.,* 16-17; *Outlook,* LXXX (Aug. 12, 1905), 893-894; *San Francisco Chronicle,* Aug. 3, 1905.

166. James L. Rodgers to F. B. Loomis, Aug. 24, 1905, State Department Archives.

167. Tseng Shao-Ching [Tseng Chu] of Fukien Province, " The Boycott against American Goods and Americans in General " (translation of an article in *Shih Pao* [*Eastern Times*] in Shanghai), *Journal of the American Asiatic Association,* v (November, 1905), 300.

168. J. L. Rodgers to F. B. Loomis, Aug. 24, 1905, State Department Archives; M. Coolidge, *Chinese Immigration,* 471.

169. Tseng Shao-Ching [Tseng Chu], *op. cit.,* 300.

170. J. L. Rodgers to F. B. Loomis, Aug. 24, 1905, State Department Archives; M. Coolidge, *Chinese Immigration,* 471.

171. American Association of China to the American Asiatic Association [May 16 (?), 1905], cablegram enclosed in John Foord to TR, May 16, 1905, quoted in " Correspondence: The Chinese Immigration Question," *Journal of the American Asiatic Association,* v (June, 1905), 132. See also James B. Reynolds to Nicholas Murray Butler, May 7, 1905, JBR to TR, May 16, 1905, TR MSS.

172. James N. Jameson to James W. Davidson, May 18, 1905, quoted in " American Association of China," *ibid.,* v (July, 1905), 165-166.

173. J. Foord to TR, May 16, 1905, F. B. Loomis to JF, May 26, 1905, quoted in *ibid.,* v (June, 1905), 132.

174. TR to Victor H. Metcalf, May 16, 1905, TR MSS. See also VHM to TR, June 7, 1905, TR MSS.

175. TR to W. W. Rockhill, May 18, 1905, TR MSS.

176. *Chicago Tribune,* May 21, 1905.

177. *San Francisco Chronicle,* June 8 and 10, 1905.

178. Charles L. Lovering for Massachusetts Cotton Mills, of Lowell, Mass., P. J. DeNormandie for Pepperell Manufacturing Company, of Biddeford, Maine, Henry L. Rand for Stark Mills, of Manchester, New Hamp., F. B. Sears for Lanett Cotton Mills, of West Point, Ga., Frederick A. Feather for the Boott Mills, of Lowell, Charles B. Amory for the Hamilton Manufacturing Company, of Lowell, and Theophilus Parsons for the Lyman Mills, of Holyoke, Mass., to TR, June 2, 1905, quoted in " The Administration of the Chinese Exclusion Laws," *Journal of the American Asiatic Association,* v (July, 1905), 167-168. Eight days later the Merchants' Exchange in New York appealed to the President for modification of the exclusion treaty.

179. *San Francisco Chronicle,* June 10, 1905; " The Administration of the Chinese Exclusion Laws," *Journal of the American Asiatic Association,* v (July, 1905), 167-168.

180. *Ibid.,* 167; *New York Tribune,* June 13, 1905.

181. See, e. g., *Chicago Tribune*, May 21, 1905.

182. TR, Reply to a Delegation of the American Asiatic Association, with a dispatch of the Washington correspondent of the *New York Evening Post*, June 15, 1905, reprinted in the *Journal of the American Asiatic Association*, v (July, 1905), 168-169. The Asiatic Association complimented Roosevelt for his understanding views. *Ibid.*, 162.

183. V. H. Metcalf to TR, June 7, 1905, TR MSS.; VHM to J. Foord, June 2, 1905, quoted in " The Administration of the Chinese Exclusion Laws," *Journal of the American Asiatic Association*, v (July, 1905), 170; J. Hay, MS. Diary, June 19, 1905, Hay MSS.

184. TR to V. H. Metcalf, June 16, 1905, TR MSS.

185. TR to V. H. Metcalf, June 12, 1905, TR MSS.

186. TR to V. H. Metcalf, June 16, 1905, TR MSS.

187. *San Francisco Chronicle*, June 16, 1905.

188. *Chicago Tribune*, June 27, 1905.

189. *San Francisco Chronicle*, June 17, 1905.

190. TR to V. H. Metcalf, June 18, 1905, TR MSS.

191. V. H. Metcalf to TR, June 24, 1905, TR to the Acting Secretary of State [A. A. Adee], June 24, 1905, TR MSS.; *New York Tribune*, June 26, 1905.

192. TR to V. H. Metcalf, June 29, 1905, TR MSS.

193. *Chicago Tribune*, June 26, 1905. Taft defended the President, too, before a Union League Club of San Francisco. *San Francisco Chronicle*, July 6, 1905.

194. *Ibid.*, June 27, 1905.

195. *Ibid.*, June 26, 1905.

196. *New York Evening Post*, June 26, 1905.

197. *Chicago Tribune*, June 29, 1905.

198. *New York Evening Post*, June 28, 1905.

199. P. Varg, *Rockhill*, 62.

200. W. W. Rockhill to the Chinese Guilds, enclosed in WWR to the Secretary of State, July 6, 1905, *Foreign Relations*, 1905, 206-207.

201. J. L. Rodgers to F. B. Loomis, June 27, 1905, State Department Archives.

202. *San Francisco Chronicle*, July 1, 1905.

203. *New York Tribune*, Aug. 22, 1905.

204. Quan Yick Nam to TR, Aug. 3, 1905, TR MSS.

205. *London Times*, July 4, 1905.

206. *New York Tribune*, July 5, 1905.

207. M. Coolidge, *Chinese Immigration*, 470.

208. *Chicago Tribune*, May 21, 1905, TR Scrapbooks.

209. W. W. Rockhill to Prince Ch'ing, June 17, 1905, *Foreign Relations*, 1905, 207.

210. [I-K'ung] Prince Ch'ing, Chief Grand Councilor, to W. W. Rockhill, July 1, 1905, *ibid.*, 207-208; WWR to J. Hay, July 1, 1905, TR MSS.

211. W. W. Rockhill to the Secretary of State, July 6 [J. Hay died July 1; E. Root was appointed July 7], 1905, *ibid.*, 205-206.

212. P. Varg, *Rockhill*, 63.

213. W. W. Rockhill to TR, July 7, 1905, TR MSS.

214. William D. Wheelwright, president of the Chamber of Commerce of Portland, Oregon, to TR, undated, quoted in " The Administration of the Chinese Exclusion Laws," *Journal of the American Asiatic Association*, v (August, 1905), 196-197.

215. *San Francisco Chronicle*, July 6, 1905.

216. *Ibid.*, July 3, 1905.

217. *Ibid.*, July 17, 1905.

218. *New York Tribune*, July 13, 1905.

219. Petition from loyal citizens of the United States residing in Canton to the President of the United States, July 17, 1905, TR MSS.

220. *North China Daily News*, July 21, 1905, enclosed in W. W. Rockhill to the Secretary of State [E. Root], July 26, 1905, *Foreign Relations*, 1905, 211.

221. *Shanghai Times*, Aug. 1, 1905, TR MSS.

222. Enclosed in J. L. Rodgers to F. B. Loomis, Aug. 17, 1905, State Department Archives.

223. J. L. Rodgers to F. B. Loomis, Aug. 11, 1905, State Department Archives.

224. J. L. Rodgers to F. B. Loomis, July 27, 1905, and poster enclosed in JLR to FBL, Aug. 17, 1905, State Department Archives.

225. *San Francisco Chronicle*, Aug. 16, 1905; *New York Tribune*, Aug. 16, 1905.

226. *Ibid.*, Aug. 2, 10, 17, 18, 22 and 25, 1905.

227. *London Times*, Aug. 11, 1905.

228. *San Francisco Chronicle*, Aug. 4, 1905.

229. *New York Tribune*, Aug. 8, 1905.

230. Herbert H. D. Pierce, third assistant secretary of State, to the American Legation, Peking, July 25, 1905, TR MSS.

231. Quoted in P. Varg, *Rockhill*, 63.

232. J. L. Rodgers to F. B. Loomis, July 27, 1905, State Department Archives.

233. Julius G. Lay to F. B. Loomis, Aug. 16, 1905, State Department Archives.

234. Samuel Gracey to the Secretary of State, Aug. 12, 1905, TR MSS.

235. J. G. Lay to F. B. Loomis, Aug. 16, 1905, State Department Archives.

236. John Fowler to H. E. Yang, Aug. 1, 1905, enclosed in JF to F. B. Loomis, Aug. 3, 1905, State Department Archives.

237. See, e. g., TR to W. W. Rockhill, Aug. 22 and 29, 1905, and Sept. 7, 1908, TR MSS.; P. Varg, *Rockhill*, 62.

238. Leslie M. Shaw to TR, Aug. 1, 1905, TR MSS.

239. TR to L. M. Shaw, Aug. 2, 1905, TR MSS.

240. W. W. Rockhill to TR, July 12, 1905, quoted in P. Varg, *Rockhill*, 63; TR to WWR, Aug. 22, 1905, TR MSS.

241. See, e. g., W. W. Rockhill to the Secretary of State [E. Root], July 14, 1905, *Foreign Relations*, 1905, 208.

242. W. W. Rockhill to J. L. Rodgers, July 18, 1905, TR MSS.

243. W. W. Rockhill to E. Root, July 25, 1905, TR MSS.

244. W. W. Rockhill to Prince Ch'ing, Aug. 7, 14, and 27, 1905, State Department Archives; WWR to TR's secretary, William Loeb, Jr., Aug. 27, 1905, TR

MSS.; WWR to E. Root, Aug. 4, 1905, quoted in Philip Jessup, *Elihu Root*, II, 46; WWR to ER, Aug. 17 and Oct. 4, 1905, TR MSS.

245. *Chefoo Daily News*, Aug. 13, 1905, reprinted in *Foreign Relations*, 1905, 216.

246. J. L. Rodgers to the Secretary of State [E. Root], Aug. 5 and 10, 1905, Rudolph Forster to TR, Aug. 5, 1905, W. W. Rockhill to B. F. Barnes, Aug. 15, 1905, WWR to ER, Aug. 26, 1905, TR MSS.

247. *New York Tribune*, Aug. 23, 25, 29, 30, and 31, 1905.

248. L. M. Shaw to TR, Aug. 1, 1905, TR MSS.

249. Prince Ch'ing to W. W. Rockhill, Aug. 26, 1905, State Department Archives and *Foreign Relations*, 1905, 222-223. See also WWR to TR, Aug. 27, 1905, WWR to E. Root, Sept. 1, 1905, TR MSS.

250. W. W. Rockhill to E. Root, Aug. 26, 1905, *Foreign Relations*, 1905, 220-221.

251. W. W. Rockhill to Prince Ch'ing, Aug. 27, 1905, *Foreign Relations*, 1905, 223-224.

252. TR to W. W. Rockhill, Aug. 29, 1905, TR MSS.

253. TR to W. W. Rockhill, Aug. 22, 1905, TR MSS.

254. J. Foord to TR, Aug. 14, 1905; B. F. Barnes to JF, Aug. 15, 1905, *Journal of the American Asiatic Association*, V (September, 1905), 231.

255. *Shih Pao [Eastern Times]*, undated, reprinted in *ibid.*, V (November, 1905), 300.

256. W. W. Rockhill to TR, Aug. 15, 1905, State Department Archives. See also WWR to the Secretary of State [E. Root], Aug. 17, 1905, State Department Archives.

257. *Outlook*, LXXX (Aug. 26, 1905), 992-993.

258. L. M. Shaw to TR, Aug. 1, 1905, TR MSS.

259. *Commercial and Financial Chronicle*, LXXX (Aug. 19, 1905), 636.

260. *Outlook*, LXXX (Aug. 26, 1905), 993.

261. Petition from loyal citizens of the United States residing in Canton to the President of the United States, July 17, 1905, TR MSS.

262. *North China Daily News*, undated, reprinted in the *Journal of the American Asiatic Association*, V (November, 1905), 301. For another and milder translation of this important edict see *Foreign Relations*, 1905, 225. See also W. W. Rockhill to E. Root, Sept. 1 and Oct. 4, 1905, TR MSS., and State Department Archives.

263. Prince Ch'ing to W. W. Rockhill, Sept. 4, 1905, *Foreign Relations*, 1905, 226.

264. George C. Perkins to TR, Aug. 30, 1905, TR MSS.

265. TR to G. C. Perkins, Aug. 31, 1905, TR MSS.

266. John Parker to F. B. Loomis, Sept. 2, 1905, TR MSS.

267. Memorandum from F. B. Loomis to TR, Sept. 2, 1905, TR MSS.; W. W. Rockhill to the Secretary of State, Aug. 17, 1905, State Dept. Archives. See also WWR to E. Root, Oct. 4, 1905, TR MSS.

268. TR to William Howard Taft, Sept. 2, 1905, TR MSS.

269. *New York Tribune*, Sept. 4, and 5, 1905.

270. HKB interview with Owen Lattimore, May, 1953; Arthur De Carle Sowerby, *Nature in Chinese Art*, 108; Soame Jenyns, *A Background to Chinese Painting*, 164; Charles A. S. Williams, *Outlines of Chinese Symbolism and Art Motives*, 404, 405.

271. James A. LeRoy, " The Outcome of the Taft Commission," *World Today*, x (January, 1906), 55-56. See also Alice Roosevelt Longworth, *Crowded Hours*, 91-92.

272. *Loc. cit.*

273. J. A. LeRoy, *op. cit.*, 55-56; *New York Tribune*, Sept. 4, 1905.

274. *Ibid.*, Sept. 5, 1905.

275. See, e. g., *ibid.*, Sept. 26, 1905.

276. *Chicago Tribune*, Sept. 28, 1905.

277. *Washington Star*, Oct. 4, 1905, TR Scrapbooks.

278. TR, Speech in Atlanta, Oct. 20, 1905, *Chicago Tribune*, Oct. 21, 1905.

279. Robert De Forest to W. Loeb, Jr., Nov. 2, 1905, TR MSS.

280. J. N. Jameson to J. L. Rodgers, Nov. 7, 1905, *Journal of the American Asiatic Association*, v (January, 1906), 357-359.

281. W. W. Rockhill to E. Root, Nov. 3, 4, 6, and 25, and Dec. 3, 23, and 29, 1905, *Foreign Relations*, 1906, 308-315; J. G. Lay to WWR, Dec. 7, 1905, in P. Varg, *Rockhill*, 67; H. V. Noyes, " What Caused the Lien-Chou Massacre? " *Chinese Recorder and Missionary Journal*, xxxvii (March, 1906), 115-120.

282. W. W. Rockhill to E. Root, Nov. 10, 1905, *Foreign Relations*, 1905, 231. See also *New York Tribune*, Nov. 2, 3, 8, 9, 10, and 12, 1905.

283. J. N. Jameson to J. L. Rodgers, Nov. 7, 1905, in *Journal of the American Asiatic Association*, v (January, 1906), 357.

284. T. Cary Friedlander, secretary of the San Francisco Merchants' Exchange, to TR, Nov. 6, 1905, TR MSS. See also TR to TCF, Nov. 23, 1905, TR MSS.

285. " Current Comment," *Journal of the American Asiatic Association*, v (December, 1905), 322. See also TR to T. C. Friedlander, Nov. 23, 1905, TR MSS.

286. TR to Charles J. Bonaparte, Nov. 15, 1905, TR MSS.

287. *Chicago Tribune*, Dec. 23, 1905.

288. *Loc. cit.*

289. Leonard Wood to TR, Dec. 13, 1905, TR MSS.

290. W. W. Rockhill to E. Root, Dec. 23, 1905, and March 9, 1906, *Foreign Relations*, 1906, 373-384, 394-398; *Chicago Tribune*, Dec. 19 and 21, 1905; *London Times*, Dec. 12-22, 1905; *New York Tribune*, Dec. 21, 1905; *San Francisco Chronicle*, Dec. 22, 1905. See also P. Varg, *Rockhill*, 67.

291. Julian Ralph to H. C. Lodge, Dec. [25 (?)], 1905, Lodge MSS.

292. *Chicago Tribune*, Dec. 23, 1905.

293. *Ibid.*, Jan. 3, 1906. So, too, believed Lyman P. Peet, missionary president of Foochow College. *Washington Post*, Feb. 11, 1906; *San Francisco Chronicle*, Feb. 11, 1906.

294. *Washington Post*, Jan. 7, 1906.

295. TR to W. H. Taft, Jan. 11, 1906, TR MSS.

296. W. W. Rockhill to TR, Jan. 11, 1906, TR MSS. See also WWR to E. Root, Nov. 6, 1905, March 7 and 17, and April 2, 1906, *Foreign Relations*, 1906, 311-313, 326-336; J. G. Lay to WWR, Dec. 7, 1905, WWR to Alfred E. Hippisley, April 21, 1906, WWR to ER, Jan. 8, Feb. 26, March 5, and April 9 and 14, 1906 in P. Varg, *Rockhill*, 66-68.

297. *New York Evening Post*, Jan. 15, 1906.

298. *New York Tribune*, Feb. 15, 1906.

299. *San Francisco Chronicle*, Feb. 22, 1906.

300. *New York Tribune*, Feb. 12, 1906.

301. *Ibid.*, March 8, 1906.

302. *San Francisco Chronicle*, Jan. 27, 1906.

303. *Chicago Tribune*, Feb. 13, 1906.

304. *Ibid.*, Feb. 19, 1906.

305. *San Francisco Chronicle*, March 1, 1906.

306. *New York Evening Post*, Feb. 9, 1906; *Washington Post*, Feb. 10, and 11, 1906.

307. *San Francisco Chronicle*, Feb. 13, 1906.

308. *Chicago Tribune*, Feb. 11, 1906.

309. *Ibid.*, Feb. 14, 1906.

310. *New York Tribune*, Feb. 6, 1906; *Washington Post*, Feb. 10, 1906.

311. *Washington Post*, Feb. 14, 1906. For a complete listing of the various regiments sent to the Philippine Islands see the *New York Evening Post*, March 1, 1906.

312. *San Francisco Chronicle*, Feb. 22, 1906.

313. *Chicago Tribune*, Feb. 10, 1906.

314. *Ibid.*, Feb. 14, 1906; *Washington Post*, Feb. 14, 1906.

315. *Chicago Tribune*, March 2, 1906; *Washington Post*, Feb. 10, 1906.

316. P. Varg, *Rockhill*, 68-69.

317. TR to L. Wood, April 2, 1906, TR MSS.

318. *New York Evening Post*, Feb. 16, 1906.

319. J. Foord, "Canards about China," *Journal of the American Asiatic Association*, VI (March, 1907), 47.

320. William Phillips to Joseph H. Choate, March 6, 1906, Choate MSS.

321. "Our Threat to China," *Nation*, LXXXII (Feb. 22, 1906), 151-152.

322. P. Varg, *Rockhill*, 68.

323. W. W. Rockhill to TR, July 7, 1905, TR MSS.

324. Gilbert Reid to J. Foord, April 11, 1906, *Journal of the American Asiatic Association*, VI (June, 1906), 132-133.

325. *New York Evening Post*, Feb. 23, 1906.

326. *San Francisco Chronicle*, Feb. 22, 1906.

327. *California Christian Advocate*, undated, quoted in the *San Francisco Chronicle*, March 1, 1906.

328. W. H. Taft, "China and Her Relations with the United States," Speech

before the American Association of China, Oct. 8, 1907, in WHT, *Present Day Problems*, 49.

329. M. Coolidge, *Chinese Immigration*, 483.

330. *San Francisco Chronicle*, Feb. 8, 1906.

CHAPTER V

1. TR, Address before the Society of Naval Architects and Marine Engineers, *New York Sun*, Nov. 13, 1897, TR Scrapbooks.

2. TR, " The Strenuous Life," Address before the Hamilton Club, April 10, 1899.

3. TR to Henry White, Nov. 27, 1907, TR MSS.

4. Brooks Adams, *America's Economic Supremacy*, 11-12.

5. *Ibid.*, 23, 25.

6. *Ibid.*, 41.

7. *Ibid.*, 196.

8. *Ibid.*, 197-198, 203, 217-219.

9. B. Adams to Henry Cabot Lodge, Oct. 26, 1901, Lodge MSS.

10. Alfred Thayer Mahan, *The Problem of Asia*, 77.

11. *Ibid.*, 44, 52.

12. *Ibid.*, 63.

13. *Ibid.*, 63, 109.

14. *Ibid.*, 116.

15. *Ibid.*, 64.

16. *Ibid.*, 120.

17. *Ibid.*, 87.

18. *Ibid.*, 165.

19. *Ibid.*, 177.

20. TR to H. C. Lodge, Nov. 28, 1896, Lodge MSS.; TR, Review of B. Adams's *The Law of Civilization and Decay* in the *Forum*, XXII (January, 1897), 587-588.

21. TR to Cecil Spring Rice, May 29 and Aug. 13, 1897, TR MSS.

22. H. C. Lodge to William B. McKinley, Oct. 22, 1900, Lodge MSS.

23. TR to Charles Arthur Moore, Feb. 14, 1898, TR MSS.

24. TR, Review of Charles W. Pearson's *National Life and Character* in the *Sewanee Review*, II (August, 1894) 363-364.

25. C. Spring Rice to TR, July 18, 1896, in CSR, *The Letters and Friendships of Sir Cecil Spring Rice*, Stephen Gwynn, ed., I, 208, hereafter cited as CSR, *Letters*. See also Nr. 6288, Freiherr Speck von Sternburg an den Grafen von Bülow, den 10. Februar 1905, *Grosse Politik*, XIX-2, 572-573.

26. TR to C. Spring Rice, Aug. 5, 1896, TR MSS.

27. C. Spring Rice to TR, Aug. 1, 1897, in CSR, *Letters*, I, 228-229.

28. TR to C. Spring Rice, Aug. 13, 1897, TR MSS. See also TR to C. Spring

Rice, May 29, 1897, TR MSS. In reviewing Elting E. Morison's *The Letters of Theodore Roosevelt* (*New York Times*, April 22, 1951), Henry F. Pringle used this letter to credit to Roosevelt fears of Russia parallel to those current in the mid-century. Actually Pringle misquoted the letter and made Roosevelt say about Russia what in reality Spring Rice had said and Roosevelt contradicted.

29. TR to Francis Cruger Moore, Feb. 5, 1898, TR MSS.; TR, " Expansion and Peace," *Independent*, LI (Dec. 21, 1899), 3403.

30. TR to George Ferdinand Becker, July 8, 1901, TR MSS.

31. TR to H. Speck von Sternburg, Aug. 28, 1900, TR MSS. See also TR to C. Spring Rice, Aug. 11, 1899, TR MSS.

32. TR to Frederic René Coudert, July 3, 1901, TR to G. F. Becker, July 8, 1901, TR MSS.

33. *Loc. cit.*

34. TR to C. Spring Rice, Feb. 2, 1904, TR to George Otto Trevelyan, March 9, 1905, TR MSS.; John Hay, MS. Diary, Jan. 15 and March 30, 1904, Hay MSS.; Allan Nevins, *Henry White: Thirty Years of American Diplomacy*, 184.

35. C. Spring Rice to TR, undated [*ca.* February-March, 1904], TR MSS.

36. See, e. g., C. Spring Rice to Edith Kermit Roosevelt, Dec. 9, 1903, and March 13 and 29, 1905, TR MSS.

37. See, e. g., George von Lengerke Meyer to TR, Feb. 21, June 9, and July 8 and 18, 1905, TR MSS.; GvonLM to H. C. Lodge, Dec. 12, 1905, Lodge MSS.; Willard Straight to TR, Oct. 15, 1906, Straight MSS. and WS to TR, Nov. 15, 1906, State Department Archives, supplied by Charles Vevier. See also Mark A. DeWolfe Howe, *George von Lengerke Meyer: His Life and Public Services*, 137-351.

38. TR to C. Spring Rice, March 19, 1904, TR MSS. See also TR to CSR, June 13, 1904, in CSR, *Letters*, I, 416-419.

39. TR to G. F. Becker, July 8, 1901, TR MSS.

40. TR to C. Spring Rice, Feb. 2, 1904, in CSR, *Letters*, I, 378.

41. TR to John E. Pillsbury, July 29, 1904, TR MSS.

42. TR to J. Hay, July 29, 1904, TR MSS.

43. TR to W. B. McKinley, April 22, 1897, TR MSS.

44. TR to Alfred T. Mahan, May 3, 1897, TR MSS.

45. TR to Francis V. Greene, Sept. 23, 1897, TR MSS.

46. *New York Tribune*, July 27, 1897, TR Scrapbooks.

47. TR to Capt. Caspar F. Goodrich, June 16, 1897, TR MSS. See also TR to Capt. Bowman H. McCalla, Aug. 2, 1897, TR MSS.

48. TR to John Davis Long, Sept. 30, 1897, TR MSS. See also TR to H. C. Lodge, Sept. 21, 1897, TR MSS.

49. TR to C. Spring Rice, Nov. 19, 1900, TR MSS.

50. TR to H. Speck von Sternburg, Nov. 19, 1900, TR to C. Spring Rice, Nov. 19, 1900, TR MSS.

51. TR to H. C. Lodge, June 16, 1905, Lodge MSS.

52. TR to C. Spring Rice, June 13, 1904, TR MSS. See also TR to John A. T. Hull, March 16, 1905, TR to G. O. Trevelyan, March 9, 1905, TR MSS.;

J. F. Rhodes, "Index Rerum," in M. A. DeW. Howe, *James Ford Rhodes,* 170.

53. TR to C. Spring Rice, June 13, 1904, TR MSS. See also TR to C. Spring Rice, March 19, 1904, TR MSS.

54. TR to C. Spring Rice, June 13, 1904, TR MSS.

55. W. Sturgis Bigelow to H. C. Lodge, Feb. 14, 1904, Lodge MSS.; George Kennan to Oscar S. Straus, Feb. 18, 1904, Straus MSS.; Nr. 5978, Freiherr Speck von Sternburg an das Auswärtige Amt, den 6. Februar 1904, *Grosse Politik,* XIX-1, 99-100; Winston B. Thorson, "Pacific Northwest Opinion on the Russo-Japanese War of 1904-1905," *Pacific Northwest Quarterly,* XXV (October, 1944), *passim.*

56. Elihu Root to TR, Feb. 15, 1904, Root MSS. See also TR to G. Kennan, May 6, 1905, TR MSS.

57. TR to J. Hay, Sept. 2, 1904, TR MSS.

58. J. Hay, MS. Diary, March 3 and June 27, 1904, Hay MSS.

59. TR to Dr. David B. Schneder, June 19, 1905, TR MSS. See also TR to J. A. T. Hull, March 16, 1905, TR to G. Kennan, May 6, 1905, TR MSS.

60. TR to C. Spring Rice, June 13, 1904, TR MSS.

61. TR to G. O. Trevelyan, May 13, 1905, TR MSS. See also TR to G. Kennan, May 6, 1905, TR MSS.

62. Nicholas Murray Butler to TR, June 2, 1903, and Jan. 12, 1904, William Loeb, Jr., to NMB, Jan. 14, 1904, J. Brander Matthews to TR, July 10, 1903, Leigh Hunt to NMB, reproduced in TR to TR Jr., March 5, 1904, TR MSS. See also NMB to TR, March 3, May 19, and Oct. 1, 1904, TR MSS.

63. TR to C. Spring Rice, March 19, 1904, TR MSS. See also Nr. 5994, H. Speck von Sternburg an den Reichskanzler Grafen von Bülow, den 9. Mai 1904, *Grosse Politik,* XIX-1, 113-114.

64. Arthur J. Balfour to C. Spring Rice, 1905 (not sent), in Blanche E. C. Dugdale, *Arthur James Balfour,* 288-290. This was an instruction never delivered because it seemed indiscreet to make official record of Balfour's knowledge of so confidential, unofficial a mission. But in conference Spring Rice was undoubtedly told verbally what it was unwise to put in writing.

65. TR to C. Spring Rice, June 13, 1904, TR MSS.

66. TR to J. Hay, Aug. 29, 1904, TR MSS.

67. TR to C. Spring Rice, June 13, 1904, TR to G. O. Trevelyan, March 9, 1905, TR MSS.

68. TR to C. Spring Rice, Dec. 27, 1904, TR MSS.

69. TR to C. Spring Rice, March 19, 1904, TR MSS.

70. J. Hay, MS. Diary, May 29, June 22, and Aug. 10, 1904, Hay MSS.; Nr. 5994, Freiherr Speck von Sternburg an den Grafen B. H. von Bülow, den 9. Mai 1904, *Grosse Politik,* XIX-1, 113-114. BHvonB to William II, Aug. 31, 1904, in *Letters of Prince von Bülow,* Frederic Whyte, trans., 72 (also quoted with Foreign Office memorandum of Aug. 24 in *La Politique Extérieure de l'Allemagne, 1870-1914* (Publications de la Société de la Guerre), traduit par

Henri Audoin, xxiv, 278-282. See also JH, MS. Diary, Jan. 1, 1905, Hay MSS.; TR to G. von L. Meyer, Feb. 6, 1905, TR MSS.

71. J. Hay, MS. Diary, Dec. 6, 1904, Hay MSS. See also Hay's proposed terms as stated to the Chinese Minister. J. Hay, MS. Diary, Feb. 23, 1905, Hay MSS.

72. G. von L. Meyer, MS. Diary, Dec. 26, 1903, quoted in M. A. DeW. Howe, *Meyer*, 81.

73. J. Hay to TR, Sept. 3, 1903, J. Hay, MS. Diary, Jan. 6, 1904, Hay MSS. See also A. Nevins, *Henry White*, 182-183.

74. J. Hay to TR, Jan. 5, 1904, JH, MS. Diary, Jan. 4, 5, and 11, 1904, JH to Joseph H. Choate, Jan. 27, 1904, Wm. Loeb, Jr., to JH, Jan. 2, 1904, Hay MSS.; A. Nevins, *Henry White*, 183-184. See also JH, MS. Diary, Jan. 10, 1904, Hay MSS.

75. TR to O. S. Straus, Feb. 9, 1904, TR MSS.

76. Francis B. Loomis to J. Hay, Dec. 21, 1903, Hay MSS.

77. J. H. Choate to J. Hay, Jan. 19, 1904, Hay MSS.; H. Speck von Sternburg to TR, Dec. 29, 1904, and Jan. 5 and 10, 1905, TR MSS.

78. J. Hay, MS. Diary, Jan. 11 and Feb. 16, 19, 21, and 22, 1904, Hay MSS.; H. Speck von Sternburg to TR, Jan. 15, 1905, TR to HSvonS, Jan. 18, 1905, TR MSS.

79. J. Hay, MS. Diary, Jan. 9 and 11 and Feb. 7, 8, and 9, 1904, Hay MSS.; TR to J. Hay, Jan. 12, 1905, E. Root to TR, Feb. 15, 1904, TR to ER, Feb. 16, 1904, TR to O. S. Straus, Feb. 9, 1904, TR MSS.; J. H. Choate to JH, Jan. 19, 1904, F. B. Loomis to JH, Feb. 6, 1904, Hay MSS.; *Washington Post*, April 6, 1905, TR Scrapbooks. See also O. S. Straus to TR, Feb. 8, 1904 (2 telegrams), TR MSS. The Russians tried to argue that from America's own point of view, backing Japan was a mistake. See, e. g., *Japan Weekly Mail*, Sept. 28, 1907.

80. J. Hay, MS. Diary, Feb. 10 and 11, 1904, Hay MSS.; Nr. 5992, Freiherr Speck von Sternburg an das Auswärtige Amt, den 21. März 1904, *Grosse Politik*, xix-1, 112-113.

81. J. Hay, MS. Diary, Jan. 11, Feb. 8, 11, 12, 13, 14, 15, 18, 19, and 21, and March 2, 1904, Hay MSS.; H. White to TR, Feb. 20, 1904, JH to J. H. Choate, Feb. 13, 1904, JH to Bellamy Storer, Feb. 13, 1904, JH to Charlemagne Tower, Feb. 10, 1904, TR MSS.; JHC to JH, Feb. 17, 1904, JH to JHC, Feb. 27, 1904, Choate MSS.; JH to JHC, Feb. 10, and 12, 1904, JHC to JH, Feb. 21, 1904, Hay MSS.; W. S. Bigelow to H. C. Lodge, Feb. 14, 1904, HW to HCL, Feb. 12, 1904, Lodge MSS.; TR to HW, Feb. 17, 1904, in A. Nevins, *Henry White*, 234, Nr. 5978, Freiherr Speck von Sternburg an das Auswärtige Amt, den 6. Februar 1904, *Grosse Politik*, xix-v, 99-100. See also the Marquess of Lansdowne (Henry C. K. Petty-Fitzmaurice) to Sir Frank Lascelles, Feb. 10, 1904, in *British Documents on the Origins of the War, 1898-1914*, George P. Gooch and Harold W. V. Temperley, eds., ii, 252; A. Whitney Griswold, *Far Eastern Policy of the United States*, 93-94.

82. J. Hay, MS. Diary, March 17, April 29, May 9, 28, and 30, 1904, and

Feb. 23 and March 2, 1905, Alvey A. Adee to TR, Aug. 23, 1904, AAA to JH, Aug. 22 and 23, JH to TR, Jan. 31, 1905, Hay MSS.; Rear Admiral Robley D. Evans to Secretary of the Navy William H. Moody, March 11, 1904, TR MSS.; JH to Count Arturo P. Cassini, Sept. 8, 1904, JH to Samuel Mather, Aug. 19, 1904, Hay MSS.; JH to H. White, May 5 and Sept. 5, 1904, Hay and White MSS.; HW to HCL, March 12, 1904, Lodge MSS.; J. H. Choate to JH, March 11, 1904, quoted in Edward S. Martin, *The Life of Joseph Hodges Choate*, II, 248; A. W. Griswold, *Far Eastern Policy*, 102-104. See also AAA to Edwin Conger, Aug. 22, 1904, Hay MSS.

83. J. Hay to the American Ambassadors to Austria, Belgium, France, Germany, Great Britain, Italy, and Portugal (Circular Telegram), Jan. 13, 1905, *Foreign Relations*, 1905, 1; TR to JH, Jan. 12 and 16, 1905, H. Speck von Sternburg to TR, Dec. 29, 1904, and Jan. 5, 1905, TR to HSvonS, Jan. 10 and 12, 1905, TR to C. Tower, Feb. 16, 1905, CT to TR, Feb. 4, 1905, TR MSS.; JH, MS. Diary, Jan. 5, 13, 18, 23, and 31, and Feb. 9 and 17, 1905, JH to TR, Jan. 19 and Feb. 3, 1905, J. H. Choate to JH, Jan. 18 and 31, 1905, Hay MSS.; Paul H. Clyde, *International Rivalries in Manchuria, 1689-1922*, 116; Tyler Dennett, *John Hay*, 408; A. W. Griswold, *Far Eastern Policy*, 102-103.

84. TR to C. Spring Rice, Dec. 27, 1904, TR MSS. See also J. Hay to TR, [Jan. 17 (?), 1905], JH to Count Cassini, Jan. 17, 1905, J. H. Choate to JH, Jan. 18, 1905, Hay MSS.

85. J. Hay, MS. Diary, Feb. 13, 1905, Hay MSS.; C. Spring Rice to E. K. Roosevelt, March 29, 1905, TR MSS.

86. TR to G. von L. Meyer, Feb. 6, 1905, TR MSS.

87. A. J. Balfour to H. C. Lodge, April 11, 1905, Lodge MSS.; Lord Lansdowne to Sir Mortimer Durand, Feb. 5, 1905, in *British Documents*, G. P. Gooch and H. W. V. Temperley, eds., II, 243; Lord Lansdowne to Edward VII, April 18, 1904, in Baron of Newton (Thomas W. Legh), *Lord Lansdowne*, 308-309.

88. J. Hay, MS. Diary, March 9 and May 5 and 29, 1904, Hay MSS.; G. von L. Meyer to TR, Jan. 28, 1905, TR MSS.; GvonLM to TR, Jan. 20, 1905, GvonLM to H. C. Lodge, March 5, 1905, in M. A. DeW. Howe, *Meyer*, 113-114, 127-128; H. Porter to JH, Jan. 21 and Feb. 18, 1904, in Elsie Mende, *An American Soldier and Diplomat, Horace Porter*, 271, 273.

89. TR to J. Hay, Jan. 12, 1905, TR to H. Speck von Sternburg, Jan. 10 and 12, 1905, HSvonS to TR, Dec. 24, 1904, and Jan. 5, 1905, TR to C. Tower, Feb. 16, 1905, CT to TR, Feb. 4 and July 13, 1905, TR MSS.; J. Hay, MS. Diary, Jan. 5 and 12 and Feb. 17, 1905, Hay MSS.; Nr. 3972, Graf von Bülow an Kaiser Wilhelm II, den 4. Januar 1904, *Grosse Politik*, XIX-1, 88-89; William II to Nicholas II, Oct. 30, 1904, in BHvonB, *Letters*, 74 (also cited in *Grosse Politik*, XIX-1, 306); Willy to Nicky, Oct. 8 and Nov. 2 and 6, 1904, *Willy-Nicky Correspondence*, in Hermann Bernstein, ed., 61, 77, 81; W. B. Thorson, " Pacific Northwest Opinion on the Russo-Japanese War of 1904-1905," *Pacific Northwest Quarterly*, XXV (October, 1944).

90. J. Hay, MS. Diary, May 28 and 29 and July 2 and 13, 1904, Hay MSS.; Nr. 6188, Graf B. H. von Bülow an den Gesandten in Tokio Grafen Emmerich

von Arco-Valley, den 14. März 1905, Nr. 6285, Freiherr Speck von Sternburg an das Aüswartige Amt, den 3. Februar 1905, *Grosse Politik*, xix-2, 413, 567-568; BHvonB to William II, Aug. 31, 1904, in BHvonB, *Letters*, 72 (also cited, with Foreign Office memorandum of Aug. 24, in *La Politique Extérieure de l'Allemagne*, xxiv, 278-282).

91. J. Hay, MS. Diary, Jan. 11 and May 9 and 28, 1904, JH to H. White, May 24, 1904, Hay MSS.; *New York Sun*, May 27, 1904, TR Scrapbooks.

92. J. Hay, MS. Diary, July 2 and Oct. 29, 1904, Hay MSS.

93. J. Hay to H. White, May 5 and Nov. 11, 1904, Robert S. McCormick to JH, May 7, 1904, JH, MS. Diary, Oct. 16, 1904, Hay MSS.

94. J. Hay, MS. Diary, Jan. 11, 1904, Hay MSS.

95. J. Hay, MS. Diary, Feb. 23, 1905, Hay MSS.; Nr. 6285, Freiherr Speck von Sternburg an das Auswärtige Amt, den 3. Februar 1905, *Grosse Politik*, xix-2, 567-568.

96. J. Hay, MS. Diary, Feb. 23, 1905, Hay MSS.; H. Speck von Sternburg to TR, Feb. 9, 1905, TR MSS.; Nr. 6190, Der Gesandte in Tokio Graf E. von Arco-Valley an Grafen von Bülow, den 16. März 1905, *Grosse Politik*, xix-2, 414.

97. Nr. 6168, Graf B. H. von Bülow an den Geschäftsträger in Petersburg Freiherrn Konrad G. von Romberg, den 12. November 1904, Nr. 6172, Der Botschafter in London Graf Paul W. von Metternich an das Auswärtige Amt, den 17. November 1904, Nr. 6173, BHvonB an KGvonR (Konzept von der Hand des Vortragenden Rats Friedrich von Holstein), den 18. November 1904, *Grosse Politik*, xix-2, 388-389, 391-392; Willy to Nicky, Nov. 2 (15) and 6 (19), 1904, in *Willy-Nicky Correspondence*, H. Bernstein, ed., 77-81; Horace N. Allen to Walter D. (?) Townsend, Nov. 17, 1904, Allen MSS.

98. H. C. Lodge, MS. Diary, March 29, 1905, Lodge MSS.

99. TR to J. Hay, March 30, 1905, H. Speck von Sternburg to TR, Dec. 29, 1904, and Jan. 5 and May 19, 1905, TR to HSvonS, Jan. 10 and 12 and March 31, 1905, TR MSS.

100. TR to H. Speck von Sternburg, March 31, 1905, TR MSS. A. J. Balfour to H. C. Lodge, April 11, 1905, Lodge MSS.

101. TR to J. Hay, March 30, 1905, TR MSS.

102. J. Hay, MS. Diary, May 29, 1904, Hay MSS.

103. *London Times*, June 12, 1905, TR Scrapbooks.

104. J. Hay, MS. Diary, Jan. 3 and Feb. 6, 1905, Hay MSS.; *Washington Post*, Jan. 3, 1905, TR Scrapbooks.

105. O. S. Straus to TR, Jan. 6, 1905, Straus MSS.; C. Spring Rice to E. K. Roosevelt, March 29, 1905, TR MSS.

106. *Washington Post*, Jan. 3, 1905, TR Scrapbooks.

107. See, e. g., J. Hay, MS. Diary, Jan. 4, 5, and 10, 1904, Hay MSS.; H. C. Lodge, MS. Diary, March 29 [1905], TR to HCL, June 16, 1905, Lodge MSS.

108. TR to H. Speck von Sternburg, March 31, 1905, HSvonS to TR, Feb. 24, May 31, and June 3 and 11, 1905, TR to H. C. Lodge, June 5 and 16, 1905, TR MSS.; *Washington Post*, June 9 and 10, 1905, TR Scrapbooks; J. Hay to

TR, Feb. 17, 1905, Hay MSS. See also Nr. 6193, Willy an Nicky, den 3. Juni 1905, *Grosse Politik*, xix-2, 420-422.

109. See, e. g., J. Hay, MS. Diary, Jan. 4 and 10, 1904, JH to TR, Jan. 5, 1904, Hay MSS.; TR to H. C. Lodge, June 5 and 16, 1905, TR to Whitelaw Reid, June 5, 1905, TR MSS.; A. W. Griswold, *Far Eastern Policy*, 117.

110. TR to J. Hay, April 2, 1905, TR to William Howard Taft, April 27 and June 3, 1905, TR to H. C. Lodge, May 15, 1905, TR MSS.; *Washington Post*, June 9, 1905, TR Scrapbooks. See also JH, MS. Diary, Jan. 4, 1905, Hay MSS.

111. J. Hay, MS. Diary, June 22, 1904, and Jan. 29, 1905, Hay MSS.; Nr. 6288, Freiherr Speck von Sternburg an Graf von Bülow, den 10. Februar 1905, *Grosse Politik*, xix-2, 572-573.

112. See, e. g., TR to H. C. Lodge, June 5 and 16 and July 11, 1905, TR MSS.

113. TR to H. C. Lodge, June 5, 1905, W. Reid to J. Hay, June 5, 1905, Lord Lansdowne to the British Embassy, June 3, 1905, TR MSS.; *Washington Post*, June 9, 1905, TR Scrapbooks. See also Evelene Peters, *Roosevelt und der Kaiser*, 140-141.

114. TR to H. C. Lodge, June 5 and 16, 1905, John Callan O'Laughlin to TR, June 9, 10, and 26, 1905, F. B. Loomis to G. von L. Meyer, June 10, 1905, Count Cassini to TR, June 3, 1905, GvonLM to TR, June 11 and 18, 1905, GvonLM to J. Hay, June 11, 1905, TR MSS.; GvonLM, Diary, June 11, 1905, in M. A. DeW. Howe, *Meyer*, 164; O. S. Straus to TR, Jan. 6, 1905, Straus MSS.; *London Morning Post*, June 12, 1905, *Washington Times*, June 4, 1905, TR Scrapbooks. See also MADeWH, *Meyer*, 168-169; JCO'L, Memorandum, June 6 or 7, 1905, TR MSS.

115. J. Hay, MS. Diary, Dec. 26, 1904, J. Hay to H. White, Jan. 23, 1905, Hay MSS.; G. von L. Meyer to H. C. Lodge, Feb. 5, 1905, Lodge MSS.; TR to O. S. Straus, Dec. 16, 1904, Straus MSS.; HCL to GvonLM, Dec. 27, 1904, and Feb. 16, 1905, HCL to HW, Jan. 23, 1905, HW to HCL, Oct. 26, 1904, Lodge MSS.; Nr. 6285, Freiherr Speck von Sternburg an das Auswärtige Amt, den 3. Februar 1905, *Grosse Politik*, xix-2, 567-568.

116. J. Hay, MS. Diary, Feb. 6, 1905, Hay MSS.

117. G. von L. Meyer to H. C. Lodge, March 5, 1905, in M. A. DeW. Howe, *Meyer*, 127-128.

118. C. Spring Rice to E. K. Roosevelt, April 26, 1905, TR MSS. See also G. von L. Meyer to H. C. Lodge, May 23/June 6, 1905, Lodge MSS.

119. William II to Prince von Bülow, July 25, 1905, in *Prince Bülow and the Kaiser: with Excerpts from the Private Correspondence Preserved in the Records of the German Foreign Office*, Oakley Williams, trans., 177; William II to TR, July [29 (?)], 1905, TR MSS.; G. von L. Meyer, Diary, May 19, 1906, M. A. DeW. Howe, *Meyer*, 284.

120. G. von L. Meyer to H. C. Lodge, March 5 and April 3, 1905, H. White to HCL, Feb. 26, 1904, Lodge MSS.; GvonLM Diary, April 4, 1905, in M. A. DeW. Howe, *Meyer*, 139.

121. J. Hay, MS. Diary, Jan. 5 and 13 and Feb. 17, 1905, Hay MSS.; H. Speck von Sternburg to TR, Dec. 29, 1904, and Jan. 5 and 15, 1905, TR to

HSvonS, Jan. 10 and 12, 1905, TR to JH, Jan. 12, 1905, C. Tower to TR. Feb. 4, 1905, TR to CT, Feb. 16, 1905, TR MSS.

122. H. Speck von Sternburg to TR, Feb. 12, 1905, TR MSS.; J. Hay, MS Diary, Feb. 13, 1905, Hay MSS.

123. H. Speck von Sternburg to TR, March 14, 1905, TR to C. Spring Rice, Nov. 1, 1905, TR MSS.

124. TR to H. Speck von Sternburg, March 31, 1905, HSvonS to TR, April 2, 1905, TR MSS.

125. H. Speck von Sternburg to TR, April 5, 1905, TR MSS.

126. William II to C. Tower, June 4, 1905, CT to TR, June 9, 1905, TR MSS.; *Washington Post*, June 4, 1905, TR Scrapbooks; E. Peters, *Roosevelt und der Kaiser*, 100. See also Willy to Nicky, July 16, 1905, *Willy-Nicky Correspondence*, H. Bernstein, ed., 110.

127. Count Cassini to TR, June 3, 1905, TR to H. C. Lodge, June 16, 1905. H. Speck von Sternburg to TR, May 31, 1905, TR MSS.; *Washington Post*. May 30 and June 2 and 3, 1905, TR Scrapbooks.

128. TR to H. C. Lodge, June 16, 1905, TR to W. Reid, June 5, 1905, H. Speck von Sternburg to TR, June 11, 1905, TR MSS.; *Washington Post*, June 4. 5, 9, and 10, 1905, TR Scrapbooks. See also TR to C. Tower, June 24, 1905. TR MSS.

129. H. Speck von Sternburg to TR, June 3, 1905, C. Tower to TR, June 9. 1905, TR to H. C. Lodge, June 5, 1905, TR MSS. Germany gave strong support to Roosevelt's efforts in the Far East. CT to TR, Feb. 4, 1905, TR MSS See also J. Hay, MS. Diary, Feb. 11, 1905, Hay MSS.

130. TR to H. Speck von Sternburg, Sept. 6, 1905, TR MSS.

131. TR to H. C. Lodge, June 5 and 16, 1905, Lodge and TR MSS.; TR to G. von L. Meyer, June 19 and July 7, 1905, TR to John St. Loe Strachey, July 27, 1905, TR to C. Tower, June 24, 1905, TR MSS.

132. J. Hay to Spencer F. Eddy, June 7, 1904, JH, MS. Diary, June 3 and 6, 1904, Hay MSS.; A. Nevins, *Henry White*, 184.

133. TR to J. Hay, April 2, 1905, TR MSS. See also TR to Seth Low, July 14, 1905, TR to G. von L. Meyer, June 19, 1905, TR to W. H. Taft, April 8, 1905, TR MSS.; TR to the American Minister in Peking, in Lord Newton, *Lansdowne*, 325; *Washington Star*, June 23, 1905, TR Scrapbooks.

134. TR to Edward VII, March 9, 1905, in Sidney Lee, *Edward VII*, II, 432-433; TR to H. C. Lodge, June 5 and 16, 1905, Lodge and TR MSS.; TR to G. von L. Meyer, June 19 and July 7, 1905, TR to Alice Roosevelt, Sept. 2, 1905, TR to J. St. Loe Strachey, July 27, 1905, TR to W. H. Taft, April 8, 1905, TR to C. Tower, June 24, 1905, TR to Andrew D. White, June 1, 1905, TR MSS. See also J. C. O'Laughlin to TR, Feb. 9, 1905, TR to G. O. Trevelyan, March 9, 1905, TR MSS.

135. TR to H. Speck von Sternburg, March 31, 1905, TR to J. Hay, April 2, 1905, TR to Alice Roosevelt, Sept. 2, 1905, TR to W. H. Taft, April 8, 1905, TR MSS.

136. TR to H. C. Lodge, June 5 and 16, 1905, TR to J. Hay, April 2, 1905,

Lodge and TR MSS.; TR to G. von L. Meyer, June 19 and July 7, 1905, TR to J. St. Loe Strachey, July 27, 1905, TR to C. Tower, June 24, 1905, TR MSS.

137. J. Hay, MS. Diary, Feb. 23 and March 16, 1905, Hay MSS.; J. C. O'Laughlin to TR, June 8, 1905, H. Speck von Sternburg to TR, March 20, 1905, TR MSS.

138. J. Hay, MS. Diary, Feb. 4 and 13, 1905, Hay MSS.; H. Speck von Sternburg to TR, Feb. 24, 1905, C. Spring Rice to E. K. Roosevelt, March 29, 1905, TR MSS.; G. von L. Meyer to TR, Feb. 21, 1905, in M. A. DeW. Howe, *Meyer*, 124.

139. J. Hay, MS. Diary, Feb. 13, 1905, Hay MSS.

140. Baron Jutaro Komura to Kotoro Takahira, handed to J. Hay, March 14 [1905], Hay MSS.

141. Lord Lansdowne to Sir Claude M. MacDonald, Jan. 29 and Feb. 5 and 7, 1904, CMMacD to Lord Lansdowne, Feb. 5, 1904, Lord Lansdowne to Sir Charles S. Scott, Feb. 8, 1904, in *British Documents*, G. P. Gooch and H. W. V. Temperley, eds., II, 240-244, 246-247, 250.

142. J. Hay, MS. Diary, Feb. 11, 1904, Hay MSS.

143. J. Hay, MS. Diary, April 21, 1904, Hay MSS.

144. J. Hay, MS. Diary, Jan. 26, 1905, Hay MSS.; TR to C. Spring Rice, May 13, 1905, TR to W. H. Taft, April 20, 1905, TR to G. O. Trevelyan, May 13, 1905, TR MSS.; Baron J. Komura to K. Takahira, summarized in WHT to TR, transmitted in B. F. Barnes to W. Loeb, Jr., April 18, 1905, TR MSS.

145. TR to W. H. Taft, April 8, 1905, J. Komura to K. Takahira, quoted in WHT to TR, transmitted in B. F. Barnes to W. Loeb, Jr., April 25, 1950, TR MSS.; W. H. Taft to Lloyd C. Griscom, April 25, 1905, Taft MSS.

146. G. von L. Meyer, Diary, April 12, 1905, in M. A. DeW. Howe, *Meyer*, 146; GvonLM to TR, April 13, 1905, TR MSS.

147. See, e. g., TR to W. H. Taft, April 8, 1905, TR MSS.

148. H. Speck von Sternburg to TR, May 19, 1905, TR MSS.; TR to A. D. White, June 1, 1905, TR MSS.

149. W. H. Taft to TR, April 5, 1905, Taft MSS.; *New York Times*, April 4, 1905, TR Scrapbooks.

150. TR to C. Spring Rice, May 13, 1905, TR to W. H. Taft, April 20, 1905, TR to G. O. Trevelyan, May 13, 1905, TR MSS.; Baron J. Komura to K. Takahira, summarized in WHT to TR, transmitted in B. F. Barnes to W. Loeb Jr., April 18, 1905, TR MSS.

151. W. H. Taft to TR, April 26, 1905, Taft MSS.; Baron J. Komura to K. Takahira, quoted in WHT to TR, transmitted in B. F. Barnes to W. Loeb, Jr., April 25, 1905, TR MSS.

152. J. Hay to Henry Adams, May 2, 1905, Hay MSS.

153. W. H. Taft to TR, May 1 and 2, 1905, Taft and TR MSS.; F. M. Huntington Wilson, *Memoirs of an Ex-Diplomat*, 115-116.

154. TR to W. H. Taft, April 27, 1905, TR MSS. See also Henry L. Stoddard, *It Costs To Be President*, 149-152.

155. Baron J. Komura to K. Takahira, May 1, 1905, Taft MSS.; W. H. Taft

to TR, May 2, 1905, TR MSS. Meantime an American adviser to the Japanese Government was giving Griscom the new and inflated terms of peace on which Japan would end the war. Lloyd C. Griscom to J. Hay, May 15, 1905, Hay MSS.

156. TR to H. C. Lodge, May 15, 1905, TR MSS. See also G. von L. Meyer to TR, May 22/June 5, 1905, in M. A. DeW. Howe, *Meyer*, 150; TR to G. von L. Meyer, May 22 and 24, 1905, TR MSS.; TR to HCL, June 16, 1905, Lodge MSS.

157. TR to G. O. Trevelyan, May 13, 1905, TR to H. C. Lodge, May 15, 1905, TR to C. Spring Rice, May 26, 1905, TR MSS.

158. TR to H. C. Lodge, June 16, 1905, K. Takahira to W. Loeb, Jr., May 31, 1905, TR MSS.; *Washington Post,* May 30 and 31, 1905, *Washington Times,* June 4, 1905, TR Scrapbooks.

159. Willy to Nicky, Oct. 8 and Nov. 2/15 and 6/19, 1904, *Willy-Nicky Correspondence,* H. Bernstein, ed., 61, 77-81. See also J. C. O'Laughlin to J. Hay, Aug. 11, 1904, Hay MSS.

160. Baron J. Komura to K. Takahira, May 31, 1905, TR to H. C. Lodge, June 5 and 16, 1905, TR MSS. The *Washington Post,* June 2, 1905, recorded conferences but has no hint of their meaning.

161. TR to H. C. Lodge, June 16, 1905, Count Cassini to TR, June 3, 1905, H. Speck von Sternburg to TR, May 31, 1905, TR MSS.; *Washington Post,* May 30 and June 2 and 3, 1905, TR Scrapbooks.

162. Count Vladimir M. Lamsdorff to Count Cassini, June 6, 1905, TR to H. C. Lodge, June 16, 1905, TR MSS.

163. J. C. O'Laughlin to TR, June 7, 8, and 9, 1905, TR MSS.; TR to H. C. Lodge, June 5 and 16, 1905, TR and Lodge MSS.; Andrew Carnegie, *Autobiography,* 368-369.

164. G. von L. Meyer to TR, July 8, 1905, in M. A. DeW. Howe, *Meyer*, 178; GvonLM to A. A. Adee, June 2, 1905, TR MSS.

165. TR, "Memo of cable sent by State Dept. to Ambassador Meyer, June 5, 1905," W. Loeb MSS.; F. B. Loomis to G. von L. Meyer, June 5, 1905, TR to H. C. Lodge, June 5 and 16, 1905, TR MSS.

166. TR to C. Spring Rice, July 24, 1905, G. von L. Meyer to the Secretary of State, May 18/31 and June 7, 1905, H. Speck von Sternburg to TR, June 11, 1905, C. Tower to TR, June 4, 5, and 9, 1905, William II to CT, June 4, 1905, TR MSS.; TR to H. C. Lodge, June 5 and 16, 1905, Lodge MSS.; William II to Prince von Bülow, July 25 and Sept. 25, 1905, in *Prince Bülow and the Kaiser,* Oakley Williams, trans., 152, 177; Nr. 6193, Wilhelm II an Nikolaus II (Eigenhändigen Konzept), 3 Juni 1905, Nicholas II to Wilhelm II [June, 1905], Nr. 6197, Fürst von Bülow an den Botschafter in Petersburg Grafen von Johann Alvensleben, den 9. Juni 1905, *Grosse Politik,* XIX-2, 420-422, 425 n., 425-426; *Willy-Nicky Correspondence,* H. Bernstein, ed., 103; *Washington Post,* June 10, 1905, TR Scrapbooks; A. W. Griswold, *Far Eastern Policy,* 117.

167. Nr. 6196, Graf von Alvensleben (St. Petersburg) an das Auswärtige Amt, den 8. Juni 1905, *Grosse Politik,* XIX-2, 424-425. See also Willy to Nicky, undated, in *Willy-Nicky Correspondence,* 103.

168. G. von L. Meyer, Diary, June 8 and 9, 1905, in M. A. DeW. Howe, *Meyer*, 163-164; GvonLM to J. Hay, June 7, 1905, GvonLM to TR, June 7, and 9, 1905, TR MSS.; *Willy-Nicky Correspondence*, 103. See also M. A. DeW. Howe, *Meyer*, 157-162.

169. TR to the Russian Government and TR to the Japanese Government, June 8, 1905, *Foreign Relations* (1905), 807-808; J. C. O'Laughlin to TR, June 8, 1905, TR MSS.; TR to H. C. Lodge, June 16, 1905, Lodge MSS.

170. G. von L. Meyer, Diary, June 10, 1905, in M. A. DeW. Howe, *Meyer*, 164; L. C. Griscom to J. Hay, June 10, 1905, TR to JH, June 12, 1905, GvonLM to TR, June 12, 1905, enclosed in TR to H. C. Lodge, June 16, 1905, TR MSS.; *Washington Post*, June 9-13, 1905, *Washington Star*, June 10, 12, and 13, 1905, *London Times*, June 12, 1905, TR Scrapbooks.

171. G. von L. Meyer, Diary, June 10, 1905, in M. A. DeW. Howe, *Meyer*, 164; GvonLM to H. C. Lodge, June 7/20, 1905, Lodge MSS. See also *Washington Post*, June 11, 1905, TR Scrapbooks; N. M. Butler to TR, June 15, 1905, TR MSS.; J. Hay to TR, June 16, 1905, Hay MSS.; H. C. Lodge to TR, June 18, 1905, Lodge MSS.

172. G. von L. Meyer, Diary, June 11, 1905, in M. A. DeW. Howe, *Meyer*, 164; C. Tower to TR, July 6, 1905, CT to J. Hay, July 13, 1905, GvonLM to JH, June 11, 1905, TR MSS.

173. *London Morning Post*, June 12, 1905. See also *London Times*, June 12, 1905, TR Scrapbooks. See also F. von Holstein to Ida von Stülpnagel-Dargitz, June 16, 1905, in FvonH, *Lebensbekenntnis in Briefen an Eine Frau*, Helmuth Rogge, ed., 240.

174. Baron J. Komura to J. Hay, March 14 [1905], Hay MSS.; TR to H. C. Lodge, June 16, 1905, TR MSS.; J. Hay, MS. Diary, Feb. 13 and June 19, 1905, L. C. Griscom to J. Hay, May 15, 1905, Hay MSS.; LCG to W. H. Taft, April 6, 1905, Taft MSS.; *London Morning Post*, June 12, 1905, TR Scrapbooks.

175. TR to H. C. Lodge, June 16, 1905, Lodge MSS.

176. Lord Lansdowne to Sir Claude O'B. Hardinge, April 3, 1905, in Lord Newton, *Lansdowne*, 322-323. See also Lord Lansdowne to Sir M. Durand, June, 1905, Hay MSS.

177. G. von L. Meyer, Diary, June 12, 13, 16, and 18, 1905, in M. A. DeW. Howe, *Meyer*, 165-167; Count A. P. Cassini to TR, June 17 and 18, 1905, TR to APC, June 15, 1905, L. C. Griscom to J. Hay, June 18 and 23, 1905, K. Kaneko to TR, June 14, 1905, Count V. M. Lamsdorff to APC, June 1/14, 1905, F. B. Loomis to LCG, June 16, 1905, FBL to GvonLM, June 14 and 15, 1905, FBL to W. Reid, June 15, 1905, TR to H. C. Lodge, June 16, 1905, GvonLM to JH, June 16 and 17, 1905, GvonLM to TR, June 16, 17, 18, 19, and 20 and July 18/Aug. 1, 1905, GvonLM to the Secretary of State, July 11, 1905, TR to GvonLM, June 16, 1905, TR to Alice Roosevelt, Sept. 2, 1905, H. Speck von Sternburg to TR, June 11, 1905, TR to O. S. Straus, June 15, 1905, TR to K. Takahira, June 13 and 15, 1905, Japanese instruction to KT, June 14, 1905, Memorandum for the Japanese Government given by the President to Minister Takahira, June 15, 1905, Memorandum of a statement made by the President to

the Russian Ambassador, June 15, 1905, TR MSS.; Nr. 6167, Aufzeichnung des Reichskanzlers Grafen von Bülow, den 2. November 1904, *Grosse Politik*, xix-2, 387-388; *Washington Star*, June 12 and 19, 1905, *Washington Post*, June 13, 14, 15, 16, 17, 19, and 20, 1905, TR Scrapbooks; TR to Kermit Roosevelt, June 14, 1905, in TR, *Letters to Kermit*, Will Irwin, ed., 106; Emile H. Dillon, *The Eclipse of Russia*, 299-300; P. H. Clyde, *International Rivalries in Manchuria*, 133-136. See also C. Tower to TR, July 6, 1905, TR MSS.; Tadasu Hayashi, *Secret Memoirs*, 230-231; M. A. DeW. Howe, *Meyer*, 167-170, 174-175; Baron Roman R. Rosen, *Forty Years of Diplomacy*, i, 259.

178. G. von L. Meyer to TR, June 18 and July 8, 18, and 19, 1905, TR to GvonLM, July 7, 1905, GvonLM to J. Hay, June 17 and 21, 1905, TR MSS.; H. C. Lodge to TR, July 25, 1905, Lodge MSS. See also M. A. DeW. Howe, *Meyer*, 168-169, 178-179, 181-183.

179. G. von L. Meyer, Diary, July 7 and 8 and Aug. 3 and 7, 1905, GvonLM to Thomas Meyer, April 3/16, 1905, GvonLM to TR, June 5, 1905, in M. A. DeW. Howe, *Meyer*, 144, 154, 177, 190-191; TR to A. P. Cassini, June 16, 1905, TR to GvonLM, June 19, 1905, GvonLM to TR, July 8 and 18 and Aug. 1 and 9, 1905, GvonLM to W. Loeb, Jr., July 3, 1905, J. C. O'Laughlin to TR, June 29, 1905, TR to W. Reid, July 7, 1905, TR MSS.; APC to TR, June 12/25, 1905, TR to H. C. Lodge, June 16, 1905, Lodge MSS.; *Washington Post*, June 22, 1905, TR Scrapbooks. See also H. Speck von Sternburg to TR, June 11, 1905, TR MSS.; M. A. DeW. Howe, *Meyer*, 189-190, 193. Military disasters and revolution at home softened Russia's resistance to making peace. O. S. Straus to TR, Jan. 6, 1905, Straus MSS.

180. G. von L. Meyer, Diary, June 30 and July 2, 3, 12, 13, and 14, 1905, GvonLM to TR, June 5, 1905, in M. A. DeW. Howe, *Meyer*, 154, 171-176, 180-181; TR to GvonLM, June 18, 1905, GvonLM to TR, June 5 and 18 and July 18 and 19, 1905, GvonLM to A. A. Adee, June 25, 1905, GvonLM to J. Hay, June 20, 21, 23, and 30, 1905, GvonLM to the Secretary of State, June 28 and July 13, 1905, J. C. O'Laughlin to TR, June 29, 1905, TR to K. Takahira, June 15, 1905, KT to TR, transmitted from the White House to W. Loeb, Jr., c/o Bishop Lawrence, June 28, 1905, Rudolph Forster to WL, Jr., July 2 and 6, 1905, WL, Jr., to RF, June 29 and July 3, 1905, C. Spring Rice to E. K. Roosevelt, Sept. 26, 1905, Memorandum of cablegrams prepared by the President to be sent by Secretary Hay to Ambassador Meyer, June 20, 23, 24, and 26, 1905, TR MSS.; WL, Jr., to J. Hay, June 20, 1905, Hay MSS.; Memorandum of statement made by TR to APC, June 15, 1905, enclosed in TR to H. C. Lodge, June 16, 1905, Lodge MSS.; *New York Tribune*, July 19, 1905, *Washington Post*, June 18, 23, and 27, and July 3, 1905, *Washington Star*, June 18 and 19, 1905, TR Scrapbooks; Baron R. R. Rosen, *Forty Years of Diplomacy*, i, 257; Alexandre Iswolsky, *Recollections of a Foreign Minister*, 6-8; E. J. Dillon, *The Eclipse of Russia*, 298.

181. G. von L. Meyer, Diary, June 30 and July 2 and 11, 1905, in M. A. DeW. Howe, *Meyer*, 171-172, 175, 180; TR to H. C. Lodge, July 11, 1905, TR to GvonLM, July 7, 1905, GvonLM to the Secretary of State, July 1, 1905, TR

to W. Reid, July 7, 1905, TR to C. Spring Rice, July 24, 1905, K. Takahira to TR, transmitted by the White House to W. Loeb, Jr., c/o Bishop Lawrence, June 28, 1905, R. Forster to W. Loeb, Jr., July 6, 1905, WL, Jr., to RF, July 1, 1905, TR MSS.; H. White to H. C. Lodge, July 29, 1905, Lodge MSS.; *New York Tribune*, July 19, 1905, *Washington Post*, June 23, 1905, *Washington Star*, June 23, 1905, TR Scrapbooks.

182. TR to W. Reid, June 30, 1905, TR MSS.

183. TR to H. C. Lodge, June 16, 1905, TR MSS. See also TR to S. Low, June 14, 1905, TR to G. von L. Meyer, June 19, 1905, TR to C. Spring Rice, July 24, 1905, TR to J. St. Loe Strachey, July 27, 1905, TR to C. Tower, June 24, 1905, TR MSS.

184. J. Hay to TR, July 21, 1904, Hay MSS.; TR to JH, July 21, 1904, TR to H. C. Lodge, June 16, 1905, TR to G. von L. Meyer, June 19, 1905, TR to W. Reid, June 30, 1905, TR MSS. See also HCL to TR, June 18, 1905, Lodge MSS.

185. TR to H. C. Lodge, June 5 and 16, 1905, Lodge and TR MSS.; TR to S. Low, June 14, 1905, TR to G. von L. Meyer, June 19 and July 7, 1905, TR to J. St. Loe Strachey, July 27, 1905, TR to C. Tower, June 24, 1905, TR MSS.

186. TR to Nicholas II, Sept. 6, 1905, TR to J. C. O'Laughlin, Aug. 31, 1905, TR to Alice Roosevelt, Sept. 2, 1905, TR MSS.

187. K. Takahira to TR, July 12, 1905, A. A. Adee to W. Loeb, Jr., July 12, 1905, WL, Jr., to R. Forster, July 11, 1905, Herbert H. D. Peirce to WL, Jr., July 13, 1905, TR MSS.; *New York Press*, July 15, 1905, *New York Sun*, July 9, 1905, *Washington Star*, July 8, 1905, TR Scrapbooks.

188. TR to Baron R. R. Rosen, July 18, 1905, RRR to B. F. Barnes, July 23, 1905, H. H. D. Peirce to W. Loeb, Jr., July 13, 1905, K. Takahira to BFB, July 29, 1905, TR MSS.; *New York Sun*, Aug. 1, 1905, *Washington Star*, July 26 and 31, 1905, TR Scrapbooks.

189. J. J. Jusserand to TR, Aug. 9, 1905, TR to Baron Rosen, July 18, 1905, K. Takahira to B. F. Barnes, July 25, 1905, TR MSS.; *New York Sun*, Aug. 1, 1905, *New York Tribune*, July 28, 1905, *Washington Post*, Aug. 5, 1905, *Washington Star*, July 31, 1905, TR Scrapbooks; Count Serge Witte, " My Visit to America and the Portsmouth Peace Conference," *World's Work*, XLI (March, 1921), 487-488.

190. G. von L. Meyer, Diary, Aug. 7, 1905, in M. A. DeW. Howe, *Meyer*, 191-192; H. H. D. Peirce to W. Loeb, Jr., July 21, 1905, HHDP to B. F. Barnes, Aug. 1, 1905, H. White to TR, Aug. 10, 1905, TR MSS.; *Washington Post*, Aug. 6, 1905, TR Scrapbooks; Baron R. R. Rosen, *Forty Years of Diplomacy*, I, 264, S. Witte, " My Visit to America . . . ," *World's Work*, XLI (March, 1921), 488; SW, *Memoirs*, A. Yarmolinsky, ed., 146.

191. Nr. 5978, H. Speck von Sternburg an das Auswärtige Amt, den 6. Februar 1904, *Grosse Politik*, XIX-1, 99-100.

192. TR to W. W. Rockhill, Aug. 29, 1905, TR MSS.; George W. Smalley, *Anglo-American Memories*, II, 363-364, John W. Burgess, *Recent Changes in*

American Constitutional Theory, 40-42. See also G. Kennan to O. S. Straus, Feb. 18, 1904, Straus MSS.

193. TR to G. von L. Meyer, July 18, 1905, TR to H. C. Lodge, July 18, 1905, TR to W. Reid, July 29, 1905, TR to C. Spring Rice, July 24, 1905, TR to J. St. Loe Strachey, July 27, 1905, TR MSS.; S. Witte, "My Visit to America," *loc. cit.*, 495.

194. TR to C. Tower, June 24, 1905, TR to G. von L. Meyer, July 18, 1905, TR to Charles W. Eliot, Aug. 16, 1905, TR MSS.

195. G. von L. Meyer, Diary, May 19, 1906, in M. A. DeW. Howe, *Meyer*, 284; H. Speck von Sternburg to TR, June 11, 1905, William II to TR, July 29, 1905, TR MSS.; William II to Prince B. H. von Bülow, July 25, 1905, in BHvonB, *Letters*, 152.

196. S. Witte, "My Visit to America," *World's Work*, XLI (March, 1921), 487.

197. TR to Corinne R. Robinson, Aug. 16, 1905, TR MSS.

198. TR to K. Kaneko, July 29, 1905, F. B. Loomis to TR, July 28, 1905, Robert S. McCormick to the Secretary of State (2 cablegrams), transmitted in R. Forster to B. F. Barnes, July 26, 1905, RSMcC to E. Root, July 26, 1905, G. von L. Meyer to the Secretary of State, July 21, 1905, J. C. O'Laughlin, memo of telephone call to TR, Aug. 3, 1905, JCO'L to TR, Aug. 9, 1905, TR to J. St. Loe Strachey, July 27, 1905, TR MSS.; Nr. 6198, Der Botschafter in Paris Fürst Hugo L. von Radolin an Fürsten von Bülow, den 25. Juli 1905, *Grosse Politik*, XIX-2, 426-428; Baron R. R. Rosen, *Forty Years of Diplomacy*, I, 262; G. W. Smalley, *Anglo-American Memories*, II, 401; S. Witte, "My Visit to America," *World's Work*, XLI (March, 1921), 495.

199. TR to K. Kaneko, July 29, 1905, KK to TR, Aug. 12, 1905, F. B. Loomis to TR, July 28, 1925, J. C. O'Laughlin to TR, Aug. 10, 1905, TR MSS.; *New York Sun*, Aug. 14, 1905, TR Scrapbooks.

200. K. Kaneko to TR, July 31, 1905, TR MSS.

201. J. C. O'Laughlin to TR, Aug. 14, 1905, TR MSS.; *New York Herald*, Aug. 30, 1905, *New York Sun*, Aug. 14, 1905, *Washington Star*, Aug. 15, 1905, TR Scrapbooks; Maxim Kovalévsky, article on the Portsmouth Conference in Russian in *Vestnik Europy*, June, 1908, pp. 473-512, digested in English in the *Springfield Republican*, Aug. 25 and Sept. 19, 1908. See also R. H. Faxon to Chester I. Long, Sept. 29, 1905, Long MSS.

202. O. S. Straus to TR, Aug. 15, 1905, TR MSS.; E. J. Dillon, *Eclipse of Russia*, 305, 307-308; Princess Catherine Radziwill, "A Russian Appreciation of Theodore Roosevelt," *Outlook*, CXXIV (Jan. 4, 1920), 19.

203. G. von L. Meyer, Diary, Aug. 10, 1905, quoted in M. A. DeW. Howe, *Meyer*, 194; E. J. Dillon, *The Eclipse of Russia*, 303-304, 310-311; S. Witte, *Memoirs*, 159. See, e. g., W. B. Thorson, "Pacific Northwest Opinion on the Russo-Japanese War of 1904-1905," *Pacific Northwest Quarterly*, XXXV (October, 1944), 318-319.

204. William II to Prince B. H. von Bülow, Sept. 27, 1905, in BHvonB, *Letters*, 178, 180; M. Kovalévsky, *op. cit.*; S. Witte, "My Visit to America,"

World's Work, XLI (April, 1921), 587; John H. Hammond, *Autobiography*, II, 466.

205. S. Witte, "My Visit to America," *loc. cit.*, 587, 589; M. Kovalévsky, *op. cit.*

206. G. von L. Meyer to TR, Aug. 9, 1905, TR MSS.; Baron R. R. Rosen, *Forty Years of Diplomacy*, I, 277.

207. *Washington Post*, Aug. 5, 1905, TR Scrapbooks. See also M. Kovalévsky, *op. cit.*

208. TR to the American Minister in Peking [1905 (?)], in Lord Newton, *Lansdowne*, 325.

209. TR to C. Spring Rice, Nov. 1, 1905, TR MSS.

210. G. von L. Meyer, Diary, Aug. 6, 1905, in M. A. DeW. Howe, *Meyer*, 192; GvonLM to A. A. Adee, July 16, 1905, GvonLM to the Secretary of State, July 21, 1905, J. C. O'Laughlin to TR, June 29 and Aug. 8, 1905, TR MSS.; William II to Prince von Bülow, Sept. 27, 1905, quoted in B. H. von Bülow, *Letters*, 178, 180; *Washington Post*, Aug. 29, 1905, TR Scrapbooks; M. Kova-lévsky, article on the Portsmouth Peace Conference in Russian in *Vestnik Europy*, June, 1908, pp. 473-513, digested in English in the *Springfield Republican*, Aug. 25 and Sept. 19, 1908; Eugene de Schelking, *Recollections of a Russian Diplomat*, 254; E. J. Dillon, *The Eclipse of Russia*, 304; J. H. Hammond, *Autobiography*, II, 466-467; T. Hayashi, *Secret Memoirs*, 232-234; A. Iswolsky, *Recollections*, 8-10; Baron R. R. Rosen, *Forty Years of Diplomacy*, I, 266; G. W. Smalley, *Anglo-American Memories*, II, 383, 389-393, 397-398, 401-402.

211. Baron R. R. Rosen, *Forty Years*, I, 262.

212. J. C. O'Laughlin to TR, Aug. 10 and 13, 1905, TR MSS.; William II to Prince B. H. von Bülow, Sept. 27, 1905, BHvonB, *Letters*, 178, 180; *New York Times*, Aug. 29, 1905, TR Scrapbooks; G. W. Smalley, *Anglo-American Memories*, II, 364-365, 401; W. B. Thorson, *Pacific Northwest Quarterly*, XXXV (October, 1944), 318-321; Eleanor Tupper and George E. McReynolds, *Japan in American Public Opinion*, 11-14.

213. S. Witte to Count Lamsdorff, Aug. 13, 1905, in S. Witte, *Memoirs*, 154. See also M. Kovalévsky, *op. cit.*

214. J. C. O'Laughlin to TR, Aug. 14, 1905, TR MSS.; *New York Sun*, Aug. 13, 1905, TR Scrapbooks; P. H. Clyde, *International Rivalries in Manchuria, 1689-1922*, 136-137.

215. G. von L. Meyer, Diary, Aug. 16, 1905, in M. A. DeW. Howe, *Meyer*, 194; J. C. O'Laughlin to TR, Aug. 13, 1905, TR to Alice Roosevelt, Sept. 2, 1905, TR MSS.; *New York Sun*, Aug. 14, 1905, *New York Tribune*, Aug. 12, 13, 14, and 15, 1905, TR Scrapbooks; Baron R. R. Rosen, *Forty Years*, I, 269; P. H. Clyde, *International Rivalries*, 134.

216. J. C. O'Laughlin to TR, Aug. 14, 1905, TR MSS.; *New York Tribune*, Aug. 12, 1905, TR Scrapbooks; M. Kovalévsky, *op. cit.*; P. H. Clyde, *International Rivalries*, 137.

217. G. von L. Meyer, Diary, Aug. 17, 1905, in M. A. DeW. Howe, *Meyer*, 195; J. C. O'Laughlin to B. F. Barnes, Aug. 19, 1905, JCO'L to TR, Aug. 20,

1905, Walter Wellman to TR, Aug. 21, 1905, TR MSS.; H. White to H. C. Lodge, Aug. 21, 1905, Lodge MSS.; *New York Herald*, Aug. 23, 1905, *New York Sun*, Aug. 17, 19, and 20, 1905, *New York Tribune*, Aug. 12, 1905, TR Scrapbooks; P. H. Clyde, *International Rivalries*, 137.

218. TR to C. W. Eliot, Aug. 16, 1905, TR MSS.; *New York Sun*, Aug. 20, 1905, TR Scrapbooks.

219. O. S. Straus to TR, Aug. 15, 1905, TR MSS.; TR to OSS, Aug. 16, 1905, Straus MSS.

220. TR to C. R. Robinson, Aug. 16, 1905, TR MSS.

221. TR to H. H. D. Peirce, Aug. 18, 1905, TR MSS.; H. White to H. C. Lodge, Aug. 21, 1905, Lodge MSS.; *New York Sun*, Aug. 19, 1905, *Washington Post*, Aug. 20, 1905, *Washington Star*, Aug. 20, 1905, TR Scrapbooks.

222. At the same time he cabled a close political associate begging him to obtain a clear decision. S. Witte to Count Lamsdorff, Aug. 17, 1905, in SW, *Memoirs*, 154; Nr. 6167, Aufzeichnung des Reichskanzlers Grafen B. H. von Bülow, den 2. November 1904, *Grosse Politik*, xix-2, 387-388; M. Kovalévsky, *op. cit.*; Vladimir K. Korostovets, *Graf Witte, der Steuermann in der Not*, 200; E. J. Dillon, *Eclipse of Russia*, 305.

223. TR to J. J. Jusserand, Aug. 21, 1905, H. Speck von Sternburg to TR, Aug. 17, 18, and 21, 1905, TR to A. H. Lee, Sept. 21, 1905, TR to C. Spring Rice, Nov. 1, 1905, TR MSS.

224. G. von L. Meyer, Diary, Aug. 18, 1905, in M. A. DeW. Howe, *Meyer*, 195; GvonLM to A. A. Adee, Aug. 18 and 20, 1905, GvonLM to E. Root, Aug. 20, 1905; Nr. 6199, Der Stellvertretende Staatsekretär des Auswärtigen Amtes Gesandter Graf von Portales an den Reichskanzler Fürsten von Bülow, den 19. August 1905, *Grosse Politik*, xix-2, 428; *Washington Post*, Aug. 20, 1905, TR Scrapbooks.

225. J. C. O'Laughlin to TR, Aug. 20, 1905, TR MSS.

226. K. Kaneko to TR, Aug. 18, 1905, TR MSS.; *New York Sun*, Aug. 20, 1905, *New York Times*, Aug. 20, 1905, *Washington Post*, Aug. 20, 1905, *Washington Star*, Aug. 20, 1905, TR Scrapbooks.

227. K. Kaneko to TR, Aug. 18, 1905, TR MSS.

228. J. C. O'Laughlin to B. F. Barnes, Aug. 19, 1905, TR MSS.; *Washington Star*, Aug. 20, 1905, TR Scrapbooks.

229. Baron Rosen to TR, Aug. 23, 1905, TR MSS.; *Washington Post*, Aug. 20, 1905, TR Scrapbooks.

230. H. C. Lodge to TR, Aug. 21, 1905, Lodge MSS.; J. C. O'Laughlin to TR, Aug. 20, 1905, W. Wellman to TR, Aug. 21, 1905, TR MSS.; *New York Herald*, Aug. 23, 1905, *New York Sun*, Aug. 23, 1905, *New York Times*, Aug. 20, 1905, *Washington Post*, Aug. 20, 1905, *Washington Star*, Aug. 22, and 23, 1905, TR Scrapbooks; Baron Rosen, *Forty Years of Diplomacy*, i, 269.

231. S. Witte, "My Visit to America," *World's Work*, xli (April, 1921), 587.

232. G. von L. Meyer to A. A. Adee, Aug. 3, 1905, GvonLM to E. Root, Aug. 3 and 7, 1905, TR MSS.

233. G. von L. Meyer, Diary, Aug. 10, 1905, in M. A. DeW. Howe, *Meyer*, 194.

234. TR to Nicholas II, transmitted in TR to G. von L. Meyer, Aug. 21, 1905, TR MSS.; TR to William J. Boise, Aug. 22, 1905, TR to J. J. Jusserand, Aug. 21, 1905, TR to H. Speck von Sternburg, Aug. 21, 1905, TR MSS.

235. TR to Nicholas II, transmitted in TR to G. von L. Meyer, Aug. 21, 1905, TR and Lodge MSS. See also TR to W. J. Boise, Aug. 22, 1905, TR to J. J. Jusserand, Aug. 21, 1905, GvonLM to E. Root, Sept. 7, 1905, TR to H. Speck von Sternburg, Aug. 21, 1905, TR to C. Spring Rice, Sept. 1, 1905, TR to S. Witte, Aug. 21, 1905, SW to TR, Aug. 9/22, 1905, TR MSS.; M. Kovalévsky, article on the Portsmouth Peace Conference in Russian in *Vestnik Europy*, June, 1908, pp. 473-512, digested in English in the *Springfield Republican*, Aug. 25 and Sept. 19, 1908; M. A. DeW. Howe, *Rhodes*, 122.

236. TR to W. J. Boise, Aug. 22, 1905, TR to J. J. Jusserand, Aug. 21, 1905, TR to K. Kaneko, Aug. 22, 1905, G. von L. Meyer to the Secretary of State, Aug. 23, 1905, TR to H. Speck von Sternburg, Aug. 21, 1905, TR MSS.; GvonLM to Mrs. Meyer, Aug. 25, 1905, in M. A. DeW. Howe, *Meyer*, 202-203; TR to H. White, Aug. 23, 1905, in A. Nevins, *Henry White*, 267; Nr. 6200, Der Reichs-kanzler Fürst von Bülow an das Auswärtige Amt, den 20. August 1905; Nr. 6201, Nikolaus II an Wilhelm II, den 23. August 1905, *Grosse Politik*, xix-2, 429, 431; William II to Nicholas II, August 24, 1905, *Letters from the Kaiser to the Czar: Copied from Government Archives in Petrograd Unpublished before 1920*, Isaac D. Levine, ed., 188-189.

237. C. Spring Rice to E. K. Roosevelt, Sept. 26, 1905; TR to W. J. Boise, Aug. 22, 1905, TR MSS.

238. Baron Rosen to TR, Aug. 23, 1905, Count V. M. Lamsdorff to G. von L. Meyer, Aug. 14/27, 1905, GvonLM to the Secretary of State, Aug. 23 and 24, 1905, TR MSS.; GvonLM to TR, Aug. 23, 1905, Lodge MSS.; VML to S. Witte, Aug. 22, 1905, in SW, *Memoirs*, 155; Nr. 6201, Nikolaus II an Wilhelm II, den 23. August 1905, *Grosse Politik*, xix-2, 430-431; *Willy-Nicky Correspondence*, H. Bernstein, ed., 125-126; *New York Sun*, Aug. 23, 1905, TR Scrapbooks; G. W. Smalley, *Anglo-American Memories*, ii, 363-364.

239. S. Witte to Count Lamsdorff, Aug. 21, 1905, in SW, *Memoirs*, 155; M. Kovalévsky, *op. cit.* See also G. W. Smalley, *Anglo-American Memories*, ii, 396, 401.

240. S. Witte to TR, Aug. 9/22, 1905, J. C. O'Laughlin to TR, Aug. 23, 1905, TR MSS.; TR to H. White, Aug. 23, 1905, in A. Nevins, *Henry White*, 267. See also W. Reid to TR, Sept. 2, 1905, TR MSS.

241. H. C. Lodge to TR, Aug. 21, 1905, Lodge MSS.

242. TR to K. Kaneko, Aug. 22, 1905, TR MSS. See also TR to W. S. Bigelow, Sept. 23, 1905, TR to W. J. Boise, Aug. 22 and 23, 1905, TR to Sir M. Durand, Aug. 22, 1905, TR to K. Kaneko, Aug. 23, 1905, TR to C. Spring Rice, Nov. 1, 1905, TR to J. St. Loe Strachey, Sept. 11, 1905, TR MSS.; TR to H. White, Aug. 23, 1905, in A. Nevins, *Henry White*, 267; Count Lamsdorff to S. Witte, Aug. 22, 1905, in SW, *Memoirs*, 155; SW, " My Visit to America," *World's Work*, xli (March, 1921), 495; G. W. Smalley, *Anglo-American Memo-*

ries, II, 364-365; E. Peters, *Roosevelt und der Kaiser,* 117-119. See also G. von L. Meyer, Diary, Nov. 13, 1903, in M. A. DeW. Howe, *Meyer,* 223.

243. TR to Sir M. Durand, Aug. 22, 1905, TR MSS.

244. K. Kaneko to TR, Aug. 23, 1905, TR to G. von L. Meyer, Sept. 1, 1905, TR MSS.; *New York Herald,* Aug. 23, 1905, TR Scrapbooks. See also TR to W. J. Boise, Aug. 22, 1905, TR MSS.

245. TR to C. Spring Rice, Sept. 1, 1905, TR MSS. See also H. C. Lodge to TR, Sept. 7, 1905, TR MSS.

246. TR to K. Kaneko, Aug. 23, 1905, TR to G. von L. Meyer, Aug. 23, 1905, TR to S. Witte, transmitted in TR to H. H. D. Peirce, Aug. 23, 1905, SW to TR, Aug. 24, 1905, TR MSS.; TR to Kermit Roosevelt, Aug. 25, 1905, in TR, *Letters to Kermit,* 109; *New York Sun,* Aug. 27, 1905, *Washington Post,* Aug. 23 and 25, 1905, TR Scrapbooks. See also KK to TR, Aug. 23, 1905, TR MSS.

247. K. Kaneko to TR, Aug. 23 and 24, 1905, TR MSS.

248. G. von L. Meyer to TR, Aug. 25 and 29, 1905, C. Spring Rice to E. K. Roosevelt, Sept. 26 and Oct. 5, 1905, J. St. Loe Strachey to TR, Sept. 1, 1905, TR MSS.; *Washington Star,* Aug. 27, 1905; G. W. Smalley, *Anglo-American Memories,* II, 363-364, M. A. DeW. Howe, *Meyer,* 197-201.

249. S. Witte to TR, Aug. 24, 1905, TR MSS. See also Vladimir K. Korostovets, *Graf Witte, der Steuermann in der Not,* 201.

250. J. J. Jusserand to TR, Aug. 25, 1905, Baron Komura to K. Kaneko, Aug. 26, 1905, enclosed in KK to TR, Aug. 26, 1905, J. C. O'Laughlin to B. F. Barnes, Aug. 27, 1905, TR MSS.; G. von L. Meyer to TR, Aug. 25 and 26, 1905, TR and Lodge MSS. See also M. A. DeW. Howe, *Meyer,* 201.

251. TR to G. von L. Meyer, Aug. 25, 1905, GvonLM to TR, Aug. 26, 1905, TR MSS.; *Washington Star,* Aug. 27, 1905, TR Scrapbooks; G. W. Smalley, *Anglo-American Memories,* II, 363-364.

252. TR, Memorandum of telephonic reply to K. Kaneko, Aug. 27, 1905, G. von L. Meyer to TR, Aug. 26, 1905, TR MSS.; Count Lamsdorff to GvonLM, enclosed in GvonLM to TR, Aug. 27, 1905, TR and Lodge MSS.

253. James Stillman to TR, Aug. 26, 1905, TR MSS.; *New York Herald,* Aug. 30, 1905, TR Scrapbooks.

254. J. C. O'Laughlin to TR, Aug. 27, 1905, JCO'L to B. F. Barnes, Aug. 27, 1905, H. H. D. Peirce to TR, Aug. 27, 1905, TR MSS.; *New York Sun,* Aug. 25, 26 and 27, 1905, *New York Tribune,* Aug. 23, 1905, *Washington Post,* Aug. 23, 1905, *Washington Star,* Aug. 27, 1905, TR Scrapbooks; S. Witte, *Memoirs,* 159; G. W. Smalley, *Anglo-American Memories,* II, 389-400.

255. J. C. O'Laughlin to TR, Aug. 27, 1905, Baron J. Komura to K. Kaneko, enclosed in KK to TR, Aug. 27, 1905, JK to KK, Aug. 28, 1905 (copy), TR MSS.; S. Witte to Count Lamsdorff, Aug. 27, 1905, in SW, *Memoirs,* 158; *New York Times,* Aug. 29, 1905, *Washington Post,* Aug. 28, 1905, TR Scrapbooks; G. W. Smalley, *Anglo-American Memories,* II, 398-400; V. K. Korostovets, *Graf Witte,* 201.

256. TR, Memorandum of telephonic reply to K. Kaneko, Aug. 27, 1905, KK

to TR, Aug. 28, 1905, Baron Komura to KK, Aug. 28, 1905 (copy), TR MSS.; G. W. Smalley, *Anglo-American Memories*, II, 396.

257. TR to William II, Aug. 27, 1905, K. Kaneko to TR, Aug. 28, 1905, Baron Hilmar von dem Bussche-Haddenhausen to W. Loeb, Jr., Aug. 30, 1905, C. Spring Rice to E. K. Roosevelt, Sept. 25, 1905, TR MSS.; Nr. 6329, Der Geschäftsträger in Washington Freiherr von dem Bussche-Haddenhausen, an das Auswärtige Amt, den 28. August 1905, *Grosse Politik*, XIX-2, 624. See also TR to J. Stillman, Aug. 28, 1905, TR MSS.

258. TR to Henri-Jacques-André Desportes de la Fosse, Aug. 27, 1905, TR MSS.

259. G. von L. Meyer to TR, Aug. 27 and 28, 1905, Baron Komura to K. Kaneko, Aug. 28, 1905, TR MSS.

260. TR, memorandum of a telephonic reply to K. Kaneko, Aug. 27, 1905, TR MSS.

261. J. C. O'Laughlin to TR, Aug. 29, 1905, TR MSS.; S. Witte to Count Lamsdorff, Aug. 29, 1905, in SW, *Memoirs*, 158-159; C. Spring Rice to E. K. Roosevelt, Oct. 5, 1905, TR MSS.; E. J. Dillon, *Eclipse of Russia*, 308-309.

262. K. Kaneko to TR, Aug. 29, 1905, C. Spring Rice to E. K. Roosevelt, Oct. 5, 1905, TR MSS.; *New York Times*, Aug. 29, 1905, *New York World*, Aug. 30, 1905, *Washington Post*, Aug. 29 and 30 and Sept. 1, 1905, *Washington Star*, Aug. 30, 1905, TR Scrapbooks; E. Peters, *Roosevelt und der Kaiser*, 117-119.

263. H. White to H. C. Lodge, July 29, 1905, Lodge MSS.; W. Loeb, Jr., to W. S. Bigelow, Sept. 25, 1905, TR to W. Reid, July 7, 1905, TR MSS.; TR to H. White, Aug. 23, 1905, in A. Nevins, *Henry White*, 267; George S. Viereck, *The Kaiser on Trial*, 285.

264. H. White to H. C. Lodge, July 29, 1905, Lodge MSS.

265. TR to C. Spring Rice, July 24, 1905, TR to William II, July 27 and Aug. 30, 1905, TR MSS.

266. J. Hay, MS. Diary, Jan. 29, 1905, Hay MSS.; C. Spring Rice to E. K. Roosevelt, Sept. 26, 1905, CSR to TR, Dec. 7, 1904, TR MSS.; Nr. 6335, Fürst B. H. von Bülow an das Auswärtige Amt, den 30. August 1905, *Grosse Politik*, XIX-2, 628; G. von L. Meyer, Diary, Sept. 7, 1905, in M. A. DeW. Howe, *Meyer*, 208-209; David Jayne Hill, *Impressions of the Kaiser*, 59; William II, *Memoirs*, Thomas R. Ybarra, trans., 200.

267. TR to C. Spring Rice, June 16 and July 24, 1905, TR to William II, Aug. 30, 1905, TR MSS.; W. H. Taft to Charles P. Taft, Aug. 18, 1907, Taft MSS.; *Washington Post*, Aug. 20, 1905, TR Scrapbooks. See also TR to H. C. Lodge, undated, in *TR-HCL Correspondence*, II, 188.

268. TR to Baron Komura, Aug. 30, 1905, TR MSS. Later he wrote a warm personal letter. TR to the Emperor of Japan, Sept. 6, 1905, TR MSS. See also H. C. Lodge to TR, Sept. 2 and 7, 1905, TR to H. H. D. Peirce, Aug. 29, 1905, TR to C. Spring Rice, Nov. 1, 1905, TR MSS.; Joseph Pulitzer to John L. Heaton, July 20, 1905, Pulitzer MSS.

269. Nr. 6896, Freiherr Speck von Sternburg an das Auswärtige Amt, den 3.

November 1905, *Grosse Politik*, xxi-1, 10; J. F. Rhodes, Memorandum of conversation with TR, Nov. 16-17, 1905, in M. A. DeW. Howe, *Rhodes*, 122-123.

270. TR to J. J. Jusserand, transmitted through H.-J.-A. Desportes de la Fosse, Aug. 29, 1905, G. von L. Meyer to TR, Dec. 6, 1905, C. Spring Rice to E. K. Roosevelt, Sept. 26, 1905, TR MSS.; GvonLM, Diary, Dec. 5, 1905, in M. A. DeW. Howe, *Meyer*, 229. See also W. B. Thorson, " Pacific Northwest Opinion on the Russo-Japanese War of 1904-1905," *Pacific Northwest Quarterly*, xxxv (October, 1944), 321-322.

271. TR to G. von L. Meyer, Sept. 1, 1905, TR to C. Spring Rice, Sept. 1, 1905, CSR to E. K. Roosevelt, July 10 and Sept. 26, 1905, W. Reid to TR, June 17, 1905, TR MSS.; M. A. DeW. Howe, *Rhodes*, 122.

272. TR to J. J. Jusserand, Aug. 21, 1905, TR MSS.

273. TR to W. J. Boise, Aug. 22, 1905, TR to Sir M. Durand, Aug. 22, 1905, TR to W. Reid, Aug. 3, 1905, WR to TR, June 17 and Aug. 15, 1905, TR to C. Spring Rice, June 16, 1905, CSR to E. K. Roosevelt, July 10, 1905, TR MSS.; Willy to Nicky, undated [September, 1905 (?)], *Willy-Nicky Correspondence*, H. Bernstein, ed., 128-129.

274. W. Reid to TR, June 17 and July 14, 1905, Lord Lansdowne to C. Spring Rice, Aug. 7, 1905, CSR to E. K. Roosevelt, July 10, 1905, TR MSS.

275. W. Reid to TR, June 17, July 14, and Aug. 15, 1905, TR to WR, Aug. 3, 1905, TR to C. Spring Rice, June 16, 1905, W. Loeb, Jr., to W. S. Bigelow, Sept. 25, 1905, Lord Lansdowne to CSR, Aug. 7, 1905, CSR to E. K. Roosevelt, July 10 and Sept. 26, 1905, TR MSS. Roosevelt put it politely that she was " foolishly reluctant to advise Japan to be reasonable." TR to H. White, Aug. 23, 1905, in A. Nevins, *Henry White*, 267. See also William II to Nicholas II, Aug. 30, 1905, *Willy-Nicky Correspondence*, H. Bernstein, ed., 128-129, and *Grosse Politik*, xix-2, 627-628; Nr. 6337, H. von dem Bussche-Haddenhausen an das Auswärtige Amt, den 19. Oktober 1905, *Grosse Politik*, xix-2, 630; Lord Newton, *Lansdowne*, 325; A. H. Lee to TR, Sept. 10, 1905, TR MSS.

276. W. Reid to TR, June 23, and Aug. 15, 1905, TR MSS.; William II to Nicholas II, Sept. 26, 1905, *Letters from the Kaiser to the Czar*, I. D. Levine, ed., 197. See also WR to TR, Aug. 17, 1905, TR MSS.

277. TR to W. Reid, July 7, 1905, WR to TR, July 14, 1905, W. Loeb, Jr., to W. S. Bigelow, Sept. 25, 1905, TR MSS.; Lord Newton, *Lansdowne*, 325. See also TR to H. White, Aug. 23, 1905, TR MSS.

278. TR to Sir M. Durand, Sept. 8, 1905, TR MSS.; A. W. Griswold, *Far Eastern Policy*, 121-122. Zabriskie, on the other hand, believed that the signing of the renewal in the early days of the conference stiffened Japan's demands. Edward H. Zabriskie, *American-Russian Rivalry*, 127n.

279. G. von L. Meyer, Diary, Sept. 19 and Nov. 29, 1905, in M. A. DeW. Howe, *Meyer*, 210-211, 224-225; H. C. Lodge to TR, Sept. 14, 1905, C. Spring Rice to E. K. Roosevelt, Oct. 5, 1905, A. H. Lee to TR, Sept. 10, 1905, TR MSS.; Sir M. Durand to TR, Aug. 31, 1905, TR to HCL, Jan. 28, 1909, Lodge MSS.; J. Pulitzer to J. L. Heaton, July 20, 1905, Pulitzer MSS.; *London World*, ca. Sept. 15-24, 1905, TR Scrapbooks; M. Kovalévsky, article on the Portsmouth

Conference in Russian in *Vestnik Europy*, June, 1908, pp. 473-512, digested in English in the *Springfield Republican*, Aug. 25 and Sept. 19, 1908; John L. Heaton, *Cobb of "The World,"* 36-37, 39; Don C. Seitz, *Joseph Pulitzer: His Life and Letters*, 299-300; G. W. Smalley, *Anglo-American Memories*, II, 401.

280. Nr. 6336, Der Botschafter in Wien Graf Karl von Wedel, an den Reichskanzler Fürsten von Bülow, den 23. September 1905, *Grosse Politik*, XIX-2, 628-629; G. von L. Meyer, Diary, Sept. 16, 1905, M. A. DeW. Howe, *Meyer*, 211-212; William II to Nicholas II, Sept. 26, 1905, in *Letters from the Kaiser to the Czar*, 197.

281. H. White to H. C. Lodge, Aug. 21 and Sept. 13, 1905, Lodge MSS.

282. Nicholas II to TR, Aug. 31, 1905, Lodge MSS. See also G. von L. Meyer to TR, Jan. 15, 1906, TR to Alice Roosevelt, Sept. 2, 1905, TR MSS.

283. William II to TR, Aug. 29, 1905, Lodge MSS. See also G. von L. Meyer, Diary, Sept. 16, 1905, in M. A. DeW. Howe, *Meyer*, 212, 218-219; Nr. 6333, Fürst B. H. von Bülow an Kaiser Wilhelm II, den 29. August 1905, Nr. 6335, BHvonB an das Auswärtige Amt, den 30. August 1905, *Grosse Politik*, XIX-2, 627-628; TR to H. C. Lodge, undated, quoted in *TR-HCL Correspondence*, II, 188. See also Maurice F. Egan, *Ten Years near the German Frontier*, 63-64.

284. Wilhelm II to Nikolaus II, Aug. 30, 1905, *Grosse Politik*, XIX-2, 627-628; W II to N II, Sept. 26, 1905, in *Letters from the Kaiser to the Czar*, 193-197; H. Speck von Sternburg to TR, Sept. 25, 1905, TR MSS.; TR to Sir M. Durand, Aug. 29, 1905, MD to TR, Aug. 31, 1905, TR MSS.

285. Baron Komura to TR, Aug. 29, 1905, TR MSS.

286. Mutsuhito to TR, Sept. 3, 1905, Lodge MSS.

287. W. Reid to TR, Sept. 2, 1905, TR MSS.

288. C. Spring Rice to E. K. Roosevelt, Sept. 26, 1905, TR MSS.; G. von L. Meyer, Diary, Sept. 7, 1905, in M. A. DeW. Howe, *Meyer*, 208-209.

289. Testimony of a British attaché in Tokyo to Lord Cromer who told Strachey. J. St. Loe Strachey to TR, Oct. 16, 1905. See also K. Kaneko to TR, Sept. 13, 1905, TR MSS.; *New York World*, Aug. 30, 1905, TR Scrapbooks.

290. C. Spring Rice to E. K. Roosevelt, Oct. 10, 1905, TR MSS.

291. Nr. 6334, Kaiser Wilhelm II an Kaiser Nikolaus II, den 30. August 1905, *Grosse Politik*, XIX-2, 627-628. See also W II to TR, Aug. 29, 1905, Lodge MSS.; Nr. 6333, Fürst B. H. von Bülow an Kaiser Wilhelm II, den 29. August 1905, *Grosse Politik*, XIX-2, 627; TR to H. C. Lodge, undated, quoted in *TR-HCL Correspondence*, II, 188; M. F. Egan, *Ten Years near the German Frontier*, 63-64.

292. K. Kaneko to TR, Aug. 29, 1905, TR MSS. See also J. C. O'Laughlin to TR, Aug. 29, 1905, TR MSS.; *New York Sun*, Aug. 30, 1905, *Washington Post*, Aug. 30, 1905, TR Scrapbooks; W. B. Thorson, "Pacific Northwest Opinion on the Russo-Japanese War of 1904-1905," *Pacific Northwest Quarterly*, XXXV (October, 1944), 321-322.

293. J. Stillman to TR, Aug. 26, 1905, TR MSS.

294. Knute Nelson to Albert J. Beveridge, July 17, 1905, Beveridge MSS.

295. H. White to H. C. Lodge, Sept. 13, 1905, Lodge MSS. See also H. White to TR, Aug. 10, 1905, TR MSS.

296. C. Spring Rice to E. K. Roosevelt, July 10, 1905, TR MSS.

297. " You have probably saved the lives of a quarter of a million men," Meyer cabled, " and have placed humanity under a lasting debt of gratitude to you." G. von L. Meyer to TR, Aug. 30, 1905, TR MSS. See also H. C. Lodge to TR, July 2, 1905, TR MSS.; M. F. Egan, *Ten Years near the German Frontier*, 63-64.

298. H. C. Lodge to TR, July 2 and 25, 1905, TR and Lodge MSS.

299. G. von L. Meyer, Diary, Aug. 31, 1905, in M. A. DeW. Howe, *Meyer*, 206; *New York Herald*, Aug. 31, 1905, TR Scrapbooks; M. F. Egan, *op. cit.*, 63-64. See also G. von L. Meyer to TR, Aug. 29, 1905, C. Spring Rice to E. K. Roosevelt, Sept. 26, 1905, TR MSS.; Baron Rosen, *Forty Years of Diplomacy*, I, 277-279.

300. Admiral Charles S. Sperry to H. N. Allen, May 7, 1907, Allen MSS.

301. L. Wood to TR, Nov. 18, 1906, TR MSS.

302. C. Spring Rice to E. K. Roosevelt, Oct. 5, 1905, H. Speck von Sternburg to TR, Oct. 16, 1905, TR MSS. See also Sir C. Hardinge to Lord Lansdowne, Oct. 5, 1905, in Lord Newton, *Lansdowne*, 326-327.

303. TR to C. Spring Rice, Nov. 1, 1905, TR MSS.

304. H. C. Lodge to TR, Sept. 14, 1905, TR to Alice Roosevelt, Sept. 2, 1905, C. Spring Rice to E. K. Roosevelt, Oct. 10, 1905, TR MSS.; *New York Herald*, Aug. 31, 1905, TR Scrapbooks; T. Hayashi, *Secret Memoirs*, 231; A. W. Griswold, *Far Eastern Policy*, 121-122; E. Tupper and G. E. McReynolds, *Japan in American Public Opinion*, 15-16.

305. TR to K. Kaneko, Sept. 2, 1905, TR MSS. See also TR to W. S. Bigelow, Sept. 23, 1905, TR MSS. See also E. Tupper and G. E. McReynolds, *op. cit.*, 14.

306. TR to H. Speck von Sternburg, Sept. 6, 1905, TR MSS.; J. Hay, MS. Diary, Jan. 26, 1905, Hay MSS.

307. TR to J. St. Loe Strachey, Sept. 11, 1905, TR to W. S. Bigelow, Sept. 23, 1905, TR MSS.

308. J. C. O'Laughlin to TR, Aug. 29, 1905, C. Spring Rice to E. K. Roosevelt, Sept. 26, 1905, TR MSS.; G. von L. Meyer to Mrs. Meyer, Aug. 31, 1905, in M. A. DeW. Howe, *Meyer*, 206-207; William II to Nicholas II, Sept. 26, 1905, in *Letters from the Kaiser to the Czar*, I. D. Levine, ed., 193-198; William to Prince B. H. von Bülow, Sept. 27, 1905, in BHvonB, *Letters*, 178, 180; *New York Herald*, Aug. 31, 1905, *New York World*, Aug. 30 and Sept. 3, 1905, *Washington Star*, Sept. 19, 1905, TR Scrapbooks; M. Kovalévsky, article on the Portsmouth Peace Conference in Russian in *Vestnik Europy*, June, 1908, pp. 473-512, digested in English in the *Springfield Republican*, Aug. 25 and Sept. 19, 1908; S. Witte, *Memoirs*, 161-162; G. W. Smalley, *Anglo-American Memories*, II, 401.

309. K. Kaneko to TR, Aug. 12, 1905, TR to KK, Aug. 22, 1905, TR to Baron Komura, Aug. 28, 1905, TR MSS.; *New York Star*, Aug. 20, 1905, *Washington Post*, Aug. 22 and Sept. 11, 1905, *Washington Star*, Aug. 15, 1905, TR Scrapbooks; G. W. Smalley, *Anglo-American Memories*, II, 401. So badly informed was the Kaiser that he thought America's " innate . . . antipathy against all coloured races " made Roosevelt anti-Japanese. William II to Nicholas II, Oct. 30, 1904, in B. H. von Bülow, *Letters*, 74-75.

310. TR to Alice Roosevelt, Sept. 2, 1905, TR to Nicholas II, Sept. 6, 1905, TR to J. C. O'Laughlin, Aug. 31, 1905, TR MSS.

311. H. C. Lodge to TR, Aug. 21, 1905, Lodge MSS.; *New York Times*, Aug. 29, 1905, TR Scrapbooks; M. Kovalévsky, *op. cit.*; S. Witte, "My Visit to America," *World's Work*, XLI (March, 1921), 495; SW, *Memoirs*, 140-142, 148, 161; G. W. Smalley, *Anglo-American Memories*, II, 364-365, 401.

312. S. Witte, "My Visit to America," *loc. cit.*, 587; G. W. Smalley, *Anglo-American Memories*, II, 364-365.

313. TR to W. W. Rockhill, Aug. 20, 1905, TR MSS.

314. TR to J. C. O'Laughlin, Aug. 31, 1905, H. C. Lodge to TR, Sept. 14, 1905, TR MSS. See also Frederick Palmer, *With My Own Eyes*, 235-236.

315. TR to C. Spring Rice, Nov. 1, 1905, TR MSS.

316. TR to Lyman Abbott, Oct. 16, 1905, TR to W. S. Bigelow, Sept. 23, 1905, W. Loeb, Jr., to WSB, Sept. 25, 1905, TR to G. Kennan, Oct. 15, 1905 (not sent), TR MSS.; Philip C. Jessup, *Elihu Root*, II, 4. See also G. von L. Meyer to TR, Aug. 29, 1905, TR MSS; Willy to Nicky, Nov. 6, 1904, *Willy-Nicky Correspondence*, H. Bernstein, ed., 79-81.

317. TR to Kermit Roosevelt, June 9, 1906, TR MSS. See also H. N. Allen to Clayton W. Everett, Nov. 10, 1904, Allen MSS.; T. Hayashi, *Secret Memoirs*, 231.

318. *Mark Twain's Autobiography*, II, 292-293. See also J. Pulitzer to J. L. Heaton, July 20, 1905, Pulitzer MSS.

319. Adolph Edwards, *The Roosevelt Panic of 1907*, 28-29.

320. J. L. Heaton, *Cobb of "The World,"* 37. See also J. Pulitzer to J. L. Heaton, July 29, 1905, Pulitzer MSS.

321. TR to Lyman Abbott, Oct. 16, 1905, TR to G. Kennan, Oct. 15, 1905 (not sent), TR MSS.

322. See, e. g., H. C. Lodge to TR, Sept. 7, 1905, Lodge MSS.; TR to W. S. Bigelow, Sept. 23, 1905, W. Reid to TR, Sept. 2, 1905, TR to K. Roosevelt, June 9, 1906, C. Spring Rice to E. K. Roosevelt, Oct. 10, 1905, TR MSS.; H. White to H. C. Lodge, Sept. 13, 1905, Lodge MSS.; E. Tupper and G. E. McReynolds, *Japan in American Opinion*, 15-16.

323. P. S. Reinsch, *World Politics*, 359.

324. L. Wood to TR, in S. Witte, "My Visit to America," *World's Work*, XLI (April, 1921), 587; J. H. Hammond, *Autobiography*, II, 466; Roosevelt's Ambassador to Austria, Bellamy Storer, felt this same way. Nr. 6336, Der Botschafter in Wien Graf K. von Wedel an Fürsten von Bülow, den 23. September 1905, *Grosse Politik*, XIX-2, 628-629. On the other hand Griswold insists: "The war ended: he did not end it . . . The . . . reason for the termination of the war was the mutual exhaustion of the two belligerents." A. W. Griswold, *Far Eastern Policy*, 117. See also H. L. Stoddard, *It Costs To Be President*, 152-163; E. Tupper and G. E. McReynolds, *op. cit.*, 15-16.

325. J. W. Burgess, *Recent Changes in American Constitutional Theory*, 40-42.

326. W. B. Thorson, "Pacific Northwest Opinion on the Russo-Japanese War of 1904-1905," *Pacific Northwest Quarterly*, xxxv (October, 1944), 322. See also Foster R. Dulles, *The Road to Teheran*, 93. TR to K. Roosevelt, June 9, 1906, TR MSS.

327. TR to J. Hay, April 2, 1905, TR to C. Spring Rice, June 16, 1905, TR MSS.

328. TR to H. C. Lodge, June 5 and 16, 1905, TR to G. von L. Meyer, June 19, 1905, TR to W. Reid, July 29, 1905, TR to C. Spring Rice, July 24, 1905, TR to A. D. White, June 1, 1905, TR MSS.; A. W. Griswold, *Far Eastern Policy*, 105.

329. TR to H. C. Lodge, June 5, 1905, TR to G. von L. Meyer, June 19, 1905, W. Reid to TR, June 17 and 23, 1905, TR to WR, July 7, 1905, TR to C. Spring Rice, June 16, 1905, TR MSS.; TR to WR, June, 1905, in Royal Cortissoz, *Reid*, II, 305; Nr. 6336, Der Botschafter in Wien Graf K. von Wedel an Fürsten von Bülow, den 23. September 1905, *Grosse Politik*, XIX-2, 628-629; M. Kovalévsky, article in *Springfield Republican*, Aug. 25 and Sept. 19, 1908, and TR Scrapbooks.

330. TR to H. C. Lodge, June 16, 1905, TR to S. Low, June 14, 1905, TR to G. von L. Meyer, June 19 and July 19, 1905, TR to W. Reid, June 30 and July 7 and July 29, 1905, TR to C. Spring Rice, June 16 and July 24, 1905, Arthur H. Lee to TR, Sept. 10, 1905, TR MSS.; A. W. Griswold, *Far Eastern Policy*, 105. See also *Washington Star*, June 20, 1905, TR Scrapbooks; Frederick Palmer, *With My Own Eyes*, 235-236.

331. TR to H. C. Lodge, June 16, 1905, Lodge MSS. See also TR to Eugene Hale, Oct. 27, 1906, TR to W. Reid, June 5, 1905, TR to J. St. Loe Strachey, Sept. 11, 1905, TR MSS.

332. TR to H. Speck von Sternburg, Aug. 28, 1900, TR MSS.; Nr. 5994, HSvonS an den Reichskanzler Grafen von Bülow, den 9. Mai, 1904, *Grosse Politik*, XIX-1, 113-114.

333. Fred H. Harrington's *God Mammon and the Japanese* contains the best and most thorough discussion and evaluation of Korean-American relations at this time. In 1908 Horace N. Allen wrote a book, *Things Korean*, that contributes little except a restatement of his views on the Russo-Japanese conflict in Korea.

334. H. N. Allen to [Edwin V.] Morgan, Oct. 5, 1902, HNA, MS. Diary, Oct. 1, 1903, HNA to Henry Collbran, July 26, 1904, and May 2, 1905, HNA to L. C. Griscom, Feb. 15, 1905, HNA to George P. Morgan, Feb. 13, 1905, HNA to James R. Morse, Aug. 30, 1904, HNA to Charles W. Needham, May 12, 1905, HNA to Edward E. Rittenhouse, May 24, 1905, HNA to William W. Rockhill, Aug. 25, 1904, HNA to Rothery, Oct. 18, 1904, HNA to E. B. Townsend, May 30, 1905, HNA to Gen. James H. Wilson, Dec. 16, 1902, EER to [Malcolm M.] Stewart, April 25, 1905, HNA to his boys, May 12, 1905. Raymond Krumm of Columbus, Ohio, a personal enemy of Allen, charged Allen with profiting personally from the business ventures to which he influenced the Koreans to grant rich concessions. Krumm even claimed that Allen got concessions for the

Japanese. Krumm later in a story in a Hearst newspaper took credit for obtaining Allen's removal. R. Krumm to J. Hay, April 21, 1904, Allen MSS.; F. H. Harrington, *op. cit.*, 85-143.

335. See, e. g., H. N. Allen to Arthur J. Brown, Oct. 30, 1902, HNA to [E. V.] Morgan, Oct. 5, 1902, Allen MSS.

336. See, e. g., H. N. Allen to his boys, Jan. 10, 1904, HNA to [E. V.] Morgan, March 2, 1904, HNA to [E. E.] Rittenhouse, May 15, 1904, HNA to Willard D. Straight, Aug. 25, 1904, HNA to J. H. Wilson, Nov. 13, 1906, Allen MSS. See also Stephen L. Selde to HNA, Nov. 22, 1905, Allen MSS.

337. H. N. Allen to J. Hay, Nov. 21 and Dec. 10, 1902, HNA to his boys, Jan. 10, 1904, HNA to J. Sloat Fassett, Oct. 9, 1902, HNA to [E. V.] Morgan, Oct. 5, 1902, HNA to W. D. Straight, Aug. 25, 1904, Allen MSS.

338. H. N. Allen to J. S. Fassett, Oct. 9, 1902, HNA to [E. V.] Morgan, Oct. 5, 1902, HNA to J. R. Morse, Aug. 30, 1904, HNA to [E. E.] Rittenhouse, May 15, 1904, HNA to W. W. Rockhill, Aug. 25, 1904, HNA to J. H. Wilson, Dec. 16, 1902, HNA, "Narrative of Facts Regarding Development of Korean Enterprises," MS. Diaries, Oct. 19, 1905, Allen MSS. See also HNA to A. J. Brown, Oct. 30, 1902, HNA to Mr. Harris, Feb. 24, 1903, Allen MSS.; N. M. Butler to TR, June 2, 1903, TR MSS.

339. H. N. Allen to J. S. Fassett, Oct. 9, 1902, Allen MSS.; L. Hunt to Jonathan P. Dolliver, March 3, 1901, Dolliver MSS.

340. H. N. Allen to J. S. Fassett, Oct. 9, 1902, HNA to J. H. Wilson, Dec. 15, 1902, Allen MSS.; N. M. Butler to TR, June 2, 1903, and Jan. 12 and May 19, 1904, J. B. Matthews to TR, July 10, 1903, L. Hunt to N. M. Butler, reproduced in TR to TR, Jr., March 5, 1904, TR MSS. See also NMB to TR, Oct. 1, 1904, TR to NMB, Oct. 3, 1904, TR MSS.

341. H. N. Allen to his boys, May 12, 1905, HNA to H. Collbran, May 1 and 2, 1905, HNA to [E. V.] Morgan, March 2, 1902, and Oct. 21, 1904, HNA to G. P. Morgan, April 28 and 30, 1905, HNA to C. W. Needham, May 12, 1905, HNA to [E. E.] Rittenhouse, May 24 and 25, 1905, HNA to W. W. Rockhill, March 21, 1905, HNA to E. B. Townsend, May 12 and 30, 1905, Allen MSS.; J. S. Fassett to Wm. Loeb, Jr., Sept. 2, 1904, TR MSS.; F. H. Harrington, *God Mammon and the Japanese*, 330.

342. H. N. Allen to J. S. Fassett, Oct. 9, 1902, HNA to [E. V.] Morgan, Sept. 2, 1902, HNA to J. H. Wilson, Dec. 16, 1902, W. W. Rockhill to HNA, June 30, 1904, Allen MSS. Allen had warned against this in Korea and had predicted Japan would be a more ruthless competitor than Russia.

343. H. N. Allen to J. H. Wilson, Dec. 16, 1902, Allen MSS.

344. H. N. Allen to [E. V.] Morgan, Sept. 2, 1902, HNA to [E. E.] Rittenhouse, May 15, 1904, HNA to W. D. Straight, Aug. 25, 1904, HNA to J. H. Wilson, Dec. 16, 1902, Allen MSS.

345. H. N. Allen to J. Hay, Nov. 21, 1902, HNA to [E. V.] Morgan, Oct. 5, 1902, Allen MSS.

346. H. N. Allen to J. S. Fassett, Oct. 9, 1902, HNA to J. R. Morse, Sept.

30, 1904, HNA to Capt. Hugh Osterhaus, Sept. 29, 1904, HNA to W. D. Straight, Aug. 25, 1904, HNA to J. H. Wilson, Dec. 16, 1902, Allen MSS.

347. H. N. Allen to H. Collbran, May 1 and 2, 1905, HNA to J. S. Fassett, Oct. 9, 1902, HNA to [E. E.] Rittenhouse, May 25, 1905, Allen MSS. See also HNA to Habe, Oct. 15, 1904, Allen MSS.; *Japan Weekly Mail*, Sept. 28, 1907.

348. H. N. Allen to H. Osterhaus, Sept. 29, 1904, HNA to Gov. George K. Nash, May 4, 1904, Allen MSS. See also HNA to W. D. Straight, Aug. 25, 1904, Allen MSS.

349. H. N. Allen, MS. Diary, Sept. 30 and Oct. 2, 1903, HNA, Memo written later, Letter Press Copy Book, vol. vii, HNA to C. W. Everett, Nov. 10, 1904, Allen MSS. See also F. H. Harrington, *God Mammon and the Japanese*, 314-318.

350. H. N. Allen to W. W. Rockhill, Jan. 4, 1904, HNA to his boys, Jan. 10, 1904, Allen MSS.

351. H. N. Allen to Gov. G. K. Nash, May 4, 1904, HNA to Yun Chi Ho, Nov. 30, 1905, Allen MSS.

352. H. N. Allen to [E. V.] Morgan, March 2, 1904, Allen MSS.

353. Herbert Croly, *Willard Straight*, 182-183; Yasaka Yakagi, *A Historical Observation of the Oriental Policy of America*.

354. J. Hay, MS. Diary, March 3, 1904, Hay MSS. See also J. S. Fassett to Wm. Loeb, Jr., Sept. 2, 1904, TR MSS.

355. H. N. Allen to [E. E.] Rittenhouse, May 15, 1904, Allen MSS. See also HNA to W. W. Rockhill, Aug. 25, 1904, Allen MSS.

356. H. N. Allen to W. W. Rockhill, May 6, 1904, HNA to E. B. Townsend, May 30, 1905, Allen MSS. See also HNA to his boys, May 12, 1905, HNA to E. V. Morgan, Sept. 2, 1902, HNA to J. H. Wilson, Dec. 16, 1902, Allen MSS.

357. L. C. Griscom to TR, Oct. 12, 1905, TR MSS.

358. TR to L. C. Griscom, Oct. 31, 1905, TR MSS.

359. See, e. g., H. N. Allen to Yun Chi Ho, Nov. 30, 1905, S. L. Selde to HNA, Nov. 22, 1905, Allen MSS.

360. J. Hay, MS. Diary, Feb. 23, 1905, Hay MSS.

361. J. Hay to TR, Jan. 26 and Feb. 27, 1905, Hay MSS.

362. H. C. Lodge to TR, June 29, 1905, TR MSS.

363. L. C. Griscom to TR, Oct. 12, 1905, TR MSS.

364. Memorandum of conversation between W. H. Taft and Count Taro Katsura, July 29, 1905; TR to J. Hay, Jan. 28, 1905, TR to C. Spring Rice, Nov. 1, 1905, TR MSS.; H. N. Allen to J. H. Wilson, Nov. 3, 1906, Allen MSS.; Y. Takagi, *A Historical Observation of the Oriental Policy of America*.

365. S. L. Selde to H. N. Allen, Nov. 22, 1905, Allen MSS. See also *Washington Post*, Nov. 30, 1905, TR Scrapbooks.

366. H. N. Allen to Gov. G. K. Nash, May 4, 1904, HNA to Durham W. Stevens, Nov. 29, 1905, Allen MSS.; J. Hay to HNA, Nov. 17, 1904, HNA to JH, Feb. 2, 1905, JH to TR, Jan. 30, 1905, Hay MSS.; Frederick A. McKenzie, *Korea's Fight for Freedom*, 88, 98-103.

367. TR to E. Root, Nov. 25, 1905, TR MSS.; Eugene A. Elliott to Harry R.

Bostwick, Dec. 10, 1905, Allen MSS. See also J. Hay to TR, Jan. 30, 1905, Hay MSS.; F. A. McKenzie, *op. cit.*, 99.

368. *New York Tribune,* Aug. 5, 1905.

369. TR to E. Root, July 29, 1907, TR MSS.

370. H. N. Allen, "Statement" [1905], Allen MSS.

371. TR to J. Hay, Jan. 28, 1905, TR MSS.

372. F. A. McKenzie, *Korea's Fight for Freedom,* 101; S. Makoto, "The World Cruise of the American Fleet during 1907-1909 and Japan," translated from the Japanese, MS. in possession of the author. This article was planned to answer a letter from the author to Professor Yasaka Takagi of the University of Tokyo asking the question: How did Japan react to the cruise of the fleet? Mr. Makoto made use of contemporary Japanese sources in his study.

373. L. C. Griscom to TR, Sept. 21, 1905, TR MSS.

374. TR to J. St. Loe Strachey, Sept. 11, 1905, TR MSS.

375. TR to H. C. Lodge, June 5, 1905, TR MSS.

376. TR to H. C. Lodge, June 5 and 6, 1905, TR MSS. See also TR to K. Roosevelt, May 12, 1907, TR to H. C. Lodge, Sept. 8, 1905, TR to Melville Stone, Sept. 12, 1904, TR MSS.; A. W. Griswold, *Far Eastern Policy,* 123; S. Makoto, "The World Cruise of the American Fleet"; William II to Prince B. H. von Bülow, Sept. 27, 1905, in BHvonB, *Letters,* 178, 180. Roosevelt also expressed these views to Assistant Secretary of State Loomis. HKB, interview with F. B. Loomis, May 8, 1940.

377. L. Wood to TR, Dec. 13, 1905, TR MSS.

378. TR to L. Wood, Jan. 22, 1906, TR MSS.; H. N. Allen to J. H. Wilson, Dec. 16, 1902, Allen MSS.; S. Makoto, "The World Cruise of the American Fleet." See also TR to J. A. T. Hull, March 16, 1905, TR MSS.

379. TR to Sir Edward Grey, Dec. 18, 1906, TR MSS.

380. HKB, interview with F. B. Loomis, May 8, 1940.

381. *Tokyo Mainichi,* July 7, 1907, in S. Makoto, "The World Cruise of the American Fleet."

382. See, e. g., TR to J. Hay, Dec. 23, 1904, TR to H. C. Lodge, Sept. 8, 1905, TR MSS. Nr. 8550, Freiherr Speck von Sternburg an den Reichskanzler Fürsten von Bülow, den 9. September 1907, *Grosse Politik,* xxv-1, 72.

383. TR to J. A. T. Hull, March 16, 1905, L. C. Griscom to TR, Sept. 21, 1905, TR to G. Kennan, May 6, 1905, TR to J. St. Loe Strachey, Sept. 11, 1905, TR MSS.

384. TR to E. Hale, Oct. 27, 1906, TR to A. H. Lee, April 8, 1908, TR MSS.

385. TR to H. C. Lodge, May 15 and June 5, 1905, Lodge MSS.

386. TR to G. Kennan, May 6, 1905, TR MSS.

387. See, e. g., TR to Lyman Abbott, Jan. 3, 1907, TR to James N. Gillett, March 11, 1907, TR to Sir E. Grey, Dec. 18, 1906, TR to Victor H. Metcalf, Nov. 27, 1906, TR to J. St. Loe Strachey, Feb. 22, 1907, TR MSS. See also Thomas A. Bailey, *Theodore Roosevelt and the Japanese-American Crisis, passim,* and J. F. Rhodes, "Index Rerum," in M. A. DeW. Howe, *Rhodes,* 170.

388. TR to A. H. Lee, Dec. 20, 1908, TR MSS.

389. HKB, interview with F. B. Loomis, May 8, 1940.

390. TR to A. H. Lee, Dec. 20, 1908, TR to E. Hale, Oct. 27, 1906, TR MSS. See also TR to G. von L. Meyer, Dec. 26, 1904, TR MSS., and TR's talk with Oscar K. Davis, Aug. 7, 1908, in OKD, *Released for Publication*, 88.

391. TR to O. S. Straus, April 10, 1906, Straus MSS. See also TR to G. O. Trevelyan, May 13, 1905, TR MSS.

392. TR to G. O. Trevelyan, Oct. 1, 1911, TR MSS.

393. Lawrence F. Abbott, *Impressions of TR*, 112-113.

394. TR to E. Root, July 13 and 23, 1907, R. D. Evans to Admiral W. H. Brownson, Aug. 17, 1907, TR to Jonathan Bourne, Jr., Aug. 13, 1907, TR to A. H. Lee, April 8, 1908, TR to H. C. Lodge, July 10, 1907, TR to Truman H. Newberry, Aug. 10, 1907, TR MSS.; *Chicago Record-Herald*, March 19, 1908, *New York Herald*, July 2, 1907, TR Scrapbooks; L. F. Abbott, *Impressions of TR*, 110-111; T. A. Bailey, "World Cruise of the American Battleship Fleet, 1907-1909," *Pacific Historical Review*, i (December, 1932), 395-403; [Samuel L. Clemens], "The President as Advertiser," Sept. 7, 1907, in *Mark Twain in Eruption*, 17; S. Makoto, "The World Cruise of the American Fleet." See also André Tardieu, "Trois Visites à M. Roosevelt," *Le Temps*, April (?), 1908, TR Scrapbooks; Finley P. Dunne, *Mr. Dooley at His Best*, 141; John J. Leary, *Talks with TR*, 11-13; Harold and Margaret Sprout, *The Rise of American Naval Power*, 265; F. M. Huntington Wilson, *Memoirs of an Ex-Diplomat*, 162-163. Mahan had early taught Roosevelt that the fleet should never be divided. TR to A. T. Mahan, Jan. 12, 1907, TR MSS.

395. J. Pulitzer to F. I. Cobb, July 8 and 10, 1907, Pulitzer MSS. (quoted in D. C. Seitz, *Pulitzer*, 311-314); JP, Memo for Mr. Heaton, August 4, 1907, Pulitzer MSS. See also TR to L. F. Abbott, Aug. 29, 1907, TR to E. Root, July 31, 1907, TR MSS.; JP to FIC, July 19, 1907, Pulitzer MSS.; *New York Herald*, July 12, 1907, TR Scrapbooks. Senator Hale, chairman of the Naval Affairs Committee, also opposed sending the fleet. H. C. Lodge to TR, Aug. 30, 1907, TR to HCL, Sept. 2, 1907, E. Hale to T. H. Newberry, July 27, 1907, TR MSS.; Max Farrand, "Theodore Roosevelt—The Man and the President," MS. in Huntington Library.

396. See, e. g., the *Jiji Shimpo*, July 11, 1907, which said, "There is nothing strange in America's establishing many bases in the Pacific area and also permanently posting large fleets there. To interpret this as an intimidation toward Japan is something that we should never dream of." "If they should happen to visit our ports," declared the *Asahi*, July 23, 1907, "we would get the chance to show the sincerity we have toward our East neighbor." Since Japan and America have had a continuous fifty years of friendship, this right-wing paper continued, "if America should at this time maneuver its fleet and try to intimidate our country, would this not be a foolish act? Since they are full of the common sense of Anglo-Saxons we cannot believe that they will do such an act." When the Democratic Convention passed anti-Japanese resolutions, the *Osaka Asahi*, August 16, 1908, proclaimed, "It is characteristic of our people, the more the other person gets excited, to become more and more calm. We look upon

these things as the wind blowing in the sky and at present are busy preparing for the fleet." " Japan is not war crazy but peace crazy," insisted the *Tokyo Asahi*, July 26, 1908. Even the right-wing *Niroku*, Dec. 8, 1907, urged a peace policy and declared that trying to dominate the world was to revert to " an old style hero " and to lag behind " the new trend of the world." Some papers thought the Japanese Government might persuade the United States not to send the fleet. See, for instance, the *Tokyo Mainichi*, July 7, 1907. " Fortunately the opinions and arguments of the Japanese newspapers are very calm and do not show any signs of getting red in the face," said the *Yomijuri*, July 11, 1907. So this conduct of America was like " pushing the air." Prominent Japanese questioned by the *New York World* were restrained. Thus Count Itagaki found the Japanese people calm. " Both countries know of the difficulties of a war," he explained, " and thus to restrain an act which will lead to war is easy." *Tokyo Mainichi*, July 8, 1907. Okuma Shigenobu, too, usually an outspoken person, refused to " believe reports that say that America wants to intimidate Japan with force." The *Evening Post*, the *Sun*, the *Times*, and the *World* defended Japan and took Roosevelt to task for sending the fleet. The newspaper comments are taken from S. Makoto, " The World Cruise of the American Fleet." See also *Niroku*, July 11, 1907, and *Nippon*, July 13, 1907, in *loc. cit*. Even when in May, 1907, a serious attack on Japanese in San Francisco occurred and some papers like the anti-government *Hochi* spoke strongly, still the pro-government *Kokumin* journal wrote: " Peace, peace, peace. If there is anything Japan needs most it is the word peace." The *Niroku*, on July 13, 1907, declared, " There is nothing so unaccountable as expecting a Japanese American war." See also *ibid.*, Aug. 22, 1907. Quotations from S. Makoto, *op. cit*. See also TR to H. C. Lodge, Sept. 2, 1907, TR MSS.; J. Pulitzer to F. I. Cobb, Aug. 4, 1907, Pulitzer MSS.

397. Baron Takahira to E. Root, March 18, 1908, TR MSS.

398. TR to T. H. Newberry, Aug. 10, 1907, TR to K. Roosevelt, Aug. 27, 1907, TR MSS.; H. C. Lodge to W. S. Bigelow, June 11, 1907, Lodge MSS.; Lincoln Steffens to Joseph Steffens, Aug. 27, 1907, in L. Steffens, *Letters*, Ella Winter and Granville Hicks, eds., I, 187-188; *Chicago Record-Herald*, March 19, 1908, *New York Herald*, July 5, 1907, *New York Press*, July 8, 1907, TR Scrapbooks; *Kokumin*, Aug. 25, 1908, *Asahi*, July 8 and 26, 1908, *Tokyo Mainichi*, July 7, 1907, *Jiji Shimpo*, July 11, 1907, *Yomijuri*, July 11, 1907, quoted in S. Makoto, " The World Cruise of the American Fleet." See, for instance, *New York Tribune*, Oct. 25, 1907, TR Scrapbooks, and Louis Morton, " Military and Naval Preparations for the Defense of the Philippines during the War Scare of 1907," *Military Affairs*, XIII (1949), 95-104. See also J. J. Leary, *Talks with TR*, 11, 13; J. F. Rhodes, " Index Rerum," in M. A. DeW. Howe, *Rhodes*, 195.

399. TR to W. Reid, March 20, 1908, TR to C. S. Sperry, March 21, 1908, TR MSS.; William II to Prince B. H. von Bülow, Dec. 30, 1907, BHvonB, *Letters*, 226-227. See also TR to Commander Andrew T. Long, Dec. 7, 1908, TR MSS.; *New York Herald*, March 22, 1908, TR Scrapbooks. For a full discussion of the many factors involved in Roosevelt's decision to send the fleet

around the world see T. A. Bailey, " World Cruise of the American Battleship Fleet, 1907-1909," *Pacific Historical Review*, I (December, 1932), 389-423. Professor Bailey suggests that the decision to send the fleet was not as Roosevelt's *Autobiography* implies a sudden decision. Rather, it had been long contemplated. TAB, " World Cruise," 389-394.

400. TR to [Thomas J.] O'Brien, Oct. 21, 1908, TR MSS.; S. Makoto, " The World Cruise of the American Fleet."

401. J. C. O'Laughlin to TR, Sept. 30, 1908, TR MSS.

402. TR to G. O. Trevelyan, Oct. 1, 1911, TR MSS.; Willy to Nicky, Dec. 28, 1907, in *Letters from the Kaiser to the Czar*, I. D. Levine, ed., 218; L. F. Abbott, *Impressions of TR*, 112-113.

403. TR to E. Root, July 23, 1907, TR MSS. See also Willy to Nicky, Dec. 28, 1907, in I. D. Levine, *op. cit.*, 218.

404. J. F. Rhodes, " Index Rerum," in M. A. DeW. Howe, *Rhodes*, 170; The Kaiser, too, thought this had prevented a war. TR to Hiram P. Collier, June 20, 1911, Charlemagne Tower to TR, Jan. 28, 1908, TR to G. O. Trevelyan, Oct. 1, 1911, TR MSS.; Arthur N. Davis, *The Kaiser as I Know Him*, 101. See also S. Makoto, " The World Cruise of the American Fleet."

405. HKB, interview with F. B. Loomis, May 8, 1940.

406. One Japanese newspaper commented: " Although it is not necessary to pay much attention to the intimidations of America, if this should develop into a race of expanding the navy it will be hard to measure its effects. What we should be concerned with is the latter problem." Quoted by S. Makoto, in " The World Cruise of the American Fleet." Professor Bailey disagrees with this point of view. He argues that the trip merely stimulated " friendlier " international relations and had little effect on naval rivalry between Japan and the United States. T. A. Bailey, " World Cruise of the American Battleship Fleet," *loc. cit.*, 417-419, 421-423.

407. See, e. g., *Japan Weekly Mail*, July 6, 1907. See, too, Ernest B. Price, *The Russo-Japanese Treaties of 1907-1916 Concerning Manchuria and Mongolia*, 26-38; *Manchuria: Treaties and Agreements* (Carnegie Endowment for International Peace, *Pamphlets*, No. 44, 1921), 107-112, 116-117 (The crucial secret clauses were still not published in this collection.); T. Hayashi, *Secret Memoirs*, 231; William R. Manning, " China and the Powers since the Boxer Movement," *American Journal of International Law*, IV (October, 1910), 881-884 (Only the public clauses were known.); C. Walter Young, *The International Relations of Manchuria* (1929), 119-120.

408. Willard D. Straight, who had served under the Chinese and as a journalist, returned for two years to Mukden, 1906-1908, as American consul-general. He was appointed Acting Chief of the Division of Far Eastern Affairs in the State Department under Roosevelt in November, 1908, but resigned in June, 1909, to go back to China as representative this time of J. P. Morgan, Kuhn, Loeb, and Company, and the First National Bank and the National City Bank of New York City. William Phillips served under Roosevelt as private secretary to Ambassador Choate in London, 1903-1905, and second secretary at the Lega-

tion in Peking, 1905-1907. In March, 1908, Roosevelt made him Chief of the State Department's Division of Far Eastern Affairs, and in December moved him up to be Third Assistant Secretary of State.

409. F. M. Huntington Wilson, *Memoirs of an Ex-Diplomat*, 115-116.

410. See, e. g., A. A. Adee to B. F. Barnes, Aug. 22, 1905, W. W. Rockhill to J. Hay, July 1, 1905, TR MSS.; *New York Tribune*, July 21, 1905, TR Scrapbooks.

CHAPTER VI

1. William II to Prince Bernard H. von Bülow, Dec. 30, 1907, in BHvonB, *Letters*, Frederick Whyte, translator, 226-227.

2. TR to Baron Hermann Speck von Sternburg, Oct. 11, 1901, TR MSS.

3. See, e. g., Cecil Spring Rice to TR, Aug. 9, 1900, TR MSS.

4. TR to C. Spring Rice, Nov. 1, 1905, TR MSS.

5. TR to Maria Longworth Storer, Oct. 28, 1899, TR MSS.

6. TR to Lawrence F. Abbott, January, 1903, TR MSS.

7. Capt. Alfred T. Mahan to TR, Dec. 27, 1904, Charlemagne Tower to John Hay, March 11, 1905, TR MSS.; J. Hay, MS. Diary, Nov. 26 and Dec. 2, 7, and 17, 1904, Joseph H. Choate to JH, Nov. 5, 1904, Hay MSS.; *New York Tribune*, Sept. 25, 1904, *Washington Star*, Dec. 23, 1904, TR Scrapbooks; JH, Circulars of Oct. 21 and Dec. 16, 1904, *Foreign Relations*, 1904, 10-14.

8. Correspondence concerning a Second Hague Peace Conference, Oct. 21, 1904, TR MSS.; TR to Elihu Root, Sept. 14, 1905, TR to Carl Schurz, Sept. 18, 1905, TR to Leslie M. Shaw, Sept. 18, 1905, TR MSS. The best discussion of the Hague Conference is found in Margaret Robinson, *Arbitration and the Hague Conferences* (1936). The Conference is also discussed in William I. Hull, *The Two Hague Conferences and Their Contributions to International Law* (1908). In *Texts of the Peace Conferences at the Hague, 1899 and 1907* (1908), James B. Scott, who was a technical delegate to the second conference and solicitor for the Department of State, printed the documents of both conferences.

9. TR to E. Root, Sept. 14, 1905, TR MSS.; *Foreign Relations*, 1905, 828-830.

10. TR to C. Schurz, Sept. 18, 1905, TR MSS. See also TR to E. Root, Sept. 14, 1905, TR MSS.

11. TR to Andrew Carnegie, Aug. 6, 1906, TR MSS.

12. *Loc. cit.*; A. Carnegie to TR, July 27 and Aug. 27, 1906, Carnegie MSS.; TR to Henry White, Aug. 14, 1906, TR MSS.

13. TR to H. White, Aug. 14, 1906, A. Carnegie to TR, Feb. 14, 1907, Whitelaw Reid to TR, Jan. 15, 1907, H. Speck von Sternburg to TR, Jan. 20, 1907, TR MSS.; A. Carnegie to David Jayne Hill, August, 1907, Carnegie MSS.; B. H. von Bülow to HSvonS, Jan. 5, 1907, in BHvonB, *Letters*, 207-208; Alexandre I. Nélidoff, Ambassadeur de Russie à Paris, le 9/22 août 1907, à Alexandre Iswolsky, in AI, *Au service de la Russie: Correspondence diplomatique, 1906-*

1911, I, 228; GvonLM, Diary, Feb. 19, 1907, M. A. deWolfe Howe, *George von Lengerke Meyer: His Life and Public Services*, 349-350.

14. TR to A. Carnegie, May 19, 1906, AC to John Morley, June 14, 1907, JM to AC, June 17 and July 18, 1906, Carnegie MSS.; TR to W. Reid, Jan. 10, 1907, AC to TR, July 27 and Aug. 27, 1906, and Feb. 14, 1907, WR to TR, Jan. 15, 1907, TR MSS.; *New York Journal of Commerce*, April 16, 1907, TR Scrapbooks.

15. TR to Wilhelm II, Jan. 8, 1907, Wilhelm II to TR, undated telegram [1907 (?)], TR MSS.; TR to A. Carnegie, May 19, 1906, Carnegie MSS.

16. See, e. g., TR to Nicholas Murray Butler, Feb. 6, 1906, TR to A. Carnegie, April 20, 1907, AC to TR, April 19, 1907, TR MSS.; C. Schurz to TR, Sept. 6, 1905, Lodge MSS.; CS, *Speeches, Correspondence, and Political Papers*, Frederic Bancroft, ed., VI, 399-400. See also TR to E. Root, July 2, 1907, TR MSS.

17. TR to N. M. Butler, Feb. 6, 1906, TR to A. Carnegie, May 19, Aug. 6, and Sept. 6, 1906, and Feb. 17 and April 5, 1907, AC to TR, July 27 and Aug. 27, 1906, TR to W. Reid, Jan. 10, 1907, TR MSS.; AC to TR, July 27 and Aug. 27, 1906, and Feb. 14, 1907, AC to J. Morley, Sept. 5, 1906, Carnegie MSS.; *New York Journal of Commerce*, April 16, 1907, TR Scrapbooks. Spring Rice agreed with him. C. Spring Rice to Edith Kermit Roosevelt, Sept. 6, 1908, TR MSS.

18. TR to John St. Loe Strachey, Sept. 11, 1905, TR MSS. See also TR to C. Schurz, Sept. 8 and 18, 1905, TR MSS.

19. TR to Charles W. Eliot, Sept. 22, 1906, TR MSS. See also TR to A. Carnegie, Aug. 6, 1906, TR MSS.

20. W. Reid to TR, Oct. 26, 1907, TR MSS.; J. H. Choate to H. White, July 17, 1907, Lodge MSS.; *Foreign Relations*, 1906, 1625-1626; Baron Roman R. Rosen, Russian Ambassador, to E. Root, April 12, 1906, ER to RRR, June 7, 1906, RRR to ER, Nov. 12, 1906, ER to RRR, Dec. 20, 1906, *ibid.*, 1906, 1629-1631, 1635-1637, 1640, 1642; ER, Instructions to the American Delegates to the Hague Conference, 1907, *ibid.*, 1907, 1133; Convention on the Recovery of Contract Debts, *ibid.*, 1907, 1199-1201; Elsie P. Mende, *An American Soldier and Diplomat: Horace Porter*, 317-320; Benjamin F. Trueblood, "The Two Hague Conferences and Their Results," *The Development of the Peace Idea and Other Essays* (1907), 136-137. For Mr. Dooley's comments see Finley Peter Dunne, *Mr. Dooley at His Best*, 144-145.

21. J. H. Choate to H. White, July 17, 1907, Lodge MSS.; TR to E. Root, Aug. 6, 1907, TR MSS.; JHC to Carrie Choate, Sept. 19, 1907, JHC to JHC, Jr., Aug. 2, 1907, Choate MSS.; JHC to CC, 1907, in Edward S. Martin, *The Life of Joseph Hodges Choate*, II, 319; A. I. Nélidoff à A. Iswolsky, le 9/22 août, 1907, in AI, *Au Service de la Russie*, I, 229; E. Root, Instructions, *Foreign Relations*, 1907, 1133-1136; Draft of a Convention Relative to the Creation of a Judicial Arbitration Court, *ibid.*, 1907, 1277-1283; B. F. Trueblood, *op. cit.*, 137-141; *New York Tribune*, April 20, 1907, TR Scrapbooks. For a full discussion see M. Robinson, *Arbitration and the Hague Peace Conferences*, 98-105.

22. R. R. Rosen to E. Root, April 12, 1906, ER to RRR, June 7, 1906, RRR

to ER, Nov. 12, 1906, ER to RRR, Dec. 20, 1906, *Foreign Relations*, 1906, 1629-1631, 1635-1637, 1640, 1642.

23. Jean Jaurès, *Oeuvres*, II, 427-428; E. Root to W. Reid, Oct. 24, 1906, Root MSS.

24. TR to Richard Bartholdt, Sept. 25, 1905, TR to W. Reid, Aug. 7, 1906, TR MSS. See also TR to A. Carnegie, May 19, 1906, Carnegie MSS.; TR to H. White, Aug. 14, 1906, TR MSS.; TR to C. Schurz, Sept. 8 and 18, 1905, Schurz MSS.

25. A. T. Mahan to TR, Dec. 27, 1904, TR MSS.

26. TR to H. White, Aug. 14 and Sept. 13, 1906, HW to TR, Aug. 29, 1906, TR MSS. See also TR to George Otto Trevelyan, Aug. 18, 1906, TR to Sir Edward Grey, Oct. 22, 1906, TR MSS.

27. TR to H. White, Sept. 13, 1906, TR MSS.

28. H. White to E. Root, March 30, 1907, in Allan Nevins, *Henry White*, 258; Count Max Montgelas, *The Case for the Central Powers*, 26-27; *Japan Weekly Mail*, July 6, 1907.

29. W. Reid to TR, Feb. 18, 1907, Sir E. Grey to TR, Feb. 12, 1907, TR MSS.; A. I. Nélidoff, Ambassadeur de Russie à Paris, La Haye, le 24 juillet/6 août 1907, à A. Iswolsky, in AI, *Au Service de la Russie*, I, 227-228; H. White to E. Root, March 30, 1907, in A. Nevins, *Henry White*, 258; *British Documents on the Origins of the War, 1898-1914*, George P. Gooch and Harold W. V. Temperley, eds., VIII, 203, 207-216; Royal Cortissoz, *The Life of Whitelaw Reid*, II, 373-375.

30. TR to G. O. Trevelyan, Sept. 9, 1906, GOT to TR, Sept. 27, 1906, TR MSS. See also TR to A. Carnegie, Sept. 6, 1906, TR MSS.; William H. Edwards, *The Tragedy of Edward VII*, 316-317.

31. TR to Sir E. Grey, Oct. 22, 1906, A. Carnegie to TR, Aug. 27, 1906, TR MSS.; AC to J. Morley, Sept. 5, 1906, Carnegie MSS.; TR to C. Schurz, Sept. 8, 1905, Schurz MSS. See also TR to H. White, Aug. 14 and Sept. 13, 1906, TR to AC, Sept. 6, 1906, and April 5, 1907, TR MSS.; Philip C. Jessup, *Elihu Root*, II, 69-73.

32. H. White to TR, Sept. 20, 1906, TR MSS.

33. A. Nevins, *Henry White*, 257; M. A. DeW. Howe, *Meyer*, 344-346.

34. TR to Sir E. Grey, Feb. 28, 1907, TR MSS.

35. *Loc. cit.* Carnegie reported Roosevelt disappointed over the Kaiser's attitude. A. Carnegie to C. Tower, Jan. 23, 1907, Carnegie MSS.

36. Sidney Lee, *Edward VII*, II, 437.

37. A. Carnegie to J. Morley, Jan. 13, 1907, Carnegie MSS.; H. White to Henry Cabot Lodge, Feb. 10, 1907, Lodge MSS.; C. Tower to TR or E. Root, Jan. 31, 1907, in P. C. Jessup, *Root*, II, 71; Burton J. Hendrick, *The Life of Andrew Carnegie*, II, 314-315, 323-324; M. A. DeW. Howe, *Meyer*, 343-346; Maurice Muret, *L'évolution belliqueuse de Guillaume II*, 147.

38. A. Carnegie to TR, July 31, 1907, Carnegie MSS.

39. A. Carnegie to C. Tower, Jan. 23, 1907, Carnegie MSS.; M. Montgelas,

The Case for the Central Powers, 26-27. See also AC to J. Morley, July 30, 1907, Carnegie MSS.

40. H. White to E. Root, undated letter, in A. Nevins, *Henry White*, 258-259.

41. Wilhelm II to TR, undated telegram [1907 (?)], TR MSS. See also S. Lee, *Edward VII*, II, 438.

42. J. Morley to A. Carnegie, Sept. 30, 1906, Carnegie MSS.

43. TR to A. Carnegie, Aug. 6, 1906, TR MSS.; G. von L. Meyer, Diary, Feb. 3, 1907, in M. A. DeW. Howe, *Meyer*, 340.

44. W. Reid to TR, May 1, 1907, TR MSS.

45. G. von L. Meyer, Diary, Feb. 3, 1907, in M. A. DeW. Howe, *Meyer*, 340.

46. W. Reid to TR, July 19, 1907, TR MSS.

47. A. Carnegie to TR, July 31, 1907, Carnegie MSS.; M. Montgelas, *op. cit.*, 26-27.

48. Admiral Charles S. Sperry to Horace N. Allen, May 7, 1907, Allen MSS.

49. Sir E. Grey to TR, Feb. 12, 1907, TR MSS.

50. S. Lee, *Edward VII*, II, 438; J. H. Choate to E. Root, June 5, 1907, Sir E. Grey to TR, Feb. 12, 1907, TR MSS.; *British Documents*, G. P. Gooch and H. W. V. Temperley, eds., VIII, 188-221, 228-241.

51. TR to Sir E. Grey, Feb. 28, 1907, TR MSS.; *St. Louis Republican*, April 14, 1907, TR Scrapbooks. See also M. A. DeW. Howe, *Meyer*, 344-346.

52. TR to Sir E. Grey, Feb. 28, 1907, TR MSS.

53. J. St. Loe Strachey to TR, Sept. 21, 1906, TR MSS.

54. A. T. Mahan to TR [December (?)], 1906, in Charles C. Taylor, *The Life of Admiral Mahan: Naval Philosopher*, 146.

55. E. Root, Instructions, *Foreign Relations*, 1907, 1135; W. Reid to TR, May 1 and June 7, 1907, TR to G. O. Trevelyan, Aug. 18, 1906, H. White to TR, March 27 and 28, 1907, TR MSS.; E. Root to A. Carnegie, June 7, 1907, Carnegie MSS.; W. H. Edwards, *Edward VII*, 316-317. See also ER to HW, Feb. 19, 1907, in P. C. Jessup, *Root*, II, 71.

56. TR to E. Root, July 2, 1907, TR MSS.

57. E. Root to TR, July 8, 1907, Root MSS. Trevelyan's account of Grey's attitude is scarcely accurate. George Macaulay Trevelyan, *Grey of Fallodon*, 206-207.

58. A. Carnegie to J. Morley, July 30, 1907, JM to AC, Oct. 6, 1906, Carnegie MSS.; TR to C. Spring Rice, Aug. 13, 1897, TR MSS. See also AC to TR, July 27, 1906, TR MSS.

59. J. H. Choate to E. Root, June 5, 1907, TR MSS.; ER to A. Carnegie, June 7, 1907, Carnegie MSS.; *Japan Weekly Mail*, July 6, 1907.

60. A. T. Mahan to TR [December (?)], 1906, in C. C. Taylor, *Mahan*, 146; E. Root, Instructions, *Foreign Relations*, 1907, 1136-1137. See also A. T. Mahan, " The Hague Conference: The Question of Immunity for Belligerent Merchant Shipping," *National Review*, XLIX (June, 1907), 521-537.

61. TR to W. Reid, July 29, 1907, WR to TR, June 7, 1907, TR MSS.; E. Root to WR, Oct. 24, 1906, Root MSS.; William D. Puleston, *Mahan*, 270. See also A. Carnegie to TR, Aug. 27, 1906, A. T. Mahan to TR, Dec. 27, 1904, TR MSS.

62. W. Reid to TR, Aug. 11, 1907, TR MSS.

63. TR to Lyman Abbott, June 8, 1905, TR to A. Carnegie, Feb. 17, 1907, TR to E. Root, Aug. 6, 1907, TR MSS.

64. TR to L. Abbott, June 8, 1905, TR to Albert Bushnell Hart, Oct. 26, 1906, TR MSS.; E. Root to W. Reid, Oct. 24, 1906, Root MSS.; A. Carnegie to J. Morley [September, 1907], Carnegie MSS.

65. TR to Sir E. Grey, Feb. 28, 1907, TR MSS. See also TR to A. Carnegie, April 5, 1907, TR to G. O. Trevelyan, Aug. 18, 1906, Ralph M. Easley to Wm. Loeb, Jr., April 25, 1907, TR MSS.; A. T. Mahan, "The Hague Conference and the Practical Aspect of War," *National Review*, XLIX (July, 1907), 688-704.

66. TR to Sir E. Grey, Oct. 22, 1906, TR MSS.; J. H. Choate to H. White, July 17, 1907, Lodge MSS.; *Washington Post*, June 29, 1907, TR Scrapbooks; JHC to JHC, Jr., May 30, 1907, in E. S. Martin, *Choate*, II, 317.

67. E. Root, Instructions, *Foreign Relations*, 1907, 1133-1136; J. H. Choate to H. White, July 17, 1907, Lodge MSS.; D. J. Hill to A. Carnegie, in B. J. Hendrick, *Carnegie*, II, 324. For a full discussion see M. Robinson, *Arbitration and the Hague Peace Conferences*, 52-67. See also D. J. Hill, *Impressions of the Kaiser*, 86-88; A. T. Mahan, "The Moral Aspect of War," *Some Neglected Aspects of War*, 24-52; B. F. Trueblood, *The Development of the Peace Idea*, 135, 139-140; "Convention on Settlement of International Disputes," *Foreign Relations*, 1907, 1181-1199.

68. F. P. Dunne, *Mr. Dooley at His Best*, 142; Elmer Ellis, *Mr. Dooley's America*, 246. See also FPD, *op. cit.*, 144-145.

69. Choate appeared to be satisfied that the Conference had accomplished enough to have been worth while, but he had had great hopes for the Conference that were none the less not fulfilled. H. White to H. C. Lodge, Oct. 30, 1907, Lodge MSS.; J. H. Choate to Mrs. [Carrie] Choate, 1907, and JHC to his son, Aug. 29, 1907, in E. S. Martin, *Choate*, II, 318-319, 320, 321-322; *Indianapolis Star*, Oct. 27, 1907, TR Scrapbooks.

70. J. H. Choate to Mrs. Choate, 1907, in E. S. Martin, *Choate*, II, 321-322; B. F. Trueblood, *op. cit.*, 141.

71. H. White to H. C. Lodge, Oct. 30, 1907, Lodge MSS.

72. G. P. Gooch, *Before the War*, II, 39.

73. See, e. g., *New York Press*, June 16, 1907, TR Scrapbooks.

74. See, e. g., *Indianapolis Star*, Oct. 27, 1907, TR Scrapbooks.

75. H. C. Lodge to H. White, undated, Lodge MSS.; E. Root, Instructions, *Foreign Relations*, 1907, 1129-1130.

76. A. T. Mahan to TR [December (?)], 1906, in C. C. Taylor, *Mahan*, 146. See also TR to C. Spring Rice, March 19, 1904, TR MSS.

77. TR to J. St. Loe Strachey, Sept. 11, 1905, TR MSS.

78. TR to G. O. Trevelyan, Sept. 9, 1906, TR MSS.

79. *Loc. cit.*

80. TR to A. Carnegie, Aug. 6, 1906, TR MSS.

81. TR to C. Schurz, Sept. 8, 1905, Schurz MSS.

82. TR to W. Reid, Aug. 7, 1906, in R. Cortissoz, *Reid*, II, 343; TR to A. Carnegie, Aug. 6 1906, TR MSS. See also J. St. Loe Strachey to TR, Sept. 21, 1906, TR MSS.

83. See, e. g., TR to W. Reid, Aug. 7, 1906, in R. Cortissoz, *Reid*, II, 343.

84. TR to G. O. Trevelyan, Sept. 9, 1906, TR to Sir E. Grey, Feb. 28, 1907, TR MSS. See also TR to C. Schurz, Sept. 8, 1905, TR to GOT, Aug. 18, 1906, TR MSS.

85. J. St. Loe Strachey to TR, Sept. 21, 1906, TR MSS.

86. TR to C. Schurz, Sept. 8, 1905, TR MSS. See also TR to A. Carnegie, Aug. 6, 1906, TR MSS.

87. TR to H. White, Aug. 14, 1906, TR MSS.

88. TR to C. Schurz, Sept. 8, 1905, TR MSS.

89. For an anti-Roosevelt, anti-American account that paints Roosevelt as conspiring with Britain in hostility to Germany see Evelene Peters, *Roosevelt und der Kaiser*, 121-153, 156. Miss Peters, an American woman studying in Berlin, did the study as her dissertation under Friedrich Meinecke and wrote from a strongly German nationalist point of view. She used *Die Grosse Politik* and other German sources extensively but among American materials had access only to obvious published collections. She believes Germany's faith in the friendship of Roosevelt misplaced. Speck von Sternburg, she feels, served his government badly. A competent and fair-minded British account is found in George P. Gooch, *History of Modern Europe, 1878-1919*, 352-366, and *Before the War: Studies in Diplomacy*, I, 53-67, 153, 156, 161-163, 168-183, 246-253, 258-259; II, 6-20. Sidney B. Fay gives a brief account in his *The Origins of the World War*, I, 184-191. A recent biography of William (Erich Eyck, *Das persönliche Regiment Wilhelms II* [1948], 366-434) treats this episode from German sources. For a complete detailed study see Eugene N. Anderson, *The First Moroccan Crisis, 1904-1906* (1930). Anderson's study, while excellent, was written from a European point of view without use of American materials that would have revealed America's rôle. Hence from the point of view of Roosevelt's part his study is inadequate.

90. Marquess of Lansdowne (Henry C. K. Petty-Fitzmaurice) to Sir H. Mortimer Durand, April 15 and May 1, 1901, HMD to Lord Lansdowne, April 13, 1901, *British Documents*, G. P. Gooch and H. W. V. Temperley, eds., II, 259-260.

91. Willy to Nicky, Oct. 30, 1904, *Letters from the Kaiser to the Czar, Copied from Government Archives in Petrograd Unpublished before 1920*, Isaac Don Levine, ed., 123; H. Speck von Sternburg to TR, Nov. 10, 1905, TR MSS.; Evelyn Baring, Earl of Cromer, to Lord Lansdowne, Nov. 27, 1903, in Thomas W. Leah, Baron of Newton, *Lord Lansdowne*, 285-286; Nr. 6896, HSvonS an das Auswärtige Amt, den 3. November 1905, *Die Grosse Politik*, XXI-1, 9, 10; G. P. Gooch, *Before the War*, I, 153, 156, 165.

92. H. C. Lodge to TR, June 29, 1905, H. Speck von Sternburg to TR, May 31 and June 22, 1905, TR MSS.; Willy to Nicky, Oct. 14, and Nov. 13, 1904, *Willy-Nicky Correspondence*, Hermann Bernstein, ed., 68-70, 86-87; Willy to

Nicky, Oct. 30, 1904, and Nov. 8, 1905, *Letters from the Kaiser to the Czar*, 123, 201; Nr. 6429, Graf B. H. von Bülow an Kaiser Wilhelm II, den 10. März 1905, Nr. 6668, BHvonB an HSvonS, den 30. Mai 1905, *Grosse Politik*, xx-1, 97-98; xx-2, 386-388; Erich Brandenburg, *From Bismarck to the World War: A History of German Foreign Policy, 1870-1914*, 209-212; Hermann von Eckardstein, *Die Isolierung Deutschlands* (*Lebenserinnerung und politischen Denkwürdigkeiten*, iii), 159-160; G. P. Gooch, *Before the War*, i, 55-56, ii, 18-20; Alexandre Iswolsky, *Recollections of a Foreign Minister*, 49-51.

93. E. g., H. C. Lodge to TR, June 29, 1905, H. Speck von Sternburg to TR, Dec. 29, 1904, C. Tower to TR, Feb. 4 and July 13, 1905, C. Spring Rice to E. K. Roosevelt, July 10, 1905, TR MSS.

94. H. Speck von Sternburg to TR, May 13, 1905, TR MSS.; Lord Cromer to Lord Lansdowne, Nov. 27, 1903, in Lord Newton, *Lansdowne*, 285-286; G. P. Gooch, *Before the War*, i, 153, 156, 165.

95. H. Speck von Sternburg to TR, Nov. 10, 1905, TR MSS.; Lord Lansdowne to Lord Cromer, Nov. 17, 1903, in Lord Newton, *Lansdowne*, 285; Nr. 6897, Fürst von Bülow an HSvonS (Konzept von der Hand des Vortragenden Rats von Holstein), den 7. November 1905, *Grosse Politik*, xx-1, 11-12; E. Peters, *Roosevelt und der Kaiser*, 122-124; G. P. Gooch, *Before the War*, i, 53-54, 161-163. See also Lord Lansdowne to Sir Frank Lascelles, April 9, 1905, in Lord Newton, *Lansdowne*, 334; HSvonS to TR, April 5, 1905, TR MSS.

96. E. Brandenburg, *From Bismarck to the World War*, 209-212; G. P. Gooch, *Before the War*, i, 53-54, 161-163.

97. *Ibid.*, i, 53-58, 168-174, 177-179, 182-183, 246-247.

98. Willy to Nicky, Oct. 30, 1904, *Letters from the Kaiser to the Czar*, I. D. Levine, ed., 123; Friedrich von Holstein, *Lebensbekenntnis in Briefen an Eine Frau*, Helmuth Rogge, ed., 239-240; H. von Eckardstein, *Die Isolierung Deutschlands*, 159-160.

99. H. C. Lodge to TR, July 2, 1905, Lodge MSS.; B. H. von Bülow to William II, April 4, 1905, BHvonB, *Letters*, 122-123; E. Brandenburg, *op. cit.*, 209-212; H. von Eckardstein, *Die Isolierung Deutschlands*, 159-160; G. P. Gooch, *History of Modern Europe*, 352-353. See also Charles W. Porter, *The Career of Théophile Delcassé*, 237.

100. B. H. von Bülow to William II, April 4, 1905, BHvonB, *Letters*, 122-123; H. von Eckardstein, *Die Isolierung Deutschlands*, 159-160; G. P. Gooch, *Before the War*, i, 65-67, 246-248. See also C. W. Porter, *Delcassé*, 237.

101. H. White to TR, Aug. 10, 1905, TR MSS.

102. H. C. Lodge to TR, July 2, 1905, Lodge MSS.; H. White to TR, Aug. 10, 1905, TR MSS.

103. W. Reid to TR, June 19, 1906, TR MSS.

104. H. Speck von Sternburg to TR, May 13, 1905, H. White to TR, Aug. 10, 1905, TR MSS.; F. von Holstein, *Lebensbekenntnis*, 239-240; G. P. Gooch, *Before the War*, i, 172-174, 177-179, 182-183, 250-253, ii, 6-7. See also W. Reid to TR, June 19, 1906, in R. Cortissoz, *Reid*, ii, 330-332.

105. H. von Eckardstein, *Die Isolierung Deutschlands*, 159-160; R. Cortissoz,

Reid, II, 326-327; S. B. Fay, *Origins of the World War*, 189; G. P. Gooch, *Before the War*, I, 67, 250-253.

106. E. Brandenburg, *From Bismarck to the World War*, 209-212; G. P. Gooch, *History of Modern Europe*, 352-353; GPG, *Before the War*, 53-54, 65-67, 168-171, 177-179, 182-183, 246-249. See also Nr. 6696, Freiherr Speck von Sternburg an das Auswärtige Amt, den 8. Juni 1905, *Grosse Politik*, XX-2, 421.

107. B. H. von Bülow to William II, March 26, 1905, BHvonB, *Letters*, 113; Nr. 6558, BHvonB and Freiherrn Speck von Sternburg, den 25. Februar 1905, *Grosse Politik*, XX-1, 257-258.

108. H. Speck von Sternburg to TR, March 7, 1905, TR MSS.; Nr. 6558, Graf von Bülow an HSvonS, den 25. Februar 1905, *Grosse Politik*, XX-1, 257-258; BHvonB to William II, April 4, 1905, *Prince Bülow and the Kaiser, with Excerpts from Their Private Correspondence*, Oakley Williams, trans., 139-140; E. Brandenburg, *From Bismarck to the World War*, 209-212; G. P. Gooch, *Before the War*, I, 248-253.

109. C. Spring Rice to E. K. Roosevelt, March 29, 1905, TR MSS.; B. H. von Bülow to William II, March 26, 1905, BHvonB, *Letters*, 109-113; BHvonB to William II, April 4, 1905, *Prince Bülow and the Kaiser*, 139-142; F. von Holstein, *Lebensbekenntnis*, 239-240; G. P. Gooch, *History of Modern Europe*, 352-353; GPG, *Before the War*, I, 54-55, 65-67, 248-250.

110. *Ibid.*, I, 250-253. See also H. Speck von Sternburg to TR, April 5, 1905, TR MSS.

111. See, e. g., H. Speck von Sternburg to TR, May 29, 1905, TR MSS.; Nr. 6719, Fürst von Bülow an den interimistischen Leiter der Gesandtschaft in Tanger Gesandten Grafen Christian F. von Tattenbach, den 20. Juni 1905, *Grosse Politik*, XX-2, 451. See also TR to W. Reid, April 28, 1906, TR MSS.

112. H. Speck von Sternburg to TR, June 11, 1905, TR MSS.; Nr. 6429, Graf von Bülow an Kaiser Wilhelm II, den 10. März 1905, *Grosse Politik*, II-1, 98; E. Brandenburg, *From Bismarck to the World War*, 209-212.

113. Nr. 6283, Der Geschäftsträger in Washington Freiherr Hilmar von dem Bussche-Haddenhausen an das Auswärtige Amt, den 20. Januar 1905, *Grosse Politik*, XIX-2, 563-564.

114. For a German account of the pre-conference controversy see Prince B. H. von Bülow, *Imperial Germany*, Marie A. Lewenz, trans., 96-97.

115. G. P. Gooch, *Before the War*, I, 250-253. See also R. Cortissoz, *Reid*, II, 327; TR to W. Reid, April 28, 1906, H. Speck von Sternburg to TR, April 5 and Nov. 10, 1905, TR MSS.; Nr. 6558, Graf B. H. von Bülow an HSvonS, den 25. Februar 1905, Nr. 6599, BHvonB an Wilhelm II., z. Z auf der Mittelmeerreise, den 4. April 1905, Nr. 6896, HSvonS an das Auswärtige Amt, den 3. November 1905, *Grosse Politik*, XX-1, 258, XX-2, 303, XXI-1, 9-10; *Prince Bülow and the Kaiser*, 139-142; C. W. Porter, *Delcassé*, 237; E. Brandenburg, *From Bismarck to the World War*, 212.

116. H. Speck von Sternburg to TR, March 6 and 7, 1905, TR MSS.; Nr. 6558, Graf von Bülow and HSvonS, den 25. Februar 1905, *Grosse Politik*, XX-1,

258; G. P. Gooch, *Before the War*, I, 248-249. See also TR to W. Reid, April 28, 1906, TR MSS.

117. J. Hay, MS. Diary, March 7, 1905, Hay MSS.; Memorandum from H. Speck von Sternburg to TR [March 6, 1905 (?)], TR MSS.; W. H. Taft to TR, April 5, 1905, Taft MSS.; B. H. von Bülow to Wilhelm II, April 4, 1905, BHvonB, *Letters*, 121-123. See also TR to HSvonS, March 7, 1905, TR MSS.

118. Nr. 6559, 6696, Freiherr Speck von Sternburg an das Auswärtige Amt, den 9. März und den 8. Juni 1905, *Grosse Politik*, xx-1, 258-259, xx-2, 421-422; G. P. Gooch, *Before the War*, I, 248-249.

119. Nr. 6559, Freiherr Speck von Sternburg an das Auswärtige Amt, den 9. März 1905, *Grosse Politik*, xx-1, 259; B. H. von Bülow to William II, April 4, 1905, BHvonB, *Letters*, 121.

120. B. H. von Bülow to Richard von Kühlman, April 3, 1905, BHvonB, *Letters*, 120; Nr. 6576, BHvonB an Wilhelm II, z. Z. in Lissabon, den 26. März 1905, Nr. 6593, BHvonB an den Geschäftsträger in Tanger RvonK, den 3. April 1905, *Grosse Politik*, xx-1, 277, xx-2, 295.

121. TR to Samuel R. Gummere, March 31, 1905, TR to State Department, April 5, 1905, TR MSS.

122. W. H. Taft to TR, April 5, 1905, Taft MSS. See also H. Speck von Sternburg to TR, April 5, 1905, TR MSS.; Nr. 6560, Graf von Bülow an HSvonS, den 11. März 1905, *Grosse Politik*, xx-1, 259-260.

123. H. Speck von Sternburg to TR, April 13, 1905, TR MSS. See also TR to W. Reid, April 28, 1906, TR MSS.

124. J. Hay, MS. Diary, Jan. 30, Feb. 2, and April 19, 1905, Hay MSS.; Francis B. Loomis to TR, April 17, 1905, TR to FBL, April 20, 1905, TR MSS. See, e. g., Nr. 7203, Wilhelm II an Fürsten von Bülow, den 7. Januar 1907, *Grosse Politik*, xxi-2, 464-465; BHvonB to William II, April 4, 1905, *Prince Bülow and the Kaiser*, 140. See also C. Spring Rice to E. K. Roosevelt, Dec. 7, 1904, TR MSS.

125. TR to H. Speck von Sternburg, April 20, 1905, HSvonS to TR, April 25, 1905, TR MSS.; Nr. 6633, HSvonS an das Auswärtige Amt, den 25. April 1905, *Grosse Politik*, xx-2, 341-342. See also TR to F. B. Loomis, April 20, 1905, FBL to TR, April 17, 1905, TR MSS.

126. TR to W. H. Taft, April 20, 1905, TR MSS.; WHT to TR, April 26, 1905, Taft MSS.; G. P. Gooch, *Before the War*, I, 55-56.

127. Nr. 6847, Der Botschafter in Paris Fürst Hugo L. von Radolin an den Grafen von Bülow, den 25. April 1905, *Grosse Politik*, xx-2, 615; G. P. Gooch, *Before the War*, I, 54-55.

128. W. H. Taft to TR, April 26, 1905, Taft MSS.; G. P. Gooch, *Before the War*, I, 55-56.

129. W. H. Taft to TR, May 1, 1905, Taft MSS.; H. White to TR, May 6, 1905, TR MSS.; G. P. Gooch, *Before the War*, I, 55-56. See also TR to W. Reid, April 28, 1906, TR MSS.

130. H. Speck von Sternburg to TR, May 29 and 31, 1905, TR MSS.; Nr. 6634, 6667, 6668, 6851, Graf von Bülow an Freiherrn H. Speck von Sternburg,

den 27. April, den 10., 25., und 30. Mai 1905, *Grosse Politik*, xx-2, 342-344, 385-388, 620-622. See also TR to W. Reid, April 28, 1906, HSvonS to TR, April 5, 1905, TR MSS.

131. H. White to TR, May 6, 1905, TR MSS.; G. P. Gooch, *Before the War*, I, 56-58.

132. H. Speck von Sternburg to TR, May 13, 29, and 31 and June 11, 1905, TR MSS.; Nr. 6851, 6667, 6668, 6856, Graf von Bülow an HSvonS, den 10., 25., und 30. Mai und den 10. Juni 1905, Nr. 6696, HSvonS an das Auswärtige Amt, den 8. Juni 1905, *Grosse Politik*, xx-2, 620-622, 385-388, 627-628, 421-422; G. P. Gooch, *Before the War*, I, 61-63. See also TR to W. Reid, April 28, 1906, TR MSS.

133. TR to W. Reid, April 28, 1906, TR MSS.

134. H. Speck von Sternburg to TR, May 13, 1905, TR MSS.; G. P. Gooch, *Before the War*, I, 55-56. See also TR to W. Reid, April 28, 1906, TR MSS.

135. H. C. Lodge to TR, May 8 and July 2, 1905, Lodge MSS.

136. J. Hay, MS. Diary, May 29, 1905, Hay MSS.

137. TR to W. Reid, April 28, 1906, TR MSS.

138. Jean Jules Jusserand à M. le Ministre des Affaires Etrangères à Paris [Théophile Delcassé], June 3, 1905, TR MSS.

139. H. Speck von Sternburg to TR, June 11, 1905, TR MSS.; Nr. 6856, Fürst von Bülow an HSvonS, den 10. Juni 1905, *Grosse Politik*, xx-2, 626-627; G. P. Gooch, *Before the War*, I, 56-63.

140. *Ibid.*, I, 61-63.

141. Lord Lansdowne to Sir F. Lascelles, April 9, 1905, Lord Newton, *Lansdowne*, 334; G. P. Gooch, *Before the War*, I, 55-56. See also H. C. Lodge to TR, June 29, 1905, W. Reid to TR, June 19, 1906, C. Spring Rice to E. K. Roosevelt, July 10, 1905, TR MSS.; GPG, *op. cit.*, I, 54-55, 65-67.

142. H. C. Lodge to TR, June 29, 1905, TR MSS. See also H. C. Lodge to TR, March 30, 1901, and June 3, 1905, W. Reid to TR, Sept. 2, 1905, TR MSS.; R. Cortissoz, *Reid*, II, 375-376.

143. W. Reid to J. Hay, June 5, 1905, TR MSS.; Nr. 6687, Graf von Bülow an Hans K. T. L. von Flotow, den 5. Juni 1905, *Grosse Politik*, xx-2, 413. See also TR to W. Reid, April 28, 1906, WR to TR, June 19, 1906, TR MSS.

144. Memorandum draft of dispatch to W. Reid, June, 1905, H. Speck von Sternburg to TR, June 11, 1905, TR MSS.; J. Hay, MS. Diary, June 7, 1905, Hay MSS.; JH to Henry Adams, June 7, 1905, in JH, *Letters and Extracts from the Diaries of John Hay*, Henry Adams, compiler, Clara Hay, ed., III, 345-346; Nr. 6696, HSvonS an das Auswärtige Amt, den 8. Juni 1905, *Grosse Politik*, xx-2, 421-422; G. P. Gooch, *History of Modern Europe*, 356-357.

145. See, e. g., J. Hay to H. Adams, June 7, 1905, in JH, *Letters and Diary*, III, 345-346; S. B. Fay, *Origins of the World War*, I, 190-191. See also H. White to TR, June 7, 1905, H. Speck von Sternburg to TR, June 18, 1905, TR MSS.; H. C. Lodge to TR, July 2, 1905, Lodge MSS.; G. P. Gooch, *Before the War*, I, 67.

146. Fürst von Bülow an Freiherrn Speck von Sternburg, den 9. Juni 1905, *Grosse Politik*, xx-2, 421 n.

147. W. Reid to TR, June 17, 1905, TR MSS.; G. P. Gooch, *Before the War*, I, 58-60.

148. *Ibid.*, I, 58-63.

149. H. White to TR, Aug. 10, 1905, TR MSS.; HW to H. C. Lodge, July 22, 1905, Lodge MSS.; G. P. Gooch, *Before the War*, I, 258.

150. H. Speck von Sternburg to TR, June 12 and 13, 1905, TR MSS.; TR to H. C. Lodge, June 16, 1905, Lodge MSS.; Nr. 6707, 6713, HSvonS an das Auswärtige Amt, den 12. und 17. Juni 1905, *Grosse Politik*, xx-2, 433-434, 442-443; G. P. Gooch, *Before the War*, I, 259.

151. TR to J. J. Jusserand, April 25, 1906, TR MSS.

152. *Loc. cit.*, JJJ à M. le Ministre des Affaires Etrangères [Pierre-Maurice Rouvier], June 16, 1905, TR MSS.; Nr. 6707, 6713, Freiherr Speck von Sternburg an das Auswärtige Amt, den 12. und 17. Juni 1905, *Grosse Politik*, xx-2, 433-434, 442-443. See also TR to W. Reid April 28, 1906, TR MSS.

153. J. J. Jusserand to P.-M. Rouvier, June 18, 1905, JJJ to TR, June 25, 1905, TR MSS. See also TR to W. Reid, April 28, 1906, TR MSS.

154. H. Speck von Sternburg to TR, June 18, 1905, TR to HSvonS, June 20, 1905, J. J. Jusserand to TR, June 25, 1905, TR MSS.; G. P. Gooch, *Before the War*, I, 259. See also TR to W. Reid, April 28, 1906, TR MSS.; E. Brandenburg, *Von Bismarck zum Weltkriege*, 195.

155. J. J. Jusserand to P.-M. Rouvier, June 23, 1905, TR MSS.

156. *Loc. cit.*; TR to H. Speck von Sternburg, June 23, 1905, TR MSS.; Nr. 6731, HSvonS an das Auswärtige Amt, den 24. Juni 1905, *Grosse Politik*, xx-2, 466-467.

157. P.-M. Rouvier to J. J. Jusserand, transmitted in JJJ to TR, June 25, 1905, TR MSS.

158. Nr. 6719, Fürst von Bülow an den interimistischen Leiter der Gesandtschaft in Tanger Gesandten Grafen C. F. von Tattenbach, z. Z. in Fes, den 20. Juni 1905, *Grosse Politik*, xx-2, 451.

159. H. Speck von Sternburg to TR, June 26 and July 24, 1905, TR MSS.; B. H. von Bülow to William II, June 25, 1905, in BHvonB, *Letters*, 138; Nr. 6732, BHvonB an Wilhelm II, den 25. Juni 1905, Nr. 6739, 6747, BHvonB an HSvonS, den 26. und 28. Juni 1905, *Grosse Politik*, xx-2, 468, 469, 475, 476, 487; Jusserand Memorial Committee, *Jusserand*, 45-46.

160. Nr. 6740, Fürst von Bülow an Wilhelm II, den 26. Juni 1905, *Grosse Politik*, xx-2, 476-478; H. Speck von Sternburg to TR, June 26, 1905, TR MSS.

161. B. H. von Bülow to William II, June 25, 1905, BHvonB, *Letters*, 137-138; Nr. 6732, BHvonB an Wilhelm II, den 25. Juni 1905, Nr. 6742, 6743, Freiherr Speck von Sternburg an das Auswärtige Amt, den 26. und 27. Juni 1905, *Grosse Politik*, xx-2, 467, 468, 479-481.

162. TR to W. Reid, April 28, 1906, TR MSS.

163. TR to H. Speck von Sternburg, June 25, 1905, J. J. Jusserand to P.-M.

Rouvier, June 23, 1905, TR MSS.; Nr. 6738, HSvonS an das Auswärtige Amt, den 25. Juni 1905, *Grosse Politik,* xx-2, 473-475.

164. H. Speck von Sternburg to TR, June 28 and July 24, 1905, TR MSS. For the wording of Bülow's instruction to HSvonS see Nr. 6744, Fürst von Bülow an HSvonS, den 27. Juni 1905, *Grosse Politik,* xx-2, 481-482.

165. H. Speck von Sternburg to TR, June 28, 1905, Wm. Loeb, Jr., to Rudolph Forster, June 30, 1905, TR to HSvonS, June 30, 1905, TR MSS.; Viscount Edward Grey of Fallodon, *Twenty-five Years, 1892-1916,* I, 118. See also TR to W. Reid, April 28, 1906, TR MSS.

166. H. White to H. C. Lodge, July 22, 1905, Lodge MSS.; TR to W. Reid, April 28, 1906, H. Speck von Sternburg to TR, June 28, 1905, TR MSS.

167. H. C. Lodge to TR, July 2 and 8 and Aug. 14, 1905, Lodge MSS.; HKB, interview with Philippe Bunau-Varilla, Paris, July, 1936; PB-V, "Theodore Roosevelt and the Kaiser in 1905," 1924, TR MSS. See also *New York Times,* Feb. 1, 1924.

168. H. Speck von Sternburg to TR, June 18, 24, and 28 and Aug. 24, 1905, TR to HSvonS, June 20 and 25, 1905, J. J. Jusserand to TR, June 25 and July 11, 1905, TR to William II, July 29, 1905, TR MSS.; TR to H. C. Lodge, July 11, 1905, HCL to TR, July 25, 1905, Lodge MSS.; B. H. von Bülow to William II, June 25, 1905, in BHvonB, *Letters,* 138-139; Nr. 6732, BHvonB an Wilhelm II, den 25. Juni 1905, Nr. 6739, BHvonB an HSvonS, den 26. Juni 1905, *Grosse Politik,* xx-2, 468, 469, 475, 476. See also G. P. Gooch, *Before the War,* I, 258-259.

169. TR to J. J. Jusserand, July 24, 1905, JJJ to TR, July 26, 1905, TR to H. Speck von Sternburg, July 24, 1905, HSvonS to TR, Aug. 21, Nov. 10, and undated [probably Nov. 22], 1905, TR to William II, July 29, 1905, TR MSS.; Alvey A. Adee to Benjamin F. Barnes, Aug. 8, 1905, State Department Archives; H. White to H. C. Lodge, Nov. 17, 1905, Lodge MSS.; Willy to Nicky, Nov. 8, 1905, in *Letters from the Kaiser to the Czar,* I. D. Levine, ed., 201-202; Nr. 6786, Fürst B. H. von Bülow an Wilhelm II, den 3. August 1905, Nr. 6896, HSvonS an das Auswärtige Amt, den 3. November 1905, Nr. 6897, BHvonB an HSvonS (Konzept von der Hand des Vortragenden Rats von Holstein), den 7. November 1905, *Grosse Politik,* xx-2, 537, xxi-1, 9-12.

170. G. P. Gooch, *Before the War,* I, 260-261, II, 6-7.

171. E. Root to H. White, Nov. 28, 1905, *Foreign Relations,* 1905, 677-680.

172. W. Reid to TR, July 14, 1905, TR MSS.

173. H. White to TR, Aug. 10, 1905, TR MSS.; George von L. Meyer, *Diary,* Jan. 10, 1906, in M. A. DeW. Howe, *Meyer,* 243-244; G. P. Gooch, *Before the War,* I, 260-261, II, 6-17.

174. Jan. 8 and 17, 1906, *Cong. Record,* 59 Cong., 1 Sess., vol. xL, part I, p. 792, part II, pp. 1069-1081; *Washington Post,* Jan. 16, 1906, TR Scrapbooks; E. Root to W. Reid, Feb. 27, 1906, in P. C. Jessup, *Root,* II, 57.

175. H. C. Lodge to H. White, Jan. 17, 1906, HCL to H. L. Higginson, Feb. 1, 1906, Lodge MSS.; *Washington Post,* Jan. 10, 16, and 25, 1906, *Washington Star,*

Jan. 23, 1906, TR Scrapbooks; H. C. Lodge, "The United States at Algeciras," *A Frontier Town and Other Essays*, 266-267, 273-274.

176. H. L. Higginson to H. C. Lodge, Jan. 26, 1906, Lodge MSS.

177. G. P. Gooch, *Before the War*, II, 17.

178. TR to J. H. Choate, Aug. 16, 1905, H. White to TR, April 8, 1906, TR MSS.

179. TR to H. White, Aug. 23, 1905, in A. Nevins, *Henry White*, 267.

180. Nr. 6896, Freiherr Speck von Sternburg an das Auswärtige Amt, den 3. November 1905, *Grosse Politik*, XXI-1, 9-10. See also P. C. Jessup, *Root*, II, 57.

181. E. Root to H. White, Nov. 28, 1905, Root MSS. See also E. Root to H. von dem Bussche-Haddenhausen, Dec. 29, 1905, TR MSS.

182. G. von L. Meyer to TR, Jan. 15, 1906, TR MSS. See also GvonLM to E. Root, [January (?)] 1906, in A. Nevins, *Henry White*, 265; John R. Carter to H. C. Lodge, Dec. 3, 1905, Lodge MSS.; G. P. Gooch, *Before the War*, II, 6-8.

183. H. Speck von Sternburg to E. Root, Jan. 8, 1906, TR MSS. See also Willy to Nicky, Nov. 8, 1905, in *Letters from the Kaiser to the Czar*, I. D. Levine, ed., 201-202.

184. G. von L. Meyer to TR, Jan. 15, 1906, TR MSS. See also GvonLM to E. Root, [January (?)] 1906, in A. Nevins, *Henry White*, 265.

185. G. von L. Meyer to TR, March 1, 1906, in M. A. DeW. Howe, *Meyer*, 264-265; GvonLM, Diary, Jan. 9, 1906, in *ibid.*, 243.

186. H. Speck von Sternburg to E. Root, Feb. 12, 1906, ER to HSvonS, Feb. 12, 1906, TR MSS.; G. von L. Meyer to H. C. Lodge, Feb. 14, 1906, in M. A. DeW. Howe, *Meyer*, 255; G. P. Gooch, *Before the War*, II, 12-14.

187. H. Speck von Sternburg to TR, Jan. 23, and 28 and Feb. 1, 1906, HSvonS to E. Root, Jan. 30 and Feb. 1, 1906, TR MSS.; Nr. 6956, 6959, 6968, 6972, Fürst von Bülow an HSvonS, den 20. (abgegangen am 21. Januar), 24., 27., und 30. Januar 1906, Nr. 6958, 6971, HSvonS an das Auswärtige Amt, den 23. und 29. Januar 1906, Nr. 6965, BHvonB an den Ersten Delegierten auf der Konferenz von Algeciras Botschafter Joseph-Marie von Radowitz, den 26. Januar 1906, Nr. 6996, J-MvonR an das AA, den 10. Februar 1906, *Grosse Politik*, XXI-1, 99-101, 105, 123-125, 127, 102, 126-127, 114-115, 155.

188. TR to G. von L. Meyer, Feb. 1, 1906, TR MSS.

189. Nr. 6989, Freiherr Speck von Sternburg an das Auswärtige Amt, den 8. Februar 1906, *Grosse Politik*, XXI-1, 147, 148.

190. H. White to H. C. Lodge, Feb. 12, 1906, Lodge MSS.; HW to TR, April 8, 1906, TR MSS.; Nr. 6990, 6996, 7004, 7072, J.-M. von Radowitz an das Auswärtige Amt, den 9., 10., und 13. Februar und den 7. März 1906, *Grosse Politik*, XXI-1, 148, 149, 155, 162-163, 258. See also Nr. 7032, J-MvonR an das AA, den 21. Februar 1906, *ibid.*, XXI-1, 204-205.

191. H. White to H. C. Lodge, Feb. 12, 1906, Lodge MSS.; Nr. 7106, Fürst von Bülow an Freiherrn Speck von Sternburg, den 16. März 1906, *Grosse Politik*, XXI-1, 295. See also *New York Times*, Feb. 14, 1906, TR Scrapbooks.

192. H. White to H. C. Lodge, Feb. 12, 1906, Lodge MSS.

193. Memorandum, Feb. 20, 1906, in *British Documents*, G. P. Gooch and H. W. V. Temperley, eds., III, 266-267.

194. G. von L. Meyer to H. C. Lodge, Feb. 14, 1906, Lodge MSS. See also GvonLM, Diary, Feb. 24, 1906, in M. A. DeW. Howe, *Meyer*, 262-263.

195. Nr. 7012, Der Erste Delegierte auf der Konferenz von Algeciras Botschafter M.-J. von Radowitz an das Auswärtige Amt, 17. Februar 1906, Nr. 7014, Der Botschafter in Wien Graf Karl von Wedel an das AA, den 18. Februar 1906, Nr. 7015, 7016, M-JvonR an das AA, den 19. Februar 1906, 7103, Der Botschafter in Rom Graf Anton von Monts de Mazin an den Fürsten von Bülow, den 11. März 1906, *Grosse Politik*, XXI-1, 173, 175-178, 289; G. P. Gooch, *Before the War*, I, 261-263.

196. G. von L. Meyer to H. C. Lodge, Feb. 14, 1906, Lodge MSS.; GvonLM, Diary, Feb. 24, 1906, in M. A. DeW. Howe, *Meyer*, 262-263.

197. H. C. Lodge to J. R. Carter, Dec. 15, 1905, HCL to H. White, Feb. 26, 1906, Lodge MSS.

198. G. von L. Meyer to H. C. Lodge, Feb. 14, 1906, Lodge MSS.

199. G. von L. Meyer, Diary, Feb. 24, 1906, in M. A. DeW. Howe, *Meyer*, 262-263; E. Root to H. Speck von Sternburg, Feb. 19, 1906, TR MSS.

200. *Loc. cit.*; Nr. 7019, HSvonS an das Auswärtige Amt, den 19. Februar 1906, *Grosse Politik*, XXI-1, 181-183; *Le Temps* (Paris) quoted in *Washington Post*, March 23, 1906, TR Scrapbooks.

201. Nr. 7019, Freiherr Speck von Sternburg an das Auswärtige Amt, den 19. Februar 1906, *Grosse Politik*, XXI-1, 183.

202. H. Speck von Sternburg to TR, Feb. 22, 1906, TR to W. Reid, April 28, 1906, TR MSS.; Nr. 7020, Fürst von Bülow an HSvonS, den 21. Februar 1906, *Grosse Politik*, XXI-1, 183, 184. See also HSvonS to E. Root, Feb. 24, 1906, TR MSS.; Nr. 7029, Der Botschafter in Petersburg Baron Wilhelm von Schoen an BHvonB, den 24. Februar 1906, Nr. 7038, HSvonS an das Auswärtige Amt, den 23. Februar 1906, *Grosse Politik*, XXI-1, 198, 199, 213; *Washington Times*, Feb. 23, 1906, TR Scrapbooks.

203. TR to W. Reid, March 1, 1906, TR MSS. See also H. von Eckardstein, *Die Isolierung Deutschlands*, 159-160.

204. G. von L. Meyer, Diary, Feb. 24, 1906, in M. A. DeW. Howe, *Meyer*, 262; Nr. 7020, Fürst von Bülow an Freiherrn Speck von Sternburg, den 21. Februar 1906, *Grosse Politik*, XXI-1, 183-184.

205. G. von L. Meyer to TR, March 1, 1906, TR MSS.

206. Nr. 7051, 7053, M.-J. von Radowitz an das Auswärtige Amt, den 3. März 1906, *Grosse Politik*, XXI-1, 233-236.

207. G. von L. Meyer, Diary, February 26, 1906, in M. A. DeW. Howe, *Meyer*, 263.

208. Nr. 7071, M.-J. von Radowitz an das Auswärtige Amt, den 7. März 1906, *Grosse Politik*, XXI-1, 257-258.

209. G. von L. Meyer to TR, March 1, 1906, TR MSS.

210. TR to William II, transmitted in E. Root to H. Speck von Sternburg,

March 7, 1906, TR MSS.; B. H. von Bülow to his brother Alfred, 1906 (?), in BHvonB, *Memoirs*, II, 253; W. Reid to TR, April 28, 1906, TR MSS.

211. Nr. 6744, Fürst von Bülow an Freiherrn Speck von Sternburg, den 27. Juni 1905, *Grosse Politik*, xx-2, 481-482.

212. E. Root to H. Speck von Sternburg, March 7, 1906, TR MSS.; Nr. 6959, Fürst von Bülow an HSvonS, den 24. Januar 1906, *Grosse Politik*, xxi-1, 105.

213. William II to TR, transmitted in H. Speck von Sternburg to TR, March 13, 1906, TR MSS.; Nr. 7093, Fürst von Bülow an HSvonS, den 12. März 1906, *Grosse Politik*, xxi-1, 277-278. See also E. Peters, *Roosevelt und der Kaiser*, 146-148.

214. TR to W. Reid, April 28, 1906, TR MSS.; Nr. 7093, William II to TR, transmitted in Fürst von Bülow an Freiherrn Speck von Sternburg, den 12. März 1906, *Grosse Politik*, xxi-1, 277.

215. H. Speck von Sternburg to TR, March 14, 1906, TR to W. Reid, April 28, 1906, TR MSS.; Nr. 7093, Fürst von Bülow an HSvonS, den 12. März 1906, *Grosse Politik*, xxi-1, 277-278.

216. Nr. 7102, Freiherr Speck von Sternburg an das Auswärtige Amt, den 14. März 1906, *Grosse Politik*, xxi-1, 285-286. See also G. P. Gooch, *History of Modern Europe*, 360, 365-366.

217. Nr. 7106, Fürst von Bülow an Freiherrn Speck von Sternburg, den 16. März 1906, *Grosse Politik*, xxi-1, 293-295.

218. The dispatch as printed says " that Germany does not wish a war " but the context makes it obvious that there is an error and that the original must have been " does wish a war " or " does not wish to avoid a war." Nr. 7112, Freiherr Speck von Sternburg an das Auswärtige Amt, den 17. März 1906, *Grosse Politik*, xxi-1, 300. See also H. von Eckardstein, *Die Isolierung Deutschlands*, 159-160.

219. Nr. 7112, Freiherr Speck von Sternburg an das Auswärtige Amt, den 17. März 1906, *Grosse Politik*, xxi-1, 300-301. See also E. Brandenburg, *Von Bismarck zum Weltkriege*, 212.

220. Nr. 7112, Freiherr Speck von Sternburg an das Auswärtige Amt, den 17. März 1906, *Grosse Politik*, xxi-1, 301-302.

221. E. Root to H. Speck von Sternburg, March 17, 1906, TR MSS.; Nr. 7112, 7115, HSvonS an das Auswärtige Amt, den 17. und den 18. März 1906, *Grosse Politik*, xxi-1, 300-301, 305-306.

222. TR to W. Reid, June 27, 1906, TR MSS.

223. Nr. 7113, Freiherr Speck von Sternburg an das Auswärtige Amt, den 18. März 1906, *Grosse Politik*, xxi-1, 302-303; TR to W. Reid, April 28, 1906, TR MSS.

224. *Le Temps* (Paris), quoted in the *Washington Post*, March 23, 1906, TR Scrapbooks.

225. Nr. 7118, Fürst von Bülow an Freiherrn Speck von Sternburg, den 19. März 1906, *Grosse Politik*, xxi-1, 309-310; TR to W. Reid, April 28, 1906, TR MSS.

226. E. Root to C. Tower, March 20, 1906, Root MSS.

227. Nr. 7121, Freiherr Speck von Sternburg an das Auswärtige Amt, den 21. März 1906, *Grosse Politik*, XXI-1, 311-312. See also Fürst B. H. von Bülow an A. von Bülow, Juli 1906, in BHvonB, *Denkwürdigkeiten*, II, 230.

228. Nr. 7126, Freiherr Speck von Sternburg an das Auswärtige Amt, den 22. März 1906, *Grosse Politik*, XXI-1, 321. See also M. A. DeW. Howe, *Rhodes*, 196-197.

229. Nr. 7130, Freiherr Speck von Sternburg an das Auswärtige Amt, den 24. März 1906, Nr. 7127, Mitteilung des österreich-ungarischen Botschafters in Berlin Graf Laszlo von Szögyény-Marich (Unsignierte und undatierte Notiz, dem Staatssekretär von Tschirschky am 23. März 1906 übergeben), Nr. 7129, Fürst von Bülow an den Ersten Delegierten auf der Konferenz von Algeciras Botschafter M.-J. von Radowitz, den 24. März 1906, *Grosse Politik*, XXI-1, 321, 323-324.

230. G. P. Gooch, *Before the War*, II, 17-20.

231. Nr. 7134, M.-J. von Radowitz an das Auswärtige Amt, den 27. März 1906, Nr. 7137, MJvonR an den Fürsten von Bülow, den 28. März 1906, *Grosse Politik*, XXI-1, 328, 330.

232. Leon V. A. Bourgeois [Ministre des Affaires Etrangères] to J. J. Jusserand, April 6, 1906, JJJ to TR, July 11, 1905, TR to W. Reid, April 28, 1906, TR MSS. See also G. P. Gooch, *History of Modern Europe*, 360, 365-366.

233. C. Tower to E. Root, Nov. 15, 1906, Lodge MSS. See also G. P. Gooch, *History of Modern Europe*, 360, 365-366.

234. B. H. von Bülow to A. von Bülow [1906 (?)], in BHvonB, *Memoirs*, II, 253.

235. H. White to TR, April 8, 1906, TR to HW, April 30, 1906, TR MSS.; C. Tower to E. Root, Nov. 15, 1906 (copy), Lodge MSS.

236. TR to J. J. Jusserand, April 25, 1906, TR MSS.

237. Fürst B. H. von Bülow an A. von Bülow, Juli 1906, BHvonB, *Denkwürdigkeiten*, II, 229-230.

238. Vagts says Roosevelt was perfectly conscious that he was giving the French the kernel of the Moroccan nut and leaving Germany only the shell. His formula, says Vagts, was: "for Germany the Conference, for France Morocco; for Germany prestige imperialism, for France and her friends real imperialism." A. Vagts, *Deutschland und die Vereinigten Staaten in der Weltpolitik*, II, 1864-1865. See also H. von Eckardstein, *Die Isolierung Deutschlands*, 162-164, 174-175; G. P. Gooch, *Before the War*, I, 261-263.

239. H. White to TR, April 8, 1906, TR MSS.; HW to H. C. Lodge, April 22, 1906, Lodge MSS. See also G. P. Gooch, *Before the War*, I, 261-263.

240. TR to J. J. Jusserand, April 25, 1906, TR MSS. For a German account of what Germany attained see B. H. von Bülow, *Imperial Germany* (1914), 99-100.

241. Joseph B. Bishop, *Theodore Roosevelt and His Time* (2 vols., 1920), I, 467-503; Eugene Anderson, *The First Moroccan Crisis* (1930); Viscount Grey of Fallodon, *Twenty-five Years, 1892-1916* (1925), II, 89.

242. Bailey, for instance, grudgingly admits that Roosevelt "did exercise some

influence," but credits "the international situation rather than the Big Stick" with being decisive. He sneers at "the President's own heroic version" without giving any evidence of having checked the Roosevelt story in the European sources. Thomas A. Bailey, *A Diplomatic History of the American People* (1950), 560-562. Pringle, indeed, pictures Roosevelt as ill-informed, unaware that Germany was not sincere in her talk of concern for "an open door." He pictures the President, too, as uninformed about the closeness of the tie between France and England and of the hostility between Germany and Britain that Pringle believes was the real menace to peace. Actually Roosevelt's policy was based on his knowledge that an Anglo-French entente would lead Germany and Russia to support each other in hostility to England, and it was one of the chief purposes of his foreign policy to heal the breach and remove the causes of distrust between Germany and England that he did know so well. Instead of using the original letters that were available to him, Pringle apparently took his account from Roosevelt's later letter to Reid as it was published in Joseph B. Bishop's *Theodore Roosevelt and His Time* (1920). There Pringle mistook a copy of a letter of Speck von Sternburg for Roosevelt's own text and hence, because Speck miswrote the name of Arthur Nicolson, British delegate at Algeciras, Pringle concluded that Roosevelt was not "too familiar with the negotiations." Henry F. Pringle, *Theodore Roosevelt* (1931), 390-397. Elting Morison in editing *The Letters of Theodore Roosevelt* (1952), v, 246-247, fell into the same error of mistaking Speck's letter for one of Roosevelt, though Morison denied that Roosevelt was not in close touch with what was happening in Europe. See also P. C. Jessup, *Root* (1938), ii, 57; John H. Latané, *A History of American Foreign Policy* (1934), 574-577; J. Fred Rippy, *America and the Strife of Europe* (1938), 178-180.

243. G. P. Gooch, *Before the War: Studies in Diplomacy* (1936), i, 17, 55-56, 248-249, 260; GPG, *History of Modern Europe, 1878-1919* (1923), 360, 365-366; Samuel F. Bemis, *A Diplomatic History of the United States* (1936), 576-580; Allan Nevins, *Henry White: Thirty Years of American Diplomacy* (1930), 261-282, especially 264, 266.

244. H. White to H. C. Lodge, June 22, 1906, Lodge MSS.

245. Viscount Grey, *Twenty-five Years*, ii, 88-89.

246. H. White to H. C. Lodge, Oct. 4, 1908, Lodge MSS.

247. TR to J. J. Jusserand, Aug. 3, 1908, TR MSS.

248. J. J. Jusserand to Stephen Pichon, Ministre des Affaires Etrangères, le 21 octobre, 1908, et le 23 janvier, 1909, No. 14, 93, Ministre des Affaires Etrangères, *Documents Diplomatiques*, 1910, Affairs du Maroc, v (1908-1910), 6, 59.

249. There are a number of treatments of the relations of Germany and the United States. The earliest good studies were Jeannette Keim, *Forty Years of German-American Political Relations* (1919) and Clara E. Schieber, *The Transformation of American Sentiment toward Germany, 1870-1914* (1923). The most comprehensive is Alfred Vagts, *Deutschland und die Vereinigten Staaten in der Weltpolitik* (1935) in two volumes. Vagts's account is based on a thorough

study of the German documents published in *Die Grosse Politik* and of the Archives of the Auswärtige Amt. William L. Langer, *The Diplomacy of Imperialism* (revised edition, 1951), and George P. Gooch, *Before the War* (1936-1938), 2 vols., give important background material. J. Fred Rippy in *The European Powers and the Spanish-American War* (1927) and *America and the Strife of Europe* (1938), Howard C. Hill in *Theodore Roosevelt and the Caribbean* (1927), and Lester B. Shippee in "Germany and the Spanish War," *American Historical Review*, xxx (July, 1925), 754-777, have used foreign language sources profitably as has A. Whitney Griswold in the portions of *The Far Eastern Policy of the United States* (1938) that deal with German-American relations. Too many Americans, however, have tried to write chiefly from sources in English. Erich Eyck, on the other hand, the most recent biographer of William, in *Das persönliche Regiment Wilhelms II* (1948), suffers in his treatment of German-American relations from lack of American sources and makes only casual reference to Roosevelt. And the usefulness of Evelene Peters, *Roosevelt und der Kaiser* (1936), in spite of her extensive use of German sources, is marred by her almost violent anti-American, anti-Roosevelt, German nationalist bias.

250. TR to G. O. Trevelyan, Oct. 1, 1911, TR MSS.

251. TR to C. Spring Rice, Aug. 13, 1897, TR MSS.

252. TR to H. C. Lodge, June 19, 1901, TR MSS. See also Andrew D. White, *Autobiography*, i, 247.

253. TR to William II, Jan. 8, 1907, TR MSS.

254. W. L. Langer, *Diplomacy of Imperialism*, 519; TR to C. Spring Rice, April 14, 1889, TR MSS.

255. W. L. Langer, *Diplomacy of Imperialism*, 517; TR to C. Spring Rice, Nov. 19, 1900, CSR to E. K. Roosevelt, Sept. 26, 1905, TR MSS.; Nr. 6288, Freiherr Speck von Sternburg an den Grafen von Bülow, den 10. Februar 1905, *Grosse Politik*, xix-2, 572-573; Paul S. Reinsch, *World Politics at the End of the Nineteenth Century as Influenced by the Oriental Situation*, 358-360.

256. See, e.g., TR to Capt. William W. Kimball, Jan. 9, 1900, John St. Loe Strachey to TR, February, 1900, TR MSS.; H. White to H. C. Lodge, July 27, 1898, Brooks Adams to HCL, Feb. 7, 1901, Lodge MSS.

257. J. Hay to H. C. Lodge, July 27, 1898, Hay MSS. See also Hiram S. Maxim to TR, Oct. 29, 1901, TR MSS.

258. TR to H. C. Lodge, Jan. 28, 1909, TR MSS.

259. H. C. Lodge to TR, March 30, 1901, TR to William II, Jan. 8, 1907, TR MSS. See also Nr. 5151, Freiherr Speck von Sternburg an das Auswärtige Amt, den 19. Februar 1903, *Grosse Politik*, xvii, 291-292.

260. TR, "National Duties," in TR, *The Strenuous Life*, 290.

261. TR to H. C. Lodge, June 19, 1901, TR MSS.

262. TR to H. Speck von Sternburg, Oct. 11, 1901, TR MSS.

263. H. C. Lodge to TR, March 30, 1901, TR MSS.

264. TR to H. C. Lodge, June 19, 1901, TR to W. Reid, July 24, 1903, TR

MSS. See also TR, "The Monroe Doctrine," *Bachelor of Arts*, II (March, 1896), 442-444; TR to J. Hay, Feb. 18, 1900, Hay MSS.

265. TR to Brooks Adams, Sept. 27, 1901, TR MSS.; BA, "Reciprocity or the Alternative," *Atlantic Monthly*, LXXXVIII (August, 1901), 145-155; TR, Annual Message, Dec. 3, 1901, in James D. Richardson, *A Compilation of the Messages and Papers of the Presidents, 1789-1907*, X, 428-429.

266. TR to O. S. Straus, Feb. 27, 1906, TR MSS.

267. TR to C. Spring Rice, April 14, 1889, TR MSS.

268. TR to Capt. Bowman H. McCalla, Aug. 3, 1897, TR MSS. See also TR to Charles A. Moore, Feb. 14, 1898, TR MSS.

269. TR to G. von L. Meyer, April 12, 1901, H. C. Lodge to TR, March 30, 1901, TR MSS. See also H. S. Maxim to TR, Oct. 29, 1901, TR MSS.

270. H. C. Lodge to TR, March 30, 1901, TR MSS.

271. TR to H. C. Lodge, March 27, 1901, TR MSS.

272. The best published account of this episode is found in H. C. Hill, *Roosevelt and the Caribbean* (1927), 106-147. Other interesting accounts are found in S. F. Bemis, *The Latin American Policy of the United States* (1943), 146-148; SFB, *A Diplomatic History* (1936), 522-525; SFB, *The United States as a World Power, 1900-1950* (1951), 52-55; H. F. Pringle, *Theodore Roosevelt* (1931), 282-289; Dexter Perkins, *Hands Off: A History of the Monroe Doctrine* (1946), 215-227; DP, *The Monroe Doctrine, 1867-1907* (1937), 319-395; J. F. Rippy, *America and the Strife of Europe* (1938), 96-97; JFR, *Latin America in World Politics* (1928), 182-199; Alfred Vagts, *Deutschland und die Vereinigten Staaten in der Weltpolitik* (2 vols., 1935), II, 1525-1635. The account that ultimately became the basis of controversy is found in William R. Thayer, *The Life and Letters of John Hay*, II, 411-417. See also the early account in *Theodore Roosevelt and His Time*, I, 221-229, by Joseph B. Bishop, who consulted Roosevelt himself as he wrote. Also useful is "Venezuelan Arbitration before the Hague Tribunal, 1903; Proceedings of the Tribunal under the Protocols . . . May 7, 1903," *U. S. Senate Documents*, 58 Cong., 3 Sess., vol. VII, doc. no. 119, ser. no. 4769, hereafter cited as "Venezuelan Arbitration."

273. TR to W. Reid, June 27, 1906, TR to C. Spring Rice, Nov. 1, 1905, TR to W. R. Thayer, Aug. 21, 1916, TR to H. White, Aug. 14, 1906, TR MSS.; Oscar K. Davis, *Released for Publication*, 88; John J. Leary, Jr., *Talks with TR*, 13-14, 42-43; E. Alexander Powell, *Yonder Lies Adventure*, 311-318; *Chicago Daily News*, Sept. 27, 1917; *New York Times*, March 21 and Sept. 28, 1917.

274. G. P. Gooch, *Before the War*, I, 24-25; *Grosse Politik*, XVII, 241 n.; Nr. 5106, Fürst von Bülow an Wilhelm II, den 20. Januar 1902, *ibid.*, 241-243.

275. *New York Times*, Nov. 21, 1901. See also, e. g., John B. Jackson to J. Hay, April 24, 1901, Hay MSS.; H. L. Higginson to H. C. Lodge, Dec. 20, 1901, Lodge MSS.

276. Lord Lansdowne to Sir Michael Herbert, Nov. 11, 1902, MH to Lansdowne, Nov. 13, 1902, in "Venezuelan Arbitration," 635-636, 638-639; Thomas C. Hansard, ed., *Parliamentary Debates*, 4th series, CXVI, 1290; British Foreign Office, *British and Foreign State Papers*, XCV (1901-1902), 1081-1082.

277. A. J. Balfour to A. Carnegie, Dec. 18, 1902, Carnegie MSS.; J. Hay, Statement on Venezuela, Dec. 16, 1901, JH to Professor George G. Wilson, Feb. 10, 1902, Hay MSS.; H. White to H. C. Lodge, Dec. 21, 1901, Lodge MSS.; Nr. 5113, Der Botschafter in London Graf Paul W. von Metternich an das Auswärtige Amt, den 13. November 1902, Nr. 5116, Der Geschäftsträger in Washington Graf Albert W. von Quadt an das AA, den 25. November 1902, *Grosse Politik*, xvii, 254, 256; [Baron Theodor von Holleben (?)] Memorandum to U. S. State Dept., Dec. 11, 1901, *Foreign Relations*, 1901, 192-194; *New York Times*, Nov. 20, 1901, TR Scrapbooks; G. P. Gooch, *Before the War*, i, 24-25; H. C. Hill, *Roosevelt and the Caribbean*, 116; A. Vagts, *Deutschland und die Vereinigten Staaten*, ii, 1537. See also Herbert W. Bowen to JH, Aug. 8, 1902, State Dept. Archives.

278. P. C. Jessup, *Root*, i, 495-496.

279. J. Hay, Statement on Venezuela, Dec. 16, 1901, JH to G. G. Wilson, Feb. 10, 1902, Hay MSS.; TR, "Annual Message," Dec. 3, 1901, J. D. Richardson, *Messages and Papers of the Presidents*, ix, 6662-6663; State Dept. Memorandum, Dec. 16, 1901, *Foreign Relations*, 1901, 195; TR to W. R. Thayer, Aug. 21, 1916, TR MSS.; P. C. Jessup, *Root*, i, 495-496; J. F. Rippy, *Latin America in World Politics*, 185.

280. Lord Lansdowne to George W. Buchanan, July 23, 1902, *British Documents*, G. P. Gooch and H. W. V. Temperley, eds., ii, 153-154; *Grosse Politik*, xvii, 242, note 1 and 243, notes 1 and 2; Canterbury, P. R. O., F. O., 80, vol. 482. memorandum undated, cited in D. Perkins, *Monroe Doctrine, 1867-1907*, 328; C. Tower to J. Hay, Jan. 28, 1903, State Department Archives; Nr. 5106 and 5107, Graf B. H. von Bülow an Wilhelm II, den 20. Januar und den 1. September 1902, Nr. 5112, BHvonB an den Botschafter in London Grafen P. W. von Metternich, den 12. November 1902, Nr. 5116, Graf A. W. von Quadt an das Auswärtige Amt, den 25. November 1902, Nr. 5117, PWvonM an das AA, den 26. November 1902, Nr. 5149, PWvonM an BHvonB, den 4. Februar 1903, *Grosse Politik*, xvii, 241-243, 245, 253, 256, 288; Johann H. von Bernstorff, *My Three Years in America*, 16-17; A. Vagts, *Deutschland und die Vereinigten Staaten*, ii, 1554-1556; H. C. Hill, *Roosevelt and the Caribbean*, 110-116; "Venezuelan Arbitration," 161; J. F. Rippy, *Latin America in World Politics*, 184, 190; G. P. Gooch, *Before the War*, i, 24-25.

281. British Foreign Office, Memorandum for communication to the German Ambassador, *British Documents*, ii, 156; Nr. 5107, 5108, 5109, Graf von Bülow an Wilhelm II, den 1. September und den 3. und 5. November 1902, Nr. 5110, 5111, Der Botschafter in London Graf P. W. von Metternich an das Auswärtige Amt, den 11. und 12. November 1902, Nr. 5114, Der Geschäftsträger in London Graf J. H. von Bernstorff an das AA, den 17. November 1902, *Grosse Politik*, xvii, 244-252, 254-255; J. F. Rippy, *Latin America in World Politics*, 184-185; H. C. Hill, *Roosevelt and the Caribbean*, 115-119; G. P. Gooch, *Before the War*, i, 24-25.

282. Lord Lansdowne to Sir F. Lascelles, Oct. 22, 1902, *British Documents*, ii, 154; H. Percival Dodge to J. Hay, Nov. 28 and Dec. 3, and 10, 1902, JH

to HPD, Dec. 5, 1902, JH to C. Tower, Dec. 12 and 16, 1902, CT to JH, Dec. 14, 17, 22, and 23, 1902, JH to H. White, Dec. 12 and 16, 1902, HW to JH, Dec. 17, 18, 19, and 20, 1902, HW to Lansdowne, Dec. 13, 1902, German memorandum for JH, Dec. 18, 1902, Proclamation by B. H. von Bülow, Dec. 20, 1902, "Ultimatum to Venezuela" as printed in the *London Times*, December, 1902, *Foreign Relations*, 1903, 417-423, 424-425, 452-455, 457-458; Nr. 5118, Der Staatssekretär des Auswärtigen Amtes Freiherr Oswald von Richthofen an den Botschafter in London Grafen P. W. von Metternich, den 5. Dezember 1902, *Grosse Politik*, xvii, 257; Nr. 5108, 5109, BHvonB an Wilhelm II, den 3. und 5. November 1902, Nr. 5110, 5111, 5113, PWvonM an das AA, den 11., 12., und 13. November 1902, Nr. 5112, BHvonB an PWvonM, den 12. November 1902, Nr. 5114, 5115, Der Geschäftsträger in London Graf von Bernstorff an das AA, den 17. und 19. November 1902, Nr. 5119, PWvonM an das AA, den 9. Dezember 1902, *Grosse Politik*, xvii, 246, 249, 250, 252, 253, 254, 255, 257; *ibid.*, xvii, 259 n.; Herbert W. Bowen to JH, July 29, Nov. 28, and Dec. 13, 1902, State Dept. Archives; G. P. Gooch, *Before the War*, i, 24-26, 236; H. C. Hill, *Roosevelt and the Caribbean*, 117-119; J. F. Rippy, *Latin America in World Politics*, 184-185.

283. J. Hay to C. Tower, Dec. 12 and 18, 1902, CT to JH, Dec. 14, 17, 18, 19, 22, 29, 1902, *Foreign Relations*, 1903, 420-424, 429-431; Nr. 5119, Der Botschafter in London Graf P. W. von Metternich an das Auswärtige Amt, den 9. Dezember 1902, Nr. 5128, Der Staatssekretär O. von Richthofen an PWvonM, den 24. Dezember 1902, Nr. 5129, Graf B. H. von Bülow an Wilhelm II, den 28. Dezember, 1902, *Grosse Politik*, xvii, 257-258, 269-270; Marquess of Lansdowne to H. White, Dec. 19, 1902, "Venezuelan Arbitration," 684; J. F. Rippy, *Latin America in World Politics*, 184-185; G. P. Gooch, *Before the War*, i, 25-26.

284. C. Tower to J. Hay, Dec. 19, 24, and 29, 1902, JH to CT, Dec. 20 and 26, 1902, JH to H. White, Dec. 26, 1902, HW to JH, Dec. 27 and 31, 1902, HW to Lord Lansdowne, Dec. 27, 1902, enclosed in HW to JH, Dec. 31, 1902, German Memorandum, Dec. 22, 1902, *Foreign Relations*, 1903, 423-424, 426-433, 463-464; Nr. 5128, Der Staatssekretär O. von Richthofen an den Botschafter in London Grafen P. W. von Metternich, den 24. Dezember 1902, Nr. 5129, Graf von Bülow an Wilhelm II, den 28. Dezember 1902, *Grosse Politik*, xvii, 269-270; Lord Lansdowne to Sir F. Lascelles, Dec. 22, 1902, and Memorandum communicated by German Embassy, Dec. 25, 1902, *British Documents*, ii, 162-163; James S. Clarkson to TR, Dec. 24, 1902, Grover Cleveland to TR, Dec. 29, 1902, JH to TR, December, 1902 (?), TR to William M. Laffan, Dec. 29, 1902, Orville H. Platt to TR, Dec. 25, 1902, TR to A. Shaw, Dec. 26, 1902, Oscar S. Straus to TR, Dec. 15, 1902, JH to Wm. Loeb, Jr., Dec. 21, 1902, TR MSS.; G. von L. Meyer, Diary, Dec. 15, 1902, in M. A. DeW. Howe, *Meyer*, 65; C. N. Goddard to William B. Allison, Dec. 22, 1902, Allison MSS.; JH to John Bigelow, Dec. 24, 1902, William H. Michael to JH, Dec. 27, 1902, JH, statement on Venezuela, February, 1903, Hay MSS.; HW to A. J. Balfour, Dec. 20, 1902, White MSS.; Lansdowne to Sir M. Herbert, Dec. 22 and 23, 1902, "Venezuelan Arbitration," 686-687, 689; Tyler Dennett, *John Hay*, 346; *Washington Star*, Dec.

20, 22, 23, and 27, 1902, TR Scrapbooks; "The Arm, Hammer and Hot Iron," *New York Sun*, Dec. 29, 1902.

285. Lord Lansdowne to G. W. Buchanan, Dec. 13, 1902, *British Documents*, II, 161; Lansdowne to Sir F. Lascelles, Dec. 18, 1902, *British and Foreign State Papers*, XCV (1901-1902), 1124-1125; H. White to J. Hay, Dec. 16, 17, and 18, 1902, *Foreign Relations*, 1903, 453, 454-455; *Washington Post*, Dec. 21, 1902, TR Scrapbooks.

286. Nr. 5133, Der Geschäftsträger in Washington Graf A. W. von Quadt an das Auswärtige Amt, den 23. Januar 1903, *Grosse Politik*, XVII, 274; British Commander-in-Chief of North America and West Indies to the Admiralty, Jan. 23, 1903, Marquess of Lansdowne to Sir F. Lascelles, Jan. 27, 1903, *British Documents*, G. P. Gooch and H. W. V. Temperley, eds., II, 165-167; *Washington Post*, Jan. 19, 22, and 27, 1903, TR Scrapbooks.

287. C. Tower to J. Hay, Jan. 17 and Feb. 19 and 21, 1903, JH to H. Speck von Sternburg, April 6, 1903, Protocol of Agreement between Venezuela and Germany . . . May 7, 1903, *Foreign Relations*, 1903, 437, 439-441.

288. Nr. 5124, Baron von Holleben an das Auswärtige Amt, den 16. Dezember 1902, Nr. 5133, Graf von Quadt an das AA, den 23. Januar 1903, *Grosse Politik*, XVII, 264, 274.

289. TR to W. R. Thayer, July 10, 1915, TR MSS.

290. A. Vagts, *Deutschland und die Vereinigten Staaten*, II, 1525-1635; S. F. Bemis, *A Diplomatic History*, 522-524; SFB, *Latin American Policy*, 145-147.

291. B. H. von Bülow to Prince Henry, Jan. 30, 1902, *Grosse Politik*, XVII, 243 n.

292. H. C. Hill, *Roosevelt and the Caribbean*, 130; W. L. Langer, *Diplomacy of Imperialism*, 519. See also Alfred L. P. Dennis, *Adventures in American Diplomacy*, 282-285.

293. TR to W. R. Thayer, Aug. 21, 1916, TR MSS.; also in WRT, *The Life and Letters of John Hay* (1915), II, 411-417.

294. See, e. g., John B. Moore, "John Hay," *Political Science Quarterly*, XXXII (March, 1917), 119-125.

295. H. C. Hill, *Roosevelt and the Caribbean*, 146.

296. H. S. Pringle, *Theodore Roosevelt*, 282-289.

297. A. Vagts, *Deutschland und die Vereinigten Staaten*, 1525-1636; D. Perkins, *America and the Two Wars*, 27-28; DP, *The Monroe Doctrine, 1867-1907*, 319-395; DP, *Hands Off*, 214-227.

298. T. A. Bailey, *A Diplomatic History*, 550-553. See also Wilfred H. Callcott, *The Caribbean Policy of the United States, 1890-1920*, 124-135; S. F. Bemis, *A Diplomatic History*, 522-525; SFB, *The Latin American Policy of the U. S.* (1936), 145-148; D. Perkins, *The Monroe Doctrine, 1867-1907*, 319-395; T. Dennett, *Hay*, 389-390. In his *Latin American Policy*, Bemis almost ignored Roosevelt's rôle and spoke of "the inordinate personal credit" that Roosevelt later took for the outcome. In his detailed account, Perkins drew heavily upon Vagts and used the German documents, but cited the Roosevelt papers only twice.

299. H. White to H. C. Lodge, Sept. 26, 1900, Lodge MSS.; TR, "The Monroe

Doctrine," *Bachelor of Arts*, II (March, 1896), 439; *Minneapolis Journal*, Sept. 2, 1901, TR Scrapbooks.

300. J. Hay to J. B. Jackson, April 10, 1901, No. 1186, MS. Instruction, Germany, XXI, 283, quoted in J. B. Moore, *A Digest of International Law*, VI, 583, and also in J. Keim, *Forty Years of German-American Political Relations*, 279-280; H. White to H. C. Lodge, Sept. 26, 1900, Lodge MSS.; D. Perkins, *The Monroe Doctrine, 1867-1907*, 312-314; J. F. Rippy, *Latin America in World Politics*, 151; A. Vagts, *Deutschland und die Vereinigten Staaten*, II, 1471-1475.

301. H. C. Lodge to TR, June 17 and 27, 1901, TR to HCL, June 19 and 29, 1901, TR MSS.; TR to H. Speck von Sternburg, July 12 and Sept. 1, 1901, HSvonS to TR, Sept. 1, 1901, TR MSS.; TR, " The Two Americas," Speech at the Opening of the Pan-American Exposition, Buffalo, May 20, 1901, in TR, *The Strenuous Life*, 234-235; D. Perkins, *The Monroe Doctrine, 1867-1907*, 320, 325-336. See also TR to C. Spring Rice, July 24, 1905, TR MSS.; *Minneapolis Journal*, Sept. 2, 1901, *New York Tribune*, Aug. 12, 1905, TR Scrapbooks.

302. TR to W. Reid, July 24, 1903, TR MSS.; D. Perkins, *The Monroe Doctrine, 1867-1907*, 320-321, 325-326, 330-337, 349, 381-387; A. Vagts, *Deutschland und die Vereinigten Staaten*, II, 1475. See also TR to J. Hay, Feb. 18, 1900, Hay MSS.; TR, " The Monroe Doctrine," *Bachelor of Arts*, II (March, 1896), 442-444.

303. TR to H. Speck von Sternburg, July 12 and Oct. 11, 1901, TR MSS.

304. TR to Capt. William S. Cowles, TR's brother-in-law, March 2, 1900, TR MSS.

305. H. C. Lodge to TR, June 17, 1901, *The Correspondence of Theodore Roosevelt and Henry Cabot Lodge, 1881-1914* (hereafter cited as *TR-HCL Correspondence*), 493.

306. TR to J. Hay, March 13, 1903, Corinne Roosevelt Robinson, TR's sister, to TR, Sept. 5, 1902, TR MSS.; *Minneapolis Journal*, Sept. 2, 1901, TR Scrapbooks.

307. TR to J. Hay, March 13, 1903, TR MSS.

308. TR to Gen. Henry M. Duffield, Feb. 20, 1905, TR to the General Staff, War Dept., Jan. 22, 1906, TR to James Roosevelt Roosevelt, July 29, 1907, TR to E. Root, Feb. 29, March 29, and Dec. 17, 1908, TR to Lt.-Col. Robert L. Howze, April 21, 1908, TR to J. J. Jusserand, Aug. 3, 1908, TR to William B. Hale, Dec. 3, 1908, TR MSS.; H. White to H. C. Lodge, March 17, 1908, Lodge MSS.; ER to W. Reid, May 22, 1908, Root MSS.; ER to A. Carnegie, Dec. 31, 1906, and Dec. 24, 1908, P. C. Jessup, *Root*, I, 497-499; *New York Tribune*, March 22, 1905, *Washington Post*, April 1 and June 24, 1908, *Washington Star*, March 21, 1905, TR Scrapbooks.

309. TR to H. Speck von Sternburg, July 12, 1901, TR MSS.

310. D. Perkins, *The Monroe Doctrine, 1867-1907*, 321-337.

311. TR to C. Spring Rice, July 24, 1905, TR MSS. See also *New York Tribune*, Aug. 11, 1905, TR Scrapbooks.

312. J. Hay, Statement on Venezuela, February, 1903, Hay MSS. See also D. Perkins, *The Monroe Doctrine*, 383-385; T. Dennett, *Hay*, 392-393.

313. Quoted from the Münsterberg MSS. at Harvard University by D. Per-

kins, *The Monroe Doctrine*, 385-386; W. R. Thayer to TR, Aug. 16, 1915, TR MSS.

314. Nr. 5151, Freiherr Speck von Sternburg an das Auswärtige Amt, den 19. Februar 1903, *Grosse Politik*, xvii, 291-292. See also D. Perkins, *The Monroe Doctrine*, 386.

315. *New York World*, April 3, 1903; TR, *Addresses and Presidential Messages, 1902-1904*, 117-120. See also D. Perkins, *The Monroe Doctrine*, 386.

316. See, e. g., W. R. Thayer to TR, Aug. 20 and 23, 1916, and Aug. 22, 1917, TR MSS.; WRT, " Bowen vs. Roosevelt: A Rejoinder," *North American Review*, ccx (September, 1919), 419-420.

317. TR to W. R. Thayer, Aug. 27, 1916, TR MSS.

318. TR to W. R. Thayer, July 10 and Aug. 8, 1915, and May 3 and 29, June 16, and Aug. 20 and 21, 1916, TR MSS.; WRT to H. White, July 17, 1915, White MSS.; WRT, " Bowen vs. Roosevelt," *loc. cit.*, 419-420.

319. TR to W. R. Thayer, Aug. 21, 1916, TR MSS.

320. TR to W. R. Thayer, Aug. 8, 1915, and Aug. 23, 1916, TR MSS.

321. TR to W. R. Thayer, May 3 and 29 and June 16, 1916, Adolph W. Callisen to Ambrose C. Richardson, in TR to WRT, Aug. 21, 1916, TR MSS.

322. TR to W. R. Thayer, May 29, June 16, and Aug. 21, 1916, Henry A. Wise Wood to Admiral George Dewey, May 22, 1916, GD to HAWW, May 23, 1916, TR MSS.; J. J. Leary, Jr., *Talks with TR*, 43. See also TR to W. Reid, June 27, 1906, TR to H. White, Aug. 14, 1906, TR MSS.

323. W. R. Thayer to TR, Aug. 20 and Sept. 2, 1916, TR to WRT, Aug. 8, 20, 21, and 23 and Sept. 6, 1916, TR MSS.

324. O. H. Platt to George G. Hill, Sept. 27, 1904, Platt MSS. See also " Editorial—' A " War Lord " Indeed,' " *New York Daily Tribune*, Sept. 14, 1904.

325. TR to C. Spring Rice, Nov. 1, 1905, TR MSS.

326. TR to W. Reid, June 27, 1906, TR MSS.

327. TR to H. White, Aug. 14, 1906, TR MSS.

328. Oscar K. Davis, *Released for Publication* (1925), 88-90. See also John Callan O'Laughlin, *Imperiled America* (1916), 63-67.

329. E. Alexander Powell, *Yonder Lies Adventure* (1932), 311-318; J. J. Leary, Jr., *Talks with TR*, 13-14. He later told the story to Leary, too. *Ibid.*, 42-43. He told slightly different stories in his speeches at the Union League Club in New York, March 20, 1917, and in Chicago, Sept. 27, 1917. *Chicago Daily News*, Sept. 27, 1917; *New York Times*, March 21 and Sept. 28, 1917.

330. H. White to J. Hay, Dec. 13, 1902, in A. Nevins, *Henry White*, 210.

331. *Grosse Politik*, xvii, 259 n.; R. Lopez Baralt to H. W. Bowen, Dec. 9, 1902, enclosed in HWB to J. Hay, Dec. 13, 1902, *Foreign Relations*, 1903, 793.

332. R. L. Baralt to H. W. Bowen, undated, enclosed in HWB to J. Hay, Dec. 11, 1902, *Foreign Relations*, 1903, 791-792.

333. J. Hay, statement on Venezuela, February, 1903, Hay MSS.; J. Hay to H. White, Dec. 12, 1902, JH to C. Tower, Dec. 12, 1902, CT to JH, Dec. 17, 1902, *Foreign Relations*, 1903, 420, 421-422, 453; *Grosse Politik*, xvii, 260 n.

334. Nr. 5120, Graf von Bülow an Wilhelm II, den 12. Dezember 1902, Nr.

5122, Der Botschafter in London Graf von Metternich an das Auswärtige Amt, den 13. Dezember 1902, *Grosse Politik*, xvii, 258-260, 261.

335. Nr. 5122, Graf von Metternich an das Auswärtige Amt, den 13. Dezember 1902, *Grosse Politik*, xvii, 261-262; G. P. Gooch, *Before the War*, i, 236; T. von Holleben an das Auswärtige Amt (?), den 13. Dezember, 1902, AA Archives, cited by A. Vagts, *Deutschland und die Vereinigten Staaten*, ii, 1569.

336. Nr. 5121, Der Staatssekretär des Auswärtigen Amtes Freiherr O. von Richthofen an Grafen von Metternich, den 14. Dezember 1902, *Grosse Politik*, xvii, 260.

337. H. White to J. Hay, Dec. 15, 1902, in A. Nevins, *Henry White*, 210. See also WH to JH, Dec. 31, 1902, in *ibid.*, 211-212.

338. Nr. 5123, Der Botschafter in London Graf von Metternich an des Auswärtige Amt, den 15. Dezember 1902, *Grosse Politik*, xvii, 262.

339. T. C. Hansard, ed., *Parliamentary Debates*, 4th series, cxvi, 1246-1287. See also J. Morley to A. Carnegie, Dec. 27, 1902, in B. J. Hendrick, *Carnegie*, ii, 182; D. Perkins, *The Monroe Doctrine, 1867-1907*, 343-344.

340. H. Speck von Sternburg to TR, Dec. 15, 1902, TR MSS.

341. J. Hay to C. Tower, Dec. 16, 1902, JH to H. White, Dec. 16, 1902, *Foreign Relations*, 1903, 421, 453.

342. Nr. 5124, Der Botschafter in Washington, Baron von Holleben an das Auswärtige Amt, den 16. Dezember 1902, *Grosse Politik*, xvii, 264. See also H. L. Higginson to H. C. Lodge, Dec. 15, 1902, Lodge MSS.; O. S. Straus to TR, Dec. 15, 1902, TR MSS.

343. Nr. 5125, Der Botschafter in London Graf P. W. von Metternich an das Auswärtige Amt, den 16. Dezember 1902, Nr. 5126, Graf von Bülow an PW vonM, den 17. Dezember 1902, *Grosse Politik*, xvii, 265-268; Marquess of Lansdowne to Sir F. Lascelles, Dec. 18, 1902, *British Documents*, G. P. Gooch and H. W. V. Temperley, eds., ii, 162; Lansdowne to Sir M. Herbert, Dec. 18, 1902, " Venezuelan Arbitration," 679; T. C. Hansard, ed., *Parliamentary Debates*, 4th series, cxvi, 1290; GPG, *Before the War*, i, 236-237. See also J. Morley to A. Carnegie, Dec. 19 and 27, 1902, in B. J. Hendrick, *Carnegie*, ii, 179-180, 182; J. Hay, statement on Venezuela, February, 1903, Hay MSS.

344. Nr. 5126, Graf von Bülow and den Grafen von Metternich, den 17. Dezember 1902, *Grosse Politik*, xvii, 266-268; Marquess of Lansdowne to Sir F. Lascelles, Dec. 18, 1902, *British Documents*, ii, 162; A. J. Balfour to A. Carnegie, Dec. 18, 1902, Carnegie MSS.; H. White to J. Hay, Dec. 17, 1902, C. Tower to JH, Dec. 18 and 19, 1902, JH to CT, Dec. 18, 1902, *Foreign Relations*, 1903, 423-424, 454; T. C. Hansard, ed., *Parliamentary Debates*, 4th series, cxvi, 1490; G. P. Gooch, *Before the War*, i, 25-26.

345. Nr. 5127, Der Geschäftsträger in Washington Graf von Quadt an das Auswärtige Amt, den 18. Dezember 1902, Nr. 5128, Der Staatssekretär des AA Freiherr von Richthofen an den Botschafter in London Grafen von Metternich den 24. Dezember 1902, *Grosse Politik*, xvii, 269-270; *Washington Post*, Dec. 19, 1902, TR Scrapbooks.

346. Marquess of Lansdowne to G. W. Buchanan, Dec. 13, 1902, *British Docu-*

ments, II, 161; Lansdowne to Sir F. Lascelles, Dec. 18, 1902, *British and Foreign State Papers,* xcv (1901-1902), 1124; Foreign Office Statement, Dec. 20, 1902, and Joint Declaration of Germany and Great Britain, enclosed in Lansdowne to FL, Dec. 22, 1902, in " Venezuelan Arbitration," 685-686; G. von L. Meyer, Diary, Dec. 24, 1902, in M. A. DeW. Howe, *Meyer,* 65; H. White to J. Hay, Dec. 17 and 18, 1902, C. Tower to JH, Dec. 19 and 22, 1902, *Foreign Relations,* 1903, 423-425, 454-455; *Washington Star,* Dec. 20, 1902, *Washington Post,* Dec. 21, 1902, TR Scrapbooks.

347. Seward W. Livermore, " Theodore Roosevelt, the American Navy, and the Venezuelan Crisis of 1902-1903," *American Historical Review,* LI (April, 1946), 456-458.

348. G. Dewey to H. A. Wise Wood, May 23, 1916, in TR to W. R. Thayer, Aug. 21, 1916, TR MSS.; J. J. Leary, Jr., *Talks with TR,* 43; S. W. Livermore, *op. cit.,* 458-462.

349. Nr. 5127, Graf von Quadt an das Auswärtige Amt, den 18. Dezember 1902, *Grosse Politik,* xvii, 269; S. W. Livermore, *op. cit.,* 464-465.

350. Rear Admiral Henry C. Taylor to William H. Moody, Secretary of the Navy, Dec. 25, 1902, Moody MSS., quoted in S. W. Livermore, *op. cit.,* 463.

351. Journal of the Commander-in-Chief [Admiral George Dewey], in S. W. Livermore, *op. cit.,* 462.

352. W. H. Moody, draft of speech, undated, Moody MSS., in S. W. Livermore, *op. cit.,* 466.

353. *New York Telegram,* March 29, 1903, TR Scrapbooks. See also J. J. Leary, Jr., *Talks with TR,* 13-14.

354. Marquess of Lansdowne to Sir M. Herbert, Nov. 11, 1902, MH to Lansdowne, Nov. 13, 1902, *British and Foreign State Papers,* xcv (1901-1902), 1081-1082, 1084; H. White to TR, Sept. 20, 1906, TR MSS.

355. H. Speck von Sternburg to TR, Nov. 21 and Dec. 15, 1902, TR to TR, Jr., Feb. 1, 1903, TR MSS.

356. J. Hay to H. White, Dec. 5, 1902, JH to H. P. Dodge, Dec. 5, 1902, *Foreign Relations,* 1903, 418, 452.

357. H. White to H. C. Lodge, Jan. 20, 1903, Lodge MSS.; HW to J. Hay, Dec. 13 and 15, 1902, in A. Nevins, *Henry White,* 210, and *Foreign Relations,* 1903, 433.

358. H. White to H. C. Lodge, Jan. 20 and Feb. 24, 1903, Lodge MSS.; HW to J. Hay, Dec. 13, 1902, in A. Nevins, *Henry White,* 210. Roosevelt later told Lodge that White had rendered valuable service. HCL to HW, Feb. 3 and March 13, 1903, White MSS.

359. Nr. 5124, Der Botschafter in Washington Baron T. von Holleben an das Auswärtige Amt, den 16. Dezember 1902, *Grosse Politik,* xvii, 264; TvonH an [das AA (?)], den 13. Dezember 1902, in A. Vagts, *Deutschland und die Vereinigten Staaten,* II, 569; White House Appointment Books, Dec. 8, 1902, TR MSS.; S. W. Livermore, " Theodore Roosevelt, The American Navy, and the Venezuelan Crisis of 1902," *American Historical Review,* LI (April, 1946), 454; W.

Loeb, Jr., to H. F. Pringle, Aug. 14, 1930, HFP, *Roosevelt*, 284-289. See also A. L. P. Dennis, *Adventures in American Diplomacy*, 290.

360. Nr. 5127, 5133, Der Geschäftsträger in Washington Graf A. W. von Quadt an das Auswärtige Amt, den 18. Dezember 1902 and 23 Januar 1903, Nr. 5140, Graf von Metternich an das AA, den 29. Januar 1903, *Grosse Politik*, XVII, 269, 274, 281; AWvonQ an das AA, den 20. und 29. Dezember 1902, Auswärtigen Amtes MSS., vol. LIX, quoted in D. Perkins, *The Monroe Doctrine, 1867-1907*, 346-347.

361. Sir H. Herbert to the Marquess of Lansdowne, Dec. 29, 1902, *British Documents*, G. P. Gooch and H. W. V. Temperley, eds., II, 163-164.

362. H. Speck von Sternburg to TR, Dec. 15, 1902, TR MSS.

363. Nr. 5120, Graf B. H. von Bülow an Kaiser Wilhelm II, den 12. Dezember 1902, *Grosse Politik*, XVII, 259-260; BHvonB to William II, Aug. 31, 1904, BHvonB, *Letters*, 72.

364. See, e. g., J. H. von Bernstorff, *My Three Years in America*, 16-17; Wolf von Schierbrand, ed., *The Kaiser's Speeches*, 121.

365. Sir M. Herbert to the Marquess of Lansdowne, Dec. 16, 1902, *British Documents*, II, 162.

366. See, e. g., A. Vagts, *Deutschland und die Vereinigten Staaten*, 1555-1556, Nr. 5116, 5127, Graf A. W. von Quadt an das Auswärtige Amt, den 25. November und den 18. Dezember 1902, *Grosse Politik*, XVII, 256, 269; AWvonQ an das AA, Dec. 20 to 29, 1902, Auswärtigen Amtes MSS., vol. LIX, quoted in D. Perkins, *The Monroe Doctrine, 1867-1907*, 346-347; H. P. Dodge to J. Hay, Dec. 3, 1902, *Foreign Relations*, 1903, 418.

367. H. Speck von Sternburg to TR, Dec. 15, 1902, TR MSS.

368. C. Tower to J. Hay, Jan. 9, 15, and 28, 1903, State Department Archives; TR to H. Speck von Sternburg, Jan. 17, 1898, July 20, 1900, and Oct. 11, 1901, HSvonS to TR, September, 1901, Nov. 8, 1901, and Dec. 15, 1902, TR to Hugo Münsterberg, Jan. 17, 1903, TR to TR, Jr., Feb. 1, 1903, TR MSS.; H. White to H. C. Lodge, Jan. 20, 1903, Lodge MSS.; "The Progress of the World," *Review of Reviews*, XXVII (February, 1903), 132; W. von Schierbrand, ed., *The Kaiser's Speeches*, 121. See also A. Nevins, *Henry White*, 212-213.

369. Cf. A. Nevins, *Henry White*, 213; J. Hay to C. Tower, Jan. 9, 1903, CT to JH, Jan. 9, 15, and 19, 1903, State Dept. Archives; A. Vagts, *Deutschland und die Vereinigten Staaten*, II, 1569; D. Perkins, *The Monroe Doctrine*, 369. See also JH to [John W.] Foster, June 23, 1900, Hay MSS.

370. H. White to J. Hay, Jan. 6 and Dec. 23 and 24, 1902, JH to HW, Dec. 20, 1902, Lord Lansdowne to HW, Jan. 5, 1903, in HW to JH, Jan. 6, 1903, C. Tower to JH, Dec. 23, 24, and 29, 1902, Jan. 6 and 8, 1903, *Foreign Relations*, 1903, 425-427, 429, 434, 457-458, 460-461, 466-467; Nr. 5130, Der Staatssekretär des Auswärtigen Amtes Freiherr von Richthofen an Grafen von Metternich, den 30. Dezember 1902, Nr. 5131, Graf von Bülow an den Grafen A. W. von Quadt, den 20. Januar 1903, Nr. 5132, 5136, AWvonQ an das AA, den 20. und 24. Januar 1903, *Grosse Politik*, XVII, 271-273, 276; *Washington Star*, Dec. 27, 1902, TR Scrapbooks; A. Nevins, *Henry White*, 212-213.

371. H. White to J. Hay, Jan. 12 and 14, 1903, *Foreign Relations*, 1903, 469-471.

372. H. White to J. Hay, Jan. 17, 1903, in A. Nevins, *Henry White*, 212; HW to JH, Jan. 26 and 30, 1903, *Foreign Relations*, 1903, 471-472.

373. H. C. Lodge to H. White, Feb. 3 and March 13, 1903, White MSS.

374. H. White to H. C. Lodge, Jan. 28, 1903, Lodge MSS.; Nr. 5133, Der Geschäftsträger in Washington Graf von Quadt an das Auswärtige Amt, den 23. Januar 1903, Nr. 5140, 5143, Der Botschafter in London Graf von Metternich an das AA, den 29. und 31. Januar 1903, *Grosse Politik*, xvii, 274, 281, 284-285; J. Hay, interview with AWvonQ, January, 1903, J. Hay, statement on Venezuela, February, 1903, Hay MSS.; British Commander-in-Chief of North America and West Indies to the Admiralty, Jan. 23, 1903, Marquess of Lansdowne to Sir F. Lascelles, Jan. 27, 1903, *British Documents*, G. P. Gooch and H. W. V. Temperley, eds., ii, 165-167; William W. Russell to J. Hay, Jan. 21, 23, and 28, 1903, State Dept. Archives; *Washington Post*, Jan. 19, 22, and 27, 1903, TR Scrapbooks. See also H. White to H. C. Lodge, Jan. 20, 1903, Lodge MSS.

375. J. Hay, interview with Count von Quadt, January, 1903, Hay MSS.

376. Nr. 5133, Der Geschäftsträger in Washington Graf von Quadt an das Auswärtige Amt, den 23. Januar 1903, *Grosse Politik*, xvii, 274.

377. Marquess of Lansdowne to Sir F. Lascelles, Jan. 22, 1903, *British Documents*, ii, 164-165; *Washington Post*, Jan. 27, 1903, TR Scrapbooks.

378. Amasa Thornton to J. Hay, Jan. 23, 1903, Hay MSS. See also William I. Buchanan to Senator W. B. Allison, Jan. 27, 1903, Allison MSS.

379. Marquess of Lansdowne to Sir F. Lascelles, Jan. 27, 1903, *British Documents*, ii, 167; Nr. 5135, Graf von Bülow an Wilhelm II, den 23. Januar 1903, Nr. 5137, 5138, 5140, Der Botschafter in London Graf von Metternich an das Auswärtige Amt, den 27. und 29. Januar 1903, Nr. 5159, Der Staatssekretär des AA Freiherr von Richthofen an den Grafen von Metternich, den 28. Januar 1903, Nr. 5141, Der Geschäftsträger in Washington Graf von Quadt an das AA, den 29. Januar 1903, *Grosse Politik*, xvii, 275-283. See also W. W. Russell to J. Hay, Feb. 20, 1903, State Dept. Archives.

380. Nr. 5140, 5143, Graf von Metternich an das Auswärtige Amt, den 29. und 31. Januar 1903, *Grosse Politik*, xvii, 281, 284-285; Lord Lansdowne to Sir F. Lascelles, Jan. 27, 1903, *British Documents*, ii, 167; H. White to Mrs. Margaret White, Jan. 29, 1903, in A. Nevins, *Henry White*, 212; G. P. Gooch, *Before the War*, i, 26-27.

381. Marquess of Lansdowne to Sir F. Lascelles, Jan. 30, 1903, *British Documents*, ii, 168; H. White to J. Hay, Feb. 3, 1903, *Foreign Relations*, 1903, 472; Nr. 5141, Der Geschäftsträger in Washington Graf von Quadt an das Auswärtige Amt, den 29. Januar 1903, *Grosse Politik*, xvii, 282-283; *Washington Post*, Jan. 30, 1903, *Washington Evening Star*, Jan. 31, 1903, TR Scrapbooks.

382. Sir M. Herbert to Lord Lansdowne, Jan. 30, 1903, Lord Newton, *Lansdowne*, 259; Nr. 5142, Der Botschafter in London Graf von Metternich an das Auswärtige Amt, den 30. Januar 1903, *Grosse Politik*, xvii, 283-284.

383. H. Adams to E. Cameron, Feb. 1, 1903, in HA, *Letters, 1892-1918*, Worthington C. Ford, ed., II, 394.

384. H. Speck von Sternburg to TR, Sept. 1, 1901, TR MSS.

385. "The Progress of the World," *Review of Reviews*, XXVII (February, 1903), 133-134; *New York Tribune*, Jan. 16, 1903.

386. *New York Herald*, Jan. 31, 1903.

387. Marquess of Lansdowne to Sir F. Lascelles, Jan. 22, 1903, *British Documents*, G. P. Gooch and H. W. V. Temperley, eds., II, 165; Nr. 5131, Graf von Bülow an den Geschäftsträger in Washington den Grafen von Quadt, den 20. Januar 1903, Nr. 5144, 5147, 5151, Freiherr Speck von Sternburg an das Auswärtige Amt, den 31. Januar 1903 und den 4. und 19. Februar 1903, *Grosse Politik*, XVII, 273, 285, 287, 291.

388. Sir M. Herbert to the Marquess of Lansdowne, Jan. 31, 1903, *British Documents*, II, 168.

389. Nr. 5145, 5151, Freiherr Speck von Sternburg an das Auswärtige Amt, den 3. und 19. Februar 1903, *Grosse Politik*, XVII, 285-286, 291; *Washington Post*, Feb. 4, 1903, TR Scrapbooks.

390. Marquess of Lansdowne to Sir F. Lascelles, Feb. 2, 4, 5, 6, and 12, 1903, Sir M. Herbert to Lansdowne, Feb. 4 and 7, 1903, Lansdowne to MH, Feb. 7, 1903, *British Documents*, II, 168-173; MH to J. Hay, Feb. 6, 1903, JH to MH, Feb. 6, 1903, H. White to JH, Feb. 3, 1903, *Foreign Relations*, 1903, 472-475; Nr. 5142, 5143, Der Botschafter in London Graf P. W. von Metternich an das Auswärtige Amt, den 30. und 31. Januar 1903, Nr. 5144, 5145, 5148, Freiherr Speck von Sternburg an das AA, den 31. Januar und den 3. und 6. Februar 1903, Nr. 5146, Graf von Bülow an PWvonM, den 4. Februar 1903, *Grosse Politik*, XVII, 283-287; G. von L. Meyer, Diary, Feb. 8, 1903, in M. A. DeW. Howe, *Meyer*, 66; JH to TR, December [1902] and Feb. 11, 1903, TR MSS.; R. S. McCormick to JH, Feb. 7, 1903, W. I. Buchanan to JH, Feb. 14, 1903, JH to HW, Feb. 9 and 16, 1903, Hay MSS.; WIB to W. B. Allison, Feb. 7, 1903, Allison MSS.; *Boston Herald*, Feb. 13, 1903, *Washington Post*, Feb. 2, 5, 6, and 11, 1903, *Washington Evening Star*, Feb. 5, 6, and 9, 1903, *Washington Times*, Feb. 2 and 3, 1903, TR Scrapbooks; Lord Newton, *Lansdowne*, 260-261.

391. H. C. Lodge to H. White, Feb. 3, 1903, White MSS.

392. Nr. 5149, Der Botschafter in London Graf von Metternich an den Grafen von Bülow, den 4. Februar 1903, *Grosse Politik*, XVII, 288-289. See also H. White to H. C. Lodge, Jan. 20 and 28 and Feb. 24, 1903, Lodge MSS.

393. Lord Newton, *Lansdowne*, 260-261; G. P. Gooch, *Before the War*, I, 26-27.

394. H. White to J. Hay, Feb. 7, 1903, George B. Cortelyou to JH, Feb. 7, 1903, Hay MSS.; W. S. Cowles to TR, Feb. 11, 1903, TR MSS.

395. J. Hay to H. White, Feb. 9, 1903, Hay MSS.; C. Tower to JH, Feb. 12, 1903, and State Dept. Memorandum, State Dept. Archives; P. W. von Metternich to [B. H. von Bülow (?)], February 11, 1903, *Grosse Politik*, XVII, 289 n. See also JH to TR, December [1902 (?)], TR MSS.

396. G. B. Cortelyou to J. Hay, Feb. 13, 1903, Hay MSS.; H. White to JH, Feb. 14, 1903, *Foreign Relations*, 1903, 475-476; Nr. 5150, Graf von Bülow an

Wilhelm II, den 14. Februar 1903, *Grosse Politik*, xvii, 289-291; *Boston Herald*, Feb. 13, 1903, *Washington Post*, Feb. 13 and 15, 1903, *Washington Star*, Feb. 17, 1903, TR Scrapbooks.

397. Nr. 5151, Freiherr Speck von Sternburg an das Auswärtige Amt, den 19. Februar 1903, *Grosse Politik*, xvii, 291-292.

398. *Loc. cit.*

399. J. Hay to H. White, March 5, 1903, in A. Nevins, *Henry White*, 214. See also JH to C. Tower, April 28, 1903, Hay MSS.; "Editorial," *Nation*, lxxvi (March 26, 1903), 241; *New York Tribune*, May 20, 1903.

400. Nr. 5151, Freiherr Speck von Sternburg an das Auswärtige Amt, den 19. Februar 1903, *Grosse Politik*, xvii, 291-292.

401. J. Hay to C. Tower, April 28, 1903, Hay MSS. See also CT to JH, Jan. 9, 1903, State Dept. Archives.

402. F. B. Loomis to TR, July 28, 1903, TR to FBL, July 29, 1903, TR MSS.; *New York Herald*, Aug. 8, 1903, TR Scrapbooks; *New York Tribune*, Aug. 8, 1903.

403. Allan Nevins came to about this conclusion in his *Henry White*, 215-216. See also J. Hay to H. White, Feb. 16, 1903, in *ibid.*, 213-214.

404. H. White to H. C. Lodge, Jan. 28, 1903, Lodge MSS.; *New York Tribune*, Aug. 12, 1905, TR Scrapbooks.

405. TR, "The Monroe Doctrine," *Bachelor of Arts*, ii (March, 1896), 437, 439; TR to A. Shaw, Dec. 26, 1902, TR MSS.; *New York Tribune*, Aug. 12, 1905, *Minneapolis Journal*, Sept. 2, 1901, TR Scrapbooks.

406. TR to H. C. Lodge, June 19, 1901, TR MSS.

407. TR to C. Spring Rice, Nov. 1, 1905, TR MSS.

408. *Loc. cit.* See also TR to William II, Jan. 8, 1907, TR MSS.; Nr. 5151, Freiherr Speck von Sternburg an das Auswärtige Amt, den 19. Februar 1903, *Grosse Politik*, xvii, 291-292.

409. C. Tower to E. Root, Nov. 15, 1906 (copy), Lodge MSS.; TR to W. H. Taft, Jan. 4, 1909, Taft MSS.; Nr. 6207, F. von Holstein an B. H. von Bülow, den 22. Juli 1905, *Grosse Politik*, xix-2, 442; BHvonB, *Imperial Germany*, 51; E. Brandenburg, *Von Bismarck zum Weltkriege*, 227. See also D. J. Hill, *Impressions of the Kaiser*, 93; BHvonB, *Denkwürdigkeiten*, i, 572-575; Paul Meinhold, *Wilhelm II: 25 Jahre Kaiser und König*, 278-279; W. von Schierbrand, ed., *The Kaiser's Speeches*, 112-114; Lloyd C. Griscom, *Diplomatically Speaking*, 299-302; Alice R. Longworth, *Crowded Hours*, 48-49, 121.

410. Entwurf zu einem Briefe Kaiser Wilhelm II an Kaiser Nikolaus II, *Grosse Politik*, xix-1, 306. See also C. Tower to J. Hay, Feb. 12, 1903, State Dept. Archives.

411. H. Speck von Sternburg, Simla, India, to TR, Sept. 1, 1901, TR MSS.

412. H. C. Lodge, MS. Diary, March 8 [1902], Lodge MSS.; TR to E. Root, Feb. 16, 1904, TR MSS. T. von Holleben to J. Hay, Feb. 28, 1902, Hay MSS.

413. H. C. Lodge, MS. Diary, March 8 [1902], TR to H. C. Lodge, Jan. 28, 1909, Lodge MSS.; TR to E. Root, Feb. 16, 1904, TR to T. von Holleben, March 10, 1902, TR MSS.

414. B. H. von Bülow to William II, Aug. 31, 1904, BHvonB, *Letters*, 72.
415. B. H. von Bülow to William II, Dec. 24, 1904, *ibid.*, 84.
416. B. H. von Bülow to William II, Dec. 26, 1904, *ibid.*, 88.
417. *Loc. cit.*
418. J. Hay, MS. Diary, Jan. 5 and 13, 1905, Hay MSS.; TR to JH, Jan. 12, 1905, H. Speck von Sternburg to TR, Dec. 29, 1904, and Jan. 5, 1905, TR to HSvonS, Jan. 10 and 12, 1905, TR to C. Tower, Feb. 16, 1905, TR MSS.; Nr. 6276, Graf von Bülow an den Geschäftsträger in Washington von dem Bussche-Haddenhausen, den 4. Januar 1905, *Grosse Politik*, xix-2, 556-557. See also *Washington Post*, April 6, 1905, TR Scrapbooks.
419. J. Hay, MS. Diary, Jan. 9-11, 13, 1905, Hay MSS.
420. C. Tower to TR, Feb. 4, 1905, TR MSS.; J. Hay, MS. Diary, Feb. 17, 1905, Hay MSS.; Nr. 5988, C. Tower an den Staatssekretär des Auswärtigen Amtes Freiherrn von Richthofen, den 16. Februar 1904, Nr. 6284, Graf von Bülow an Freiherrn H. Speck von Sternburg, den 20. Januar 1905, Nr. 6285, HSvonS an das AA, den 3. Februar 1905, *Grosse Politik*, xix-1, 190, xix-2, 564, 567-568.
421. C. Tower to TR, July 13, 1905, TR to CT, July 27, 1905, TR MSS.
422. William II to B. H. von Bülow, Dec. 30, 1907, BHvonB, *Letters*, 227.
423. J. Hay, MS. Diary, Nov. 5, 1904, Hay MSS.
424. TR to William II, May 6, 1908. See also TR to H. Speck von Sternburg, April 3, 1905, C. Spring Rice to E. K. Roosevelt, March 29, 1905, TR MSS.; TR to W. Reid, undated, WR to TR, June 19, 1906, in R. Cortissoz, *Reid*, ii, 330.
425. M. A. DeW. Howe, *Meyer*, 211-219; G. von L. Meyer to TR, March 3, 1905, TR MSS.
426. TR to J. Hay, April 2, 1905, TR MSS. See also Maurice F. Egan, *Ten Years near the German Frontier*, 63-64.
427. See, e. g., A. R. Longworth, *Crowded Hours*, 122; C. Tower to TR, Jan. 28, 1908, TR MSS.; B. H. von Bülow, *Denkwürdigkeiten*, i, 573-574.
428. TR to A. H. Lee, Oct. 17, 1908, TR to W. Reid, Jan. 6, 1909, TR to E. Root, Aug. 8, 1908, TR to C. Spring Rice, May 13, 1905, TR to W. H. Taft, April 8 and 20, 1905, TR MSS.; Arthur N. Davis, *The Kaiser as I Know Him* (1918), 99-104.
429. TR to J. J. Jusserand, Aug. 21, 1905, TR MSS.
430. TR to William II, Jan. 8, 1907, TR MSS.
431. TR to C. Spring Rice, Sept. 1, 1905, TR MSS.
432. W. H. Taft to Charles P. Taft, Aug. 18, 1903, Taft. MSS.; TR to William II, Jan. 8, 1907, TR MSS. See also TR to WHT, Jan. 4, 1909, Taft MSS.
433. TR to William II, Jan. 8, 1907, TR MSS.
434. TR to William II, April 4 and Dec. 26, 1908, TR MSS. See also TR to C. Tower, July 27, 1905, TR MSS.
435. Lord Lansdowne, however, professed to believe the United States understood Germany perfectly. Lansdowne to Sir F. Lascelles, April 9, 1905, Lord

Newton, *Lansdowne*, 334. See also C. Spring Rice to E. K. Roosevelt, March 29, 1905, TR MSS.

436. TR to H. C. Lodge, May 15, 1905, TR MSS.

437. TR to C. Spring Rice, May 13, 1905, TR MSS. See also TR to William II, May 5, 1908, TR to H. Speck von Sternburg, April 3, 1905, CSR to E. K. Roosevelt, March 29, 1905, TR MSS.; TR to W. Reid, undated, WR to TR, June 19, 1906, in R. Cortissoz, *Reid*, II, 330-333.

438. Sir Edward Grey to TR, Dec. 4, 1905, TR MSS.

439. TR to C. Spring Rice, May 13, 1905, TR MSS. See also TR to CSR, Nov. 19, 1907, TR MSS.

440. See, e. g., TR to G. von L. Meyer, May 22, 1905, TR to W. Reid, Sept. 19, 1905, TR MSS.

441. See, e. g., Nr. 6285, Freiherr Speck von Sternburg an das Auswärtige Amt, den 3. Februar 1905, *Grosse Politik*, XIX-2, 567.

442. H. C. Lodge, MS. Diary, March 6, 1905, Lodge MSS.; TR to J. St. Loe Strachey, Feb. 22, 1907, TR MSS. See also Willy to Nicky, Oct. 14, 1904, *Willy-Nicky Correspondence*, H. Bernstein, ed., 68-70; C. Spring Rice to TR, Dec. 7, 1904, TR MSS.

443. TR to J. Hay, April 2, 1905, TR MSS. " Each nation is working itself up to a condition of desperate hatred of each other from sheer fear of each other. The Kaiser is dead sure England intends to attack him. The English Government and a large share of the English people are equally sure that Germany intends to attack England." TR to W. H. Taft, April 20, 1905, TR MSS. See also Willy to Nicky, Oct. 14 and Nov. 13, 1904, *Willy-Nicky Correspondence*, H. Bernstein, ed., 68-70, 86-87.

444. TR to C. Spring Rice, May 13 and 26, 1905, TR MSS.

445. TR to C. Spring Rice, Nov. 1, 1905, TR MSS.

446. TR to C. Spring Rice, May 13, 1905, TR MSS.

447. TR to C. Spring Rice, Nov. 1, 1905, TR MSS.

448. See, e. g., A. Carnegie to TR, May 12, 1908, TR MSS.; B. H. von Bülow, *Memoirs*, I, 153-154; R. Cortissoz, *Reid*, II, 346; H. von Eckardstein, *Die Isolierung Deutschlands*, 173-174; E. Peters, *Roosevelt und der Kaiser*, 6-9; Stuart P. Sherman, " Roosevelt and the National Psychology," *Americans* (1922), 280-281; George S. Viereck, *The Kaiser on Trial*, 41.

449. Ambassador von Holleben told of a conversation in which the Kaiser had said this. George W. Smalley, *Anglo-American Memories*, II, 356-357.

450. Nicholas Murray Butler, *Across the Busy Years*, II, 60.

451. S. Lee, *Edward VII*, II, 435-436.

452. J. Morley to A. Carnegie, Dec. 3, 1907, Carnegie MSS.; JM to J. Bryce, Jan. 6, 1908, Herbert A. L. Fisher, *James Bryce*, II, 93.

453. Charles Seymour, ed., *The Intimate Papers of Colonel House*, I, 254.

454. TR to W. Reid, Dec. 4, 1908, TR MSS.; R. Cortissoz, *Reid*, II, 346.

455. TR to G. O. Trevelyan, Oct. 1, 1911, TR MSS. See also O. K. Davis, *Released for Publication*, 88.

456. G. von L. Meyer to H. C. Lodge, March 5, 1905, Lodge MSS. See also

B. H. von Bülow, *Denkwürdigkeiten*, I, 572-573; N. M. Butler, *Across the Busy Years*, II, 64; M. F. Egan, *Ten Years near the German Frontier*, 63; G. S. Viereck, *The Kaiser on Trial*, 285-286; A. D. White, *Autobiography*, II, 202; *New York World*, June 27, 1903, *Washington Star*, Dec. 9, 1904, TR Scrapbooks. See also A. N. Davis, *The Kaiser as I Know Him*, 101.

457. TR to C. Spring Rice, May 26, 1905, TR MSS.

458. S. B. Fay, *Origins of the World War*, I, 190-191.

459. TR to H. Speck von Sternburg, Nov. 27, 1899, TR to C. Spring Rice, July 3, 1901, TR MSS.

460. TR to A. Carnegie, July 15, 1907, TR to W. Reid, Dec. 4, 1908, TR MSS.

461. TR to W. H. Taft, April 8, 1905, TR to W. Reid, Dec. 4, 1904, TR MSS. See also H. C. Lodge, MS. Diary, March 6, 1905, Lodge MSS.; TR to A. H. Lee, Oct. 17, 1908, TR to H. C. Lodge, May 15, 1905, C. Spring Rice to E. K. Roosevelt, March 29, 1905, TR MSS.; B. H. von Bülow, *Memoirs*, III, 60.

462. TR to C. W. Eliot, July 24, 1905, TR MSS. See also C. Spring Rice to E. K. Roosevelt, March 29, 1905, TR MSS.; TR to W. Reid, undated, in R. Cortissoz, *Reid*, II, 332.

463. TR to C. Spring Rice, May 13, 1905, TR MSS.

464. TR to H. White, Aug. 14, 1906, TR MSS.

465. B. H. von Bülow to Theobald von Bethmann Hollweg, Sept. 28, 1909, BHvonB, *Letters*, 329.

466. A. N. Davis, *The Kaiser as I Know Him*, 102.

467. TR to K. Takahira, May 17, 1905, TR MSS.

468. *London Daily Telegraph*, Oct. 28, 1908; J. L. Bashford, "The Berlin Crisis," *Nineteenth Century*, LXIV (December, 1908), 908-923; W. Reid to TR, Nov. 24, 1908, TR MSS.

469. TR to Kermit Roosevelt, Nov. 22, 1908, TR MSS.; A. Carnegie to TR, Nov. 15, 1908, Carnegie MSS.; E. Eyck, *Das persönliche Regiment Wilhelms II*, 492-502.

470. TR to E. Root, Aug. 8, 1908, TR to A. H. Lee, Oct. 17, 1908, TR to TR, Jr., Nov. 20, 1908, TR MSS. See also O. K. Davis, *Released for Publication*, 84, 87-88, William B. Hale to William C. Reick, July 19, 1908, in *ibid.*, 82-83; TR to W. Reid, Jan. 6, 1909, TR MSS.

471. TR to E. Root, Aug. 8, 1908, TR MSS.

472. B. H. von Bülow, *Memoirs*, I, 153-154, 357; BHvonB, *Denkwürdigkeiten*, I, 305, 573-574.

473. TR to A. H. Lee, Oct. 17, 1908, TR MSS. See also W. Reid to TR. Nov. 24, 1908, TR MSS.

474. TR to G. O. Trevelyan, Oct. 1, 1911, TR MSS.; Burrie [W. S.] Swift to Ella Swift, July 8, 1910, Swift MSS.; Archie Butt to Clara Butt, June 30, 1910, *Taft and Roosevelt: The Intimate Letters of Archie Butt*, 421-422; H. [Kellett (?)] Chambers, interview ca. 1920. The interviewing of people close to TR was done about 1920 by J. B. French, Hermann Hagedorn, and Marcus L. Hansen, who deposited their interview notes at Roosevelt House.

475. TR to A. H. Lee, Oct. 17, 1908, TR MSS. See also A. Carnegie to TR, Nov. 15, 1908, Carnegie MSS.

476. H. von Eckardstein, *Die Isolierung Deutschlands*, 175-176.

CONCLUSION

1. TR, " The Romanoff Scylla and the Bolshevist Charybdis," *Metropolitan*, XLIX (December, 1918), 66-67.

2. Brooks Adams to Henry Cabot Lodge, Oct. 14, 1900, Lodge MSS.

3. TR to Hermann Speck von Sternburg, Oct. 11, 1901, TR MSS. See also TR to Cecil Spring Rice, May 29, 1897, TR to Anna Roosevelt Cowles, Dec. 17, 1899, TR MSS.

4. TR to George Ferdinand Becker, July 8, 1901, TR MSS. See also TR to C. Spring Rice, Aug. 11, 1899, TR MSS.

5. TR to G. F. Becker, July 8, 1901, TR MSS.

6. TR to Lyman Abbott, Sept. 7, 1908, TR MSS.

7. TR to William II, Jan. 8, 1907, TR MSS.

8. TR to William Bayard Hale, Dec. 3, 1908, TR MSS.

9. TR to Sir Harry H. Johnston, Dec. 4, 1908, TR MSS.

10. James Bryce, " The Policy of Annexation for America," *Forum*, XXIV (December, 1897), 388, 391-392.

11. TR to Whitelaw Reid, Sept. 3, 1908, TR MSS.

12. TR to Henry White, April 2 [1910], White MSS.

13. TR to Silas McBee, Aug. 27, 1907, TR MSS.

14. James Bryce, " The Policy of Annexation for America," *Forum*, XXIV (December, 1897), 391-392.

15. Andrew Carnegie to TR, April 10, 1907, TR MSS.

16. William James to the *Boston Evening Transcript*, March 1, 1899, in Ralph Barton Perry, *The Thought and Character of William James*, 245-246.

17. Joseph A. Schumpeter leaned to this interpretation of early twentieth-century expansionism in a little volume he wrote in 1919. *Zur Sociologie der Imperialismen* (1919) translated into English in 1951 by Heinz Norden under the title *Imperialism and Social Class*.

Index